ENTREPRENEURIAL FINANCE

Second Edition

Richard L. Smith
Claremont Graduate University

Janet Kiholm Smith
Claremont McKenna College

www.wiley.com/college/smith

Acquisitions Editor	Leslie Kraham
Project Editor	Cindy Rhoads
Editorial Assistant	Jessica Bartelt
Marketing Manager	David Woodbury
Senior Production Editor	Kelly Tavares
Production Editor	Sarah Wolfman-Robichaud
Illustration Editor	Benjamin Reece
Cover Design	Jennifer Fisher
Cover Image	© Getty Images

This book was set in Palatino by Leyh Publishing, LLC and printed and bound by
R. R. Donnelley & Sons Company, Inc. The cover was printed by The Lehigh Press.

This book is printed on acid-free paper.∞

ISBN:978-0-471-23072-4
WIE ISBN: 978-0-471-45221-8

Printed in the United States of America

10 9 8 7 6

To Erin and Kelly

Preface

History abounds with examples of extraordinary entrepreneurs whose new ideas and products changed the world. Many people are enamored with the idea of creating new products and services and starting businesses. Of course, these new ventures require financing, and accompanying the interest in venture creation is broad interest in venture capital markets, investment banking, and other careers related to new venture financing, deal structuring, and harvesting. Anyone who works in or around a university environment surely has encountered the enthusiasm surrounding new ventures and entrepreneurship.

One of our motivations for writing this book is to nurture interest in new ventures. Another is to empower students and practitioners to be successful in developing and financing the ideas they bring to the market. Our overriding orientation is to apply the theory and methods of finance and economics to the emerging field of entrepreneurial finance. Application of financial economic theory to corporate finance is highly developed and analytically sophisticated. Many of the tools and methods of corporate finance are applicable to new venture finance. However, applying them correctly often is challenging. This book fills a gap by extending and building upon financial economic principles to focus on the difficult and important financial problems associated with incubating and growing new ventures.

While a discipline-based approach to entrepreneurial finance is innovative and useful, it is at its infancy. The subject area is dynamic, and the amount of new research on the topic is expanding in a seemingly exponential way! We invite comments and suggestions from readers as to how best to update the material in the book and on the Web site to reflect the new contributions and insights that business people and academic researchers are generating.

INTENDED AUDIENCE

We designed the book primarily for students who have previously taken a course in finance and principles of microeconomics. For those with limited training in these fields, or for those who would like a refresher, we have included Web-based tutorials and appendices. Hence, the book is appropriate for MBA students, advanced undergraduates in business and economics, and Executive MBA students. In our own teaching, we have used the material with students

A NEW COPY OF THIS BOOK INCLUDES FREE ACCESS TO *Venture*.**SIM**™: A FINANCIAL ASSESSMENT TOOL

A Web link from the book's companion Web site for a six-month license to simulation software *Venture*.**SIM**™ is included. We use simulation to study alternative new venture strategies, to assess financial needs, to assess risk and expected cash flows as elements of valuation, and to compare different deal structures and contract terms.

Venture.**SIM**™ is an application utility for financial modeling. The simulator allows users to build uncertainty and chance into financial spreadsheet models. The user can simulate scenarios involving decision trees to determine the most probable outcome and the uncertainty of the outcomes. Results can be used in the valuation templates also available on the book's companion Web site. *Venture*.**SIM**™ can also be used for financial planning in the corporate finance and derivatives arenas.

Throughout the text there are problems and sections that include a *Venture*.**SIM**™ icon signifying that these particular problems can be solved using this simulation software.

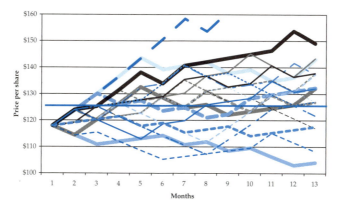

Figure 5-1 Simulation of 12 months of a stock price diffusion process

The figure shows the results of 20 random sequences of returns for a stock that trades monthly. The Excel spreadsheet that generated these results also generates the values of puts and calls on the underlying stock, and can be used to simulate the effects of different assumptions.

Unconditional Simulation Results

Trials 300

Venture.**SIM**™

Output	Average	Median	Standard Deviation	Skewness	Percentiles				
					Minimum	25%	50%	75%	Maximum
1 Market Size	3,217,592	3,125,748	1,030,772	0.3321	1,125,794	2,452,174	3,125,748	3,944,959	5,827,140
2 Unit Sales	318,658	305,911	103,264	0.2320	101,365	240,041	305,911	392,507	500,000
3 Total Present Value	1,085,056	1,003,019	662,507	0.6682	(325,430)	598,105	1,003,019	1,460,043	3,232,787
4 Entrepreneur's Share	0.65	0.65	0.02	(0.3826)	0.57	0.64	0.65	0.67	0.71
5 NPValue to Entrepreneur	304,522	252,092	427,485	0.6360	(608,649)	(8,162)	252,092	553,485	1,609,254

Figure 5-3 Illustrative output of *Venture*.**SIM**™

The figure shows the output generated from *Venture.SIM*™, using the unconditional simulator. To see the output table, please refer to the Web site version of this figure. Results are compiled for the five variables listed in the table and are based on 300 iterations of the model for the large restaurant.

ENTREPRENEURIAL FINANCE

Second Edition

at all three levels. In addition, our experience is that the book is useful to entrepreneurs, practicing venture capitalists, business angels, consultants, and others who have an interest in using more rigorous analytical approaches to new venture financing and deal structuring.

A NOTE ABOUT THE WEB SITE AND INTERNET RESOURCES

The Web site includes a variety of resources that are integral to the text. Much of the book ties into software, spreadsheets, templates, simulation applications, and interactive lab tutorials that are available to download from the book's Web site. A Web link from the book companion Web site to simulation software *Venture.SIM* is also included. We use simulation to study alternative new venture strategies, to assess financial needs, to assess risk and expected cash flows as elements of valuation, and to compare different deal structures and contract terms.

The Web site also contains electronic versions of many of the figures in the book, an online test bank, and several templates that allow you to study your own new venture valuation questions. Lab tutorials that cover many of the more difficult technical applications of the text, as well as essential background, are available to download.

In preparing the text, we have avoided including material that becomes obsolete quickly and material that is easy to find on the Internet. The Web site includes links to information sources that are relevant to the subject matter of most chapters.

A NOTE TO INSTRUCTORS

Instructors who teach corporate finance and valuation courses, and those who teach entrepreneurship courses with a strong finance component, should have no trouble making the transition to *Entrepreneurial Finance*. The first chapter contains an outline of the book, and, as a starting point, identifies conceptual and practical differences between corporate finance and entrepreneurial finance. As noted, the book is discipline-based and stresses application. Generally, we look at new venture financing decisions through the lens of their effects on value to the entrepreneur or to an outside investor.

The major changes in the second edition include: more end-of-chapter problems (and solutions); an online test bank; additional international material and comparisons. The valuation chapters (8-11, 13) are organized so they can be used with or without simulation techniques. Sections of chapters that make use of simulation are marked accordingly. In this edition we are able to rely more on market data to estimate cost of capital for entrepreneurs and investors. As with the first edition, technical tutorials and appendices are provided on the Web site, allowing instructors to preserve class time for discussion of concepts and applications. We have added more interactive cases to complement chapter material. Most cases include downloadable Excel files. Some cases include teaching notes and solutions.

We have found that applying financial economic theory to new venture finance topics is intellectually challenging and sometimes difficult. We welcome comments and suggestions on improving the pedagogy and the organization of the material.

ACKNOWLEDGMENTS

In preparing the first and second editions of the book, we have benefited from numerous comments that we received from colleagues, students, venture capitalists, business angels, entrepreneurs, and friends. Several reviewers provided detailed chapter-by-chapter comments that helped sharpen the presentation. They include Carol Billingham (Central Michigan University), Sanjai Bhagat (University of Colorado), Glenn Hubbard (Columbia University), Frank Kerins (Washington State University, Vancouver), James Nelson (Florida State University), Bill Petty (Baylor University), Steven R. Scheff (Florida Gulf Coast University), James Seward (University of Wisconsin, Madison), Jeffrey Sohl (University of New Hampshire), and Howard Van Auken (Iowa State University). Thanks also to the reviewers who commented on various chapters: Robin Anderson (University of Nebraska), Alan Atkinson (Northern Arizona University), Carol Marie Boyer (Clarkson University), Nathan Cox (Golden Gate University), Ronald Crowe (Jacksonville University), David Culpepper (Millsaps College), Daniel Donoghue (DePaul University and Piper Jaffray), Samuel Gray (New Mexico State University), Fernando Fabre (Universidad Anahuac del Sur), Thomas Hellmann (Stanford), William C. Hudson (St. Cloud University), Steve Kaplan (University of Chicago), Jill Kickul (DePaul University), Kenji Kutsuna (Kobe University), Daniel McConaughy (California State University Northridge), Edward Rogoff (Baruch College), Chip Ruscher (University of Arizona), Bob Schwartz (University of Texas), Nikhil Varaiya (San Diego State University), and Edward Williams (Rice University), and to our many colleagues at the Claremont Colleges.

A number of practitioners, including venture capitalists, venture funds managers, entrepreneurs, and angel investors were very generous in sharing their experiences and providing ideas for cases and other book material. Special thanks to Andy Horowitz, John Sibert, Richard Sudek, Luann Bergsund, Luis Villalobos, John Kensey, Kazuhiko Yamamoto, Yoshinori Bunya, and Thomas Gephart. In particular, their insights on valuation practices and deal negotiations, and their willingness to challenge academic theory, have added institutional richness to the book.

We also are grateful to Leslie Kraham, editor of the Wiley series in economics and finance, Cindy Rhoads, project editor, and Jessica Bartelt, editorial assistant, for their help in completing the project.

Richard L. Smith
Janet Kiholm Smith
Claremont, California
August 2003

Author Biographies

Richard Smith is Professor of Financial Management at the Peter F. Drucker Graduate School of Management, Claremont Graduate University, where he teaches courses on new venture finance, and strategic risk management. He also is Director of the Venture Finance Institute at Claremont. Professor Smith has served on several boards that are responsible for investing on behalf of pension funds and university endowments, and has consulted extensively for venture capitalists, business angels, entrepreneurs, and government, on matters involving investment, valuation, financial contracting, securities litigation, and antitrust.

Janet Kiholm Smith is the Von Tobel Professor of Economics at Claremont McKenna College, where she teaches courses on the economics of strategy and industrial organization. She currently serves on the College's investment committee and consults on matters related to working capital management, the economics of contracts, and antitrust. She is the author of numerous journal articles, including publications in *Journal of Legal Studies, Journal of Finance, Journal of Corporate Finance, Journal of Financial and Quantitative Analysis, Journal of Law and Economics,* and *Journal of Law, Economics and Organization.*

Contents

PART 2 FINANCIAL ASPECTS OF STRATEGIC AND BUSINESS PLANNING

PART 3 FINANCIAL FORECASTING

PART 4 VALUATION

PART ◆ 5   ORGANIZATIONAL DESIGN AND FINANCIAL CONTRACTING

Chapter 16   Harvesting   546

PART ◆ 7   CONCLUSION

Chapter 17   The Future of Entrepreneurial Finance: A Global Perspective   585

Index   615

Introduction

What distinguishes the successful entrepreneur and promoter from other people is precisely the fact that he does not let himself be guided by what was and is, but arranges his affairs on the ground of his opinion about the future. He sees the past and present as other people do; but he judges the future in a different way. (*Human Action*, Ludwig von Mises, 1966)

Learning Objectives

After reading this chapter you should:

- Understand how entrepreneurial finance differs from corporate finance.
- Understand that the objective of maximizing value for the entrepreneur is central to the study of entrepreneurial finance.
- Be able to describe the evolution of thinking about entrepreneurship.
- Be able to describe the process of new venture formation from inception of the idea to harvesting of the investment.
- Recognize that studying entrepreneurial finance leads to better investment and financing decisions and increases the potential for establishing a successful venture.

Thousands of business ventures are started every year. Most fail within a short period. Of those that survive, most achieve only meager success, some achieve rates of return high enough to justify the initial investment, and a few achieve phenomenal success. What distinguishes the successes from the failures? There is not just one answer. A new venture based on a good idea can fail because of poor implementation or bad luck. One that is based on a bad idea can fail despite excellent implementation. Many that survive, but do not thrive, should not have been undertaken. Sometimes, even when a venture is hugely successful, early financing mistakes prevent the entrepreneur from sharing in the rewards.

INTERNET RESOURCES FOR THIS BOOK

This book is accompanied by a significant amount of supporting material that we have placed on the Internet. Among other things, the Web site contains custom software that complements the book, as well as soft copies of most of the figures. It also contains a glossary of the technical terms related to entrepreneurial finance and lab tutorials that can be used for review or to gain hands-on experience with new tools and concepts. The site contains links to a variety of information sources relevant to entrepreneurial finance, a series of case applications of chapter material, and other features. The Web site is designed to make learning and practicing entrepreneurial finance easier and to help you keep up with developments in the field.

This would be a good time to visit the site, and open the "First Time Visitor" link. You can access the *Entrepreneurial Finance* Web site through the John Wiley & Sons home page, at *www.wiley.com*. The complete link to the *Entrepreneurial Finance* site is *www.wiley.com/college/smith*.

This is a book on financial decision making for new ventures. Our goal is to help students, prospective entrepreneurs, and investors think more clearly about the conditions under which an idea is worth pursuing and about how to apply the tools of financial economic theory in ways that add to the expected value of an undertaking.

1.1 THE ENTREPRENEUR

Just as corporate finance concerns financial decision making by managers of public corporations, entrepreneurial finance concerns financial decision making by entrepreneurs who are undertaking new ventures. There are important distinctions between the responsibilities and decisions that face managers of public corporations and those that face entrepreneurs.

To understand the distinctions it is useful to begin with an understanding of what is meant by the term entrepreneur. The term is of French origin, and its literal translation is simply "undertaker," in the sense of one who undertakes to do something. The English banker, Richard Cantillon, in the early 1700s coined the use of the word in a managerial context. He emphasized the notion of the entrepreneur as a bearer or "undertaker" of risk, particularly with respect to provision of capital. This early usage, however, does not adequately characterize our current understanding of what it means to be an entrepreneur. Clearly, risk-bearing is an aspect of entrepreneurship, but risk also is borne by capital providers who may have no direct involvement in managing the venture, and by employees who have no financial capital invested.

J. B. Say, a French economist, in the early 1800s characterized the entrepreneur as a person who seeks to shift economic resources from areas of low to high productivity. Although Say's notion points us in a useful direction, it is too general. Most purposeful human activity can be described as shifting economic resources to higher valued uses (or attempting to do so).[1]

The contributions of Cantillon and Say gained renewed attention in the early 1900s through the writings of two other economists. Frank Knight (1921) conceived of the entrepreneur as a manager of uncertainty, "With uncertainty present, . . . the primary problem or function is deciding what to do and how to do it." To Knight the entrepreneurial function of directing resources in the presence of uncertainty (and realizing a reward for performing successfully) is an unavoidable aspect of the ordering of economic activity. In contrast, Joseph Schumpeter

◆   **The Failure Record of New Ventures**

Starting a new venture entails significant risk of failure. During the first half of the 1990s, an average of 903,000 new businesses were created in the United States each year. The average number of business terminations during the same period was 818,000 per year, resulting in annual net new business formations of 85,000. As these statistics show, most new ventures eventually are terminated. The number terminated with financial loss to creditors, however, is comparatively small—only 10 percent of all terminations. The remainder, voluntary terminations, involve cases where the business was closed for inadequate profitability or where the owner simply decided to exit.

These statistics, however, do not reveal much about the life expectancy of a new venture. Based on data compiled from sources published during the 1980s, Timmons (1999) reports 23.7 percent of new ventures failed within two years of inception, 51.7 percent within four years, and 62.7 percent within six years. Timmons cites economic factors and financial troubles as the primary causes of failure. Together these factors accounted for 85.8 percent of failures. Other causes include owner neglect and inexperience. Focusing just on business terminations involving financial loss to creditors, Case (1997) draws on Dun and Bradstreet's *Business Failure Record,* (1994) to report that 40 percent of such failures occur during the first five years and 67 percent occur during the first ten. Collectively, these results suggest that the first three to five years are the most critical for determining whether a venture will succeed or fail.

Sources: The State of Small Business: A Report on the President, 1994 (Washington, D.C.: U.S. Government Printing Office, 1995). Timmons, J. A., "The Entrepreneurial Process," *New Venture Creation.* 5th ed.

(1934), viewed the entrepreneur as actively seeking out opportunities to innovate. In his view, the entrepreneur is the driver of economic progress, continuously seeking to disturb the status quo in a quest for profits from deliberate and risky efforts to combine society's resources in valuable ways that are not yet perceived by others.[2]

Current use of the term *entrepreneurship* derives from these views and from more recent thinking by such management scholars as Peter Drucker (1985), who describes entrepreneurs as individuals who "create something new, something different; they change or transmute values." Today, entrepreneurship is most often described as the pursuit of opportunities to combine and re-deploy resources, without regard to current ownership or control of those resources. This notion clearly draws on the definition offered by Schumpeter, but seeks to add structure by recognizing that the entrepreneur does not regard current control of resources as a constraint. Thinking of entrepreneurship in this way suggests a multistep process. First, the entrepreneur must perceive an opportunity to create value by re-deploying society's resources. Second, the entrepreneur must devise a strategy for marshaling control of the necessary resources. Third, he or she must implement a plan of action to bring about the change. And fourth, the entrepreneur must harvest the rewards that accrue from the innovation.

The listing seems to suggest that successful innovation necessarily yields a reward. This, of course, is far from true. To be successful, an entrepreneur needs to maintain a clear focus on how strategic choices and implementation decisions are likely to affect rewards.

1.2 FINANCE AND THE ENTREPRENEUR

Often we hear entrepreneurs described as visionaries, too caught up in the excitement of their ideas to get involved in the mundane tasks of planning a course of action that is important to ultimate success. But take a closer look. Most entrepreneurs are involved in small and basic enterprises—small manufacturing, wholesaling, or retailing operations. They are not so much driven by the idea as by the desire to make themselves better off. The visionary, at the other extreme, may not be focused on personal gain, but if the venture is successful, is likely to devote considerable effort to lining up and managing the financing that will enable the venture to grow.

Regardless of their desires or their lack of interest in accumulating personal wealth, few entrepreneurs can afford to ignore financing. In fact, being caught up in the vision and ignoring the details of implementation is a danger sign to prospective investors. A common view of venture capital investors is that good ideas are easy to find, but that people who can implement the ideas are hard to find. To quote one successful venture capitalist, "Good ideas and good products are a dime a dozen. Good execution and good management—in a word, good people—are rare."[3]

A useful distinction can be drawn between institutional finance and finance as a structured approach to decision making. Many books on small business finance are institutional in nature. They identify the different sources of financing that may be available to small business and report statistical data on the extent of use. Although we present information on financing sources, our focus is on financial decision making. The domain of the financial decision-making paradigm is resource allocation. The range of decisions that can be approached using the finance paradigm is much broader than may be apparent at first glance. For example, the choice of organizational form (e.g., sole proprietorship, partnership, or corporation) can be construed as a financial investment decision. Is the expected value higher for the entrepreneur if the venture is organized as a proprietorship or a corporation? Similarly, issues like the choices of scale and scope of a business venture can be analyzed as financial investment decisions.

1.3 THE FINANCE PARADIGM

The guiding principles of financial decision making can be stated succinctly as: (a) more of a good is preferred to less; (b) present wealth is preferred to future wealth; and, (c) safe assets are preferred to risky assets. We formalize and rely heavily on these principles when we consider the subject of valuation.

We consider two distinct kinds of decisions. Investment decisions concern acquisition (or sale) of assets. In an accounting sense, these decisions relate to the left-hand side of the balance sheet. The assets that are acquired can be either tangible like a machine or intangible like a patent, or simply an option to take some action in the future. The objective of investment decision making is to acquire assets that are worth more than they cost. The worth, or value, of an investment depends on its ability to generate cash flows for the investors in the future and on the riskiness of those cash flows.

The other kind of decision that we consider is financing. In contrast to investment decisions, financing decisions concern the right-hand side of the balance sheet. Given the decision to acquire an asset, what is the most desirable way to structure the ownership or to finance the acquisition? How much of the entrepreneur's money should be used as compared to money provided by other investors? What should be the nature of the financial claims of the investors—how much debt versus equity, or would some hybrid like preferred stock be better?

At this point, it may seem that there is not much difference between new venture finance and what you may already have learned in a traditional course in corporate finance. Clearly, the finance paradigm is no different for new ventures than for large public corporations. However, as you will see, financial decision making in the context of a new venture is much different.

Many of the decisions we examine can also be evaluated using other paradigms from management, strategy, or marketing. Thus, you can think of entrepreneurial finance as one of several approaches to making entrepreneurial decisions. Our objective is to help you learn how to use the financial approach. We think you will see that the tools of finance are powerful and can contribute substantially to the value of a new venture.

1.4   WHAT MAKES ENTREPRENEURIAL FINANCE DIFFERENT FROM CORPORATE FINANCE?

Why, if you are interested in entrepreneurship, is it useful to study entrepreneurial finance, particularly if you already have studied corporate finance? And why, if you are interested in finance, but not particularly in entrepreneurship, is studying entrepreneurial finance useful?

The answer is that the focus on entrepreneurship and early-stage ventures dramatically changes the ways in which the essential features of the finance paradigm must be applied. The basic course in corporate finance is not well-suited for evaluating investment and financing decisions in a new venture or privately held business setting. The techniques of entrepreneurial finance—such as thinking about investment opportunities as portfolios of real options—while they are particularly useful in a new venture setting, are also relevant in the context of a large public corporation. However, they normally receive little attention in courses on corporate finance.

Entrepreneurial finance differs from corporate finance in many ways. At this early stage, we highlight the eight most important differences:

- The nonseparability of investment decisions and financing decisions.
- The role of diversification of risk as a determinant of investment value.
- The extent of managerial involvement by outside investors.
- The effects of information problems on the firm's ability to undertake a project.
- The role of contracting to resolve incentive problems.
- The importance of options as determinants of value.
- The importance of harvesting as an aspect of valuation and the investment decision.
- The focus on maximizing value for the entrepreneur as distinct from maximizing value for shareholders.

Interdependence between Investment and Financing Decisions

In corporate finance, students learn that investment and financing decisions are largely independent and, for the most part, can be made separately. That is, the manager makes the decision of which assets to acquire by comparing the return on the investment to the market rate of interest for projects of equivalent risk. The manager does not need to consider, simultaneously, how the investment will be financed or whether the firm's shareholders value high-dividend payouts or prefer capital gains.[4]

Of course, investment and financing decisions are not completely independent in large public corporations. For example, tax savings from debt financing may increase the net present value (NPV) of a project. However, these types of interactions are fairly simple and usually are addressed by making incremental adjustments to the net present value of an investment as if it were financed entirely with equity.[5]

The interactions between investment and financing decisions are more complex for a private business than for a public corporation. Among other things, appropriate application of the finance paradigm implies that the value placed on a new venture will be very different for the entrepreneur than for many outside investors.[6] This difference in value arises because of differences in required rates of return between entrepreneurs and outside investors. Because the entrepreneur usually is compelled to invest a significant amount of time and financial capital in a venture, simple adjustments to the NPV cannot be used to address the divergence of valuations between the entrepreneur and the market.

More generally, some investment choices are possible only if certain financing choices are made. For example, rapid growth may only be possible with substantial outside financing, whereas if the same project were undertaken by an established large corporation, it might be possible to finance the entire project with internally generated funds. The link between investment choices and financing choices creates complexity that does not arise in corporate finance.

Figure 1-1 provides a graphical illustration of how the divergence of valuations between the market and the entrepreneur can give rise to different decisions of whether or not to invest in a project. For a venture like the one illustrated in the figure, the entrepreneur would only be willing to invest if a substantial fraction of the total investment could be raised from outside investors who valued the venture based on the market rate of interest.

Diversifiable Risk and Investment Value

The advances of modern portfolio theory lead to the conclusion that cost of capital depends not on total project risk, but on the component of project risk that cannot be avoided through diversification.[7] That conclusion from corporate finance relies on the assumption that investors can diversify at low cost. Although the assumption holds for many of the outside investors in new ventures, it does not hold for the entrepreneur. In fact, the entrepreneur often is compelled to invest almost exclusively in the venture. This difference between entrepreneurs and outside investors, in the ability to diversify, results in the project value being different for the entrepreneur than for outside investors.

A number of additional implications follow from this fundamental difference between the entrepreneur and outside investors. For example, because of the difference, project value depends on the relative ownership shares of the entrepreneur and outside investors. Furthermore, even when the entrepreneur and outside investors have identical expectations regarding the future performance of a project, the overall value of the project depends on how risk is allocated between the parties.

These conclusions are different from the conclusions that arise in a public corporation setting. In that setting diversifiable risk does not affect value. Allocation of ownership claims among different groups of investors, though it affects the required returns of each group due to the way nondiversifiable risk is allocated, does not affect the overall required return of the business.[8] This conclusion sometimes is referred to as the principle of value additivity or the law of conservation of value.

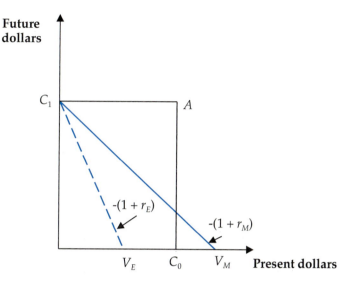

Figure 1-1   Entrepreneurial investment and financing decisions are not separable.

The horizontal axis is present dollars, and the vertical axis is future dollars. Venture A is a one-period investment opportunity that requires an investment of C_0 today and is expected to return C_1 in the future. In the corporate finance setting, investors can trade financial claims to the venture at the market rate of interest, r_M. Venture A has a positive net present value to a public corporation because the present value of C_1 is V_M, which is greater than C_0. If venture A is a nonmarket asset that depends on involvement of an entrepreneur, the entrepreneur may be unable to sell the financial claims. In that case, value depends on the entrepreneur's willingness to forego current consumption. The entrepreneur, using a discount rate of r_E, would reject venture A unless it could be financed substantially by others on terms more favorable to the entrepreneur.

In corporate finance, value additivity implies that allocation of financial claims does not affect the decision to accept a project. But for new ventures, because entrepreneurs and outside investors view risk differently, they ascribe different values to the same risky asset. As a result, value additivity does not hold. Consequently, the way ownership is shared between the entrepreneur and outside investors can determine whether a project is worth undertaking.

Managerial Involvement of Outside Investors

In public corporations, investors generally are passive and do not contribute managerial services. In contrast, outside investors in new ventures frequently do provide services that contribute to venture success. This is particularly true of venture capitalists and business angel investors. Normally, venture capitalists and angels do not charge explicitly for their services. Rather, they seek to recover the cost of their services by increasing the ownership stakes they take.

This bundling of compensation for the managerial and financing functions of the venture capitalist is another reason that the investment and financing decisions cannot be separated. The bundling together of investment and managerial involvement of outside investors like venture capitalists causes them to seek ways of closing out their ownership positions and to seek ownership rights that facilitate their ability to do so.

Information Problems and Contract Design

To this point, we have identified differences between public corporation finance and entrepreneurial finance that arise even when inside and outside investors agree about expected future cash flows (and know that they agree). Differences also arise from the magnitude and importance of the information problem between inside and outside investors. Although information gaps exist between insiders and outsiders of public corporations, the gaps need not materially affect the investment decisions of public corporation managers. Public corporations generally can, and usually do, make investment decisions without much immediate regard to how outside investors perceive the value of the investment. Most corporate projects are small relative to the overall value of the corporation. Investors in corporations look not to the individual projects for returns, but to the overall performance of the corporation.[9]

Because the normal pattern of financing in large corporations is to expand by retaining earnings and through low-risk debt, outside investors have little control over investment decisions. The managers act accordingly. Generally, at least in the short run, they do not need to convince anyone but themselves that a project is worth undertaking. The situation is much different in the case of a start-up that requires outside financing. In the latter case, outside investors are looking specifically to the venture to realize a return. Consequently, the entrepreneur bears a heavy burden of trying to convince outsiders of the value of the project. If the entrepreneur is unable to do so, the project will not go forward. This is in sharp contrast to the corporate setting, where "selling" specific projects to investors is not necessary.

Often, there is no easy way for an entrepreneur to communicate his or her true beliefs about the potential for success of a venture. From a financial perspective, this places considerable emphasis on preparing a well-thought-out and well-researched business plan and on designing financial contracts with outside investors in ways that signal the entrepreneur's confidence in the venture. Signaling of managerial beliefs, while it occurs in the corporate setting, is oriented toward helping outsiders value their existing investments, and does not play much of a role in the efforts of most firms to raise capital for new projects. In fact, the corporate finance literature suggests that public corporations often are organized and capitalized intentionally to limit the needs of managers to convince outside investors of the value of new projects.[10] Sometimes it is suggested that public corporations would benefit from adopting financial policies that compel them to act more like start-ups in their dealings with outside investors.[11]

Incentive Alignment and Contract Design

Clearly, incentive contracting plays a role in the large public corporation. On the positive side, managerial stock options and performance bonuses are intended to align the interests of managers and investors. On the negative side, debt covenants and similar provisions are designed to discourage reliance on risky debt financing, which can lead to inefficient investment decisions and other problems associated with heavy reliance on risky debt.[12] The issues are similar for start-up businesses, but reliance on incentive contracts is, in some respects, more compelling.

In contrast to the managers of a public corporation, the entrepreneur generally is kept on a short leash by investors. Whereas corporate CEOs can be selected based on track records of achievement, entrepreneurs often can provide little evidence of their abilities to convert good ideas into successful businesses.

Although most outside investors would like to rely heavily on the experience and track records of entrepreneurs, there are compelling reasons to find ways of investing in the projects of entrepreneurs who cannot demonstrate prior success. An investor who is good at identifying the untested entrepreneurs who are likely to succeed can participate profitably in new ventures that would be rejected by a less astute investor. The result is that outside investors use a variety of contractual devices to improve upon their abilities to identify high-quality entrepreneurs and to motivate them.

Contract terms are designed to motivate entrepreneurs to develop their ideas quickly, to guarantee that the entrepreneur stops spending resources on an idea after its potential is found to be unacceptable, and to make certain that ineffective management does not cause the venture to fail. Staging of investments, termination options, and other contractual devices transfer substantial control over ultimate success to the outside investors. From the perspective of the entrepreneur, it is important to ensure that the incentives of investors to stop investing or to make other changes are compatible with the entrepreneur's interests.

The Importance of Real Options

In corporate finance, students learn that projects can be valued by forecasting cash flows and discounting them back to NPV. Even in the corporate setting, this is an oversimplification. In reality, most investing involves a process of acquiring, retaining, exercising, and abandoning options.[13] In fact, a common criticism of the NPV approach is that it fails to take account of the option values associated with a project. The criticism is misdirected because careful implementation of the NPV approach does take account of option values. Nonetheless, the common practice of ignoring options in corporate investment decisions suggests that they often are of secondary importance.

The values of real options associated with an investment depend on the level of uncertainty surrounding the investment. Particularly for routine investment decisions, such as capital replacement and some kinds of expansion decisions, uncertainty may not be very high. In those cases, the importance of valuing the embedded options is limited. For other kinds of projects, such as investments in research and development and decisions to invest in a new industry, uncertainty is likely to be very high, adding to the importance of considering the values of embedded options. The options might include, for example, the option to abandon the project if it does not appear to be developing according to expectations, the option to expand the scope or scale of investment if the market opportunity appears to warrant doing so, or the option to wait before investing. For these kinds of decisions, corporate managers in industries where the option values are likely to be substantial may try to value the options explicitly.[14] More often, they try to make subjective adjustments when assessing the NPV of the project.

Nowhere is the importance of option values more central than for a start-up business. In fact, a new venture can be viewed most accurately as a portfolio of real options, some controlled by the entrepreneur and others controlled by outside investors. Staging of capital infusions, abandonment of the project, acceleration of the growth rate, and a variety of other choices all involve real options and contribute to the need for an investment decision-making approach that focuses on recognizing and valuing the real options.[15]

Harvesting the Investment

In corporate finance, investment opportunities are evaluated based on ability to generate free cash flow beyond what is needed to maintain the investment and provide for its growth. The free cash flow may be distributed to investors or retained by the corporation to help finance other opportunities. Normally, the investment decision does not depend on when free cash flows are distributed to investors, except that it usually is assumed that the corporation will not retain cash it cannot invest economically.

Investors in corporations purchase stock in public markets. They realize returns in the form of dividends (the distributed net free cash flows from all investments of the corporation during a period of time) and from capital gains realized by re-selling the shares of stock to other investors. The investors' decisions to sell are essentially independent of a company's investment activities. In their decisions to invest, investors normally give little consideration to when they will sell or to valuation and costs associated with selling.

Investing in new ventures is different. New venture investments normally are not liquid and often do not generate any significant free cash flow for several years. Most investors in new ventures, and many entrepreneurs, have finite investment horizons. To realize the returns on their investments, a liquidity event must occur (such as a public offering of equity by the venture or private acquisition of the venture for cash or freely tradable shares of the acquirer). Such liquidity events are the main ways investors in new ventures harvest and realize the returns on their investments. Because of the importance of liquidity events, they generally are explicitly forecast. The forecasts are formally factored into valuation of the investment.

Value to the Entrepreneur

The final difference between start-ups and public corporations is the focus on the entrepreneur. In the public corporation, the focus of decision making is on investment returns to shareholders. Management is viewed as an agent of the shareholders, who are the residual claimants on corporate earnings. In a start-up business that is structured as a corporation, shareholders' claims on the residual are proportional to their fractions of equity ownership. But in a fundamental sense, the true residual claimant is the entrepreneur. In the corporate setting, maximum shareholder value is the most frequently espoused financial objective. In contrast, the objective of the entrepreneur, in deciding whether to pursue the venture and how to structure the financing, is to maximize the value of the financial claims and other benefits that the entrepreneur is able to retain as the business grows.

It is easy to envision cases where an objective of maximizing share value would not be in the entrepreneur's best interest. This is particularly true if the entrepreneur is unable to convince outside investors of the true value of the project and would therefore have to give up too large a fraction of ownership, or if the entrepreneur values other considerations besides share value. Among other considerations are the salary of the entrepreneur and the satisfaction the entrepreneur may derive from self-employment or from creating something new.

1.5 WHY STUDY ENTREPRENEURIAL FINANCE?

Whether you see yourself as an entrepreneur or a corporate financial manager, a solid understanding of entrepreneurial finance can help you make better decisions. But there is a more pragmatic reason to master the subject. Even though most business students aspire initially to positions in large corporations, a large percentage gravitate over time toward entrepreneurial positions. At the 1997 New York University Conference on the Economics of Small Business Finance, for example, it was reported that more than 50 percent of all MBA students move into positions in entrepreneurship within a few years of completing their degrees. Couple this with an estimate that 63 percent of new businesses fail within six years, and the value of understanding new venture finance becomes clear. Perhaps more telling, even for the businesses that survive, the entrepreneur may not. By one estimate, after 80 months of operation, in 80 percent of start-up businesses in Silicon Valley, a nonfounder had been appointed CEO.[16]

How can the hazards and pitfalls of forming new ventures be avoided? We believe the answer is to understand and use the best available decision-making tools and methods. A new venture should not be undertaken unless the expected reward is high enough to compensate for the value of other foregone opportunities. Investing personal resources and time in a venture that should never have been pursued is just as serious an error as failing to invest in a good venture. Both kinds of errors are common.

We are not alone in the view that understanding finance is important to entrepreneurial success. Hood and Young (1993) surveyed 100 chief executives from the *Inc. Magazine* list of the nation's most successful publicly held entrepreneurial firms for the years 1979–1989. Respondents indicated that knowledge of finance and cash management is the single most important area of knowledge for an entrepreneur to have.

Furthermore, the original design of the business, including both its product market orientation and the structure of contractual relationships among the entrepreneur, employees, and outside investors, has a great deal to do with the expected return to the entrepreneur and with the risk that the business will not survive. This tradeoff of risk and return is not easy to assess intuitively. This is another area where the analytical methodology of new venture finance adds considerable value.

Even the best projections, however, can prove to be overly optimistic as the future unfolds. It is important to base the decision to continue or abandon on the same kind of rigorous analysis that was used in making the original decision to enter. It is all too easy to continue investing time and resources on a venture that is destined for mediocre performance or to give up on a venture that has experienced a temporary setback.

Finally, in many cases it is possible to separate the entrepreneurial function from the management function of a start-up venture. It is a rare individual who is good at both *seeing an opportunity* to add value through innovation and *managing the venture* that is intended to capitalize on the opportunity. Careful design at the outset helps assure that a business does not fail just because the visionary was not well suited to manage the day-to-day operations. Conversely, careful design can help assure that the entrepreneur does not lose control unnecessarily.

1.6   THE OBJECTIVE: MAXIMUM VALUE FOR THE ENTREPRENEUR

To the nineteenth-century economist, J. B. Say, an entrepreneur creates value for society by shifting resources from areas of low productivity to areas of higher productivity. Schumpeter, however, makes clear that the entrepreneur's motivation is not so much to make society better off as it is to make the entrepreneur better off. This is our orientation as well. We expect that the entrepreneurial function will create value for society, but we assume that prospective entrepreneurs are driven by self-interest.

Clearly, outside investors, consumers, and other stakeholders also will try to capture as much of the gain as possible. Although each party is expected to benefit, competition in the product market and in the market for financing limits those gains. In contrast, the entrepreneur controls a unique asset (the innovation). If it truly is both valuable and unique, the entrepreneur should be able to capture a significant fraction of the social gain.

Throughout this book, we look at the venture from the perspective of an entrepreneur who is seeking to maximize value for himself or herself. The entrepreneur faces many choices of how best to develop the project and can be expected to have a different appetite for risk and expected return than would outside investors. Accordingly, the entrepreneur cannot simply rely on investor recommendations concerning how best to develop the project. Rather, he or she must consider the range of product market strategies and available financing opportunities and select the one that offers the most attractive combination of risk and expected return for the entrepreneur.

Although the lessons of this book are developed from the perspective of the entrepreneur, they are no less valuable for prospective outside investors. All of the analysis could be reformulated around the objective of maximizing value for an investor, such as a venture capitalist or business angel. Moreover, the investor can benefit from a better understanding of how the entrepreneur views the economics of the project under consideration. And because the entrepreneur can benefit from understanding how an investor would view the project, we study value from both perspectives.

1.7 THE PROCESS OF NEW VENTURE FORMATION

In Figure 1-2 we provide a diagrammatic integration of the principles we have discussed in this chapter. The diagram traces the process of new venture formation from perception of the opportunity to harvesting, with an emphasis on key financial decisions. Although the formality of the process varies from case to case, the fundamental process is appropriate for any new venture.

As implied by the diagram, once an opportunity is recognized, some nonfinancial activities can begin immediately. Filing for patents, searching for personnel, assessing the size of the market, and identifying actual and potential competitors are examples of activities that need to be done regardless of any decisions about development strategy.

From a decision-making standpoint, the entrepreneur's first action is to generate a short list of realistic alternative development strategies related to the opportunity. For some kinds of ventures, only one development strategy may be feasible. For others, it should be possible to represent the array of alternatives with a small number of discrete strategic scenarios.

For each strategic scenario, the entrepreneur needs to identify a limited set of real options for implementation. These real options are choices such as "start now" or "wait until the potential for the opportunity to succeed becomes clearer."

Given the strategic scenarios and the implementation options, the next step is to construct a financial model of the venture, complete with carefully researched assumptions about the market and the venture. The model should enable the entrepreneur to assess the financing requirements of each implementation option and to evaluate each choice, with an emphasis on value to the entrepreneur.

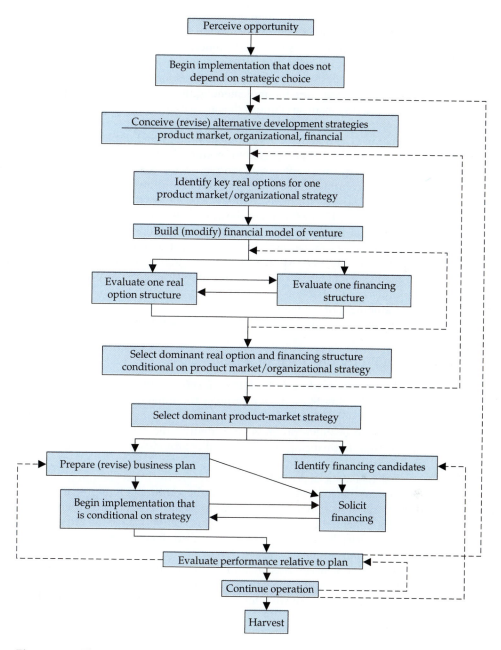

Figure 1-2 The entrepreneurship process

This analysis is done for one real option structure at a time, matched with one financing structure (with assumed availability of financing). The real option structure and financing structure are interdependent. So the entrepreneur needs to search for the most valuable financing structure to complement a particular real option structure.

Based on analysis of the various structures for one strategic scenario, the entrepreneur selects a dominant structure for implementing the strategic scenario. The other alternatives can be ignored. The dominant structure is the one with the highest present value for the entrepreneur. The same process needs to be repeated for other real option structures and for the other strategic scenarios. The dominant development strategy and implementation plan emerges from this process as the one that is expected to produce the highest value for the entrepreneur.

The strategy and implementation plan is the core of the business plan that the entrepreneur uses to control and monitor progress of the venture and to solicit outside funding. At this point, it makes sense for the entrepreneur to engage in implementation activities that are specific to the plan. Up to this point, however, all the work that has been done is based on the conjecture that the entrepreneur can attract an outside investor.

Performance evaluation is a continuous process. If implementation and financing results comport generally with expectations, then all that is necessary is to periodically refine and update the business plan. If not, then the entire strategy is suspect and the entrepreneur should revisit the overall strategic plan, considering alternatives ranging from major changes of focus to abandonment of the venture.

The final stage, for a venture that is successful, is harvesting.

1.8 ORGANIZATION OF THE BOOK

We address new venture finance from inception of the idea to harvesting. In the remainder of Part 1, "Getting Started," we provide some institutional background on new venture financing that will be used throughout the text. In particular, we discuss the practice of using milestones to evaluate progress; and identify the stages of new venture development, and their relation to financing sources. We also provide an overview of the deal structure of new venture financing.

Part 2, "Financial Aspects of Strategic and Business Planning," stresses the importance of formulating the strategy for developing the venture before preparing the business plan. The plan can serve several purposes, including a means of benchmarking future performance and a tool for soliciting outside financing. This section makes the important connection between entrepreneurial finance and strategy. We also develop and demonstrate the use of decision trees to examine strategic choices. A new venture can be thought of as a portfolio of real options (abandonment, expansion, and delay). In this section we introduce analytical and practical tools for examining the values of different options. The section begins with a chapter on the business plan where we offer a rational and systematic conceptual approach to developing the plan.

In Part 3, "Financial Forecasting," we cover methods of financial forecasting, and techniques for projecting cash flows and assessing financial needs. The material in this section is practical and essential. We make the point that uncertainty about the future, rather than reducing the value of financial planning, makes good financial planning critical. We do not look at assessment of financial needs from the traditional perspective of making sure that the entrepreneur secures enough financing to avoid running out of cash. Instead, we discuss the topic from the perspective of adding value for the entrepreneur, recognizing that raising less capital now will enable the entrepreneur to retain a larger share of ownership and preserve the opportunity to attract lower cost financing later if the venture is successful. Issues related to working capital policy are also addressed in this section.

The focus of Part 4, "Valuation," is on learning to value new venture investment opportunities and on the financial claims related to those opportunities. A central and unique aspect of the book is recognizing that the value of a venture can be much different for an outside investor than it is for the entrepreneur. We examine valuation from both perspectives. In some cases, the material in this section is very challenging. We provide a series of spreadsheets to help with implementation.

Part 5, "Organizational Design and Financial Contracting," demonstrates how organizational design choices and financial contracting provisions can create value for the entrepreneur and for the investor. We consider how the differences in risk-tolerance between investors and entrepreneurs create opportunities for enhancing value by using contractual provisions that optimally allocate ownership share and risk among the parties to the contract. As an aspect of this section, we review the economic approach to contracts and demonstrate how the contracting framework relates to new venture formation and financing. Coverage in the section includes risk allocation, incentive alignment, signaling, and reputation. With the valuation methodology already established, we return to the view of projects as bundles of real options and use the methodology to study the value of different strategic alternatives for developing the venture. The material in this section leads to some important implications for structuring ownership of the venture. We fit the earlier work on assessing financial needs into the contracting framework, beginning with a scenario where an outside investor agrees with the entrepreneur about the likely development of the venture. We then extend it to the more realistic case where the outside investor is concerned that the entrepreneur may be unduly optimistic or may have concealed negative information.

The relation between contract structure and financial flexibility of the venture is an important aspect of Part 5. Although the section is firmly grounded in financial economic theory, our objective is to develop your ability to apply the theory to real-world opportunities.

Part 6, "Financing and Harvesting Choices," considers alternative means of financing new ventures and alternative ways to harvest the investment. In the first chapter of the section, we study the venture capital industry, including partnership agreements, and contractual provisions that are common in venture capital financing. We examine alternative sources of financing in the second chapter of the section, including informal sources, government programs, franchising, and corporate involvement in venture financing. Our goal is to avoid an institutional treatment of the industry and to concentrate more on why the industry is organized as it is and on building an understanding of the reasons for the different orientations of different financing sources. An important aspect of this section is consideration of how engaging different kinds of financing partners can affect the value of the venture for the entrepreneur. The section also includes consideration of financial distress and turn-around financing.

Harvesting is the realization of investment return by the entrepreneur and outside investors. The orientation is on the choice of harvesting alternatives: initial public offering (IPO), merger or acquisition, employee stock ownership plan (ESOP), and so on. We devote specific attention to the IPO process and the role of the investment banker.

Part 7, "Conclusion," contains the final chapter of the text. The chapter includes a review of what you will have learned, and identifies some unresolved issues. It also contains forward-looking discussions of the future of entrepreneurial activity, including prospects for international expansion, and areas of fruitful research.

1.9 SUMMARY

An entrepreneur is a person who sees an opportunity to redirect resources from lower to higher valued uses and acts on the opportunity without being hindered by current ownership of the resources. A new venture is a business that the entrepreneur organizes in order to capitalize on the opportunity.

Entrepreneurial finance applies the basic tools of financial economic theory to decision making by entrepreneurs and others involved in new ventures. Although the same basic tools underlie corporate finance, there are important differences between new venture finance and corporate finance as to how the tools apply. The more important distinctions include the following:

- Decision making in public corporations is delegated to the firm's managers by its shareholders. The managers of public corporations are responsible for maximizing value for the shareholders. Decision making in new ventures is vested in the entrepreneur, who may decide to raise capital by offering ownership shares to outside investors. In contrast to public corporations, these outside investors frequently share managerial responsibility, as well as offering other services to the firm. In a new venture, the entrepreneur's objective is to maximize the value of the entrepreneur's interest in the venture.

- In public corporations, investment decisions are based on the principle that outside investors can diversify to limit exposure to risk. In contrast, the entrepreneur is compelled to make a highly specific investment in the new venture and is unlikely to be able to diversify fully. As a result, the entrepreneur and outside investors will reach different conclusions about the value of a new venture, even if they have the same beliefs about future financial performance. The differences in valuation give rise to substantial opportunities to add value to the project by using contract provisions to allocate ownership share and risk.

- In contrast to the basic proposition from corporate finance that financing and investing decisions can be separated, in new venture finance these decisions cannot be separated. Decision models used in new venture finance must take into account the interrelationships between financing and investment decisions.

- Although information problems between insiders and outsiders of public corporations can be significant, the information problems facing participants in a new venture are potentially more severe and differ in several ways from those of public corporations. These information problems give rise to complex contracting issues for the entrepreneur and outside investors.

- Because uncertainties about the potential for success and direction of future development generally are greater for new ventures than for established corporations, it is more important to base new venture investment decisions on the effects of real options on the value of the venture.

The implications of the distinctive aspects of new venture finance will be explored throughout the book.

QUESTIONS AND PROBLEMS

1. Think of some of the decisions that a prospective entrepreneur must make. Do you think applying financial economic theory to these decisions can enhance the expected value of a new venture for the entrepreneur? Why or why not?

2. What is meant by "harvesting"? Does it necessarily mean that the ownership interest is sold? If not, how else might harvesting occur? Why do you think harvesting is an important aspect of the entrepreneurial process?

3. Entrepreneurs care about the total risk of a project, whereas most outside investors care only about the risk that cannot be eliminated by diversifying. Given this difference, who would value a prospective new venture more highly? (Assume all parties agree about the expected future cash flows of the venture.) What opportunities can you see for an entrepreneur to benefit by bringing in an outside investor, even if the entrepreneur has sufficient wealth to fund the entire project?

4. Venture capitalists generally are actively involved with the ventures in which they invest. How might the active involvement benefit the venture capitalist? How might it benefit the entrepreneur?

5. Suppose, as the entrepreneur of a prospective new venture, that you find you are much more optimistic about the future prospects for the venture than is the venture capitalist whom you are trying to convince to invest in the project. Assuming you are confident that your optimism is well founded, can you think of any ways to structure the financing contract with the venture capitalist that would make the venture capitalist more comfortable with your projections?

6. How do you think an entrepreneur might benefit by limiting the amount of cash that an outside investor contributes up-front and by giving the investor the right to abandon the project without making any subsequent investments? Compare this to a scenario where the outside investor makes an up-front contribution of all the cash that the venture might require.

7. Why do you think greater uncertainty about the future is likely to increase the importance of real options as determinants of project value?

8. Why might an objective of maximizing value for the entrepreneur result in different decisions than an objective of maximizing shareholder value?

9. Despite the evidence that a large proportion of new ventures fail, most entrepreneurs believe they will succeed. In fact, evidence suggests that entrepreneurs tend to be more optimistic than they should be based on the actual performance of ventures. As a prospective entrepreneur, what could you do to help assure that your expectations for success are realistic? Given that outside investors know that entrepreneurs tend to be overly optimistic, what do you think you could do to convey to an investor that your projections are realistic?

10. What does it mean to say that a prospective entrepreneur should not pursue a new venture opportunity unless the opportunity is more valuable than alternative uses of the time and money the entrepreneur would need to commit? Do you agree with the statement? What kinds of considerations might reasonably enter into the entrepreneur's assessment of value?

11. How might a venture capitalist or angel investor benefit by understanding what a prospective entrepreneur believes about the risk and potential returns of an opportunity? How might the entrepreneur benefit by understanding the beliefs of prospective investors?

12. Briefly describe an entrepreneurial opportunity that is of interest to you. Using Figure 1-2:
    a. What kinds of implementation activities could you begin to work on even before you have settled on a strategy for developing the venture?
    b. What alternative development strategies might make sense for pursuing the opportunity?
    c. For one of the development strategies, what real options might bear importantly on the value of the opportunity?
    d. For the same development strategy, what do you think might be appropriate ways to finance the venture?

    For each of these questions, explain your reasoning.

NOTES

1. Kirzner (1979) discusses early views of entrepreneurship.
2. Bull and Willard (1994) survey recent definitions of entrepreneurship and conclude that most are fairly simple permutations of, or otherwise strongly derivative from, Schumpeter's view.
3. Rock (1992).
4. See, for example, Brealey and Myers (2003) for elaboration of the separation principle. Separability of investment and financing decisions derives from the early work of Fisher (1930) and Hirschleifer (1958).
5. See Myers (1974).
6. Throughout this book we use the term *outside investor* to distinguish between the entrepreneur and other investors in the venture. An outside investor may be actively involved in the venture or passive and may be an insider in the sense of one who has access to inside information about the venture.
7. The pioneering contributions underlying this conclusion are the work of Markowitz (1952) on portfolio theory and of Sharpe (1964) and Lintner (1965) on the Capital Asset Pricing Model.
8. This is the implication of the path-breaking work of Modigliani and Miller (1958). Using different reasoning, Miller (1977) extends their conclusion to apply in the presence of corporate and personal taxes.
9. Myers and Majluf (1984) analyze the effects of information differences between managers and investors and conclude that corporations tend to deal with the problem by maintaining financial slack in various forms, including unused low-risk borrowing capacity. Corporations may sometimes forego good investments if information problems are substantial and the lack of financial slack would necessitate raising capital by issuing risky debt or equity.
10. See Myers and Majluf (1984).
11. Jensen (1986, 1989) proposes that, in order to subject their investment decisions to more rigorous scrutiny by investors, corporations should employ capital structures and dividend policies that compel them to distribute much of their free cash flow to investors. Doing so forces the corporation to seek new risky capital in order to fund new investment opportunities.
12. See Jensen and Meckling (1976) on the agency cost of debt.
13. For the original work on valuing options, see Black and Scholes (1973), and Merton (1973).

Merton and Scholes won the 1997 Nobel Prize in economics for their work on option theory. (Black's work was recognized, but the prize is not awarded posthumously.)

14. Nichols (1994) describes the investment option valuation practice of Merck.

15. For review of how real options affect investment decisions, see Mason and Merton (1985), and Kester (1984).

16. Hannan, Burton, and Baron (1998).

REFERENCES AND ADDITIONAL READING

BHIDE, AMAR. *"The Origin and Evolution of New Business."* Oxford: Oxford University Press, 2000.

BLACK, FISHER, AND MYRON SCHOLES. "The Pricing of Options and Corporate Liabilities." *Journal of Political Economy* 81 (May–June 1973): 637–654.

BREALEY, RICHARD A., AND STEWART C. MYERS. *Principles of Corporate Finance.* 7th ed. New York: Irwin-McGraw-Hill, 2003.

BULL, IVAN, AND GARY WILLARD. "Towards a Theory of Entrepreneurship." *Journal of Business Venturing* 8 (1993): 183–195.

DRUCKER, PETER F. *Innovation and Entrepreneurship: Practice and Principles.* New York: HarperCollins, 1985.

FISHER, IRVING. *The Theory of Interest.* New York: Macmillan, 1930.

HANNAN, M., M.D. BURTON, AND J. BARON. "Inertia and Change in Early Years: Employment Relations in Young, High-Technology Firms." Mimeo, Graduate School of Business, Stanford University, 1998.

HIRSCHLEIFER, JACK. "On the Theory of Optimal Investment Decision." *Journal of Political Economy* 66 (1958): 329–352.

HOOD, JACQUELINE, AND JOHN YOUNG. "Entrepreneurship's Requisite Areas of Development: A Survey of Top Executives in Successful Entrepreneurial Firms." *Journal of Business Venturing* 8 (1993): 115–131.

JENSEN, MICHAEL C. "The Agency Cost of Free Cash Flow, Corporate Finance and Takeovers." *American Economic Review* 76 (May 1986): 323–329.

JENSEN, MICHAEL C. "The Eclipse of the Public Corporation." *Harvard Business Review* 67 (September–October 1989): 61–74.

JENSEN, MICHAEL C., AND WILLIAM H. MECKLING. "Theory of the Firm: Managerial Behavior, Agency Costs and Capital Structure." *Journal of Financial Economics* 3 (1976): 305–360.

KESTER, W. CARL. "Today's Options for Tomorrow's Growth." *Harvard Business Review* 62 (March–April 1984): 153–160.

KIRZNER, ISRAEL M. *Perception, Opportunity, and Profit.* Chicago: University of Chicago Press, 1979.

KNIGHT, FRANK H. *Risk, Uncertainty, and Profit.* New York: Houghton Mifflin, 1921.

LINTNER, JOHN. "The Valuation of Risk Assets and the Selection of Risky Investments in Stock Portfolios and Capital Budgets." *Review of Economics and Statistics* 47 (February 1965): 13–37.

MARKOWITZ, HARRY M. "Portfolio Selection." *Journal of Finance* 7 (March 1952): 77–91.

MARTIN, DOLORES T. "Alternative Views of Mengerian Entrepreneurship." *History of Political Economy* 11 (2) (Summer 1979).

MASON, SCOTT P., AND ROBERT C. MERTON. "The Role of Contingent Claims Analysis in Corporate Finance." In *Recent Advances in Corporate Finance,* edited by Edward I. Altman and Marti G. Subrahmanyan. Homewood, IL: Irwin, 1985.

MERTON, ROBERT C. "Theory of Rational Option Pricing." *Bell Journal of Economics and Management Science* 4 (Spring 1973): 141-183.

MILLER, MERTON H. "Debt and Taxes." *Journal of Finance* 32 (May 1977): 261–276.

MODIGLIANI, FRANCO, AND MERTON H. MILLER. "Cost of Capital, Corporation Finance and the Theory of Investment." *American Economic Review* 48 (June 1958): 261–297.

MYERS, STEWART C. "Interactions of Corporate Financing and Investment Decision—Implications for Capital Budgeting. *Journal of Finance* 29 (March 1974): 1–25.

MYERS, STEWART C., AND N. S. MAJLUF. "Corporate Financing and Investment Decisions When Firms Have Information Investors Do Not Have." *Journal of Financial Economics* 13 (June 1984): 187–222.

NICHOLS, NANCY A. "Scientific Management at Merck." *Harvard Business Review* 72 (January–February 1994): 88–91.

ROCK, ARTHUR. "Strategy vs. Tactics from a Venture Capitalist." In *The Entrepreneurial Venture*, edited by William A. Sahlman and Howard H. Stevenson. Boston: Harvard Business School Press, 1992.

SAHLMAN, WILLIAM A. "Entrepreneurial Finance—Course Introduction." *Harvard Business School Note* 9–288–004 (August 1997).

SCHUMPETER, JOSEPH A. 1934. *The Theory of Economic Development*. Cambridge, MA: Harvard University Press, 1934.

SHARPE, WILLIAM F. "Capital Asset Prices: A Theory of Market Equilibrium Under Conditions of Risk." *Journal of Finance* 19 (September 1964): 425–442.

TIMMONS, JEFFREY A. *New Venture Creation*. 5th ed. Chicago: Irwin-McGraw-Hill, 1999.

VON MISES, LUDWIG. *Human Action*. 3rd rev. ed. Chicago: Henry Regnery Co., 1966.

An Overview of New Venture Financing

Money is the seed of money, and the first guinea is sometimes more difficult to acquire than the second million. (Jean Jacques Rousseau)

Learning Objectives

After reading this chapter you should:

- Be able to recognize and use terminology commonly adopted by participants in the market for new venture financing.
- Understand some of the considerations that influence the choice of organizational form of the venture.
- Understand the value of tying new venture financing to milestones that mark the progress of the venture.
- Recognize the distinguishing characteristics of the various stages of new venture development.
- Be able to identify the financing sources available to a new venture and understand some of the factors that tend to favor one source over another.
- Recognize the basic attributes of the various financing sources and when each source is likely to be available.
- Be able to identify the key elements of deal structure and the basic functions they serve.

Economic history abounds with examples of entrepreneurs who develop ingenious ideas that transform markets and societies. The printing press, automobile, microchip, satellites, and recombinant DNA are just a few of the inventions that have changed the course of history. But how are these great ideas and inventions financed and brought to market? In this chapter, we introduce the taxonomy of new venture development and provide an overview of the new venture financing sources. We also outline the elements of the financial relationship between the entrepreneur and an outside investor.

The choice of financing method is pivotal to whether an idea or product reaches the market quickly and successfully. Financing decisions during the early stages of new venture development also dramatically affect the value the entrepreneur derives from the endeavor. It takes skill and creativity to raise cash for a venture that has a limited history and an uncertain future, and to do so on terms that benefit the entrepreneur.

2.1 THE ROCKET ANALOGY

Practitioners often draw an analogy between undertaking a venture and launching a rocket. They refer to "launching" a venture in the same way that they would to launching a rocket. Just as with complex rockets, the venture proceeds in "stages." Each stage offers the opportunity to terminate or make minor mid-course corrections. Because most new ventures do not generate sufficient cash to cover operating costs or provide for future growth, they must be "fueled" by an initial supply of cash. The normal intent is to fuel the venture with enough cash at each "stage" of development so that it is able to reach the next stage. At that point, it is hoped the venture will be able to raise additional cash on terms that are more favorable. Continuing the rocket analogy, the rate at which cash is consumed during one stage often is referred to as the venture's "burn rate," which normally is computed monthly.

The rocket analogy is not perfect. When a rocket is launched it carries all of its stages, and there is sufficient fuel in each to advance it to the next. A new venture, in contrast, does not raise all of the necessary capital up-front. Rather, there are stations along the way where the venture expects to refuel. By raising capital in stages, the entrepreneur can potentially own a larger share of the venture at the end. Imagine how much smaller a rocket could be if there were a series of space stations along the way where the rocket could take on additional fuel.

Another difference between rockets and new ventures concerns the specificity of the objective. When a rocket is launched, the objective is clear and does not change. Mid-course corrections occur only because the rocket has strayed off course. In contrast, with a new venture, a mid-course change of direction can result from a changed objective. At the time of the launch, the objective cannot be as clearly defined. Over time, as the backers of the venture learn more about the market and the potential success of their efforts, it may become apparent that a change of direction would lead to higher value.

External Financing and the Bell Telephone Company

Ingenuity of financing is often key to new venture success. Consider, for example, the invention of the telephone by Alexander Graham Bell.

Bell did not have an easy start. Almost from the beginning he relied on outside financing to bring his ideas to market. Two angel investors, attorney Gardiner Green Hubbard and leather merchant Thomas Sanders, helped to underwrite early experiments on the telephone. Even after Bell was successful in inventing the telephone, he spent several years in litigation defending his patent.

Bell Telephone Co. had its start in 1877 with the objective of mass-producing telephones. The marketing and financing issues facing the company were difficult. At the time of the founding, there was no ready demand for telephones. A telephone is only helpful if someone answers on the other end. For the company to protect its strategic advantage and benefit from mass-producing telephones, a broad network of telephone lines had to be built quickly.

The financing problem was solved with the advice of Hubbard, the financial manager qua angel investor of Bell Telephone.* Hubbard proposed that the company sell franchises to local telephone service providers, who would be responsible for developing the network of telephone lines. Franchising allowed telephone technology to spread rapidly and networks to be developed. The royalties were used to finance manufacturing of the telephones and the subsequent acquisition of Western Electric Company, a manufacturer of communications equipment.

Not until Bell expanded into long-distance service did the company become entrenched as the dominant producer and service provider in the market. Bell Co. organized around its long-distance subsidiary, American Telephone & Telegraph, and entered into an alliance with a syndicate of bankers who provided funds for growth. Except for a small shareholding, Alexander Graham Bell, the entrepreneur, was out of the picture completely by 1881, four years after the company was formed.

---

*Hubbard's assumption of the role of financial manager is an early example of the active involvement of an angel investor in the operations of the venture, a pattern that is common in the current market.

Sources: Charles R. Geisst, *Wall Street, A History* (New York: Cambridge University Press, 1997); Susan Rosegrant and David R. Lampe, *Route 128: Lessons from Boston's High Tech Community* (New York: Basic Books, 1992).

2.2 CHOOSING THE ORGANIZATIONAL FORM

One of the earliest decisions an entrepreneur must make concerns the organizational form of the venture. The choice has important implications for a variety of factors, including taxes, liability, succession, and ability to attract financing and employees. Figure 2-1 identifies some of the more common organizational forms in the U.S.

The choice of organizational form can be addressed most effectively by using criteria such as those in Figure 2-1 to exclude alternatives. You might, for example, begin with the question of whether or not the venture is intended to generate profits for investors. The organizational forms listed in the figure are all for-profit forms. However, many economic enterprises, such as churches, foundations, and many universities, are not intended to be profit-making ventures.

Common Organizational Forms in the U.S.

Organizational Form	Ownership Rules	Tax Treatment	Liability	Transferability of Ownership	Financial Capacity
Sole proprietorship	A single owner	Earnings pass through to owner	Owner is liable for business debts.	Only through sale of the business	Limited by financial capacity of owner.
Partnership	Two or more co-owners	Earnings pass through, flexibility concerning allocation of gains and losses.	Each partner is fully liable for business debts.	Partnership interests may be transferable through sale, subject to approval of other partners.	Limited by combined financial capacity of the partners. Partners may disagree about borrowing to support the venture.
Limited-liability partnership	Two or more co-owners	Earnings pass through, flexibility concerning allocation of gains and losses.	Liability of partners is limited to the extent of their investments.	Partnership interests may be transferable through sale, subject to approval of other partners.	Limited by combined financial capacity of the partners. Partners may disagree about borrowing to support the venture.
Limited partnership	General partner(s) with control and limited partners who are passive investors	Earnings pass through, flexibility concerning allocation of gains and losses.	Each general partner is fully liable for business debts. Limited partners are liable to the extent of their investments.	Partnership interests may be transferable through sale, subject to approval of other partners.	Limited by combined financial capacity of the partners. Limited partners may have substantial financial capacity.
S corporation	Up to 75 share-holders, one class of stock	Earnings pass through to owners	Liability of shareholders is limited to the extent of their investments.	Shares are transferable without approval of other investors as long as guidelines and SEC rules are adhered to.	Limited by constraint on maximum number of shareholders
C corporation	Unlimited numbers of shareholders and classes of stock	Taxable to the corporation when earned and to shareholder when realized.	Liability of shareholders is limited to the extent of their investments.	Shares are transferable without approval of other investors as long as guidelines and SEC rules are adhered to. Registered shares of public corporations are freely transferable	Unlimited, since number of investors is not limited.

Figure 2-1 Common organizational forms in the U.S.

The distinction between for-profit and not-for-profit enterprises often is not very clear. Currently, for-profit and not-for-profit universities compete for students, and for-profit and not-for-profit medical care providers compete for patients. Entities occasionally convert from not-for-profit to for-profit status, or not-for-profit entities are acquired by for-profit entities. Factors that bear on the choice are complex. They relate to the ability to attract funding from particular sources, or by methods such as tax-deductible donations. Not-for-profit entities can accumulate wealth tax-free. Converting to for-profit status may enable owners to withdraw capital while avoiding substantial tax liability.

Assuming a venture is to be operated for profit, the next question could relate to long-run capital needs. C corporations and limited partnerships can raise very large amounts of money from passive investors. The other forms all restrict capital-raising ability by effectively limiting the number of investors or limiting investment to parties who are actively involved. The important distinctions between a C corporation and a limited partnership relate to transferability of ownership and tax treatment of earnings. A C corporation, particularly if it is public, can most easily raise capital from diverse groups of investors, and facilitates transfer of ownership. A public corporation has the additional benefit of an established and verifiable market value for its shares. Such shares can serve as the currency in a variety of business transactions. Limited partnership interests are less easily transferable. However, limited partnership avoids taxation of earnings at the corporate level and facilitates structures that allocate taxable gains and losses most effectively to partners. Both forms offer limited liability to investors who are not actively involved in management. Limited liability is essential to large-scale fund-raising from investors who do not wish to be actively involved.

If raising large amounts of capital is not important, a venture may be organized as a partnership. Doing so subjects the partners to unlimited liability but enables earnings to flow through to the partners untaxed at the level of the venture. Sometimes the number of partners can become so large and the activities so diffuse that the pure partnership form is an impediment to growth. In that case, a limited liability partnership can preserve the tax advantages and still offer some protection against liability. As a practical matter, the protection from liability can break down if partners act negligently in monitoring the activities of the venture.

An S corporation affords the tax advantages of partnership, while, at the same time, facilitating a limited amount of capital-raising from a small number of passive investors, owing to their limited-liability status.

The list in Figure 2-1 is, by no means exhaustive. A professional corporation, for example, is similar to a limited liability partnership in terms of its effect on investor liability but is somewhat different with respect to ownership transferability and taxation. A cooperative works much like a partnership to share the costs of a common activity. Cooperatives are not-for-profit entities but often are intended to enhance the profits of participants in the cooperative. C&H Sugar, for example, is a cooperative organized for marketing sugar. Its members are sugar refiners. A joint venture is like a partnership, where the participants team up to carry out a specific narrow activity, often for a finite period of time or with a specific objective.

The choice of organizational form is of strategic importance to a new venture. Sole proprietorships and small partnerships often are easy to convert to other forms, but as the venture grows and more parties become involved, the ability to transition from one form to another decreases. Thus, it is important to select organizational form in light of overall strategic orientation.

2.3   INFORMATION PROBLEMS FACING THE ENTREPRENEUR AND INVESTORS

Three basic information problems characterize the market for financing new ventures. First, the entrepreneur's information about the value of the opportunity may be incomplete and uncertain. Second, information about the value of the idea and the ability of the entrepreneur is held asymmetrically: The entrepreneur may have more accurate information about the idea's technological merit, whereas outside investors may have superior information about economic value. The entrepreneur probably knows more about his or her own abilities, managerial skills, and commitment than does an outsider. Asymmetry of information leads to the third problem—risk of appropriation of intellectual property. How can an entrepreneur convince prospective investors of the merits of the project without risking appropriation? An untried entrepreneur cannot merely assert the existence of a valuable idea and expect to be believed. But disclosing the idea opens the entrepreneur to the risk of appropriation.

These problems give rise to some unique features in the market for entrepreneurial finance. First, since information is highly uncertain and asymmetrically held, outside investors want to see tangible evidence that both reduces uncertainty about the market potential and reveals the entrepreneur's abilities. The demand for better information gives rise to the institution of milestones. Milestones are specific and verifiable performance benchmarks. Examples include completion of clinical tests, production of a prototype, and initiation of sales.

The second feature, closely related to milestones, is staging of financing. When entrepreneurs receive commitments of funds, the funds are not normally invested up-front. Rather, they are staged and linked to achieving milestones. Financing one stage does not commit an investor to finance additional stages. Indeed, the source of financing often is different at each stage. Thus, staging reflects the common-sense idea of "wait and see."

Reliance on staging tied to milestones may appear to serve only the interest of the outside investors, since many nascent entrepreneurs seek as much cash up-front as possible. But this perception is wrong. With the right investment partner and a good project, staging is in the interest of the entrepreneur. Investor concerns about the project and about the entrepreneur make early investment capital expensive, for a large fraction of ownership must be exchanged for a small amount of investment capital. The entrepreneur's willingness to predicate outside investment on attainment of milestones makes it much more likely that the entrepreneur can attract investment in the first place, and that the entrepreneur can retain significant ownership.

Staging can benefit both parties even if the venture fails. Once it becomes apparent that failure is likely, both parties are positioned to make clean breaks and to stop investing time and capital in the venture. Conditioning investment on objective measures of performance identifies the decision points of when to renegotiate the financing or withdraw from the venture. Without milestones, the entrepreneur (and outside investors) may erroneously believe things are progressing well and, rather than exiting and finding a better opportunity, may overinvest.

The third information problem is the entrepreneur's concern appropriation of intellectual property. Entrepreneurs often seek assurances that their ideas are secure with those to whom they are presented. The frequent practice of asking investors to sign confidentiality agreements, as a condition of receiving a copy of the entrepreneur's business plan, is a highly imperfect solution. Also, many venture capitalists and business angels refuse to sign these agreements because if the information leaks from any source, there may be messy legal implications.[1] The reputation of the outside investor for trustworthiness is far more important to the entrepreneur than is a signature on a confidentiality agreement.

2.4 MEASURING PROGRESS WITH MILESTONES

Rather than thinking of staging in terms of intervals such as months or years, orienting around milestones is more useful. Although it is possible, even at an early stage, to forecast free cash flows (i.e., cash flows that are available to investors) and to discount them to NPV, uncertainty is extremely high. As a result, raising capital at a very early stage is difficult. Reliance on milestones enables the parties to postpone financial commitments until they are needed, and to base infusions on the levels of risk and expected return that exist at the time of investment.

Each milestone also functions as a working hypothesis about the venture. Understanding the reasons for failing to meet a milestone is important. Suppose, for example, an entrepreneur believes or "hypothesizes" that a prototype of the idea can be completed in six months. If, instead, prototype completion takes nine months, the delay is an indication that some aspects of the venture need to be reexamined. There are several reasons why a milestone may not be met. Perhaps the entrepreneur underestimated the technical difficulties. Alternatively, the entrepreneur may have mismanaged the project. In either case, milestones enable the entrepreneur and outside investors to sharpen their expectations about ultimate success or failure. Milestones also help identify ways to enhance the expected benefits of the project.

Appropriate milestones differ with circumstances. For some kinds of ventures, the first significant milestone is concept testing. The objective of concept testing is to do enough fieldwork to determine whether a market opportunity exists and whether there is enough upside potential to warrant continued investment. Reaching this milestone helps resolve some of the uncertainty and contributes to convergence of expectations between the entrepreneur and outside investors.

A second milestone might be the completion of a prototype. Normally, a prototype is an early-stage working model of the envisioned product. Completing the prototype forces the entrepreneur to anticipate and encounter a variety of issues related to product development. By doing so, the entrepreneur is likely to gain increased understanding of technological bottlenecks, manufacturing costs, and materials availability. In addition to resolving uncertainties about the product, reaching this milestone may help establish the first-mover advantage of the entrepreneur, so that control over development of the idea is easier to retain. It also provides early tangible evidence of the entrepreneur's managerial ability.

A number of milestones may be appropriate for particular projects. Block and MacMillan (1992) identify ten, including the two we have already discussed. The particular nature of the venture determines which milestones provide the most potential to assess progress and facilitate the venture's development. The nature of the venture also determines the order in which the various milestones are likely to be reached. The key is to select milestones that resolve uncertainty about potential success.

2.5 STAGES OF NEW VENTURE DEVELOPMENT

Although there is no typical "life cycle" for a new venture, firms do go through stages of development. They come into existence. They may undergo stages of rapid growth, slow growth, or stagnation, which parallel many living organisms; and they may fail. But a firm can go through these stages in any order and can go through one or more stages a number of times. A firm can even fail more than once.

With this caveat in mind, Figure 2-2 offers a representation of the stages of new venture development. To avoid overgeneralizing, the figure represents a high-tech, single-product venture for a product that gains rapid market acceptance after it is introduced. The horizontal axis measures time, and the vertical axis is dollars. Time zero represents initiation of sales. The three curves in the figure are sales revenue, net income, and cash flow available to investors. Sales revenue and net income are measured in the conventional ways for a firm that uses accrual-based accounting. Cash flow available to investors is defined in the figure as cash flow from operations after tax and before interest expense, less the net investment in working capital and new investment in fixed assets that is needed to achieve the revenue levels. If cash flow available to investors is negative, the venture must finance the shortfall. If cash flow available to investors is positive, the firm can use the surplus to pay returns to investors, including interest payments on debt, debt redemption, dividends, and share repurchase.

The figure reflects five fundamentally distinct stages of new venture development.[2] During the development stage, the entrepreneur has not yet begun to invest in the infrastructure

Some Possible Milestones for New Venture Planning

Milestones are verifiable achievements that help to resolve uncertainties about the likely success of a venture. The list of appropriate milestones depends on the nature of the venture. The following ten are examples suggested by Zenas Block and Ian MacMillan (1992).

- Completion of Concept and Product Testing. Is there a real market opportunity? What is the market? How should the product be priced, distributed, and so on?
- Completion of a Prototype. Can the product be manufactured? What facilities are needed? How costly is manufacturing? How long does production require?
- First Financing. Can we convince others of the value of the concept and the strength of our team? Can enough money be raised to carry the venture to the next milestone?
- Completion of Initial Plant Tests. What materials are best suited to the product? What training is needed? How reliable is the production process?
- Market Testing. Will customers buy the product? Are the early assumptions about the opportunity still supported? What level of sales can be achieved?
- Production Start-up. Are operations working as expected? How can the manufacturing process be fine-tuned?
- Bellwether Sale. What can be learned from the first important sale about how best to manufacture, distribute, and market the product?
- First Competitive Action. How are competitors reacting? Is the reaction different than anticipated? What should be done to position the venture in light of competitive reaction?
- First Redesign or Redirection. In the event of such a change, has the market responded to the change in the way that was expected? If not, why not?
- First Significant Price Change. How is the change expected to affect sales and profitability? Is there a way to make a small-scale test of the effects before fully implementing a price change?

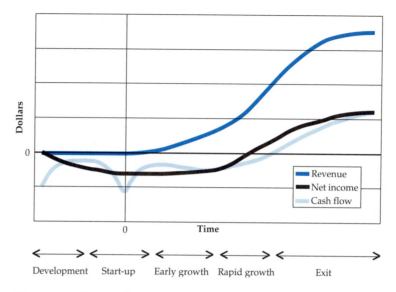

Figure 2-2   Stages of new venture development

The figure reflects five stages that are typical of new venture development. During the development stage, the venture generates no revenues, net income is negative, and cash flow is negative. Start-up begins when the firm acquires the facilities, equipment, and employees required to produce the product. During early growth, revenue is growing, but both net income and cash flow available to investors are negative. Rapid growth is the last stage during which external financing is required. During exit, the rate of growth declines to the point where cash flow available to investors is positive.

needed to initiate production and sale of the product. The venture generates no revenues during this period. Net income is negative and may be increasingly negative, as the number of people involved in product development increases. Cash flow initially is very negative, as the firm invests in the capital equipment needed for development. Under existing accounting conventions, firms must record the depreciation expense of equipment over time. As a result, net income is not as negative as cash flow.

The second stage is start-up. The demarcation between development and start-up is when the firm begins to acquire the facilities, equipment, and employees required to produce the product.[3] The decline in cash flow leading into start-up reflects investment in production equipment, facilities, and net working capital.

Revenue is growing (possibly rapidly) in the third stage. Both net income and cash flow available to investors are negative. Cash flow exceeds net income, essentially because periodic depreciation expenses are larger than the increase of investment in working capital and fixed assets needed to support the growth of revenue. This is referred to as the early growth stage because, although growth may be rapid in percentage terms, the base from which we calculate revenue growth is low. Thus, cash flow available to investors exceeds net income.

There is no clear line of demarcation between the early growth stage and the rapid growth stage. However, many new ventures experience growth in the early stage but fizzle out before they achieve a level of sales that is sufficient to sustain the business. Hence, entrepreneurs can benefit by being tuned in to signs that the venture has reached the rapid growth stage. As shown in the figure, net revenues are increasing at an increasing rate. (The slope of the revenue curve increases.) More importantly, rapid growth puts heavy demands on the entrepreneur to locate the financing needed to sustain the corresponding growth of working capital and fixed assets. The rapid growth stage of the venture is the last one during which external financing is required. During this stage, if the venture is to survive, net income becomes positive, so the venture can benefit immediately from the tax deductibility of interest payments on debt financing.

During exit, the venture's rate of growth declines to the point where cash flow available to investors is positive. The venture is able to provide returns to debt and equity investors without the need to increase outside financing. This is an obvious point for investors to harvest, although earlier harvesting can be accomplished by selling the investment interests to others.

It sometimes is convenient to employ looser terminology than the five stages described here. It is common, for example, to refer to financing during development and start-up as early-stage financing and financing during the growth stages as later-stage financing.

2.6 SEQUENCE OF NEW VENTURE FINANCING

It should be evident that the stages in Figure 2-2 correspond roughly to measurable milestones. A correspondence also exists between the milestones and the opportunities to attract outside financing. At an early stage, the entrepreneur looks for ways to finance the venture from personal savings and borrowing where repayment does not depend on success. Many successful ventures have been bootstrapped with very little financial capital. Bootstrap techniques include, for example, drawing down savings accounts, taking out second mortgages, using the credit lines of multiple credit cards, and borrowing on life insurance policies.

In one sense, bootstrapping is not a form of new venture financing. Rather, the entrepreneur is financing the venture from personal resources. There is no fundamental difference between drawing down personal savings balances to finance the venture, and running up credit card balances for that purpose. A provider of bootstrap financing does not perceive that an investment is being made in the venture. Instead, willingness to lend is based on the credit history and reputation of the entrepreneur or on other assets that can serve as collateral.

Although bootstrapping can work as a short-run financing tactic, it normally cannot be a source of permanent financing. Credit card loans eventually must be repaid, and a growing venture can quickly exhaust the entrepreneur's ability to bootstrap. The more likely scenario is that the entrepreneur must turn to outside financing that is based on the merits of the venture. Depending on the stage of development, outside investors may include family members, friends, business angels, banks, venture capitalists, and a variety of others.

Customary venture financing taxonomy reflects the correspondence between financing choices and development stages.[4] The earliest external financing is known as seed financing. Seed financing consists of relatively small amounts of money to support exploration of a concept. It may cover such things as the cost of assessing the size of a market and preparing the business plan. The principal risk exposures of seed financing are risks of discovery. For example, during this phase the entrepreneur may discover that no significant market exists or that an existing competitor controls essential technology.

For high-technology ventures, seed financing may provide initial funds for research and development. In cases where research and development efforts are expensive and protracted, R&D financing could be required beyond what is typically regarded as seed financing. The critical risk exposure at this point is the risk of unsuccessful development efforts.

Start-up financing covers activities from later research and development to initiation of sales. Generally, start-up financing is provided when a concept appears to be worth pursuing, key members of the team are in place, and most of the risks related to development have been resolved. At this point, actual production has not yet begun, and the main risk exposure is related to whether a cost-effective manufacturing technology can be put in place.

First-stage financing is provided to a company that has initiated production and is generating revenues but normally has not yet achieved profitability. Development activities are completed to the point where the firm has a marketable product, but substantial uncertainty remains as to achievable sales and profitability. The critical element of risk at this point is marketing risk, the question of whether the venture can reach a level of sales sufficient to attract and compensate investors.

Second-stage financing supports continuing growth of a venture that is operating around the breakeven point of profitability. Operating cash flows may also be near breakeven, but because of rapid growth, the venture is still a consumer of cash. The operations of the venture are not generating sufficient cash flow to support planned expansion. Uncertainty remains about ultimate market potential and profitability. As the venture grows, competitive reactions and the ability of managers to position the venture gain increasing importance.

In practice, a venture may go through even more stages of growth financing. Third-stage financing is fairly common, and even fourth stage is not unusual. The limiting factors on the number of times the venture can "go to the well" are practicality and the desire of the investor to maintain a close monitoring relationship. The downside of increasing the number of stages, particularly if the investments are being made by a venture capitalist or someone else with fiduciary responsibility, is that each unplanned-for round of financing reduces the ownership share of the entrepreneur and every stage requires a valuation. One venture we know of went through 16 stages of venture capital-backed financing, with a valuation at each stage.

Mezzanine financing (frequently, debt financing) is used to support major expansion of a profitable business. Because of continuing market uncertainty and the possible actions of competitors, the debt typically is high-risk. Bridge financing is temporary financing, particularly between later-stage financing rounds and harvesting. It usually can be arranged quickly, and allows the firm time to arrange permanent financing, possibly in the public market. Another use of bridge financing is to facilitate a leveraged buyout (LBO) or a management buyout (MBO) of the business. At this point, the venture is at the exit stage, where the founders and other investors will attempt to "harvest" their investments. Harvesting techniques include taking the company public with an initial public offering (IPO), or arranging for a buyout.

2.7   SOURCES OF NEW VENTURE FINANCING

A menu of likely new venture financing sources appears in Figure 2-3. The suitability of the various alternatives changes as the firm matures.

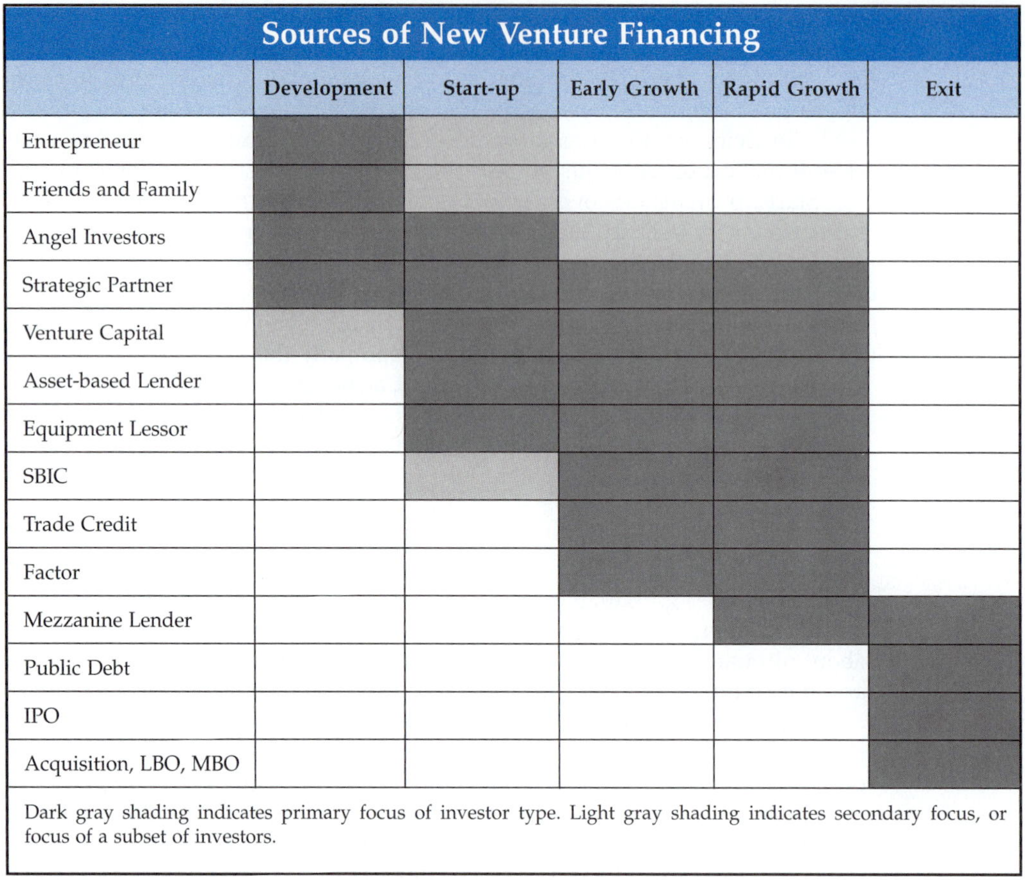

Sources of New Venture Financing					
	Development	Start-up	Early Growth	Rapid Growth	Exit
Entrepreneur	■	□			
Friends and Family	■	□			
Angel Investors	■	■	■	□	
Strategic Partner	■	■	■	■	
Venture Capital	□	■	■	■	
Asset-based Lender		■	■	■	
Equipment Lessor		■	■	■	
SBIC		□	■	■	
Trade Credit			■	■	
Factor			■	■	
Mezzanine Lender				■	■
Public Debt					■
IPO					■
Acquisition, LBO, MBO					■

Dark gray shading indicates primary focus of investor type. Light gray shading indicates secondary focus, or focus of a subset of investors.

Figure 2-3 Sources of new venture financing

Self, Friends, and Family

The obvious starting point for the entrepreneur is to use personal resources to advance the project to a point where third-party financing is feasible. The entrepreneur's resources include not only personal savings and assets, but also debt capacity. The relevant measure of debt capacity is one based on the entrepreneur's earnings in existing employment plus the market value of assets that can be liquidated to service the debt. Stories of entrepreneurs whose earliest financing was achieved by "maxing out" credit card borrowing and by taking out second mortgages on their homes are not uncommon. Because these sources do not depend on project value, personal debt capacity gives the entrepreneur access to a limited amount of outside capital without the risk of losing control.

Family members and friends have one important advantage relative to conventional financiers. Family and friends have years of experience with the entrepreneur and most likely have a sense of the entrepreneur's reliability, trustworthiness, and ability to handle adversity.

There are no precise data available on the extent to which personal finances of the entrepreneur, family, and friends are employed in the new venture process. Yet, numerous ventures are legendary for their success in spite of getting started with bootstrap financing. Steve Jobs and his partner, Steve Wozniak, sold a Volkswagen and a programmable calculator to raise $1350 to build the first Apple PC in a garage. Bill Gates tells of his start when he and his partner, Paul Allen, started their venture from Gates's dorm room at Harvard in 1975 and later relocated to a hotel room in Albuquerque, New Mexico.[5] They funded the start-up from savings and took a shoestring operation to a company with 47,600 employees and more than $28 billion in sales. On the other hand, there are many more ventures that began by bootstrapping but failed miserably. Some undoubtedly were based on good ideas but were underfinanced.

Angel Financing

For ventures based on concepts that require lengthy development efforts, the earliest source of outside financing often is informal and is provided by high-net-worth individuals rather than organized financial institutions. The so-called angels, or business angels, generally are free-lancers interested in investing relatively small amounts of money, $25,000 to $500,000, in early-stage projects.[6]

Angel investors often provide seed capital to develop an idea to the point where formal outside financing becomes feasible. Investors at this stage generally accept investment horizons of 5 to 10 years. They seek to add value by identifying ventures with high potential for success and helping them progress. Angel investors usually hope to realize a return by taking equity in the venture. The most common exit for angel investors in a successful firm is sale of the firm to another company or sale of equity to the public following an IPO. Most estimates put the amount of angel capital invested in recent years in the United States at about $10–20 billion annually, exclusive of money from friends and family.[7]

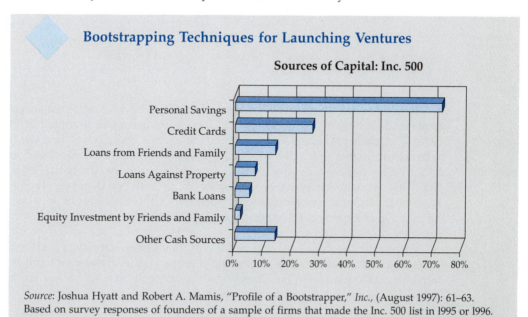

Bootstrapping Techniques for Launching Ventures

Sources of Capital: Inc. 500

Source: Joshua Hyatt and Robert A. Mamis, "Profile of a Bootstrapper," *Inc.*, (August 1997): 61–63. Based on survey responses of founders of a sample of firms that made the Inc. 500 list in 1995 or 1996.

Note: Percentages add to more than 100 percent because respondents may indicate more than one source.

(Continues)

(Continued)

Other legendary examples of bootstrapping include:

- Lillian Vernon. She started her mail-order company in 1951 with $2,000 in cash that she and her husband had received as wedding gifts. For $495 she purchased a partial-page ad for monogrammed leather handbags in *Seventeen Magazine.* The ad generated $32,000 in orders by the end of the year. In 2002, her company had 1,400 employees and posted sales of $260 million. Lillian Vernon publishes eight catalogues, with mail distribution of more than 162 million.

- Paychex, Inc. Founder Tom Golisano bootstrapped expansion of this small-business service provider through joint ventures and franchise agreements. In 2002, the business had 125 locations, with 7,400 employees and annual sales of $955 million. Paychex was founded in 1971 and went public in 1983.

- Black and Decker. The company was started for $1,200 in 1910. Early products included a milk bottle cap machine, a vest-pocket adding machine, and a candy dipping machine. In 1916, the company invested in the first portable electric drill. Company sales in 2001 were $4.3 billion, with 22,700 employees. Black and Decker ranks 377 in the Fortune 500.

- Hewlett-Packard Co. Bill Hewlett and Dave Packard began working together in a garage with an initial investment of $538. Their first product was an improvement on existing oscillator technology, and their first customer helped generate the cash to spur growth. The customer, Walt Disney, purchased eight of the oscillators for use in producing *Fantasia,* which was released in 1940. By 2001, before its acquisition of Compaq, Hewlett-Packard had 86,200 employees and revenues of $45.2 billion. The company ranked 28 in the Fortune 500.

Source: Compiled from Hofman, "Desperation Capitalism: A Bootstrappers' Hall of Fame," *Inc.,* August 1997, and Hoover's Online database, *http://www.hoovers.com/.*

In many cases, angel investors are individuals who have achieved success as entrepreneurs and are seeking to build on that success by becoming involved in other new ventures. The market for angel financing tends to operate casually, on the basis of contacts and referrals. Investors generally specialize in technologies they understand and in projects located close to home. Because of their varied backgrounds, the nature of angel participation varies widely. Some angels participate in less than one deal per year, on average; others participate in four or more. Many work solo. Others are part of angel networks.[8] Since many have entrepreneurial experience, they can be good sources of information concerning financing and strategy.

Angel investors have been around for centuries. Queen Isabella backed the Columbus ventures. Two Boston-area angels backed the inventions of Alexander Graham Bell in 1874 and later put up money to start Bell Telephone.[9] Laurence Rockefeller backed Eddie Rickenbacker and the development of Eastern Airlines in the 1930s.

Venture Capital Investors

For financing requirements beyond seed capital, the entrepreneur can turn to organized providers of venture capital. Most venture capital firms invest on behalf of venture capital funds. A fund is

International Patterns of New Venture Financing

While the U.S. is, by far, the largest market for new venture financing, venture capital and business angel investing is spreading throughout the world. The figure below shows estimates of the dollar amounts of formal domestic venture capital and informal business angel financing in a number of countries. The data in the figure are developed from two separate studies of different but overlapping sets of countries. Thus, for example, Belgium was included in the estimates of venture capital financing but not in estimates of business angel financing, whereas Argentina was included in estimates of business angel financing but not in estimates of venture capital financing. Overall, the data suggest that angel financing activity is higher than formal venture capital financing. Developed countries tend to have higher levels of venture capital financing. Variations in venture capital financing levels depend on whether enabling infrastructure exists to foster the organization of formal venture capital funds and to provide financing to the funds, such as presence of pension funds that can invest in non-public equity, established public capital markets, and tax structures that allow pass-through of earnings. Such infrastructure is more prevalent in developed economies than among emerging economies. Emerging economies like Argentina and Mexico are more heavily dependent on business angel financing, often provided through family relationships.

Whereas the established economies show significant levels of venture capital investment, the nature of the investment varies greatly across countries. In some cases, banks predominate venture capital investment and the funds target later-stage ventures that are generating cash flow or where the entrepreneur can demonstrate a means of repayment, even if the venture is not successful.

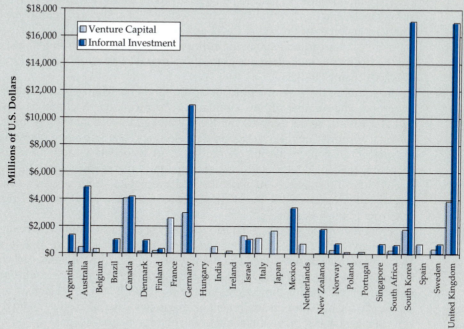

Source: Global Entrepreneurship Monitor 2001 Summary Report, Reynolds, Camp, Bygrave, Autio, and Hay (London Business School and Babson College), 2002.

a portfolio of investments in several entrepreneurial ventures. Each fund is organized as a limited partnership. In a venture capital limited partnership, the venture capitalist is the general partner and controls the fund's activities. The venture capital firm normally has expertise in identifying and nurturing promising new ventures. Investors in the fund are the limited partners. Investors monitor the fund's progress and attend annual meetings but cannot be involved in the fund's day-to-day operations if they are to retain limited liability and passive investor status. In contrast, the general partner is involved, at a strategic level, in the operations of the portfolio companies. Venture capital funds have predetermined, finite lifetimes (usually 10 years, with extensions often allowed). The larger venture capital firms establish new funds every two to five years.

Because of the limited life of the venture capital fund, the responsibilities of the general partner change over time. When a new fund is organized, the limited partners make commitments of the amount of capital they are willing to provide and the general partner actively seeks investment opportunities. The financial commitments of the limited partners are drawn down by the venture capitalist over the first few years. This approach, of drawing down commitments over time and providing financing in stages, facilitates the financing of new ventures as they are identified. It also provides additional staged financing to ventures that have received earlier support from the fund. Then follows a period when the primary activity of the venture capitalist is to monitor the progress of ventures in the portfolio and to assist with management transitions and other activities that contribute to success. Later, the focus of the general partner turns to harvesting. Venture capital funds target investments that they hope can be harvested within three to seven years. Ideally, during that period a portfolio company will reach a sufficient level of development so that its shares of stock can be sold in an initial public offering or an established company can acquire the venture.

The limited partners tend to be large diversified investors such as insurance companies, endowments, and pension funds. Figure 2-4 shows the sources of venture capital commitments from various types of limited partners and compares those sources in the current market versus two decades earlier. As shown, institutions such as pension funds, insurance companies, and endowments contributed significantly more to venture capital funds in the period 1997–2001 than 1979–1983.

In addition, the investment focus of the funds has changed. As venture capital funding has grown, the number of new company investments has declined as a percentage of total capital invested. Venture capital funds have moved toward later-stage investments. Based on National Venture Capital Association data, seed and start-up stage investment declined from 19.4 percent of venture capital commitments in 1980-1984 to only 4.4 percent in 1997–2001. Offsetting this shift, later stage investments and leveraged buyouts have grown in importance. More information on particular venture capital funds, average size of investment, investment criteria (stages financed), portfolio companies, and industry preferences is available from published sources.[10]

From the entrepreneur's perspective, a number of factors aid in determining whether venture capital is appropriate and which venture capital firm to select. First, timing is important. The venture must be developed to a point where the venture capitalist can expect to add value. Whereas the limited partners contribute capital, the general partner contributes expertise. Venture capitalists monitor the progress of firms, sit on boards of directors, and mete out infusions of financing based on attainment of milestones. They also often retain the right to appoint key managers and remove members of the entrepreneurial team.

Second, the venture must be in an industry about which the venture capitalist has expertise. Figure 2-5 shows the industries in which venture capital funds typically invest. Although

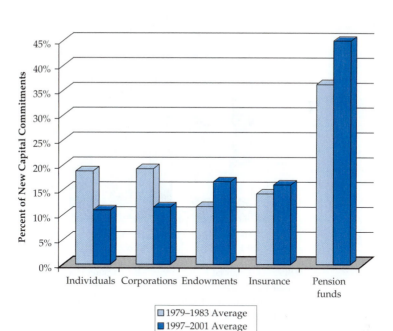

Source: National Venture Capital Association 2002 Yearbook, Thompson Financial
Venture Economics, 2002.

Figure 2-4   Venture capital commitments by limited partner type

the majority of investments are in high-technology fields, investments occasionally are made in low-tech industries such as healthcare, consumer products, and retailing.

Third, for the same reason that venture capital firms tend to focus investments on industries where their expertise is most valuable, they also tend to concentrate in particular geographic areas. The information in Figure 2-6 provides an indication of the geographic concentration. As shown, large fractions of venture capital investments are made in two geographic regions—the Boston area and Silicon Valley in northern California. Geographic concentration has changed little over time despite the efforts of many regions to foster entrepreneurial activity.

Fourth, the investment horizon and investment objectives of venture capital funds make some projects better suited than others. Venture capital funds seek equity or equity-like returns, and the finite life of the fund constrains the investment horizon. As a result, venture capital investors are interested in projects that do not generate much cash flow early on but offer the potential for very rapid growth over a period of a few years. Hence, venture capitalists are not likely to take interest in projects that generate positive cash flows quickly, yet have limited growth potential, or those that are likely to be harvested outside of a three-to-eight year window.

There is little to be gained by seeking funding from a venture capital firm that does not have a geographic presence in the area. The same is true for one that does not have expertise

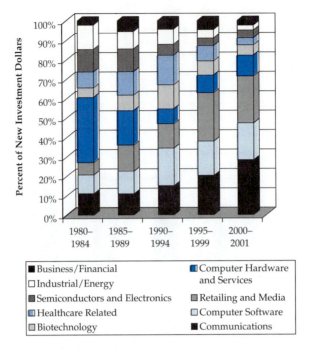

Figure 2-5   Venture capital investments by industry

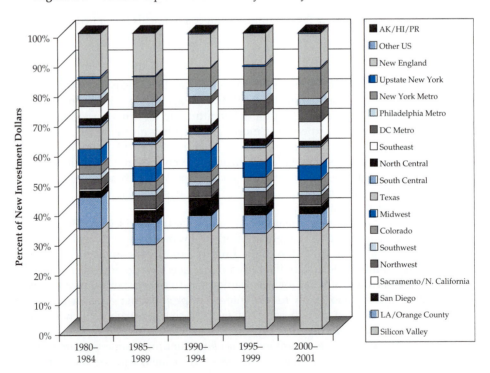

Figure 2-6   Venture capital investments by region

in the entrepreneur's industry, or one that is specialized in a stage of development that is different from that of the venture, or one that is not actively searching for new investments at the time.

Corporate Venturing

Corporations provide financing to new ventures in various ways. In addition to their own internally-managed projects, some corporations operate and provide financing to proprietary venture capital funds that invest in companies that are external to the corporation. In some cases, the fund acts like other venture capital funds, seeking investment opportunities with financial return as the sole objective. In other cases, the fund is a vehicle for advancing the corporation's product-market strategy and selects investments on the basis of how the ventures relate to the corporation's core business.[11] In addition, corporations sometimes invest directly in independent ventures, acting as strategic partners.

Small Business Investment Companies

As an enterprise matures, the entrepreneur is able to attract financing that increasingly has the characteristics of debt. For a number of years the federal government, through the Small Business Administration (SBA), has sought to stimulate formation and development of new ventures by providing a financing subsidy on financing. Most of the financing is provided through Small Business Investment Companies (SBICs). SBIC financing usually takes the form of interest-bearing loans that are guaranteed by the SBA. Recently, however, the program has broadened to enable financing that has much more of an equity quality. In 2000, approximately $12.1 billion in new loans were guaranteed or made directly by the SBA.[12] SBICs have invested in such winners as Federal Express, Cray Research, and Teledyne.

SBICs are privately owned and managed, for-profit organizations that are licensed by the SBA. With their own capital (raised from private sources including banks, corporations, individuals, and others) and with funds borrowed at favorable rates through the federal government, SBICs provide capital to new and established small businesses. Because of government support, the capital that the SBICs invest is obtained at below-market rates of interest. An SBIC therefore can pass along some of these savings to entrepreneurs wishing to borrow.[13] Although SBICs are involved in financing at about the same stages as venture capitalists, the normal interest-bearing structure of the financing makes it better suited for firms with more limited growth potential and the ability to achieve profitable operations quickly.

Small Business Innovation Research Program

If the venture involves technology, several government agencies sponsor grants under the auspices of the SBIR program (Small Business Innovation Research). Participants include the departments of Agriculture, Commerce, Defense, Education, Energy, Health and Human Services, NASA, and the National Science Foundation. SBIR Plan I research grants provide seed capital and funding up to $50,000 to determine the feasibility of a project. Plan II grants go up to $500,000 of R&D financing to develop specific technologies and products.

Ex-Im Bank

The Export-Import Bank of the United States helps export companies through the Working Capital Guarantee Program. The Ex-Im Bank makes working capital guarantees to small and medium-sized companies. Although providers of financing buy or use receivables to secure loans, the Ex-Im Bank takes one step back and finances the purchase orders of the firm. In effect, the program allows these firms to finance the cost of goods sold. The Bank issues a guarantee to the bank that makes the loan. If the company fails, the Ex-Im Bank pays the lender 90 percent of the principal.

Trade Credit

Trade credit is the largest source of external short-term financing for firms in the United States.[14] Such financing arises whenever a business makes a purchase from a supplier that offers trade credit. For example, if a venture buys supplies on terms of "net 30," that means that the venture receives the supplies right away but does not need to pay for them for 30 days. In effect, the venture receives a zero interest loan for 30 days; after 30 days the bill is past due. Whenever a firm buys on credit, it receives financing for some time period depending on the terms of the trade credit offer. On the other hand, whenever a firm extends trade credit, it generates an account receivable. The difference between accounts receivable and accounts payable is net trade credit. Net trade credit defines the position of the firm in terms of whether trade credit functions as a source or a use of financing.

Trade credit can be very expensive. For example, 2/10 net 30 are common terms that offer the buyer a 2 percent discount if the invoice is paid within 10 days; otherwise the full payment is due in 30 days. If the buying firm decides to take the credit and forego the 2 percent discount, there is a sizable opportunity cost. In effect, the firm borrows the invoiced amount for 20 days. The implicit interest rate on such a loan is 44 percent per annum.[15] Obviously, managers of any new venture must consider this opportunity cost in making a decision of whether to use the credit or take the discount. If bank loans are not available, or only available at a higher interest rate, foregoing the discount may make sense.

Entrepreneurs managing new ventures may not have much discretion over the ability to make use of trade credit. Credit terms and availability are determined by competition and tend to be uniform in a given industry. A venture that is competing against established firms may find that it must offer credit to its customers to get them to try the product, whereas its suppliers may insist on receiving cash until the venture has proven itself.

Factoring

When a business offers trade credit, it generates accounts receivable. In lieu of borrowing to finance the receivables, the venture may be able to "sell" the accounts receivable to a factor— a specialist who buys accounts receivable and manages credit collection. Factoring comes in two basic types: with and without recourse. If factoring is without recourse and a customer does not pay its bill, the factor absorbs the loss. Factoring with recourse means that if the customer does not pay on time, the factor has "recourse" to the seller and can collect from the seller directly. Most factoring is done with notification, so the customer knows that the seller has sold its receivables. Usually, this means the customer is instructed to pay its bill directly to the factor. Factors that provide collection, insurance, and finance are known as "old-line" factors. The factor typically advances 75 to 90 percent of the face value of receivables. When the full amount is collected, the factor remits back to the company the remaining 10 to 25 percent, less fees. For most companies the fee is around 1.5 percent of the amount financed. There also is an interest charge on the amount financed. Although the fee may seem high, in practice it is a competitive price and may be attractive to a cash-poor new venture until it grows to the size that makes integrating the collections function more economical.

Asset-based Lenders

Asset-based lenders, or "secured lenders," provide debt capital to businesses that have accumulated assets that can serve as collateral. The lender is not relying on the cash flow stream of the business for repayment. Instead, the lender relies on the ability to liquidate business assets, if necessary, for debt servicing. Loans may be secured by accounts receivable, inventory, equipment (depending on liquidation value), and other assets with verifiable market values.

Mezzanine Capital

Mezzanine financing usually refers to capital raised after the firm has established a record of positive net income, with revenues approaching $10 million or more. This type of financing generally is a hybrid that has characteristics of senior debt and common equity. A common type of mezzanine financing is subordinated debt with an equity "sweetener" of warrants. A warrant is a long-term call option that is issued by a firm. Warrants entitle the holder to buy shares of the firm's common stock at a stated price for cash. For example, each $1,000 bond might have 20 stock purchase warrants attached that permit the purchase of shares at $5 each. Such bonds often are callable in order to give the issuing firm the ability to replace them with other debt on more favorable terms. The call feature may be important since mezzanine financing typically is high-risk and therefore can be expensive. Many venture capital firms are involved in mezzanine financing, as well as early stage equity financing.

Private Placements

A private placement is a sale of equity or debt securities to a small number of investors (angel investors, venture capital firms, and others) by means other than public issue. One advantage is that the venture avoids the complex, ongoing reporting that is required under the SEC Acts if it were to raise capital via public offering. In addition, an entrepreneur can use private placement to limit the number of people who gain access to information about the venture.

Sometimes, a firm would like to raise a specific amount of capital quickly and would prefer to avoid the cost and time required to complete a public offering. This can be accomplished by a private placement of debt or equity. Prospective equity investors or lenders are identified by the company's management team, by the venture capitalist, or by an investment banker who is working in the capacity of an advisor to the venture. The private placement market generally is more attractive than the public market for small equity or debt issues, or for debt issues backed by complex security arrangements.

Several types of investors may find a private placement appealing. First, when a venture capitalist invests in a firm in exchange for equity, it is on the receiving end of an equity private placement. Second, stakeholders in the new venture, including distributors, retailers, franchises (if any), suppliers, and so on, are potential investors. Third, insurance companies and pension funds, high-net worth individuals, and foreign investors invest in private equity. Institutional investors like insurance companies and pension funds are candidates for buying debt issues.

Usually the equity is structured in the form of convertible preferred stock. The preferred stock typically converts to common at an IPO. Privately placed debt may have some advantages relative to a public issue. As with equity, the costs of a private placement tend to be lower and the placement quicker. It also is possible to negotiate greater flexibility in the terms than would be possible in a public offering.

A significant advantage of a privately placed issue is that it may permit better monitoring. A public placement normally has a large number of investors. The resulting diffuse ownership structure leads to free riding in terms of investor interest in monitoring the company. In contrast, if a debt or equity issue is placed privately, ownership of the securities is concentrated and there are significant incentives to monitor company management.

IPOs

An initial public offering, commonly known as an IPO, raises capital through federally registered equity shares. As discussed earlier, an IPO is a convenient exit mechanism for venture capitalists and other private placement investors. The importance of venture capital in the IPO market has become clear over the past decade or so. Venture capital-backed firms have accounted for about 30 percent of the number and total market value of all IPO companies. In industries like biotechnology, computers, and software, the fraction of venture capital-backed firms is higher.[16]

The IPO market is volatile. Issuers and underwriters often try to time IPOs to reach the market after periods of substantial marketwide price appreciation. They sometimes withdraw planned IPOs or refrain from issuing after marketwide price declines. As a result, there are "good years" and "bad years" for the IPO market. Figure 2-7 shows the relation between stock market performance and new issue activity measured as the percent change in dollar value of equity issues compared with the previous year. As the figure shows, new issue activity tends to rise in years when the S&P 500 Index has increased and to fall when the value of the Index has declined.[17]

Under what conditions does it make sense to raise capital or harvest an investment via an IPO? Public issue provides a way for early-stage investors to realize the gains on their investments, to achieve liquidity, and to diversify.[18] It also provides a market-determined valuation of the firm that can be used as a basis for negotiating merger and acquisition transactions. In cases where the venture track record is clear, large amounts of capital are needed, and the firm lacks synergies that would favor private sale, an IPO may bring a higher share price than a private placement. Public ownership also provides a way to create equity incentives for employees. Finally, a publicly traded firm is able to raise additional capital more quickly and more cheaply than if it were not public.

On the cost side, an IPO is expensive in terms of time and costs of compliance with SEC regulations and reporting requirements. Scarce managerial time must be diverted from the business and devoted to the IPO process. The presence of a visible stock price may induce management to be unduly concerned with short-term fluctuations in stock price. On the other hand, the stock price is a barometer of market expectations, and can provide useful information on how investors expect economic events and managerial decisions to affect future earnings.

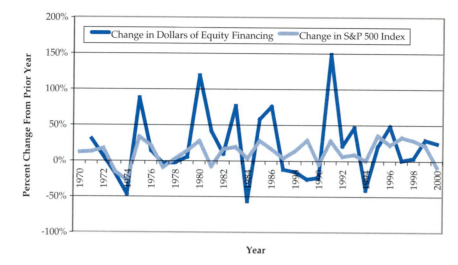

Source: Federal Reserve Bulletin, Daily Stock Price Record: New York Stock Exchange, Statistical Abstract of the United States (various issues).

Figure 2-7   How changes in the stock market relate to new equity capital raising

The figure shows the correspondence between year-to-year changes in the value of the S&P 500 Index and year-to-year changes in the amount of new equity financing by public offering. Increases in public offering activity generally correspond to increases in the value of the S&P 500 Index.

Public Debt

Small firms, and especially new firms, do not have much access to the bond market. Investment banking firms seldom underwrite bond issues smaller than $10 million in gross proceeds and virtually never do so for noninvestment-grade debt. So unless a firm has a substantial asset base and is in need of a significant amount of capital, it is not likely to be able to arrange a bond issue. New ventures are more likely to be successful borrowing from commercial banks, life insurance companies, or the SBA.

Debt financing may make sense for a rapidly growing venture. There are two primary reasons for using debt to finance growth. First, because the interest is tax deductible, debt may be less expensive than equity for a firm that has consistent earnings and limited use of non-debt tax shelters.[19] In contrast, dividends on preferred or common equity are paid from after-tax profits. Second, debtholders usually cannot vote. Therefore, equity owners do not lose voting control if debt is raised. On the other hand, debt is a contractual obligation so that in the event of bankruptcy, bondholders have priority over equity owners.

Later-Stage Financing Alternatives

The list of financing sources could be extended considerably. Other possibilities identified in Figure 2-3 include leveraged buyout (LBO) or management buyout (MBO). There are also alternatives like leasing and franchising that do not fit neatly into a simple hierarchy of financing sources.

These alternatives are addressed later in the text when we turn to the issue of how early-stage investors harvest their investments and when we look in more detail at the choice of new venture financing.

2.8   THE DEAL

A central aspect of an entrepreneur's attempt to raise resources is negotiation of the deal with the owner of the resources.[20] The deal defines the allocation of risk and returns and defines other rights and obligations of the entrepreneur and the outside investor. A well-structured deal has the potential to create value for the entrepreneur and to provide the investor with a return that compensates for the risk.

Because every new venture is different, the arrangements between the entrepreneur and investors defy generalization. Nonetheless, certain elements and documents are common. First, it is common for the parties to reflect their understanding of the agreement in a term sheet. The term sheet reflects an agreed-on valuation, and sets out the amount of the investment that is to be made, as well as the ownership claims the investor receives in exchange for the investment. In addition, the term sheet may identify some of the options, rights, and responsibilities of each party. For example, the investor may have the right to make appointments to the board of directors and, under some conditions, may have the right to withdraw from the project or to terminate the entrepreneur. The entrepreneur may have the right to call on the investor for additional funds in the event that certain milestones are achieved or to acquire additional shares through the exercise of stock options.

The valuation of the venture, though it may not be stated formally in the term sheet, is key to the negotiation. Consider a simple deal where an outside investor contributes $1 million of capital in exchange for 400,000 shares of common stock and where the entrepreneur retains 600,000 shares. Effectively, the investor is acquiring the shares for a price of $2.50 per share. The term post-money valuation refers to the total value of the venture that is implied by multiplying $2.50 by the entire 1 million shares. So, in this case the post-money valuation (sometimes referred to as capitalization) is $2.5 million. Pre-money valuation is the implied value of the venture before the investment. In this case, the pre-money valuation is $1.5 million (i.e., the post-money valuation less the $1 million investment). This sometimes is referred to as an investment in "plain vanilla equity." The post-money valuation is a measure of the value of the venture to the outside investor. The entrepreneur may have different beliefs about value, and those beliefs affect the negotiation, but they do not appear in the term sheet.

When the investor is interested in something other than plain vanilla equity, post-money valuation is not an accurate measure of what the venture is worth. Suppose, in the above example, the investor pays $2.50 per share, but the shares are preferred stock that can be converted to common at a later date. Because the owner of preferred shares has a prior claim to common stockholders (i.e., the entrepreneur) in the event of bankruptcy, the post-money valuation as calculated above overstates value. In fact, the more rights the entrepreneur is willing to surrender to the investor, the more the investor is willing to pay for the shares. The result is a higher "valuation," both post-money and pre-money, but in reality value is not necessarily increased. Rather, it is transferred from the entrepreneur to the investor.

For now, it is important only to recognize that the ultimate concern of the entrepreneur is not the post-money valuation of the venture, but the true value to the entrepreneur of the entrepreneur's ownership interest. Many entrepreneurs make the mistake of focusing on post-money valuation and ignore the value of the "sweeteners" and other rights promised to the investor, that affect the post-money valuation. Accordingly, it does not make sense for the entrepreneur to negotiate pre- or post-money valuation at the same time that ownership rights are negotiated.

Once the parties believe they have reached an understanding on the terms of the investment, the next step is to prepare a formal investment agreement. The investment agreement is a contract between the entrepreneur and the investor. With the term sheet as a starting point, the investment agreement formally sets out the terms and conditions of the investment, including any options, rights, or contingencies retained by either party. In addition, the investment agreement sets out a comprehensive list of representations and warranties of the entrepreneur, as well as a list of covenants and undertakings.

Representations and warranties are intended to protect the investor from the possibility that the entrepreneur has not disclosed some material fact, which would affect valuation or willingness to invest. Obvious examples relate to ownership of the tangible and intangible assets, absence of litigation, and accuracy of the financial statements.

Covenants and undertakings are intended to ensure that the investor's capital is used in the manner envisioned at the time of the agreement. Affirmative covenants are actions the entrepreneur agrees to perform in exchange for receiving the investment. For example, the entrepreneur might agree that the investor can make certain appointments to the board, approve annual budgets, be provided with regular financial statements, or expect that certain financial ratios will be maintained. Negative covenants are actions the entrepreneur agrees not to do. Among others, the entrepreneur may agree that, without the investor's consent, the entrepreneur will not change the nature of the business, issue additional securities, increase employee compensation, or enter into competition with the venture.

In addition, the investment agreement may define the rights of the parties that relate to liquidation of their investments or participation in future investments. For example, it is common for investors to have some form of registration rights that may be exercised if the company makes a public offering. Registered shares are freely tradable, whereas unregistered shares are not. Piggyback registration rights give the investors the right to have their shares included in any registration of shares by the venture. Demand registration rights give the investors the ability to force the venture to register their shares and, effectively, to force the company to go public. Registration rights may be coupled with a forced buyout provision that obligates the entrepreneur to buy out the investors if the venture does not go public or if a buyer is not found within a specified period.

On the flip side, the investment agreement may grant the investor rights to participate in future financings. Common examples of such rights include: a right of prior negotiation, which means the entrepreneur must negotiate future financing with the investor before looking elsewhere for capital; a right of first refusal, which means that the investor has the right to meet any outside offer to provide additional financing; and a preemptive right, which means the investor has a right to maintain its fractional ownership share by participating in subsequent sales as an investor.

Because the parties negotiate the term sheet, whereas attorneys prepare the investment agreement, the parties may not have given much consideration to the various provisions of the investment agreement. Although many of the provisions may seem innocuous, eminently reasonable, or simply boilerplate, they should not be taken lightly. If the relationship between the entrepreneur and the investor ever breaks down, the investor will try to use those provisions for leverage with the entrepreneur and as a means to recover some of the investment. It is important to think through the implications of each provision and to understand what

Antidilution Ratchet Provisions

A ratchet provision protects the investor from dilution of value in the event of a subsequent round of financing at a lower valuation. The mechanism can be implemented in various ways, but the net effect is the same. Here are two possibilities.

CONVERTIBLE PREFERRED STOCK OR DEBT WITH FLOATING CONVERSION PRICE

The investor receives convertible securities with a conversion price that is tied to post-money valuation. As long as subsequent financing is at a valuation per share that is at least as high, the securities will convert to common stock at the stated conversion price. In this case, the ratchet provision protects against dilution by reducing the conversion price to equal the lowest price (full ratchet) or weighted average price (weighted ratchet) in subsequent rounds of financing.

WARRANTS OR RIGHTS TO ACQUIRE ADDITIONAL SHARES

The initially issued securities are either convertible at a set price or are common shares. To protect the investor against dilution, the investor also has a right to receive enough warrants to buy additional common shares at a nominal price (e.g., one cent per share), so that the investor's average cost per common share is equal to the lowest price (full ratchet) or weighted average price (weighted ratchet) in subsequent rounds of financing.

may happen if the venture performs better or worse than expected, or if there is reason to change the focus of the venture in a material way.

Some provisions that are not intended to be problematic can turn out to be so. A good case in point is a ratchet or antidilution provision. A ratchet is designed to protect the outside investor from the possibility of a lower valuation in a subsequent round of financing. If the valuation declines from what the investor paid, a "full" ratchet provision gives the investor enough new shares for free so that the investor's average cost per share is the same as the cost to a new investor. A "weighted" ratchet is less onerous. It gives the investor the ability to acquire additional shares such that the investor's cost per share is the same as the weighted average price of subsequently issued shares. An investor who has a ratchet can be expected to demand a smaller fraction of ownership in exchange for a given level of investment. However, existence of a ratchet also makes raising subsequent financing more difficult.

Suppose an investor contributes $3 per share to a new venture and that in the next financing round the highest any investor is willing to pay is $2 per share. If the original investor has a full ratchet and the next round is priced at $2 per share, then the original investor gets one new share for free for every two shares of initial investment. The average cost per share for the investor is reduced to $2. But if the original investor gets more shares for free, then the new investor will not value the deal at $2. The price must be lower to compensate for dilution of value caused by the ratchet. If the initial investment is large enough and the decline in value is great enough, there may be no positive price at which new capital can be raised. Some ratchet agreements recognize this problem and limit the potential dilution effect of the ratchet.

Although the overriding purpose of the investment agreement is to protect the investor, it also is the result of negotiation. In exchange for protecting the investor, the entrepreneur gains by being able to attract investment capital on terms that involve giving up less of the ownership of the venture. Sahlman (1988) discusses some of the characteristics of successful deals. Among the more important characteristics are simplicity of the deal, robustness in the face of deviations from projections, and adaptability in response to unforeseen developments. Well-structured deals also provide appropriate incentives for the parties and do not make future capital-raising too difficult. On a more qualitative level, a good deal structure improves the chances of new venture success, and the provisions of the deal reveal information about the capabilities, commitment, and beliefs of the parties. Because any formal agreement can be abused, the single most important contributor to the success of a deal is that it is based more on trust than on legal formalism.

2.9   SUMMARY

Investing in new ventures is much different from investing in the shares of a public company. Because of the high degree of uncertainty about the potential for survival and success of a venture, financing commitments tend to be made in stages related to development of the venture. Customarily, new venture development is described in terms of milestones that correspond to significant resolutions of uncertainty. The list of appropriate milestones differs across ventures. New venture development is divided into five specific stages: development, start-up, early growth, rapid growth, and exit. The boundaries between stages can be defined in terms of revenue, revenue growth, net income, and cash flow available to investors.

Appropriate forms of financing depend on the stage of new venture development. Financing begins with seed capital. High-tech ventures with long development stages may require specific R&D financing. Start-up financing provides funds to initiate operations. First-, second-, and possibly third-stage financing are used to finance growth before the venture is profitable. Mezzanine financing and other forms of debt financing are best suited for ventures generating taxable income. Finally, exit financing, including buyout financing and public debt or equity issues, is designed to enable early-stage investors to realize the returns on their investments.

A correspondence also exists between the stage of financing and the source. At the earliest stages of development, most ventures are financed by the entrepreneur, family, and friends. As the concept takes shape and development activity progresses, the firm gains increasing access to financing from business angels and possibly venture capital investors. SBICs also are willing to finance early-stage ventures and, along with lenders, provide financing for more advanced ventures. As the venture matures, financing with trade credit and factoring of accounts receivable become increasingly available. At the harvesting stage, public issues normally are undertaken by ventures that have developed significant track records of market success.

The deal between the entrepreneur and the investor normally is described first in the form of a term sheet and may later be set out in a formal investment agreement. The investment agreement describes the conditions under which investment will be made and is used by the entrepreneur and the investor to protect the investor and increase the ability of the entrepreneur to raise investment capital.

QUESTIONS AND PROBLEMS

1. Use the Internet to locate some Web sites of venture capital firms and business angel groups. Based on your search, what are the characteristics of investments sought by these two types of investors? What are the main differences in investment characteristics between the types? What differences in investment objectives, if any, do you see within each type?

2. In some activities, such as education and healthcare, for-profit and not-for-profit enterprises compete with each other. What do you think it means for an enterprise to be organized as not-for-profit? Why do you think not-for-profits sometimes compete aggressively for business? As a prospective entrepreneur of a venture that could be organized as either, what factors do you think should bear on the choice? Explain.

3. What is the meaning of "limited liability" in terms of total risk and risk allocation? If equity investors in a venture have limited liability, and the venture fails, how might the failure affect the equity investors, creditors, employees, suppliers, and customers? Do you think it would matter to the other stakeholders whether equity investors have limited liability? Why or why not?

4. The following table contains financial information from the business plan of a new venture that makes a portable device that uses Laser technology for measuring distances with great precision, LaserGolf, Inc. The information in the table is in thousands of dollars and is measured over intervals of six months.

Month	6	12	18	24	30	36	42	48	54	60
Sales	0	0	100	500	1,000	2,500	5,000	10,000	12,000	15,000
Profit	(200)	(300)	(500)	(200)	100	300	700	2,000	2,500	3,500
Cash Flow*	(1,000)	(500)	(2,000)	(1,000)	(500)	(100)	300	1,000	2,000	3,000

*Equals cash flow available to investors.

Using the information, how would you propose to identify the stages of new venture development? How much cash is the venture expected to need in total? How would you suggest staging the infusions of cash? Why? Would your proposal for staging be different if you were advising the entrepreneur as opposed to a prospective investor? What would you suggest as useful milestones for evaluating progress? What kinds of investors are best suited for investing at the various stages of development? Suppose that after your group makes an initial investment in the venture prior to month 18, the venture fails to achieve the next milestone you had agreed upon with the entrepreneur for making the next cash infusion. What would you do? Why?

5. An existing biotechnology venture is seeking an infusion of $5 million to carry it to the next milestone. The company has a prototype of a device for using ultrasound to shatter kidney stones. The $5 million is needed to complete the testing required for FDA approval. An investor is proposing to provide the capital in exchange for 2 million shares of common stock. Alternatively, the investor will accept 1.8 million shares of preferred stock, convertible to common on a 1 for 1 basis, or the investor will accept 1.5 million convertible preferred shares, along with warrants to acquire an additional 1.5 million shares for

a nominal price. The warrants can only be exercised if the venture fails to achieve the revenue level projected by the entrepreneur two years after the investment. In any case, the entrepreneur would own 2.5 million shares of common stock. Compute the pre- and post-money valuations for each scenario. If you were the entrepreneur, what factors would you want to consider in deciding which of the offers to accept? If you were the investor, how would you interpret the entrepreneur's choice?

6. In a previous round of financing for a resort spa, an investor contributed $2 million in exchange for 1 million shares of common stock. The entrepreneur retained ownership of 2 million shares. Because of massive construction cost overruns and delays, things have not gone well for the spa since the investment. The venture needs another $1 million, with which the entrepreneur hopes to complete development. However, the existing investment agreement includes a ratchet provision for the prior investor. Under the terms of the ratchet, the investor will receive enough new shares for free so that the investor's average cost per share is the same as that of any new investor.

   a. Suppose that in the absence of the ratchet provision a new investor would be will-ing to accept 1.25 million shares in exchange for the $1 million investment. Compute the post-money valuation of the venture.

   b. Now, based on the valuation in part (a), giving effect to the ratchet provision, what price per share would the new investor seek, and how many new shares would the existing investor receive?

   c. Suppose the ratchet agreement has a floor that limits the average cost of the exist-ing investor to a minimum of $1 per share. How would that limitation affect the price per share for the new investor and the number of new shares going to the exist-ing investor?

   d. What fraction of the equity would the entrepreneur end up retaining under each of the three scenarios?

7. Define "term sheet" and "investment agreement." What are the differences between the two?

8. Search the Internet or print media sources to find a prospective invention that may lead to a marketable product in the future (*Popular Science* is a good source, among others: www.popsci.com).

   a. Briefly describe the product.

   b. As a potential investor, identify four milestones that you might want to use as bases for staging your investment and evaluating the progress of the venture.

   c. Referring to Figure 2-2, identify the stage of development at which each milestone would be appropriate.

   d. Based on your reading of the chapter, what types of financing would you select for the new product and for which development stage(s) would you employ each financ-ing type? Explain.

9. Hacker Inc., a software developer, is considering a financing deal with an investor. The investor and Hacker have agreed on a $2 million investment for 2 million shares of the com-pany. The post-money valuation is $10 million. Hacker has developed promising gaming software to use with popular game consoles, but has been stymied by the closed architec-ture of the most popular consoles. If the architecture opens up and interest in the software takes off, Hacker will need considerably more money to continue its line of software.

    a. Design a ratchet provision, to include in the investment agreement, which will protect the investor against dilution in subsequent rounds of financing.

    b. Why would Hacker's entrepreneurs agree to the provision?

    c. What are the costs, direct and indirect of such an antidilution provision? Explain.

10. Why do you think convertible preferred stock is so common in investment deals between entrepreneurs and venture capital investors? Why not use common stock? Why not use convertible debt?

11. When would you organize as an S Corporation instead of a C Corporation?

12. As an entrepreneur, when would you seek business angel financing as opposed to venture capital financing?

13. Explain the advantages of basing financing on attainment of milestones. What problems might milestones create?

NOTES

1. Entrepreneurs often "number" the business plans so that they can keep track of the identities of those who have copies. This attempt at control, however, is impossible to monitor, given easy access to copying machines. Gates (1995) discusses aspects of protecting and pricing intellectual property in information-based industries. Concern with software piracy led to Microsoft's early adoption of its software licensing strategy (p. 41).

2. The descriptions of stages of development vary somewhat from one source to another. We adhere generally to the taxonomy used by Wetzel (1979) and presented in Timmons (1999). However, we introduce definable boundaries between the various stages.

3. A venture that licenses production and sale to another firm in exchange for a fee does not directly incur the costs of acquiring these productive resources, but the license fee or royalty must be structured to compensate the other firm for doing so.

4. The terminology is derived from *Pratt's Guide to Venture Capital Sources* (1993). Also see Bygrave (1997) and Sahlman (1990).

5. Gates (1995).

6. There are a few angels who may commit to significantly larger amounts ($250,000 to $2.5 million). Angels in this category are rare but include people like Mitch Kapor, founder of Lotus, and Paul Allen, co-founder with Bill Gates of Microsoft.

7. Based on an estimate of Freear, Sohl, and Wetzel presented in a panel discussion on Angel Financing, New York University conference on Entrepreneurship and Small Business Finance, 1997. They estimate that there are around 250,000 angels in the United States who invest in approximately 30,000 firms annually and invest from $10–$20 billion. By way of comparison, the dollar volume of public equity issues averaged over $50 billion per year over the period 1990–1995. Also see Wetzel (1984) and Sohl (1999).

8. Examples of prominent angel groups in large urban areas are the "Tech Coast Angels" in the Los Angeles/Orange County area; "Breakfast Club" in the Boston area; and the "Band of Angels" in the Silicon Valley. The Tech Coast Angels indicate the following venture characteristics as investment criteria: a technology focus; market opportunity sufficiently large to create a business with $50–$100 million in annual revenues; a well-articulated strategy; proprietary technology or other strong barriers to entry; management with relevant and successful experience (not necessarily a complete team); Southern California location; capital needs of $1–2

million to accomplish significant milestones and to attract the next level of funding—usually institutional venture capital; an exit strategy; and a desire for advice and coaching.

9. See Rosegrant and Lampe's (1992) history of the Route 128 venture capital region.

10. See, for example, the *National Venture Capital Association 2002 Yearbook.* The book Web site contains links to other information sources.

11. Chesbrough (2002) compares strategic and financial rationales for corporate venture capital and concludes that the financial rationale has tended not to produce the results the corporations hoped to achieve.

12. U.S. Department of Commerce *Statistical Abstract of the United States,* 2001, p. 492.

13. The most popular type of SBA loan is the 7-A loan, whereby an SBIC makes a loan up to the approved amount (generally less than $750,000) for the financing of working capital, equipment purchase, or purchase of real estate. The SBA guarantees up to 90 percent of the amount of the outstanding loan. The rate charged usually is not more than 2.75 percent above the prime loan rate, and the rate is adjusted quarterly to market rates. Other types of loans are available and are described on the SBA Web page.

14. Petersen and Rajan (1997)

15. The effective annual rate is calculated as $(1 + \text{discount percent})^{365/\text{credit period}} - 1$.

16. See Gompers (1995), Barry, Muscarella, Peavy, and Vetsuypens (l990) and Lin and Smith (1998).

17. The correlation between the two series is .51 and is significant at the .01 level.

18. Early-stage investors are often precluded from selling shares they own in or during the IPO. For the most part, they harvest by selling in the public market after the offering and after the shares have been trading for several months.

19. Whether the tax effect is sufficient to result in a net benefit is an empirical question. Because interest payments are taxable to recipients, the benefits are less than might, at first, appear. A firm that cannot fully exploit the debt tax shelter may actually increase its cost of capital by overreliance on debt financing. See Miller (1977) and DeAngelo and Masulis (1980).

20. Discussion is drawn partly from "Deal Structure," *Harvard Business School Note* (9–384–186); rev. 8/88.

REFERENCES AND ADDITIONAL READING

AVERY, ROBERT B., RAPHAEL BOSTIC, AND KATHERINE SAMOLYK. "The Role of Personal Wealth in Small Business Finance." *Journal of Banking and Finance* 22 (1998): 1019–1061.

BARRY, CHRIS, CHRISTOPHER MUSCARELLA, JOHN PEAVY, AND MICHAEL VETSUYPENS. "The Role of Venture Capital in the Creation of Public Companies: Evidence from the Going Public Process." *Journal of Financial Economics* 27 (1990): 447–472.

BERGER, ALLEN N. AND GREGORY F. UDELL. "The Economics of Small Business Finance: The Roles of Private Equity and Debt Markets in the Financial Growth Cycle." *Journal of Banking and Finance* 22 (1998): 613–673.

BHIDÉ, AMAR. "Bootstrap Finance: The Art of Start-ups." *Harvard Business Review* (November–December 1992): 109–118.

BLOCK, ZENAS, AND IAN C. MACMILLAN. "Milestones for Successful Venture Planning." In *The Entrepreneurial Venture,* edited by W. A. Sahlman and H. H. Stevenson. Boston: Harvard Business School Publications, 1992.

BYGRAVE, WILLIAM D., ed. *The Portable MBA in Entrepreneurship.* 2nd ed. New York: John Wiley & Sons, Inc., 1997.

CHESBROUGH, HENRY W. "Making Sense of Corporate Venture Capital." *Harvard Business Review* (March 2002): 90–99.

COVENEY, PATRICK AND KARL MOORE. *Business Angels.* Chichester: John Wiley and Sons 1998.

DEANGELO, HARRY, AND RONALD MASULIS. "Optimal Capital Structure under Corporate and Personal Taxation." *Journal of Financial Economics* 13, no. 2 (1980): 3–30.

FREEAR, JOHN, JEFFREY SOHL, AND WILLIAM WETZEL, JR. "Angels and Non-Angels: Are There Differences?" *Journal of Business Venturing* 8 (1994): 109–123

GARNER, DANIEL R., ROBERT R. OWEN, AND ROBERT P. CONWAY. *The Ernst & Young Guide to Raising Capital.* New York: John Wiley & Sons, 1991.

GATES, BILL. *The Road Ahead.* New York: Viking, 1995.

GEISST, CHARLES R. *Wall Street, A History.* New York: Cambridge University Press, 1997.

GOMPERS, PAUL. "Optimal Investment, Monitoring, and the Staging of Venture Capital." *Journal of Finance* 50 (1995): 1461–1489.

GOMPERS, PAUL AND JOSH LERNER, "The Venture Capital Revolution." *Journal of Economic Perspectives* 15 (2001): 145–168.

LIN, TIMOTHY H., AND RICHARD L. SMITH. "Insider Reputation and Selling Decisions: The Unwinding of Venture Capital Investments During Equity IPOs." *Journal of Corporate Finance.* 4 (1998): 241–263.

MILLER, MERTON. "Debt and Taxes." *Journal of Finance* 32, no. 2 (1977): 261–275.

National Venture Capital Association 2002 Yearbook. Newark, NJ: Thompson Financial Venture Economics, 2002.

PETERSEN, MITCHELL A., AND RAGHURAN G. RAJAN. "Trade Credit: Theories and Evidence." *Review of Financial Studies* 10, no. 5 (Fall 1997): 661–691

Pratt's Guide to Venture Capital Sources, edited by D. Schutt. New York: Venture Economics Publishing (annual).

REMEY, DONALD P. "Mezzanine Financing: A Flexible Source of Growth Capital." In *Pratt's Guide to Venture Capital Sources,* edited by D. Schutt. New York: Venture Economics Publishing, 1993, pp. 84–86.

ROSEGRANT, SUSAN AND DAVID R. LAMPE. *Route 128: Lessons from Boston's High-Tech Community.* New York: Basic Books, 1992.

SAHLMAN, WILLIAM A. "Note on Financial Contracting: Deals." *Harvard Business School Note* 288-014 (1988).

SAHLMAN, WILLIAM A. "The Structure and Governance of Venture Capital Organizations." *Journal of Financial Economics* 27 (1990): 473–521.

SOHL, JEFFERY E. "The Early-Stage Equity Market in the USA." *Venture Capital* (1999): 101–120.

TIMMONS, JEFFREY A. *New Venture Creation.* 5th ed. Chicago: Irwin-McGraw-Hill, 1999.

TULLER, LAWRENCE W. *The Complete Book of Raising Capital.* New York: McGraw-Hill, 1994.

WETZEL, WILLIAM H. *The Cost and Availability of Credit and Risk Capital in New England. A Region's Struggling Savior: Small Business in New England.* Edited by J. A. Timmons and D. E. Gumpert. Waltham, MA: Small Business Foundation of America, 1979.

WETZEL, WILLIAM H, JR. "Angels and Risk Capital." *Sloan Management Review* 24, no. 4 (Summer 1984) 23–24.

The Business Plan

A brilliant idea is a job half done. (PriceWaterhouse)

Learning Objectives

After reading this chapter you should:

- Understand how and why business plans of new ventures differ from those of established businesses.

- Be able to determine what to include in the business plan and what to leave out.

- Understand how strategic planning is related to the business plan.

- Know how to use milestones and financial projections to manage and evaluate the progress of a new venture.

- Recognize the importance of using the business plan to provide evidence of the entrepreneur's commitment and capability.

- Recognize the potential to use financial information to facilitate negotiation between the entrepreneur and outside investors.

- Understand how a business plan can be tailored to meet the needs of specific kinds of investors.

- Know what is meant by due diligence, and why due diligence is important for both parties.

A business plan for a new venture is a document that describes the critical internal and external elements involved in starting the venture. Typically, the plan summarizes the proposed venture and overriding strategy, and provides details on the operations, financing, marketing, and management. Most fundamentally, the plan is the embodiment of a set of hypotheses about a perceived opportunity and what is expected to result if the opportunity is pursued in a particular way.

In Chapter 1 we described entrepreneurship as a four-step process: recognizing an opportunity, developing a strategy for pursuing the opportunity, implementing the strategy, and harvesting the investment. The business plan is a bridge between strategy and implementation. Ideally, the entrepreneur will have settled on a strategy before preparing the plan. We introduce the business plan now because the necessary elements of the plan provide a structure that is useful for studying new venture finance. As we progress to strategic planning, financial planning, valuation, and harvesting you will better understand how all of these pieces relate to the business plan.

3.1 WHY BUSINESS PLANS OF NEW VENTURES ARE DIFFERENT

Business plans for new and early-stage ventures differ in fundamental ways from plans for established businesses. A key difference is the precision with which projections can be made. Although every plan is based on a set of assumptions about the future, the bases for the assumptions are likely to be much more reliable for an established business than for a start-up. For example, sales projections for an established business generally can be based on prior experience, whereas those for a new venture must be based on conjecture, economic modeling, and analogy to other ventures.

A practical implication of the lack of a track record that can be used as a benchmark is that the appropriate amount of investment in planning is likely to be greater for a new venture. The established firm may be able to project future performance accurately and convincingly based on simple extrapolations and inferences drawn from experience. In contrast, the accuracy and credibility of a new venture plan depends on a number of critical assumptions: How long will it take to develop a marketable product? If development efforts are successful, how much will the product cost to manufacture, and at what price can it be sold? How large is the market, and what share can the venture expect to achieve? These kinds of questions, critical to the new venture plan, must be answered using the best available data and reasoning. As a consequence, convincing plans are likely to require more substantial investments of time and effort than the plans of established businesses.[1]

In businesses where the planning objectives can be specified with relative accuracy and where deviations from projections can be traced to specific factors, it is common for the plan to serve as a basis for performance evaluation and management compensation. For a new venture, use of the plan for such a purpose is not a good idea. Actual sales may be less than projected for a variety reasons, only one of which is the effectiveness of the person responsible for the selling efforts. Stated differently, for an established business it may be valid to reconcile attained sales with planned sales by taking the position that the assumptions in the plan are accurate and deviations reflect the amount or quality of effort to achieve the target. For an early-stage venture it is more likely that the effort was reasonable but (with hindsight) the assumptions in the plan are too optimistic.

Another difference between the plans of new ventures and established businesses is the degree of external reliance on the plan. For an established business the plan may be strictly an internal document. Decisions by outsiders, such as the decision to continue to extend financing, are likely to be based on experience with management, track record of the business, and current financial health. Outsiders are not likely to depend significantly on review of the business plan. For a start-up the reverse is true. Consequently, the business plan must be prepared with an expectation that it will be scrutinized by outsiders who may not be very familiar with the business. Many things that are unnecessary in the plan of an established venture are essential in a plan that is relied on by outsiders.

The important distinction is between business plans designed for internal planning and those designed for attracting investment. From this perspective, there is little difference between a new venture that is competing for funds from venture capitalists and a new venture within an established business that is competing for funds against other new ventures and against continued investment in the ongoing activities of the business. The plan must inspire the confidence of managers responsible for funding the venture in much the same way that the plan of an independent new venture must inspire the confidence of outside investors.

A final distinction is that the breadth of coverage is likely to be greater for the business plan of a start-up than for an established business. The product market normally is the primary focus of the plan of an established business. That is, the plan is likely to concentrate on such matters as marketing efforts, sales projections, new product introductions, and product cost and pricing. In contrast, the business plan of a new venture (in addition to addressing marketing issues) must pay significant attention to the organizational and financial aspects of the venture. Organizational aspects include descriptions of the people responsible for implementation and discussion of issues related to organizational design, such as vertical integration and product distribution. Financial aspects go beyond pro forma projections of profitability to include cash flow projections, valuation, and ownership structure.

For an established business, most of the organizational and financial questions already are resolved and are built into the existing design of the business. As Block and MacMillan (1993) note, the nature of the business already is defined, assumptions about the future are based on experience, members of the team already have learned how to work together, and the important risks already have been identified. More fundamentally, for established businesses, previous decisions about the design of the organization and its financing operate as constraints on direction and rate of future growth. As a result, product market aspects of the plan are viewed in the context of existing organizational and financial structures. Only if the enterprise is considering a major departure from the status quo does it become important to broaden the focus of the plan.

New ventures are different because their plans are unconstrained by previous decisions. Questions of financing, organizational design, and product market strategy all are open. The plan needs to reflect simultaneous consideration of all three.

The distinction between simultaneous consideration and sequential consideration is fundamental. Figure 3-1 illustrates how sequential consideration of strategic questions constrains attainable value. In the figure, four different product market alternatives are considered, along with four financing options. Each cell in the figure represents a combination of product market and financing choice. The amount in the cell is the assumed net present value (NPV) to the entrepreneur that is associated with that combination of choices. The assumed most valuable combination in the figure is a strategy of large-scale entry and slow sales

Alternative Product Market and Financing Choices Net Present Value to the Entrepreneur				
	Financing Choice			
Product Market Choice	Entrepreneur	Entrepreneur + Debt	Entrepreneur + Equity	Entrepreneur + Debt + Equity
Small Scale–Slow Growth	$100	$40	$ 30	$ 10
Small Scale–Rapid Growth	$ 60	$80	$ 20	$ 90
Large Scale–Slow Growth	$ 60	$50	**$120**	$ 70
Large Scale–Rapid Growth	$ 20	$40	$ 80	$100

Figure 3-1 Alternative product market and financing choices: net present value to the entrepreneur

The figure shows the NPV to the entrepreneur of various combinations of product market and financing choices. If choices are made sequentially, the entrepreneur's decision is constrained by the first choice. If the choices are evaluated concurrently, the entrepreneur is assured of selecting the highest-valued combination.

growth, coupled with financing provided by the entrepreneur and an outside equity investor. However, suppose the entrepreneur were to settle first on small-scale entry and slow growth in the product market, and then look for the best financing alternative. The best financing alternative in that case would be for the entrepreneur to finance the entire project. However, the NPV of the choice is not as high as the first-best alternative of large-scale entry with slow growth and reliance on outside equity financing.

3.2 MAKE THE PLAN FIT THE PURPOSE

Business plans are developed for a variety of reasons. Attracting outside funding is the one that receives most of the entrepreneur's attention. Business plans also are used to attract key personnel and to set out benchmarks against which the progress can be measured.

Although it is common to speak of the plan as if it were a single document, the document that is most appropriate for attracting financing is unlikely to be the same one that is most appropriate for attracting key employees or for setting out benchmarks for growth. Although the coverages of plans written for these different purposes overlap, there are aspects of each that are not useful for inclusion in the others. A key employment prospect, for example, may not be very interested in the details of proposed venture financing. Conversely, a venture capitalist may find little of interest in highly technical details that could be appropriate to include in a plan written to attract an engineer.[2] Depending on the extent of overlap, it makes sense to consider preparing separate plans for separate uses. In each case, the plan can focus on the information most useful for the intended purpose.

By using more than one plan, the entrepreneur can focus the presentation in constructive ways. This does not mean that any version of the plan should present a distorted picture of the entrepreneur's vision or expectations. In fact, if different versions are used for different purposes, it is important that they be consistent with each other. The benchmarks in a plan used by the entrepreneur to monitor and assess progress should be consistent with the projections that appear in a plan shown to prospective providers of financing.

3.3 IS TOO MUCH ATTENTION DEVOTED TO THE BUSINESS PLAN?

The business plan is easily the most talked about, written about, taught about, and studied aspect of new venture formation. Most textbooks (including this one) devote at least one chapter to the business plan. Universities offer full semester courses on business plan preparation, and prospective entrepreneurs can attend seminars on the subject of preparing a business plan. In addition, venture forums throughout the United States hold regular sessions where business plans are presented and critiqued.

With all the attention, one could easily conclude that the business plan is the *sine qua non* of new venture success. This is hardly the case. A venture with an obviously valuable product can thrive and even attract funding without a formal plan. Conversely, an elaborate and polished business plan cannot salvage a venture that is not fundamentally sound. Like most things to which the entrepreneur can devote effort, the business plan contributes to success *on the margin*. A carefully thought out plan can contribute to the value of a venture, but is unlikely to be the critical determinant of success or failure.

As for the question of whether business planning receives too much attention, the answer is, "it depends." Commitment of significant effort to planning can pay off in many ways. Probably the most important payoff is better and faster decision making. A well-thought-out plan can help the entrepreneur decide whether the venture is worth pursuing, and, if so, how. It can also provide early warning of problems, enabling the entrepreneur to react and the venture to adapt to what is learned. But much of the attention that is directed toward preparing the business plan is concerned not so much with planning as with attracting funding. It is easy to overinvest in learning about how to use the plan for marketing the venture to prospective investors.

Adherence to a few basic principles can contribute much more to effectiveness of the plan for raising capital than can adherence to an elaborate and exhaustive outline of a business plan. Such outlines are available from a variety of Internet and other sources. Our basic point is that a plan that does a good job of meeting the needs of the entrepreneur for effective decision making can, with basic modification, serve also as a vehicle for raising funding or attracting key employees. In keeping with this principle, we examine the plan, first, as an aid to decision making, and, second, as a vehicle for attracting financing.

3.4 PLAN FIRST—WRITE SECOND

Many prospective entrepreneurs regard preparing the business plan as the first step in the process of starting a venture. They envision a process where, once an opportunity is perceived, the plan is used to gain external validation that the entrepreneur's judgment about the opportunity is correct. But as Timmons (1999) points out, "relying on raising money as an indication that an idea is sound is a cart-before-the-horse approach, which usually results in rejection." Perhaps more importantly, writing and circulating a business plan too early can be a costly mistake, even if the entrepreneur eventually is successful in attracting funding. Simply stated, it is important to plan the venture before preparing the formal plan.

Most business plans set out the entrepreneur's vision of how the venture can succeed. The plan may commit the entrepreneur to a strategy for developing the venture and to a course of action for implementing the strategy. One of the risks in preparing and circulating the plan too early is that the entrepreneur may default into a course of action that is not as valuable as a foregone alternative. Before the plan is written and circulated, the entrepreneur has a number of real options for how to develop the venture. It is important to recognize that these options exist and that by committing to a particular plan some of them will be given up.

Looking again at Figure 3-1, suppose that without analyzing the implications of the different choices, the entrepreneur settles on small-scale entry and slow growth in the product market, and decides to seek outside equity as a means of validating the idea. If outside investors recognize that the entrepreneur could easily have pursued small-scale entry and slow growth without any outside financing, they may interpret efforts to raise funding as evidence that the entrepreneur lacks confidence in the venture. If the entrepreneur does not lack confidence, then the skepticism of outside investors leads them to demand too large of an ownership fraction in exchange for their investment.

Suppose the entrepreneur postpones strategic planning until after the deal is set, and then discovers that large-scale entry with slow growth would have been a higher valued strategy. Perhaps the entrepreneur can go back to the investors and try to change the deal. But even if the change is possible, it will require renegotiation and the expected value to the entrepreneur can never be as high as if the entrepreneur had studied the alternatives first and written the business plan accordingly.

Although most new venture strategies are revised as the venture progresses, such adjustments are not costless. The adjustments tend to be incremental refinements rather than radical redirections. Some courses of action, once they are committed to, are too costly to change. In other cases, the option to approach the market in a different way may expire before the entrepreneur has a chance to refocus the venture.

Of course, any commitment of resources to a particular plan of action limits flexibility. If, for example, you build a factory in California, it would be costly to change your mind and decide that New York would be a better location. But here we are concerned with something more subtle, a loss of flexibility that arises from reliance on outside financing. Almost any outside financing comes with limitations on how it can be used, and even on how the other resources of the venture can be used. Commonly, those limitations are tied to the business plan that was presented to the investors. Even if it is clear to the entrepreneur that a change of plans would be good for the venture, the change often cannot be made unless the investors also are convinced. Yet convincing them is likely to be difficult, particularly if they have not been involved in the operation of the venture. The surest way to limit this problem is to plan the venture before presenting a business plan to investors.

3.5 STRATEGIC PLANNING AND THE BUSINESS PLAN

Strategic decisions are complex, and the relative values of different strategies often are not intuitive. Hence, there is value in systematic analysis of strategic alternatives. Such analysis can be a formal and detailed consideration of the alternatives, or it can be more casual, but systematic, nonetheless. The advantages of careful planning are numerous: orientation toward measurable goals, better understanding of the risks and expected rewards, enhanced ability to recognize and diagnose problems, and quicker and more deliberate reaction to new developments. The principal limitations are that the environment may be changing too rapidly for extensive planning, that inflexibility may result from rigid adherence to plans, and that time devoted to planning is taken away from time devoted to acting.[3]

Although strategic planning is important, comparisons of strategic alternatives do not belong in the business plan. Rather, the plan is developed to facilitate implementation of the single strategy that is selected. We expect that the entrepreneur will conduct the analysis of strategic alternatives with a focus on maximizing value *for the entrepreneur.* The business plan, most likely, will not be written to highlight this focus, especially if it is used to attract financing. Accordingly, there is no reason to present details of the analysis to prospective investors or others who might read the plan.

The above discussion does not mean that the entrepreneur can avoid negotiating with investors over strategic direction. Sophisticated investors will do their own analysis and may regard a different strategy as being in their best interest. In that case the entrepreneur will have to revisit the strategic analysis and may end up modifying the plan to better fit the objective of outside investors.

Nor does it mean that the entrepreneur should sacrifice valuable flexibility by making the plan artificially narrow and constraining. Strategic planning, the topic of the next chapter, compares and values alternative courses of action. Selecting a strategy, in part, on the basis of its ability to preserve flexibility, is one consideration.

3.6   WHAT TO INCLUDE

Unlike many books that address the topic of business plan preparation, we do not devote much space to listing or discussing the specific elements that can or should be included. There are countless sources of this kind of information.[4] The Small Business Administration (SBA), for example, publishes a series of templates for business plans of various types of ventures (manufacturing, retail, etc.) and provides an Internet tutorial on preparing a plan.

Our approach is different, and is focused on helping you determine what to include in the plan and what to leave out. Our suggestions are:

1. Focus on the purpose(s) and uses of the plan and include whatever information about the management team, product, marketing plan, and so on, is relevant and material.

2. Write the plan in such a way that the audience is neither overloaded with unnecessary information nor left to speculate or search elsewhere for answers to important questions.

3. Be certain that key assumptions are identified and recognized as assumptions.

4. Identify the critical elements for success or failure of the venture.

5. Delineate important milestones that can help users of the plan make early decisions about the success of the venture and the need to modify assumptions, expectations, tactics, and possibly strategy.

6. Include financial projections that can be used to test the plan.

Plans designed for internal use can help to secure employee commitments to critical goals and focus organizational effort on clearly articulated targets. A plan enables the entrepreneur to identify and react to problems and future developments more quickly than otherwise would be possible. The plan reflects expectations about such factors as when product development efforts will be completed, when the product will be ready to market, product cost and unit price, and rate of sales growth. Each of these expectations is an hypothesis about the venture.

As the venture progresses, these hypotheses are tested. In general, meeting the expectations set out in the plan would lead to no revision of expectations and probably no change of

Outline for a Business Plan

No single outline is appropriate for every new venture. The following outline covers most of the areas that are appropriate to include in a business plan to be used for attracting outside investment.

Table of Contents

Executive Summary

I. Background and Purpose of Venture—Includes the venture history and current condition, describes the concept, and sets out the objectives and financing being sought.

II. Market Analysis—Contains a description of the market, including size, trends, and key customer groups. Presents results of market testing or market research. Describes the competitive environment, including any regulatory restrictions. Identifies distribution and marketing strategy and sources of competitive advantage related to marketing. Uses the above factors to develop a sales forecast. Identifies critical marketing risks.

III. Products and Services—Contains a detailed product description, including life cycle, intellectual property issues, and status of development efforts. Identifies sources of competitive advantage related to the product or service. Identifies critical product-related risks.

IV. Development, Production, and Operations—Describes the status of research and development efforts and what remains to be done to achieve a marketable product. Sets out a time line for reaching start-up. Describes the status of production efforts. Identifies perceived competitive advantages related to development or operations. Identifies critical risks of development and operations.

V. Organization and Management—Identifies key personnel, status of hiring efforts, and future staffing requirements. Identifies capabilities that are needed, their availability, and anticipated compensation. Identifies sources of competitive advantage related to management and staffing. Identifies critical staffing risks.

VI. Ownership and Control—Describes legal and control structure. Gives details of managerial ownership, proposed ownership of outside investors, and composition of board of directors.

VII. Financial Information—Reports current and historical financial status. Sets out total funding requirements over time and includes pro forma financial statements for an appropriate period. Identifies critical assumptions underlying the financial projections and gives support for the assumptions.

Appendices—Resumes of team members, product photos or drawings, references, market studies, relevant publications, patents and significant contracts, production flowchart, pricing information, start-up cost schedule, staffing plan, detailed financial statements.

direction. However, failure to achieve a milestone or financial projection signals the need to reexamine expectations and reevaluate the merits of the venture. The entrepreneur needs to understand why the projection was not achieved and, based on that new understanding, to reassess the opportunity and the relative merits of going forward, redirecting effort, or abandoning the venture entirely.

The milestones and financial projections in a business plan also are important to outside investors. Achievement of a stated projection helps build confidence in the venture and adds to the willingness of investors to continue to fund the venture. Failure to achieve a projection signals the need to reevaluate initial decisions to invest.

Clearly, it is easier to attract investors with a plan that sets out definite financial projections and milestones than with a plan that is vague. By making the plan specific, the entrepreneur invites oversight and evaluation and provides an easy mechanism for investors to use for re-valuing or abandoning their investments. Furthermore, investors can easily use the milestones and projections to test the beliefs of the entrepreneur.

Aside from factual and quantitative information, any plan used to attract investor interest should contain evidence of three things:

1. Evidence that the entrepreneur understands the technology, market, risks, needs, and potential rewards of the proposed venture and the soundness of the idea.
2. Evidence of the qualifications of the people involved in the venture, and in particular that they can implement the plan and can function as effective members of a team.
3. Evidence that key personnel are committed to the venture.

Direct representations by the entrepreneur that she understands the market and the opportunity, and has assembled a well-functioning team of people who are committed to the venture, will not suffice. Rather, to be credible, the information must be communicated indirectly. Thus, virtually every section of a plan that is to be used for raising capital must convey specific information to prospective investors and signal the knowledge, capability, and commitment of the entrepreneur and other members of the team. The investor will be looking for evidence of sunk investment, reputation, and certification to help gauge knowledge, capability, and commitment.

Evidence of Credible Commitment

Entrepreneurs often prepare and circulate business plans in an effort to test investor interest. The entrepreneur, in such a case, is operating with the perception that the critical success factor is that outside investors will come forth with funding. Obviously, this approach of looking for investors before committing to the project reduces risk for the entrepreneur. Unfortunately, it also drastically reduces the potential for getting the project funded. Any experienced venture capital investor will report that in a year's time they see many good ideas but fund very few of them. Given the size of the market, there is no scarcity of good ideas. What is scarce are capable and committed people, without whom the ideas are worth very little.[5]

Although a good idea is a necessary ingredient of a plan, investors are looking for evidence that the entrepreneur (along with key members of the team) is committed to the venture. The most convincing evidence of commitment is the investment of effort and capital that the entrepreneur already has made in the venture and for which a return cannot be realized unless the venture goes forward and is successful. There are many ways of demonstrating such investments. The key element for their functioning as credible commitments is that they are "sunk," meaning that they are not recoverable or will not generate a return for the entrepreneur unless the entrepreneur continues to commit effort.[6]

An investment that is not recoverable is referred to in economics as a sunk cost. All sunk costs also are fixed costs, but fixed costs and sunk costs are distinct economic concepts. A fixed cost is one that does not vary with output but may be recoverable if the project for which it was incurred is terminated. A sunk cost is a fixed cost that is not recoverable. For example, investment in a locomotive is a fixed cost, but because the locomotive can be moved from one location to another and can be sold for its market value, the market value of the locomotive is not sunk. In contrast, the railroad track connecting two locations (and with trivial salvage value) is both fixed and sunk, as its use is specific to the two locations.

To illustrate how sunk costs can signal commitment, consider the description of the competitive environment that is contained in most business plans. Clearly, the investor wants to know something about the competitive environment, though a sophisticated venture capital investor is likely to know quite a bit already. More importantly, the investor wants to know that the entrepreneur understands the competitive environment. That knowledge may be important in its own right, but also signals that the entrepreneur has invested in learning about the environment. Such an investment is valuable only if the entrepreneur goes forward with a venture where knowledge of the industry is useful. The entrepreneur's investment in learning about the industry is sunk and contributes to the credibility of the entrepreneur's commitment. It follows that a perfunctory description of competitors in the industry, that could be developed easily from public sources, does not signal that the entrepreneur is committed to the venture.

More generally, concrete and deliberate actions such as prototype development, product test marketing, and significant investments in software design can demonstrate the entrepreneur's commitment. Similarly, payment of wages or consulting fees for work related to the venture can signal commitment. These are direct investments in the success of the venture. Other kinds of less direct action can also demonstrate commitment. For example, resigning from existing employment can signal commitment even though no direct investment has been made in the venture.

The fact that either kind of action can signal commitment underscores the point that it is not the action, per se, that matters but the irreversibility of the action. Test marketing expenses are only of value if the venture attempts to market the product. Similarly, payment of consulting fees to assist with preparation of the business plan is of value only if the plan is used to initiate the venture. The loss of salary that comes with resignation of current employment is credible as a signal only if the entrepreneur would have difficulty finding new employment of equal value.

Timing of resignation also is an important factor in assessing credibility. Burning bridges with an existing employer to search for a new venture opportunity, with no clear opportunity in mind, may help motivate a prospective entrepreneur to intensify the search. However, it does very little to signal the entrepreneur's commitment to, or confidence in, the venture that ultimately is selected. How can the investor in such a case determine whether the entrepreneur is truly attracted to the opportunity or is merely settling on one that appears to be the best candidate from a list of not-so-attractive possibilities?[7]

Two final comments are in order on the subject of credible commitments. First, although a sunk cost is evidence of commitment, it is not evidence of the entrepreneur's current beliefs. Because the sunk cost is not recoverable, except by going forward with the venture, it carries no opportunity cost. Consequently, the size of the sunk cost bears no immediate relationship to what the entrepreneur thinks the project is worth. True, at the time the investments were made, the entrepreneur would only have made them based on the belief that the project would be worth enough to compensate for the investments. But those beliefs are likely to change during the early stages of new venture development. The bottom line is that if the outside investor is trying to assess current beliefs, it is necessary to look at something other than a sunk cost.

Credible Commitments of Entrepreneurs

Credibility requires finding a way to prevent going back.
Avinash Dixit and Barry Nalebuff (1991)

For an entrepreneur, credibility is important for attracting capital, employees, and customers, and for discouraging prospective rivals. There are various ways of establishing credibility. Among others, the entrepreneur can: use prior behavior to develop a reputation upon which others can rely; contract to limit choice; or close off avenues of retreat.

CORTEZ—BURNING BRIDGES TO PREVENT RETREAT

In his search for the Seven Cities of Gold, when Cortez arrived in Mexico, he ordered that all of his ships be burned or disabled. The action sent a clear message to his small army of soldiers, and to the much larger native population of Central America, that Cortez would succeed in the quest or he and his army would die trying.

LEE IACOCCA—CONTRACTING TO SIGNAL COMMITMENT AND CONFIDENCE IN A TURN-AROUND

When Iacocca took over as CEO of the bankrupt Chrysler Corporation, he contracted to receive compensation of $1 per year. The balance of his compensation was paid in the form of stock options, with an exercise price set at the then prevailing market price of Chrysler stock. The deal sent a message to employees, customers, and investors that Iacocca was confident of success, and helped to restore public confidence in the company.

JEFFREY BEZOS—CONTRACTING AND BRIDGE BURNING TOGETHER

When, at age 31, Bezos founded Amazon.com, it was not because he had nothing better to do. In fact, he abandoned the career path of a rising star in the New York investment community to move to Seattle and become an Internet vendor. As additional evidence of commitment, Bezos contracted to receive a salary that was much lower than he could earn in alternative employment.

A COUNTER EXAMPLE—THE VALUE OF "WORKING WITHOUT A NET"

A biotech entrepreneur we know of was seeking to raise a minimum of $1 million in a private placement. The capital was needed to complete product testing before a marketable product could be developed. Being a cautious individual, the entrepreneur retained his well-paid position with a pharmaceuticals manufacturer while he sought the funds. After several months of frustrating and unsuccessful efforts to raise the capital, he finally resigned from his existing position. In response to the demonstration of commitment, the project was funded quickly by several investors.

HERBERT H. DOW—PERSISTENCE GIVING RISE TO REPUTATION

In 1889, at age 23, Dow became interested in the prospect of extracting bromide from the brine water that was a byproduct of oil drilling in his resident state of Ohio. To pursue the idea, he established the Canton Chemical Company, which failed in less than one year, because of undercapitalization. In 1890, with stronger financial backing, he established Midland Chemical Company and achieved success. He then shifted his efforts to developing a process for extracting chlorine from brine. When his initial effort resulted in an explosion, financial backers withdrew. In 1895 he launched the Dow Process Company to continue the effort but lost financial backing within a few months. In 1896, he tried again and was successful. The Dow Chemical Company was formed in 1897 to commercialize the success.

Source: Based, in part, on information from A. Hallett and D. Hallett, *Entrepreneur Magazine Encyclopedia of Entrepreneurs,* (New York: John Wiley & Sons, Inc., 1997).

The second point is related. The credibility of an entrepreneur's commitment can be undermined by the entrepreneur's intent to draw cash out of the venture in a way that is unrelated to success. Consider a draw by the entrepreneur, or salary paid to the entrepreneur, that is large relative to the entrepreneur's continuing investment. Such payments may suggest that the entrepreneur is continuing to promote the project not because of its market potential, but because attracting outside investment to cover the entrepreneur's draw is a way to recoup past losses even though the project is not worth pursuing. The ambiguity can be avoided by making sure the draw is smaller than the salary and benefits that the entrepreneur could generate in alternative employment.

Evidence of Reputation and Certification

Experienced entrepreneurs sometimes attract outside investment without needing to make credible demonstrations of commitment.[8] What is it, in such cases, that investors are relying on to justify their investments? Investors in such cases must expect that the entrepreneur will be effective at implementation. The track record of a successful entrepreneur can be sufficient to attract investors, even though they may have difficulty explaining why they feel comfortable relying on the track record.[9] Later in the text we'll explore the connection between past success and reputation, and we'll see other ways that reputation is important in entrepreneurial settings.[10]

What about the first-time entrepreneur who has yet to establish a reputation, or an entrepreneur whose track record is less than perfect? We've already seen that the entrepreneur may be able to make a credible commitment to the venture, but without a reputation, the commitment alone may not be sufficient to attract the interest of investors. One solution is to rely on the reputations of others. Those reputations sometimes can be used by the entrepreneur as a means of certification. Important suppliers or customers who have publicly committed to transact with the venture can provide the level of certification that is important for attracting investment, as can relational partners who become involved in implementing the business plan.[11] In addition, establishing a reputable board of advisors can help to certify the viability and uniqueness of the technology upon which the product or business concept is based.

3.7 CONFIDENTIALITY

A difficult tension exists for the entrepreneur who needs to attract outside funding. Do you disclose your good ideas fully in the plan and run the risk of having them appropriated by others, or do you hold back critical information and run the risk of having the plan ignored? Ideally, you do neither. It is unlikely that a plan will attract much interest from investors if they cannot understand clearly what the entrepreneur proposes to do.

For ideas that cannot be protected by existing intellectual property laws, appropriation is avoided in two ways. The first is to deal with investors who have reputations sufficient to keep them from appropriating good ideas. An investor who plans to continue involvement with new ventures cannot afford to develop a reputation for stealing ideas.[12] The second is for the entrepreneur to have enough of a head start before circulating the plan so that appropriation is not in the economic interest of anyone who sees the plan. The significance of the head start

Track Records and Business Plans

Investors in new ventures use various bits of information to predict success. The entrepreneur's track record contains information that is difficult to reflect in the business plan. A track record of success in previous ventures speaks to the character of the entrepreneur, even to the point where formal articulation of a business plan may lose importance for the investor.

SEYMOUR R. CRAY—A TRACK RECORD OF SUCCESS

Born in Wisconsin in 1925, Cray completed his education in electronic engineering and mathematics in 1951 and went to work for Engineering Research Associates as a computer designer. When that company was sold to Sperry Rand Corporation in 1957, Cray and William Norris, the founder of Engineering Research Associates, formed Control Data Corporation to design and manufacture the first computer using transistors instead of vacuum tubes. Cray left Control Data in 1972 (after which Control Data languished) and established Cray Research to build the world's most powerful supercomputer. The first commercial order of the CRAY-1 was made six years later, in 1978. Based on his track record of success at Control Data, Cray was able to attract financing through the development stages. The financing included an IPO in 1976, two years before the company's first commercial order.

MITCH KAPOR—LOTUS DEVELOPMENT CORPORATION

In 1982, Kapor was seeking investment capital for Lotus Development Corporation. He approached only one group of investors, and did so with a business plan that was fragmentary and incomplete. Nevertheless, his efforts to attract funding were successful. Kapor's first involvement with computer programming came shortly after he completed college. His first product, Tiny Troll, was designed to perform statistical analysis on an Apple II computer. The product, though not a financial success, inspired Kapor to a full-time career in software development. After making a major contribution to VisiCalc, an early computer spreadsheet application, he went on to found Lotus Development Corporation. Sevin Rosen Partners, a venture capital firm, invested in Lotus primarily on the basis of Kapor's track record.

H. WAYNE HUIZENGA—WASTE MANAGEMENT, BLOCKBUSTER VIDEO, REPUBLIC SERVICES, AND AUTONATION

Huizenga began his entrepreneurial career as a trash collector. Starting with one truck, he formed Waste Management a few years later, and within a decade annual sales were in excess of $1 billion. In the mid-1980s Huizenga turned his attention to home video. Leveraging on past success, he arranged an $18 million financing of Blockbuster Video. The company had grown to more than 1,000 stores by 1989 and over 4,500 by 1994. After selling Blockbuster to Viacom, Huizenga dramatically leveraged the operations of an ongoing waste collection business, Republic Services, into a diversified effort to consolidate many aspects of automobile retailing and service. The venture, AutoNation, been able to raise substantial amounts of capital based almost entirely on his earlier successes. While the ultimate success of AutoNation remains an open issue, it is noteworthy that the venture's stock price has not followed the overall market. After reaching a high of about $38 per share in early 1997, the price declined to about $7 by the end of 2000. As of mid-2002, the stock price had risen to about $11.

Source: A. Hallett and D. Hallet, *Entrepreneur Magazine Encyclopedia of Entrepreneurs* (New York: John Wiley & Sons, Inc., 1997).

Certification in Business Plans

An entrepreneur who lacks a track record of success and cannot use the business plan to communicate fully the potential value of an opportunity, still can use the reputations of large customers, suppliers, board members, or others to certify the venture.

H. ROSS PEROT—ELECTRONIC DATA SYSTEMS, INC.

After a successful sales career with IBM, at age 32 Perot used $1,000 in savings to launch Electronic Data Systems as a provider of software development services to large owners of IBM computers. He quickly landed a consulting contract with Blue Cross/Blue Shield of Texas that covered only basic operating expenses. In less than a year, based on that first contract, he had secured more profitable contracts with Collins Radio and Frito-Lay. Leveraging from its client base of strong customers, EDS went public a few years later.

DAVID W. THOMPSON—ORBITAL SCIENCES CORPORATION

Launching satellites is a business that usually is pursued by such major corporations as Hughes Aircraft and TRW. The exception is Orbital Sciences Corporation, a venture formed by David Thompson in 1982 to build satellite launch vehicles. Since then, it has expanded into satellite production and GPS navigation systems. As of mid-2002, the company had annual revenue of $451 million. How could a start-up like Orbital Sciences raise the large amounts of capital needed to compete in the business of launching satellites? The answer, in part, is a high-powered board of directors that includes a former U.S. senator and Apollo Astronaut, former NASA administrator and president of Northrop Corporation (now Northrup Gruman), a former secretary of the Air Force, and the chairman of the M.I.T. Department of Aeronautics and Astronautics. Orbital Sciences leveraged the reputation of its board to subcontract manufacturing to companies such as Martin Marietta Corporation (now Lockheed Martin).

Sources: A. Hallett and D. Hallett, *Entrepreneur Magazine Encyclopedia of Entrepreneurs* (New York: John Wiley & Sons, Inc., 1997), Robert Acker, "Bootstrapping Your Way into the Satellite Business," *Tales from Successful Entrepreneurs,* compiled by Amar Bhidé, Harvard Business School 9–396–050, August 1995, Hoovers Online, Yahoo Financial.

may be that a prospective rival could not expect to beat the entrepreneur to the market. Alternatively, the entrepreneur's sunk investment could reduce the incremental cost of going ahead with the project to a point where, even if someone else were to enter the market quickly with a similar product, the entrepreneur still would choose to go forward.

3.8 FINANCIAL ASPECTS OF THE BUSINESS PLAN

Views differ about what kind of financial information to include in the business plan. A number of writers are critical of plans that rely heavily on detailed financial projections. Commenting on what they refer to as the Planning/Performance Paradox, Block and MacMillan remark, "All the concrete numbers and detailed analyses contained in the typical business plan belie the fact that forecasting the performance of nascent ventures is even harder than predicting the weather."[13] Even more critically, Sahlman singles out financial projections as unimportant to a good business plan.

What's wrong with most business plans? The answer is relatively straightforward. Most waste too much ink on numbers and devote too little to the information that really matters to intelligent investors. As every seasoned investor knows, financial projections for a new company—especially detailed, month-by-month projections that stretch out for more than a year—are an act of imagination. An entrepreneurial venture faces too many unknowns to predict revenues, let alone profits. Moreover, few if any entrepreneurs correctly anticipate how much capital and time will be required to accomplish their objectives. Typically, they are wildly optimistic, padding their projections. Investors know about the padding effect and therefore discount the figures in business plans. These maneuvers create a vicious circle of inaccuracy that benefits no one.[14]

The substance of these criticisms is that there is far too much uncertainty involved in a new venture to justify placing very much reliance on financial projections.

To an extent, we agree. The financial projections are not likely to be very important if the fundamentals are not established. It is easy to include too much financial information in the plan. Of necessity, the financial planning process generates a large volume of detailed accounting data. Projections usually must be made monthly or even weekly and must cover a period of several years. But it is not necessary, and may not be desirable, to include detailed month-by-month projections in the plan. It makes more sense to highlight the projected financial condition of the venture around a few critical milestones. Just because a projection has been generated for every month does not imply that all of the projections should find their way into the plan.

Comments on the difficulties of accurate forecasting fail to recognize that forecasts can be a powerful instrument for both performance review and for contracting with outside investors. When the future is easy to predict, planning for the future is not particularly difficult or interesting. Financing arrangements can be initiated to meet the expected cash needs of the venture, and minor deviations from expectations can be dealt with quickly. When uncertainty is great, monthly, or even weekly projections of sales and profits have their greatest value in plans designed for internal use. By comparing actual with projected income statement and balance sheet categories, the entrepreneur can learn more quickly whether the business is developing as planned or whether some type of corrective action is needed. Given that additional financing can take several months to arrange, monthly forecasting and frequent review affords greater control than if the venture were attempting to operate with only annual financial data.

The more uncertain the future, the more important it is to develop a financial model that can project both expectations about the future and the uncertainty about the future. Ventures that are subject to great uncertainty generally require more time and effort when actual performance differs from expectations. For example, if cash flows are below expectations, it is likely to take more time to secure additional outside financing. Also, the greater the uncertainty, the larger the liquidity cushion the venture needs.

On the other hand, monthly projections are not of much use to an outside investor who is trying to decide whether to invest in the venture. For that decision, annual information is likely to be all that is needed, though once the decision to invest is made, monthly information is useful for monitoring performance.

Are the financial projections so fanciful that they are not useful? Clearly, they are useful as a basis for attracting investors.[15] The projections provide an important mechanism that the entrepreneur and investors can use to signal their beliefs about the value of the venture. Suppose, for example, that the business plan includes a projection of sales and net income that the outside investor believes is overly optimistic. Perhaps the entrepreneur actually believes the projections and perhaps not. Conversely, the entrepreneur may be unsure of whether the investor is really skeptical of the projections or is just posturing in order to achieve more favorable terms for investing.

A common way of reaching agreement is to negotiate a structure that uses warrants to tie ownership to actual performance. A warrant is a long-term option to acquire more shares, usually for a nominal price. In this case, the investor might agree to invest but make the ownership share contingent on how well the venture does in meeting its revenue and income targets. More specifically, the investor might end up with a 20 percent share if performance meets or exceeds projections, but the investor might also be issued enough warrants so that ownership share could rise to as much as 40 percent if actual performance were only 50 percent or less of projected performance.[16]

Such a contract does a variety of things. First, if the entrepreneur truly expects to achieve the targets, agreeing to use warrants is a credible way of expressing the belief. Conversely, if the *investor* believes actual performance will fall short of the projection, tying ownership to performance enables the entrepreneur to keep more of the ownership if the investor is proven wrong. Finally, warrants strengthen the entrepreneur's incentive to try to achieve the projected results.

Beyond the benefit that explicit financial projections afford as an anchor for negotiating financing contract terms, a less tangible benefit is that making the projections helps the entrepreneur understand some of the subtleties of the financial aspects of the venture. Among other things, the entrepreneur gains increased understanding of the cost structure, the overall need for financing, how future growth and financing needs are related, and, to an extent, how the outside investor views the venture. Many deals are not consummated because the entrepreneur and the investor do not agree about value. Financial modeling can serve as a reality check for the entrepreneur and can help ensure that agreement can be reached.

With respect to the scope of projections, it makes sense to think in terms of a financial model of the venture. If the modeling is done well, the entrepreneur should be able to generate forecasts of sales, income, balance sheet accounts, and financial needs. Beyond these, the entrepreneur should be able to use the information to arrive at an estimate of value. Collectively, this information should enable the entrepreneur to put forward a plan for capitalizing the venture. Depending on the nature of the business, it may be appropriate to include additional information, such as a hiring plan or a schedule of planned capital acquisitions.

Finally, the prospective investor can use financial projections as a basis for deciding how much to invest and to decide on ownership share and other contractual terms. It makes little sense for the entrepreneur to enter the negotiation without the ability to assess the financing terms that are offered by prospective investors. Without a financial model of the venture, accurately assessing the effects of financing terms is not possible.

3.9 TARGETING THE INVESTORS

Business plans that are intended for use in raising capital must address the needs of investors. Those needs differ, depending on the type of investor and the form of financing.

If the entrepreneur is seeking equity financing, most investors expect to see an indication of the terms the entrepreneur considers reasonable. This might be in the form of a share of equity the investor would receive, together with the amount of funding being sought. Together, these terms imply a valuation. Alternatively, the entrepreneur might suggest a valuation directly. The entrepreneur's proposed terms are a starting point for negotiations with

Using Warrants or Conversion Terms to Signal Beliefs

The entrepreneur can use contingent claims that are tied to a venture's attainment of performance targets to signal confidence in projections. Contingent claims also can be used by outside investors to test the confidence of the entrepreneur. Contingent claims also shift risk of poor performance from the investor to the entrepreneur but preserve the investor's ability to participate in success. The following are examples of the different ways performance contingencies can be implemented.

CONTINGENT WARRANTS

A new venture raises $10 million by issuing 4 million shares. In addition, the investor receives warrants to acquire 1 million more shares at no cost if sales revenue in two years is less than 75 percent of the projection in the business plan and an additional 1 million if sales revenue is less than 50 percent of projected revenue. The entrepreneur retains 5.5 million shares.

The effect of the contingent warrants is shown in the following table. As the venture fails to achieve its revenue targets, valuation declines and outside investor shares increase. If the venture's performance is less than 50 percent of projected performance, the outside investor ends up with majority ownership. Unless there is a provision to the contrary, the investor will be able to terminate the entrepreneur or restructure the venture.

% of Target Achieved	Investor's Shares	Average Cost per Share	Pre-Money Valuation	Post-Money Valuation	Investor Ownership (%)
≥75%	4,000,000	$2.50	$13,750,000	$23,750,000	42.1%
≥50%	5,000,000	$2.00	$11,000,000	$21,000,000	47.6%
<50%	6,000,000	$1.67	$ 9,166,667	$19,166,667	52.2%

CONVERTIBLE SECURITIES WITH A CONTINGENT CONVERSION PRICE

The same results as in the above table can be achieved by issuing convertible securities and tying the conversion price to attained performance. In this case, the $10 million investment would be convertible to 4 million shares of common stock if at least 75 percent of projected performance was achieved, 5 million shares if at least 50 percent was achieved, and 6 million shares if less than 50 percent was achieved.

the investor. Most investors take the position that a realistic valuation by the entrepreneur is an important indication of whether a deal is achievable. Failure to include such information can suggest that the entrepreneur will be hard to deal with or is incapable of carrying out an efficient negotiation. A very high valuation, compared to the expectations of the investor, can suggest that the parties would have trouble agreeing on terms.

In contrast, if the entrepreneur seeks debt financing, the concern of the creditor is not valuation. Rather, it is whether the venture can be expected to generate the cash flows that are necessary to service the debt and whether the venture (or the entrepreneur) has capital assets that can be used to secure the debt. Thus, a business plan used for debt financing can appropriately include a proposed repayment schedule and information on how the debt would be repaid if the venture were to perform below projections. That is, the concern of the creditor is not so much with valuation of the enterprise as it is with risk of default. Only if the debt is very risky or includes equity sweeteners is the investor likely to be concerned with valuation.

If the entrepreneur hopes to raise funds from multiple individual investors, it is important to recognize that there is little opportunity, outside of the business plan (or financing proposal), for negotiation of terms. Investors expect to participate on equal terms with each other, and each investor is likely to want assurance that committed capital will not be expended unless enough capital is raised to enable the entrepreneur to go forward with the venture. Accordingly, such a business plan normally must include a specific financing proposal that is essentially a "take-it or leave-it" offer and may provide that investment commitments are contingent on achieving a threshold level of funding.

3.10 DUE DILIGENCE

Venture capitalists and others who manage investments have a responsibility to take reasonable steps to assure that their investment decisions are based on information that is accurate and comprehensive. Due diligence is the process of assembling and verifying the information related to an investment decision, whether on behalf of others or oneself.[17]

The business plan is an important input to due diligence. The entrepreneur can anticipate that any material representation in the plan will be subject to verification by the investor or an agent of the investor. Otherwise the claims will be included among the representations and warranties of the entrepreneur. An entrepreneur can enhance the likelihood of funding by using the plan and supporting information to facilitate due diligence.

Due diligence is a two-way street. Just as prospective investors investigate the venture and the entrepreneur, the entrepreneur should investigate investors. For most new ventures, the relationship between the entrepreneur and the investor is ongoing. The entrepreneur can examine the track records of prospective investors and use the experiences of other entrepreneurs to assess the likely contribution of the investor to the venture, the flexibility of the investor in response to unanticipated developments, and so on.

3.11 UPDATING THE BUSINESS PLAN

Developing the business plan is not a once-and-for-all exercise. As the venture develops, some of the assumptions on which the initial projections are based will prove to be incorrect. The projections will have to be modified in light of actual experience, and it may be appropriate to reassess overall strategy. Revising the plan does not imply that the original planning exercise was a failure. In fact, existence of the plan enables the entrepreneur to diagnose the problems and opportunities that may lead to revisions. Revising the plan is important for the same reasons. The revised plan will contain a new set of projections and milestones that the entrepreneur can use to benchmark progress.

3.12 SUMMARY

The business plan of a new venture is a plan for implementing a particular strategy. The plan relies on a series of assumptions about the opportunity. These assumptions provide the foundation for predictions of what will happen if the opportunity is pursued in a particular way. From the perspective of new venture finance, the business plan reduces the risk of failure. It is a tool for diagnosing problems swiftly, so that investment capital is not misallocated and corrective actions can be taken. In addition, the plan is a vehicle for raising external financing.

Business plans for new ventures differ from those of established firms in four basic ways. First, the attainable precision of the forecast is less for a new venture. Second, entrepreneurs usually must invest more time and energy in planning, partly because the entrepreneur must develop from scratch the forecasting approach and key assumptions that underlie the projections. Third, external reliance on the plan is greater for a new venture. Fourth, for a new venture the plan must reflect simultaneous thinking about organization, product market, and financial strategies. For example, the plan must evaluate, at least implicitly, the financing method and organizational form that are best suited for a scenario of rapid product market growth versus slower growth. In contrast, an existing business effectively has already committed to one or more of these components of strategy.

The content of a new venture business plan is dictated by the functions of the plan. It may make sense to prepare several versions, depending on objectives. Plans that are used for control of the venture need to identify the key assumptions on which performance expectations are based. They also need to delineate important milestones and set out financial projections that can be used to test the assumptions on which the plan is based.

Plans that are used to attract funding have an additional burden. To be effective, such plans need to provide credible evidence that the entrepreneur and other members of the team understand the opportunity and that they are capable of developing the venture and are committed to doing so. Typically, this information is conveyed through sunk costs, reputations of the participants, and certification by others, such as key trading partners or recognized investors.

Although new ventures are fraught with uncertainty, that uncertainty does not diminish the need to include financial projections in the plan. If anything, the more uncertain the future, the more important it is to include such projections and even to model the level of uncertainty into the new venture forecast. Financial forecasts not only provide a means of diagnosing whether the venture is developing according to plan, they also serve as the basis for contracting when entrepreneurs and investors disagree about the potential for the venture.

QUESTIONS AND PROBLEMS

1. How do sunk costs affect decisions? What is the difference between a sunk cost and a fixed cost?

2. Identify the sunk costs, if any, in each of the following, and explain how they affect the decision:

   a. A student who is one year from completing an MBA degree is considering going to law school.

   b. A person who owns a house in Los Angeles receives a job offer in Boston.

   c. Your company's copier, which cost $5,000, breaks and will cost $1,500 to repair. New copiers sell for $6,000.

   d. You were planning to buy a new suit for $500 and got a $150 traffic ticket on the way to the mall.

3. "Every new venture is an industrial experiment, with the assumptions as hypotheses. The experiment must be designed to ensure that the hypotheses are tested." What does this statement imply for new ventures? Do you agree with it?

4. "It is foolish to put a lot of effort into preparing the business plan. Everyone knows that the financial projections in the business plan of a new venture bear almost no relation to what actually will happen." What do you think?

5. According to the business plan, sales of the venture are expected to reach $1.5 million over the first 12 months of operation, and the venture is projected to be breaking even by year-end. As a prospective investor, how would your decision to invest, and the terms for investing change, if:
    a. In reality, as of year-end, the venture had yet to make its first sale?
    b. In reality, first-year sales reached $4 million, with $800,000 in net income?
    c. In reality, sales and profitability are almost exactly in line with projections?

6. "The environment in which we operate is changing so rapidly and is so unpredictable that we cannot afford to devote time to preparing a business plan." What do you think?

7. Using the Internet, see what information you can find that would be helpful for preparing a business plan for: a new housewares retailing business venture; an inflight electronic mail service; a new manufacturer of golf clubs.

8. "The more personal wealth an entrepreneur has sunk into developing an idea, the more convinced we are that the idea is worth pursuing." Do you agree? Why or why not?

9. Explain how the financial projections in a business plan might be used by the entrepreneur and by a prospective investor.

10. "Certification sounds like a good idea, but it costs too much. If I try to bring in a supplier or major customer as an investor, they always want a large share of the equity or some other arrangement that lowers the value of the opportunity. I would rather keep shopping the plan around until I find an investor who sees the true value of the idea." Evaluate.

11. You are seeking to raise $10 million of venture capital to finance a new enterprise. Your financial projections suggest that the return on investment is likely to be very high. You know that venture capital investors are skeptical of the projections of entrepreneurs, and routinely discount the projections heavily. What steps might you take to convey to prospective investors your high level of confidence in the financial projections?

12. You are considering investing in a new venture that has a patented method for manufacturing DVD disks that the entrepreneur claims will have a significant cost advantage over existing technology. Your main concern is that you believe the entrepreneur is overly optimistic about the potential for success of the venture and, as a result, will be unwilling to give up enough equity to make investing worthwhile. Generally, you agree with the entrepreneur about the high rate of growth of the DVD market that is projected in the business plan. However, you are concerned that the entrepreneur has overestimated the attainable market share of the venture and the extent of cost saving the patented technology can achieve. How could you structure the financing arrangement with the entrepreneur so that if the projections about market share and cost advantage in the plan are correct, the entrepreneur keeps the fraction of ownership that she is seeking, but where the share is reduced if these elements of the plan are not met? The structure you design should be one where you continue to bear the risk of the uncertain size of the DVD market.

13. "I've invested so much time and money in this venture that I'm not giving it up now." Evaluate.

14. How might a business plan differ in content if the entrepreneur is seeking debt financing versus equity financing? Explain.

15. Identify ways in which a technical board of advisors might help an entrepreneur secure financing? When would it not make sense to build a technical board of advisors? Explain.

16. A fellow student, JW, has launched a clothing company. He has developed 10 designs for young men's slacks, shorts, and polo shirts. He has a contractual relationship with a clothing manufacturer in Korea, and has secured and filled an order from Blarney's in NY for four of his ten designs. JW is seeking an angel investor. Which of the following would be useful as milestones for rounds of equity financing? Explain.

    a. Entrepreneur finishes college and enrolls in an MBA program.

    b. Entrepreneur receives $200,000 from his parents to support his business activities.

    c. Entrepreneur adds a women's clothing line.

    d. Entrepreneur opens a store in Santa Monica featuring his designs.

    e. Blarney's places a new order worth $500,000 in revenue.

    f. What types of milestones would you suggest if you were writing the term sheet?

17. The following are some commonly used provisions in debt contracts between borrowers and bank lenders. Identify how each of these provisions limits future financing choices for the borrower and explain why. Can you draw a parallel with provisions you might find in financing arrangements between venture capitalists and entrepreneurs? Explain. If any of the terms are unfamiliar to you, research them on the Internet or in other sources.

    a. A loan can be secured with collateral, possibly including accounts receivable, inventory, and other assets.

    b. A term loan can be linked to acquisition of specific assets.

    c. A bank can refuse a draw on a line of credit.

    d. A lender can require that future borrowing be subordinated to the loan from the bank.

    e. A lender can require the entrepreneur to personally guarantee the loan.

    f. The lender can require that the borrower maintain a specified minimum level of liquidity, as evidenced by net working capital, cash balances, or in other ways.

    g. The term of the loan can be set to correspond to anticipated timing of business receipts of cash.

NOTES

1. Sykes and Dunham (1992) examine differences in the business plans of new ventures and established firms, with a primary focus on developing and testing critical assumptions.

2. In a study of the business plan evaluation processes of venture capital investors, Hall and Hofer (1993) find that reviewers reached a go/no go decision in an average of less than six minutes on initial screening.

3. See Drucker (1964) for further discussion of the value of planning.

4. See, for example, Baty (1990), Schilit (1990), Gumpert (1996), Scarborough and Zimmerer (1993), and Hisrich (1995).

5. See Sahlman (1997) for related discussion.

6. See Williamson (1985) and Ghemawat (1991) for a discussion of the economics of commitment and the role of sunk costs. Besanko, Dranove, and Shanley (1999) provide a brief formal model of how sunk investments encourage a firm to stay with its existing technology.

7. Levesque and MacCrimmon (1997) report on one study of the owners of *Inc.* magazine's list of fastest-growing companies. The study found that, on average, the entrepreneurs kept their existing jobs for four months beyond the founding of the new venture. Levesque and Mac-Crimmon offer a theoretical model of the choice of when to resign, based on the tolerance for continuing to work and the marginal productivity of devoting effort to the venture. They indicate that timing is often affected by the entrepreneur's need for cash to defray living expenses or to help fund the venture. The evidence generally is consistent with a view that resignations tend to occur at a point when the entrepreneur perceives the specific opportunity to be more attractive than continued current employment, and when resignation would lend credibility to the entrepreneur's capital-raising efforts.

8. Wright, Robbie, and Ennew (1997) study venture capital investment decisions and find a strong preference to invest in projects of entrepreneurs who have played major roles in previous successful ventures.

9. Bhidé and Stevenson (1989) discuss the value of the entrepreneur's track record for attracting stakeholders to a new venture.

10. For an overview on the role of reputation and reputation formation, see Milgrom and Roberts (1992). Klein and Leffler (1981) provide a formal analysis of reputation formation, the role of sunk investment as a bonding mechanism, and the effect of reputational capital on product price. See also Kreps and Wilson (1982).

11. A formal model of certification, applied to new issue underwriting, is presented in Booth and Smith (1986). See Fiet (1995) for application to venture capital.

12. Lin and Smith (1998) use several indicators of venture capitalist reputation, including age of the firm and number of deals in which the firm is the lead venture capital investor. Often it is obvious that the venture capital firm has a sufficient stake in the industry to be conscientious about protecting its reputation.

13. Block and MacMillan (1993), p. 163.

14. Sahlman (1997).

15. In fact, fanciful projections can signal to investors that the entrepreneur does not understand the opportunity. See Brodsky (1998) for some illustrations of how investors are likely to react to business plans based on assumptions that are not well-founded.

16. The same result can be achieved by issuing convertible securities where the conversion price depends on the venture's attainment of its performance targets.

17. See Harvey and Lusch (1995) for a brief review of the due diligence process.

REFERENCES AND ADDITIONAL READING

BATY, GORDON. *Entrepreneurship for the Nineties.* Englewood Cliffs, NJ: Prentice Hall, 1990.

BESANKO, DAVID, DAVID DRANOVE, AND MARK SHANLEY. *Economics of Strategy* 2nd ed. New York: John Wiley & Sons, Inc., 1999.

BHIDE, AMAR, AND HOWARD STEVENSON. "Note on Attracting Stakeholders." *Harvard Business School Publishing* 9–389–139, 1989.

BLOCK, ZENAS, AND IAN MACMILLAN. *Corporate Venturing.* Cambridge, MA: Harvard Business School Press, 1993.

BOOTH, JAMES R., AND RICHARD L. SMITH. "Capital Raising, Underwriting, and the Certification Hypothesis." *Journal of Financial Economics* 15 (1986): 261–281.

BRODSKY, NORM. "Due Diligence." *Inc.* (February 1998): 25–26.

CAMP, JUSTIN J. *Venture Capital Due Diligence.* New York: John Wiley & Sons, 2002.

DIXIT, AVINASH, AND BARRY NALEBUFF. *Thinking Strategically.* New York: W. W. Norton, 1991.

DRUCKER, PETER F. *Managing for Results.* New York: Harper and Row, 1964.

FIET, JAMES. "Reliance upon Informants in the Venture Capital Industry." *Journal of Business Venturing* 10 (May 1995): 197–223.

GHEMAWAT, PANKAJ. *Commitment: The Dynamics of Strategy.* New York: Free Press, 1991.

GUMPERT, DAVID. *How to Really Create a Successful Business Plan.* Boston: Goldhirsch Group, Inc., 1996.

HALL, JOHN, AND CHARLES HOFER. "New Venture Evaluation." *Journal of Business Venturing* 8 (1993): 25–42.

HARVEY, MICHAEL G., AND ROBERT F. LUSCH. "Expanding the Nature and Scope of Due Diligence." *Journal of Business Venturing* 10 (January 1995): 1–22.

HISRICH, ROBERT. *Entrepreneurship: Starting, Developing, and Managing a New Enterprise.* Homewood, IL: Richard D. Irwin, 1995.

KLEIN, BENJAMIN, AND KEITH B. LEFFLER. "The Role of Market Forces in Assuring Contractual Performance." *Journal of Political Economy* 89 (1981): 615–641.

KREPS, DAVID M., AND ROBERT WILSON. "Reputation and Imperfect Information." *Journal of Economic Theory* 27 (August 1982): 253–279.

LEVESQUE, MOREN, AND KENNETH R. MACCRIMMON. "On the Interaction of Time and Money Invested in New Ventures." *Entrepreneurship Theory and Practice* 22 (Winter 1997): 89–110.

LIN, TIMOTHY, AND RICHARD SMITH. "Insider Reputation and Selling Decisions: The Unwinding of Venture Capital Investments During Equity IPOs." *Journal of Corporate Finance* 4 (1998): 241–263.

MILGROM, PAUL, AND JOHN ROBERTS. *Economics, Organization, and Management.* Englewood Cliffs, NJ: Prentice-Hall, 1992.

SAHLMAN, WILLIAM A. "How to Write a Great Business Plan." *Harvard Business Review* (July–August 1997): 98–108.

SCARBOROUGH, NORMAN, AND THOMAS ZIMMERER. *Effective Small Business Management.* New York: Macmillan, 1993.

SCHILIT, KEITH. *The Entrepreneur's Guide to Preparing a Winning Business Plan and Raising Venture Capital.* Englewood Cliffs, NJ: Prentice-Hall, 1990.

SYKES, HOLLISTER, AND DAVID DUNHAM. "Critical Assumption Planning: A Practical Tool for Managing Business Development Risk. *Journal of Business Venturing* 7 (1992): 413–424.

TIMMONS, JEFFRY. "A Business Plan Is More Than a Financing Device." *Harvard Business Review* 58 (March–April 1980): 28–34.

TIMMONS, JEFFRY. *New Venture Creation.* 5th ed. Chicago: Irwin, 1999, Chapter 11.

WILLIAMSON, OLIVER. *The Economic Institutions of Capitalism.* New York: Free Press, 1985.

WRIGHT, MIKE, KEN ROBBIE, AND CHRISTINE ENNEW. "Venture Capitalists and Serial Entrepreneurs." *Journal of Business Venturing* 12 (May 1997): 227–249.

New Venture Strategy

Risk is inherent in the commitment of present resources to future expectations . . . The main goal of management science must be to enable business to take the right risk. (Peter Drucker, 1973)

Learning Objectives

After reading this chapter you should:

- Understand what makes a decision strategic.
- Understand the interrelationships between financing decisions and other aspects of new venture strategy.
- Be able to explain how strategic decisions are related to the entrepreneur's objective of value-maximization.
- Recognize the real options reflected in strategic alternatives.
- Understand how to use decision trees to identify and evaluate real options.
- Understand how to use game trees when strategic choices depend on rival reactions.

The strategic plan of a new venture is a plan for advancing an opportunity to a successful business venture. Any such plan must be developed with a particular objective in mind. What does the entrepreneur hope to achieve? Given the objective, the plan seeks to define a course of action designed to achieve it.[1] In our view, a strategic plan has three critical dimensions: a product-market strategy, an organizational strategy, and a financial strategy. These three are reflected in the plan and are highly interrelated. It is essential for the entrepreneur to design an overall strategy that recognizes the interrelationships.

This chapter establishes the basics of strategic planning in an entrepreneurial setting and develops a framework for evaluating alternative strategies.[2] The framework we propose is one that combines decision trees (or game trees) and investment valuation to compare alternative strategies. The framework begins with identifying the objective and strategic alternatives for achieving it. The alternatives are essentially structures of real options that can be described and evaluated as the branches of a decision tree. We begin with an example from business history that illustrates the importance of financing choices in the overall design of new venture strategy.

4.1   HENRY FORD AND THE MODEL T

In the early 1900s, more than 100 different firms were manufacturing and selling automobiles in the United States.[3] Now there are only two domestic manufacturers: General Motors and Ford. Most of the attrition occurred during the early decades, offsetting the meteoric growth of Ford Motor Company.[4] From 1908 through 1921, the U.S. market share of Ford had risen steadily to 60 percent, and half of the automobiles operating in the world were Fords.[5] It looked, at the time, as if Ford soon would become the sole U.S. manufacturer.

Why did Henry Ford succeed in the early years of the industry when so many other entrepreneurs failed? Surely, we all know the answer (that we have read and heard about before). Ford succeeded because he chose a strategy of mass production and his rivals did not. As he stated to one of his partners in 1903,"The way to make automobiles is to make one automobile like another automobile, to make them all alike—just like one pin is like another pin when it comes from a pin factory."[6]

But this must be an incomplete explanation. Henry Ford did not invent mass production.[7] Eli Whitney, for example, began mass-producing rifles with interchangeable parts in 1798. Moreover, Adam Smith (in the famous pin factory example to which Ford implicitly refers) recognized the economic benefits of specialization and mass production in *The Wealth of Nations* in 1776, more than a century before Ford began to manufacture automobiles.

Surely, by the 1900s, it did not take a genius to recognize the cost saving that mass production could bring. A piece of the puzzle is missing, and that piece is Ford's innovative marketing and financing plan. In the early stages of the industry, to limit up-front costs, automobiles were being manufactured one by one, often to order, and using generic tools and parts. Accordingly, the capital commitments of most manufacturers were negligible. Mass production, on the other hand, requires a major capital investment. Standardized parts must be inventoried; several automobiles must be in production at the same time by a team of employees; efficient production requires investment in customized tools and parts; and finished goods must be inventoried for future sale.

Henry Ford's true genius was in perceiving the vast market for sales of low-priced automobiles, recognizing that low cost could be achieved through high-volume mass production, and in *solving the financing problem*. Without financing, he could never have produced the Model T and sold it profitably for less than $500 (while competitors were attempting to charge hundreds more).

How did Ford finance his new venture? He limited capital commitments by purchasing parts from others and performing only the assembly operation himself. He purchased parts on credit, assembled automobiles quickly and sold them to his dealers for cash. By quickly building a large dealer network (attracting dealers because of his ability to sell at a price well below the competition), he was able to exploit the efficiencies of large-scale mass production. The strategy quickly began to generate positive cash flow, which was used to upgrade the assembly line and integrate upstream from assembling into manufacturing. By applying the same techniques to parts manufacturing, he was able to achieve additional efficiencies so that by 1916, the retail price of a Model T had declined to $360, down 58 percent from its initial 1908 price of $850.

The Model T is a compelling example of the important role that financial strategy can play in the success of a new venture. However, business strategy must be dynamic and responsive to changes in the competitive environment. Why, despite its domination of the automobile industry in the early 1920s, did the Ford Motor Company ultimately falter and end up in second place among domestic producers? The answer is that Henry Ford would not depart from the strategy that had been so successful in the early years, even though the economics of the industry had changed. Ford continued to produce the Model T from 1908 through 1927 with no substantial improvements to design or performance. Ford's strategic focus was 100 percent on cost minimization. Consumers could buy any car they wanted "as long as it is black."

Meanwhile, competitors who had managed to survive the intense price competition from Ford had also moved into mass production, but with more of a view toward the changing tastes of consumers. Those companies made tradeoffs between cost reduction through large-scale mass production and product quality and styling. As a result, General Motors, in particular, was able to achieve most of the cost savings while offering automobiles that outperformed the Model T and catered to consumer demand for styling.[8] Model T sales declined rapidly after 1921, as the market share of General Motors climbed.

Finally, in 1927 Ford Motor Company was compelled by competitive pressure to discontinue the Model T but failed to adjust its strategy to a market where cost was only one dimension of competition. At that time, Ford introduced the Model A, which it attempted to sell without modification for several years. The ultimate result was the same, but the end came more quickly. When the Model A was introduced, Ford immediately regained some of its lost share, but the gains were eroded quickly, as competitors continued to improve and differentiate their products and Ford did not.

In the competitive struggle between Ford and General Motors, financing took a less important position than in the early days of the industry. Both companies were well established and could easily raise financing for whatever product-market strategy they chose to pursue. This second episode illustrates a general principle that is an important motivation for this book: The link between product-market strategy and financing strategy is much more acute for entrepreneurial ventures than for established large businesses.

4.2 WHAT MAKES A PLAN OR DECISION STRATEGIC?

What is a strategic plan? Perceptions differ. To some, it is a broad plan for achieving a particular objective. Others regard the term in a more militaristic or game theoretic context, emphasizing strategy as a broad plan for defeating or out-competing rivals. Our view comports with the former definition in that, particularly for a start-up, there may be little reason to focus on competition against particular rivals. Regardless of the specific definition, it is useful to distinguish strategic decisions from other decisions along several dimensions.

First, *strategic decisions are consequential.* Unlike the decision of which way to drive home from work, a strategic decision involves substantial commitment of time and resources. Strategic decisions are of sufficient magnitude and importance that they are rare, and little precedent exists on which to base them.

Second, *strategic decisions are both active and reactive.* The decision is made in a competitive setting with regard to the possible actions and reactions of others who may have competing or complementary objectives. In selecting among alternatives, the decision maker must take into consideration the choices that may already have been made by others whose objectives overlap and must recognize that others may react to the decision. The decision of when, where, and how to locate a retail store is strategic in this sense. The decision maker must consider the habits of the prospective customers, likely decisions of rivals, and how the store's presence might affect the actions of both prospective customers and rivals.

Third, *strategic decisions limit the range of future actions that are possible.* In other words, a strategic decision is not costlessly reversible. If a wrong course of action is selected, the decision maker cannot simply retract the move. Investments made to pursue the first course of action are, to some extent, sunk. Sunk investments limit flexibility because the full cost of proceeding in a new direction must be compared to only the incremental cost of continuing in the same direction. As a consequence, an initial wrong strategic choice is one from which the decision maker can never fully recover.

The early actions of Ford satisfy these criteria. First, the decision to appeal to the mass market was a deliberate choice to reject the prevailing view, that the automobile was a luxury. Had Ford produced a customized luxury vehicle, he would have been unable to realize economies of mass production. Could he have hedged his bet by producing vehicles appropriate for both the mass market and the high end? Probably not. Attempting to reach both would require using two different manufacturing processes; send confusing marketing messages; and undercut Ford's ability to attract financing from the dealer network.

Second, given the large number of small manufacturers in the early automobile industry, Ford *initially* did not need to be concerned that other manufacturers would react to his entry. He did, however, need to be concerned with how they would react to his unprecedented success. Manufacturers of higher priced automobiles, acting as a group, sought to foreclose him from the industry by refusing to grant Ford licensing rights to use a patent that was argued to control the automobile technology. The rivals also ran ads critical of the assembly-line technology. Ford managed to turn the attacks to his benefit.[9] Subsequently, other manufacturers, like General Motors, imitated aspects of his success with mass production, eventually forcing the Ford Motor Company to abandon an element of Henry Ford's initial strategy and move to annual model changes.

Third, Ford's commitment to one model, the Model T, was costly to reverse. It required abandoning other models, investing in large-capacity facilities, and purchasing large specialized inventories. These investments left Ford little choice but to price aggressively and to maintain capacity utilization at a high level.

4.3   FINANCIAL STRATEGY

Financial strategic choices have the same three elements. A financing choice, such as the decision to finance a new investment with debt, can limit future financing choices in a variety of ways. For example, contractual provisions (or covenants) of the debt agreement may restrict the firm's ability to redeem the debt and replace it with equity capital or other debt. Existing debt financing may also limit financing sources available for new projects. And debt service requirements may limit the firm's ability to undertake new projects that would generate negative cash flows in the short-run.

Competitive interdependencies also are present. Financing choices that are costly to reverse or change involve sunk investments in arranging the financing. In such cases, a firm's financing choices may credibly commit the firm to a particular course of action that is observable by competitors, suppliers, customers, employees, and stockholders. Such credible commitments can influence the actions of these groups. For example, securing project financing to develop a new shopping center can discourage others from moving ahead with plans to develop centers of their own in the same geographic market. Conversely, announcement of intent to develop a shopping center, if not backed by a credible commitment of some sort, could touch off a scramble among rivals to be first in the market.

The scope of financial strategy is quite broad. It goes beyond the simple debt-versus-equity financing decision and includes such considerations as the connections between financing choices and growth, flexibility, and control. In addition, we define financial strategy to include such choices as the use of financial contracts to address or overcome informational asymmetries between entrepreneurs and investors, and to better align the incentives of entrepreneurs and employees with investor interests.

4.4 PRODUCT-MARKET, FINANCIAL, AND ORGANIZATIONAL STRATEGY

Financial strategic decisions are interdependent with product-market and organizational strategic decisions. The potential for success is greatest when the decisions are in harmony. The early experience of the Ford Motor Company illustrates this point. The product-market strategy of Ford emphasized high-volume, low-product-priced marketing. The complementary organizational strategy involved a focus of manufacturing efforts on final assembly rather than upstream integration into manufacturing of component parts. The financial strategy overlaps both. By focusing on final assembly, Ford reduced its need for early-stage capital. It also could take advantage of vendor financing (trade credit) for the parts it purchased. By selling to dealers for cash, it shifted the burden of carrying finished goods inventory to the dealers. It is unlikely that Ford's product-market strategy could have been achieved without the complementary financial and organizational strategies.

Figure 4-1 provides a general framework for thinking about how the various components of strategy fit together. Financial strategy defines the type and timing of financing. Strategic decisions include: the amount of outside financing as opposed to financing provided by the entrepreneur, the target capital structure of the venture, the staging of cash infusions, and so on. Product-market strategy involves the targeted sales growth rate, product price, level of product quality, how to differentiate the product, whether to produce multiple products, and the like. Organizational strategy defines the horizontal and vertical boundaries of the firm, in whom decision-making authority within the firm resides, and so forth.[10]

As an illustration of the relations displayed in Figure 4-1, suppose, based on an investigation of the product-market, a decision maker were to conclude that rapid sales growth was the preferred strategy. By growing rapidly, the firm might discourage entry of rivals, might secure a defensibly large market share, and so on. However, the strategic choice to grow rapidly commits the firm to a limited array of financing options. Growth requires capital, and rapid growth usually requires external capital. The firm could choose to operate with a high degree of financial leverage, in which case it might sacrifice product-market and organizational flexibility, or it might turn to the market for equity capital, in which case, challenges to control are more likely to arise.

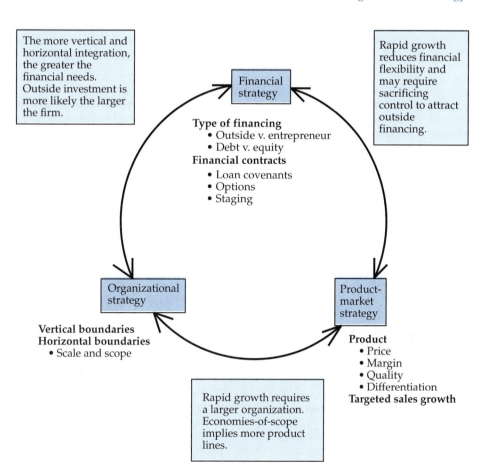

The more vertical and horizontal integration, the greater the financial needs. Outside investment is more likely the larger the firm.

Rapid growth reduces financial flexibility and may require sacrificing control to attract outside financing.

Financial strategy

Type of financing
- Outside v. entrepreneur
- Debt v. equity

Financial contracts
- Loan covenants
- Options
- Staging

Organizational strategy

Product-market strategy

Vertical boundaries
Horizontal boundaries
- Scale and scope

Product
- Price
- Margin
- Quality
- Differentiation

Targeted sales growth

Rapid growth requires a larger organization. Economies-of-scope implies more product lines.

Figure 4-1   The interdependent components of strategy

It does not make sense to settle on a product-market strategy without considering how that choice restricts financing options. It also makes little sense to place product-market strategy ahead of financing in the decision hierarchy. As illustrated in the previous chapter, in Figure 3-1, while it may be possible to settle on a financing option that makes the product-market strategy choice viable, sequencing the two decisions can lead to second-best outcomes. Even though rapid growth may appear to be attractive for dealing with the product market, the entrepreneur might be better off if the firm were to grow more slowly and maintain a higher level of organizational flexibility.[11]

Similarly, there are interactions between financial and organizational strategy and between product-market and organizational strategy. Examples of interactions appear on the outside of Figure 4-1. You can probably think of others, particularly in the context of specific examples.

Financial strategic choices arise in businesses of all types, sizes, and ages. However, nowhere are the strategic issues more acute than for new ventures. The interdependencies between product-market, organizational, and financial decisions can weaken in large, well-established organizations. If a large company contemplates a strategy of rapid growth in a market that accounts for a small fraction of its total activity, that decision does not necessarily commit the company to a highly leveraged capital structure or to the need to raise equity capital by selling stock. In such a case, investors may not be harmed if the investing and financing decisions are treated as separate.

There are, however, clear cases where, even in large organizations, the link between investing and financing remains important. These tend to be cases where financial strategy has the potential to come before product-market strategy. For example, a large company may attempt to limit collective bargaining demands by committing to a highly leveraged capital structure on the theory that excessive wage demands would threaten firm survival and hence the employees' jobs. Although this is one potential effect, high leverage can also deprive the firm of product-market flexibility, threatening its survival no less effectively.

Our point is that product-market, organizational, and financial decisions need to be viewed simultaneously. This forces the decision maker not to arbitrarily narrow the opportunity set of possible actions. Simultaneous consideration helps guarantee that the first-best overall strategy is not overlooked. Thinking about product-market, organizational, and financial strategies as simultaneous rather than sequential choices takes us beyond the limits of intuitive decision making.[12] Evaluating the choices simultaneously requires more formal analysis. Accordingly, an important aspect of this chapter is to develop an analytical framework for strategic decision making. We use decision trees and game trees as devices to structure thinking about the interplay between simultaneous and sequential decisions, and to identify and evaluate alternative strategies.

4.5 DECIDING ON THE OBJECTIVE

The first step in developing the analytical framework for strategic planning is to specify an objective. For this purpose, we rely on the guiding principle of microeconomics—that individuals are rational utility maximizers. This means that if a person is confronted with a decision, such as whether to go to a movie or out to dinner, the individual tries to predict which of the two will be more satisfying and chooses accordingly. Making rational choices is a forward-looking concept. Rationality does not mean that the choice is always right *ex post*, but just that it is *expected* to be right given the information available at the time.

The principle of utility maximization applies to entrepreneurial decisions. A prospective entrepreneur considers a variety of actions and selects the one that is expected to result in the highest level of satisfaction *for the entrepreneur*. A number of qualitative factors bear on the choice. A person who is relatively risk-tolerant is more willing to abandon secure employment in pursuit of a new venture than is a person who places a high value on security. A person who enjoys work-related challenges is more willing to start a new venture than one who values leisure time. These are the prospective entrepreneur's personal preferences, and little can be done in a formal way to assess the highly individualized qualitative tradeoffs. But analysis can help entrepreneurs do a better job of identifying and evaluating the tradeoffs.

For many entrepreneurs, the decisions to proceed with a new venture or continue in current employment, and of how to develop the venture, are made on the basis of intuition or "gut-feel." Yet the decision to undertake a new venture, and if so, how to proceed, is not one where intuition is likely to lead to the best outcome. Of course, like the example of Ford Motor Company in the early days of the automobile industry, there are many successful ventures where the entrepreneur's intuitive choice resulted in a huge payoff. But like Ford's later experience with the Model A and the hundreds of early entrants to automobile manufacturing, there are many more examples where intuition resulted in failure.

Formal strategic planning reduces the importance of intuition in the decision process, so that prospective entrepreneurs can make more informed decisions. To achieve this, we must begin with an objective that can be measured. As stated in Chapter 1, we assume that the entrepreneur's objective is maximum value of the venture to the entrepreneur. Thus, 40 percent ownership of a $5 million business is more valuable than 15 percent of a $10 million business. It is not the overall value of the business that should influence the entrepreneur's strategic choices, but the value of the entrepreneur's interest.[13]

This does not mean the entrepreneur "should" substitute value-maximization for utility-maximization as the ultimate determinant of the choice. Once the quantitative value of the entrepreneur's interest is determined, it is easier for the entrepreneur to assess the qualitative tradeoffs that arise from such factors as the value of control or security. Suppose, as an entrepreneur, you are confronted with two choices by a prospective investor. Under one, you would retain control and under the other you would not.[14] In exchange for relinquishing control, however, you would receive additional compensation having a present value of $100,000. You can then ask yourself whether retaining control is worth a $100,000 reduction in the value of your interest in the venture.[15]

On one level, the objective function of the entrepreneur is likely to be complex. McMahan and Stanger (1995), for example, suggest eight elements that the financial objective function of a small enterprise can include. The entrepreneur is likely to be concerned with financial return on effort and investment. Risk is an important consideration for new ventures, and, in contrast to public corporations, both systematic and nonsystematic risk are relevant. Beyond these, entrepreneurial decisions are likely to be influenced by their effects on the liquidity, diversification, and flexibility of the venture; by transferability of ownership; and by the effects on control and the entrepreneur's accountability to others.

At a more fundamental level, the primary determinant of value is the tradeoff between risk and expected return. Factors such as liquidity, diversification, transferability, and flexibility are taken into consideration through their effects on expected return and risk. The value of control is an additional qualitative factor that goes beyond the objective assessment of present value.

As a final note, the principle of value-maximization does not mean that a venture is exploitative of either consumers or employees. A viable venture must offer a product or service that is attractive enough to draw consumers away from alternative purchases. Similarly, compensation packages must be sufficient to attract employees away from other positions.

4.6 IDENTIFYING THE ALTERNATIVES

Suppose, while working in your current position, you have perfected a technology for making calorie-free ice cream that actually tastes good. You are trying to decide whether to resign and start a venture that will employ the technology. Should you decide to proceed, there are a number of other decisions to be made. To keep matters simple, in the product market you must choose between a high-margin, slow-growth approach and a low-margin, high-growth approach. With respect to organizational design, you need to choose between entering only at the manufacturing level and contracting for distribution, or entering into both manufacturing and distribution. Of course, more complexity could be added. For example, we could consider variations in the kind and intensity of marketing effort, or different distribution channels, such as grocery stores or branded ice cream stores. Let's suppose that the nonintegrated approach involves selling through grocery stores and the integrated approach involves a network of branded ice cream stores.

Figure 4-2 shows the implications of product-market and organizational choices for financing needs. If the entrepreneur decides to enter only manufacturing and pursue a slow-growth product-market strategy, the entrepreneur's own resources are sufficient to fund the initial investment. The growth rate is determined by the operating cash flows of the business. With one-level entry and a plan of rapid growth, the entrepreneur must rely on outside financing to supplement the financing available through operating cash flow. If the entrepreneur decides to enter both manufacturing and distribution, the initial investment is too large for the entrepreneur alone to make, and additional outside financing is required at the start-up stage. With both vertical integration and rapid growth, outside financing is needed for both start-up and to sustain growth.

Even in this simple illustration, the product-market and organizational decisions limit the financing options. If entry is at two stages, available outside financing is likely to have the characteristics of equity. The entrepreneur may have to sacrifice voting control or give other control rights to providers of financing. With rapid growth, the financing needs occur after the business is established. In the early stages, equity-like claims still may be required, but the fraction of ownership that must be relinquished is likely to be less than if funding is required at the outset. As the business grows and begins to generate taxable income, debt financing becomes a more realistic and attractive possibility. In addition, there are other alternatives, such as franchising of distribution outlets and equipment leasing, that may have advantages over either equity or debt. A well-thought-out strategic plan takes such alternatives into consideration.

Financial Implications of Product-market and Organizational Strategic Choices			
		Product-market Choice	
		Slow growth	Rapid growth
Organizational Choice	One-level entry	Initially financed by entrepreneur, growth financed with operating cash flows	Initially financed by entrepreneur, growth financed with operating cash flows and outside financing
	Integrated entry	Initial financing includes outside equity, growth financed with operating cash flows	Initial financing includes outside equity, growth financed with operating cash flows and outside financing

Figure 4-2 Financial implications of product-market and organizational strategic choices

Product-market and organizational strategic choices are interdependent with financing choices. One-level entry combined with slow growth minimizes immediate and ongoing needs for external financing. Integrated entry and rapid growth normally require higher levels of immediate and ongoing external financing.

4.7 RECOGNIZING REAL OPTIONS

Strategic planning is not a one-time exercise. With the passage of time, original targets will be exceeded or not met, and new developments, such as changes in the economy or actions of competitors, will make the initial plan obsolete. A sensible approach to planning recognizes that the future holds surprises. It follows that, rather than planning a single immutable course of action, it is more useful to select the strategy that offers the highest expected value for the entrepreneur, in light of the flexibility that the strategy affords for dealing with surprises. Opportunities to abandon a venture, expand it, or change direction in a fundamental way are real options. You can think of the focus of the strategic planning as deciding which real options to acquire, retain, and abandon at key decision points.[16]

Describing Decision Rights as Options

An option is simply the right to make a decision in the future. In the stock market, a call option is a right to buy a share of stock at some future date for a price that is established today.[17] The right to buy a share of Microsoft common stock any time during the next three months at a price of $110 is a call option with an exercise price of $110, and where the underlying asset is a share of Microsoft common stock.

The value of an option depends on several factors. A call option gains value if the market price of the underlying asset rises, and loses value if the price of the asset falls. Suppose that Microsoft is selling for about $118 per share. If the price of Microsoft stock goes to $125, the value of the right to buy the stock for a fixed exercise price will increase. It follows that call options with low exercise prices are more valuable than those with high exercise prices. The right to buy Microsoft for $100 per share obviously is more valuable than the right to buy for $110.

The other factors that affect option values are the volatility (or risk) of the underlying asset, time to option expiration, and the time value of money. Since option risk is one-sided, the more volatile the underlying asset, the higher the value of an option on the asset. Suppose, over the next three months, Microsoft is equally likely to increase in value to $140 or to decline in value to $100. If the price of Microsoft stock increases to $140, a call at $110 will be in the money and can be exercised to acquire the stock for a saving of $30. If the price of Microsoft falls to $100, the call is out of the money and will not be exercised. Thus, buying a call option limits the downside risk of investing in Microsoft but preserves the potential for gain. Because the exposure to risk is one-sided, an option is more valuable the higher the risk of the underlying asset. Because volatility increases with time to expiration, long-term options are more valuable.

The time value of money affects option values because buying an option works like borrowing. If you buy a call, you do not have to come up with the money to exercise the option until you decide to do so. That is different from buying the stock outright, where you would have to pay the full price today. Accordingly, buying an option is like borrowing the exercise price without having to pay interest. Because the value of not having to pay interest is greater the higher the interest rate for borrowing, call options increase in value with increases in the cost of money.[18]

A put option is the antithesis of a call. It is the right to sell an underlying asset during a specified period at a specified exercise price. If the owner of a put decides to exercise, he or she receives the exercise price, whereas the owner of a share of stock receives whatever the stock is selling for at the time. In contrast to calls, puts gain value when underlying asset values are low and when exercise prices are high. A put on Microsoft at $110 is more valuable if Microsoft is selling for $80 than $90. It is also more valuable than a put at $100. However, like a call option, a put option is more valuable when the underlying asset is riskier. Because the owner of a put is effectively lending the exercise price without charging interest, a put option is less valuable if the cost of money is high (i.e., more interest income is foregone).

Calls and puts can be either bought or sold. The seller (or writer) of a call is obligated to deliver the underlying asset in exchange for the exercise price if the call is exercised. The writer of a put is obligated to buy the underlying asset at the exercise price if the put is exercised. Puts and calls can be used to allocate the risk of investing in the underlying asset. For example, an investor in Microsoft common stock, who buys a put option, has reallocated the downside risk to the writer of the option. In this case, the stockholder is hedged against the downside risk, and the writer of the put is acting as an insurer. The writer of the put may or may not be hedged as well.

Comparisons Between Real Options and Financial Options

Puts and calls on Microsoft common stock are financial options. The underlying asset is a financial asset, and exercising or not exercising a financial option does not affect the value of the underlying asset. In several respects, real options are similar to financial options. Just as the values of financial options increase with the riskiness of the underlying asset and time to expiration of the option, so do the values of real options increase with these factors. The values of real options are also affected by the difference between the exercise price and the underlying asset value in ways that are similar to how financial options are affected.[19]

Yet, real options differ from financial options in important ways. First, the markets for financial options are often complete, meaning that calls and puts on an underlying share of stock are available with the same exercise price and expiration date, the underlying stock is freely traded, and riskless borrowing is possible. If the market is complete, the value of an option can be determined by appealing to the ability of investors to risklessly arbitrage pricing disparities.[20] In contrast, real option markets are not complete. The formal models used to value financial options can overstate the values of real options owing to lack of a ready market for the options or the underlying assets.

Second, real options often are interdependent in ways that make the application of formal option pricing models difficult or inappropriate. Financial options can be bought and sold separately, and the values of financial options can be calculated without regard to other options that may exist. The value of a portfolio of financial options is simply the sum of the values of the individual options. Real options, in contrast, often are interdependent, and the decision to exercise one may have implications for the values of others. Consequently, the value of a portfolio of real options usually cannot be determined by simply adding up the values of the individual options.

The term, *real options,* is used to stress the similarity to financial options, while preserving the notion that there also are important differences. Returning to the calorie-free ice cream example, once you have developed the technology to manufacture the ice cream, you have options to benefit from the technology in many ways. Some of those ways, as already discussed, are reflected in Figure 4-2. You also have the option to do none of those things and, instead, continue working in your existing position. In addition, you have the option to delay and, for example, start the venture next year (though in an environment that will have changed, including the possibility that someone else may act before you do). Once you begin the venture, depending on the contractual arrangements you make for outside financing, you may have the option to abandon it if things do not work out as expected.

The alternative courses of action in the previous paragraph are real options. A useful strategic plan is one designed around the values of these real options. The plan must be sufficient to carry the venture from one key decision point to the next, at which time it is important to review the options. Depending on the conclusions of that review, it may be necessary to revise the plan. Normally, the decision points correspond to the milestones we discussed in Chapter 2. Because strategic planning must consider the values of real options, it is useful to incorporate formal decision analysis techniques into plan design.

Examples of Real Options

Category of Option	Description	Examples
Option to defer	The option to wait before taking an action until more is known or timing is expected to be more favorable.	When to harvest a stand of trees, introduce a new product, or replace an existing piece of equipment.
Option to expand or contract	The option to increase the scale of an operation in response to high demand or reduce the scale in response to low demand.	Adding or subtracting to the daily flights on an existing airline connection, adding memory to a computer, or scaling back production.
Option to abandon	The option to discontinue an operation and liquidate the assets.	Discontinuation of a research project, closing a store, or resigning from current employment.
Option to stage investment	The option to commit investment in stages instead of all at once gives rise to a series of abandonment options. Each stage is an option on the value of the subsequent stages.	Staging of research and development projects, staging of financial commitments, or staging of expansion of a development project.
Option to switch inputs or outputs	The option to alter the mix of inputs or outputs of a production process in response to market prices.	The output mix of refined crude oil products, or the substitution between coal and natural gas to produce electricity.
Option to grow	The option to expand the scope of activities to take advantage of newly perceived opportunities.	Extension of brand names to new products, marketing a new product through existing distribution channels.

Source: Adapted from L. Trigeorgis, *Real Options* (Cambridge, MA: MIT Press, 1996), pp. 2–3.

4.8 STRATEGIC DECISION ANALYSIS AND DECISION TREES

A decision tree is a way to conceptualize strategic alternatives. The process of constructing a decision tree imposes discipline on the evaluation process and helps the entrepreneur identify relevant real options and points at which critical decisions must be made. It also enables the entrepreneur to assess, in a structured way, the connections between decisions made today and the value of the venture in the future.

We use a simple example to illustrate the use of decision trees to describe real options and to evaluate strategic alternatives. Let us suppose an entrepreneur is considering investing in a restaurant. For simplicity, the entrepreneur assumes that potential demand for the restaurant may be high, medium, or low. Corresponding to the level of expected demand, the entrepreneur is considering building a large restaurant, a small restaurant, or not entering the business at this time. The cost of the large restaurant is $750,000. The cost of the small restaurant is $600,000. The entrepreneur has $400,000 to invest and plans to bring in an outside investor for the balance. The investor requires 1 percent of the equity for each $10,000 invested, resulting in a 35 percent interest in the larger restaurant or a 20 percent interest in the smaller one. The entrepreneur retains the balance of ownership.

Naturally, the large restaurant has the potential to generate more revenue, but it also necessitates a higher level of fixed operating expenses. The present values of future cash flows under different states of the world reflect these economies. If the high-demand state occurs, the limited capacity of the small restaurant limits its value. Accordingly, in the high-demand state, we assume that the entrepreneur expects the present value of future cash flows of the large restaurant to be $1.5 million, and the present value of the small restaurant is expected to be $800,000. If the intermediate-demand state occurs, the present values of future cash flows of both the large and the small restaurants are expected to be $800,000. In the low-demand state, the present value of the large restaurant is $300,000 and the present value of the small restaurant is $400,000. The difference is due to the higher fixed cost of the large restaurant.[21]

If the investment is a one-time accept-reject decision, then Figure 4-3 represents the choices in the form of a decision tree. The square in the diagram represents the one decision point, as we currently are viewing the choices. The circles represent outcomes that are beyond the entrepreneur's control. They reflect states of the world. You can think of "Nature" as "choosing" a state of the world, and each state has a probability associated with it. In Figure 4-3, the entrepreneur has simplified the decision problem by thinking in terms of three states of the world and has estimated the probability of each state. At the time the entrepreneur is deciding whether to invest and in what sort of restaurant, the probability of high demand is 30 percent, the probability of intermediate demand is 50 percent, and the probability of low demand is 20 percent. Finally, the solid circles in the figure are terminal nodes. Next to each is the net present value of the profits the entrepreneur expects if the corresponding branch is selected and the specified state of the world is realized. Thus, for example, if the large restaurant is built and the high-demand state is realized, the entrepreneur will invest $400,000 in return for 65 percent of a restaurant with a total present value of $1.5 million. The resulting NPV (conditional on the large restaurant and high demand) of the entrepreneur's investment is $575,000.

In our simple example, the entrepreneur decides how to invest by multiplying each state-contingent payoff by the probability of that state's occurrence and the entrepreneur's fractional ownership interest (.65 or .80) and then subtracting the investment of the entrepreneur.

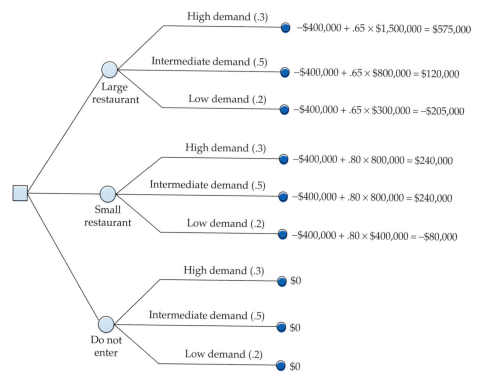

Figure 4-3   Accept-reject decision to invest in restaurant business

With a one-time accept/reject decision, the entrepreneur cannot anticipate the level of product demand that will be realized. The investment decision and choice of level of investment are made in light of existing uncertainty, by maximizing expected net present value.

The result of the calculation is the NPV of that choice to the entrepreneur, given what the entrepreneur knows at the time the decision is made.[22] Thus, if the large restaurant is selected, the expected payoff to the entrepreneur is as follows:

$$\text{Payoff} = .65 \times (.3 \times 1,500,000 + .5 \times 800,000 + .2 \times 300,000) = \$591,500.$$

As this amount exceeds the entrepreneur's $400,000 investment by $191,500 (the NPV of the choice), it is better than the choice of not investing at all. By a similar calculation, the payoff to the entrepreneur from investing in the small restaurant is $576,000, an NPV of $176,000. Because the large restaurant offers a higher NPV, that choice is better than investing in the small restaurant.

Ex post, it may turn out that building the large restaurant is the wrong decision. If demand turns out to be intermediate, the small restaurant is more valuable to the entrepreneur. If demand turns out to be low, not entering is better than either of the other choices. At the time of the decision, however, the entrepreneur cannot know which state the world will attain.

Given what is known, and the relative probabilities of the different states, building the large restaurant is the best alternative.

In Figure 4-3, the decision facing the entrepreneur is a once-and-for-all choice. There are no real options reflected in the figure. However, suppose the actual decision is more complicated. We now want to expand the range of possibilities by considering three types of real options: (1) the option to wait, (2) the option to invest more, and (3) the option to abandon.

The Option to Wait to Invest

Suppose that by not investing immediately the entrepreneur can learn more about which state of the world is likely to occur, but that waiting increases the likelihood of entry by competitors so that the payoffs in the various states are reduced. For simplicity, assume that by waiting the entrepreneur will be able to determine the state with certainty so that in each state, the highest valued (for the entrepreneur) size of restaurant can be built.

The option to wait sometimes is referred to as a learning option. Rarely do investment opportunities involve now-or-never choices. Waiting can add value because uncertainty is reduced or because waiting defers expenditures of resources until they are more immediately needed. The offsetting cost is that waiting may encourage others to enter the market or market conditions may change.[23] The option to wait is a call option. As with any call option, its value is higher if the level of uncertainty is high and if waiting will materially reduce the uncertainty.

In the context of our example, waiting could allow the population of the market served by the restaurant to grow, but could also attract more competition. Because of the likelihood of competitive entry, we assume that the present value of the large restaurant declines to $1.3 million, and the present value of the small restaurant declines to $700,000.[24] To examine, in an overly simplified way, the value of the option to wait, we compare the value today of that alternative against the value of investing today (where we already have determined that building the large restaurant is the higher valued choice).

Figure 4-4 modifies Figure 4-3 to reflect the option to delay investing until uncertainty about market demand is resolved. Conditional on the high-demand state, the NPV to the entrepreneur of waiting and then investing in the large restaurant is $445,000 (net of the $400,000 investment), and the NPV of investing in the small restaurant if the intermediate-demand state occurs is $160,000. Also, by waiting, the entrepreneur avoids the potential mistake of investing, only to find out that the low-demand state has been realized. Because, at present, we do not know which of the three states will occur, we can only compare the expected value that would result from waiting against the most favorable alternative that does not involve waiting. The expected NPV of waiting is simply the probability weighted average of the three possible outcomes (.3 × $445,000 + .5 × $160,000 + .2 × $0) or $213,500. Because this value is greater than the $191,500 NPV that is expected under the most favorable immediate strategy (investing today in the large restaurant), it is better to wait. In this case, the option to delay investment adds $22,000 to the value of the project. The $22,000 difference is a rough measure of the value of the real option.

The Option to Add to the Initial Investment

A second kind of option is the option to increase the amount of the investment after the initial investment has been made, that is, an expansion option. Suppose that after an initial investment of $600,000 in the small restaurant (including $400,000 by the entrepreneur), the restaurant can be expanded to the large size by investing an additional $200,000. Assume that the $200,000

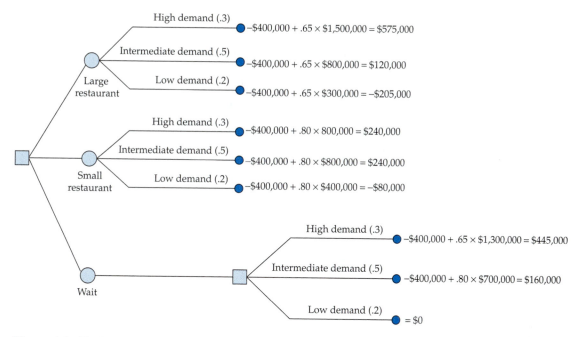

High demand (.3)
−$400,000 + .65 × $1,500,000 = $575,000

Intermediate demand (.5)
−$400,000 + .65 × $800,000 = $120,000

Large restaurant

Low demand (.2)
−$400,000 + .65 × $300,000 = −$205,000

High demand (.3)
−$400,000 + .80 × 800,000 = $240,000

Intermediate demand (.5)
−$400,000 + .80 × $800,000 = $240,000

Small restaurant

Low demand (.2)
−$400,000 + .80 × $400,000 = −$80,000

High demand (.3)
−$400,000 + .65 × $1,300,000 = $445,000

Intermediate demand (.5)
−$400,000 + .80 × $700,000 = $160,000

Wait

Low demand (.2)
= $0

Figure 4-4 Decision tree for investing in a restaurant business, with the option to delay investing until uncertainty about market demand is resolved

Not investing today may preserve an option to wait until more information is known about the true state of demand.

(if needed) comes from the outside investor but on more favorable terms because the second investment is delayed until uncertainty about the future state of the world is resolved. So the investment is less risky. Specifically, the second $200,000 is raised in exchange for a 10 percent ownership share (1 percent of the equity for each $20,000 invested), bringing the outside investor's total to 30 percent in the event of expansion. Because the initial investment is sufficient to establish a market presence, we assume that the present value of the large restaurant is $1.4 million. This value is higher than if no immediate investment is made but lower than if the large restaurant is built today.

What is the value of the option to expand after the initial investment is made? Figure 4-5 modifies Figure 4-3 to reflect this option. As the problem is structured, if the large restaurant is chosen initially, the option is foregone. If the small restaurant is built and the high-demand state is realized, the entrepreneur can either expand or not. Expanding increases the entrepreneur's NPV to $580,000 ($980,000 less the original $400,000 investment by the entrepreneur). Not expanding leaves the NPV at $240,000, as in Figure 4-3.

Clearly, expansion is better if the high-demand state is realized, but is it a good idea to invest in the small restaurant first and wait to see what happens to demand?

The answer in this case is yes. The NPV from investing initially in the small restaurant and expanding only if the high-demand state is realized is as follows:

$$\text{NPV} = .3 \times \$580,000 + .5 \times \$240,000 - .2 \times \$80,000 = \$278,000$$

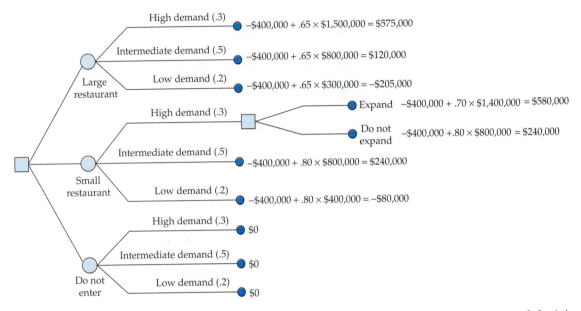

Figure 4-5 Decision tree for investing in a restaurant business, allowing for the option to expand the initial investment

Some investment decisions allow flexibility in reacting to new information. The option to expand capacity is an example.

The entrepreneur would compare this with the $191,500 NPV of investing initially in the large-scale restaurant and with the $213,500 NPV from waiting to invest until after it is known which state of the world arises (Figure 4-4). Expansion is not a good idea if the intermediate-demand state is realized because investing in that case reduces the entrepreneur's ownership share without increasing the value of the venture. Hence, according to these calculations, the NPV from investing immediately in a small restaurant (preserving the option to expand) is higher than from investing in a large restaurant, and higher than from waiting to invest in the small restaurant.

The important point is that ignoring the option to expand would have led the entrepreneur to select a less valuable strategy. In some cases, a project can be passed up entirely because of the failure to recognize that initial investments sometimes create valuable options that can be exercised in the future if the environment is right. Also, you should recognize that the waiting option and the expansion option are mutually exclusive. The entrepreneur cannot acquire both. This is different from financial options, which can each be bought or sold piecemeal and can be held in any combination.

The Option to Abandon the Venture

The final type of option we consider is an abandonment option, the option to abandon the venture if things do not work out as well as expected. Suppose the restaurant facility, large or small, has alternative use as office space. If converted to office space (for a negligible net expenditure), we assume that the present value of the large restaurant would be $600,000 and the

Techniques for Reasoning through Decision Trees

A decision tree identifies a sequence of decisions in which the range of available choices is limited by previous decisions and the best decision depends on which state of the world is realized. Decision trees are used for comparing the values of different strategies. The decision maker is uncertain about which state of the world will be realized but knows or estimates the probabilities of the different states. In addition, the decision maker estimates the net present value of a choice conditional on which future state is realized.

A few simple techniques can ensure that the decision tree you construct accurately reflects the important choices you face and helps value the choices correctly.

- **Focus on the most important decisions:** It is easy to overly complicate the analysis by thinking of the choices in too much detail or with too much complexity. Because the number of branches in a decision tree expands geometrically, decision-tree analysis can become intractable rapidly. Focusing on a few critical decisions and a few discrete choices is all that usually is needed or useful (e.g., make or buy, borrow or issue equity, grow rapidly or slowly).

- **Construct the tree by reasoning forward:** Sequencing is chronological. You need to keep track of how one choice limits the options for subsequent decisions. Determine the choices available to you today. For each of those, determine the choices that would be available at the next decision point, and so on. Decisions that are simultaneous can be represented as more branches emanating from the same node. For example, scale of entry (large or small) and rate of growth (rapid or slow) can be represented as four branches from the same point (large scale with rapid growth, etc.).

- **At each decision point, keep track of what you know and what you don't know:** If you are trying to decide on the best scale of entry today and what is best depends on the level of future demand (a state of the world that is uncertain today) you can only base today's decision on expected future demand.

- **Evaluate the choices by calculating backward:** Start with the last decision point (the terminal node) and compare the values of the alternatives that emanate from that node. Identify the highest-valued alternative and eliminate the rest. For example if, conditional on high demand, you would choose to expand, then you do not need to keep track of the other choices that you would not pursue. Move to the next decision point and evaluate the choices considering only the highest-valued branches from the subsequent node.

- **Select the branch with the highest expected value:** The process of backward induction, working from the best future decision conditional of choices made previously, leads to a set of valuations that reflect the values of the embedded options in the decision process.

value of the small restaurant would be $300,000.[25] You can see from the numbers that the option to abandon the small restaurant is worthless. This is so because a small restaurant, even in the low-demand state, has a present value of $400,000, which is more than its present value as office space. But the option does have value for the large restaurant, because $600,000 is more than the $300,000 present value as a restaurant in the low-demand state.

Is the value of the option to abandon the large restaurant (by converting it to office space) enough to tip the balance in favor of building the large restaurant? The entrepreneur would realize a 65 percent share of $600,000 or $390,000. The net present value to the entrepreneur from investing immediately in the large restaurant is as follows:

$$NPV = -\$400,000 + .3 \times \$975,000 + .5 \times \$520,000 + .2 \times \$390,000 = \$230,500.$$

This amount is less than the value of the strategy of initially investing in the small restaurant, with the option to expand, but it is higher than any of the other alternatives. If the option to expand did not exist, then investing in the large-scale restaurant with recognition of the abandonment option would be the preferred strategy. It would exceed the NPV of the next best alternative—waiting until the state of the world is realized—by $17,000.

Bailing out of a project is not something most entrepreneurs want to consider. After all, who wants to plan for failure? However, the option to abandon a venture that does not work out as well as expected can be critical to value. Test pilots of new aircraft normally take along parachutes in case something goes wrong, and would otherwise be much less interested in trying new designs. The same should be true of entrepreneurs. Thinking about what can be done to abandon a venture if it proves to be unsuccessful can significantly reduce risk for the entrepreneur, and can increase the potential for identifying ventures that should be undertaken.

4.9   RIVAL REACTIONS AND GAME TREES

Decision-tree analysis is used to value strategic alternatives. However, such analysis does not explicitly incorporate the reactions of rivals. For example, consider a new venture that offers an innovative line of athletic shoes. Its entry strategy in terms of introductory price, advertising expenditures, geographic scope, and so on, may depend critically on how it expects incumbent firms to react. The new firm may decide to enter with an aggressive pricing strategy, making the assumption that incumbents will keep their prices constant. But if incumbents react by pricing aggressively, then the effectiveness of the entrant's pricing strategy is reduced.

Rival reactions are likely to affect decision making in settings where there are only a few competitors. This is so because decisions of the various firms can be highly interdependent. Rival reactions are not at issue in perfectly competitive markets because other firms will not react specifically to entry of a new rival. For a small venture entering a large market, it may make sense to think of the market as perfectly competitive. Also, rival reactions are not an issue for a new venture that offers a unique product and therefore has monopoly power (and anticipates no entry), because the firm can make decisions independently of other firms.

How do firms decide what to do in highly interdependent environments? One way to evaluate rival reactions is to assign probabilities to their actions and to use a decision tree to evaluate the choices. This approach is not likely to yield reliable results because the probabilities are subjective and effectively yield a weighted average reaction from among the various possibilities, whereas the actual reaction will be one choice or another. There is a better way to think about the decision when rival reactions are important. The alternative is to model the reactions of the rivals and to determine what reaction would be in the best interest of each rival. The underlying reasoning is that a firm's actions depend on expected rival reactions and rival reactions depend on the firm's action. Each firm is assumed to behave rationally by trying to maximize its value. The objective is to select the strategy that maximizes value given what you believe your rival will do.

Accordingly, strategic interactions can be modeled by relying on the contributions of game theory.[26] Game theory is a branch of economics concerned with analysis of optimal decision making when all decision makers are aware that their actions affect each other's behavior and take these interactions into account.[27] They are assumed to behave in a self-interested, rational way. To illustrate the uses of game theory in formulating strategy, we need to introduce some new terminology. A game consists of a set of players, an order of play, the information set available to the players, the set of actions available to each player, and the payoff schedule that results from the actions of the players. The players are simply decision makers such as an entrepreneur, a firm manager, a venture capitalist, or a rival. The players are called on to make decisions at various points in a game (decision nodes). In a decision tree, the decisions are based on Nature's actions that are determined by fixed probabilities and are not strategic. However, in a game-theoretic setting, player actions are strategic and driven by rationality. The sequence in which decisions are made is the order of play. If all players make their decisions one at a time in a sequence, then the game is a sequential-move game. If the decisions are made at one time, then the game is a simultaneous-move game.

A sequential-move game can be analyzed with a game tree.[28] A game tree is a joint decision tree for the players and is composed of nodes and branches like a decision tree. Each node represents a decision point for one player. Each branch represents a possible action at that point.

Consider a common problem of a prospective entrepreneur. Kelly is interested in quitting her job and opening her own bar, Kelly's Bar, in the small town where she lives. Her options are to: (1) enter with a large bar (ENTER LARGE), (2) enter with a small bar (ENTER SMALL), and (3) wait (WAIT) to see if the town's economy will support another bar. She has done a thorough job of estimating the costs and revenues associated with the two establishment sizes. Her biggest concern is a rumor that a national franchiser, Erin, is considering opening a pub in the town. Kelly's decision depends on the two actions available to the rival, Erin's Pub, Inc. Since Erin's Pub is a business format franchise (one size only), Erin is considering two options: (1) enter (ENTER) or (2) do not enter (STAY OUT).

The decisions are illustrated in the game tree in Figure 4-6. The payoffs for both players are expressed in terms of NPV. For our purposes, suppose that the game is sequential and that by acting quickly, Kelly can make the first move. Thus, the first decision node (working left to right) belongs to Kelly. The middle three decision nodes belong to Erin. If Kelly chooses large-scale entry, then Erin's Pub makes a $100,000 loss if Erin elects to enter, and $0 if Erin elects to stay out. In this case, Erin's rational choice is to stay out. If Kelly chooses small-scale entry, then Erin's Pub earns a $200,000 profit if Erin chooses to enter the market and $0 if Erin decides to stay out. The rational decision for Erin in this case is to enter. Finally, if Kelly is uncomfortable acting quickly, she can decide to wait for the market to develop further. In this case, Erin must decide between entering and staying out without knowing what Kelly is going to do. If Erin enters, she earns $100,000, $210,000, or $300,000, depending on Kelly's decision to enter large, enter small, or stay out, respectively.

If Erin finds herself on the branch of the game tree where Kelly has decided to wait, then clearly Erin would prefer to enter because all choices associated with an entry strategy generate positive profits for Erin's Pub. Hence, Kelly can "prune" the bottom branch of the decision tree. If Kelly decides to wait, she knows Erin will enter, as Erin is better off by entering if Kelly decides to wait. There is, therefore, no reason for Kelly to analyze her choices conditional on Kelly waiting and Erin deciding not to enter.

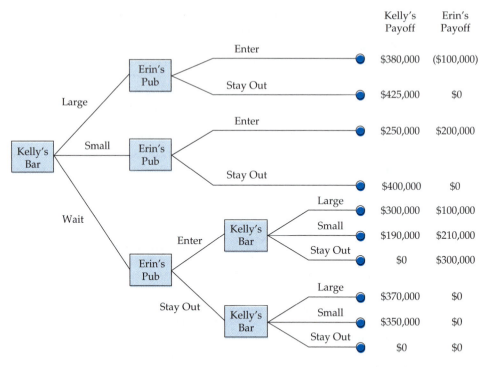

	Kelly's Payoff	Erin's Payoff

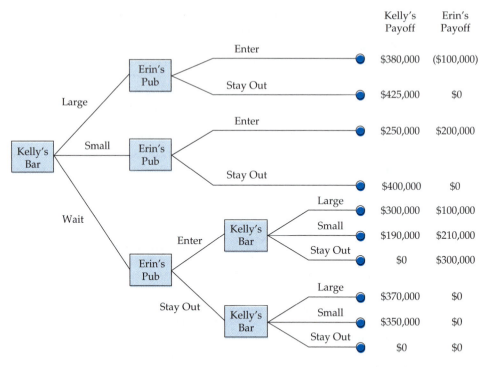

Figure 4-6 Entry decision game tree

In this sequential-move game, Kelly is the first mover. Kelly assumes Erin will react rationally to Kelly's investment decision. Kelly can select the choice that maximizes value for her, in light of Erin's expected reaction.

Examining the remaining branches, we can adopt the same technique used with the decision tree, of backward induction. We use the algorithm, "think forward and calculate back," to solve the decision problem. Start at the terminal decision nodes that display the NPVs of the various alternatives for the two parties. We reason that the rational strategy for Erin is to enter if Kelly selects small-scale entry or if Kelly decides to wait, and to stay out if Kelly selects large-scale entry. Knowing that these will be Erin's rational responses (because they maximize NPV for Erin), Kelly then selects her optimal strategy. Kelly prefers large-scale entry rather than small-scale entry or waiting. Given Erin's expected reaction of staying out of the market, Kelly expects to earn $425,000 in profits.

Nash Equilibrium

What we have described is a noncooperative game. In a noncooperative game, the players cannot enter into binding, enforceable agreements with each other. Any solution of a noncooperative game must be a Nash equilibrium.[29] A Nash equilibrium is a collection of strategies, one for each player, such that each player's strategy is optimal given the strategy of the other player(s). The Nash equilibrium in our example is the pair of strategies such that (1) Kelly's strategy maximizes her profit, given Erin's strategy and (2) Erin's strategy maximizes her profit, given Kelly's strategy.

In the entry-decision game, the Nash Equilibrium is (Kelly: ENTER LARGE, Erin: STAY OUT). That is, Kelly does not wait to see whether Erin's Pub opens; instead, she enters at a scale that makes it unprofitable for Erin's Pub to open. Both parties maximize their profits given the other player's action. If each party expects the other to choose its Nash equilibrium strategy, then both will. In other words, in equilibrium, expected behavior and actual behavior are the same.

Prisoner's Dilemma

The preceding result is interesting because in equilibrium neither party has an incentive to change strategy. But notice that the result does not maximize the combined profits of both players. Erin and Kelly would do better if they could both agree to enter and Kelly would agree to enter with the small version of her bar. In this case, the combined value equals $450,000. This is more than the $425,000 Kelly would earn from the best noncooperative strategy (where Erin does not enter). The rational noncooperative pursuit of self-interest leads to a result that is not in the players' collective interest.

This conflict between what is in the rational self-interest of individual participants and what is in their collective interest is an example of a prisoner's dilemma, a concept we will return to later in the context of deal negotiation. In that discussion, we focus on the use of contracting to avoid prisoner's dilemma problems that may arise when entrepreneurs negotiate with outside investors.

Tensions Between Maintaining Flexibility and Committing

Game theory is instructive because it forces you to think about a business situation from the perspective of your competitors, customers, suppliers, and investors, as well as from your own. The game tree is useful for thinking about tradeoffs between the value of maintaining flexibility (real options) and the value of committing to a more limited course of action. As indicated by the game tree, even though the option to wait has value, the net present value of the

Games Entrepreneurs Play

Strategic "games" include a large class of activities in which a decision maker takes into account the actions and reactions of others. Bridge, chess, dating, and war are all strategic games. Strategic games commonly played by entrepreneurs include the following:

- An entrepreneur who is preparing a business plan must decide how much optimism to build into the projections that are included in the plan. In doing so, the entrepreneur must recognize that the investor may counter with a proposed deal that ties the entrepreneur's return to the venture's ability to achieve the projections.

- An entrepreneur must decide whether to bring in a vertically integrated company as a distributor and strategic partner, or risk the possibility that the corporation will independently develop a competing product.

- An entrepreneur must decide how much control over the venture to forsake in exchange for securing funding. If the entrepreneur is unwilling to give up control, a prospective investor might decide to forego the opportunity.

- A new venture's management must decide whether to patent a product idea now and risk "copycat" entry of rivals, or maintain the idea as a trade secret.

strategy of committing first to a large-scale bar is greater than the net present value associated with the option to wait. You can see this by examining the payoffs to Kelly in terminal nodes emanating from the bottom branch of the tree. If Kelly waits to see what Erin will do, then the best Kelly can hope for is that Erin will enter and Kelly will still have the ability to open a large bar. If she waits and opens a large bar, her profit is $300,000, which is $125,000 lower than if she commits right away to open a large bar (foreclosing Erin's entry). It is important for any new business venture to consider the values of the various types of imbedded real options that it may have. But it also is important to see that early commitment to a course of action can preempt or limit rival reactions in the best interest of the new venture.

4.10 SUMMARY

Strategic decisions involve major commitments that limit the range of future actions a new venture can take. Comprehensive strategic planning involves product-market and organizational choices that are highly interrelated with financing choices. By considering all three simultaneously, the entrepreneur can be assured of identifying the strategic alternative that yields the highest expected value for the entrepreneur.

A new venture can be thought of as a portfolio of real options, including, among others, the options to delay investing, to expand the size of the investment, and to abandon the investment. Strategic planning is a process of identifying these real options and comparing the values of alternative combinations of real options.

Decision tree analysis provides a framework for identifying and describing strategic alternatives and for identifying and managing the real options that are embedded in any new venture. The different branches of the tree describe the interplay between alternative strategic choices and uncertain states of the world. By starting at the ends of the branches, determining the highest-valued choice at each stage, and eliminating the other branches from further consideration, it is possible to identify the strategic alternative today that is expected to result in the highest overall value of the project. Game tree analysis is a useful extension of decision trees when the reactions of other parties to specific strategic choices are important. Game theory forces the entrepreneur to think about a business decision from the perspectives of others who will be affected by the decision.

QUESTIONS AND PROBLEMS

1. What is an abandonment option? In what ways might an entrepreneur benefit by agreeing to give an outside investor the option to abandon a venture?

2. You can acquire an existing business for $2 million. You are uncertain about future demand. There is a 40 percent chance of high demand, in which case the present value of the business will be $3 million. There is a 25 percent chance of moderate demand, and the associated present value is $1.5 million. Finally, there is a 35 percent chance of low demand, in which case the present value is $1 million. What is the net present value of the business? Should you invest or not? Explain.

3. Suppose that if you buy the business described in question 2, you can expand the business by investing another $500,000, in which case the present value of the business would be $4 million in the high-demand state and $2.5 million in the moderate demand state. Draw a decision tree to reflect the option to expand. Evaluate the alternatives. What is

the net present value of the business if you consider the option to expand? How valuable is the option to expand?

4. Consider question 2 again, and suppose that the market value of the assets of the business would have a present value of $1.8 million if the business were to be liquidated. Draw a decision tree to reflect the abandonment option. Evaluate the alternatives. What is the net present value of the business if you consider the abandonment option? How valuable is the option to abandon?

5. Reevaluate the investment opportunity in question 2, incorporating both the expansion opportunity from question 3 and the abandonment option from question 4. Draw the decision tree incorporating both options. Are the values of the expansion and abandonment options additive? Why or why not?

6. Suppose that by committing to invest $3 million today, you can acquire a research project that has a 30 percent chance of success at the end of the first year. If it is not successful at that point, the probability of success in the second year is 40 percent, and if it is not successful at the end of the second year, the probability of success at the end of the third year is 20 percent. In the event of success at any point, the project will generate cash flows worth $4 million. If the project is unsuccessful, it is worth zero. Find the cumulative probability of success and determine the net present value of the project.

7. In contrast to question 6, suppose that if you spend $1 million today on the research project, there is a 30 percent chance of success at year-end and a 70 percent chance of no success. At that point, you can decide to invest another $1 million to continue the project. If you do invest, the probability of success at the end of the second year is 40 percent and the probability of no success is 60 percent. Finally, if you invest another $1 million in the project (if you still have not achieved success), the probability of success falls to 20 percent and the probability of failure rises to 80 percent. Conditional on success at any stage, the project is expected to generate cash flows worth $4 million.

   a. Draw a decision tree to reflect the structure of decisions the entrepreneur must consider.

   b. Evaluate the decision tree. Is the project worth pursuing? If so, which is the best course of action for the decision maker?

   c. Compare the values in questions 6 and 7. How valuable is the staging option? Explain how staging is related to abandonment options. Would you expect a series of abandonment options to be additive? Explain.

8. Having accumulated 7,000 points at a casino night fund-raiser for your school, you are in the lead. The closest contender has accumulated only 4,000 points. At the end of the evening there will be an auction, where the grand prize is a two-day yacht trip with Michael Bloomberg. The other prizes are all of trivial value. The master of ceremonies announces that there is time for one more bet, and you are at the roulette table, as is the runner-up. Assume that you both would like to win the trip. Support your reasoning with game trees.

   a. Suppose you hold on to 5,000 points and bet 2,000 on black. What should your rival do?

   b. Suppose your rival goes first and bets everything on red. What should you do?

   c. Suppose your rival offers to split the prize evenly with you if you both agree not to bet. What should you do? How does your answer depend on whether you would bet first, your opponent would bet first, or you both would have to bet at the same time?

d. All things considered, would you rather be the first mover, the second mover, or both bet at the same time?

9. Which of the following decisions are "strategic?" Explain your reasoning.

a. An owner of a nursery decides to buy an option on a parcel of land that is contiguous to his nursery.

b. The nursery owner exercises the option and buys the land.

c. The nursery owner decides to carry palm trees.

d. The nursery owner expands his staff by 10 employees.

e. The nursery owner builds a greenhouse on the plot of land he purchased.

10. Explain how trade credit can be used to shift part of the financing burden to others?

11. From the perspective of the entrepreneur explain, in general terms:

a. The strategic considerations that would tend to favor small-scale entry over large scale entry.

b. The strategic considerations that would tend to favor rapid growth.

c. The strategic considerations that would tend to favor vertical integration into manufacturing as well as distribution.

d. The strategic considerations that would tend to favor outside equity financing instead of debt.

In each case, be sure to focus on the value of the entrepreneur's interest in the venture rather than the entire venture, taking into consideration the interdependencies among product-market, organizational, and financial strategic choices. Try to support your reasoning with some specific examples.

12. Redo the real options analysis of the restaurant model in Section 4.8 assuming that the probability of high demand is 40 percent and the probability of low demand is 30 percent. All other assumptions are unchanged.

a. Calculate or examine how this change affects the values of the accept-reject decision and the various alternatives involving the real options to wait, expand, and abandon.

b. What are the approximate values of the various options?

c. Based on the analysis, what is the best strategy to pursue? Assume that the option to abandon the small restaurant can be acquired costlessly, but that the option to abandon the large restaurant would cost $17,000 (the incremental values computed in Section 4.8).

d. Why do you think increases in the probabilities of the high and low demand states change the values in the way that they do?

e. What can you say about how the values of real options depend on risk levels?

13. Suppose, as the restaurant entrepreneur in Section 4.8, you believe the outside investor should be willing to accept a lower fraction of equity in the case that the option to wait before investing is exercised. Specifically, because the investor will know the true state of

nature, you believe the investor should be willing to accept 1 percent of the equity for each $20,000 he invests (just like with the expansion option, but for the investor's entire investment). All other assumptions are unchanged.

a. Reevaluate the waiting option.

b. How, if at all, does this change the conclusions about the best strategy for you to follow?

14. Consider the game-tree analysis in Section 4.9.

a. Suppose Kelly is uncertain of how Erin will react to her decisions. Kelly believes that, conditional on Kelly's decisions, there is a 70 percent probability that Erin will make the right choice, based on the assumptions in Figure 4-6, and a 30 percent that Erin will make the wrong choice. How does this affect the expected values of Kelly's strategies to enter with a large bar, a small bar, or wait? How, if at all, does this affect Kelly's optimal strategy? (Ignore the possible effects of this risk change on the conditional present values shown in Figure 4-6).

b. Suppose Kelly believes Erin will ignore Kelly's initial decision. Rather, there is a 70 percent chance that Erin will enter no matter what Kelly does. What is the best strategic course of action for Kelly to follow? Comment on how game trees and decision trees differ from each other. (Ignore the possible effects of this risk change on the conditional present values shown in Figure 4-6).

NOTES

1. By "course of action," we do not mean a rigid set of plans that will be adhered to steadfastly, regardless of future events. In fact, as discussed by Mintzberg (1994), an important aspect of strategic planning is incorporating an appropriate level of flexibility to deal with the inability to forecast the future with precision and to deal with unexpected events.

2. Detailed coverage of techniques of strategic planning is outside the scope of this text. Useful background on this topic is provided by Porter (1980). For specific applications to formulation of new venture strategy, see Cooper (1979) and Vesper (1980). For economic perspectives on strategy formulation see Spulber (1992, 1994) and Williamson (1994).

3. Turnover also was high. In July 1909, *Motor* magazine reported that 639 firms had been engaged in the industry up to that time.

4. By 1927, the number of manufacturers had fallen to 44. See Rae (1965).

5. Rae (1965) reports that the increase in market share coincides with Ford's decision to abandon all other models and concentrate exclusively on the Model T.

6. Ford made this remark in 1903 to one of the partners in his venture, John W. Anderson. See Rae (1965), p. 59.

7. Ford implemented conveyor-belt assembly lines in 1913–1914 after visiting the Chicago slaughterhouses. He watched cow carcasses being "dismembered" as they were carried along the line. He reasoned that the technique could be applied to automobiles—but the other way around, by assembling components and building an entire vehicle.

8. To execute its consumer-focused strategy; General Motors had to solve management problems to which solutions Ford was unprepared to respond. To offer product variety efficiently, General Motors had to be able to monitor production, ordering, and inventory on a timely basis. It

did so under the direction of Alfred Sloan, by designing an information system that remained the operating standard of the industry for decades. For an insightful discussion, see Norton (1997).

9. Ford successfully and publicly fought the validity of the Selden Patent in court. See Smith (1979).

10. See Stearns, Carter, Reynolds, and Williams (1995) for an examination of the relation between new venture survival and strategic choices of location and focus.

11. Hammond (1994) outlines the debate in strategic management regarding whether organizational structure follows strategy or whether product-market strategic choices dictate organizational structure. Our point is that framing the problem in either way can lead to second-best decisions.

12. Hammond, Keeney, and Raiffa (1998) offer a survey of the pitfalls of decision making that is guided by intuition or misapplication of more systematic approaches.

13. For an established public corporation, Rappaport (1991) argues that the appropriate focus of strategic planning is on creation of shareholder value.

14. Control and share of ownership are two separate things. Equity shares can have differential voting rights, and contingencies can be agreed to that allocate control to different parties under different conditions. The separation is addressed more fully in later chapters relating to design of financing contracts.

15. Bhidé (1994) notes that a variety of factors in addition to present value can influence the suitability of an investment. He cautions against over-analyzing opportunities, based, in part, on the prospect that the opportunity may disappear while the analysis is being completed. While overanalyzing should be avoided, many (if not most) entrepreneurs err in the opposite direction.

16. Amram and Kulatilaka (1999) illustrate application of real options approaches to new venture investing and other decisions. See Chen, Kensinger, and Conover (1998), Childs, Ott, and Triantis (1998) and Loch and Bode-Greuel (2001) for specific applications. Dixit and Pindyck (1995) provide a useful perspective on treating and valuing investment decisions as options. Luehrman (1998b) and Kim and Sanders (2001) discuss strategic decision making in terms of real options.

17. Discussion in this section is intended to review the basics of options and option valuation. If you have not already been introduced to options, Appendix 4A on the Web site contains a somewhat more complete overview. Most corporate finance or investments texts can be used for a more comprehensive introduction.

18. Because, for financial options, it often is possible to use options to form a riskless investment, the appropriate cost of money is the risk-free rate of interest.

19. Luehrman (1998a) describes how simple investment opportunities can be valued as real options using financial option valuation methods.

20. See Appendix 4A on the text Web site for elaboration of this point.

21. These are values from the perspective of the entrepreneur, and are not necessarily the same as values to an outside investor. Because the focus in this chapter is on learning to recognize and compare real options, we are abstracting from other aspects of the strategic analysis. We address methods of forecasting future cash flows and discounting them to present value in later

chapters. For now, the present values are provided without getting into the mechanics of fore-casting and valuing cash flows or valuing real options.

22. As the entrepreneur is selecting the strategy, we do not consider the total net present value of the restaurant or the net present value to the outside investor.

23. As an aspect of a theory of entrepreneurship, Baumol (1993) studies the optimal rate of innovation using the tradeoff between delaying introduction of new products as a means of improving their quality, and the risk that a competitor will enter first.

24. An analogy for a financial option is that the owner of a call option is not entitled to receive the dividends on the underlying share of stock. If the dividends are large, compared with the overall value of the stock, the value of the call is diminished. The same principle applies to real options. Where the likelihood of being preempted is high, the option to wait may not be very valuable.

25. Because the present values are lower than the initial investments, which we assume would have been similar to the restaurant investments, the decision to produce office space would not have been pursued initially and does not need to be in the first node of the decision tree. But once the restaurant investment is sunk, if the market opportunity does not develop as expected, then the option to convert to an alternative use can be valuable.

26. Discussion of game theory and use of game trees in this section is basic. For a more comprehensive discussion, see Bierman, Fernandez, and Fernandez (1997).

27. See Dixit and Nalebuff (1991) for a practical introduction to developing strategy in a game-theoretic context.

28. Simultaneous-move games usually are analyzed using payoff matrices that display the players' outcomes for the simultaneous choices. We illustrate use of payoff matrices later in the text.

29. The concept of a Nash equilibrium is named in honor of John Nash, a Princeton mathematician who was a pioneer of game theory.

REFERENCES AND ADDITIONAL READING

AMRAM, MARTHA, AND NALIN KULATILAKA. *Real Options: Managing Strategic Investment in an Uncertain World.* Boston: Harvard Business School Press, 1999.

BAUMOL, WILLIAM J. "Formal Entrepreneurship Theory in Economics: Existence and Bounds." *Journal of Business Venturing* 8 (May 1993): 197–210.

BHIDÉ, AMAR. "How Entrepreneurs Craft Strategies that Work." *Harvard Business Review* 76 (March–April 1994): 150–161.

BIERMAN, HAROLD S., LOUIS FERNANDEZ AND LUIZ FERNANDEZ. *Game Theory with Economic Applications.* Reading, MA: Addison-Wesley, 1997.

BREALEY, RICHARD, AND STEWART MYERS. *Principles of Corporate Finance.* 7th ed. New York: McGraw-Hill, 2003.

CHEN, ANDREW H., JOHN W. KENSINGER, AND JAMES A. CONOVER. "Valuing Flexible Manufacturing Facilities as Options." *Quarterly Review of Economics and Finance* 38 (1998): 651–674.

CHILDS, PAUL D., STEVEN H. OTT, AND ALEXANDER J TRIANTIS. "Capital Budgeting for Interrelated Projects: A Real Options Approach." *Journal of Financial and Quantitative Analysis* 33 (1998): 305–334.

COOPER, ARNOLD. "Strategic Management: New Ventures and Small Business." In *Strategic Management*. Edited by Dan E. Schendel and Charles W. Hofer. Boston: Little Brown & Co., 1979, pp. 316–327.

DIXIT, AVINASH, AND BARRY NALEBUFF. *Thinking Strategically.* New York: W. W. Norton, 1991.

DIXIT, AVINASH, AND ROBERT PINDYCK. "The Options Approach to Capital Investment." *Harvard Business Review* (May–June 1995):

DRUCKER, PETER F. "The Manager and Management Science." In *Management: Tasks, Responsibilities, Practices.* New York: Harper & Row, 1973.

HAMMOND, JOHN S., RALPH L. KEENEY, AND HOWARD RAIFFA. "The Hidden Traps in Decision Making." *Harvard Business Review* (September–October 1998): 47–58.

HAMMOND, THOMAS. "Structure, Strategy, and the Agenda of the Firm." In *Fundamental Issues in Strategy.* Edited by Richard Rumelt, Dan E. Schendel, and David J. Teece. Cambridge, MA: Harvard Business School Press, 1994, pp. 9–154.

KIM, YONG JIN., AND G. LAWRENCE SANDERS. "Strategic Actions in Information Technology Investment Based on Real Option Theory." *Decision Support Systems.* 33 (2001): 1–11.

LOCH, CHRISTOPH H., AND KERSTIN BODE-GREUEL. "Evaluating Growth Options as Sources of Value for Pharmaceutical Research Projects." *R&D Management* 31 (2001): 231–248.

LUEHRMAN, TIMOTHY A. "Investment Opportunities as Real Options: Getting Started with the Numbers." *Harvard Business Review* (July–August 1998a): 51–67.

LUEHRMAN, TIMOTHY A. "Strategy as a Portfolio of Real Options." *Harvard Business Review* (September–October 1998b): 89–99.

MCMAHAN, RICHARD G. P., AND ANTHONY M. J. STANGER. "Understanding the Small Enterprise Financial Objective Function." *Entrepreneurship Theory and Practice* 19 (Summer 1995): 21–40.

MAGEE, J. "How to Use Decision Trees in Capital Investment." *Harvard Business Review* 42 (September–October 1964): 79–96.

MINTZBERG, HENRY. "The Fall and Rise of Strategic Planning." *Harvard Business Review* (January–February 1994): 107–114.

MYERS, STEWART. "Finance Theory and Financial Strategy." *Midland Corporate Finance Journal* 5, no. 1 (1987): 6–13.

NORTON, SETH. "Information and Competitive Advantage, the Rise of General Motors." *Journal of Law and Economics* (April 1997): 245–260.

PORTER, MICHAEL. *Competitive Strategy.* New York: Free Press, 1980.

RAE, JOHN. *The American Automobile.* Chicago: University of Chicago Press, 1965.

RAPPAPORT, ALFRED. "Selecting Strategies that Create Shareholder Value." *Strategy, Seeking and Securing Competitive Advantage.* Edited by Cynthia Montgomery and Michael Porter. Cambridge, MA: Harvard University Press, 1991, pp. 379–399.

SANDBERG, WILLIAM, AND CHARLES HOFER W. "A Strategic Management Perspective on the Determinants of New Venture Success." *Journal of Business Venturing* (1985): 204–237.

SMITH, RICHARD. The United States Automobile Industry: Three Studies of Industry Conduct and Structural Change. University of California at Los Angeles, 1979.

SPULBER, DANIEL. "Economic Analysis and Management Strategy: A Survey." *Journal of Economics and Management Strategy* 1 (1992): 535–574.

SPULBER, DANIEL. "Economic Analysis and Management Strategy: A Survey Continued." *Journal of Economics and Management Strategy* 1 (1994): 355–406.

STEARNS, TIMOTHY, M., NANCY M. CARTER, PAUL D. REYNOLDS, AND MARY L. WILLIAMS. "New Firm Survival: Industry, Strategy, and Location." *Journal of Business Venturing* 10 (January 1995): 23–42.

TRIGEORGIS, LENOS. *Real Options: Managerial Flexibility and Strategy in Resource Allocation.* Cambridge, MA: MIT Press, 1996.

VESPER, KARL. *New Venture Strategies.* Englewood Cliffs, NJ: Prentice-Hall, 1980.

WILLIAMSON, OLIVER. "Strategizing, Economizing, and Economic Organization." In *Fundamental Issues in Strategy.* Edited by Richard P. Rumelt, Dan E. Schendel, and David J. Teece. Cambridge, MA: Harvard Business School Press 1994, pp. 361–401.

Developing Business Strategy Using Simulation

To me all kinds of business decisions are options. (Judy Lewent, CFO, Merck and Co.[1])

Learning Objectives

After reading the chapter you should:

- Understand the advantages of using simulation to evaluate scenarios described by decision trees.
- Understand the steps involved in developing a simulation model for a new venture.
- Be able to make better strategic decisions by using and evaluating the statistical information produced by a simulation model.
- Apply simulation techniques to evaluate common real options that face new ventures.

Decision trees are used to identify strategic alternatives and to examine the sensitivity of expected value to discrete changes in individual variables, one at a time. In Chapter 4, we used decision tree analysis with discrete possibilities for future states of the world to see how the expected value of a restaurant venture changed if we switched between a large restaurant and a small one. We also used it to evaluate the effects of options, such as an option to abandon in the event that demand turned out to be lower than expected. But without going through many tedious calculations of alternative scenarios, we could not determine how sensitive the value of the restaurant was to fluctuations in demand. Nor could we determine the range of possibilities over which it would have been desirable to expand the small restaurant. Furthermore, if some of the factors that determine value are statistically correlated with each other, then our estimate of the value of the restaurant could be biased.

To deal with the limitations of decision trees, we introduce simulation and demonstrate its use for evaluating real options embedded in strategic choices. In a general sense, a simulation is a representation of the behavior of a complex system through the use of another system. Usually, the other system is a computer, but you could also carry out a simulation manually. In fact, discrete scenario analysis is a primitive form of simulation. For our purpose, the complex system to be simulated is the future performance of a new venture. Simulation takes into consideration uncertainty about the environment, the venture itself, and possibly even the reactions of rivals.

The normal way to represent uncertainty in a simulation model is to describe each element of uncertainty as a statistical distribution, e.g., a normal distribution or a uniform distribution. To simulate the future of the venture, a random draw is made from each statistical distribution, and the combined effect is computed. You might, for example, be interested in projecting the level of net income for a venture at the end of five years, given four sources of uncertainty: the economy, the market's reaction to the product, cost of production, and development lead time. If you simulate the future of the venture one time, the result is a prediction of net income in five years, given specific outcomes for each source of uncertainty.

A single prediction is not likely to be very helpful, but with a computer it is possible to run hundreds, or even thousands of iterations of the simulation model and to aggregate the data from the iterations. Not only does averaging the results improve the accuracy of the prediction, but the dispersion of outcomes around the average serves as a measure of the aggregate effect of all the various sources of uncertainty that are built into the model.

As a management tool, simulation has been around for over three decades. David Hertz and McKinsey & Co. first advocated using simulation for investment decision making in 1968. For a variety of reasons, the technique was slow to catch on. Among the early impediments were confusion about the correct way to apply simulation to investment decision making, lack of low-cost computational capacity, lack of data useful for calibrating uncertainty, and lack of user-friendly software. In spite of the difficulties, companies like Merck have been using simulation to analyze investment decisions for a number of years.[2] Each of the early impediments either has been, or is being, removed. Appropriate application methods for investment decisions have been developed, computational capacity is inexpensive and fast, appropriate software is inexpensive, and data are becoming increasingly available.[3] Furthermore, the growing recognition of the value of viewing investments as portfolios of options suggests greater reliance on simulation.

Applications of Simulation to Entrepreneurial Finance

- **Strategy formulation:** An entrepreneur is considering a risky opportunity to develop an amusement park and knows that incorporating options to abandon or to change the nature of the venture can reduce the risk and potentially make the project more valuable. Simulation can be used to study the effects of different option structures on risk and the value of the opportunity.

- **Deal structure:** An entrepreneur and an investor are negotiating investment terms. The investor is willing to accept common stock but wants a large share of total equity in exchange. The entrepreneur would like to add sweeteners to the investor's financial claims and reduce the fraction of ownership the investor receives. Simulation can be used to evaluate the effects of various deal structures on the value of the entrepreneur's position and on the value of the investor's position.

- **Risk allocation:** An entrepreneur and an investor have different tolerances for bearing the risk of a new venture to build snow shovels equipped with cardiac monitors. The entrepreneur is more risk-averse than the investor. Simulation can be used to design a deal structure that shifts more of the risk to the investor, raising the overall value of the opportunity.

- **Contingent claims:** An investor is not convinced by the financial projections of an entrepreneur who wants to produce and market golf balls equipped with location sensors. The entrepreneur is willing to accept financial claims that make the entrepreneur's ownership share contingent on success. Simulation can be used to design a deal structure that is attractive to both parties.

- **Cash needs:** An entrepreneur is trying to determine the total amount of financing that is needed for a prospective new venture to sell subscriptions to a news service. The service will deliver a CD each morning, which is customized to the interests and commuting time of the subscriber. The entrepreneur knows that if the venture performs worse than expected, the need for financing will be greater. Simulation can be used to examine the relation between attained performance and total financial need.

- **Staging investment:** A venture capitalist is interested in investing in a project but would like to stage the investment so that progress can be evaluated at critical milestones. There is uncertainty about when the next milestone can be achieved and about the cost of achieving it. Simulation can be used to help the venture capitalist decide on an amount to invest, so that the potential for achieving the milestone is reasonable and the potential for overinvesting in a project that will never succeed is limited.

- **Valuation:** An investor is trying to value an opportunity to participate in a new venture and knows that the value of the investment depends not just on the expected return but on the riskiness of the return. Simulation can be used to determine the expected return, the riskiness of the return, and the value of the investment.

Nowhere is the case for using simulation more compelling than for decision making about new ventures. In this chapter, we apply simulation to the problem of designing new venture strategy. Later in the text, we use it in other ways. Among them, we apply simulation to the complex problem of business valuation and use it as a tool for designing efficient contracts between the entrepreneur and outside investors.[4]

5.1 SIMULATION—AN ILLUSTRATION

To begin with a simple illustration of how simulation works, suppose you are considering starting a new parcel delivery service to capitalize on the demand for delivery of purchases made on the Internet. As an aspect of evaluating the opportunity, you must determine the number of cubic feet of warehouse space you should lease in order to handle the December activity peak. You believe the warehouse must be capable of handling 5000 boxes per day. In addition, you know that, on average, boxes are 2 feet high, 1.5 feet wide, and 1.5 feet deep. Using this information, you might estimate the warehouse space requirement as 4.5 cubic feet per box ($2 \times 1.5 \times 1.5$), times 5000 boxes, or 22,500 cubic feet.

   This would be a fine estimate if all boxes were the same size or if the different dimensions of the boxes were not correlated with each other. But suppose the dimensions are correlated so that there are actually three different sizes of boxes: 1 foot by 1 foot by 1 foot, 2 feet by 1.5 feet by 1.5 feet, and 3 feet by 2 feet by 2 feet. Each size of box is equally likely to be received and stored. The area of the small box is 1.0 cubic foot, the medium box is 4.5 cubic feet, and the large box is 12.0 cubic feet. This makes the average size per box not 4.5 cubic feet, but 5.83 cubic feet. If you need to store 5000 boxes and there are exactly as many of each size, you will need 29,150 cubic feet of space. The original estimate is too low by almost 30 percent.

   Beyond this, you must allow for the fact that the mix of boxes will vary from day to day. You cannot simply assume that each day you will receive one-third of each size. Perhaps you could decide on a very conservative approach and contract for enough space to hold 5000 of the 12 cubic foot boxes. But that course of action is certain to be wasteful in that much of the space will never be used.

   How can you determine an amount of space that is adequate for the venture's needs most of the time, but does not end up wasting money? Simulation can be used to address this concern.

   Simulation is designed to study the behavior of complex systems. In this case, the system to be simulated actually is not very complex. It is the total volume of boxes that need to be stored each day. Every simulation problem requires a model of the system. This decision can be examined by first modeling the volume of a single box as follows:

$$\text{Volume} = \text{Height} \times \text{Width} \times \text{Depth}.$$

The model of the system is simply the volume of the box multiplied by 5000 boxes per day.

   Because the boxes come in three heights (1, 2, and 3 feet) that are equally likely to arrive, a function can be specified that describes the uncertainty as a discrete probability distribution of heights:

$$\text{Expected height} = 1/3 \times 1' + 1/3 \times 2' + 1/3 \times 3'.$$

There is no need to calculate the expected height since we already know that multiplying the expected values of height, width, and depth together gives a biased estimate of average volume. Instead, the known relationships of height to the other two dimensions can be used to determine volume. Thus, if height is 1 foot, then width and depth are each 1 foot, so volume is 1 cubic foot. But if height is 3 feet, then width and depth are each 2 feet, so volume is 12 feet.

The main challenge is to determine the optimal amount of warehouse space, given that the average volume per box on any given day is uncertain. Using simulation software, we asked the computer to select at random 5000 boxes such that, each time, the probability of drawing a box of any of the three given sizes remains at one-third. The first time we ran the simulation the computer returned a value of 5.977 cubic feet as the average volume per box for the 5000 boxes. This is a random result for one day's use of the warehouse. We then arbitrarily ran the simulation 16 more times (16 more days). Over all 17 days, the average volume per box was in a range between 5.681 and 5.998 cubic feet.

Now, suppose you want to lease enough space so that you can expect to meet the venture's needs on at least 95 percent of the days. The central limit theorem can be used, together with the sample mean and standard deviation from the 17 trials, to estimate the critical value where the available warehouse space is adequate. The mean from the sample is 5.87 cubic feet, and the standard deviation across the 17 simulated days is 0.09 cubic feet. Assuming the distribution of outcomes is normal, a value two standard deviations above the mean volume per box, or 6.05 cubic feet, will be sufficient 95 percent of the time.[5] Thus, you should lease 30,250 cubic feet of storage space. This is about 1000 cubic feet more than if you had selected based on the average volume per box, but almost 30,000 cubic feet less than if you provided for the highly unlikely event that all boxes on a day would measure 12 cubic feet.

The example could be enriched in several ways. What if there were uncertainty about the number of boxes that would need to be stored each day? What if there were more variation in the sizes of boxes? What if boxes of different sizes do not stack together perfectly so that some of the space cannot be filled? Issues such as these are all candidates for simulation.

5.2   SIMULATING THE VALUE OF AN OPTION

Because options are important to the value of a new venture and to the values of the financial claims that make up the deal structure, it is useful to see how simulation can be used to value options. To begin, consider how options can be used in financial markets. Suppose an underlying share of stock currently sells for a price of $118 and that calls and puts that expire in one year are available with an exercise price of $125 per share of the underlying common stock. To keep the illustration simple, suppose that securities trade monthly. We assume, initially, that the expected return for investing in the stock is the risk-free rate of interest of 0.3 percent per month (3.66 percent per year), but in any given month there is a 0.3 probability that the return is 4 percent lower and a 0.3 probability that it is 4 percent higher. Figure 5-1 shows the results of simulating this stock price model 20 times, over a period of 12 months, beginning from an initial price of $118, but with an expected return of 1 percent per month. Each line in the figure is a random draw from the possible price paths of the share of stock.

We used a computer simulation model to estimate the expected value of the stock at the end of 12 months and, more importantly, the standard deviation of annual returns for investing in the stock. Given that the risk-free rate of interest is 3.66 percent per year, the true (theoretically correct) expected value of the stock at the end of one year is $122.32.[6] With 10,000 iterations of the simulation model, the estimate of expected value turned out to be $122.23, very close to the true expected value. The estimated standard deviation of ending stock prices from the simulation was $13.49 or 11.43 percent of the initial stock price, also very close to the theoretically correct value.

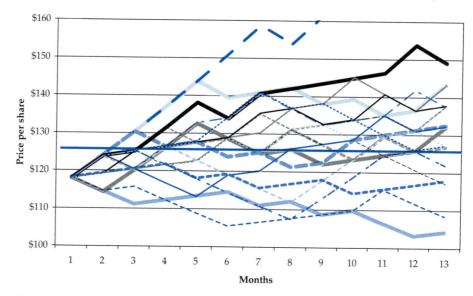

Figure 5-1 Simulation of 12 months of stock price performance (20 random trials)

The figure shows the results of 20 random sequences of returns for a stock that trades monthly. The Excel spreadsheet that generated these results also generates the values of puts and calls on the underlying stock, and can be used to simulate the effects of different assumptions.

A call option has value at expiration if the price of the underlying asset is above the exercise price of the option. The value of the call, at expiration, is the excess of the stock price over the exercise price. In the simulation, the call was in-the-money 43.3 percent of the time. Over all 10,000 iterations, the average ending value of the call was $4.21. If the risk-free rate of interest is used to determine the present value of the call option, the result is $4.05. Conversely to a call, a put option has value at expiration if the price of the underlying asset is below the exercise price. The value of the put, at expiration, is the excess of the exercise price over the price of the stock. In the simulation, the put was in-the-money 56.7 percent of the time and had an average ending value of $6.97, a present value of $6.71.

How do the simulated values compare to the values that can be derived from option theory using the Black-Scholes Option Pricing Model (OPM)? Using the true expected return and the estimated standard deviation, according to the OPM, the call is worth about $3.95 and the put is worth about $6.45. As you can see, the simulated values are close to the theoretical values. The main reasons the differences are more than trivial are that the distribution of possible stock prices in the simulation is not quite a normal distribution, which is the assumed distribution of the OPM, and that the simulated standard deviation is slightly higher than the theoretical standard deviation.

If the OPM and simulation yield such similar values, why do we bother with simulation? In part, the answer is that often the true expected return and standard deviation of returns are not known, and must be estimated by simulation. Beyond that, the other assumptions of the OPM generally are not satisfied when real options are being valued. To illustrate the problem, suppose $118 is the value of a share in a new venture that is expected to appreciate at the rate of 1 percent per month (or 12.68 percent per year) as shown in the figure.[7] How valuable would a call option on the underlying share of stock be, if all of the other assumptions from the previous example still hold (i.e., the risk-free rate is 3.66 percent and the actual monthly return can be 4 percent higher or lower than the expected return)?

In this case, if the riskless rate were used to discount the option cash flows, the simulated value of the call at expiration would be $10.62 and the simulated value of a put at the same exercise price would be $2.63. Compared with the previous example, the call value would be higher and the put value would be lower. Because the values of the options at expiration are different, the present values also will be different. However, this is not the answer you would get from the Black Scholes OPM. In that model, the values of the options do not depend on the expected rate of price appreciation of the underlying asset. This implication of the Black Scholes model is justified on the basis of market completeness and continuous trading.[8] Unfortunately, there is no agreement on the appropriate discount rate to use for determining the present value of a real option when the assumptions of the OPM are not satisfied.

We will return to this issue later in the text, when we examine the valuation of real options. The point for now is that you can use simulation to study the effects of real options on the value of a new venture, as well as on the values of the financial claims included in the deal structure. Simulation has advantages over theoretical option pricing because financial markets related to new ventures are incomplete and because many real options are interdependent.

5.3   USING SIMULATION TO EVALUATE A STRATEGY

Now that we have seen some simple illustrations of simulation, let's reexamine the restaurant venture. Our purpose is to see how simulation can improve the evaluation of strategic alternatives that include real options.

Simulation involves six distinct steps: (1) identifying the strategies to be evaluated; (2) establishing the criteria for evaluating the alternatives; (3) modeling the strategies to which simulation is applied; (4) specifying the assumptions and uncertainties that influence the value of each strategy; (5) running the simulation; and (6) analyzing and evaluating the results.

Identifying Strategic Alternatives

When simulation is used to evaluate strategic alternatives, the normal practice is to compare simulation results that are generated from different models of the venture, where each model is designed to incorporate a particular set of strategic choices. We might, for example, develop separate models of the large and small restaurants and compare the simulated values of the two strategies to see which is better.

Limiting some choices to a few discrete possibilities (e.g., a large restaurant or a small one) maintains the tractability of the analysis. Thus, although a restaurant can be any size, it may be that the important questions can be answered by looking at only a few possibilities, such as large or small. The effects of including real options (like waiting, abandoning, and expanding) can be studied by making minor modifications to the two basic models.

Choosing Evaluation Criteria

The choice of evaluation criteria depends on the nature of the business and the focus of the simulation. A not-for-profit entity may have an objective of serving as many clients as possible with a given resource base. A political party may seek to win as many legislative seats as possible. A public official may simply want to select the strategy that has the least potential of generating negative newspaper headlines. For a public corporation, maximizing shareholder value is the most sensible overall objective, though subsidiary objectives could be articulated to keep customers and employees happy. A marketing department that does not have responsibility for pricing might focus more narrowly on market share as an objective. For an entrepreneur, as we have stated previously, it makes sense to focus on maximizing the value of the entrepreneur's interest in the venture. Outside investors will, of course, want to maximize the net present values of their own investments.

A simulation model must be designed to produce information relevant to the criteria against which alternative strategies will be judged. Accordingly, for the entrepreneur's strategic decisions about establishing a new restaurant venture, the simulation model must generate information about the NPVs of the various alternatives, so the entrepreneur can use simulation results to make the best decision.[9]

Modeling the Problem

We use the large restaurant strategy to illustrate the design and operation of a simulation model. As in Chapter 4, the appropriate risky discount rate (or rates) to be used by the entrepreneur is already determined and is implicit. For now, prices and costs are expressed in such a way that it is unnecessary to deal explicitly with time value.

In setting up the model of the large restaurant, it is necessary to specify mathematically how the entrepreneur's operational decisions contribute to the present value of cash flows. We begin by determining the present value of the restaurant as if it were owned entirely by the entrepreneur and then adjusting that value downward to reflect the fractional ownership interest of outside investors. The present value of the restaurant can be stated in terms of present valued streams of cash flows:

$$\text{PV Cash Flow} = \text{PV(Revenues} - \text{Cash Expenses} - \text{Depreciation)} \times (1 - \text{Tax Rate})$$
$$+ \text{PV Depreciation.}$$

Because the business will be privately held, the owner should be able to avoid corporate-level taxes, so we apply a corporate tax rate of zero. Accordingly, the above expression simplifies to:

$$\text{PV Cash Flow} = \text{PV Revenues} - \text{PV Cash Expenses.}$$

To model the restaurant business, we need to specify the underlying determinants of revenues and cash expenses. On the revenue side, the concerns are price and unit sales. The demand side of unit sales, in turn, can be described as the product of total market size and the restaurant's potential market share. We model unit sales to include a capacity constraint. If demand exceeds the constraint, then the constrained quantity is what is sold. Otherwise, sales volume depends on market demand. Thus,

$$\text{PV Revenues} = \text{PV Unit Price} \times \text{Unit Sales,}$$
$$\text{Unit Sales} = \text{Lesser of Demand Quantity or Capacity,}$$
$$\text{Demand Quantity} = \text{Market Size} \times \text{Potential Market Share,}$$
$$\text{Capacity} = \text{An assumed maximum value.}$$

For simplicity, in this illustration we aggregate market size and market share over the expected life of the restaurant. We model the present value of cash expenses in a similar fashion, but includes both a fixed and a variable cash expense component, where the variable component depends on unit variable cost and unit sales. Thus,

$$\text{PV Cash Expenses} = \text{PV Unit Cost} \times \text{Unit Sales} + \text{PV Fixed Costs.}$$

The above structure determines the present value of the restaurant as if it were owned entirely by the entrepreneur. But in this venture, the entrepreneur is willing to commit only part of the required investment capital. The balance must be raised from an outside source. To determine the value of the restaurant to the entrepreneur, we need to know the fractional share of ownership that the entrepreneur retains. This depends on how much the outside investor contributes and how much equity the investor receives for the contribution. The present value of the entrepreneur's interest in the restaurant can be specified as follows:

$$\text{PV Entrepreneur Interest} = \text{PV Cash Flow} - \text{PV Outside Investor Interest,}$$

where all of the present values are expressed from the perspective of the entrepreneur.[10] The value of the outside investor interest can be expressed as:

$$\text{PV Outside Investor Interest} = \text{PV Cash Flow} \times (\text{Total Investment} - \text{Entrepreneur Investment})$$
$$\times \text{Percent Equity per Dollar Invested}$$

Finally, the net present value of the entrepreneur's investment is:

$$\text{NPV Entrepreneur Interest} = \text{PV Entrepreneur Interest} - \text{Entrepreneur Investment}$$

This completes the model of the entrepreneur's interest. Clearly, a more complex model could be developed by specifying the determinants, in equation form, of some of the terms in the above equations. For example, we could break fixed cost into components or define market size in terms of underlying economic factors like population growth and family income. However, the returns from adding complexity diminish rapidly. Although it is useful to think about the complex relationships that ultimately drive success or failure, a parsimonious model that is focused on key relationships is likely to yield results that are just as useful as a model that is more complex.

Specifying the Assumptions and Describing the Uncertainties

For the simulation to work, each variable in the model must be specified as either an assumed value or mathematical expression, or an assumed statistical process that will generate a value. No matter how carefully you model the venture, the model can only be as good as its assumptions. Assumptions should be based on data, experience, or careful reasoning. If the model is to be shared with outside parties, each assumption must be defensible. As forecasting is the subject of the next two chapters, we will skip discussion of the bases for our assumptions at this point. Nonetheless, you should consider how to generate the information to support the key assumptions of the model.

Figure 5-2 is a table that shows our assumptions for the model of the large restaurant.[11] These assumptions parallel the more limited assumptions used earlier for the decision tree analysis. For example, we assumed earlier that each meal served would contribute $5 toward covering fixed costs or toward the net cash flows of the venture. In the simulation model, the expected contribution margin is still $5, but the average price and cost of a meal are subject to uncertainty and can fluctuate around the expected values. The expected price is $10 per meal, and the uncertainty is characterized as a normal distribution with a standard deviation of $1. Similarly, the expected cost is $5, with a standard deviation of $0.6.

For reasons that become apparent later, we use a two-step process to determine market size. Suppose that during the first year, the entrepreneur receives information about market size. Though incomplete, this information serves as a preliminary estimate of the actual size of the market. To characterize market size in the simulation model, we use a triangular distribution with maximum size of 6 million meals (over the life of the restaurant), minimum size of 1 million meals, and most likely size of 2.6 million meals.[12] The actual size of the market is equal to the realization of the first-year estimate plus a random error. The notion behind including the error is that the first-year demand information helps to clarify the future but does not resolve it entirely. In this case, we assume the error to be normally distributed with a mean of zero and a standard deviation of 100,000 meals. Market share is determined using a similar two-step process. If the product of market size and market share exceeds restaurant capacity, then sales volume is constrained not to exceed capacity. Otherwise, demand determines unit sales volume.

Assumptions and Statistical Processes of the Large Restaurant Model	
Variable	Assumption
PV Unit Price of a meal	Normal Distribution ($\mu = \$10$, $\sigma = \$1$)
PV Unit Cost of a meal	Normal Distribution ($\mu = \$5$, $\sigma = \$0.6$)
Market Size Estimate (after first year)	Triangular Distribution (6, 2.6, 1 million units)
Market Size	Normal Dist. (μ = Estimate, $\sigma = 100,000$)
Market Share Estimate (after first year)	Normal Distribution ($\mu = 10\%$, $\sigma = 1\%$)
Market Share	Normal Distribution (μ = Estimate, $\sigma = 0.3\%$)
Capacity	500,000
PV Fixed Costs	Normal Dist. ($\mu = \$500,000$, $\sigma = \$50,000$)
Total Investment	Normal Dist. ($\mu = \$750,000$, $\sigma = \$25,000$)
Entrepreneur Investment	$400,000
Percent Equity Per Dollar Invested	1% per $10,000 of outside investment

Figure 5-2 Assumptions and statistical processes of the large restaurant model

Unconditional Simulation Results

Trials 300

Venture.SIM™

Output	Average	Median	Standard Deviation	Skewness		Minimum	25%	Percentiles 50%	75%	Maximum
1 Market Size	3,217,592	3,125,748	1,030,772	0.3321		1,125,794	2,452,174	3,125,748	3,944,959	5,827,140
2 Unit Sales	318,658	305,911	103,264	0.2320		101,365	240,041	305,911	392,507	500,000
3 Total Present Value	1,085,056	1,003,019	662,507	0.6682		(325,430)	598,105	1,003,019	1,460,043	3,232,787
4 Entrepreneur's Share	0.65	0.65	0.02	(0.3826)		0.57	0.64	0.65	0.67	0.71
5 NPValue to Entrepreneur	304,522	252,092	427,485	0.6360		(608,649)	(8,162)	252,092	553,485	1,609,254

Figure 5-3 Unconditional simulation results

The figure shows the output generated from *Venture.SIM™*, using the unconditional simulator. To see the output table, please refer to the Web site version of this figure. Results are compiled for the five variables listed in the table and are based on 300 iterations of the model for the large restaurant.

We also allow uncertainty about both the level of fixed costs and the size of the total investment that is required to construct the restaurant. Because the entrepreneur's investment is limited to $400,000, this makes the amount of outside investment uncertain. The outside investor receives 1 percent of the equity for each $10,000 of capital invested.

You probably can think of other ways of setting up the model and may question some of our assumptions. For the simulation model to be useful, it is important for the entrepreneur to give a lot of thought to the assumptions. If they are specified arbitrarily, no one will have much confidence in the results. The entrepreneur can make use of a variety of information sources to improve the quality of assumptions about uncertainty. These include such resources as government and industry publications and actual experience of similar ventures.[13]

In addition, breaking down the model more finely sometimes is useful, so variables that are easier to estimate can be substituted for those that are difficult to estimate directly. For example, it may be easier to estimate and describe the uncertainty about the population growth of an area and the number of meals consumed per capita in restaurants than to estimate the size of the market directly. You could then derive expected market size, and the uncertainty of market size, as the product of the two underlying variables.

Running the Simulation

With the model complete and the assumptions specified, the simulation is ready to run. A variety of software packages are available for this purpose.[14] To illustrate the usefulness of simulation, we focus on five variables in the model: market size, unit sales, present value of the venture, the entrepreneur's ownership share, and the net present value to the entrepreneur. Figure 5-3 is a table of simulation statistics for these variables based on running 300 iterations of the model. Each time the model is run, the computer makes a random draw from each of the distributions that describe the uncertainty of the variables in the model. Thus, simulation differs from sensitivity analysis by allowing us to examine the net effects of changing a number of variables at the same time.

The expected net present value of the venture for the entrepreneur is indicated in Figure 5-3 to be $304,522, indicating that the investment is worth making. This is the average of the NPVs to the entrepreneur from 300 iterations of the model. However, based on inspection of the individual trials, there is about a 25 percent chance that the venture will be a net loser (in present value terms) for the entrepreneur. The minimum figure in the "Net Present Value to Entrepreneur" column shows that there is even a small chance that the entrepreneur will lose more than the initial $400,000 investment.[15] The expected ownership share of the entrepreneur is 65 percent, with a range of 57 to 71 percent. Thus, despite the potential for cost over-runs in the initial construction, the entrepreneur always ends up with a controlling interest.

Remember that we use a two-step process to simulate market size. First, to generate an estimate of the size of the market, a draw is made from a triangular distribution, and then a normally distributed random error is added to that to find the true size of the market. Figure 5-4a is a histogram that illustrates the net effect of the two-step process on market size. The basic shape of the distribution is still triangular, and not symmetrical, so that the peak of the distribution is below the mean. Because we ran only 300 iterations of the model, the overall shape is quite irregular. In Figure 5-4b, you can see the result of running 5000 iterations. The interplay of the triangular and normal distributions is clearer in this figure.

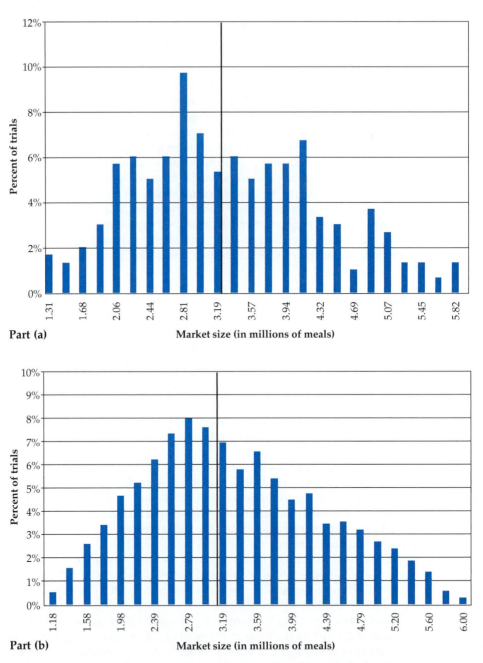

Part (a) — Market size (in millions of meals)

Part (b) — Market size (in millions of meals)

Figure 5-4 Distribution of market size estimates generated by simulation

(a) The figure shows the results of 300 iterations of the simulation of market size. (b) This figure is in contrast to Figure 5-4*a*. It shows the effect of increasing the number of iterations in the simulation to 5000. The shape of the sampling distribution conforms closely to the underlying triangular distribution assumed in the simulation.

Figure 5-5 shows the effect of the capacity constraint on total unit sales. Were it not for the constraint, the distribution of unit sales would look much like the distribution of market size. Instead, there are a number of iterations (about 9 percent of them) in which the constraint is binding and only 500,000 meals are sold.

How many iterations of the model are needed in order to make a correct investment decision? One way to find out is to look at a graph of the rate of convergence of the model. Figure 5-6 shows the convergence of estimates of the net present value of the entrepreneur's investment. Convergence is illustrated in the figure by plotting the average value of the variable for all the iterations up to a given number. The point on the far left of the figure reflects only the first iteration of the model, and the point on the right reflects the average of all 300 iterations. You can see that after about 80 iterations, the expected net present value of the entrepreneur's investment does not change very much.

How many iterations are enough? If the entrepreneur's choice is either investing in the large restaurant now or doing nothing, then a few iterations are sufficient to determine that the venture has a positive net present value. But if the entrepreneur is trying to compare different alternatives, such as choosing between the large and small restaurants, more iterations of the model may be necessary. Figure 5-3 shows that with 300 iterations the standard error of the estimate for the value of the entrepreneur's investment is $24,681. This means there is about a 65 percent probability that the true mean value of the entrepreneur's investment is between $279,841 and $329,203 (i.e., $304,522 + or − $24,681), and about a 95 percent probability that the true mean is in the range of $304,522 + or − (2 × $24,681).[16] Adding more iterations reduces the standard error of the estimate of the mean value, so that better decisions can be

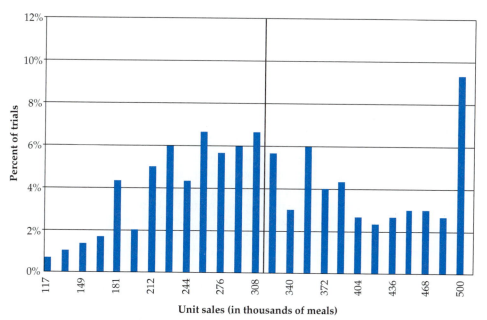

Figure 5-5   Histogram of unit sales simulation results

The figure illustrates the effect of the capacity constraint at 500,000 meals on total unit sales of the larger restaurant. Results are based on a simulation of 300 iterations of the model.

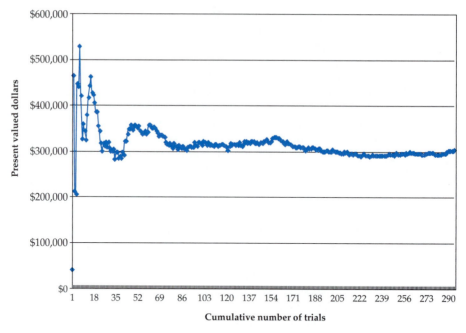

Figure 5-6   Convergence of net present value to entrepreneur

The figure shows the rate of convergence of the estimate of NPV of the large restaurant. After about 80 iterations, the simulated estimate of NPV is quite stable, even though individual iterations are subject to considerable uncertainty.

made even when the differences between values of alternative strategies are small. Although not shown, at 5000 iterations the standard error is reduced to $6,005.

Analyzing the Results

The final step in using simulation is to use the results as a basis for making a decision. If the choice were simply between building the large restaurant and doing nothing, the positive NPV of the large restaurant would be sufficient to conclude that the investment should be made. Most real decisions, however, are more complicated. They involve comparing several different alternatives and may require that inferences be drawn about alternative scenarios that have not been formally analyzed (such as an intermediate-size restaurant). For such decisions, it may be necessary to develop several simulation models with alternative assumptions and to compare the results of the different simulations. This is the focus of the next section.

5.4   COMPARING STRATEGIC CHOICES WITH SIMULATION

Now that the exercise of simulating the large restaurant is complete, we can turn to our primary objective—the use of simulation to compare strategic alternatives and to examine the values of real options. To do so, we use the same set of alternatives for establishing the restaurant venture as in Chapter 4. The branches of the decision trees from that chapter represent alternative scenarios concerning the decisions of the entrepreneur. To recap, the following possibilities were considered:

- Build the large restaurant immediately.
- Build a small restaurant immediately.
- Wait for more information on demand and build whichever size is appropriate, in light of that information.
- Build the small restaurant now, and expand if demand is sufficient.
- Build the large restaurant now and abandon it if demand is insufficient.
- Build the small restaurant now and abandon it if demand is insufficient.

To this list, more complex alternative scenarios can be added that combine the options to wait, expand, and/or abandon.

We begin by comparing the large restaurant to the simple alternative of investing in the small restaurant. The small restaurant is modeled by making a few modifications to the large restaurant model. Specifically, the expected value of fixed costs is reduced from $500,000 to $400,000. Second, a capacity limitation of 260,000 meals is imposed, instead of 500,000. Third, the expected cost of acquiring the restaurant is reduced from $750,000 to $600,000.

Using the same number of iterations (300) as for the large restaurant, we find that the expected net present value of the entrepreneur's $400,000 investment is $235,100. This is substantially less than the $304,500 value of the large restaurant. Strictly on the basis of NPV, the entrepreneur should select the large restaurant.

Are there any considerations that would shift the balance in favor of the small restaurant? One possibility is that the entrepreneur does not want to accept the downside risk of the project. Although the initial investment is $400,000, in the event of a loss the entrepreneur may be compelled to draw on her other resources beyond those originally committed. To gain a sense of the risk exposure, the standard deviations of values of the two restaurants can be compared. As it turns out, the small restaurant has a smaller standard deviation of expected net present value. But since the expected return is also lower, this does not appear to help. The simulated worst case values of both restaurants are similar: –$608,600 for the large and –$585,800 for the small.

How about differences in the ownership interest that the entrepreneur can retain? The expected ownership share of the entrepreneur is 65 percent for the large restaurant and 80 percent for the small, and the worst case ownership shares are similar for both at 57 percent. Conceivably, the difference in expected ownership share is enough to lead the entrepreneur to favor the small restaurant. In either case, the entrepreneur can retain voting control.[17] But the expected 80 percent interest that results from selecting the small restaurant may afford greater flexibility if the entrepreneur wants to use the restaurant as a launching pad for additional activities. Offsetting the difference in share of ownership, the large restaurant generates more cash for the entrepreneur, so that flexibility for taking on other activities is achieved in that way.

How much is the higher level of expected ownership worth to the entrepreneur? It might make sense for the entrepreneur to think more carefully about the value of flexibility acquired through stock ownership as compared to cash flow. One could also consider the possibility of contracting in advance for terms that enable the entrepreneur to repurchase stock from the outside investor. Simulation can be used to design reasonable contract terms of this sort. We consider these contracting issues later in the text.

The Option to Abandon

The analysis, thus far, examines two very simple strategic scenarios—a once-and-for-all investment in either a large or small restaurant. No real-world venture is that simple. It usually is possible, for example, to abandon a venture if actual results are discouraging enough.

How does factoring in the abandonment option change the values of the two restaurants? In the case of the large restaurant, we assume (as we did in the previous chapter) that the alternative use value of the building is $600,000.[18] In the terminology of finance, the entrepreneur has a put option with an exercise value of $600,000. As the simulation model is constructed, the exercise date is the date when true demand for the restaurant is known with certainty. The simulation model can be used to calculate the expected present value of continuing to operate the restaurant, conditional on the true state of demand. If this value were less than $600,000, then an entrepreneur, who was seeking to maximize the value of the investment, would exercise the option to abandon the project.

To estimate the value of the abandonment option, we ran 300 iterations of the large restaurant model, modified to include the option to abandon. The resulting estimate of NPV to the entrepreneur is $331,600. Comparing this to the earlier value of $304,500 for the large restaurant, it appears that the option is worth about $27,100 to the entrepreneur.[19]

When we evaluate the abandonment option of the small restaurant, we find that it is worth about $18,200 to the entrepreneur. Expected net present value increases from $235,100 to $253,300. This calculation is based on an abandonment value of $300,000 for the small restaurant. Based on the simulation results, presence of the abandonment option does not alter the initial decision to invest in the large restaurant instead of the small. However, investment in either one is more attractive when it includes an abandonment option.

As the problem is structured, the abandonment option is costless to the entrepreneur. But what if it were not? Suppose some locations have high values as office space, but others do not. The locations that afford valuable options are likely to sell for more because options usually are not free. To see how much the entrepreneur should be willing to pay (in terms of a location premium) for the option to abandon, we would need to run the model again. The answer is not obvious since the entrepreneur is contributing only $400,000. The outside investor would be contributing the full premium, but only sharing the increased value based on fractional ownership. Also, because the option raises the expected value of the venture, shouldn't the entrepreneur be able to convince the investor to take a smaller equity position per dollar of capital contributed? If your intuition does not lead quickly to the answers to these questions, then you should begin to recognize the value of simulation.

You may also recognize that the model can be used to value options that are more complex than the simple one-time option to abandon. In reality, the restaurant owner never knows demand with certainty. Each year is different from the years before. The abandonment option does not disappear just because it is not exercised at the end of the first year. With a simulation model that covers several years, we could estimate the value of a complex abandonment option that would give the entrepreneur the option to abandon at the end of each year. If the option is exercised, that is the end of the process. If not, the option for that year expires, but options to abandon in the future continue to exert a positive influence on the value of the business.

Let's look in more detail at the values of the small and large restaurants with options to abandon. In Figure 5-7, the individual outcomes of 600 iterations of the simulation model for the small restaurant are plotted. The horizontal axis in the figure is the expected number of

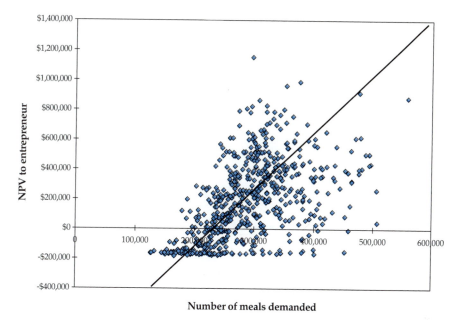

Figure 5-7   Small restaurant–NPV to entrepreneur
The figure shows the sample distribution of the entrepreneur's NPV from 600 iterations of the simulation model for investing in the small restaurant. The effect of the abandonment option is reflected in the figure by the lower bound of negative NPVs.

meals the restaurant serves over its useful life. You can see from the figure that the outcomes tend to be dispersed around the upward sloping-line that is drawn in the figure and that the lowest value for the entrepreneur is around –$175,000, which reflects the loss limitation provided by the abandonment option.

To see the option quality of the strategy more clearly, in Figure 5-8 we remove all of the uncertainty about prices and costs by using the mean values of those distributions, so that the only random variable is the level of demand. In addition, demand is modeled so that all of the uncertainty is resolved after the first year. The pattern in the figure can be represented as a combination of three securities. First, the upward-sloping portion of the value function shows that, by building the restaurant, the entrepreneur acquires a long position in the demand for meals in the market. The floor at a value of about –$175,000 reflects the abandonment option. Figure 5-8 shows that, in effect, the entrepreneur is hedged against low demand by acquiring an abandonment (put) option, which is valuable at demand levels below about 140,000 meals. Finally, by building a restaurant that is too small to serve the highest conceivable level of demand, the entrepreneur has, in effect, sold a call option on demand in excess of what the restaurant can serve. That is, by limiting capacity (and building a smaller, less expensive restaurant), the entrepreneur has left open an opportunity for someone else to enter the market in the event demand turns out to be high. The implicit proceeds from sale of the call option on high demand are reflected in the figure as a reduction in the cost of the restaurant compared with the alternative of building a much larger one that can serve the highest conceivable level of demand.

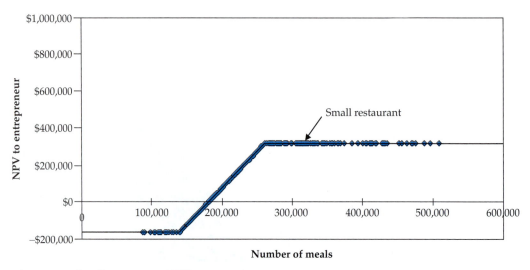

Figure 5-8 Small restaurant–NPV to entrepreneur

The figure shows the combined effects of capacity constraints and abandonment options for the small restaurant, leaving out the other sources of uncertainty.

As a step toward assessing the differences between the small and large restaurants, in Figure 5-9, we overlay the value function of the small restaurant with the same kind of function for the large one. It may surprise you to see that the large restaurant is more valuable to the entrepreneur than the small one if demand for meals turns out to be low (less than about 175,000 meals). This occurs because the large restaurant requires $150,000 more in outside investment, but increases the abandonment value by $300,000.[20] Although the outside investor pays the entire cost increment between the small and large restaurants, most of the increase in abandonment value accrues to the entrepreneur. Over the demand range from 175,000 to about 300,000 meals, the small restaurant is more valuable for the entrepreneur. Generally, over that range the restaurant is capable of serving all or nearly all of the demand but at lower cost than the large restaurant. Beyond demand of 300,000 meals, the extra capacity of the large restaurant makes it more valuable than the small one.

Figure 5-9 makes the choice appear simple. As long as we know the true demand and can strip away the uncertainties about other factors like prices and costs, it is obvious which of the two restaurants should be built. Unfortunately, we cannot simply remove those uncertainties. Nor can we be certain about the level of demand. However, the simulation results can be used to help determine which of the two restaurants has the higher NPV. This is what we did earlier in this subsection. In the next two subsections, we examine alternative strategies that resolve some of the uncertainty or deal with it in a more effective way.

The Option to Wait

Another choice that is available to the entrepreneur is to wait to build either the large or small restaurant until after the estimate of market size has been generated. As we did in Chapter 4, we assume that delaying investment invites competitive entry, so that the expected share of market

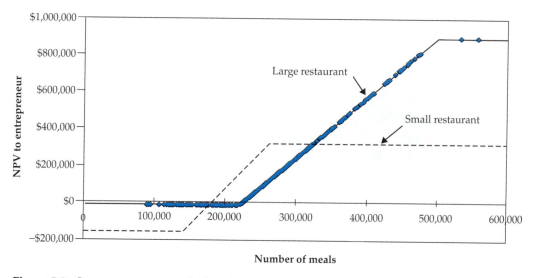

Figure 5-9 Large restaurant overlaid with small–NPV to entrepreneur

The figure shows the combined effects of capacity constraints and abandonment options for the large and small restaurants, leaving out the other sources of uncertainty.

for the entrepreneur's restaurant is reduced. Furthermore, if the investment is postponed for more than one year, it is clear to the entrepreneur that the opportunity to invest is lost. Because the entrepreneur invests only $400,000, but can do so in either the large or small restaurant, the entrepreneur has a complex call option on an uncertain share of the value of a restaurant of uncertain size. The option is a call on the expected value to the entrepreneur of either the large or the small restaurant, whichever value is greater. The exercise price of the option is $400,000, and the option expires after one year. Notice that if the entrepreneur decides to invest, an option is acquired to abandon the venture once the true level of demand is established. Should one or the other of the two investments be made, the entrepreneur will exercise the abandonment (put) option if the expected value of the restaurant is less than its value in alternative use.

Figure 5-10 is the branch of the decision tree that faces the entrepreneur if a decision is made to wait before investing. The three-pronged choice after the demand estimate is received reflects a complex call option. The binary choices, once true demand is learned, reflect the abandonment options.

At this point, the entrepreneur cannot know which, if any, of the options will be exercised. The only issue is whether the option of waiting to decide whether to invest is more valuable than the highest-valued immediate investment alternative (in this case, more valuable than building the large restaurant with option to abandon). When we simulated the model represented by the decision tree in Figure 5-10, the resulting expected value was $274,505. This strategy for developing the venture has a higher expected value than the $253,300 value of building the small restaurant immediately, but a lower expected value than the $331,600 value of the large restaurant. As the model is structured, the main reason the option to wait does not add value relative to the large restaurant alternative is that waiting is assumed to encourage competitive entry, which reduces the entrepreneur's market share in the event that the large restaurant is built. The expected loss of market share can be thought

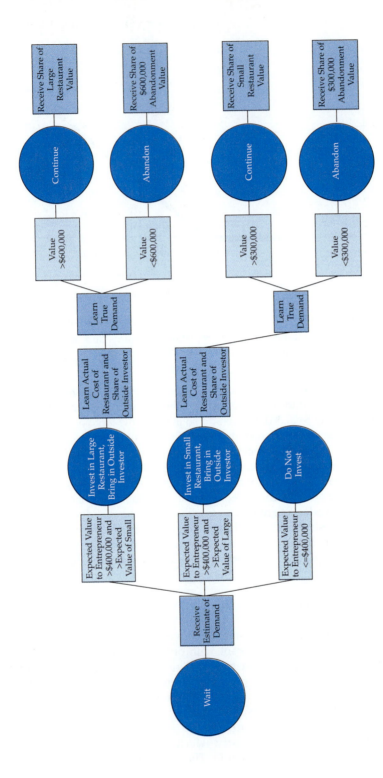

Figure 5-10 Decision tree for restaurant investment conditional on deciding to delay investing. The entrepreneur's decisions are represented by circles. Information received by the entrepreneur is represented by rectangles.

of as the cost of acquiring the option to delay investing. For the large restaurant, the cost of acquiring the option, measured in terms of the expected loss of future business, is more than the increase in value that results from learning more about actual demand.

As it turns out, the abandonment option is not very valuable in conjunction with the option to delay. This is because most of the uncertainty about future sales is resolved when the initial estimate is received at the end of the first year. Accordingly, the option to abandon is almost never exercised when the option to delay investing is employed. Generally, we should expect that when combinations of options are used, their values will not be additive. This means that formal analyses of option values are unlikely to be of much use when one is attempting to develop a venture strategy that involves selecting from among various real options that may be available. On the other hand, techniques such as simulation or other numerical evaluation methods are extremely valuable. Because the values of individual options diminish as more choices are added, we do not need to be overly complicated or complete in describing and modeling the strategic alternatives. A parsimonious model that captures the main strategic choices is capable of generating an accurate estimate of the expected value of a project.

The Option to Invest More

Finally, recall from Chapter 4 that if the small restaurant is built immediately, the entrepreneur acquires an option to expand in the event that demand is sufficient to justify the large restaurant. In effect, the small restaurant is built, and at the end of the first year the entrepreneur receives an estimate of demand. Based on the estimate, the entrepreneur decides to expand the restaurant or maintain it at its current size. The option to expand is a call option on additional capacity. Although the entrepreneur does not need to invest anything further to exercise the option, the cost is in the form of a reduction in the entrepreneur's ownership share needed to compensate for the additional outside investment. Furthermore, the model is structured to reflect an expectation that the overall cost of building the large restaurant in stages would be higher than building it all at once. The higher construction cost is the cost of the call option on expanded capacity.

In Chapter 4, we assumed only three discrete levels of demand: high, medium, and low. The large restaurant would be built if the high-demand state was expected, but not otherwise. This is not necessarily the best course of action. When demand is allowed to vary continuously, and the initial estimate of demand is uncertain, the best course of action is not clear. Simulation helps evaluate the range of expected demand levels over which exercising the option to expand would add value to the small restaurant. Figure 5-11 shows the branch of the decision tree facing the entrepreneur who decides to invest initially in the small restaurant. The option to expand is evaluated by comparing the expected value of the expanded restaurant with the expected value of the small restaurant over a range of critical values for expected unit sales. Waiting to expand until after more information about market demand is obtained reduces the risk of the outside investment that is required for expansion. Because the risk of investing at this point is lower, we assume that the outside investor receives 1 percent of the equity for each $20,000 invested in expansion. Again, the entrepreneur has an option to abandon the venture once true demand becomes known.

Our purpose is to determine the value of a strategy of investing small at first and waiting to see the market response before a larger investment is made. Earlier, with the option to delay investing, we set up the simulation to always select the choice with the highest

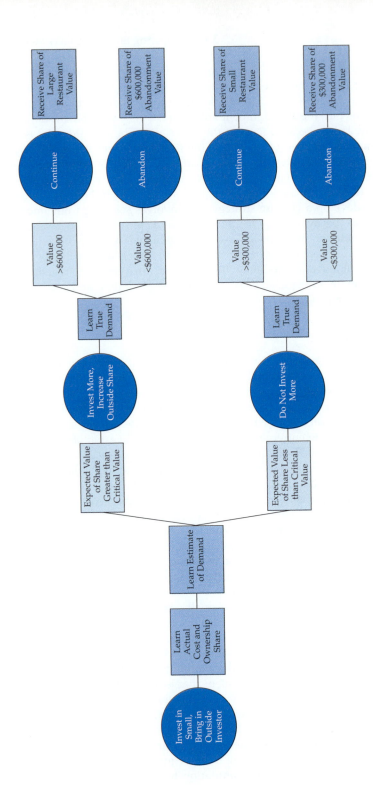

Figure 5-11 Decision tree for investment in small restaurant with option to expand. The entrepreneur's decisions are represented by circles. Information received by the entrepreneur is represented by rectangles.

◆ Using Simulation at Merck

The pharmaceutical industry is complex and uncertain. The uncertainty arises from numerous sources: health care reform, emergence of the generic drug market, tort litigation, as well as the uncertainty inherent in developing, testing, and marketing new drugs. Investing in development of new drugs has much in common with entrepreneurial investment in new ventures. Uncertainty is very high, and the firm faces many opportunities to abandon or modify its development efforts.

Rather than relying on static, single-point estimates of the future for research and development investment decision making, Merck develops models that use probability distributions for numerous variables. Under the direction of CFO Judy Lewent, Merck developed the Research Planning Model that integrates principles of economics, finance, statistics, and computer science to produce quantitative analyses of specific strategic decisions that Merck faces. The model, using Monte Carlo simulation, synthesizes probability distributions for key variables such as revenues, cash flow, return-on-investment and net present value. The output of the model is a frequency distribution showing the probability that a project's NPV exceeds a certain level. Summary statistics, such as standard deviation, can be computed and then used in other analyses, such as to price an option to delay. The model simulates risk and return, project by project (prior to commitment of funds), and simulates the contribution of R&D to performance of the entire corporation. The model's inputs include scientific and therapeutic variables, capital expenditures, production and selling costs, product prices and quantities, and macroeconomic variables. For each variable, the model uses ranges of possibilities rather than point estimates (e.g., "optimistic", "moderate," and "pessimistic" scenarios).

To demonstrate, consider how the model could be used to evaluate a drug research project. Merck's CFO, Lewent, describes it this way:

> We may know at the beginning of a project that there is a market for a specific treatment that includes many thousands of people, and once we reach a certain point in the process, we may know that a certain compound may be effective. But we still aren't 100% certain that the compound will prove so safe and effective that it can be turned into a drug. So we have to ask ourselves, "Do we continue to invest?" Those are the kinds of decisions we face every day. And these aren't investments that easily lend themselves to traditional financial analysis. Remember that we need to make huge investments now and may not see a profit for 10 to 15 years. In that kind of situation, a traditional analysis that factors in the time value of money may not fully capture the strategic value of an investment in research, because the positive cash flows are severely discounted when they are analyzed over a very long time frame. As a result, the volatility or risk isn't properly valued.

How then does Merck evaluate such an investment?

> Option analysis, like the kind used to value stock options, provides a more flexible approach to valuation of our research investments . . . because it allows us to evaluate those investments at successive stages of a project.

Merck takes a systematic and formal approach to modeling risks associated with R&D, manufacturing, and marketing. As an example, in considering a new drug's market potential, a scientific or medical constraint might be the expected time for FDA approval. The range of possible time frames can be modeled and described in terms of short, medium, and long. The sooner the drug is approved, the sooner it can be brought to market. By drawing from the range of possibilities and simulating cash flows based on alternative assumptions, it is possible to synthesize probability distributions for output variables. The output variables are the staple measures of finance: revenue, cash flow, net present value, and return-on-investment.

Source: Drawn from: Nancy A. Nichols, "Scientific Management at Merck: An Interview with CFO Judy Lewent," *Harvard Business Review* (January–February 1994): 89–99.

expected value. Instead, this time we examine different critical values for the decision to expand and compare the values for this strategy to the alternative of investing immediately in the large restaurant.

Using the simulation model, we evaluated options to expand at critical values of expected demand ranging from 200,000 units to 500,000 units, in 20,000 unit increments. Although exercising the option to expand would benefit the entrepreneur over the entire range, compared with staying with the small restaurant, the benefit to the entrepreneur from expanding when expected demand is low comes at the expense of the outside investor. This is because at low levels of sales it is better to abandon the restaurant. Bringing in an outside investor under such conditions effectively subsidizes part of the entrepreneur's losses. An outside investor is unlikely to enter into such arrangements. Accordingly, we limit the option to expand to the range of expected demand levels where the investor derives a positive expected net present value from the project (assuming the investor values project cash flows using the same discount rate as the entrepreneur). Using the simulation model, we determined that with this constraint the option can only be exercised if expected demand reaches at least 300,000 units. At this level, the option to expand increases the value of the entrepreneur's position to about $432,000, or about $100,000 higher than building the large restaurant initially and $179,000 more than limiting the investment to the small restaurant.

Is a decision rule of exercising the option to expand if expected demand exceeds 300,000 meals the best one for the entrepreneur, or would some other critical value be better? Using the model, we found that expected net present value is roughly constant up to a critical value of about 340,000 meals. At that level, the simulation model returned a value of $428,000 for the entrepreneur. But the expected ownership share increases from 74.6 percent to 75.8 percent. The increase in expected ownership share arises because raising the critical value reduces the probability that the entrepreneur will exercise the option to expand. Accordingly, we settled on a strategy of exercising the option only if expected demand exceeds 340,000 meals.

Why does the option to expand create so much value for the entrepreneur, even though it increases the cost of the large restaurant? The main reason is that it reduces the uncertainty of part of the second stage of outside investment so that the investor is willing to accept a smaller equity stake in exchange for contributed capital. This is an important lesson and one that will be explored in greater detail later. By staging the needs for outside capital, the entrepreneur can offer the investor a safer bet and can retain a larger share of the venture as a result.

5.5   SUMMARY

The objective of strategic planning for a new venture is to develop a framework for maximizing value for the entrepreneur. By this criterion, success depends on making good assessments of the risks and uncertainties of the prospective venture and on developing a new venture strategy that anticipates the need to adapt to new information as it arrives. An effective framework is one that helps the entrepreneur decide whether to undertake the venture in the first place, promotes effective negotiation with providers of outside financing, and encourages value-maximizing decisions.

Simulation is a powerful tool for evaluating the critical decisions that a prospective entrepreneur faces, and it can add substantial value to the venture and to the ownership stake of the entrepreneur. There are six steps to implementing a simulation for strategic purposes. First, identify the important strategic alternatives, possibly by representing them in a decision tree. Second, decide on the criteria for evaluating the choices, such as net present value of the entrepreneur's investment. Third, develop a model of each strategy that can be used to evaluate the various options facing the entrepreneur and specify mathematically how the decisions of the entrepreneur contribute to the evaluation criteria. Fourth, specify the assumptions of the model and describe the uncertainties. Fifth, run simulation. Sixth, interpret the results.

These steps are generally stated propositions. The best way to appreciate the value of simulation is to work through specific examples.

QUESTIONS AND PROBLEMS

Note: You should be familiar with using *Venture.SIM*™ before attempting these problems. If you are not familiar with it, please refer to the simulation tutorial.

1. You have spent the last six months developing a new product for treatment of arthritis. You believe a breakthrough could occur at any time during the next eight months and that the probability of success in any given month is about 10 percent. If you do not succeed within that period, you have decided to abandon the project. In the event that your efforts are successful, the clinical testing required for FDA approval will take six to ten additional months from the time of development success. Based on prior experience, if development efforts are successful, there is an 80 percent probability that approval will be granted. Notice of approval or disapproval in any month is equally likely. During development, your venture has been consuming cash at an average rate of $30,000 per month. You estimate that in any given month there is a 30 percent probability that the cost will be only $20,000 and a 20 percent probability that it will be $45,000. The cost of financing the venture will be much lower once FDA approval is obtained. The problem is that you need additional financing right now.

   a. Suppose you want to provide enough financing for the worst case outcome. How much money should you raise?

   b. Using a simulation model, determine how much you should raise now so that the probability of running out of money before the FDA acts is 25 percent.

   c. Suppose the cost of financing would also be lower after development was completed. How could you use simulation to determine the best way to stage the financing of the venture? What factors would affect your choice of when and how much capital to raise?

2. An entrepreneur who would like to open a restaurant has approached you. By coincidence, it is the same entrepreneur whose decisions we have been studying in this chapter. The entrepreneur is offering 1 percent of the equity of the venture for each $10,000 you invest and will contribute $400,000 to the project. Suppose you agree with the entrepreneur's assumptions, as set out in Figure 5-2 for the large restaurant and elsewhere in the chapter for the small restaurant, including the PV assumptions. Use simulation to examine the opportunity from your perspective instead of the entrepreneur's.

   a. What is the NPV of your investment in the large restaurant if there are no options and investment is immediate?

   b. What is the NPV of your investment in the small restaurant if there are no options and investment is immediate?

   c. How do the abandonment options with exercise values of $600,000 for the large and $300,000 for the small restaurant affect the NPVs of your prospective investments?

    d. Suppose, in order to acquire an abandonment option for either restaurant, the expected cost is $20,000 higher (which you would pay in exchange for an additional 2 percent of the equity). Would you want the entrepreneur to acquire the option?

    e. Suppose the entrepreneur proposes to build the small restaurant initially, and if expected demand turns out to be more than 300,000 meals, to expand capacity to the same as the large restaurant. The cost of expanding is $300,000, and the entrepreneur proposes that you contribute this in exchange for an additional 15 percent of the equity. Based on the simulation, would you want to accept this proposal? Why or why not? Is there another alternative under which the entrepreneur could exercise the expansion option that you would find more attractive?

3. The monthly standard deviation of the S&P 500 Index is 6.8 percent. The expected return for investing in the Index is 1.0 percent each month.

    a. Suppose you invest $100 in the Index today:

        (1) Use simulation to estimate the expected value of the stock at the end of three months and the standard deviation of the ending value (at that point).

        (2) What are the estimates of expected value and standard deviation at the end of nine months?

    b. Suppose, instead of investing $100 in the Index, you are interested in a call option on an underlying $100 claim on the Index (i.e., the underlying claim has a market value of $100, the same as in part a.

        (1) What is the expected value in three months of a three-month call option with an exercise price of $100, and what is the corresponding standard deviation of possible values?

        (2) What is the expected value in nine months of a nine-month call option with an exercise price of $100, and what is the standard deviation?

        (3) What is the expected value in nine months of a nine-month call option on an underlying Index value of $100 if the exercise price is $80?

4. Think about an aspect of your current situation (possibly related to your career, education, or personal life).

    a. What are the most important decisions you will have to make as you go forward?

    b. Try describing the alternatives in terms of a decision tree.

    c. What real options are reflected in the choices you will have to make?

    d. The outcomes of the different branches of the tree should be describable in terms such as dollars, utility, and happiness. See if you can write a model, similar to the one in the chapter, that describes how the outcomes relate to your possible choices.

    e. Now, supposing that you wanted to simulate the results of your decisions, how might you go about specifying the assumptions of your model?

    f. If you feel ambitious, try setting up the model in an Excel spreadsheet and use simulation to evaluate the choices. (Feel free to take some liberties with the specific assumptions.)

5. Refer to the restaurant example in the chapter. "If the investor is astute, the terms of the deal will be different for the large restaurant than for the small one." Why and how do you think they might be different?

6. The origin of the term "real options" is traceable to Professor Stewart Myers ("Determinants of Capital Borrowing," 5 *Journal of Financial Economics*, 1977), who noted that many corporate real assets can be viewed as call options. What do you think he means? Why might it be useful to think of corporate real assets as call options? Provide examples to illustrate your answer. Try to identify, at least conceptually, the underlying asset, the exercise price, and the expiration date.

7. Reevaluate the storage space needed in the box example in Section 5.1. However, instead of 5000 boxes per day, you expect from 4000 to 6000 per day. The actual number will be drawn from a uniform distribution over this range. What is the maximum size of warehouse you will need? Estimate the size that would be sufficient 95 percent of the days. How does this compare to the estimate in the text of the size that would be sufficient 95 percent of the days? What do you think accounts for the difference in size?

8. The common stock of Unron is selling today for $50 per share. The stock is expected to appreciate at a rate of 1.0 percent per month with a standard deviation of 15.0 percent per month. As an Unron employee, you have just been awarded executive stock options to acquire 1000 shares. The options have an exercise price of $50 but cannot be sold or exercised for 5 years (60 months). The monthly risk-free rate is 0.3 percent. Construct a spreadsheet to simulate the price of Unron stock at the end of the five years and the value of the call option at expiration. Run the simulation and plot the results for the stock price. How likely is the option to be in the money at expiration? What is the expected stock price in five years? What is the expected value of the call option at that time? As you cannot trade the options, you cannot use conventional option pricing models to determine their value. What is the present value of the options if you discount their expiration-date value by 1.0 percent per month? What is it if you discount by the risk-free rate?

9. Download the Black-Scholes Option Value Template from the text Web site and use it to value the following options on Unron stock (see problem 8):

   a. One-year calls with exercise price of $50.

   b. One-year calls with exercise price of $40.

   c. One-year puts with the same exercise prices.

   d. Six-month calls and puts with the same exercise prices.

   e. For one-year puts and calls with exercise price of $50, how does value change if the risk-free rate increases to 0.5 percent per month?

   f. For one-year puts and calls with exercise price of $50, how does value change if the monthly standard deviation decreases to 10 percent?

   Discuss the consistency of your findings with the principles of option valuation.

10. For the restaurant example in the chapter, evaluate the combined effects of the following assumption changes on the values of the large and small restaurants and the effects of the various options on value: (i) The standard deviation of meal prices is $2. (ii) The

preliminary market size estimate has a triangular distribution with (8, 2.6, and 0.5 million units). (iii) The preliminary estimate of market share has a standard deviation of 2 percent. How do these assumptions of increased risk affect the optimal strategy? Why do you think the effects are as you find them to be?

11. For the restaurant example in the chapter, evaluate the combined effects of the following assumption changes on the values of the large and small restaurants and the effects of the various options on value: (i) The expected variable cost per meal is $4. (ii) Expected fixed cost of the large restaurant is $750,000. (iii) Expected fixed cost of the small restaurant is $600,000. How do these assumptions about the variable and fixed cost structures affect the optimal strategy? Why do you think the effects are as you find them to be?

NOTES

1. From an interview appearing in Nichols (1994).

2. See Nichols (1994).

3. A variety of software packages are available for running simulations on personal computers. Some are freestanding data and decision analysis programs. Others function as add-ins to Excel. Some simulation software employs random sampling to generate the iterations. Others use "Monte Carlo" variance reduction techniques in an effort to generate more accurate predictions of expected outcomes and distributions of outcomes with fewer iterations. As computational speed has increased, the cost- and time-saving rationale for Monte Carlo simulation has diminished in importance. To most simulation users, differences among the approaches are not observable. You may or may not be using Monte Carlo methods. The simulation software that accompanies this book is an Excel add-in that does not use Monte Carlo methods.

4. See Stevenson et al. (1987) for an application of simulation techniques to changes in investment patterns of venture capital funds. They simulate a multistage investment process based on a large number of funds, all operating under a common set of assumptions. They use models to examine the impact of management and venture capital industry practices on fund results.

5. Alternatively, it would be possible to run the simulation many more times and determine by inspection the 95th percentile of average daily volume per box.

6. By going to the Excel file for this figure, you can see the effects of simulation and assumptions on calculating the value of the option.

7. The shares of a new venture are not freely tradable, so the "no arbitrage" condition of the OPM is not satisfied.

8. Theoretically based options valuation models address this in a variety of ways, including by adjusting the probability distribution of outcomes to mimic the distribution expected under risk neutrality.

9. Later in the text we use simulation to generate information about the cash flows the entrepreneur or investor will receive. We compute the present value of the cash flows in a separate step that does not require simulation. In this chapter, we abstract from the extra level of complexity and focus on NPV directly.

10. Later in the text, we will allow for the possibility that the present value to the entrepreneur can be different from the present value to an outside investor.

11. The Internet site contains a copy of the Excel simulation model of the restaurant incorporating the assumptions described here. Separate simulation models are constructed to reflect the various real option structures for the large restaurant and for the small restaurant. All can be studied on the Internet site.

12. Most simulation software enables the user to select from a comprehensive array of statistical distributions. It is up to the user to select and calibrate a distribution that provides an accurate representation of future uncertainty. We use a triangular distribution to describe market size partly because it is an easy way to provide for a high degree of uncertainty about market size but avoid the possibility of simulated values that are negative. (Negative market size does not make sense.)

13. Chapter 6 covers methods of financial forecasting, including where to find and how to use publicly available information in financial models. An appendix to Chapter 6 identifies a number of data sources, including many that are accessible online.

14. We have experimented with *CrystalBall, @Risk, Insight,* and the proprietary *Venture.SIM* simulation software that is available to users of this text. The simulation results in this chapter are generated using *Venture.SIM™.*

15. A loss of more than the initial investment is possible only if the entrepreneur makes subsequent investments (such as by taking a reduced salary) that also are lost, or makes personal guarantees to investors or suppliers, beyond the $400,000 investment.

16. The standard error equals the standard deviation (from Figure 5-3) divided by the square root of the number of iterations. Confidence intervals are derived using the properties of a normal distribution, that approximately 65 percent of the distribution is within one standard deviation of the mean and about 95 percent is within two standard deviations.

17. There is, of course, no requirement that share of ownership be the same as share of control. In this example, however, we assume that all shares have equal voting rights.

18. We do not allow for any uncertainty about this value, but with simulation we could easily do so.

19. Because the option changes the riskiness of the project, it also may affect the discount rate that is appropriate for valuing future cash flows. Again, discounting is an issue we will address later in the text.

20. If the investor is astute, the terms of the deal will be different for the large restaurant than for the small one, in part because the entrepreneur gets more benefit from the abandonment option of the large restaurant.

REFERENCES AND ADDITIONAL READING

BELL, DAVID, AND ARTHUR SCHLEIFER, JR. *Decision Making under Uncertainty.* Cambridge, MA: Course Technology, Inc., 1995.

HERTZ, DAVID B. "Investment Policies that Pay Off." *Harvard Business Review* 46 (January–February 1968): 96–108.

HERTZ, DAVID B. "Risk Analysis in Capital Investment." *Harvard Business Review* 57 (September–October 1979): 169–181.

NICHOLS, NANCY A. "Scientific Management at Merck: An Interview with CFO Judy Lewent." *Harvard Business Review* (January–February 1994): 89–99.

STEVENSON, HOWARD H., DANIEL F. MUZYKA, AND JEFFREY A. TIMMONS. "Venture Capital in Transition: A Monte-Carlo Simulation of Changes in Investment Patterns." *Journal of Business Venturing* 2 (1987): 103–121.

CHAPTER

6

Methods of Financial Forecasting

The more successful a new venture is, the more dangerous is lack of financial foresight. (Peter Drucker, *Innovation and Entrepreneurship*, 1985)

Learning Objectives

In this chapter you will:

- Learn the elements of the cash flow cycle.
- Understand the critical determinants of a firm's financial needs.
- Understand how working capital policies are established and how they influence financial needs.
- Learn how to prepare a sales forecast for an established firm.
- Learn how to prepare a sales forecast for a new venture.
- Develop and prepare a pro forma analysis to build a financial model of a venture that integrates income statement, balance sheet, and cash flow items.
- Identify and use publicly available data sources to provide an objective basis for the assumptions underlying the financial model.

Many entrepreneurs of profitable and rapidly growing ventures are puzzled that they never seem to have enough cash to finance ongoing operations. Financial forecasting is a critical element of the planning for a new venture, particularly if the entrepreneur may require outside financial support. Even if the entrepreneur expects to be able to finance the entire venture, however, financial forecasting adds value in a number of ways.

The principal benefits of a good financial forecast are: First, financial forecasting is a disciplined way to evaluate how much cash the business is likely to require and how much might be required if the venture develops at a different rate than expected. Second, financial forecasting provides a basis for estimating the value of the venture so that an objective comparison can be made between the value of pursuing the venture and the value of the entrepreneur's other opportunities. Third, financial forecasting helps the entrepreneur compare strategic alternatives and select the one with the highest expected value. Fourth, if

INTERNET RESOURCES FOR THIS CHAPTER

The Excel spreadsheets for the figures in the chapter provide a way for you to study the integration of financial statements. For example, by changing key assumptions, you can see how the income statement and balance sheet are related and how they interact to determine cash needs. The "Integrated Financial Statements Template" in Appendix 6A on the Web site includes an Excel spreadsheet that can be downloaded and used as a starting point for generating a set of pro forma statements for a venture. The statements can be used to help assess financing needs and to study the effects of different financing decisions. Appendix 6B on the Web site also identifies some of the data sources that commonly are used in business forecasting, including a number of sources that are accessible on the Internet. A case application is included to provide exposure to forecasting data and methods.

outside capital is required, financial forecasting helps prospective investors perceive the merits of the venture and helps the entrepreneur negotiate an appropriate financial interest. Finally, a financial forecast can be used as a benchmark against which to compare actual performance, thereby providing early warning if the venture is not developing as expected. The forecast enables the entrepreneur to make timely decisions to arrange for additional financing or possibly to abandon the venture.

In this chapter we introduce the basics of financial forecasting. We look first at the cash flow cycle of a business venture. The cash flow cycle identifies the four key determinants of financial needs: minimum efficient scale, profitability, cash flow, and sales growth. We then use a simple example to explain the process of pro forma analysis, and we discuss how the financial statements of the venture are related to each other and why the sales forecast is the foundation for pro forma analysis. Once the structure of the forecast is established, we shift the focus to the critical element of forecasting—specifying the assumptions that underlie the financial model. These assumptions are what make the forecast more than just an exercise and make it credible to investors. In this context, we discuss forecasting techniques and information sources. The chapter concludes with an example of the use of pro forma analysis to forecast financial needs. In Chapter 7 we use the forecasting methods developed here as part of the process for assessing financial needs, and we do so in the context of strategic decision making. In Chapters 8 and 9 we use the financial forecast as a basis for valuation.

6.1 THE CASH FLOW CYCLE

At a high level of abstraction, a business venture is like a machine that converts cash today into cash in the future. All of the physical capital of the business, as well as the employees and even the goods or services that are produced and sold, are simply inputs to the venture's technology for producing cash. A prospective entrepreneur hopes the venture represents a technology that is particularly good at converting present into future cash, so that a small investment of cash and effort today can be expected to yield a large cash payoff in the future.

The technologies of business ventures for producing cash display a number of common features. These common features are represented diagrammatically in Figure 6-1. You can think of the venture as originating as a pool of cash that is supplied by infusions in the form of equity investments and possibly debt. As the venture commences operations, the cash is expended, to acquire and pay for various resources: fixed assets, materials, and employees. These resources are used to produce an inventory of finished goods. Sales of finished goods may be carried out on a cash basis, a credit basis, or a combination. Credit sales generate accounts receivable, which are converted to cash over time through the venture's collection process. Ending cash may be distributed to equity investors (in the form of dividends or possibly share repurchase), to

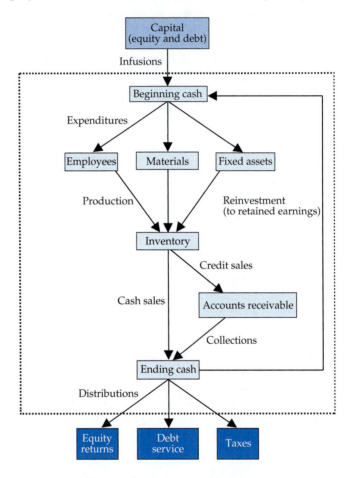

Figure 6-1 The cash flow cycle of a business venture

The cash flow cycle traces a simplified flow of cash through a venture. Ventures use cash infusions from investors and cash retained from the previous period to acquire productive inputs. The inventory that is produced is sold for cash or credit. Cash sales and collections of receivables combine to yield the ending cash balance. The venture can retain this balance, distribute it to investors, or pay tax obligations. The figure does not illustrate timing differences between expense recognition and cash outflow related to the various productive resources. A more comprehensive diagram would address these timing issues by providing for wages payable, accounts payable, and depreciation expenses.

creditors (in the form of interest payments and principal repayments), and some may go to meet tax obligations of the business. Any cash that is not distributed is retained by the venture and is available for reinvestment during the next period.

The figure illustrates the flow of cash through the venture, including the conversion of cash into inventory through the production process and back into cash through the selling effort.[1] The distinction between cash and credit sales is useful. Normally, accountants recognize income at the time a sale is made, regardless of whether the sale is for cash or on credit. The existence of credit sales (that generate accounts receivable but not immediate cash) is one reason net income is not equivalent to net cash flow. Selling on credit is only one of several factors that contribute to the difference. Any time there is a difference between the timing of revenue or expense recognition on the company's books and the timing of cash inflow or outflow, a disparity will exist between net income and net cash flow. It is important for the entrepreneur to distinguish between accounting income and cash flow, and that highly profitable ventures can have significant negative cash flows over long periods.

The figure also indicates that there is a relationship between financing choices and the cash flow cycle. This is most apparent in the choice of how to allocate ending cash. A venture that uses debt financing normally is obligated to make debt service payments according to a specific schedule. Such payments reduce the cash the venture can retain to finance ongoing operations, and limit the ability of the enterprise to grow without additional infusions of capital. In the next chapter we study the connection between financial policy choices and growth, an issue that is important to any new venture.

6.2 CRITICAL DETERMINANTS OF FINANCIAL NEEDS

Our objective in this chapter is to develop the use of financial forecasting as a tool for assessing the financing needs of a venture. The cash flow cycle illustrated in Figure 6-1 demonstrates that financial needs depend on a number of factors. Here we highlight four determinants of financial needs: minimum efficient scale, profitability, cash flow, and the growth rate of sales.

Minimum Efficient Scale

Every business uses a combination of inputs to produce the goods or services it sells. In Figure 6-1 we group these inputs under the broad headings of employees, materials, and fixed assets. Capital-intensive businesses require high levels of fixed assets compared to the other inputs. Petroleum refining, for example, is a highly capital-intensive business, as are many manufacturing businesses that are designed around assembly lines (like automobile manufacturing) or flow processes (like pulp and paper milling). Such businesses generally have large initial capital needs partly because the entire investment must be made before production can begin and partly because such investments usually are not easy to expand, so that the initial investment must be of a scale that is appropriate for the long run. In contrast, a mail-order business can involve almost no capital investment. In some cases, the business does not even need to acquire the items it advertises for sale until after orders are received. Clearly, the resources required to start up a capital-intensive business are much greater than those needed to start up a labor-intensive business like mail order.

In economic terms, economies of scale exist if long-run average cost falls as the volume of output per unit of time increases. If entering an industry would require making some fixed investments, such as committing to a particular production technology, then usually it would be important for an entrant to select the technology that would enable it to reach the minimum point on the long-run average cost curve. Not doing so would place the firm at a permanent competitive disadvantage.

In Figure 6-2, we illustrate the long-run average cost curve for a manufacturing business. The figure shows that as a manufacturer's intended production increases, the manufacturer's long-run average cost falls and is at a minimum over the range of output Q to Q^*. A firm's production is subject to economies of scale if a proportionate increase in all inputs results in a more than proportionate increase in output. For example, inputs double, and output more than doubles. There are several reasons average cost might fall until output level Q is reached: for example, the firm may be able to buy inputs at a quantity discount; or may be able to use fixed assets like managerial skills more efficiently. However, as the figure shows, economies of scale do not continue indefinitely.

Figure 6-2 also illustrates the concept of minimum efficient scale (MES). MES is the smallest level of output for which average cost is at a minimum. For the cost curve in the figure, MES corresponds to output level Q. If a prospective new venture faces competition, then the venture will need at least enough cash to enable it to enter with sufficient capacity to produce at minimum efficient scale. Entering with an investment in fixed factors designed to produce at a scale less than Q would mean that the venture would have higher long-run average costs than its competitors. However, some new ventures face little competition (at least in the short run), provided they have created a unique product with no close substitutes. For such a venture, the requirement to enter the market at MES is lessened.

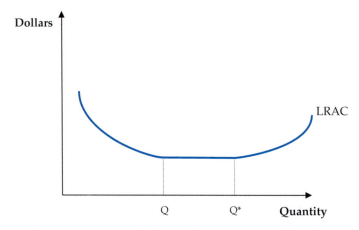

Figure 6-2 Manufacturer's long-run per unit cost (LRAC)

The long-run average cost (LRAC) curve shows the minimum cost of producing at each level of output, assuming all inputs are variable. In the long run, a venture can be designed to produce as efficiently as possible at any given level of output. The negative sloping portion of the curve reflects economies of scale. Scale economies are exhausted at output level Q, the minimum efficient scale (MES) at which the lowest possible cost of production per unit is achieved. Beyond Q^*, increases in scale are inefficient and result in higher unit cost. To operate profitably in a competitive market, a venture normally must be designed for productive capacity between Q and Q^*.

Determining the MES of a venture is complicated by the substantial investments in intangible assets that sometimes are required. Research-oriented ventures generally do not require large investments in physical capital but may require substantial investments in research and development before they are able to generate any significant revenues. Similarly, in some industries competition requires that substantial investments be made in brand name and reputation. Such investments increase the minimum efficient scale the firm must attain. Not surprisingly, individual entrepreneurs may not be willing, or able, to make the large initial investments required to achieve MES in capital-intensive industries. Such investments are more likely to be undertaken by large, established businesses.

Profitability

Profitability reduces financial needs. All else being equal, the more profitable a venture, the lower the need for external financing. A business that is immediately profitable may be capable of providing internal financing to meet most of its needs. Consulting practices, for example, often have high margins of profit compared to variable costs, as well as low initial capital requirements. It is not surprising that many entrepreneurs start such businesses without any significant effort to line up outside financing.

Cash Flow

It may seem obvious that firm profitability reduces the demand for external financing. However, high profitability sometimes goes along with other factors that increase the demand for financing. As Figure 6-1 illustrates by distinguishing between cash and credit sales, profitability is not the same thing as cash flow. James Stancill notes, "Any company, no matter how big or small, moves on cash not profits. You can't pay bills with profits, only cash. You can't pay employees with profits, only cash."[2] A profitable business that sells on credit may not collect its receivables for several months, whereas a business that sells for cash may be less profitable but be better able to finance its operations internally. The operating cash flows of a business depend on several factors in addition to profitability. Among these are factors such as buying inventory on credit, and timing of payments to employees. Other things being equal, ventures that sell for cash and purchase inputs on credit have lower needs for other means of financing.

Another important cause of the distinction between cash flow and profit is that capital equipment normally cannot be reported as an expense on the income statement in the period when it is purchased. Instead, the purchase is reflected in the balance sheet as a capital asset. The value of the asset is "expensed" over several years (subject to the conventions of the tax laws). Thus, a $100,000 machine that is depreciated on a straight-line basis over four years has the following effects on cash flow and profitability. Acquisition results in a $100,000 negative cash flow at the time of payment for the machine but does not affect reported profit. Depreciating the machine over four years reduces reported profit by $25,000 in each year that the depreciation expense is claimed but does not reduce operating cash flow. Focusing on profitability rather than cash flow understates the need for financing when the machine is acquired and overstates it in the years when the machine is being depreciated.

Sales Growth

Ventures that are profitable and growing rapidly often encounter difficulties generating enough cash to finance the ongoing operations. The financing difficulty arises because growth requires increasing investment of capital. As the business expands, more of the company's resources

Forecasting Profitability

Profitability can be projected directly or indirectly. Direct estimation involves using data on the actual profitability to infer future profitability. If the venture is an established company, the forecast can be based on the historical experience of the venture. If it is a new venture, or a venture that is growing rapidly, historical profitability is unlikely to be very informative. Instead, the forecast can be based on evidence of profitability for other established businesses that are expected to be comparable. Normally, profitability estimates are benchmarked to sales, assets, or some other factor that is perceived to bear a stable relation to profitability.

Indirect approaches to forecasting profitability involve making direct estimates of costs of sales and deriving the estimate of profitability as a residual value. Often an indirect approach is easier and more reliable. One argument in favor of an indirect approach is that some important components of total cost bear strong relationships to sales, whereas others may be substantially fixed. When it is reasonable to classify costs as either fixed or variable, an indirect forecast of profitability may be easier to develop and more defensible than a direct forecast. In addition, some of the information that is used in an indirect forecast can be generated even if the venture has no operating track record and there are few good comparable firms. Materials costs, labor costs, and many of the fixed asset costs can be estimated from information that is relatively easy to generate.

must be allocated to inventories, wage increases, investments in equipment, and so on. If the venture's growth rate is high relative to profitability, then internally generated cash flows will not be sufficient, and the entrepreneur will be compelled to turn to outside sources of financing. In Chapter 7, we look more systematically at the relation between profitability and the ability to support growth internally.

6.3   WORKING CAPITAL, GROWTH, AND FINANCIAL NEEDS

The term *working capital* applies to the current assets of a venture that are integral to its operations. The most important components of working capital usually are inventory, accounts receivable, and cash. Normally, because of the cash flow cycle, a relationship exists between actual or planned sales and the levels of the various working capital accounts. A business that sells from inventory must have enough of it on hand to fill the orders as they arrive. Because the timing of demand is not perfectly predictable and as cost savings are sometimes associated with purchasing in volume, the business normally will try to carry enough inventory, on average, to supply expected demand for several days or weeks. A manufacturer also may need to carry an inventory of raw materials. Similarly, if the business sells on credit, the balance of accounts receivable will be driven by the level of sales and by how quickly the receivables are collected. Many businesses also find it necessary to carry some normal level of cash balance, which balance also depends on the level of sales.

Some working capital transactions generate financing that often is referred to as spontaneous. The level of spontaneous financing is determined automatically by the level of sales in the context of the existing working capital policies of the business and of its suppliers. Spontaneous financing can be changed in deliberate ways by changing working capital management practice. Usually, the most important sources of spontaneous financing are inventory that is purchased on

> ### ◆ Factors That Increase a Firm's Cash Needs
>
> Comparisons across different types of ventures yield general principles that illustrate how financial needs are affected by specific variables. Each of these principles represents a "partial effect." That is, holding all other factors constant, it represents the impact of a particular factor on a firm's financial requirements?
>
> - Ventures with high minimum efficient scale require larger amounts of capital.
> - Ventures low profit margins require larger amounts of capital.
> - Ventures with high rates of sales growth require larger amounts of capital.
> - The more the firm relies on depreciation of assets and the less on expensing, the greater the firm's financial needs.
> - Ventures expecting low levels of cash flow require larger amounts of capital.
> - The more trade credit a venture offers (accounts receivable as a fraction of assets is high), the greater the firm's financial needs.
> - The less trade credit a venture uses (accounts payable as a fraction of assets is low), the greater the firm's financial needs.

terms (which gives rise to accounts payable) and wages that are paid in arrears (which gives rise to wages payable). A business can deliberately change the extent of reliance on accounts payable as a financing source by changing the rate at which it pays for its inventory and wages.

Working Capital Financing

The net working capital of a business is the difference between the sum of the current asset categories of working capital and the spontaneous current liabilities.[3] If the balance of net working capital is positive (assets exceed liabilities), that balance must be financed in some way. If it is negative, then the productive activities of the venture are not only self-financing, they also generate financing for other assets.

For most businesses, the balance of net working capital is positive and additional financing is required. For such a firm, the larger the business grows, the more it requires financing of net working capital. On the other hand, some ventures are able to finance growth by relying partly on their working capital policies. A business that carries little inventory and sells for cash, but purchases on terms, is likely to have a negative net working capital balance (current liabilities exceed current assets). The more rapidly the venture grows, the more it can rely on spontaneously generated financing.

Figure 6-3 is a schematic that shows how working capital policy choices contribute to the size of the net working capital position that must be financed. The various policy choices are represented in the shaded boxes on the left and in the center of the figure. The financial results of those policies are shown in the two shaded columns on the right. These columns conform to the current asset and current liability accounts of the venture. The amount of net working capital (for which financing is required) is shown at the bottom of the figure. The numbers included in the figure as an illustration are representative of a manufacturing venture that carries significant inventories, offers trade credit, and purchases inventory on terms. The result of the specific assumptions is a positive financing need that is equal to about 48 days' sales.[4]

Working Capital Policy

As Figure 6-3 shows, a company's working capital position is not the result of a single policy choice. Some of the choices are easily recognizable as aspects of working capital policy, others are not. Furthermore, the effects of individual policy choices are interdependent in ways that are not emphasized in the figure.

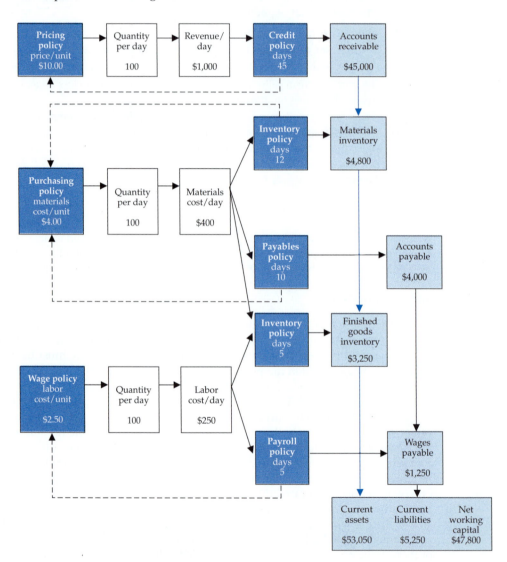

Figure 6-3 Financing needs and working capital policy

The figure is a template for assessing the effects of working capital policies on financial needs. It can be used to examine how working capital policies interact to determine the balances of current asset and current liability accounts. Current assets must be financed, but current liabilities are a spontaneous source of financing. Net working capital is the excess of current assets over current liabilities.

Pricing Policy   Pricing policy is intended as a generic descriptor of decisions related to product positioning, pricing, and marketing. Collectively, these decisions are key determinants of the expected quantity of sales of the venture. We emphasize pricing in the figure because the effective price (along with quantity of sales) is influenced by credit policy. If, for example, a venture sells on trade credit terms that include a discount for prompt payment, then the price used in the calculation should be the average expected price, which is the net of trade discounts that are expected to be taken and of expected default losses. With cash sales, the price is not discounted and there is no risk that a buyer will default. On the other hand, the quantity of sales is likely to be higher if the venture offers credit.

Credit Policy   Given that credit policy influences the effective average price and quantity of sales, how should a business establish an appropriate policy? Figure 6-3 suggests that a policy of selling on cash only terms would reduce the amount required to finance net working capital. But minimizing the need for financing usually is not consistent with maximizing value. It could make sense to evaluate the effect of some alternative credit policy scenarios on profitability and economic value. Suppose you were to sell only for cash—what would be the likely effect on sales? If you accept credit cards as a way of providing credit, how much would expected unit sales increase, and what is the expected effect on average net price? As credit card sales are quickly converted to cash, the credit period would be very short, or zero. Finally, suppose you were to offer credit and integrate the firm into the credit management function. How would that affect price and quantity, and how quickly would you expect to collect accounts receivable?

As a practical matter, new and small businesses often have limited ability to determine their own credit policies. Smaller and less well-established businesses are more likely than others to offer terms that include delayed payment. Customers of such businesses often demand opportunities to verify the quality of the seller's product before they pay. Also, although trade credit terms vary greatly across industries, they tend to be similar within an industry. Thus, in an industry where offering delayed payment terms is common, a new or small business generally must offer terms consistent with the general practice. In an industry where cash payment is common, a new or small business still may find it is important to offer delayed payment as a means of assuring product quality and delivery.[5]

Purchasing and Inventory Policies   Purchasing policy is our rubric for choices that affect cost of materials. Choices of materials, negotiations with suppliers, and similar considerations affect the cost of materials per unit produced. Inventory policy relates to the average number of days of inventory the business seeks to maintain in raw materials and in finished goods. Inventory policy affects average cost of materials indirectly, because maintaining large average inventories may enable the business to take advantage of purchase quantity discounts. Purchasing and inventory policies interact with sales quantity to determine the value of materials inventory.

Payables Policy   Payables policy concerns the extent of reliance on delaying payment for materials as a means of financing. Vendors generally require cash payment or offer deferred payment either with or without a discount for prompt payment. Normally, a purchaser would be expected to delay payment, as long as doing so did not affect purchase price. The policy decision is whether to take advantage of discounts for prompt payment. Doing so reduces the effective cost of materials, as suggested by the feedback loop in the figure, but also reduces the balance of accounts payable, giving rise to a need for additional financing. Generally, discounts for prompt payment are large enough that a business with alternative means of financing available to it would not routinely choose to pay after the discount period.[6]

Determining Working Capital Policy

Most new ventures are compelled to adopt working capital policies that are consistent with industry norms. To be competitive, the venture needs to offer trade credit terms that are typical for the industry, or possibly even more generous. As the venture probably purchases materials from the same industries as do its competitors, it is likely to face similar terms for payment and similar discounts for prompt payment. It also is probably similar to other firms in the industry with respect to the combined effects of quantity discounts and the value of maintaining inventory. Because it competes for labor in the same market, the venture may need to adopt a similar payroll policy.

If the venture is in an industry with other competitors of similar size, working capital policies can be developed by observing the practices and results of the others. Information on standard operating ratios, such as accounts receivable to sales, accounts payable to cost of goods, and inventory to cost of goods is available by industry from a number of public sources. Such information can be a useful basis for formulating working capital policy.

For a venture that is not easily classified into an industry, the data can still be used by searching for information on industries that are similar in terms of such factors as size and reputation of the firms. Beyond this, policy choices depend on fundamental considerations, such as reputation of the venture, its suppliers, and its customers, verifiability of product quality, and the economic cost of being short of inventory.

Wage and Payroll Policies   Wage policy relates to decisions such as offering a high wage rate to limit turnover and motivate employees, or a low rate that increases turnover. Depending on the importance of experience on the job, motivation, availability of new employees, and similar considerations, average labor cost per unit could be lower by either approach. The average labor and materials costs per unit comprise the cost of a unit of finished goods. They interact with finished goods inventory policy to determine the value of finished goods inventory.

Payroll policy relates to frequency of payroll and timing of payroll, relative to timing of productive activity by employees. The balance of wages payable as a source of spontaneous financing is increased by paying in arrears and by paying less frequently (e.g., biweekly instead of weekly). Payroll policy affects wages indirectly. Wage payments that are substantially in arrears may necessitate higher wage rates. Wage and payroll policies interact with sales quantity to determine the balance of wages payable.

6.4   PRO FORMA ANALYSIS

Working capital policy is only one of many factors that affect the profitability, financing needs, and economic value. Assessing the combined effects of these factors requires forecasting tools and techniques that incorporate the complex interrelationships among the factors. Pro forma analysis is the most widely used method of financial forecasting, and the method that is most useful for new venture finance. Pro forma analysis is simply a prediction of how the venture's financial statements will look in the future. Underlying the forecast are assumptions that together make up a financial model of the venture. These assumptions combine with another set of assumptions that reflect expectations about the economy and the market, to yield a forecast of performance.

A simple example illustrates the relation between the assumptions and the forecast. Suppose a venture begins today, with total assets of $1 million and no debt. We assume that each dollar of assets at the beginning of a year is capable of supporting $2 million of sales during the year and that each dollar of sales is expected to generate $.10 in net income. To keep things simple, all sales are for cash and economic depreciation is equal to accounting depreciation. These assumptions constitute our financial model of the venture. Now, suppose market demand during the first year is just sufficient to be achieved by the sales capabilities of the firm and that demand is expected to grow at an annual rate of 6 percent. This is a simple model of the economy, including a description of how the economy relates to the venture.

How is such a firm expected to progress? Beginning at time zero, the venture has total assets of $1 million (all equity), and no sales revenue. During the first year, the venture is expected to generate sales of $2 million and result in net income (and cash flow) of $200,000. The firm can retain all of this income or distribute some of it to the entrepreneur as a dividend. Because the model of the economy implies that demand will be 6 percent higher next year, the venture needs to retain enough earnings to support $2.12 million in sales during the second year. Accordingly, it can retain $60,000 of the $200,000 and distribute the remaining $140,000 to the entrepreneur. So, at the end of the first year the venture is expected to have $1,060,000 in assets. With that asset base, it is expected to generate sales of $2,120,000, and profits of $212,000. Moving ahead to the second year and providing again for 6 percent growth, the venture retains $63,600 and distributes $148,400. At the end of the second year, the venture is expected to have assets of $1,123,600.

We can easily incorporate these assumptions into a spreadsheet.[7] Doing so enables us to extend the pro forma analysis for additional years. Figure 6-4 shows the result through the first five years of operation.

Although the spreadsheet in Figure 6-4 does not look much like the typical financial statements that you may be used to seeing, the interplay between balance sheet and income statement accounts is evident. Start with the stock of beginning assets (a balance sheet account, which, in this example, also equals equity). The stock of assets determines the level of sales for the subsequent year. Sales is a flow variable and appears in the income statement, as does net income. From there, the allocation is made between dividends and retained earnings for the year. Retained earnings for the year is added to the existing balance of retained earnings in the balance sheet.

Five-year Pro Forma Analysis for a Simple Business Venture					
Year	**Beginning Assets**	**Sales**	**Net Income**	**Retained Earnings**	**Dividends**	**Ending Assets**
1	$1,000,000	$2,000,000	$200,000	$60,000	$140,000	$1,060,000
2	$1,060,000	$2,120,000	$212,000	$63,600	$148,400	$1,123,600
3	$1,123,600	$2,247,200	$224,720	$67,416	$157,304	$1,191,016
4	$1,191,016	$2,382,032	$238,203	$71,461	$166,742	$1,262,477
5	$1,262,477	$2,524,954	$252,495	$75,749	$176,747	$1,338,226

Assumptions:
Sales = 2 × Beginning Assets
Net Income = Sales × 0.1
Retained Earnings = Beginning Assets × 0.06
Dividends = Net Income − Retained Earnings
Ending Assets = Beginning Assets + Retained Earnings

Figure 6-4   Five-year pro forma analysis for a simple business venture

In this example, given the equivalency of net income and cash flow, the figure also embodies a rudimentary flow of funds statement. Net income equals net cash inflow, and the net outflows are to retained earnings (new investment in assets) and to dividends. Finally, from the perspective of the entrepreneur, you can see that the initial investment of $1 million is expected to generate an increasing stream of dividends during the five years, with a book value of assets of about $1,338,000 at the end of year 5.

An integrated financial forecast is one that links, by formula, the projected income statement, balance sheet, cash flows and assumptions that underlie the model.[8] The formulas are part of the assumptions that underlie the forecast. These assumptions specify attainable sales, profitability, cash flow, and resource needs. The beginning balance sheet and sales forecast are determined simultaneously. The income statement is a product of the sales forecast, beginning assets and liabilities, and the assumptions related to the income statement. The cash flow statement is derived from the income statement and from assumptions about such factors as the accounts receivable collection period and payment practices. In addition, new financing activities and asset acquisitions affect cash flow. The cash flow needs of the venture must be financed by increases in balance sheet liabilities or equity. The financial statements are linked over time since the ending balance sheet from one period is the beginning balance sheet for the next.

6.5 FORECASTING SALES

To anticipate long-run financing requirements, we need a method for linking product-market performance to financing. The sales forecast is the customary link. This is because once the venture reaches the stage where it is producing and selling a viable product, sales growth is the primary driver of financing requirements. For any given pattern of desired or expected future sales, we can work back to determine the cash flows from operations that are expected to be available for future investment. Using estimates of the productivity of assets, in terms of their ability to support sales, we can also work back to determine expected external financing needs.

Four key questions must be answered in the sales forecast of a new venture:

- When will the venture begin to generate revenues?
- Once revenues are being generated, how rapidly will they grow?
- Over what span of time (3 years, 5 years, 10 years, etc.) should the forecast be made?
- What is an appropriate forecasting interval (weekly, monthly, annually, etc.)?

For now, we set aside the problem of forecasting product development costs. However, the timing of product development activities does need to be factored into the sales forecast. If you expect that two years of development effort will be required before the product can be marketed, then two years of zero sales should be included in the forecast.

The span of time that should be covered by the forecast depends on how the forecast is to be used. If the forecast is made for the purpose of assessing financial needs, it should cover a long enough period so that by the end, the venture is expected to attract follow-on financing based on its track record. If the forecast is made to determine the value of the venture, the period must be long enough to carry the venture to a point where harvesting opportunities are likely to develop.

The appropriate forecast interval depends on the planning period of the venture. For assessing financial needs of an early-stage venture, forecast intervals of one year are too long. Many such ventures, after all, do not even survive the first year. If there is to be hope of survival, the entrepreneur needs to project cash needs over much shorter intervals so that financing can be arranged on a timely basis. Furthermore, the important milestones that help the entrepreneur gauge whether the venture is on track are unlikely to be annual. On the other hand, daily or even weekly forecasts are unlikely to be of much value either. Departures from projected results for short-interval forecasts are certain to be highly variable. As a result, the entrepreneur is likely to aggregate the data into longer intervals to get a better sense of how the venture is doing. Generally, an interval of about a month provides a good balance of timeliness and reliability.

Forecasting Sales of an Established Business

Commonly, an established business develops a sales forecast based on its prior experience or track record. For example, the organization might project that sales will grow at the average rate of the previous five years. A more sophisticated approach might take into consideration the trend in the rate of sales growth (as opposed to the average), or the forecast could be tied to changes in underlying economic and demographic factors. In this section, we illustrate simple forecasting approaches for businesses with track records.

Suppose that for an existing business we observe the following levels of sales and macroeconomic information for the previous six years:

Year	−6	−5	−4	−3	−2	−1
Sales (millions)	$2.0	$2.4	$2.7	$2.6	$2.6	$2.9
Sales growth		+20%	+12.5%	−3.7%	0%	+11.5%
Inflation		+3%	+6%	+7%	+4%	+2%
Change in real GDP		+3%	+1.5%	−1%	−1%	+2%

So, for example, from six years ago to five years ago sales increased from $2.0 million to $2.4 million, a 20 percent increase. During the same year, the inflation rate for the industry was 3 percent, and real gross domestic product increased 3 percent.

One approach to forecasting sales is to extrapolate the average historical growth rate. In this case, the simple average of the five sales growth rates in the table is 8.06 percent. However, the range during the five years is from −3.7 percent to 20 percent. Knowing that the historical average is 8.06 is useful, but the high degree of uncertainty about the rate in any given year can be problematic, particularly if management is deciding on questions such as how much financing to arrange to cover the next year of operations. Clearly, a more precise estimate would be desirable. One way to improve the sales forecast may be to make it in real (inflation-adjusted) terms rather than nominal terms, especially if price increases for the venture track the inflation index well and if inflation forecasts are available publicly.[9] By subtracting the inflation rate from the sales growth rate, we can express the sales growth rate in real terms.

Year	−6	−5	−4	−3	−2	−1
Sales growth		+20%	+12.5%	−3.7%	0%	+11.5%
Inflation		+3%	+6%	+7%	+4%	+2%
Real sales growth		+17%	+6.5%	−10.7%	−4%	+9.5%

The simple average of the real rate of sales growth over the period is 3.66 percent.

In one sense, we have not improved the accuracy of the forecast very much by expressing it in real terms. The range in real terms, -10.7 percent to 17 percent, is wider than it is in nominal terms. However, the real numbers may provide a more accurate characterization of uncertainty. It is useful to consider other alternatives as well. A reasonable forecast of growth may be achieved by using historical nominal growth rates (assuming that expected future inflation is the average of past inflation rates). Alternatively, it may be more accurate to add the historical average real growth rate to a current forecast of inflation.

We can illustrate the difference between forecasting in real terms and nominal terms. Suppose that publicly available forecasts for next year are for an inflation rate around 1.0 percent. If the 1.0 percent rate is used to project sales growth, then we forecast that sales are expected to increase by 4.66 percent (the 3.66 percent average real growth plus the 1.0 percent inflation). Had the nominal growth rate been used, we would forecast sales growth of 8.06 percent, no matter what the rate of inflation was expected to be. Which forecast is better? The answer depends on how the inflation rate is expected to affect sales. If the product price tends to follow the inflation rate, then a forecast based on expected inflation is likely to be better than simple trend extrapolation.

Even though the preferred method of forecasting takes expected inflation into account, the most useful method of stating a pro forma income statement usually is in nominal terms. If, in your judgment, the sales forecast ought to be generated in real terms, then when formulating the pro forma statements, it is better to take the inflation-adjusted sales numbers and express them in nominal terms again. This is helpful for practical reasons. Managers are accustomed to nominal measures, and some income statement items like depreciation are fixed in nominal terms. Also, interest rates are quoted in nominal terms. Regardless of which approach is used—real or nominal—it is critical that the treatment be consistent. All items that appear in the pro forma income statement and balance sheet should be either in nominal terms or real terms. Thus, if the sales forecast is expressed in real terms and some expense items (such as rent) are fixed in nominal terms, those items must be deflated at the expected inflation rate to reflect the expected future real costs.

Another technique for improving forecast accuracy is to weight the historical observations of sales growth so that the more recent experience receives greater weight. There are many reasons to expect that this will result in a more accurate forecast, but the general point is that the future probably will be more like the recent past than the more distant past. With enough historical data and appropriate software, one could use the computer to determine the weights on prior year sales that yield the (statistically) best estimates of sales in later years.[10] In the context of our example, five years of data are not enough to support a formal analysis of the appropriate weightings. Accordingly, we use a simple judgmental approach of applying a weight factor of 5/15 to the real growth rate of sales in the most recent year, 4/15 to the prior year, and so on. The following table shows the weight factors applied to the real sales growth rates. Note that the weight factors over five years sum to one (15/15).

Year	−6	−5	−4	−3	−2	−1
Real sales growth		+17%	+6.5%	−10.7%	−4%	+9.5%
Weight factor		1/15	2/15	3/15	4/15	5/15
Weighted growth		+1.13%	+0.87%	−2.14%	−1.07%	+3.17%

The resulting forecast of real sales growth is 1.96 percent, the sum of the numbers in the last row of the table. The forecast is below the simple average forecast of 3.66 percent, in large part because the high growth in year –5 is accorded much less weight in the average than are the negative growth rates in years –2 and –3.

In the above forecast, the weights placed on historical returns are linearly related to each other. Exponential smoothing is an alternative weighting scheme that is easy to apply and can work well when historical data are limited. The simplest form of the exponential smoothing model is stated as:

$$Forecast_{T + 1} = \alpha \times Actual_T + (1 - \alpha) \times Forecast_T \tag{6.1}$$

where α is a weighting factor between zero and one. As the period T forecast is estimated in the same way, actual results of earlier periods are reflected implicitly in the $T + 1$ forecast through the previous forecast. The term *exponential smoothing* signifies that, when equation (6.1) is used, the weights applied to earlier results decrease exponentially.

The relative importance of recent, and not so recent, results to the forecast is determined by the weight factor. A high value of α is used if recent results are believed to be an important predictor of future results. A lower value increases the importance of less recent results. If α is high, the forecast adjusts quickly to new results. In the extreme, if α is equal to 1, then the next period's forecast is equal to this period's result. If α is low, the forecast adjusts gradually. These general properties also apply if a linear smoothing approach is used.

If exponential smoothing is used to generate a forecast from the above table, and α is set at 0.2, the resulting forecast is for 7.5 percent real growth in sales, compared to a 4.4 percent growth forecast that results when α is set at 0.6. The higher forecast arises because $\alpha = 0.2$ places more weight on the high growth that occurred in the first year.

Year	−5	−4	−3	−2	−1	Forecast
Real sales growth	+17%	+6.5%	−10.7%	−4%	+9.5%	?
Forecast with α is .2		+17%	+14.9%	+9.8%	+7.0%	+7.5%
Forecast with α is .6		+17%	+10.7%	−2.1%	−3.3%	+4.4%

The averaging approaches to sales forecasting that we have discussed thus far are examples of naïve forecasting methods. They extrapolate the existing trends without consideration of underlying economic forces. More elaborate naïve models can be developed by augmenting the above approaches to deal with factors like seasonality, or with a growth rate that is expected to decline systematically over time. Also, in some cases, it may be more reliable to forecast levels instead of percentage changes.

Admittedly, our focus on real rather than nominal sales is a slight departure from naïve forecasting, as it does bring the inflation rate into play in a fundamental way. However, beyond that, the underlying economic forces are ignored. Perhaps we could generate a more accurate forecast by trying to identify the economic factors that affect the level of sales. These forces might be macroeconomic variables such as the growth rate of gross domestic product (GDP). They might be socioeconomic, such as the population growth rate or the average age of the population. Or they could be industry-specific, such as industry sales growth rate, emergence of new competitors, or product innovations.

The table we used to initiate this discussion of forecasting methods includes information on the change in real gross domestic product as a macroeconomic factor that potentially affects the sales growth of the business. Using a computer to examine the statistical relationship between sales growth and real GDP, we find that the real sales growth rate of the business is about five times as volatile as the GDP and that the two are highly correlated with each other.[11] Based, more simply, on visual inspection of the relationship, the expected growth of sales that is generated by multiplying GDP by five is very close to the actual growth rate.

Year	−5	−4	−3	−2	−1
Change in real GDP	+3%	+1.5%	−1%	−1%	+2%
Expected sales growth (×5)	+15%	+7.5%	−5%	−5%	+10%
Real sales growth	+17%	+6.5%	−10.7%	−4%	+9.5%
Difference	+2%	−1%	−5.7%	+1%	−0.5%

This table shows that, once the historical growth rate of GDP is known, it is possible to estimate the historical growth rate of sales with considerable accuracy. But how can this relationship be used to forecast the growth rate of sales in the future? To rely on this relationship for forecasting, we must be able to assume correctly that the relationship that existed in the past is expected to persist. This is an issue of judgment. It does not make sense to search arbitrarily for variables that appear to have been related to sales growth in the past. Instead, it is important to think critically about the factors that are likely to influence sales growth, and then use past information to test the strength of the relationship. Furthermore, it is not helpful to identify relationships between sales and other factors that are, themselves, equally hard to forecast. In the case of factors like GDP, however, public forecasts are abundant and can be employed easily.

Forecasting Sales of a New Venture

Developing a sales forecast for a new venture is more difficult, and the result is likely to be much less certain. Because the venture is new, there is no track record that can be used to develop the sales forecast. How, then, is the entrepreneur to arrive at a forecast for a product that may not yet exist, where the full scope of applications is not yet known, and where actions and reactions of potential competitors are yet to be seen? Rather than allowing these concerns to become overwhelming, it is important to search for simplicity. We consider two approaches.

Yardsticks   An approach that is useful for many new ventures is to identify reasonable yardstick ventures for which public (and possibly nonpublic) data are available. A yardstick is an established firm that is comparable to the entrepreneur's venture in some important dimensions but not necessarily all dimensions. Actual comparability often does not need to be very close. Certainly, it is not necessary that a yardstick firm be producing the same product. Comparability can be evaluated by considering factors such as: the expected market for the product; distribution channels; uniqueness of the product relative to existing substitutes; and manufacturing technology.

One advantage of the yardstick approach is data availability. Hundreds of small companies go public every year. In the process, they supply a great deal of information about the period before the company was public. Companies that make initial public offerings are ideal candidates for assessing optimistic but realistic sales growth potential. The fact that they have chosen to issue equity publicly suggests that, from a financing standpoint, they are often firms that have grown so rapidly that outside equity financing became important for growth. By studying the experiences of yardstick companies, the entrepreneur obtains data and other information on the various stages of growth of new ventures and their changing financing needs.

In many cases, the offering prospectus of a public company contains enough historical data to measure sales growth over a number of years during which the company was private. In some cases there is enough historical information that it is possible to infer the length of the development period before the company was able to market a product successfully.

Financial information from yardstick companies has value beyond just forecasting. The prospectus also contains information on how those companies met their financing needs before going public. Thus, each company can serve as a case study, providing insights to the financing choices the entrepreneur faces. In addition, the companies' financial statements can aid in formulating the assumptions the entrepreneur needs to make in projecting the financial statements of the new venture.

Copies of prospectuses can be obtained from various sources, including the issuing company, the underwriter, and the Securities and Exchange Commission (SEC). The SEC maintains an electronic file of prospectuses and other corporate submissions on its EDGAR database.[12]

How can the sales information from yardstick companies be used to generate a sales forecast? The techniques are fundamentally the same as they are for an established business that is attempting to generate a forecast based on its own historical sales. The historical experience of an existing business is simply one yardstick that is likely to be particularly good, as many of the factors that cause variations in sales growth rates are effectively held constant by using the firm's own history. For a new venture, this convenient sales record is not available, but the task is the same—to use historical sales experience (of other firms) to generate a forecast.

Fundamental Analysis   Fundamental analysis of the market is an alternative to the yardstick approach. Typically, the analysis starts with an estimate of the aggregate size of the relevant market. For example, the entrepreneur might begin by defining the geographic trade area that the venture would be able to serve, recognizing that the area might grow over time if the business were to expand or add locations. Within the trade area, the next step is to estimate the number of potential customers and the buying characteristics of a typical customer. How frequently does a typical customer make purchases? What are the size and composition of a typical purchase? From this base, the entrepreneur can estimate the size of the market in terms of annual units or revenue.

What Can You Learn from a Prospectus?

Radica Games Yardstick Analysis

You have an idea for a new hand-held action computer game for adults, GameMan. It is difficult to assess demand for the product because most hand-held games are designed for children and most adult computer games are designed for laptops and desktop computers. However, several companies could be appropriate yardsticks. One company, Radica Games, recently issued shares in an IPO and has a product with some of the same characteristics as yours. The first page of the prospectus for Radica Games, Ltd. is displayed below. Radica (the company) "designs, develops, and manufactures and distributes a variety of non-gambling casino theme games." The company's principal products include hand-held and tabletop electronic poker, blackjack, slot, and keno games, tabletop mechanical slot machines, and so on. All of these are designed to simulate games in casinos. The games retail for prices ranging from $9.95 to $99.95. The company designs and sells its products in the United States but procures its supplies from a manufacturer in the People's Republic of China. It sells to retailers who serve a broad spectrum of customers, including Target, WalMart, Walgreens, Best, and Macy's.

So far, so good, since your plans include trying to attract similar retailers and you have already made contacts with suppliers in Asia.

The prospectus shows the following:

Income Statement and Balance Sheet (selected items)

	Year Ended October 31 (in thousands)				
	1989	1990	1991	1992	1993
Income Statement Data					
Net Sales	$4,682	$4,222	$5,154	$9,853	$32,505
Gross Profit	1,779	1,750	2,352	4,519	16,420
R&D	164	208	129	158	652
Operating income	343	310	953	1,939	11,002
Balance Sheet Data					
Working capital	$ (189)	$ (141)	$ 536	$ 1,887	$ 7,687
Total assets	2,377	2,131	2,096	5,755	21,826
Shareholder equity	504	692	1,460	3,187	10,365

How do you evaluate whether the company is a reasonable yardstick company? After all, several aspects of the company's experience may not provide a good approximation of what your firm can expect. For example, the company's latest three-year growth rate is very high: net sales grew 670 percent, and operating income increased 3,449 percent. It is unlikely that your venture will grow at the same rate. On the other hand, for assessing financial needs, your planning should provide for an optimistic scenario of growth, along with other scenarios, and this company's experience provides evidence that can be used to benchmark an optimistic growth rate scenario. A more serious problem with the prospectus is that there is no information on the development period and there is only sparse information on the predecessor company responsible for developing the early stages of the venture. This suggests you

(Continues)

(Continued)

will need to look elsewhere for this information. Your planning will benefit from a concerted effort to collect a small sample of yardstick companies.

Still, you can use a lot of the information from the prospectus. You have the basis for calibrating some of the assumptions for your financial model including:

- Over a five-year period for which data are available, Radica's cost of goods sold declined as a percentage of sales from a high of 62 percent to 49 percent. The average over the period was 55 percent. This suggests that a 45 to 50 percent gross profit margin is a reasonable assumption.
- Operating expenses represent, on average, 23.8 percent of net sales
- R&D expenses represent, on average, 2.9 percent of net sales.
- The company does not sell any of its products on consignment, and accepts returns only for defective merchandise. The product has a one-year warranty, and the warranty costs prior to going public were less than 0.4 percent of sales.
- Annual salaries of management totaled $180,000 exclusive of stock options.
- Risk factors mentioned in the prospectus include: risks of manufacturing in China (including the risk of China losing Most Favored Nation Status in the U.S.); dependence on a processing agreement and on local government; dependence on product appeal and new product introductions; the company's limited range of products; lack of assurance of continued growth or adequate management of growth; increased working capital requirements associated with a change in distribution methods; dependence on major customers; dependence on suppliers and subcontractors; concentrated manufacturing facilities; seasonality; and competition.
- During the most recent three-year period, the company was able to finance its rapid expansion primarily through cash flow from operations. It was able to achieve this expansion "by using subcontractors in China, relying on distributors, including . . . distributors who carried inventory and customer receivables for product sales, and as a result of the availability of seasonal trade financing secured by shareholder guarantees and cash." The company did not rely on venture capital.

In addition, there is a discussion in the prospectus of supply sources for components, including some of the same ones you will need: semiconductor chips and molded plastic parts. There also is a discussion of lead times for ordering, as well as an indication of the number of suppliers that the company uses for each of the inputs. This information may raise some questions that you have not thought about before. For example, you learn that the company's supplier only maintains approximately two months of supply of semiconductor chips. This suggests the supplier may constrain production of products on short notice.

Sales estimates for the venture can be generated either from the demand side or the supply side. The demand-side approach tries to determine how much consumers in the market would be willing to buy from the venture, assuming the venture has adequate capacity to supply all of the demand. The demand-side forecast begins with an estimate of the market share that the venture would be able to capture, depending on such demand-related factors as number of competitors, pricing, location, and intensity of marketing efforts. For products that are unique, initial market share is easy to estimate (100 percent), but the size of the market is difficult to judge, and the rate of market share erosion due to competitive entry will depend on defensibility of the entrepreneur's position. For a more traditional venture, market size may be easy to estimate (published estimates may even exist), but market share is more uncertain and the reactions of competitors may be important.

In contrast, the supply-side approach tries to determine how fast the venture can grow, given managerial, financial, and other resource constraints. Relevant questions include: What are the resource requirements to develop the product? to produce the product? to distribute the product? to finance growth? Possible supply-side constraints include limits on access to raw materials, financing, and technology. There also may be constraints on the ability to hire and train employees. Managing growth always is difficult. The point is that, even if demand is expected to increase rapidly, the venture's growth rate may be limited on the supply side.

When the supply-side and demand-side approaches are combined, the expected rate of growth of the venture will be whichever is slower. Slow-growth scenarios normally are constrained by the limits of market demand, whereas rapid-growth scenarios normally are constrained by the organization's ability to manage growth. One advantage of the yardstick approach is that, because it is based on the actual experience of other firms, it implicitly considers both supply-side and demand-side factors.[13]

Whether based on yardsticks, fundamental analysis, or a combination, it is important that projections be realistic and credible. Fundamental analysis is likely to be subject to greatest potential for wild speculation. Consider the sales forecast of a proposed fast-food chain, the Bunny Hutch: "Assume each person in America eats one bunny burger one night per week; at $1.00 per bunny burger. That's $10 million per week."[14] Projections made by experienced individuals with established reputations or by objective third parties are more likely to be realistic and credible than those made by an entrepreneur, who is enamored of the idea in the first place. The best substitute for relying on an independent expert projection is to base the analysis on solid reasoning and well-supported and documented assumptions.

6.6   ESTIMATING UNCERTAINTY

For a new or early-stage venture, efforts to forecast sales and other results may seem futile. After all, the probability that actual performance will turn out to be much like the forecast is very low. Nonetheless, forecasting performance is probably more important for a business with an uncertain future than for a business that has grown steadily for years and is expected to continue to grow.

For a venture with an uncertain future, the forecast of expected performance is simply a way to anchor a forecast of uncertainty. For many purposes, the forecast of uncertainty is far more important. For example, as we demonstrate in Chapter 7, the financial needs of a venture depend heavily on uncertainty. Failure to allow for such possibilities as development delays and lower-than-expected profitability can result in critical financing errors. In addition, failure to assess the level of uncertainty can result in serious strategic errors.

In this section, we introduce some simple approaches for estimating uncertainty. We use and expand on these approaches in Chapter 7 and elsewhere in the text.

Assessing Risk on the Basis of Experience

The methods discussed earlier for forecasting sales can also be used to develop estimates of forecast uncertainty. One simple approach is to generate a baseline trend for a variable of interest, such as sales, during an historical period, and then estimate uncertainty as the historical standard deviation of differences between actual and expected values.

◆   **Fundamental Determinants of Sales Revenue**

Demand-side Considerations:

- What geographic market will the venture serve?
- How many potential customers are in the market?
- How rapidly is the market growing?
- How much, in terms of quantity, is a typical customer expected to purchase during a forecast period?
- How are purchase amounts likely to change in the future?
- What is the expected average price of the venture's product?
- How good is the venture's product compared to the products of competitors?
- How aggressively and effectively, compared to competitors, will the venture promote its product?
- How are competitors likely to react to the venture?
- Who else is considering entering the market, and how likely are they to do so?
- In light of the above, what market share is the venture likely to be able to achieve?

Supply-side Considerations:

- How much can the venture effectively produce, market, and distribute, given its existing resources?
- How rapidly can the venture add and integrate the resources that would be needed for expansion of output?

To illustrate, the following table shows actual and expected sales growth rates from the previous example.

Year	−5	−4	−3	−2	−1
Sales growth	+20%	+12.5%	−3.7%	0%	+11.5%
Expected sales growth	+8.06%	+8.06%	+8.06%	+8.06%	+8.06%
Deviation from expected	+11.94%	+4.44%	−11.76%	−8.06%	+3.44%

The uncertainty of sales growth can be estimated as the standard deviation of differences between historical actual and expected growth rates. In this example, the standard deviation of differences between actual and expected growth rates is 9.71 percent. Thus, the forecast for next year could be expected sales growth of 8.06 percent, with a standard deviation of 9.71 percent.

For a venture that does not have a track record, uncertainty is greater and is more difficult to estimate. One approach is to base the estimate on the experience of other companies that are similar in important respects. Another way to estimate uncertainty is to envision alternative realistic scenarios for the venture and to develop projections consistent with each. An estimate of uncertainty can be developed by applying weight factors to the different scenarios.

Developing Alternative Scenarios

Prospectuses of public companies and other public data can help you make a reasonable forecast of a success scenario. The success scenario may be the one that is most important for trying to determine how much financing you will need. But for other purposes, it is important to develop a more comprehensive reasonable forecast of uncertainty. Value, for example, depends more on expected performance and uncertainty than it does on the performance under a success scenario.

What can you do to develop scenarios that reasonably represent the uncertainty of a new venture? For simple businesses like retail shops and restaurants, the realistic range of actual performance is not broad. For those it may be possible to rely on information from public sources, some of which we describe below. But what about a business with tremendous potential as well as tremendous uncertainty?

Recently, we were contacted by a research professor from a leading university medical school. The professor was working on an AIDS treatment that appeared to have considerable promise but is in need of venture funding to carry out the next phase of testing. The professor's question was, "How can I figure out how much my idea and the related patents are worth?" The answer depends partly on expected future cash flows and uncertainty of the cash flows.

Defining a success scenario for the sales forecast is not difficult. Public information is sufficient to estimate the current and expected number of people who would be candidates for treatment, and quantity sales can be converted to revenues based on prevailing prices for proprietary treatments for other life-threatening ailments. But it is hard to imagine a project that is subject to more uncertainty. How likely is it that the development efforts will be successful and that the patent holder will be permitted to sell the product for a price that is unconstrained by some form of government intervention? More importantly, how many other AIDS research projects are underway, and what is the likelihood that one or more of them will be successful either sooner or later than the one being evaluated?

One way to come to terms with the uncertainty is to try to define a small number of realistic scenarios in addition to the success scenario. Some of the possibilities are: a scenario where development efforts are successful but the product faces a weak level of competition from other successful development efforts; or one where successful development efforts are offset by development of strong competing products; or one where development efforts are not successful and the project is abandoned. The challenge for the entrepreneur is to flesh out the alternative scenarios with realistic assumptions of their effects on product price and quantity and realistic assessments of their relative probabilities. Defining a small number of realistic scenarios helps to focus the research effort and points toward the kinds of information that will be most useful.

6.7 FORECASTING INCOME STATEMENT AND BALANCE SHEET INFORMATION

Once the sales forecast is developed, the next step is to use the sales numbers as a baseline for developing pro forma financial statements. Ultimately, we are concerned not with forecasting income, but with cash flows from operations. However, to project operating cash flows, it is necessary to work through the income statement and balance sheet.

How does a company with no track record develop a pro forma income statement? More specifically, how can the entrepreneur estimate the key relationships in the income statement, such as gross profit as a percentage of sales or labor cost as a percentage of sales? For a new venture, it again is useful to rely on data for public companies that are comparable (see the Radica Games example above). Note, however, that the dimensions of comparability that are most critical for projecting the rate of sales growth often are not the ones that are most critical for projecting income. Critical income statement relationships are likely to be sensitive to factors such as business size, intensity of competition in the product market, and capital intensity of the production process. These factors may have less of a bearing on the rate of sales growth.

It is useful for some purposes to classify expense items as fixed, variable, or semivariable. However, caution is in order. Some sources provide lists of expenses that typically are regarded as fixed and others that are expected to vary with output. The simplistic treatment of expenses as either fixed or variable leads to an inference that the profitability of a venture increases continuously with increases in sales, particularly for a business with high fixed costs. But before accepting the classifications of expenses as fixed or variable, it is a good idea to take a look at the actual expense levels of businesses of different sizes. Few expenses are truly fixed, and others may vary more than proportionately with changes in sales. Consequently, assuming that variable expenses will change in proportion to sales and that fixed expenses will not change is likely to overstate the potential profitability associated with sales growth.

Early in this chapter, we discussed the importance of economies of scale as a factor affecting financial needs. Economies of scale and MES result from the interplay between fixed and variable expenses. In many industries, beyond a certain minimal size, we do not find much of a connection between scale and profitability. A useful test of the importance of scale is to look at the distribution of sizes of companies that are surviving and competing with each other. If the companies are generally small, or if there is a broad mix of companies of different sizes, then scale economies probably are not very important, regardless of any simplistic classification of expenses as either fixed or variable. On the other hand, if the companies are all large, then scale probably is an important factor. The point is that assumptions about the cost structure of the venture should be consistent with reality. Although it may not be possible to find data for established businesses that are exactly like the venture under consideration, good analogies to established industries can improve projections of profitability.

6.8   INFORMATION SOURCES

There are a number of good places to search for data useful for projecting sales, income, and cash flow. One source already mentioned is the prospectuses of firms making initial public offerings. If comparable firms can be located, then yardstick income statement relationships can be estimated and incorporated into the assumptions underlying the financial forecast. For most businesses, however, it is likely that only a few prospectuses of comparable firms can be found. In working with comparable firm data, it is important to understand why the financial ratios vary for apparently similar companies. Understanding these differences may require additional research regarding the companies. Also, it is important to recognize that the data on comparable firms that are most useful for sales forecasting may not be the best ones for forecasting income statement and balance sheet relationships.

One likely source of information is the Risk Management Associates (RMA) *Annual Statement Studies* (formerly "Robert Morris Associates"). RMA compiles financial data from information that is supplied by credit customers of banks. Using the data, it reports a number of income statement and balance sheet relationships by industry. These compilations are published annually and are available at most large public libraries. Reporting companies are classified by four-digit SIC code so that it is possible to locate one or more industry grouping that

Estimating Minimum Efficient Scale (MES)

The MES of firms in an industry sometimes can be evaluated using the survivor test developed by Nobel prize-winning economist, George Stigler. Stigler reasons that firms or plants that survive and contribute an increasing fraction of an industry's output over time are likely to be of efficient size; those that supply a declining share are likely to be "too large" or "too small." As Stigler observes, MES is determined by several factors, not just production economies. Minimum efficient size "is one that meets any or all problems that the entrepreneur actually faces: strained labor relations, rapid innovation, government regulation, unstable foreign markets, and what not."*

Several techniques have been used to estimate MES. Hibdon and Mueller (1990) study petroleum refining. They divided plants into different size categories based on the proportion of total industry capacity produced by each plant. They calculate the share accounted for by each size category and analyze what happened to this share and to the number of refineries in each size category over the period 1947 to 1984. As they conclude, "The average cost curve has a pronounced negative slope at small capacities, a mildly positive slope at the largest sizes, and is relatively flat over the very wide range of in between sizes." The cost curve in Figure 6-2 has a shape like the one suggested by the study.

For an entrepreneur considering a new venture in an existing industry, it is wise to examine available data on the actual sizes of firms in the industry. Such information provides an indication of typical firm size and the minimum size required for entry. It also helps the entrepreneur gain a better understanding of the structure of the industry, as defined by the number and size distribution of the firms.

The following table illustrates the type of firm-size data that are available from public sources. The table shows the percentage of firms producing in various size classes for three industries: paint manufacturing, building contractors, and personal services.

*See Stigler (1958), p. 56.

Industry Comparison of Percentages of Firms Producing in Various Size Classes

Industry	Size of Assets in Thousands of Dollars							
	Under 100	100 to 250	251 to 500	501 to 1,000	1,001 to 5,000	5,001 to 10,000	10,001 to 25,000	25,001 and over
Paints & allied products (SIC 2850)			9.82%	17.64%	51.35%	10.67%	6.83%	3.70%
General building contractors (SIC 1510)	54.18%	15.77%	11.11%	8.50%	8.67%	1.13%	0.44%	0.18%
Personal Services (SIC 7200)	68.42%	16.27%	6.70%	5.15%	3.22%	0.12%	0.01%	0.02%

Source: Almanac of Business & Industrial Financial Ratios (1997). Based on accounting period July 1993–June 1994. For contractors and paint manufacturers, the data are for corporations with and without net income; for personal service firms, data are for corporations with net income.

◆ **General Rules of Financial Forecasting**

- Build and support a schedule of assumptions.
- Begin with a forecast of sales.
- In forecasting sales, consider forecasting in real terms if sales growth is expected to track the inflation rate.
- If using historical data to forecast for an established firm, consider a weighting scheme that puts more weight on the firm's most recent experience.
- If forecasting for a new venture, identify several "yardstick" firms that can be used to develop underlying assumptions regarding expected performance.
- Integrate, by way of formulas, the pro forma balance sheet, income statement and cash flow variables.
- The time span covered by the forecast depends on how the forecast is to be used. If used for assessing financial needs, the time span should cover the period until the firm is expected to attract follow-on financing. If used for determining the value of the venture, the time span should take the venture to the point of harvesting.
- The time interval of the forecast (month, quarter, etc.) depends on the planning horizon. For new ventures, a monthly interval is usually a good choice.
- Test the reasonableness of the model by thinking through the relations among line items across financial statements.
- Try a basic "what if" analysis to see if the results are consistent with theory. For example, if cash sales growth is reduced and accounts receivable falls, then cash needs should fall. Ask yourself whether the magnitudes of the changes make sense.
- Try a basic sensitivity analysis to make sure that the model yields reasonable results when magnitudes and growth rates of key variables change.

serves as a benchmark. Often the data for hundreds of individual companies are reflected in the RMA report for an industry. In addition to grouping by industry, RMA also reports within industry groupings by firm size. An attractive aspect of the RMA data is that the sample includes a large number of small, nonpublic companies. Although the tax reduction strategies of closely held businesses can distort some of the income statement relationships, much of the data is quite useful. Other information sources include: Prentice-Hall, Inc. *Almanac of Business and Industry Financial Ratios;* Dun and Bradstreet, Inc., *Industry Norms and Key Business Ratios;* the annual *Corporate Income and Unincorporated Income* publications of the Internal Revenue Service; and U.S. Department of Commerce, *Quarterly Financial Report for Manufacturing, Mining and Trade Corporations.* These sources contain a myriad of financial information at the industry level, and sometimes the information is stratified by firm size.

In addition, trade associations and investment services such as the *Value Line Investment Survey* and the *Standard and Poor's Analysts Handbook* publish industry-level data. Moody's and Standard and Poor's report data for individual public companies. Increasingly, financial reports of individual companies are available on the Securities and Exchange Commission's EDGAR database and through on-line services such as Yahoo Financial, Hoover's, and Lexis/Nexis. To locate other sources, consult the Gale Research, Inc., *Encyclopedia of Business Information Sources* and the Funk and Scott, *F&S Business News Index.* Appendix B to the chapter appears on the Web site and contains a compilation of information sources and Internet links.

6.9 BUILDING A FINANCIAL MODEL: AN ILLUSTRATION

To see how the sales forecast and forecasts of the financial statements relate to each other, suppose we are considering a new medical technology venture called NewCompany. We've done the background research described above and, based on the research, have generated a set of assumptions that are appropriate for the venture. These assumptions are detailed in Figure 6-5.

Generating the Sales Forecast   The obvious place to begin the pro forma analysis is with the forecast of sales. Because this is a new venture, we decided to use a forecasting interval of one

---

NewCompany Assumptions

1. Development will require 18 months, during which period no sales will be made.

2. Initial sales of $10,000 in the 19th month.

3. Sales will grow 8 percent per month in real terms for three years and at the inflation rate thereafter.

4. Cash operating expenses during the development period of $15,000 per month, plus inflation.

5. Inflation at 9 percent per year (0.75 percent per month).

6. A $200,000 production facility will come on line at the end of month 18. The facility is to be leased with monthly payments of $3,000, and is expected to be adequate for the first five years of operation.

7. A gross profit of 60 percent of sales revenue (net of any trade discounts) on materials costs.

8. Selling expenses of 15 percent of sales.

9. Administrative expenses of $2,000 per month beginning in month 19, growing at the inflation rate, plus 15 percent of sales (Included in development period operating expense total).

10. Entrepreneur's salary of $3,000 per month through the first full year of sales (included in initial operating expenses), increasing thereafter by $500 per month.

11. Corporate tax rate of 45 percent. No loss carry forward.

12. All sales are for credit. The average collection period is 45 days. No discount for prompt payment.

13. The inventory turnover rate is 5 times per year, measured against ending inventory.

14. The company desires to maintain the greater of 30 days' sales in cash or $10,000.

15. All materials are purchased on credit, with terms of 2/10 net 30. The company anticipates paying in time to receive the discount. The payables period is 10 days.

16. The entrepreneur borrows any funds necessary at a rate of 1 percent per month.

17. Initial investment by the entrepreneur of $200,000. Additional financing by borrowing on a line of credit.

Figure 6-5   NewCompany assumptions

month. As shown in the assumptions detailed in Figure 6-5, based on a (hypothetical) study of other similar ventures we have assumed that the venture will have no sales for the first 18 months. Based on the study and the characteristics of the market for NewCompany's product, initial sales of $10,000 are expected in the nineteenth month. Following that, sales are expected to grow 8 percent per month in real terms for three years. After the third year of sales, no further real sales growth is expected.

Overlaying the pattern of real sales growth is an expected inflation rate of 9 percent per year, which we derived from information sources containing macroeconomic projections. This raises the question of whether it is better to make the forecast in real or nominal terms. The most important consideration is to be consistent in the treatment of revenues and expenses as either real or nominal values. Because our other assumptions include a mix of costs that are fixed in nominal terms (rent and the salary of the entrepreneur) and others that are fixed in real terms, we cannot escape dealing with the forecast of inflation in some way. We've decided to develop the analysis in nominal terms, in part because income taxes are calculated on nominal income and could be difficult to forecast in real terms. Because of the expected rapid growth rate during the first three years of operation, monthly sales are expected to increase from $10,000 in month 19 to almost $230,000 per month by the end of the fifth year after start of operation.

Developing the Financial Projections   The process of working through the assumptions in Figure 6-5 to derive an estimate of cash requirements is a bit complicated and tedious. So bear with us as we work through the NewCompany example. Figure 6-6 contains the pro forma balance sheet and income statement on a monthly basis from the start of product development through the first five years of operations. Also in the figure are monthly analyses of the sources and uses of funds for the venture.

Given the expected development period of 18 months, we project financial needs through month 78. To avoid overloading you with accounting numbers, the financial statements are highly simplified (but appropriate for the venture), and only selected months are shown in Figure 6-6. We selected the months to include in the figure because they correspond to major milestones: development, initiation of external financing, start of revenue-generating operation, attainment of profitable operation, attainment of positive free cash flow (the end of rapid growth), and the end of five years of operation. We now work through the statements chronologically, highlighting the months shown.

Modeling the Development Stage   Under the heading for month 0, Figure 6-6 shows the beginning balance sheet. Based on the assumptions in Figure 6-5, NewCompany has only one asset, cash, all of which the entrepreneur invests in the venture in the form of equity. Development activity begins in month 1 and, as reflected in the income statement, costs $15,000 in addition to the $3,000 salary of the owner.[15] The sources and uses of funds analysis for month 0 reflect the total of $18,000 net loss from operations. Because the company owns no depreciable assets and has no accruals, this is equivalent to the cash flow from operations. During the development stage, the company has no current assets or liabilities, so the negative cash flow from operations is equivalent to net funds used in operating activities. The negative cash flow reduces the company's cash balance by $18,000, but because the remaining total of $182,000 is more than the minimum $10,000 that the entrepreneur wants to have on hand, the venture requires no new financing at this point.

Except for changes due to inflation, the statements for months 2 through 10 are similar to those for month 1. Over this period, the company's cash continues to erode but is always sufficient to cover the minimum cash constraint. The figure shows the expected status of the venture

NewCompany—Pro Forma Balance Sheet

Month	0	1	10	11	18	19	20	39	40	54	55	56	78
Cash	$200,000	$182,000	$14,835	$10,000	$10,000	$10,000	$10,000	$49,740	$54,122	$176,498	$192,047	$193,488	$228,058
Accounts Receivable	$0	$0	$0	$0	$0	$10,000	$15,881	$78,992	$85,952	$280,296	$289,511	$291,683	$343,797
Inventory	$0	$0	$0	$0	$24,000	$26,114	$28,415	$141,337	$153,789	$464,371	$467,853	$471,362	$555,579
Total Current Assets	$200,000	$182,000	$14,835	$10,000	$34,000	$46,114	$54,296	$270,070	$293,863	$921,165	$949,412	$956,533	$1,127,434
Other Assets	$0	$0	$0	$0	$0	$0	$0	$0	$0	$0	$0	$0	$0
Total Assets	$200,000	$182,000	$14,835	$10,000	$34,000	$46,114	$54,296	$270,070	$293,863	$921,165	$949,412	$956,533	$1,127,434
Accounts Payable	$0	$0	$0	$0	$8,000	$24,705	$26,881	$133,708	$145,488	$462,066	$465,531	$469,023	$552,822
Short Term Debt	$0	$0	$0	$0	$0	$0	$0	$0	$0	$0	$0	$0	$0
Total Current Liabilities	$0	$0	$0	$0	$8,000	$24,705	$26,881	$133,708	$145,488	$462,066	$465,531	$469,023	$552,822
Long Term Debt (Credit Line)	$0	$0	$14,835	$14,329	$173,116	$175,257	$187,765	$365,133	$376,775	$585,187	$592,877	$579,502	$281,931
Total Liabilities	$0	$0	$14,835	$14,329	$181,116	$199,961	$214,646	$498,841	$522,263	$1,047,253	$1,058,408	$1,048,525	$834,753
Equity	$200,000	$182,000	$14,835	($4,329)	($147,116)	($153,847)	($160,350)	($228,772)	($228,400)	($126,088)	($108,996)	($91,992)	$292,681
Total Liabilities and Equity	$200,000	$182,000	$14,835	$10,000	$34,000	$46,114	$54,296	$270,070	$293,863	$921,165	$949,412	$956,533	$1,127,434

NewCompany—Pro Forma Income Statement

Month	1	10	11	18	19	20	39	40	54	55	56	78
Sales	$0	$0	$0	$0	$10,000	$10,881	$54,122	$58,890	$192,047	$193,488	$194,939	$229,768
Cost of Goods Sold	$0	$0	$0	$0	$4,000	$4,352	$21,649	$23,556	$76,819	$77,395	$77,976	$91,907
Gross Profit	$0	$0	$0	$0	$6,000	$6,529	$32,473	$35,334	$115,228	$116,093	$116,963	$137,861
Selling Expenses	$0	$0	$0	$0	$1,500	$1,632	$8,118	$8,834	$28,807	$29,023	$29,241	$34,465
Administrative Expenses	$0	$0	$0	$0	$3,500	$3,647	$10,441	$11,173	$31,405	$31,640	$31,878	$37,573
Lease Expense	$0	$0	$0	$0	$3,000	$3,000	$3,000	$3,000	$3,000	$3,000	$3,000	$3,000
Operating Expenses	$15,000	$16,043	$16,164	$17,032	$8,000	$8,279	$21,559	$23,007	$63,212	$63,664	$64,119	$75,038
Owner's Salary	$3,000	$3,000	$3,000	$3,000	$3,000	$3,000	$7,500	$8,000	$15,000	$15,500	$16,000	$27,000
Total Expense Before Interest and Tax	$18,000	$19,043	$19,164	$20,032	$11,000	$11,279	$29,059	$31,007	$78,212	$79,164	$80,119	$102,038
Operating Income	($18,000)	($19,043)	($19,164)	($20,032)	($5,000)	($4,751)	$3,414	$4,327	$37,016	$36,929	$36,845	$35,822
Interest Expense	$0	$0	$0	$1,357	$1,731	$1,753	$3,540	$3,651	$5,879	$5,852	$5,929	$2,957
Net Taxable Income	($18,000)	($19,043)	($19,164)	($21,389)	($6,731)	($6,503)	($125)	$676	$31,137	$31,077	$30,916	$32,865
Income Tax	$0	$0	$0	$0	$0	$0	$0	$304	$14,012	$13,985	$13,912	$14,789
Net Income	($18,000)	($19,043)	($19,164)	($21,389)	($6,731)	($6,503)	($125)	$372	$17,126	$17,092	$17,004	$18,076

NewCompany—Pro Forma Sources and Uses of Funds

Month	1	10	11	18	19	20	39	40	54	55	56	78
Net Income	($18,000)	($19,043)	($19,164)	($21,389)	($6,731)	($6,503)	($125)	$372	$17,126	$17,092	$17,004	$18,076
Depreciation Expense	$0	$0	$0	$0	$0	$0	$0	$0	$0	$0	$0	$0
Operating Cash Flow	($18,000)	($19,043)	($19,164)	($21,389)	($6,731)	($6,503)	($125)	$372	$17,126	$17,092	$17,004	$18,076
Changes in Current Assets												
Accounts Receivable	$0	$0	$0	$0	$10,000	$5,881	$6,396	$6,959	$22,695	$9,215	$2,171	$2,559
Inventory	$0	$0	$0	$24,000	$2,114	$2,301	$11,444	$12,452	$3,457	$3,483	$3,509	$4,136
Changes in Current Liabilities												
Accounts Payable	$0	$0	$0	$8,000	$16,705	$2,176	$10,826	$11,780	$26,031	$3,465	$3,491	$4,115
Net Funds Used in Operating Activities	($18,000)	($19,043)	($19,164)	($37,389)	$2,141	$12,508	$7,139	$7,260	($17,005)	($7,860)	($14,815)	($15,496)
Beginning Cash Balance	$200,000	$33,878	$14,835	$10,000	$10,000	$10,000	$45,713	$49,740	$162,207	$176,498	$192,047	$226,360
Minimum Cash Balance	$10,000	$10,000	$10,000	$10,000	$10,000	$10,000	$49,740	$54,122	$176,498	$192,047	$193,488	$228,058
New Financing Needed	$0	$0	$14,329	$37,389	$2,141	$12,508	$11,166	$11,642	$2,715	$7,689	$13,375	$0
Debt Repayment	$0	$0	$0	$0	$0	$0	$0	$0	$0	$0	$0	$13,798
Cumulative New Financing Needed	$0	$14,835	$14,329	$173,116	$175,257	$187,765	$365,133	$376,775	$585,187	$592,877	$579,502	$281,931
Surplus Cash	$172,000	$4,835	$0	$0	$0	$0	$0	$0	$0	$0	$0	$0

Figure 6-6 NewCompany integrated financial statements. NewCompany pro forma statements are generated based on the assumptions in Figure 6-5. To see the complete projections, download the Excel file. Examine the cell formulas to see how the assumptions are incorporated in the model and how the financial statements are integrated.

at the end of month 10. At that point, the company has exhausted its original cash, and the statements reflect that, from an accounting perspective, the equity of the owner is almost gone.

If we were to construct financial statements in terms of economic value, those statements would look much different. Assuming that the development activities are progressing, we would find that the expenditures during the first 10 months are actually capital investments in an intangible asset. The value of this asset, though not reflected in the accounting book value of the venture, is an element of its economic value. Clearly, the company's ability to raise outside funding depends on the economic value of the venture as perceived by prospective investors. In the NewCompany example, we assume that perceived economic value, together with any guarantees provided by the entrepreneur, is sufficient to convince a lender to make a long-term loan commitment to the venture.

Beginning in month 11, the initial cash reserve of the venture is no longer sufficient to fully fund the operation and maintain the cash balance at the minimum desired by the entrepreneur and shown in Figure 6-6. In that month, net funds used by the venture total $19,164, against an initial cash balance of only $14,835. To cover the cash needs and maintain an ending cash balance of $10,000, the entrepreneur must raise $14,329 in outside financing. We have assumed that the venture is able to raise the needed funds in the form of debt. We have structured the loan such that interest on the month 11 debt balance is paid in month 12, and so on. The balance sheet for month 11 reflects this new borrowing. It also shows a negative balance for the accounting value of equity. The negative balance simply means that all of the owner's initial capital has been spent, plus part of what was loaned. If the economic value of the venture is high enough, the negative balance in the equity account should not concern us. In fact, many new ventures have negative accounting equity but still have positive economic value.

Modeling the Start-up   In month 18, the company must begin to prepare for the sales that are expected to begin in month 19. Accordingly, consistent with the assumptions in Figure 6-5, it begins to acquire inventory on credit. The sources and uses analysis shows the increase in inventory as a use of funds and the increase in accounts payable as a source. By this point, the company's total financing needs are expected to reach $173,116. Sales commence in month 19, but because all sales are on account, no cash is generated. Month 20 reflects the collection of 15 days worth of receivables for month 19 (offset by the increase in receivables from new sales during month 20). At this point, the venture is not yet profitable, showing a loss of $6,503 for the month. Because of the rapid growth, cash flow is even more negative—increases in current assets exceed increases in current liabilities by about $6,000 for the month.

Achieving Profitability   The venture is expected to reach profitable operations in month 40. However, rapid growth and the commensurate need to increase business assets faster than spontaneous increases in liabilities (the growth of accounts payable) results in a flow of funds that is still negative. Including the requirement for increased cash balances to support growth, the venture is expected to need an additional $11,642 in funding in month 40, bringing total borrowing at that point to $376,775.

Achieving Stable Growth   Month 54 is expected to be the last month of rapid sales growth. Because of the slowdown, months 54 through 56 reflect a transition. By the end of that three-month period, the venture is generating a level of net income (and operating cash flow) that is more than sufficient to cover its increased financial needs. Accordingly, in Figure 6-6 we allocate the excess, the free cash flow, toward debt repayment. The pattern of positive free cash flows that are allocated to debt service continues through to month 78, the last month of our pro forma analysis.

Developing Accounts Receivable Policy Assumptions

The following table, constructed from the *Almanac of Business and Industry,* provides an example of how to support an assumption regarding accounts receivable policy. Suppose you have secured patents to produce a new type of varnish for home use. You are building a financial model for a paint manufacturing plant. You expect that the firm will be in $1 million–$5 million range, in terms of asset value. According to the table, for established firms in the industry, accounts receivable as a function of total revenue averages around 13 percent. That implies that it takes on average 47 days to collect receivables (365 × .13). Because you expect to adopt trade credit terms and policies that conform to those in the industry, this number seems reasonable for your financial model.

This assumption serves to integrate the financial model. Because forecasted sales revenue is included in the income statement and accounts receivable, a balance sheet item is generated based on the revenue forecast. Suppose you want to determine the impact of an increase in time to collection. If collections drop off, cash flows will be negatively impacted. However, without an integrated financial model and with no change in sales revenue projections, a "stand-alone" financial model would show no change in the income statement.

As discussed above, firms with larger net receivables (accounts receivable less doubtful accounts) have lower cash flow and greater financial needs, other things being the same, than firms that have fewer credit sales. Notice how net receivables, as a function of average total revenue, varies across firm size categories for the three industries listed in the table. The data document a well-established statistical observation that larger firms tend to offer more trade credit, thereby generating more accounts receivable, than smaller firms.

Industry Comparison of Net Receivables as a Percentage of Average Total Revenues for Firms Producing in Various Size Classes

	Size of Assets in Thousands of Dollars							
	Under 100	100 to 250	251 to 500	501 to 1,000	1,001 to 5,000	5,001 to 10,000	10,001 to 25,000	25,001 and over
Paints & allied products (SIC 2850)			11.17%	11.54%	13.28%	14.48%	11.77%	59.71%
General building contractors (SIC 1510)	1.83%	4.55%	6.14%	8.26%	12.23%	14.00%	15.73%	68.60%
Personal Services (SIC 7200)	1.13%	5.03	7.09%	8.41%	11.21%	10.60%	13.64%	7.40%

Source: Almanac of Business & Industrial Financial Ratios (1997). Based on accounting period July 1993–June 1994. For contractors and paint manufacturers, the data are for corporations with and without net income; for personal service firms, data are for corporations with net income.

Measuring Financing Needs   As the figure shows, the need for external financing peaks at slightly under $600,000 in month 54 and declines to about $280,000 by month 78. As of month 55, equity is still negative in an accounting sense but has been increasing since month 40, when the venture is expected to begin profitable operation. The negative balance of book equity is not a problem as long as the venture's economic value exceeds its liabilities. Given that the venture is highly profitable and growing rapidly as of month 40, the negative accounting value of equity does not pose a problem. Indeed, by month 78, the venture is in the black, with positive equity and a steadily declining debt burden.

If the entrepreneur decides to proceed and if everything goes according to plan, the venture will need about $600,000 in outside financing. Furthermore, the need for outside financing materializes during the development stage, before any revenue is generated and before the venture is expected to achieve profitability. Although it is not necessary, or even desirable, to raise all of the required financing at the outset, the entrepreneur does need to be able to anticipate the need for funding.

What about Uncertainty?   The pro forma analysis provokes a number of interesting questions. For example, how might things change if some of the assumptions prove to be wrong (as they undoubtedly will)? What would be different if the entrepreneur were to put more equity into the deal, or if the outside financing were raised in the form of equity, or if it were raised in stages as the plans of the venture began to materialize? Finally, how should the entrepreneur select from among the various financing options that may be available? More generally, how does uncertainty affect the financing needs of the venture and its economic value? We begin to explore these issues in the next chapter.

6.10   SUMMARY

Financial forecasting adds discipline to the way an entrepreneur thinks about the venture. Not only does forecasting help determine cash needs and the timing of those needs, it also helps determine the value of the venture. A forecast can be an important marketing tool if it convinces prospective investors of the merits of the project and provides some specific performance benchmarks.

Every forecasting project is unique, but preparing a credible and useful financial forecast requires several key ingredients. The first is to understand the cash flow cycle and how various business factors increase or decrease the firm's demand for cash. The critical determinants of financial needs are minimum efficient scale, profitability, cash flow, and sales growth. Every financial forecast must link expectations for performance in the product market to the implications for financial performance. The second ingredient, the sales forecast, provides such a link. The third ingredient is a careful specification of a schedule of assumptions that underlie the sales forecast and the financial model. These assumptions should be backed by research and, as far as possible, by objective data.

Numerous data sources can be used to develop assumptions. For established businesses, forecasts should consider the impact of macroeconomic variables that are known to affect sales and normally should reflect a weighting scheme that gives more weight to recent experience. Two possible approaches may be used to forecast sales for a new venture. A reasonable way to forecast is to base the sales forecast and the underlying financial ratios on a collection of firms that serve as yardsticks from which to deduce performance expectations. An alternative is to develop a fundamental analysis of the expected market for the new venture by estimating the market demand for the product and by considering supply-side constraints that may limit growth. The financial model should reflect a solid understanding of the product and the industry.

An integrated, well-formulated financial model is an important decision-making tool for an entrepreneur. This is especially true for evaluating the impact of changes in the business environment. The financial model allows the entrepreneur to conduct "what if" analysis: What if sales are 10 percent lower than expected? What if bad debts amount to a much more significant fraction of receivables? What if product development time doubles relative to expectations and sales are delayed by an extra year?

QUESTIONS AND PROBLEMS

1. A new venture is expected to require a capital investment of $2.5 million and an investment of $200,000 in initial working capital. The capital investment can be depreciated over a five-year period, on a straight-line basis. During the first year of operation, the venture is projected to achieve sales of $800,000. The sales level is projected to triple in the second year, double in the third year, and increase by 50 percent in the fourth year. No additional capital investment is needed during the first five years. The projected gross profit margin is 60 percent, and operating expenses, other than depreciation, are projected to be $500,000 per year, plus 15 percent of sales. The venture is subject to a corporate tax rate of 35 percent, and losses from prior years can be carried forward in computing the tax liability. Based on industry norms and the expected growth rate of sales, the venture is expected to need ending cash equal to 5 percent of sales for the year, ending accounts receivable equal to 30 percent of annual sales, ending inventory equal to 10 percent of annual sales, and ending accounts payable equal to 10 percent of the cost of sales.
    a. Using a spreadsheet, project the net income, cash flow, and ending balance sheet of the venture for each year, assuming that no debt financing is used. (You may wish to begin with the Integrated Financial Statements Template in Appendix 6A.)
    b. Contrast the net income of the venture with the annual cash flows. How do the factors of capital intensity, profitability, sales growth, and cash flow affect the financial needs of the venture?
2. Using the spreadsheet from problem 1, examine how each of the following changes to the assumptions would affect net income and cash flows. Assume that the other assumptions from problem 1 are unchanged.
    a. The sales growth (percentage increase) in each year is only half as much as expected.
    b. The gross margin is 40 percent of sales revenue.
    c. Inventory is 30 percent of ending sales.
    d. The initial capital investment in the venture is $4 million.
3. A new venture requires an initial capital investment of $2 million. Similar ventures in the same industry have been able to achieve sales levels of 60 to 100 percent of assets, with profitability on sales of from 10 to 30 percent. Demand for the venture's product is expected to grow at a rate of 2 to 13 percent per year.
    a. Using the midpoints of the ranges, develop a pro forma forecast of the venture for five years, assuming sales growth matches the growth of market demand. How much free cash is the venture expected to generate in each year, or how much additional financing is needed in each year?

b. Develop a "worst case" pro forma analysis for five years, assuming all of the uncertainties turn out at the low ends of the ranges. How does this affect the ability of the venture to distribute cash or the need to raise additional capital?

c. Develop a "best case" pro forma analysis assuming the uncertainties are resolved at the high end of the range, and evaluate the cash needs or disbursement capabilities of the venture under those conditions.

d. Suppose you want to develop a pro forma analysis of the worst case in terms of the financial needs of the venture. How would you use the information about the uncertainties of the various assumptions to do so?

4. Suppose that for an existing business we observe the following levels of sales and macroeconomic information for the previous six years:

Year	−6	−5	−4	−3	−2	−1
Sales (millions)	$1.2	$1.8	$1.6	$2.4	$2.8	$2.6
Inflation		+6%	+4%	+5%	+3%	+1%
Change in real GDP		+3%	−2%	2%	1%	−1%

Use the information in the table to generate sales forecasts for years 0 and 1 by the following approaches.

a. Trend extrapolation applied to nominal sales levels.

b. Trend extrapolation based on nominal percentage growth rates of sales.

c. Trend extrapolation applied to nominal sales, with greater weight on the more recent data.

d. Trend extrapolation based on real percentage growth rates in sales.

e. Trend extrapolation based on the relationship between the real sales growth rate and the annual change in real GDP. The forecast of real GDP for year zero is 2.5 percent, and for year one, it is the average from the past five years.

f. Based only on the information in the table and the results of your calculations, which approach do you think will do the best job of forecasting sales for this venture? Why?

5. You have developed and patented a new kind of felt for the outer coating of tennis balls that never wears out but, remarkably, does not affect how the balls play. To capitalize on the innovation, you also have developed new tennis ball packaging that will enable players to repressurize the container after each use. As a result, the tennis balls you plan to manufacture can last up to five times as long (in terms of playing time) as traditional tennis balls. Because of the innovations, you need to sell the balls for three times the current price of tennis balls.

a. Develop a simple model of the market for tennis balls and explain how you might go about calibrating the various assumptions you must make in order to estimate the total size of the market.

b. Certain "purists" and people who only want to play with clean tennis balls are unlikely to switch from traditional tennis balls. Many other individuals play only rarely. And existing manufacturers may respond to your entry by cutting prices. Develop a model of your share of the market for tennis balls. How might you calibrate the assumptions of the model?

6. Think of a product you would be interested in developing, that can serve as the basis for a new venture. What are the critical assumptions on which success of the venture depends?

    a. Use the Internet to collect information on public companies that are comparable in some ways, such as from prospectuses and annual reports. Identify the information from these sources that you can use to help calibrate the critical assumptions in a financial model of your venture.

    b. Look up some sources of financial data for industries that are comparable, in some ways, to the one you are considering. Explain how the information from these sources can be used to calibrate a financial model of the prospective venture.

7. Use the following assumptions to develop a five-year set of pro forma statements. Make any additional assumptions you need. (You may want to use the template from Appendix 6-A).

    a. The entrepreneur has $300,000 to invest in the venture, will raise an additional $150,000 from family members in exchange for equity, and will borrow $200,000 in the form of long-term debt. A total of $600,000 will be invested in fixed assets that can be depreciated on a straight-line basis over five years. The balance of initial investments will be held as cash. New capital investments are needed each year to maintain net fixed assets equal to 1.2 times expected sales in the subsequent year.

    b. Expected sales during the first year is $250,000. Sales are expected to double each year for the next two years, to increase by 50 percent in the fourth year, and to increase by 20 percent in the fifth and sixth years.

    c. Based on industry data, cost of goods sold is expected to be 25 percent of sales, selling expense is expected to be 12 percent of sales, and general and administrative expense is expected to be $100,000 plus 7 percent of sales. There are no other material operating expenses. The above figures exclude depreciation expenses.

    d. The interest rate on debt is expected to be 9 percent, and revenue from short-term investment of cash is expected to be negligible.

    e. The corporate tax rate is 35 percent. There is no tax loss carry forward.

    f. Typical experience in the industry for ventures that are growing rapidly is that accounts receivable equals 20 percent of ending sales; inventory is 15 percent of cost of goods sold; accounts payable is 8 percent of cost of goods sold; wages payable is 5 percent of cost of goods sold; and taxes payable is negligible.

    g. The venture needs to maintain a cash balance equal to the lesser of 20 percent of annual sales or $50,000.

    h. If additional financing is needed, the entrepreneur hopes to use long-term debt to the extent that profitability is sufficient to cover interest expense (so that the full tax advantage of debt financing is realized).

8. Download the Working Capital Policy Template and use it to contrast the effects of the following policies on net working capital (use the assumptions reflected in Figure 6-3 as a starting point). Evaluate the impact of each of these changes on the firm's gross profit (Revenue − Materials Cost − Labor Cost) per day and the firm's need for financing of its net working capital.

    a. Product demand is inelastic, so that a $1 price increase is expected to reduce quantity per day to 95 units. Product demand is elastic, so that a $1 price increase is expected to reduce quantity per day to 80 units.

    b. The company sells only for cash so that quantity per day is expected to decline to 90 units. The company sells only for cash, but reduces product price to $9.50, so that quantity per day is expected not to change.

c. The company increases its target materials inventory to 20 days, and its target finished goods inventory to 15 days. As a result, the company is able to more-reliably respond to orders. Therefore, quantity of sales per day is expected to increase to 105 units.

d. The company plans to pay its payables in 30 days. As a result, cost of materials is expected to increase to $4.10.

e. The company changes to paying monthly so that the average wages payable balance is for 15 days of work. To offset, it expects it will need to increase wages to $2.60 per unit.

9. Consider the following pattern of historical sales growth rates of a venture that began operation seven years ago:

Year −6	Year −5	Year −4	Year −3	Year −2	Year −1
223%	127%	174%	59%	90%	43%

Use exponential smoothing to derive year-zero sales growth forecasts. Consider some values of α between 0.2 and 0.8 and generate forecasts for growth from year −1 to year 0. Assume the forecast for year-6 equals the actual for year −6. Given the pattern of generally decreasing growth rates, what do you think of exponential smoothing as a technique for forecasting sales growth? What problem do you see? Do similar problems apply to naïve forecasting techniques discussed in the chapter? Can you think of any way to use naïve forecasting approaches to project the year-zero sales for this company?

10. Download a copy of Figure 6-6 and use it to address the following (you may need to "unhide" the hidden columns in the figure):

a. How much initial cash from equity investors would NewCompany need so that it would not be expected to draw on its line of credit during the entire 78 months of the pro forma statements?

b. How much initial cash from equity investors would the company need so that it would not be expected to draw on its line of credit until the 25th month (the 7th month after start-up)?

c. How much initial cash from equity would the company need in order to avoid borrowing if the monthly rate of real sales growth during the first three years after start-up is 5 percent instead of 8 percent?

d. How much initial cash from equity would the company need in order to avoid borrowing if the gross profit margin is 50 percent instead of 60 percent?

e. How much initial cash from equity would the company need in order to avoid borrowing: (i) if the it must purchase materials for cash; (ii) if the average collection period is two months instead of 45 days; (iii) if both changes are made?

NOTES

1. Cash flow cycles for other kinds of firms are similar. Wholesale and retail distribution businesses, for example, generate revenue by purchasing and reselling inventory.

2. See Stancill (1987), p. 38.

3. As a practical matter, net working capital usually is defined as all current assets less all current liabilities. However, some current assets, such as marketable securities, may not be

central to operation of the venture, and some current liabilities, such as notes payable, do not arise spontaneously from the productive activities of the business.

4. Figure 6-3 is an Excel spreadsheet. By downloading it, you can study how changing various aspects of working capital policy would affect the amount of financing required.

5. See Ng, Smith, and Smith (1999) for supporting evidence.

6. Smith (1987) interprets credit terms with significant discounts for prompt payment as a device the seller can use to gain timely information about the financial health of its customers.

7. Appendix A to this chapter, on the Web site, contains a reasonably general template that can be used to develop pro forma statements for a new venture. The spreadsheet template can be downloaded and modified by users of the text.

8. For maximum usefulness, pro forma statements normally should be constructed under GAAP (generally accepted accounting principles). GAAP include the rules, conventions, and procedures that define how firms should maintain records and prepare financial reports. In the United States these rules and procedures are based on guidelines used by the Financial Accounting Standards Board (FASB). Because GAAP systems differ across countries, it is important to adjust for differences when comparing financial statements prepared under different systems.

9. There is an important distinction between a forecast of sales and a forecast of profit. Even though public forecasts of inflation may be helpful for refining the sales forecast, profit depends on a mix of factors, some of which depend on inflation and some of which are fixed in nominal terms (depreciation expense, for example). Whether it is better to forecast profits in real or nominal terms depends on how these factors balance out. The most important consideration for forecasting profit is to be consistent in the treatment of inflation. Copeland et al. (1996) argue that nominal forecasts are preferred for valuation purposes. This is because most managers think in terms of nominal measures and because interest rates generally are quoted in nominal rather than in real terms. Also, historical financial statements are stated in nominal terms.

10. Using a standard statistical package, such as is available in Excel, sales levels or growth rates in one period can be regressed on several lagged values of sales levels or growth rates (the prior year, two years prior, etc.). The coefficients from the regression can then be used in conjunction with historical sales data to project future sales or sales growth.

11. Using Excel to regress sales growth on the change in GDP, the following linear model results:

$$\text{Expected growth in sales} = 3.34\% + 5.24 \times (\text{Change in GDP}), r^2 = 0.95.$$

12. The EDGAR Web site address is *www.sec.gov/edgar.shtml*. Prospectuses of new issues are normally posted to the site within a few days of filing.

13. For many kinds of ventures, the search for comparable information is greatly simplified by the existence of published information that sets out the financial characteristics of a sample of firms in the industry. Generally, however, because of data aggregation, it is difficult to use this information to estimate the growth rate of sales for firms in the sample.

14. Quoted in Silver (1994), p. 20.

15. We treat owner's salary as a separate category because the amount is discretionary.

REFERENCES AND ADDITIONAL READINGS

COPELAND, TOM, TIM KOLLER, AND JACK MURRIN. *Valuation.* 2d ed. New York: John Wiley & Sons, 1996.

DRUCKER, PETER F. *Innovation and Entrepreneurship: Practice and Principles.* New York: HarperCollins, 1985.

HIBDON, JAMES, AND MICHAEL J. MUELLER. "Economies of Scale in Petroleum Refining, 1847–1984: A Survivor Principle-Time Series Analysis." *Review of Industrial Organization* 5 (1990): 25–44.

MIAN, SHEHZAD L. AND CLIFFORD W. SMITH, JR. "Accounts-Receivable Management Policy: Theory and Evidence." *Journal of Finance* 47 (1992): 169–200.

NG, CHEE, JANET KIHOLM SMITH, AND RICHARD SMITH. "Evidence on the Determinants of Credit Terms Used in Interfirm Trade." *Journal of Finance* 54: (June 1999): 1109–1129.

RONSTADT, BOB. "Financial Projections: How to Do Them the Right Way." in *The Portable MBA in Entrepreneurship.* Edited by William D. Bygrave. New York: John Wiley & Sons, 1997.

SILVER, DAVID A. *The Venture Capital Sourcebook.* Chicago: Probus Publishing Company, 1994.

SMITH, JANET KIHOLM. "Trade Credit and Informational Asymmetry." *Journal of Finance* 42 (1987): 863–872.

STANCILL, JAMES M. "When Is There Cash in Cash Flow?" *Harvard Business Review* (March–April 1987): 38–49.

STIGLER, GEORGE J. "The Economies of Scale." *Journal of Law and Economics* 1 (October 1958): 54–71.

Assessing Financial Needs

Necessity never made a good bargain. (Attributed to Ben Franklin)

Learning Objectives

After reading this chapter, you should:

- Understand how the sustainable growth model is derived and apply it to determine financing requirements.
- Be able to determine how the choice of financing facilitates the entrepreneur's abilities to respond to product-market success or failure and to retain significant ownership.
- Understand how to use a cash-flow breakeven analysis to assess financial needs.
- Be able to apply scenario analysis to assess financing needs.
- Be able to apply simulation techniques to assess financing needs.
- Recognize when each type of analysis is appropriate for assessing cash needs.

It takes money to start a business, sometimes lots of it. For a manufacturing venture, equipment and facilities must be purchased or leased, materials must be acquired, employees must be hired, and merchandise must be produced—all before the business begins to generate any revenue. If the venture offers trade credit terms, there is an additional delay before revenues are converted into cash. Most ventures require some level of up-front investment, and many do not generate positive net operating cash flows for several months or even a few years.

An entrepreneur needs to have a good sense of how much cash is required to carry the venture to the point where it becomes self-sustaining, as well as a good sense of when the cash infusions are likely to be needed. An entrepreneur who does not evaluate the cash needs of the venture runs a variety of unnecessary risks. Most fundamentally, the venture may fail, not because the idea is bad, but simply because the entrepreneur does not anticipate the cash needs far enough in advance to do anything about them. Or the venture may succeed, but only after outside investors make such large infusions of cash that the entrepreneur ends up with very little to show for the capital and effort she expended. Or, even if the total cash needs are not large, the entrepreneur's failure to anticipate them can result in an adverse negotiating

INTERNET RESOURCES FOR THIS CHAPTER

In this chapter we introduce simulation as a technique for studying how uncertainty affects financial needs. If you have not already installed *Venture.SIM™*, this would be a good time to do so. Even if you already have some familiarity with simulation, we recommend that you review the Simulation Tutorial and work through the basics of using the simulation feature in Excel. For applications in this chapter, and the next few, you should be familiar with the Unconditional Simulator in *Venture.SIM™*. The tutorial shows how to develop a simple spreadsheet financial model that incorporates uncertainty. The Web site also contains a soft copy of the Excel spreadsheet that is used in the simulation study of financial needs discussed toward the end of the chapter. Exploring the spreadsheet should help you to begin thinking about the importance of modeling uncertainty and about some ways to do so. The site also includes a case application on assessing financial needs.

position in which investors have all of the bargaining leverage. This adverse negotiation position can arise because of urgency of need or because original financing agreements constrain the entrepreneur's ability to raise cash in the future.[1]

"Do not run out of cash" is a common admonition to entrepreneurs. Jim Stancill, for example, refers to his first law of entrepreneurship: "If you want to fly to financial paradise, have enough gas to make the trip, as there are no service stations along the way."[2] Warnings such as this suggest that a very large cash cushion should be secured before the venture is undertaken.

But having too much cash can be as bad as having too little. An entrepreneur who is excessively cautious may find that raising "enough" cash up-front is not feasible. Even if the financing can be arranged, it comes at a price, and the entrepreneur may be compelled to give up far more of the value of the venture than is necessary or desirable. Although the venture cannot survive without cash, the objective is not simply survival. Rather, it is to finance the venture in a way that yields the highest expected value for the entrepreneur. We do not address valuation until later in the text, but financial needs have a direct bearing on overall value and on the value of the entrepreneur's ownership interest.

As a general principle, an entrepreneur who expects the venture to succeed can benefit by raising only enough cash to carry the venture to the next milestone. At that point, risk to outside investors will be lower and easier to assess. The venture probably will be able to raise capital on more favorable terms. The question of interest in this chapter is how the amount of cash raised now affects the likelihood that the venture can reach the next milestone. In later chapters, we link this issue to valuation.[3]

Hence, the objective of this chapter is to enable the entrepreneur to answer the question, "How much money do I need?" In previous chapters, we described the strategic planning process, in which the entrepreneur compares the expected values of future cash flows of strategic alternatives. After selecting the strategy that is expected to generate the highest value, the entrepreneur prepares the business plan that includes a projection of cash flows and financial needs. However, we side-stepped the problem of how to generate the financial information required for comparing strategic alternatives. Accordingly, in this chapter we build on the forecasting tools from Chapter 6 to focus on methods of assessing financial needs.

We first present the sustainable growth model. The model can help the entrepreneur determine the venture's sustainable growth rate and evaluate whether a particular level of initial financing is sufficient to sustain a desired growth rate with internally generated funds. If not, then financing policies related to use of debt or additional equity and distribution of dividends must be reevaluated. Cash flow breakeven analysis is another evaluation tool. It can be used to assess the amount of initial investment a venture needs to achieve a level of cash flow sufficient to maintain its operations (the cash flow breakeven point).

Later in the chapter, we use scenario analysis and simulation to focus on how uncertainty affects financial needs. Scenario analysis and simulation can be used to assess the effects of alternative sales levels, prices, fixed costs, and variable costs on cash needs. Decisions that face entrepreneurs are complicated by high levels of uncertainty. Scenario analysis and simulation are alternative ways to study the effects of uncertainty. Additional insights can be derived from the sustainable growth model and cash flow breakeven analysis when they are coupled with methods of assessing the effects of uncertainty on financial needs.

7.1 SUSTAINABLE GROWTH AS A STARTING POINT

The first step in projecting the financial needs of a nascent venture is to develop a financial model of the venture that relates investment to cash flows. By changing a few key assumptions in the model, the financial implications of the entrepreneur's strategic choices can be examined. A good starting point is to explore the conditions under which, following an initial investment, the cash flow of the venture is sufficient to sustain growth.

Suppose an entrepreneur, Gill Bates, is considering investing in a venture that markets and supports an on-line board game, "Policy Wonks." He believes that, as the venture grows, assets, debt financing, sales, and net income will all grow in fixed proportion to each other. Thus, the level of sales the venture can achieve is a constant percentage of assets, and net income is

---

◆ Differing Schools of Thought on Early-Stage Financing*

Arguments in favor of raising as much money as possible:

- Liquidity is a cushion against unexpected setbacks.
- Liquidity affords flexibility to pursue unexpected opportunities.
- Liquidity makes obtaining credit from lenders and suppliers easier.
- Liquidity is comforting for the entrepreneur and key employees.

Arguments in favor of raising as little money as possible:

- Limiting investment limits the loss if the venture fails.
- Limiting investment disciplines the entrepreneur to focus on the objective.
- Limiting investment causes the entrepreneur to develop cash-management skill.
- Limiting investment preserves more of the ownership for the entrepreneur.

The different views are not actually in conflict. In deciding how much outside investment to seek and how much liquidity to maintain, all of the factors must be considered.

---

*Based partly on Baty (1990).

a constant percentage of sales. Bates is prepared to make an initial investment in equity, but prefers not to raise additional outside equity to support growth. Based on only this information, we use the sustainable growth model to explore how the cash flow cycle of the venture contributes to the growth rate it can sustain. The answer depends on three key financial policy decisions: whether to raise additional equity over time, how much financial leverage to employ, and what fraction of earnings to pay out to investors.

Given the assumptions, the sustainable growth rate is described by a simple model.[4] The growth rate is defined as

$$g = \frac{\Delta E}{E} \tag{7.1}$$

where g represents the percentage growth rate of equity from one year to the next, E is the level of equity at the beginning of the year, and ΔE is the change in equity during the year. The sustainable growth rate is designated as g^*. Given the assumption that Bates does not want to raise any additional equity after the initial investment, the change in equity is

$$\Delta E = NI \times R \tag{7.2}$$

where NI is net income after tax in dollars and R (the retention ratio) is the fraction of net income that is retained in the venture as opposed to being paid out to investors. Equation (7.2) states, for example, that if a business generates \$100,000 in net income and retains 60 percent of net income (paying out the balance), the book value of equity increases by \$60,000. Dividing both sides of the equation by the level of equity at the beginning of the year yields

$$g = \frac{NI}{E} \times R \quad \text{or} \quad ROE \times R \tag{7.3}$$

Return on equity, or ROE, is a simple measure of the profitability of the equity investment. From Eq. (7.3), the growth rate of equity depends on the rate of return on equity and the earnings retention (payout) policy. All else being equal, the lower the retention rate, the lower the growth rate.

To examine the relation between the venture growth rate and the policy decisions of the entrepreneur, we restate return on equity as

$$ROE = \frac{NI}{E} = \frac{NI}{S} \times \frac{S}{A} \times \frac{A}{E} \quad \text{or} \quad ROS \times Turnover \times Leverage, \tag{7.4}$$

where S is sales and A is assets. Thus, the return on equity is the product of the profit margin or rate of return on sales (NI/S or ROS), the asset turnover ratio or operating leverage of the venture (S/A or $Turnover$), and the financial leverage of the venture (A/E or $Leverage$). The equation suggests that a venture can address the profitability of its equity investment in several ways. It can try to improve the profit margin on sales; it can try to increase the amount of sales that are supported by its asset base; and it can rely more heavily on debt. In the sustainable growth context, we assume that the selling efforts are as effective as they can be and that the venture is using its assets efficiently to generate sales. The financial leverage ratio, however, is a policy choice that can affect the sustainable growth rate.

Substituting Eq. (7.4) into Eq. (7.3) yields the sustainable growth model,

$$g^* = \frac{NI}{S} \times \frac{S}{A} \times \frac{A}{E} \times R \tag{7.5}$$

The model reflects the assumption that, as the venture grows, assets, debt financing, sales, and net income grow proportionately.

It now is possible to show the connection between the sustainable growth model and venture cash flows. First, recognize that profits, measured as net income after tax, are not independent of financial leverage policy. To see the interdependence, as well as the tax shelter associated with debt financing, we restate net income as

$$NI = (EBIT - r(A - E))(1 - t) \tag{7.6}$$

where $EBIT$ is net income before interest and taxes, $A - E$ is the amount of debt financing, r is the interest rate on debt financing, and t is the corporate tax rate. Also, the sustainable growth model assumes that the accounting treatment of depreciation expense corresponds to economic depreciation so that the annual cash flows related to depreciation are sufficient to maintain the productivity of the assets of the venture.

Substituting Eq. (7.6) into Eq. (7.5) yields

$$g^* = \frac{(EBIT - r(A - E))(1 - t)}{S} \times \frac{S}{A} \times \frac{A}{E} \times R \tag{7.7}$$

The model in Eq. (7.7) can be used to see how the sustainable growth rate of the venture varies in response to the policy choices facing Gill Bates. Suppose that, for strategic reasons, he believes the venture should be targeted to achieve sales of $2.5 million by the end of the fifth year. Assume further that he identifies targets for the operating leverage ratio (of 2.0), the ratio of EBIT to sales (of .10), and the corporate tax rate is 35 percent.

Bates is considering an initial equity investment of $500,000 and plans to use no debt financing. For the first five years he is willing to retain all earnings in the business. Suppose Bates approaches you, a consultant, and asks you to determine whether these financial policies would enable the venture to achieve the targeted level of sales in the fifth year.

You determine that, under the assumed conditions and policies, the sustainable growth rate, g^*, is:

$$g^* = .1(1 - .35) \times 2.0 \times 1.0 \times 1.0 = .13 \quad \text{or} \quad 13 \text{ percent.} \tag{7.8}$$

The venture can grow at an annual rate of 13 percent without having to seek additional equity or debt financing. With initial capitalization of $500,000 and the operating leverage ratio of 2.0, first-year sales of $1 million could be supported. Starting from this base and with compounded growth of 13 percent for five years, the venture could sustain sales of $1.842 million by the fifth year. This is well below the $2.5 million sales target.

Now that you've delivered the bad news to Mr. Bates, you discuss with him the policy choices he faces. First, you suggest an increase in the size of the initial equity investment. Using Eq. (7.7), you solve for the investment required for a sustainable growth rate of

13 percent and the sales target of $2.5 million. The answer is that Bates would need to invest $678,000 to achieve the year-5 sales target. However, as Bates is willing to invest only $500,000, he would need to raise the balance of the equity ($178,000) from outside sources.

Another alternative is for Bates to revisit the policy against using debt financing. Because the venture is expected to generate taxable income immediately, using some debt might be preferred to raising outside equity. In the context of the sustainable growth model, the way to consider the debt policy is to focus on the leveraging decision. The question: What financial leverage ratio would enable the venture to begin with $500,000 in equity and achieve sales of $2.5 million by the fifth year? Assume that, over the relevant range of leverage choices, the interest rate on debt financing is 10 percent. To determine the solution, you again use Eq. (7.7) and experiment with various debt-to-equity ratios until you find the one that makes these targets achievable.[5] It turns out that a debt-to-equity ratio of 26 percent works (initial borrowing of $130,000).

One aspect of Eq. (7.7) that may not be clear is that increasing the financial leverage ratio increases the sustainable growth rate. The venture can achieve its year-5 target with either $178,000 of outside equity or $130,000 of outside debt. Hence, the sustainable growth rate is greater with debt financing than with equity. In Figure 7-1 we plot the sustainable growth rate as a function of financial leverage. To see why the growth rate increases with leverage, look back at Eq. (7.7). The growth rate depends on the ratio of net income after tax to assets. As long as the after-tax cost of debt is less than the return on assets, adding leverage increases the sustainable growth rate.

Sustainable Growth Model Definitions

g	The annual percentage growth rate of equity.
g^*	The sustainable annual percentage growth rate of equity, given the company's leverage and dividend policies and no additional outside equity financing.
E	The level of equity book value in dollars at the beginning of a year.
ΔE	The dollar-valued change in equity book value during the year.
NI	Net income after tax for the year, expressed in dollars.
R	The earnings retention rate, that is, the fraction of net income after tax that is retained in the venture and not distributed to investors.
ROE	The accounting rate of return on equity, that is, net income after tax, divided by equity.
S	Sales revenue for the year.
A	Book value of total assets at the beginning of the year.
ROS	The accounting rate of return on sales, that is, the ratio of net income after tax to sales revenue.
$Turnover$	The ratio of sales revenue for the year to total assets at the beginning of the year.
$Leverage$	The ratio of beginning assets to beginning equity.
$EBIT$	Accounting net income for the year, before interest and income taxes.
r	The effective interest rate on debt financing (all nonequity financing).
t	The corporate income tax rate.

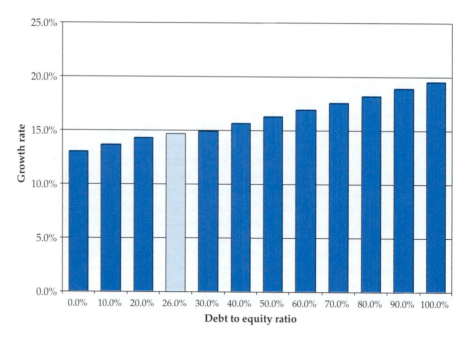

Figure 7-1   Relation between financial leverage and sustainable growth

Because of the tax deductibility of interest expense, adding financial leverage increases the sustainable growth rate. This conclusion assumes that the rate of return on assets is greater than the after-tax interest rate on debt financing. Under the assumptions stated in the text, at a debt to equity ratio of 26.0 percent, the venture can sustain growth at a rate that enables it to reach sales of $2.5 million in the fifth year of operation.

Assuming that Bates is correct in his strategy of setting a sales target of $2.5 million by the end of five years, what would you advise him to do? Is it better to raise equity from outside investors, or is it better to borrow? You are still a step or two away from being able to answer this fundamental question. Without knowing more, you cannot determine the fraction of the equity the entrepreneur would need to give up in exchange for the $178,000 in outside equity. That will depend on the value the investor places on the venture. Nor can you determine the value of the remaining equity to the entrepreneur. So before you can decide between debt and equity, you need to know how to value investment in the venture, a topic we shall address in the next few chapters.

The important lesson for now is that the entrepreneur's financing decision can have a dramatic effect on the growth rate the venture can achieve and the speed with which it can reach its targets. The choice of new venture strategy cannot be made without considering financing alternatives.

7.2 ASSESSING FINANCIAL NEEDS WHEN GROWTH IS NOT SUSTAINABLE

Product-market growth that is either too rapid or too slow is not sustainable and is problematic for an entrepreneur. Growth that is too slow threatens venture survival; this threat comes from competition in the product market. Growth that is too rapid threatens both control and survival; this threat comes from the capital market.

Long-run survival depends on achieving a level of sales that is sufficient for financial viability. In some product markets, survival and profitability depend on rapidly attaining a substantial market position. Computer software is a good example of a market in which long-run survival can depend less on product quality than on the ability to achieve a substantial market position quickly. The reason is that for many software packages, such as word processing and spreadsheet programs and video games, there are important network externalities. Rather than relying on user manuals or calls to help lines, consumers tend to rely on pooling of their individual knowledge and experience to solve technical problems. Because of network externalities, a software manufacturer who does not achieve substantial market share quickly may be driven from the market. In some cases, network externalities are sufficiently important to consumers that a dominant product can hold competitors in abeyance, even those with products that are superior technically and available at lower prices.

In other cases, rapid growth is not essential for survival but may still be an element of the entrepreneur's aspiration. Without careful analysis, it is easy to equate rapid growth with financial success. But as the sustainable growth model implies, nothing could be further from the truth. There are countless examples of rapid growth ultimately destroying a venture. There are other examples where the venture survives, but growth results in loss of control for the entrepreneur. The challenge is to identify and implement a viable product-market strategy that produces value for the entrepreneur. Careful assessment of financial needs is central to the decision.

7.3   PLANNING FOR PRODUCT MARKET UNCERTAINTY

Long-run financial planning is critical for assessing the benefits and threats of rapid growth. The financial planning process begins with tentative selection of a product-market strategy that includes a growth objective. We refer to this as a conjectural product-market strategy. The strategy is only a conjecture at this point because financing considerations are yet to be evaluated. Financing considerations can lead the entrepreneur to reject what may appear to be the best product-market strategy in favor of one that is expected to be less effective in the product market but more valuable for the entrepreneur.

In the preceding discussion of sustainable growth, the conjectural product-market strategy was a simple one—to achieve a sales level of $2.5 million in five years. Given the amount the entrepreneur was able to invest, the product-market strategy could not be achieved without outside financing. Whether it would be advantageous for the entrepreneur to pursue the financing or reevaluate the product-market strategy depends on which approach would maximize value for the entrepreneur.[6]

We cover valuation in the next few chapters. For now we highlight the problem of providing sufficient financial slack so that the entrepreneur can deal with unanticipated success or failure in the product market. Financial slack is liquidity that would enable the venture to deal with surprises without the need to raise additional capital. Financial slack is available in various forms, including, for example, cash flow from operations, excess cash or other liquid assets, or an unused line of credit.

Planning for Product-Market Success

Ironically, unexpected product-market success is a threat to new venture survival and control. Entrepreneurs often want their ventures to grow at whatever rate the product market will permit. But growth and profitability are not equivalent. In fact, the entrepreneur of a venture that is both profitable and growing rapidly can face a threat to control. Accordingly, for the purpose of assessing long-run financial needs, it is important to deal with the risk of unexpected product-market success.

If a venture is profitable and, more importantly, is generating cash in excess of capital replacement requirements, it can finance growth internally. This is the lesson of the sustainable growth model. Excess operating cash flow is an important source of investment capital. For a venture that is debt-free, ability to finance growth internally is approximately equal to the venture's after-tax rate of return on assets. If that return is, for example, 8 percent, then the organization is capable of growing assets at a rate of approximately 8 percent by relying exclusively on internally generated funds. Growth more rapid than 8 percent requires external funding.[7] The larger the gap between actual growth and sustainable growth, the greater the need for external funding.

Conversely, if the after-tax return on assets exceeds the growth rate of assets, the organization generates free cash flow. Free cash flow is the excess of cash flow over the amount that reasonably is required to deal with uncertainty. Free cash flow that is retained by the venture does not contribute to its value. Accordingly, to achieve maximum value for investors, a venture that generates free cash flow should distribute the surplus funds. Dividends, share repurchase, and debt repayment all are means of distributing free cash flow.

Unexpected product-market success compels the entrepreneur to both reexamine the product-market strategy and explore alternatives for outside financing. However, arranging new financing takes time, particularly for an early-stage venture. Furthermore, the need to invest time in seeking financing comes at a critical point, when rapid growth is likely to generate a host of organizational challenges. Fortunately, with financial planning, the entrepreneur can prepare, in advance, for a scenario involving growth more rapid than expected.

Although rapid growth usually increases the need for external financing, it normally does not increase the need for initial financing. At the start-up stage, the potential for success is uncertain. Some of the uncertainty is resolved if the venture grows and is profitable. As a result, financing at a later stage is likely to be available on more favorable terms. Still, in structuring initial financing, the entrepreneur must anticipate that growth requires financing. He or she must have a sense of how the necessary capital would be raised. In negotiating the initial rounds, the entrepreneur would want to preserve the option of raising additional funding if the growth rate justified doing so.

Some current financing decisions can cause problems if the venture needs more funds at a later stage. Loan contracts, for instance, sometimes contain covenants that preclude raising additional funds without the lender's approval. The lender's interests may be contrary to the entrepreneur's. Some equity financing structures can cause similar difficulties. The antidilution provisions of outside equity claims can impair the venture's ability to raise capital, particularly where the venture has run into problems and needs cash to get through them. By limiting the venture's ability to raise funds in the future in these ways, the entrepreneur can lower the apparent cost of financing. But if the venture grows rapidly or runs into difficulties, those earlier decisions can be a significant threat. Before committing to such a provision, the entrepreneur should assess the implications if the venture grows at a different rate than expected.

Planning for Unexpected Failure

Once a venture is established and is generating positive cash flows, unexpected slow growth does not pose a very serious problem. If the actual growth rate is lower than expected, but still high, the venture may be able to reduce its reliance on externally supplied capital. If the growth rate is less than what can be financed internally, then the resulting free cash flow can fund new investments or distributions to investors.

A more serious problem arises if unexpected poor performance is encountered before the organization has reached financial viability. For example, if product development takes longer than expected or sales growth is less than expected and the attained level of sales is below what is needed to generate funds for capital replacement, then the organization must depend on external financing to a greater extent than expected. This is a particularly serious problem because a venture that has not achieved financial viability and has not met expectations will have difficulty raising capital.

This is a precarious situation for an entrepreneur, and loss of control in these circumstances is common, though often avoidable. A forward-looking entrepreneur can manage the risk by maintaining financial slack and preserving the ability to raise additional capital in the event growth is slower than expected.

High-Tech, High-Growth Innovation

Some of the most challenging financing problems are associated with a product innovation that requires a long and expensive development period followed by rapid sales growth. Negative cash flows in such cases can extend over many years and last through both the development stage and the rapid growth stage. The venture does not begin to generate free cash flow for investors until the growth rate slows to a point where operating cash flows are more than sufficient to fund growth. The NewCompany model in Chapter 6 had these characteristics. We extend the model later in this chapter.

The pattern of long development lead times followed by rapid sales growth is characteristic of many high-tech innovations (pharmaceuticals, biotechnology, and some electronics, for example). It is not surprising, therefore, that large, well-established companies perform much of this development activity. Such companies can draw on their existing financing capabilities without the need to convince outside investors of the merits of a specific project.

7.4   CASH FLOW BREAKEVEN ANALYSIS

Much is written about breakeven analysis in accounting and finance textbooks. Not all of it is flattering, primarily because the traditional accounting approach to breakeven analysis ignores the time value of money and focuses on accounting net income rather than cash flow.[8] Thus, even though a capital outlay may have been made at the beginning of a project, the accounting approach seeks a breakeven point that is based on the accounting treatment of depreciation expense. As the approach does not factor in the opportunity cost of invested capital, it is not well suited for investment decision making.

For assessing financial needs, however, one type of breakeven analysis can provide insight: cash flow breakeven analysis. Cash flow breakeven analysis addresses the question, "What level of sales generates operating cash inflows that are sufficient to cover operating cash outflows?" The cash flow breakeven point is where the venture achieves a level of sales high enough to maintain its operations at the current level, without additional investment. At the breakeven point, cash inflows are sufficient to maintain and replace current assets. The accounting approach generates data that can be used to construct a cash flow breakeven analysis.[12]

In conjunction with a forecast of sales, finding the cash flow breakeven point helps the entrepreneur assess initial financing needs. This financing enables the venture to generate a sales

A Menu of Cash Flow Breakeven Points

NET INCOME OR NET INCOME BEFORE TAX

Net income before tax is a measure of earnings after payment of all cash and noncash expenses, including interest expense on debt. The breakeven point allows for replacing existing assets and continuing to make interest payments. Thus, it is a stable breakeven level, which takes capital structure into consideration.

EARNINGS BEFORE INTEREST AND TAXES (EBIT)

EBIT is a measure of earnings available to all claimants on the firm's earnings (stockholders, creditors, and governments). For a venture without debt financing, EBIT and Net Income breakeven points are equivalent. EBIT understates operating cash flow because some expense items (especially depreciation and amortization) do not involve cash outlays. One argument in favor of EBIT is that by not adding back depreciation, a provision for capital replacement is being made implicitly.

EARNINGS BEFORE INTEREST AND TAXES, PLUS DEPRECIATION AND AMORTIZATION (EBITDA)

EBITDA is a measure of operating cash flow that does not provide for capital replacement. The measure starts with EBIT and adds back noncash expenses. At this point, the venture has positive operating cash flows, but replacement capital would need to be financed. Such financing would have to be over and above existing financing. Because EBITDA is not sustainable unless the venture takes on additional financing to replace depreciating capital, it is essentially a short-run cash flow breakeven concept.

FREE CASH FLOW (FCF)

The FCF breakeven point occurs when the venture has sufficient cash flow from operations to provide not only for capital replacement, but also for new investments in equipment, intangible assets, and working capital necessary to achieve future sales objectives. Free cash flow is available for debt repayment, distribution to investors, or pursuit of other opportunities. For most ventures, FCF breakeven is likely to be realized when the growth rate of the venture slows to a point where new investments of these kinds are small compared to their base levels.

level and accompanying cash inflows that are sufficient to "break even," such that cash outflows are covered and the venture can maintain its level of operation. Once a breakeven model is constructed, the entrepreneur can use it to determine how initial cash needs depend on sales levels, sales growth, product prices, fixed costs, variable costs, and noncash revenues and expenses. Breakeven analysis can be used to conduct a variety of "what if" or sensitivity analyses.

An Illustration

Consider the launching of a new magazine for aspiring writers. Like other magazines, *Ink* will derive its revenues from two primary sources: subscriptions and advertising. The publisher expects that *Ink* will be similar to other magazines in that both the amount and price of advertising in the magazine depend on the size of the subscriber base. The production values of the magazine are also expected to increase with the subscriber base. With these considerations, Figure 7-2 shows the revenues, expenses, income, and cash flows of *Ink* at various subscriber levels.

Three different levels of circulation (in addition to the start-up level of zero) are listed in the figure. Subscription revenue is computed at the rate of $15 per subscription. At higher circulation levels, advertising revenue per subscription increases but does so at a decreasing rate.

The expenses of a magazine include primarily circulation, production, editorial, and administrative expenses. To varying extents, each of these can include variable and fixed components. For the purpose of breakeven analysis, the expenses are aggregated in Figure 7-2 as either variable or fixed.

Because we are concerned with the cash flow breakeven point, accounting net income must be adjusted to take account of noncash expenses and to provide for capital replacement at the given subscriber level. In the figure, we distinguish between capital expenditures needed to launch the magazine but nonrecurring, and recurring expenditures. The nonrecurring capital expenditures can include those made to acquire lists of potential subscribers and other tangible or intangible assets that do not have to be replaced after the magazine is launched. Such outlays are reflected in depreciation expenses for several years after the launch. The figure is based on an assumption that the assets acquired to launch the venture are still being

Annual Revenues, Expenses and Cash Flows of *Ink* Magazine at Various Circulation Levels
(all figures in thousands)

Number of Subscribers	0	250	400	550
Revenues				
Subscriptions	$0	$3,750	$6,000	$8,250
Advertising	$0	$2,250	$4,650	$7,350
Total	$0	$6,000	$10,650	$15,600
Expenses				
Variable Expenses	$0	$5,500	$9,175	$12,625
Fixed Expenses	$2,700	$2,700	$2,700	$2,700
Total	$2,700	$8,200	$11,875	$15,325
Income				
Operating Income	($2,700)	($2,200)	($1,225)	$275
Taxes (40%)	($1,080)	($880)	($490)	$110
Net Income	($1,620)	($1,320)	($735)	$165
Cash Flows				
Net Income	($1,620)	($1,320)	($735)	$165
Depr.—nonrecurring investments	$650	$650	$650	$650
Depr.—recurring investments	$0	$250	$300	$350
Capital Replacement	$0	($250)	($300)	($350)
Net Cash Flow	($970)	($670)	($85)	$815

Figure 7-2 Annual revenues, expenses, and cash flows of *Ink* magazine at various circulation levels

depreciated. Recurring expenditures are for office equipment, computers, and other assets required in the business of magazine publishing. Because the cash flow breakeven point is examined as a steady state, we assume that depreciation expenses for such assets are exactly offset by outlays for new assets.

Usually, breakeven analysis assumes that revenue increases in proportion to unit sales and that all costs can be neatly classified as either fixed or variable. The result is that the contribution margin to profit, that is, the difference between unit revenue and unit variable cost, is constant. So it is easy to find the breakeven point by dividing total fixed cost by the contribution margin per unit. You can use the same principles to find the cash flow breakeven point.

The problem facing the publisher of *Ink* is more complicated than the usual breakeven analysis. Both advertising revenue per subscription and variable expenses per subscription are nonlinear with changes in the number of subscriptions. Consequently, the contribution margin per subscription is not constant.

We use the information in Figure 7-2 to calculate the contribution margins to net income and cash flow of subscription sales at various output levels.[9] Figure 7-3 show the results of those calculations. In the top half of the figure, revenues and expenses are averaged over all subscriptions up to the particular level of subscriptions. Thus, at 400,000 subscribers, revenue per subscription is $26.63, much of which comes from advertising, and variable expenses per subscription are $22.94, resulting in an average contribution margin of $3.69 per subscription. Because the contribution margins at subscription levels of 250,000 or 550,000 differ, it is not possible to simply use the $3.69 figure to find the breakeven point of either cash flows or net income.

The top half of the figure also does not reveal the value of adding incremental subscribers. Suppose, for example, that by spending $4 per new subscriber (say, through selectively discounting subscription prices), the venture could add 50,000 subscribers to a base of 400,000. The top half of the figure suggests that doing so would be a mistake. But that is an incorrect inference. In the bottom half of Figure 7-3, contribution margins are computed for incremental subscriptions. Over the range from 400,000 to 550,000 subscriptions, the average contribution margin is $6.50. Thus, discounting the price by $4 to selected new subscribers would actually make the venture more profitable and increase cash flow.

In Figure 7-4, we present the breakeven analysis in graphical form. In the figure, the results from Figure 7-2 are smoothed to address the nonlinear contribution margins. In addition, the difference between a cash flow breakeven point and a net income breakeven point is illustrated. Because we assume the venture is equity-financed, the net income and EBIT breakeven points are the same. Using the traditional accounting approach, the net income breakeven point is about 530,000 subscriptions. However, for a company that has nonrecurring noncash expenses, this overstates the cash flow breakeven point. Cash flow breakeven occurs at about 420,000 subscribers. Thus, focusing on net income or EBIT could lead to a wrong investment decision. If it was believed that the subscriber base would not reach 530,000 very quickly, the project could be rejected incorrectly.

In defense of the accounting approach, the difference between the cash flow breakeven point and the net income breakeven point can be slight. For *Ink*, the difference arises only because some of the initial investment is nonrecurring. Once that investment is fully depreciated, fixed expense in the income statement will be lower, and the breakeven point will be about 450,000 in terms of either net income or cash flow.[10] In fact, the accounting approach of focusing on EBIT or net income works well whenever the steady state includes depreciation expenses and replacement investments that are approximately offsetting.

Net Income and Cash Flow Contribution Margins of *Ink* Magazine at Various Circulation Levels			
Number of Subscribers (thousands)	250	400	550
Average over All Subscribers			
Revenue per Subscription			
Subscriptions	$15.00	$15.00	$15.00
Advertising	$9.00	$11.63	$13.36
Total	$24.00	$26.63	$28.36
Expenses per Subscription			
Variable Expenses	$22.00	$22.94	$22.95
Contribution to Net Income	**$2.00**	**$3.69**	**$5.41**
Average over Increment of Subscribers	0–250	250–400	400–550
Revenue per Subscription			
Subscriptions	$15.00	$15.00	$15.00
Advertising	$9.00	$16.00	$18.00
Total	$24.00	$31.00	$33.00
Expenses per Subscription			
Variable Expense	$22.00	$24.50	$23.00
Contribution to Net Income	**$2.00**	**$6.50**	**$10.00**

Figure 7-3   Net income and cash flow contribution margins of *Ink* magazine at various circulation levels

Revenues and expenses under the heading, "Average Over All Subscribers," are calculated for the number of subscriptions shown at the top of each column. Revenues and expenses under the heading, "Average Over Increment of Subscribers," are calculated for the increments of zero to 250,000 subscribers, 250,000 to 400,000 subscribers, and 400,000 to 550,000 subscribers. Contribution to Net Income is calculated as total revenue per subscriber, less variable expense per subscriber, and is shown for all subscribers up to the stated level and for incremental subscribers. Because incremental contribution margins are different from average contribution margins, decisions about the value of additional subscriptions must be based on the incremental margins.

Using Breakeven Analysis to Project Financial Needs

Using breakeven analysis to assess financial needs requires another step. Financial need depends on two things: one is the time until breakeven is reached, and the other is the financing required to cover the shortfalls until that time. Thus, to estimate the amount of financing required, we combine breakeven analysis with a sales forecast. For example, in the case of *Ink* magazine, it might be expected that first-year subscriptions would be 100,000, second-year would be 300,000, and third-year would be 600,000. We use the chart in Figure 7-4 to estimate annual cash needs. Based on the chart, the shortfalls in the first and second years, respectively, are about $750,000 and $500,000, or a total of $1,250,000. In the third year, the venture is expected to generate positive cash flows of $75,000.[11]

The cumulative cash shortfall of $1,250,000, implied for the first two years by the breakeven analysis, does not tell the full story. The shortfalls are steady-state shortfalls, but as the venture

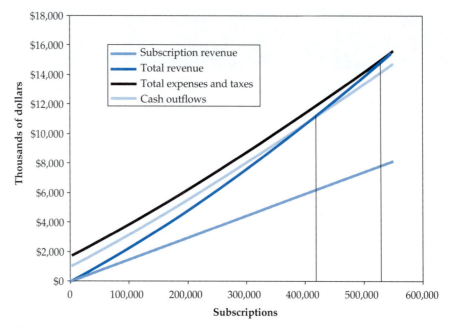

Figure 7-4 *Ink* magazine breakeven chart

The figure shows total revenues, expenses, and cash outflows by number of subscriptions. Although the growth rate of subscription revenue is linear, growth rates of total revenues, expenses, and cash flows are nonlinear. Because of the nonlinearity, incremental contribution margins are different from average contribution margins. The venture achieves net income breakeven when total revenue equals total expenses and taxes, at approximately 530,000 subscriptions. Because some of the initial capital expenditures are nonrecurring, the venture achieves breakeven cash flow at a lower level, when total revenue intersects cash outflows. The venture achieves cash flow breakeven at approximately 420,000 subscribers.

is expected to grow, it is not in steady state. Further, the total does not include the initial investment outlay to acquire capital assets that are being depreciated. A more comprehensive estimate would provide for investment in the capital asset base needed to produce the magazine, as well as for the working capital needed to support operations.[12] Even though growth beyond the cash flow breakeven point may require additional investment, the fact that breakeven is achieved makes securing additional financing less difficult.

Present-value Breakeven Analysis

It is important to keep in mind the limitations of cash flow breakeven analysis. It is useful because it enables the entrepreneur to get a better feel for the venture by providing a way to assess how sales levels, prices, fixed costs, and variable costs affect cash needs. However, the analysis does not contribute much insight to the investment decision. It is not a valuation technique and does not use the present value concepts that are central to investment decision making.

For investment decision making, a modified form of breakeven analysis can determine the level of sales where the present value of revenues is sufficient to cover the present value of cash outflows (both cash expenses and investment outlays). This type of analysis, present-value breakeven analysis, helps answer the question, "What level of sales is needed to justify investing?" It is best suited for projects where revenue and expense streams can be described as level annuities. The present-value approach is most helpful for capital budgeting and investment decisions. It is unlikely to be of much help for assessing cash needs.[13]

7.5 ASSESSING FINANCIAL NEEDS WITH SCENARIO ANALYSIS

Because the future is uncertain, the financing decision should consider both the expected future of the venture and uncertainty. Accordingly, methods of assessing financial needs under conditions of uncertainty are particularly valuable.

Scenario analysis is one simple approach to incorporating uncertainty into projections of financial needs. A scenario describes one possible realistic version of the future in a complex way and represents a single resolution of a list of sources of uncertainty.[14] For example, a scenario could be that overall growth of the product market is slowed by recession and that competitors react by reducing prices and advertising more aggressively. A scenario analysis reflects these factors formally in the assumptions of the model. The financial information for *Ink* magazine in Figures 7-2 through 7-4 is based on one scenario of what is "most likely" to occur.

An entrepreneur can use alternative scenarios of sale revenue, cost, and other factors to generate alternative projections of financial needs. One might, for example, consider a "most likely" scenario, a "best case," and a "worst case" with respect to financing needs. Other scenarios also are possible. For ventures with lengthy product development periods, it can be helpful to consider a scenario in which product introduction is slow, sales grow slowly and are not initially profitable, and another in which sales growth is rapid and more profitable but product development is still slow.

The key to forecasting long-run financial needs is developing a model that links product-market performance to financing requirements. We saw in Chapter 6, as well as through the sustainable growth model and cash flow breakeven analysis, how this can be done. The general approach to forecasting financial needs is a "backing-out" approach. That is, for any given pattern of desired or expected sales, costs, and resulting profitability, we can "reason back" to determine expected cash flows available for future investment. Using estimates of the efficiency of assets, in terms of their ability to support sales, we reason back to estimate external financing needs.

Because our concern in this chapter is the adequacy of financing, the most important sales scenario is not based on what is most likely to occur. Rather, it is a realistic "worst case" forecast, where the worst case is defined not as least profitable, but as a case that requires heaviest reliance on external financing. This is likely to be a case where development time is longer than expected; where development expense is higher than expected; and where sales growth is more rapid and less profitable than expected.

Scenario analysis can be developed in much the same way as decision tree analysis. For example, Figure 7-5 describes 18 scenarios of sales growth, cost, and revenue for *Ink* magazine. Each scenario involves differing assumptions concerning sales growth, advertising revenue, and production cost, as detailed in the notes to the figure. The decision maker is faced with an issue of how much initial financing to secure, and wants to apply scenario analysis to a cash flow breakeven study. Although there are 18 scenarios in the figure, some are more realistic than others are. The remainder of this analysis focuses on four scenarios.

The first is a success scenario. The magazine is a hit. Sales grow more rapidly than expected, and advertisers are attracted to the magazine. The combination of these factors results

Ink Magazine Scenario Analysis			
Subscription Growth Rate[1]	Variable Cost[2]	Advertising Revenue[3]	Projected Cash Shortfall[4]
High Growth	High Cost	High Revenue	
		Low Revenue	
	Expected Cost	High Revenue	
		Low Revenue	
	Low Cost	High Revenue	$375,000
		Low Revenue	
Expected Growth	High Cost	High Revenue	
		Low Revenue	
	Expected Cost	High Revenue	$750,000
		Low Revenue	$2,250,000
	Low Cost	High Revenue	
		Low Revenue	
Low Growth	High Cost	High Revenue	
		Low Revenue	$3,250,000[5]
	Expected Cost	High Revenue	
		Low Revenue	
	Low Cost	High Revenue	
		Low Revenue	

[1]Expected subscriptions are 100,000 the first year, 300,000 the second year, and 600,000 the third year. High growth is 20 percent above expected and low growth is 20 percent below.

[2]Expected variable cost per subscription is as shown on an incremental basis in figure 7-4. High cost is 10 percent above expected variable cost and low cost is 10 percent below.

[3]High advertising revenue per subscription is 15 percent above incremental advertising revenue per subscription as shown in figure 7-4, and low advertising revenue is 15 percent below.

[4]Projected cash shortfalls have not been discounted to present value. If financing is staged to match cash needs, discounting is not necessary. If financing is received in advance of anticipated need, projected cash shortfalls can be discounted at the rate the venture can earn by investing the funds until they are required. For the purpose of an investment decision, a different discount rate would be appropriate.

[5]Cash shortfall for this scenario is for the first three years only. The actual shortfall extends beyond the third year.

Figure 7-5 *Ink* magazine scenario analysis

The figure identifies 18 possible scenarios with respect to growth rate of subscriptions, variable cost per subscription, and advertising revenue. Total financing needs (projected cash shortfalls) are estimated for four of the scenarios.

in low variable cost per subscription and advertising revenue per subscription that is higher than expected. When the information in Figures 7-2 and 7-3 is modified to reflect the revenue and cost changes, a new breakeven chart can be generated and the annual cash shortfalls can be evaluated at the projected low sales levels. The resulting estimate of the cumulative cash shortfall is $375,000, well below the projection based on the "most likely" scenario in Figure 7-4 (when everything comes out as expected).

The other extreme is a failure scenario. Aspiring writers (the target readership) are not attracted to *Ink.* As a result, neither are advertisers. Sales growth is slow, variable cost per subscription is higher than expected and advertising revenue per subscription is lower. The resulting cumulative cash shortfall for the first three years is projected to be $3.25 million, far more than under the expected scenario. Conceivably, the venture would continue to generate negative cash flows for even longer.

The last two scenarios represent a sensitivity analysis of the effect of varying assumptions about advertising revenues upward or downward by 15 percent, compared to the most likely scenario. Figure 7-5 shows that varying the assumption about advertising revenue over this range results in a $1.5 million swing in financial need.

The information in Figure 7-5 is relevant to how much financing the entrepreneur should try to line up before initiating the venture, but does not fully resolve the issue. Should the entrepreneur arrange for enough financing to cover the failure scenario? For at least two reasons, probably not. First, we have not assessed the present value of the opportunity. Given the weak performance in the failure scenario, it may make sense from an investment perspective to abandon the venture if *Ink* is not well received by its target market. Second, very early-stage financing is expensive owing to high uncertainty. Accordingly, lining up all of the financing at the outset reduces the entrepreneur's ownership stake if the venture is a success. The entrepreneur needs to think about a contingency plan for raising financing or abandoning the venture if the magazine proves to be a failure, but does not need to lock up all of the financing commitments at the beginning.

7.6   SIMULATION OF FINANCING REQUIREMENTS: AN ILLUSTRATION

Simulation is a more comprehensive approach for incorporating uncertainty into a decision. To see how simulation can be used to assess financial needs, we reconsider NewCompany, the high-tech start-up, in Chapter 6. Refer to Figure 6-6, which contains the pro forma financial statements for the venture. Those statements are generated on the basis of what is expected to occur. With performance conforming to expectations, the need for outside financing peaks at about $593,000 in month 55.

But what if NewCompany does not develop as expected? Product development, for example, could take more or less time than expected, and costs during the development period could be more or less than expected. In addition, there is uncertainty about the rate of sales growth once development starts and about when the period of rapid sales growth ends. Also, expense levels, both in absolute terms and in relation to contemporaneous sales, are subject to uncertainty. With a few simple modifications to the spreadsheet in Figure 6-6, these sources of uncertainty can be incorporated into the pro forma analysis.[15]

It is not important that you study the financial model in detail, but you should investigate the ways that uncertainty is introduced by examining the cell formulas. The modifications we made to Figure 6-6 are simple ones designed to reflect some of the different kinds of uncertainty a venture like NewCompany could face. Our more specific purpose in this chapter is to see how uncertainty affects financing needs and how simulation can be used to study financing choices.

The following is a brief summary of the changes we made to build uncertainty into the model. The discussion is intended only to illustrate some ways of modeling financial uncertainty and some considerations that could affect the specific assumptions of a model.

Uncertainty about Development Timing

To reflect development-time uncertainty, we revised the spreadsheet model of NewCompany so development is completed no sooner than the ninth month after the start of the venture. We structured the model so the probability of development is highest during the period from

How Long Will Product Development Take?

When product development efforts are expensive and timing of development success is uncertain, the financial needs of a venture depend critically on development timing. A venture that runs out of cash before reaching a significant milestone in the development process (completion of a prototype, completion of preliminary testing, etc.) is likely to face considerable difficulty lining up additional financing.* To a significant degree, the difficulty arises because failure to achieve the milestone suggests to investors that the entrepreneur's projections are overly optimistic in other ways as well.

There is no general rule to determine how long development of a new product takes, but that doesn't mean it cannot be estimated reasonably. In some cases, engineering studies or regulatory reports are helpful, as are experiences of comparable ventures. Innovations in new drugs provide an interesting example of products with protracted, variable, and unpredictable development horizons, due, in part, to regulatory hurdles. The example is a good one because the government keeps records of all new drug applications. Since the Prescription Drug User Fee Act (PDUFA) was passed in 1992, new drug approval times have been reduced (from a median of 22 months in 1992 to 12 months in 1999, with an increase in year 2000 to 15.6 months). However, for assessing cash needs, the median is not enough. It also is important to estimate the uncertainty of development time.

The chart following provides information regarding a sample of all new drug applications that were approved in the year 2000. The data illustrate regulatory histories and cycles for individual products approved in 2000. A horizontal bar represents the experience for an approved application. As shown, two of the new drugs approved in 2000 were first submitted in 1996, a four-year process; six were submitted in 1997; six in 1998, ten in 1999, and three were submitted and approved in 2000. The chart shows the breakdown of development timing, including, in some cases, lengthy sponsor response times.

One problem with the data is that all of the drugs in the chart were approved. Many others are not approved. It is important not to sample only successful ventures to estimate timing, as doing so would impart a selection bias to the estimate. Fortunately, the FDA Web site (fda.gov) also has data on drug applications that are not approved.

---

*Start-Up, by Jerry Kaplan (1994), is an insightful review of the financial difficulties encountered by a high-technology venture in the computer industry, as it struggled to raise enough cash to carry it from one milestone to the next.

(Continues)

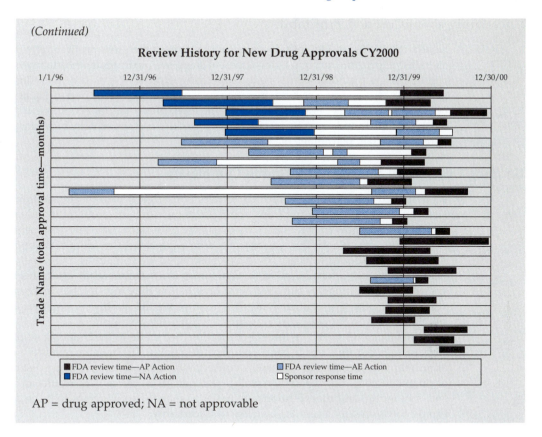

(Continued)

Review History for New Drug Approvals CY2000

Trade Name (total approval time—months)

AP = drug approved; NA = not approvable

month 9 through month 24 (where the cumulative probability reaches about 84 percent). During the next 12 months the cumulative probability rises to about 87 percent, and through month 78 it rises to about 89 percent. Thus, there is a residual probability of about 11 percent that development is not completed even after 78 months of effort.

Uncertainty about the Rate of Sales Growth

In the revised NewCompany model, we also allow for uncertainty about the rate of sales growth. We model sales in each month to depend on sales in the previous month, adjusted for the expected rate of sales growth and by a random component tied to the level of sales in the previous month. This structure treats sales levels over time as a random walk, where the best forecast of sales in the next period is the level of sales in the current period, adjusted for expected growth. The net effect is that if the level of sales in one period is unexpectedly high (or low), that change is treated as a permanent shift that raises (or lowers) expected sales level in all subsequent periods. An alternative specification would allow for some degree of reversion toward the trend. In that case, the forecast for the next period depends on past sales levels for several prior periods. Other specifications can be designed to reflect seasonal patterns or other regularities of the growth rate. The experience of comparable ventures can again help determine what assumption to make.

Uncertainty about Cost and Profitability

Finally, the revised model introduces uncertainty about the gross profit margin and the level of operating expenses. During the development stage, we incorporate uncertainty of development cost by adding a random component to operating expense. We assume a random walk similar to that for sales revenue, where operating expense in the current period equals operating expense in the previous period, adjusted for inflation, plus a random component. Once development is complete and revenue is positive, we introduce cost uncertainty by making cost of goods sold an uncertain percentage of sales.

Gauging Uncertainty and Avoiding Undue Complexity

As described in Chapter 6, published sources offer a great deal of information that provides a reasonable basis for assumptions about static measures of profitability. Ideally, we would like to estimate how profit levels vary over time with sales. Data sources such as *RMA Statement Studies*, provide profit measures based on aggregated firm data at one point in time. In practice, a time-series forecast could be constructed by combining this type of information with longer-term information from companies with comparable attributes. Fundamental analysis of the companies can shed light on whether they are suitable "comparables" of the venture. The objective of such analysis is to improve the quality of assumptions used in the simulation and to provide a way of substantiating the assumptions.

As you can tell from the three modifications we made to the model, a simulation that incorporates uncertainty can become complicated quickly. The benefits of adding complexity diminish rapidly once the key elements of uncertainty are modeled. There are distinct advantages of a parsimonious model based on well-researched assumptions. The results are more tractable and convincing, and modifications are easier to make. This suggests that the decision maker should focus on only a few key sources of uncertainty.

Results of the Simulation

The NewCompany simulation model is designed so the venture has a large line of credit. Any time the venture runs short of cash, borrowing is automatic. Any time the venture generates free cash flow, repayment of the loan is automatic. If the venture is able to repay its debt and has cash left over, the surplus is invested at a market rate of interest and carried forward to the final month of the simulation. The cumulative cash surplus can then be used as an element of a scorecard, so to speak, of how well the venture does in a particular iteration of the model.

Figure 7-6 graphically displays some of the results of a simulation for NewCompany in which all of the above uncertainty factors are allowed to vary. The figure shows cumulative frequency distributions of required external financing (in the form of borrowing) at the end of each of the first five years (measured in months) after initiation of the venture. The results in the figure are generated without the possibility of second-stage equity financing. The horizontal axis in the figure is the required amount of external financing, and the vertical axis is the percentage of iterations from the simulation. Thus, a point on the cumulative frequency distribution for a particular year indicates the percentage of iterations where the amount of financing required did not exceed the corresponding dollar amount from the horizontal axis. For each year, the figure also shows the mean of the distribution. For example, the distribution at the end of the first year shows that the mean of required external financing is about $29,000. The probability is about 15 percent that no outside financing will be required in the

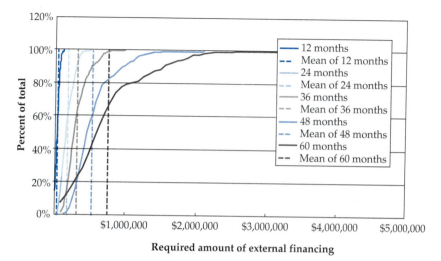

Figure 7-6 NewCompany cumulative frequency distributions of financing needs at various times

The figure shows simulation results for NewCompany. The simulation run assesses total financing needs over time. The financial model used in the simulation allows the company to borrow additional funds whenever it is short of cash and to repay the loan whenever it has excess cash. Results plotted in the figure are the cumulative frequency distributions of debt in the venture's balance sheet as of the end of each of the first five years of the financial model. The average level of required financing increases each year. However, by the fifth year, some simulated outcomes are sufficiently profitable that loans are paid off and the venture accumulates a cash surplus. About 22 percent of the time, financing that is required in the fifth year is less than financing that is required in the fourth year.

first year. By inspecting individual iterations from the model, we determined that the outcomes where no external financing is required in the first year correspond to scenarios where development is completed earlier than expected and monthly development costs are lower than expected. At the other extreme, the maximum need during the first year is about $110,000 and is associated with unexpectedly high monthly development costs.

Figure 7-6 shows that external financing requirements generally are increasing over the first five years, reaching a mean of about $700,000 by the fifth year. In general, low financing requirements are associated with a short development period, followed by slow but profitable sales growth, whereas high financing requirements are associated with a long development period and rapid, but not highly profitable, sales growth. The figure also shows that there is a reasonable chance that external financing requirements are lower at the end of the fifth year than at the ends of some of the previous years (i.e., the venture is able to repay some of the outstanding debt). There is even a small chance that the venture is able to repay all of its debt by that point. The outcomes with full repayment by the fifth year are associated with a combination of a short development period, profitable sales, and an early end of the rapid expansion phase. Although these outcomes look good for the creditor, because of the early termination of the rapid-growth stage they are not necessarily the best ones for the entrepreneur or for equity investors. Keep in mind that we are not yet looking at value, but only at the venture's ability to finance its activities and repay its debt.

Interpreting the Simulation Results

The information in Figure 7-6 can be viewed in the context of the entrepreneur's planning horizon. Given that the venture could require as much as $110,000 of outside financing by the end of the first year, it is a good idea for the entrepreneur to have a sense of how the financing could be raised. In the model, we structured the outside financing as a loan commitment that the entrepreneur draws against as needed and repays as free cash flow becomes available. Loan commitments, however, take time to arrange, and it is unlikely that any lender would make a large commitment to a venture with no track record and no cash flow. From a planning perspective, it is sensible to build-in several months of lead-time for making financing arrangements and to recognize the realistic limits of the venture's ability to borrow.

The forecasts of more distant financial needs serve a different function. There is no particular urgency for the entrepreneur to arrange financing that is not needed for several years. However, the longer-term analysis is relevant to consideration of how early-stage financing should be arranged. If things go according to expectations, NewCompany will need about $700,000 by the end of the fifth year. But it could need considerably more. Accordingly, early-stage financing should not be on terms that make later-stage financing difficult to arrange. It is important for the entrepreneur to examine carefully the covenants and restrictions associated with any early-stage financing plan, and to make sure they do not make the venture hostage to the investor later on. Conversely, there may be some covenants and restrictions to which the entrepreneur can agree. By agreeing to restrictions that will not be binding if the venture develops according to expectations, the entrepreneur can communicate confidence in the financial projections.

In the worst case, Figure 7-6 suggests that NewCompany could need to raise almost $4 million in outside financing. However, this is not very likely, and the need for so much external financing is associated with outcomes in which the venture has been unable to complete product development or where the actual rate of sales growth is very high and profitability is modest. The first situation could lead the entrepreneur to abandon the venture anyway (an option we have not built into the pro forma analysis). The second would enable the entrepreneur to raise additional financing later, based on its track record. The probability is very high that the venture would not need more than about $2 million by the end of the fifth year. Thus, in structuring early-stage financing, it is not important, or even desirable, to provide for the highest conceivable level of future financial needs.

In the best case (from a financing perspective), the venture generates sufficient cash by the end of the fifth year to repay all of its prior borrowing. This possibility has implications for structuring early-stage financing. Figure 7-6 suggests that external financing needs are transitory. If they are, the entrepreneur should consider the choice between permanent and temporary financing. The simulation is based on temporary debt financing. More permanent debt financing would enable the entrepreneur to draw more cash from the venture at an earlier stage. Had outside equity financing been used, it would make sense to consider incorporating an option to redeem the shares on pre-agreed terms.[16]

7.7   HOW MUCH MONEY DO YOU NEED?

As the NewCompany simulation is modeled, financing is automatic whenever the venture needs money. But this is not how new venture financing usually works. We just set it up this way as a starting point to help us determine how much money the venture might need. New-Company appears to be worth pursuing but requires outside investment. The question the entrepreneur inevitably must face from outside investors and be prepared to answer is, "How much money do you need?"

The entrepreneur should anticipate the question and may want to incorporate a response in the business plan that is used to attract investors. Alternatively, the plan may provide only a general indication of need. The entrepreneur must be prepared to offer a more specific answer when the question actually is raised. The entrepreneur's ability to answer specifically, thoughtfully, and directly is one test investors use in deciding whether it is worthwhile to begin negotiating.

To answer, the entrepreneur must do some careful thinking and analysis. Most entrepreneurs intuitively would like to have enough cash on hand to carry the venture to a point where cash flows from operations are sufficient to finance further growth. The amount desired intuitively includes a healthy cushion in case things do not work out as expected. The problem with this way of thinking is that the entrepreneur is unlikely to be able to raise this amount of financing at the outset. By asking for too much, the entrepreneur runs a risk of chasing off investors. Even if doing so is possible, the cost, in terms of ownership rights given to investors, is likely to be unacceptable to the entrepreneur.

The question is difficult to answer in part because it is compound. The investor is really asking three things: "How much do you need to initiate the project? How much, ultimately, do you think you will need? And when do you expect to need it?" The entrepreneur should respond to all three.

To provide an overview on how much outside equity to seek, we start with three principles:

- First, the entrepreneur does not need to raise capital now to cover cash needs for scenarios in which the business is thriving. If such a scenario is realized, the entrepreneur will not have trouble raising additional funds later on more favorable terms.

- Second, the entrepreneur does not need to raise initial capital that will only be needed if the venture proves to be unsuccessful. There is no reason to seek financing to cover scenarios where operating losses are expected to continue, with little prospect of significant improvement.

- Third, the entrepreneur does not need to raise initial capital that will not be needed until after a significant milestone is passed. In fact, attempting to raise the funds before they are needed signals that the entrepreneur is not confident.

Using Simulation to Examine Alternative Financing Arrangements

We now return to the specifics of the NewCompany model and apply these three principles. As a starting point, consider the possibility that the entrepreneur would like to raise enough cash at the outset to ensure that the venture continues to operate for the full six and one-half years of the model. Using the model, and assuming initial cash is raised as equity and that idle cash earns a return of 4 percent per year, we modified the assumptions by increasing the initial cash investment to $3 million (including the original funds of the entrepreneur). It turns out that $3 million is sufficient in about 99.2 percent of the simulated outcomes. This is consistent with the results in Figure 7-6, which indicate a very low probability of needing more than $3 million by the fifth year. But raising all of the cash up-front is unlikely to be feasible, and even if it were, the entrepreneur would have to give up more ownership than is necessary. Figure 7-7 is a summary of the simulation results with varying choices of the amount of initial financing.

In the NewCompany example, with $3 million of initial capital (Scenario 1 in Figure 7-7), we found only four outcomes from a sample of 500 where the venture did not have enough cash. All four were outcomes in which the venture had failed to complete product development by the ending month of the simulation. Although, at this time, we are not ready to delve into valuation, we can use net income in the last month as a simple indicator of whether, in a particular outcome, the venture has proven to be worth pursuing. The higher the ending net income, the more valuable the venture is likely to be.

Our simulation experiment with $3 million of initial investment generated many outcomes in which the venture failed to complete development by month 78. In fact, this occurred in 10.2 percent of the outcomes. For another 13 percent, sales revenue by month 78 was positive, but the venture had not yet reached breakeven in terms of net income. These scenarios may be worth continuing inasmuch as they probably will eventually generate positive income and cash flow. But an investor who is trying to decide, at the outset, whether to invest is unlikely to ascribe much value to those outcomes. The payoffs are too far in the future and too uncertain.

The implication of these results is that $3 million is too large an initial investment. It provides full financing in too many simulated outcomes in which development is not completed or which have low values. An additional point that bears on this conclusion is that, with $3 million of initial financing, in most outcomes the venture has far more cash than it needs. In fact, on average over the outcomes, the venture had over $1.86 million more cash than it required. This average is computed at the point where, for each outcome, surplus cash is at a minimum.

If $3 million is too much, how much is enough? To help find an answer, we ran the simulation again, but this time we used $2 million as the initial investment (Scenario 2). With the lower initial investment, there are many more outcomes in which the initial investment was not enough to carry the venture through the full 78 months of the simulation. Altogether, the venture would have needed additional financing about 17.4 percent of the time. Of this group, 11.2 percent of the total were outcomes with "no development" by month 78; 1.2 percent were outcomes with "slow development" and had not yet reached breakeven by month 78; and 3.0 percent were high-growth outcomes in which additional capital would have been needed to sustain the growth.[17] In none of the no-development or slow-development outcomes did the venture run out of initial cash before month 61, well after the product development stage was likely to have been completed. Average surplus cash with this level of initial financing was $0.94 million. The $2 million of initial financing was sufficient to fully fund NewCompany operations for 78 months in 82.6 percent of the cases, including 1.4 percent in which development was not completed, and 11.4 percent with income still negative by month 78.

With $1 million of initial investment (Scenario 3), the venture ran out of initial cash in 40.4 percent of the outcomes (12.2 percent with no sales by month 78, 4.4 percent with low sales, and 23.8 percent with high growth where additional cash was needed). The earliest point where

NewCompany Simulation Results for Alternative Financing Decisions
(In each case, results are based on 500 iterations of the model.)

Financing Scenario Description/ Simulation Results	Scenario 1: $3 million of initial investment capital in the form of equity	Scenario 2: $2 million of initial investment capital in the form of equity	Scenario 3: $1 million of initial investment capital in the form of equity	Scenario 4: $500 thousand of initial investment capital in the form of equity
Number of iterations where additional financing is needed to cover operations through month 78	Total = 4 Development not complete = 4 Net income still negative = 0 High-growth = 0	Total = 87 Development not complete = 56 Net income still negative = 6 High-growth = 15	Total = 202 Development not complete = 61 Net income still negative = 22 High-growth = 119	Total = 481 Development not complete = 58 Net income still negative = 65 High-growth = 127
Number of iterations where additional financing is not needed to cover operations through month 78	Total = 496 Development not complete = 51 Net income still negative = 65	Total = 413 Development not complete = 7 Net income still negative = 57	Total = 298 Development not complete = 0 Net income still negative = 50	Total = 19 Development not complete = 0 Net income still negative = 4
Average minimum level of surplus cash	$1.86 million	$.94 million	$.17 million	$.08 million
Earliest "out of cash" point for no-development or slow-development iterations	Month 76	Month 61	Month 38	Out of cash by month 25 or sooner in 25 iterations

Figure 7-7 NewCompany simulation results for alternative financing decisions

The figure shows results of simulating the performance of NewCompany with different amounts of initial equity. The simulation shows the conditions under which the starting equity investment is adequate compared to when additional financing is required. The model is used to find a level of initial financing such that the venture is likely to reach its next milestone (completion of product development) without running out of cash, but where the amount of initial financing is low enough that the venture cannot operate without additional financing if the probability of failure becomes high.

the venture ran out of initial cash was month 38, still well beyond the point where development was likely to have occurred. Average surplus cash was only $.17 million. However, the level of initial investment was still too high to screen out many of the outcomes with either slow growth or low profitability, as 10 percent of the outcomes were of these types.

Finally, we considered an initial investment of $500,000 (Scenario 4). The venture ran out of initial cash 96.2 percent of the time, including 11.6 percent with no development and 13 percent with low sales by month 78. The screen missed only four slow-growth outcomes. In 5 percent of the outcomes, the venture ran out of initial cash by month 25 or sooner, the point after which development was likely to have been completed.

To evaluate whether an initial cash investment of $500,000 is too high or too low, we ran the simulation again and studied the relation between development timing and running out of initial cash. Figure 7-8 shows graphically the relation between development timing and the point where the venture's initial cash level is at a minimum. The diagonal line in the figure divides the area so that above the line are points where development occurs before the minimum initial cash level is reached and points below the line are those where the minimum cash point occurs first. In all but about 5 percent of the cases, the minimum cash level is zero (i.e., the venture runs out of initial cash 95 percent of the time).

If the venture runs out of initial cash after development is complete, the entrepreneur can use the degree of development success to attract additional funds and the investors can use the same information to decide whether to make an additional investment. If initial cash is exhausted before the development milestone is reached, the entrepreneur is likely to have difficulty attracting additional capital and the existing investors will have to decide whether to put more money into the venture in the face of its limited development success. It is apparent from Figure 7-8 that in most of the simulated outcomes the results tend toward the extremes. Either development is complete well before the minimum cash point is reached or development occurs well after the minimum, if at all.

The following table contains a breakdown of the outcomes from the simulation according to whether NewCompany runs out of initial cash before development is complete, compared to either running out of cash after development or not running out.

Ultimate Development Success in Relation to Whether the NewCompany Venture Runs Out of Initial Cash Before Development Is Complete

	Total	Development Not Completed	Slow Growth	Moderate Growth	High Growth
Runs out before development complete	14.6%	11.0%	3.0%	0.6%	0.0%
Runs out after or does not run out	85.4%	0.0%	9.4%	54.8%	21.2%

The table shows that in 85.4 percent of the outcomes the venture did not run out of initial cash before development was complete. Furthermore, the venture did not run out of cash before development was completed in any of the high-growth outcomes, or for most of the moderate-growth outcomes. Conversely, the venture did run out of initial cash before development was complete in all cases in which development efforts ultimately were not successful and for about one-fourth of the slow-growth outcomes. Thus, from the perspective of the outside investor,

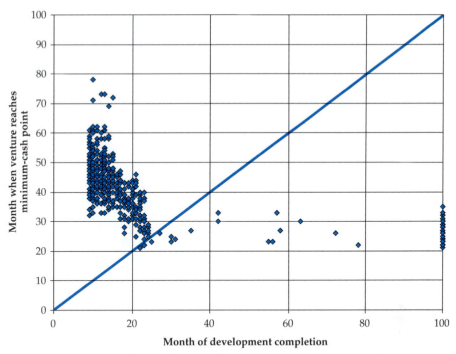

Figure 7-8 NewCompany: minimum cash point to development completion point

The figure shows the results of 500 iterations of the NewCompany simulation. The horizontal axis is the month when product development is completed, and the vertical axis is the month when the venture reaches its minimum point of available initial cash. The diagonal line divides the space into an upper region, where development is successful before the minimum cash point is reached, and a lower region, where the venture runs out of initial cash before development is complete. In cases where development occurs first, minimum cash occurs either because the growth rate of sales is very rapid or because profitability is low. Successful development provides a basis for seeking additional financing, particularly if the shortage of cash is due to rapid growth. In cases where the minimum-cash point is reached before development, the venture runs short of cash because development is taking significantly longer than expected. In these cases, the venture would have difficulty raising funds to continue development efforts.

making an initial investment of $500,000 enables the investor to base a second-stage investment decision on actual development success (and, in some cases, on market success) for almost all of the more attractive outcomes. For all of the no-development outcomes, staging the investment at this level of initial funding gives the investor an opportunity to make a subsequent investment decision before development is complete. Deciding not to invest additional funds at that point would exclude only a few of the slow- or moderate-growth outcomes.

An initial investment of $500,000 appears to be in the interest of the outside investor. Another consideration is that the investor may want to preserve the option of investing additional cash after development is completed. Failure to incorporate such an option would give the entrepreneur an opportunity to negotiate with third parties who did not invest in the first stage. Because the option to make a second-stage investment is valuable, granting the option to the first-stage investor should enable the entrepreneur to retain a larger fraction of the equity in the initial round.[18]

Is the initial investment a good one from the entrepreneur's perspective, or is the $500,000 too limiting? The answer depends on whether the entrepreneur will want to pursue the venture even if development is not completed by the time the venture runs out of cash. The arrangement should be acceptable if (given the high probability of failure at that point, and the limited up-side potential) the entrepreneur would not want to proceed. If the $500,000 is not attractive to the entrepreneur because of the risk of shutting down a viable venture, then some refinement of the agreement might be warranted. Feasible refinements could involve specifying additional milestones, with smaller incremental investments, or other contracting devices. We take up these concerns later in the text.

7.8 ASSESSING FINANCIAL NEEDS WITH STAGED INVESTMENT

Suppose the investor commits to a first-stage investment in NewCompany, with the expectation that, if development is successful, the venture will need additional funds. How much cash is the venture likely to need in the second round? To answer, we again use the simulation model with $500,000 of initial investment. Because the preceding analysis indicated that this amount normally would be sufficient to carry the venture through the twenty-fifth month, we modified the model so that additional cash would be invested at the twenty-fifth month in the event that development had been completed by that time.[19] If so, we assume a second-stage investment of $500,000. As, for NewCompany, the second-stage investment makes financial viability likely, we also allow the venture to borrow after development is complete and the second round of equity financing has been made.

Figure 7-9 illustrates a sample outcome from the simulation model, revised to include the second-stage investment in the event that development is successful by the twenty-fifth month. In the figure, development is successful, and NewCompany receives the second round of financing. The figure shows the time series pattern of sales revenue, net income, and cumulative surplus cash over the period covered by the simulation.

The result of these modifications to the model is that the venture failed to achieve development in time for second-stage financing in 16.4 percent of the runs. These included 10.4 percent in which development never was achieved and 6 percent where development was slow. For the 83.6 percent of the runs with second-stage investments, all had achieved sales by month 78, with ending monthly sales averaging $605,000, against which average borrowing was $184,000. This compares to average sales of $75,000 and average additional financing needs of $1,890,000 for the 16.4 percent of the outcomes in which no second-stage investment is made.

Clearly, staging can add to the overall value by reducing the total investment in scenarios where development does not go well. It would be possible to improve the expected results by designing in more flexibility about the timing and size of the second-stage investment. Such refinements would still involve commitments in the $500,000 range for the second stage.

7.9 SUMMARY

There are a number of analytical techniques for assessing financial needs. They range from the comparatively simple sustainable growth model and cash flow breakeven analysis to more complex methods that involve scenario analysis and simulation to study how uncertainty affects financial needs.

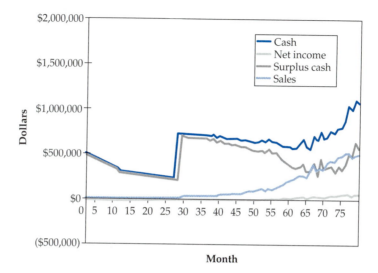

Figure 7-9 NewCompany cash sufficiency analysis

This figure shows one simulated scenario for the NewCompany venture, with $500,000 in initial equity and an additional investment of $500,000 in month 25. The second round of financing occurs only if product development efforts are successful. The illustrated scenario is one in which development is successful but product sales growth is slow. Consequently, in this scenario the cash surplus stays positive, and the $500,000 investment turns out to be more than the venture requires.

The value of the sustainable growth model is that it links a venture's ability to finance growth from operations to a few policy decisions. For any given growth objective, the model can help the entrepreneur understand when growth can be financed from operations and how much will need to be financed externally.

Cash flow breakeven analysis considers financial needs in a different way. On one level, the technique helps determine the level of sales a venture must achieve to finance its operations from cash flow. At that point, the venture is viable on a cash flow basis, but growth beyond the breakeven point would require additional capital. On another level, by combining cash flow breakeven analysis with a sales forecast, the entrepreneur can estimate the investment needed to sustain the venture until the breakeven point is reached.

Scenario analysis is a nonspecific approach to studying the effects of uncertainty. When the technique is applied to assessing financial needs, the objective is to gain an understanding of how those needs are different over a range of realistic scenarios. Scenario analysis can be combined easily with other methods of assessing financial needs. That is, the sustainable growth rate or cash flow breakeven point can be evaluated over a range of realistic scenarios to improve understanding of financial needs.

Simulation is by far the most powerful analytical tool for evaluating financial needs. Beginning with a firmly based financial model, the effects of key aspects of uncertainty can be evaluated simultaneously. Skillful application of simulation can help the entrepreneur or an outside investor design a financial structure that, while it preserves the potential for success, does so with a limited amount of investment capital. At the same time, the financial structure enables the entrepreneur and investors to avoid overinvesting once it becomes apparent that success is unlikely. By using simulation, it is simple to study the effects of subtle, but significant, changes in financing provisions.

QUESTIONS AND PROBLEMS

1. As a result of a merger, Mike Bloom has just received a golden handshake of $5 million from his former partners. Rather than taking a comfortable early retirement, he has decided to try to leverage the payment into something even more valuable. His plan is to use the money to start a new financial information service, and he is willing to invest all of the money, if necessary. His goal is to realize an annual return of $8 million per year beginning in five years. The $8 million is to be measured as his share of venture net income after tax.

    Bloom expects that each dollar invested in the venture can support $3 in annual sales and that the before-tax return on sales will average 15 percent per year if only equity financing is used. Debt financing is expected to cost 8 percent per year, and the corporate tax rate is 30 percent. Bloom plans to draw no investment income from the venture until the end of the fifth year. After that, he expects to be able to take his share of net income as a distribution each year.

    a. Can Bloom achieve his return objective by using debt financing? If so, what capital structure policy (with stable leverage ratio) will enable him to do so?

    b. Suppose an outside investor is interested in participating in the venture by contributing equity capital at the initiation of the venture. Doing so would enable the venture to start up on a larger scale. The investor wants 1 percent of total equity for each $250,000 of investment. Can Bloom achieve his objective using outside equity financing? If so, how much outside financing is needed?

    c. In the event that either debt or equity could be used to meet the objective, what other considerations should affect the choice? In particular, how might you expect issues of control and risk to bear on the decision?

2. What is the difference between a breakeven point measured in terms of net income and one measured in terms of cash flow? What factors would cause the two to be similar? What factors would cause them to be different?

3. Lillian Jordan is considering using some of the cash generated from her mail-order business to open a retail store. The fixed investment in the store is expected to be $3.5 million. The investment can be depreciated over five years, after which point annual expenditures of $300,000 will be sufficient to maintain the facility. These outlays can be expensed in the years they are made. The required investment in net working capital is expected to be 25 percent of annual sales. Variable cost is estimated to be 35 percent of sales.

    a. If annual fixed costs other than depreciation total $600,000, what is the cash flow breakeven point during the first five years? What is it after the fifth year? How does the cash flow breakeven point compare to the breakeven point of net income?

    b. Suppose Lillian projects first-year sales of $1 million, second-year sales of $4 million, and sales after the second year of $1.8 million. How much of an investment will be required to undertake the project? How much surplus cash is the venture expected to generate each year in the first six years of operation?

4. Look back at problem 1.

    a. How does the sustainable growth rate of the venture with all equity financing change under the scenario where the service is very well-received by the financial community, so that each dollar of investment can support $3.75 worth of sales and the profitability of sales is 20 percent? What does this do to the amount of equity financing that is required to achieve the objective?

    b. How are your conclusions affected by a scenario in which the product is not very well-received, so that each dollar of investment supports only $2.50 worth of sales and the profitability of sales is 10 percent?

    c. How are your conclusions in parts (a) and (b) affected if outside debt financing is used instead of equity.

    d. Do the results of the scenario analysis affect your perceptions of the relative merits of debt or equity financing in this case? If so, how, and why?

5. Look back at problem 3 and develop a 10-year simulation model that incorporates the following elements of uncertainty.

- The level of sales in the first year is uncertain. The expected level is $1 million, and the uncertainty can be represented as a normal distribution with a standard deviation of $100,000.

- The level of sales in the second year is expected to be $3 million above the level in the first year. The uncertainty about the actual growth can be represented as a normal distribution with a standard deviation of $200,000.

- The level of sales in the third year is expected to be $1.2 million below the level in the second year, with a standard deviation of actual growth of $200,000.

- After the third year, expected sales is equal to sales in the prior year, with uncertainty about the level being represented as a standard deviation of $75,000.

- The magnitude of the initial fixed investment is uncertain, with a standard deviation of $200,000 around the mean from problem 3.

- Working capital requirements increase when sales are higher than expected and decline if sales are lower than expected, but not to the same extent as the base investment in net working capital. The required level of net working capital is 25 percent of expected sales, plus 10 percent of the difference between actual and expected sales in any year (where the expected level of sales is determined based on actual sales in the prior year).

- When demand is high, more merchandise can be sold with a full markup. When it is low, more discounting is required. The uncertainty of variable cost can be represented as a standard deviation of 2 percent applied to 35 percent of expected sales, plus 50 percent of the difference between actual and expected sales.

- All other assumptions are the same as in problem 3.

    a. Use the simulation model to estimate expected surplus cash in each of the first five years of operation. Be sure to include the amount of initial investment and required increases in net working capital. How much investment capital is needed each year (0 through 5), if performance is as expected? How much is needed each year to cover the results in 75 percent of the outcomes?

    b.   Are there any outcomes in your analysis in which the venture fails to achieve positive cash flow by year 6 and beyond? If so, and if Lillian would want to abandon the venture as soon as it becomes apparent that positive cash flows after year five are unlikely, how much initial investment capital is needed to pursue the venture? What criteria would you recommend for deciding whether to abandon the venture to meet this objective? Be as creative as you can in designing a response to this question.

6.   Look back at the asset-driven models of performance in problems 1 and 4. Suppose the probability of the scenario in problem 1 is 0.4, and the probabilities of the optimistic and pessimistic scenarios in problem 4 (a) and (b) are each 0.3.

    a.   Consider an inside equity investment of $5 million and initial outside equity levels of $0, $5 million (for 20 percent of total equity), $10 million (for 40 percent of total equity), and $15 million (for 60 percent of total equity). If all net income can be distributed beginning in year five, how does the entrepreneur fair in each scenario with each level of outside equity investment? What is the expected distribution to the entrepreneur? Which level of outside equity financing do you favor and why? (Plan your Excel work carefully, so you can easily explore these alternative strategies.)

    b.   Consider an initial inside equity investment of $5 million, and debt to equity ratios of 0:1, 0.2:1, 0.4:1, and 0.6:1. If all net income can be distributed beginning in year five, how does the entrepreneur fair in each scenario with each level of outside debt investment? What is the expected distribution to the entrepreneur? Which level of outside debt financing do you favor and why?

    c.   Considering your answers in parts (a) and (b), do you favor equity or debt financing. Why? What, if any, changes in performance expectations would lead you to prefer the other form of outside financing (e.g., debt instead of equity)? Why?

7.   EBIT/Sales = 5 percent, Sales/Assets = 2, Assets/Equity = 2, the dividend payout ratio = 0.3, the interest rate on debt = 10 percent, and the tax rate = 40 percent.

    a.   What is the sustainable growth rate?

    b.   How does the sustainable growth rate change in response to reducing any of the above ratios or percentages by one-half (e.g., EBIT/Sales = 2.5 percent)?

    c.   How does the sustainable growth rate change in response to increasing any of the above ratios or percentages by one-half (e.g., EBIT/Sales = 7.5 percent)?

    d.   Do some changes have greater impacts on the sustainable growth rate than others? Are the effects linear or nonlinear? Explain your findings.

8.   Refer back to problem 7. Suppose EBIT/Sales has an expected value of 5 percent with a standard deviation of 3 percent, Sales/Assets has an expected value of 2 with a standard deviation of 0.3, the interest rate is expected to be 10 percent with a standard deviation of 1 percent, and the tax rate is 40 percent if net taxable income is positive but zero if net income is negative.

    a.   Build a simulation model of the sustainable growth rate. Set up the model so the leverage ratio and payout ratio are policy choices and dividend yield (the ratio of dividend payout to equity investment) is the objective.

b. Simulate the model with the initial assumptions to determine the expected sustainable growth rate and its standard deviation.

c. Using the leverage ratio and payout ratio as policy choices, try to design a policy that maximizes the expected value of the dividend yield.

d. Using the leverage ratio and payout ratio as policy choices, try to design a policy that provides an expected dividend yield of three percent with the lowest risk (as measured by the standard deviation of dividend yield from the simulation).

9. Consider the Ink magazine example in Section 7.4. Suppose that, instead of $15, the price per subscription is only $8. At the level of 250,000 subscribers, advertising revenue is expected to be $9 per subscription; at 400,000 subscribers, it is expected to be $15 per subscription; and at 550,000 subscriptions, it is expected to be $18 per subscription. Average variable expenses are expected to be $22 per subscription at 250,000 subscribers, $20 per subscriber at 400,000 subscribers, and $18 at 550,000 subscribers. Other assumptions, those pertaining to fixed expenses, tax rate, depreciation, and capital replacement, are as shown in Figure 7-2.

a. Revise Figures 7-2 and 7-3 to reflect the new assumptions.

b. Use the graphical technique discussed in Section 7.4 to estimate the venture's expected operating cash needs in each of the first three years, assuming that the venture expects 300,000 subscribers in the first year, 400,000 in the second year, and 500,000 in the third year. (Keep in mind that this estimate does not include the initial investment or investments in working capital necessitated by growth).

10. Reconsider problem 9. Suppose the level of subscribers in each of the first three years could be 30 percent higher or lower than the expected level; variable cost per subscription in each year could be 20 percent higher or lower than the expected level; and advertising revenue per subscription in each year could be 20 percent higher or lower than expected. Construct a scenario analysis to assess the sensitivity of annual operating cash needs to these variations in performance.

11. Download Figure 7-9 and go to the worksheet that contains the financial model (the "New-Company Simulation" tab). Prepare the spreadsheet for a new analysis by editing the cells shaded in red in the worksheet. First, find the "Development Success Test" in month 25 and disable it (you can do this easily by setting the conditional second-round investment to "0" even if development is successful. Second, find the "Initiate Sales Binary Flag" row and change the assumption so that before month 13 the flag has a value of zero; from month 13 through month 48 the flag in each month is a binary variable with a 5 percent chance of returning a "1" and is otherwise zero; and after month 48 the flag has a value of zero. This change means the development efforts will take at least one year, after the year, there is a 5 percent chance of success in each month (conditional on no success in the a prior month), and after month 48 development is not worth pursuing.

a. Redo the kind of analysis illustrated in Figure 7-7, testing various levels of initial cash and examining the scenarios where the venture runs out of cash versus those where it does not. Try to find a level of initial investment where development has a good chance of being successful but that does not provide excessive financing in scenarios where the venture does not do well or where it does so well that additional financing would be easy to get.

b. Based on your analysis in part (a), move the development Success Test to an appropriate month and try to determine an appropriate amount for the second-round investment.

Don't be surprised if you cannot find a sharp line of demarcation between good and bad outcomes. The assumption changes in this problem make the optimal financing choice less clear than in the text example.

NOTES

1. Cooper, Gimeno-Gascon, and Woo (1994) find evidence that both initial human capital and initial financial capital contribute to new venture survival and growth.

2. Stancill (1992) clarifies that initial financing should be adequate to advance the venture to the point where a significant milestone has been achieved so that second-round financing is possible.

3. Sahlman (1992) provides an overview of some issues related to assessing financial needs and valuation.

4. See Higgins (1995) and Donaldson (1991) for additional discussion of sustainable growth.

5. The Goal Seek tool in Excel can carry out the trial and error search for you.

6. The same question could be examined from the perspective of an investor and the same issues would arise, but the conclusions could be somewhat different.

7. For clarity, and because the distinction is important when we address valuation, we distinguish between funds that are generated from outside sources and funds that are generated from external sources. Sources of funding other than the entrepreneur are referred to throughout the text as outside financing sources. These include venture capitalists, lenders, and angels. Funds can be generated internally from operations or externally from new investment. External sources include new investment by both the entrepreneur and outside investors.

8. In the accounting approach, the breakeven point is the level of sales where the total contribution margin over all units sold equals total fixed cost. The contribution margin is the difference between price and variable cost. So, for example, if the price is $20 per unit and variable cost is $16, the contribution margin is $4 per unit. With total fixed cost of $700,000, the breakeven point is 43,750 units, or $175,000 in sales. See Reinhardt (1973) for a case study involving breakeven analysis.

9. In this illustration, we are not assuming any debt financing. Consequently, the net income breakeven point is the same as the EBIT breakeven point.

10. The new breakeven point is estimated by assuming all other revenue and expense items are unchanged and re-computing net income after tax.

11. Projected cash shortfalls have not been discounted to present value. If financing is staged to match cash needs, discounting is not necessary. If financing is received in advance, projected cash shortfalls can be discounted at the interest rate the venture can earn by investing the funds until they are required. For the purpose of an investment decision, a different discount rate would be appropriate.

12. The magazine publishing business is somewhat unusual in that rapid growth can actually reduce financing needs. Because magazine subscriptions usually are paid annually, in advance of publication, and advertising receivables are of much shorter duration, current liabilities can

exceed current assets and net working capital can be negative. An increase in a negative net working capital balance is a source of funds. Hence, growth can reduce cash needs.

13. See Brealey and Myers (2003) for an illustration of present-value breakeven analysis.

14. Scenario analysis is different from sensitivity analysis. Sensitivity analysis is used to examine the effects of changing variables one-at-a-time.

15. The Internet site for this text contains a copy of the Excel spreadsheet used in the simulation. You can use the spreadsheet to examine how the assumptions are reflected in the model and to experiment with alternative assumptions. The spreadsheet also provides for financing to be staged.

16. Preferred stock issues sometimes incorporate such call provisions.

17. We classify ventures as "high growth" based on the rate of increase in sales after development is complete. Scenarios with high sales growth and profitable operations are likely to be able to finance growth with later-stage financing. Running out of cash from the initial round is not of particular concern for these outcomes.

18. Note, however, that first right of refusal options such as this can cause difficulties if the entrepreneur wants, or needs, to look elsewhere for second-round funding. Other investors are usually reticent to undertake serious due diligence if an existing investor can simply agree to meet their offer.

19. This modified version of the model is the one available on the Web site.

REFERENCES AND ADDITIONAL READING

BATY, GORDON. *Entrepreneurship in the Nineties.* 5th edition, Englewood Cliffs, NJ: Prentice-Hall, 1990.

BREALEY, RICHARD, AND STEWART MYERS. *Principles of Corporate Finance.* 7th edition, New York: McGraw-Hill, 2003.

COOPER, ARNOLD C., F. JAVIER GIMENO-GASCON, AND CAROLYN Y. WOO. "Initial Human and Financial Capital as Predictors of New Venture Performance." *Journal of Business Venturing* 9 (1994): 371–390.

DONALDSON, GORDON. "Financial Goals and Strategic Consequences." In *Strategy, Seeking and Securing Competitive Advantage.* Edited by Cynthia Montgomery and Michael Porter. Cambridge, MA: Harvard Business School Press, 1991.

HIGGINS, ROBERT C. *Analysis for Financial Managers.* Chicago: Irwin, 1995.

KAPLAN, JERRY. *Startup.* New York: Penguin Books, 1994.

REINHARDT, UWE E. "Break-even Analysis for Lockheed TriStar: An Application of Financial Theory." *Journal of Finance* 28 (1973): 821–838.

SAHLMAN, WILLIAM A. "The Financial Perspective: What Should Entrepreneurs Know?" In *The Entrepreneurial Venture.* Edited by William A. Sahlman and Howard H. Stevenson. Cambridge, MA: Harvard Business School Press, 1992.

STANCILL, JAMES M. "How Much Money Does Your New Venture Need?" In *Launching the New Venture.* Edited by William A. Sahlman and Howard H. Stevenson. Boston: Harvard Business School Publications, 1992.

The Framework of New Venture Valuation

My ventures are not in one bottom trusted, Nor in one place; Nor is my whole estate
Upon the fortune of this present year; Therefore, my merchandise makes me not sad.
(William Shakespeare, *Merchant of Venice*, Act 1, Scene 1)

Learning Objectives

After reading this chapter you will be able to:

- Recognize the difference between the "hurdle rates" often used by investors to value new ventures and the realized rates of return.

- Explain why hurdle rates generally are much higher than realized rates of return.

- Understand that the hurdle rate is not the opportunity cost of capital for investment.

- Use the Capital Asset Pricing Model (CAPM) to determine the opportunity cost of capital.

- Use either the risk-adjusted discount rate form or the certainty equivalent form of the CAPM to value a financial claim.

- Recognize the limitations of the CAPM, particularly as they relate to valuing new ventures.

- Understand the differences between the CAPM and Option Pricing Model (OPM), and reconcile their use for valuing financial claims on new ventures.

- Recognize that in a competitive capital market, investors in new ventures cannot expect to earn returns on diversifiable risk.

- Understand that the entrepreneur and the outside investor can strike a better deal if both realize that their valuations are likely to differ and recognize the sources of the differences.

How do venture capitalists and other outside investors select the projects in which to invest? And how do they settle on the ownership stakes, terms, and conditions they require in exchange for investing? There are no simple answers to these questions. Certainly, the perceived value of

INTERNET RESOURCES FOR THIS CHAPTER

In this chapter we introduce and discuss several different asset pricing models that are used to value financial and real assets. If you wish to learn more about the different models, the Web site contains links to sources with relevant information. As we go forward, the mathematics of time value and basic statistics are important tools. If you would like a refresher on approaches to computing present value, you can download Appendix 8A and the tutorial on the Mathematics of Time Value, and work through the problems and exercises. If you would like to review the statistics we will be using, you can download Appendix 8B and work through the statistics tutorial.

the concept and capabilities of the entrepreneur are critical hurdles to investing. No venture will be funded unless an investor sees the merits of the concept and regards the entrepreneur as capable of implementing it or of working with the investor to build a capable team.

In addition, there are issues of "fit" and timing. Is the project one in which the investor can contribute to overall value? Does the investor have the financial and organizational capacity to take on another project? The answers to these questions depend on the particular expertise of the investor and on whether, at the time, the investor is looking for new projects or is fully committed to existing projects. We address issues of fit and timing later in the text when we examine how different types of investors operate and the functions they perform.

The concern of this chapter is more specific. We analyze, at a conceptual level, how investors value new venture investment opportunities. In Chapter 9 we look more pragmatically at the specific methods investors use. In Chapter 10 we consider valuation from the perspective of the entrepreneur and examine how differences in the risk tolerance of investors and entrepreneurs give rise to opportunities to design financial contracts that enhance the investment value of an opportunity.

8.1 PERSPECTIVES ON VALUATION OF NEW VENTURES

The value of any investment depends on its ability to generate future cash flows, as well as on investor assessments of, and attitudes toward, the riskiness of the future cash flows. Two aspects of valuation make investment decisions about entrepreneurial projects particularly difficult. First, the future cash flows of a prospective new venture, although they are a fundamental determinant of value, are very difficult to estimate. Second, the discount rates appropriate for estimating the present value of the future cash flows are difficult to estimate.

In spite of the near impossibility of precision, earnings or cash flow forecasts appear in most business plans, and forecasts are made and studied by venture capitalists and other investors who are shopping for deals. In the previous chapter, we presented several approaches for forecasting performance and for using the forecast information to estimate financial needs. Those same approaches can be used to estimate the future cash flow returns to investors and to quantify uncertainty. In addition, the problem of determining an appropriate discount rate is addressed routinely by venture capitalists and other outside investors. As you will see, financial economic theory provides considerable guidance for estimating discount rates that are appropriate for new ventures.

In an area as competitive and complex as investing in new ventures, the importance of good decision-making methods cannot be overemphasized. One indicator of the potential for good decision making to add value is the variation of investment performance of venture capital funds. Venture Economics reports that the internal rate of return (IRR) of funds formed between 1969 and 1996 ranged from less than –50 to more than 100 percent per year. About half of the funds generated returns in the zero to 20 percent range.[1] Low rates of return can result from unfortunate timing, bad luck, and unforeseeable negative events. However, the important reasons for low rates of return are valuation mistakes and deal structuring mistakes. Both of these problems can be avoided (or, at least, minimized) by using decision-making methods that give the investor a competitive advantage over its rivals in both project selection and deal structuring.

In 1995, Charles Tschampion, managing director of the General Motors pension fund, remarked, "Investment management is not art, not science, it's engineering."[2] His point is that the business of investment management has moved away from an emphasis on stock selection and toward investment decision making based on an objective of efficiently trading off the risks and returns of individual investments in the context of a diversified portfolio of investments.

Compared to investing in the stock market, investing in new ventures is at a more primitive stage. But the market is changing. New venture investment decisions are becoming increasingly sophisticated. As documented earlier in the text, investments in venture capital funds are made predominantly by institutions that employ sophisticated money managers. Although the money managers base the majority of their investment decisions on the principles of market efficiency, they continue to seek out opportunities to invest in new markets, where it still may be possible to add value by tactical selection of individual investments.

The arrival of professional investment managers to venture capital investing has changed the market in fundamental ways. Most important for our purpose is the changing way investment opportunities are valued by outside investors. In time, we can expect that those changes will affect the ways entrepreneurs evaluate projects. Because the market is changing, some of the approaches and rules of thumb that have been used historically for investing in new ventures no longer can be relied upon to identify projects that are likely to yield acceptable rates of return.

8.2 MYTHS ABOUT NEW VENTURE VALUATION

Past practice has generated four myths about new venture investing. Because of the way the market is changing, the myths no longer serve the interest of either the entrepreneur or the investor. We begin the study of new venture valuation by examining these myths. Following that, we present an overview of valuation theory, as it applies to new venture investing. Much of the material on valuation is derived from the fundamentals of portfolio theory.

Myth 1: Beauty Is in the Eye of the Beholder.

Over a decade ago, Gordon Baty (1990) wrote, "Pricing a new company's stock is much like pricing any other glamour item (such as perfume, paintings, rare coins) where appeal is based on emotional, as well as analytical considerations."[3] However, given the significant increase in professional management of investments in new ventures, this notion no longer rings true. Professional investment managers recognize the economic tradeoff between cash flow and risk and are not influenced by the "emotional considerations" of an investment. To the managers of investment funds, the particular product market focus of the venture is only important for what it portends for cash flows and for how the risk of the venture fits into the investor's portfolio. Certainly, investment managers differ about the values they place on ventures in different industries. But these differences reflect varying, but informed, expectations about future cash flows the investors will receive, rather than any "psychic" value that may come from investing in a particular venture.

We know of an entrepreneur who is working on two new products. One promises a cure for glaucoma, a disease that leads to blindness for many people every year and where existing treatments are inadequate. The other is an implant that works somewhat like PRK surgery to improve vision for people who are near-sighted. In terms of the "feel good" nature of the products, the glaucoma treatment seems much more socially beneficial. As the entrepreneur noted, however, "Our investors do not care about the social good that the product does. They care about return on investment, and there are many more people who would like to get rid of their eye glasses than people who would be customers for the glaucoma product." This is not meant to be an indictment of new venture investing. In fact, it is the process of capitalism at work. Flows of investment capital are guided by consumer demand. If investors perceive that demand for the glaucoma product is sufficient to cover the cost of development, then that, too, will be funded.

Myth 2: The Future Is Anybody's Guess.

This is a more reasonable-sounding version of Myth 1. The claim is that, even though cash flow is what matters, future cash flows are so uncertain that forecasting them is not of much value. Often it is argued that an entrepreneurial venture faces too many unknowns to predict revenues with any precision. Forecasting cash flows is even more challenging.

Although new venture forecasts are subject to great uncertainty, rather than making the forecast worthless, uncertainty makes forecasting critical. In particular, it is important to try to understand the extent and nature of the uncertainty. It is true that a single-scenario forecast for a new venture is not likely to be of much value. However, scenario analysis and simulation are of considerable practical value for understanding and dealing with the risks and for valuing the venture.

Both the entrepreneur and potential investors gain important information from forecasts of future cash flows. Regardless of whether the forecasts are formal or not, the investment decisions hinge on the adequacy of future cash flows compared to the cost of the investment.

Myth 3: Investors Demand Very High Rates of Return to Compensate for the Risks They Are Taking.

New ventures are high-risk investments that tie up the investor's capital for several years, with no easy means of exit. These considerations have led to a broadly held perception that the required rates of return are very high. On this subject, Michael Roberts and Howard Stevenson write, "In order to compensate for the high risk of their investments, give their own investors a handsome return, and make a profit for themselves, venture firms seek a high rate of return. Target returns of 50% or 60% are not uncommon."[4] Stanley Rich and David Gumpert offer a similar view. They state, "Because risk and reward are closely related, investors believe companies with fully developed products and proven management teams should yield between 35% and 40% on their investment, while those with incomplete products and management teams are expected to bring in 60% annual compounded returns."[5] Jeffrey Timmons provides a more comprehensive summary that echoes the same point:

Rates of Return (ROR) Sought by Venture Capital Investors

Stage	Annual ROR%	Typical Expected Holding Period (Years)
Seed and start-up	50–100% or more	More than 10
First stage	40–60%	5–10
Second stage	30–40%	4–7
Expansion	20–30%	3–5
Bridge and mezzanine	20–30%	1–3
LBOs	30–50%	3–5
Turnarounds	50%+	3–5

Source: Jeffrey A. Timmons, *New Venture Creation*, 5th ed. (Chicago: Irwin, 1999), p. 465.

Scholars and others who remark on the high rates of return base their statements on historical practice, generally asking venture capital investors to identify the rates they apply when discounting the projected cash flows of proposed new ventures. Approaching the question in this way, they find the rates typically are quite high.

An alternative way to estimate required rates of return is to examine, over a long period of years, the actual average returns for investing in new ventures. Such evidence tells a much different story. For example, in a 1976 study of 92 venture capital firms, the average return during the 1960s and early 1970s was 14 percent.[6] Another study from the same year examines returns before management fees for a sample of over 100 investments by venture capital firms made from 1960 through 1968, and finds an average return through 1975 of 23 percent, before deducting management fees.[7] A reasonable adjustment for fees results in a net return of 18 to 19 percent. A 1987 study of the stock price performance of public venture capital firms over the period from 1959 through 1985 finds an average return of 16 percent.[8] The highest average rate of return, 27 percent, is from a 1983 study of the stock price performance of 11 venture capital firms over a short period of five years, from 1974 through 1979.[9]

A more recent study uses data compiled by Venture Economics, Inc. to examine annual internal rates of return of venture capital funds from 1974 through 1989. Over that 16-year period, the maximum return on a capitalization-weighted basis was 32 percent. The minimum was a negative return of 3 percent. The compound annual return over the entire period was approximately 13.5 percent.[11] The latest available data reveal that the internal rate of return (IRR) performance of venture capital funds over the past decade has roughly paralleled the performance of the stock market. The 20-year holding period venture capital IRR ending in mid-2002 was 16.9 percent, most of which was generated in the late 1990s and partially offset by negative returns in the most recent years. Returns to investments in venture capital funds in Europe and Japan were similar over this period, averaging 14.4 percent in Japan and 14.2 percent in Europe.[11]

To summarize, the evidence of actual returns from investing in new ventures suggests that the typical returns are in the mid to high teens. Higher rates can be found for short periods, but the overall performance is nothing like the 30 to even as high as 100 percent returns that are often mentioned.

How can the common practice of using very high rates to value individual projects be reconciled with the evidence that over many years the average realized return for investing in new ventures has been much lower? Do investors suffer from chronic unfounded optimism so that actual returns have been disappointingly low? Or is there another interpretation of the evidence, one that does not rely on biased decision-making methods? Surely if rates of return in the neighborhood of 60 percent could be expected, capital would flood the new venture market, driving the returns to levels that are more consistent with those for other forms of investment.

The reality is that true required rates of return are much closer to the range documented in the empirical studies than to the very high rates that sometimes are sought by investors when they evaluate individual projects. Later in the chapter we examine how required rates of return are determined. We also offer a reconciliation of the above statements and evidence that places the statements in a more useful context and demonstrates that the actual required rates are much lower. The point for now is that the contradiction is more apparent than real.

Myth 4: The Outside Investor Determines the Value of the Venture.

Some writers contend that it is pointless for the entrepreneur to undertake a valuation. They argue that investors do not accept the entrepreneur's valuation anyway, so the entrepreneur's efforts are better spent in other ways. The problem with this view is that it fails to recognize the pivotal role that valuation plays in reaching agreement between the entrepreneur and the investor and the role it can play in helping the entrepreneur decide whether to undertake the venture.

It is true that outside investors commonly prepare their own valuations based on their own research and assumptions. However, there is more to new venture financing negotiations than a simple exchange of cash for a percentage of the equity. In the context of a financing negotiation, valuation is important to the entrepreneur for three reasons. First, the entrepreneur can better understand how the venture is likely to be valued by prospective investors. Second, the entrepreneur can better understand what the venture should be worth to herself and how that differs from value to the investor. Third, the entrepreneur needs to understand how alternative deal structures affect overall value and the values of the financial claims of the investors and the entrepreneur.

By estimating the value to prospective investors, the entrepreneur can gain a sense of how much ownership must be exchanged for a certain amount of financing. Because the overall value to investors depends, in part, on product-market and organizational strategy, the entrepreneur can use a valuation model to examine strategic alternatives from the perspective of investors. For this purpose, the entrepreneur should base the valuation on projections and assumptions that investors are likely to use.[12]

Venture capital investors report that many of their negotiations fail. They fail not because the idea is bad or the entrepreneur is the wrong person to carry it out. Rather, they fail because the entrepreneur does not have a clear sense of what the outside investor requires in order to make the deal attractive. Good working knowledge of valuation can help the entrepreneur avoid a breakdown of negotiations.

For a variety of reasons, the entrepreneur is likely to place a different value on the opportunity than would outside investors. Most importantly, the entrepreneur can be expected to have a different attitude toward the risk and may also be more optimistic about the prospects for the venture.[13] Hence, valuation can help the entrepreneur compare alternative strategies and assess whether the venture is worth pursuing.

In addition, valuation can help the entrepreneur avoid conceptual errors that impair the ability to secure financing. For example, entrepreneurs sometimes try to seek financing based on their sunk investments, rather than the potential for the venture to generate cash flows. Because the investor's concern is future cash flows, an entrepreneur's efforts to recover sunk investment through the financing terms can result in failure of negotiations.

Finally, the deal structure can enhance the overall value of the venture and can be used to allocate value between the entrepreneur and investors. Among other things, the parties are concerned with determining milestones to which the investor's financing commitments can be anchored. The ownership claims held by the entrepreneur and by investors often are complex and involve arrays of rights, options, and obligations. Complexity makes valuing the financial claims difficult.

The entrepreneur might expect that competition among prospective investors can eliminate the need to value complex financial claims. This expectation is incorrect. Even if several investors are vying to participate in a venture, they probably will seek different structures of ownership claims and propose different financing commitments. Without the ability to study the valuation consequences of different proposals, choosing the best alternative can be problematic for the entrepreneur.

Furthermore, even if, in the early stages of negotiation, several potential investors court the entrepreneur, the negotiation can become bilateral when later rounds of financing are sought. In a bilateral negotiation, the entrepreneur is less able to rely on market forces to produce favorable allocations of value. One reason for the shift to bilateral negotiation is that the investor who finances the first round gains an information advantage over others in later

The Many Uses of Valuation

Business valuation is one of the most challenging, yet consequential, types of analysis an entrepreneur undertakes. Valuation is not a one-time occurrence. In fact, many different kinds of events can trigger the need for a valuation. Among the triggers are the following:

- Strategic planning—The choice of strategy depends on how each alternative contributes to value.
- Estate planning—Estate tax liability depends on market value. For a nonpublic venture, market value must be estimated.
- Partnership formation and dissolution—The fractional interest that is assigned to a new partner is likely to depend on a valuation, and partnership agreements often include reciprocal buyout provisions, where buyout offers depend on valuation.
- Initial public offering (IPO)—The price at which new shares are offered to investors depends on the value of the venture.
- Stock options and employee stock ownership plans (ESOPs)—Contributions to ESOPs and the terms of stock option arrangements depend on the value of the venture.
- Mezzanine financing—Mezzanine debt often includes equity "sweeteners," such as warrants. The value of such sweeteners depends on the value of the underlying venture.
- Negotiating a merger or sale of the venture—The terms of exchange depend on the value of the venture and the value of financial claims that are exchanged for ownership of the venture.

rounds of financing. A second reason is that financing provisions agreed to in the first round may give the investor an advantage over others in later rounds.

8.3 AN OVERVIEW OF VALUATION METHODS

The value of any investment is the present value of its future cash flows. Although a variety of methods exist for estimating value, they all are attempting to measure, either directly or indirectly, the present worth of the right to receive future cash flows.

Valuation is guided by two fundamental principles: that a dollar today is worth more than a dollar received in the future; and that a safe dollar is worth more than a gamble with an expected payoff of one dollar. Thus, the present value of any investment depends on the timing of expected cash flows and on the riskiness of the cash flows.

In this chapter we describe two methods for estimating present value. The first commonly is referred to as the risk-adjusted discount rate (RADR) method. The second is referred to as the certainty equivalent cash flow (CEQ) method. If the methods are applied in a consistent manner, they will yield identical estimates of present value. However, the information that is needed to implement the two methods differs. Thus, availability of information is the primary determinant of which to use.

The RADR method is used most commonly in corporate finance because it is convenient and because the information requirements are satisfied by using data on comparable public firms. In the RADR method, an expected future cash flow is converted to present value by applying a discount rate that reflects both the time value of money and the riskiness of the future cash flow. We refer to this as the risk-adjusted discount rate method because consideration of how risk affects the value is built into the discount rate that is applied to the expected cash flow. For a particular project, j, that yields an uncertain cash flow at time, t, the appropriate discount rate for valuing the expected cash flow can be stated as follows:

$$r_{jt} = r_{Ft} + RP_{jt} \tag{8.1}$$

where r_{Ft} is the required rate of return (or cost of capital) for investing in a risk-free asset that would pay off at the same time as the cash flow that is being valued, and RP_{jt} is a risk adjustment to the discount rate. The risk adjustment depends, in some fashion, on the riskiness of the future cash flow.

To use the RADR method, you must be able to forecast expected future cash flows, estimate the risk-free rate, and estimate the appropriate risk premium to include in the discount rate. The primary impediment to using the RADR method for valuing a new venture is that the appropriate risk premium is difficult to estimate, particularly if public market data for comparable projects is not available.

In the CEQ method, instead of adjusting the discount rate, the risk adjustment is made directly to the cash flow. Then the risk-adjusted (or certainty equivalent) cash flow is converted to present value by discounting at the risk-free rate. Thus, if C_{jt} is the expected future cash flow of asset j at time t, the certainty equivalent cash flow, $CE(C_{jt})$, can be described as follows:

$$CE(C_{jt}) = C_{jt} - RD_{jt} \tag{8.2}$$

where RD_{jt} is the dollar-valued discount to C_{jt} that is required to convert the risky expected cash flow to its certainty equivalent.

To use the CEQ method, it is again necessary to forecast the expected future cash flow and the risk-free rate. But instead of estimating the percentage risk premium to apply to the discount rate, it is necessary to estimate the dollar-valued risk discount to apply to the expected cash flow. It turns out that for new ventures it is often easier to estimate the dollar-valued risk discount than the percentage risk premium. In the subsequent discussions we examine both approaches.

8.4   VALUATION BY THE RISK-ADJUSTED DISCOUNT RATE METHOD

Under the RADR method, expected future cash flows are discounted to present value using a discount factor that reflects the time value of money and the riskiness of the future cash flows. The present value, PV_j, of an investment that offers a series of expected future cash flows, C_{jt}, is given as

$$PV_j = \sum_t \frac{C_{jt}}{(1 + r_t)^t} \tag{8.3}$$

In Eq. (8.3), r_t is the risk-adjusted discount rate that is appropriate for computing the present value of an expected future cash flow at time t. The expression is general in that it allows for cash flows to be received at any time and for the cost of capital to be specific to the period in which the flow is expected.

Our purpose in this subsection is to provide the background necessary for application of Eq. (8.3) to the problem of valuing an investment. We provide conceptual answers to two questions. First, what cash flows are appropriate to include in the valuation model? Second, what is the RADR or cost of capital that is appropriate for valuing each expected cash flow?

Identifying Relevant Cash Flows

On a conceptual level, determining the cash flows to include in a valuation is straightforward. They are the cash flows the investor can expect to receive in exchange for investing. The first step for identifying the relevant cash flows is to determine exactly what asset is being valued. For our purpose, the asset may be the entire venture, or it may be a particular financial claim on the venture, such as common stock, preferred stock, debt, or an option.

The second step is to determine the cash flows investors in the asset can expect to receive. A share of stock, for example, yields cash flows in the form of dividends. An investor who owns the shares for a finite period, of course, does not receive the entire dividend stream but receives a lump-sum payment when the shares are sold. Because that payment depends on the stream of dividends from that point forward, implicitly the dividend cash flows are being valued, even by an investor who plans to sell the shares in the near future.[14] Debt is expected to yield a stream of interest payments and eventual repayment of principal. If the debt is risky, the interest payments and principal repayment to be valued are not those specified in the debt contract. Rather, they are the cash flows that are expected to be received, recognizing that the borrower may default on the obligation. If the asset to be valued is an option, the relevant cash flows depend on the probability of the option being exercised and the cash flows that are expected to be received in the event of exercise.

In a valuation conducted on behalf of an individual who is involved in the venture, relevant cash flows include the value of expected compensation, to the extent that the value of the compensation exceeds the value of expected compensation in the best alternative employment. Sometimes an investor in a new venture (such as a venture capitalist) takes on a managerial or advisory role. In this case, the cash flows to be valued should be adjusted for the opportunity cost of the investor's time.[15]

For valuation, it is important that the relevant cash flows be identified correctly. As an aid to identification, Figure 8-1 includes examples of cash flows that are appropriate for valuing debt and equity claims. The first group of concepts in the figure are expected cash flows, assuming the actual capital structure. In addition, the figure identifies two measures of hypothetical cash flows that sometimes are used to estimate value. Contractual cash flow to creditors is different from expected cash flow to creditors because default risk and the potential for early repayment are ignored in contractual cash flow. We include this definition in Figure 8-1 to emphasize the difference between expected cash flows and contractual cash flows. Unlevered free cash flow is a measure of expected cash flow on total assets assuming no debt financing. The fundamental difference between unlevered free cash flow and expected cash flow to all investors is the difference between taxes under the actual capital structure and theoretical taxes as if the venture were unlevered.

Some informal valuation approaches are based on a narrower concept of operating cash flows—EBIT plus depreciation expense and amortization expense (EBITDA). While EBITDA is convenient to compute, it does not provide for capital replacement or expected growth. Consequently, EBITDA is not a measure of the cash flows investors can expect to receive.

Measures of Expected Cash Flow
Expected Cash Flow with Actual Financing
Operating Cash Flow   Operating Cash Flow = EBIT + Depreciation Expense − Capital Expenditures − Increase in NWC
Cash Flow to All Investors (both stockholders and creditors)   Total Capital Cash Flow = Operating Cash Flow − Actual Taxes
Cash Flow to Creditors (expected, in light of default risk, potential prepayment, potential additional borrowing)   Debt Cash Flow = Expected Interest Payments + Expected Net Debt Service
Cash Flow to Stockholders (residual, in light of expected cash flows to creditors)   Equity Cash Flow = Operating Cash Flow − Expected Interest Payments − Expected Net Debt Service − Actual Taxes
Other Measures of Cash Flow
Contractual Cash Flow to Creditors (assuming no default or prepayment)   Contractual Cash Flows to Creditors = Contractual Interest Payments + Contractual Net Debt Service
Unlevered Free Cash Flow (expected if no debt financing)   Unlevered Free Cash Flow = Operating Cash Flow − Theoretical Taxes as Unlevered
Earnings Before Interest and Taxes plus Non-Cash Expenses (EBITDA)   EBITDA = EBIT + Depreciation Expense (and Amortization Expense)
NOTES: EBIT = Earnings Before Interest and Taxes, NWC = Net Working Capital, EBIAT = Earnings Before Interest and After Taxes

Figure 8-1 Measures of expected cash flows

Determining the Outside Investor's Cost of Capital

Identifying the relevant cash flows is Part One of the valuation process. Part Two is determining the cost of capital. The cost of capital used in Eq. (8.3) to discount the future cash flows has two components. The first is the cost of capital for investing in a risk-free asset that would pay off at the same time as the project. The second is a risk premium that depends on the riskiness of the expected future cash flow of the project.

Equation (8.1) is useful because it sometimes is easier to estimate r_{Ft} and RP_{jt} than to estimate the risky discount rate, r_{jt}, directly. A simple way of estimating r_{Ft} is to examine currently available returns on zero coupon government bonds of similar duration. Estimating the risk premium is more difficult. First, we need a measure of risk, and, second, we need a metric to determine the risk premium associated with a given level of risk.

The Measure of Risk   The measure of risk that has become the norm for investment valuation is the standard deviation of holding-period returns.[16] A holding-period return is a rate of return, expressed as a percentage, that is measured from the point of investment to the point when the return is realized. Take, for example, a common stock. Its holding-period return consists of two parts, a dividend yield and a capital gain (or loss). A share of stock that is purchased for $20 and pays a $1 dividend at the end of a one year holding period and then is sold for $22 has a 15 percent holding-period return, consisting of a 5 percent dividend yield (i.e., $1/$20) and 10 percent capital appreciation (i.e., $2/$20). Uncertainty about how large the dividend will be and about the price at which the shares can be sold in the future are the risks the investor faces. Describing those risks in terms of a standard deviation of holding-period returns brings us one step closer to determining cost of capital. Later, we will examine some techniques for estimating the standard deviation of holding-period returns.

The Price for Bearing Risk   How do we go from measuring risk to ascribing a price for bearing risk? To answer, we must distinguish between the entrepreneur and prospective investors in a new venture. For prospective investors, we follow the standard corporate finance approach to estimating the risk premium. The following assumptions underlie our reliance on the standard approach:

- There is active competition to invest capital in new ventures.
- Investors view new venture investing as an alternative to other investment opportunities.
- Investors assess the risk of a project based on its contribution to the risk of a diversified portfolio of assets.
- Investors are able to allocate their wealth across a large number of investments, so that the fraction of wealth committed to any single investment can be quite small.
- Illiquidity does not affect the investor's valuation of new venture investment.

At first, it might appear that the risk premium demanded by an outside investor would depend on the investor's appetite for bearing risk. Risk-tolerant investors prefer to hold risky instead of safe assets, in exchange for a small differential in expected return. Highly risk-averse investors prefer to hold safe assets unless the expected return for bearing risk is very high. This suggests that sorting should occur, so that the more risk-tolerant investors are the ones who invest in the riskier assets. If so, then the return premia for bearing risk will be different for different investors. The problem of investment valuation would then be individualized, difficult, and subjective. However, despite individual differences in risk preference, financial economic theory provides a solution to the problem of pricing risk. The solution does not depend on the idiosyncratic risk-tolerances of individual investors.

The logic is as follows. Suppose investors agree about the degree of risk and the expected holding-period return characteristics of all risky assets, including how the holding-period returns of different assets correlate with each other. Given those beliefs, it is possible to determine the feasible set of all combinations of risk and expected return that can be achieved by investing in various mixtures (or portfolios) of the risky assets. If, for example, there were only two risky assets, investors could form portfolios by allocating their wealth between the two in different weights (all to one or the other, half to each, and so on). Each portfolio would offer a particular combination of risk and expected return. The principle is the same when the number of risky assets is increased. Figure 8-2 includes an illustration of the feasible set of risk and return combinations for a market that includes several risky assets.

Each point in the feasible set represents a risk-and-return combination that can be achieved in at least one way—by investing in a combination of the risky assets. From the feasible set of portfolios, it is possible to identify a subset that includes only those combinations that offer the highest expected return for a given level of risk. This group of portfolios is known as the efficient set because it includes only the portfolios that maximize expected return, given the level of risk. The other portfolios are uninteresting because in a risk-return sense (standard deviation of returns and mean return) they are dominated by portfolios that are members of the efficient set. Because all investors are assumed to agree about which portfolios are on the efficient frontier, they will only invest in those portfolios. The particular portfolio that each investor selects depends on the investor's tolerance of bearing risk.

Figure 8-2 shows the efficient frontier as a heavily shaded boundary of the feasible set and illustrates the different investment decisions that would be made by risk-tolerant and highly risk-averse investors. It is apparent from the figure that investors with different tolerance for risk are attracted to different risk-and-return tradeoffs. We still are left with the problem identified above: that portfolios on the efficient frontier do not exhibit a single price for bearing risk. An investor's price for bearing risk is measured by the slope of a line where the investor's indifference curve is tangent to the efficient frontier. Because the slope of such a line is greater at the point of tangency for a highly risk-averse investor than for a risk-tolerant investor, there is no single price for bearing risk in Figure 8-2. As a result, the risk premium in Eq. (8.1) would be different for different investors.

Now, suppose that, in addition to risky assets, the investor also can invest in a risk-free asset with the same holding period. When investors are able to allocate their wealth between risky assets and the risk-free asset, only one of the portfolios from the efficient set of risky assets remains efficient. All other risky portfolios are dominated, again in a risk-return sense, by portfolios that combine the risk-free asset with one particular portfolio of risky assets. Under the assumptions of the model, because all investors agree about the risk and expected returns of the assets available in the market, they also agree about the portfolio of risky assets that is most efficient. It follows that the portfolio must include all risky assets that exist in the market in the weights that exist in the market. That portfolio is known as the market portfolio and has a particular level of risk, σ_M, and expected return, r_M, associated with it.[17]

The decision problem facing investors is different than if there were no risk-free asset. Investors who are risk-averse compared to the market level of risk and return can reduce risk most efficiently by dividing their investment capital between the market portfolio and the risk-free asset. Doing so enables them to achieve risk-and-return combinations along the line

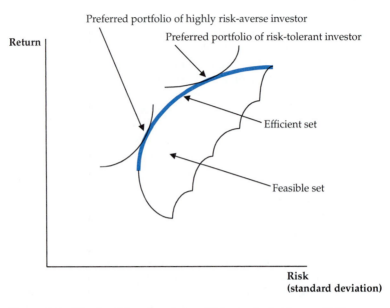

Figure 8-2 The feasible set and the efficient set of risky portfolios

The feasible set of risky portfolios represents all attainable combinations of risk and expected return that can be achieved by investing only in risky assets. The efficient set is a subset of the feasible set. It includes only the portfolios that offer the highest expected return for any given level of risk. The curves that are tangent to the efficient set are indifference curves of a relatively risk-averse and a relatively risk-tolerant investor. Each investor chooses the risky portfolio that offers the highest utility combination of risk and expected return. The points of tangency represent these choices. The more risk-tolerant investor is willing to take on more risk for a small improvement in expected return, whereas the more risk-averse investor requires a greater increase in expected return to compensate for a small increase in risk.

segment between the market portfolio and the risk-free asset. Those who are risk-tolerant compared to the market level of risk can improve their expected returns most efficiently by borrowing at the risk-free rate and investing the proceeds plus additional capital in the market portfolio. By doing so, they can achieve risk-and-return combinations along the extension of the line segment that connects the market portfolio and the risk-free asset.

Figure 8-3 shows how introducing a risk-free asset leads to identification of the market portfolio. The attainable set of combinations of the risk-free asset and the market portfolio is a straight line, the position of which is defined by the locations of the risk-free asset and the market portfolio in terms of expected return and standard deviation of returns. This line is known as the capital market line (CML). The CML includes all of the combinations of the risk-free asset and market portfolio. The figure shows how the investment choices of risk-averse and risk-tolerant investors are altered by inclusion of the risk-free asset. In contrast to the result in Figure 8-2, all investors now trade off risk and expected return at the same rate. The slope of the CML is the rate at which risk and return are traded off.

Risk Preferences and Indifference Maps

Indifference curves, sometimes called utility curves, are a convenient graphical device for describing the preferences of individuals. Most often we see indifference curves used to describe the way an individual values the tradeoff between two consumer goods, such as beer and pretzels or hamburger and french fries. One of the most common applications of using indifference curves in finance is to depict graphically the way an individual investor trades off the risk of an investment with the expected return of the investment.

Points along a single indifference curve between investment risk and expected return represent different risk-return combinations that generate the same level of utility for the investor. Higher levels of utility are represented by higher indifference curves so that risk-return combinations on U_3 are preferred to those on U_2, U_2 combinations are preferred to U_1 combinations, and so on. This graphical feature reflects the common-sense idea that investors seek high returns and low risk. The more risk-averse an investor, the steeper the indifference curve at any given point.

Indifference maps for two investors, Abby and Emma, are overlaid in the illustration below. Both are risk-averse, but Abby is less risk-averse than Emma. To see how this difference in taste for bearing risk is reflected in the map, consider the implicit tradeoff each is willing to make in terms of the increase in expected return that each requires for taking on additional risk. The point (r_0,σ_0) represents a specific combination of risk and expected return. For Abby, the point lies on the indifference curve labeled U_2^A. For Emma, the point lies on the indifference curve labeled U_2^E. Each investor regards other points along the same indifference curve as equally attractive.

The upward slopes of the curves indicate that each values high returns and safety of returns. The steeper slope of Emma's indifference curves indicates that she is more risk-averse than Abby.

To see the effects of differences in risk aversion, consider how much of an increase in return each investor requires for shifting from point (r_0,σ_0) to a higher level of risk, designated as σ_1. Compared to the initial investment, Emma requires an increase in expected return to r_1^E, whereas Abby, the less risk-averse investor, requires an increase to only r_1^A.

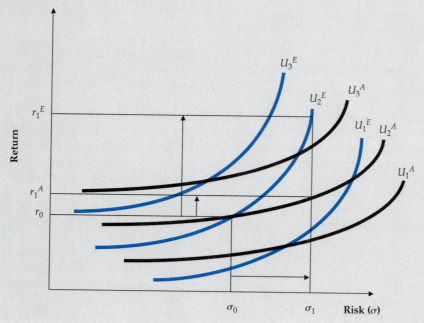

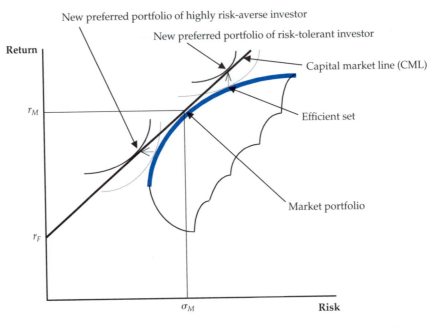

Figure 8-3 The efficient set, the market portfolio, and the capital market line

Introduction of a riskless asset gives rise to two-fund separation. All investors are better off investing in combinations of the riskless asset and a single market portfolio than selecting other portfolios from the efficient set. The set of attainable combinations of risk and expected return from combining the riskless asset and the market portfolio is the line in the figure labeled the "Capital Market Line." Both risk-tolerant and highly risk-averse investors can achieve higher levels of utility by investing in the market and the riskless asset than by limiting themselves to portfolios of only risky assets. The point of tangency of the highest achievable indifference curves with the capital market line represents the preferred portfolio. At those points, both investors trade off risk and expected return at the same rate. All investors agree on the market price for bearing risk.

Portfolio Theory and the Capital Asset Pricing Model An important insight from Figure 8-3 is that risky portfolios with the same expected return can have different degrees of risk (different standard deviations of returns). If investors are risk-averse, how is it possible that a very risky asset can have the same expected return as another asset with much lower risk? The answer is that, if investors can diversify then only risk that cannot be eliminated by diversification can affect the expected return.

The total risk of any asset can be partitioned into a component that is attributable to the overall uncertainty of the market for risky assets and a component that is uncorrelated with overall market uncertainty. The uncorrelated component is risk that is not important to an investor who is able to diversify. Because of diversification, the unexpected positive and negative returns of different investments tend to cancel each other out. In a portfolio with a very large number of assets, this component of risk can be virtually eliminated. On the other hand, diversification does not affect the component of risk that is due to the overall market. This component determines the risk premium for an investor who is able to diversify. Thus, in Figure 8-3, portfolios with the same expected return but different standard deviations of returns have the same amount of nondiversifiable risk but different amounts of diversifiable risk.

Figure 8-4 demonstrates the principle that the risk of a portfolio varies as a function of the number of randomly selected securities. As shown, the total risk of the portfolio is composed of diversifiable (nonsystematic) and nondiversifiable (systematic) risk. By holding more securities, diversifiable risk approaches zero. Thus, total risk approaches the risk of the market.

Investing in a well-diversified portfolio is not difficult, even for a small investor. An investor can diversify by investing in a stock market fund that is designed to match the performance of a standard market index, such as the S&P 500. It follows that investors cannot demand high expected rates of return because of their voluntary decisions not to diversify.

The basic point is that the expected return on a risky asset depends on risk that is not diversifiable. When we search for a market price for bearing risk, the appropriate focus is on risk that cannot be avoided by diversifying. The nondiversifiable component of risk is known as beta (β) risk, or market risk. By convention, the beta risk of the market portfolio is defined as one unit of risk. The risk-free asset, by definition, has no risk and therefore no beta risk (i.e., it has a beta of zero). A portfolio that has nondiversifiable risk that is half as great as the market has a beta of 0.5, and so on. Figure 8-5 shows a plot of the relation between beta risk and expected return. Different portfolios, with different amounts of total risk, but equal amounts of beta risk, have the same expected return. Accordingly, all such portfolios plot at the same

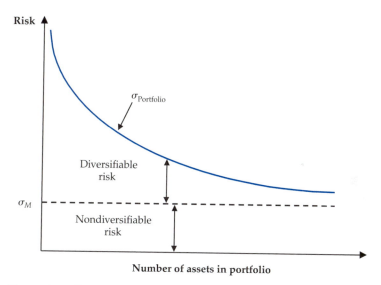

Figure 8-4 How portfolio risk depends on the number of assets in the portfolio

The total risk of an asset can be divided into a systematic component and a nonsystematic component. The systematic component depends on correlation of asset returns with overall returns of the market. The nonsystematic component is uncorrelated with the overall market. As assets are added to a portfolio, diversification reduces the total risk of the portfolio. The reduction affects nonsystematic risk but does not affect the systematic component of risk.

point in the figure. The sloping line in Figure 8-5 is known as the security market line (SML) because all risky market assets must plot on the line. The result is a single price for bearing nondiversifiable risk. We refer to the difference between the expected return on the market portfolio and the return on a risk-free asset as the market risk premium.

The relation represented graphically in Figure 8-5 is known as the Capital Asset Pricing Model (CAPM).[18] The algebraic description of the CAPM is:

$$r_j = r_F + \beta_j(r_M - r_F). \tag{8.4}$$

In Eq. (8.4), the market risk premium is defined as $r_M - r_F$. The CAPM offers a measure of the risk premium on any risky asset, j, as $\beta_j(r_M - r_F)$, where β_j is the beta risk of the asset.

The value of β_j, the beta risk of the jth asset, depends on its nondiversifiable risk. Specifically, β_j is measured as follows:

$$\beta_j = \frac{Cov(r_j, r_M)}{\sigma_M^2} = \frac{\rho(r_j, r_M)\sigma_j}{\sigma_M} \tag{8.5}$$

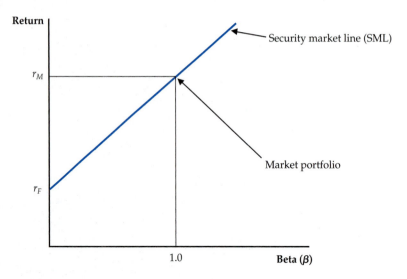

Figure 8-5 The capital asset pricing model

The Capital Asset Pricing Model (CAPM) describes the required return on an asset as a function of its nondiversifiable or "beta" risk. The market portfolio is defined to have a beta of 1.0. The riskless asset earns the risk-free rate. The difference between the expected rate of return on the market portfolio and the risk-free rate is the market price of risk. The CAPM is represented by the line that describes the attainable combinations of expected return and beta risk by combining the market portfolio and the riskless asset. If the CAPM correctly describes investor behavior, then all market assets will offer risk and expected return combinations that plot on the line. Accordingly, the line is known as the Security Market Line (SML).

In Eq. (8.5), $Cov(r_j, r_M)$ is the covariance of holding-period returns of asset j with the market, $\rho(r_j, r_M)$ is the correlation coefficient of holding-period returns between the asset and the market, σ_M^2 is the variance of market returns, and σ_M and σ_j are the standard deviations of returns for the market and for asset j. Equations (8.4) and (8.5) identify the information necessary for using the CAPM as a means to estimate the required rate of return on an investment. To estimate the risk premium for use in the RADR model, you must be able to estimate the beta of the asset and the market risk premium. As an alternative to estimating beta directly, the estimate can be calculated from estimates of the standard deviations of holding-period returns for both the asset and the market and an estimate of the correlation between asset returns and market returns. In Chapter 9 we examine methods for estimating the information needed to use the RADR method.

Given its focus on nondiversifiable risk, the CAPM is appropriate when investors are able to diversify at low cost. Clearly, the typical investors in new ventures (pension plans, endowment, and insurance companies) are able to do so. Public corporations may not be diversified, but the investors who own their shares are free to diversify their investments. Those investors should not require an increase in expected return for bearing underdiversified risk. Other kinds of investors in new ventures may find diversification more difficult to achieve. In particular, private corporations and high-net-worth individuals may be compelled to hold portfolios that are not well diversified. If they must compete with investors who are well diversified, such investors cannot expect to be compensated for underdiversification.

Valuing Financial Claims   In Figure 8-1, we listed several definitions of cash flows associated with specific financial claims. Correct valuation depends on correctly matching the cash flows with the discount rate. In Figure 8-6 we identify the discount rates that correspond to the financial claims listed in Figure 8-1.

In general, under the RADR method, expected cash flows are discounted to present value using a discount rate that is based on the risk of the cash flows. The tax deductibility of interest payments is a complicating factor because taxes may affect both the cash flows and the discount rate. Therefore, it is important to make sure that cash flow assumptions and discount rate assumptions are consistent. One way to achieve consistency is to estimate expected after-tax cash flows given the target capital structure and to discount those flows at a rate that is not adjusted for the tax deductibility of interest expense. By this approach, any tax benefit is incorporated as an adjustment to cash flows and not to the discount factor. The other way to achieve consistency is to estimate theoretical cash flows as if the venture were financed without debt and then discount those cash flows using a discount rate that is based on the benefit of the debt tax shelter at the target capital structure. By this approach, the tax benefit (if any) of debt financing is incorporated in the discount factor and not in the cash flow. In principle, either approach can yield a correct estimate, but the net tax advantage is difficult to determine directly. The preferred approach depends on ease of estimation and availability of information.

Techniques for estimating the discount rates and information sources are discussed in Chapter 9.

8.5 VALUATION BY THE CERTAINTY EQUIVALENT METHOD

It sometimes is difficult to use the RADR form of the CAPM to value real investment opportunities with risky cash flows. The model requires that risk be measured as the standard deviation of holding-period returns. However, even if we can estimate the expected cash flows of a project and the riskiness (i.e., standard deviation) of those cash flows, we cannot deter-

Matching Cash Flows to Discount Rates for Various Financial Claims			
Financial Claim	**Cash Flow**	**Discount Rate**	**Comment**
Cash Flows to Creditors	Debt Cash Flow	$r_D = r_F + \beta_D(r_M - r_F)$	The cost of capital for debt depends on the extent to which debt service payments are subject to market risk.
Cash Flows to Stockholders	Equity Cash Flow	$r_E = r_F + \beta_E(r_M - r_F)$	The cost of capital for equity depends not on the total risk of equity, but on the market component of the risk.
Cash Flows to All Investors	Total Capital Cash Flow with Actual Financing	$r_A = r_F + \beta_A(r_M - r_F)$	The required rate of return on assets is used to value cash flows that are expected to be received by all claimants given the target capital structure. The effect of tax deductibility of interest payments is reflected in the cash flows.
Unlevered Free Cash Flows to All Investors	Total Capital Cash Flow with All Equity Financing	$WACC = (D/V)(1 - t^*)r_D + (E/V)r_E$	The Weighted Average Cost of Capital (WACC) is used to value hypothetical cash flows as if the venture were financed entirely with equity. D and E are market values of debt and equity, $V = D + E$. The tax benefit of debt financing is an adjustment to the cost of debt capital. The correct tax adjustment is not the corporate tax rate, but the net advantage of debt financing, giving consideration to the off-setting effects of personal taxes.

Figure 8-6   Matching cash flows to discount rates for various financial claims

mine the expected holding-period return or the standard deviation of holding-period returns without knowing the cost or value of the project.

Difficulties of Using the RADR Method

To see the nature of the problem, consider a simple wager that will pay either $1 or $2, with equal probability. We can easily determine that the risk of the bet (in terms of the standard deviation of the payoff cash flows) is $0.50.[19] But what about the standard deviation of holding-period returns? Suppose the wager can be acquired by paying $1.25. If so, the $2 payment is a return of 60 percent and the $1 payment is a return of negative 20 percent. Thus, the expected return is 20 percent and the standard deviation of holding-period returns is 40 percent.[20] But what if the wager can be acquired for $1.50. In this case, the $2 payment is a return of 33.3 percent and the $1 payment is a return of negative 33.3 percent. The expected return is zero, and the standard deviation of holding-period returns is 33.3 percent. Thus, the standard deviation of holding-period returns depends on the cost of the wager.

You can see that applying the conventional RADR form of the CAPM is challenging when it is being used to value real assets. The problem is an inherent simultaneity. To value the expected cash flows, you need to know the discount rate, but the discount rate depends on the standard deviation of holding-period returns, which, in turn depends on the value of the project. Suppose the question you are trying to answer is, "How much should I be willing to pay?" Using the RADR form of the CAPM, you can only find an answer by making repeated guesses about the value; computing the resulting holding-period returns and cost of capital; valuing the cash flows; and checking to see whether your guess about the value is the same as the value you compute. If it is, you are finished. You have found both the correct discount rate and the present value of the future cash flows. If you can acquire the cash flows for less than the computed present value, the difference is the NPV of the investment. If your guess about value is different than the computed value, then both the discount rate and the computed value are wrong and you need to guess again.

Take another look at the wager described above. Suppose it can be acquired for $1.25. The CAPM can be used to find out whether the wager is worth taking. Assume that if you accept the bet, the payoff will be received one year later. Assume, further, that the riskless rate of interest is 4 percent; the market risk premium is 6 percent; the standard deviation of holding-period returns of the market portfolio is 20 percent; and the correlation between the payoff of the bet and the return you could earn by investing in the market portfolio is 0.6.

If you pay $1.25 for the wager and compute the beta of the wager based on the corresponding 40 percent standard deviation of holding-period returns, using Eq. (8.5), the estimate of beta is 1.20. The resulting required rate of return, from Eq. (8.4), is 11.2 percent. Because, at a cost of $1.25, the bet has an expected return of 20 percent, it is clear at this point that the NPV of the bet is positive. In fact, if you use 11.2 percent as the discount rate to estimate the present value of the expected $1.50 payoff, the result is about $1.349.

Does the above calculation mean that the NPV of the wager is $0.099 (i.e., $1.349 − $1.25)? The answer is "no." To see this, suppose you pay $1.349 to acquire the wager. At this price, the holding-period returns is either 48.1 percent (if $2 is received) or negative 25.9 percent (if $1 is received). The standard deviation of holding-period returns is now 38.6 percent. Because the standard deviation changes, the beta estimate changes. This, in turn, changes the estimate of the required rate of return and, ultimately, the present value of the wager. The new estimate of present value is $1.352. Granted, in this example, the difference is very small. But a variety of factors that are typical of new ventures can make the differences in estimated value large. Many iterations of this type of calculation may be needed before a reliable estimate of NPV is derived by the RADR approach.[21]

In corporate settings, it is customary to finesse the problem by analogizing the investment decision to an existing market asset that is publicly traded. If that can be done, a two-step approach can be used. First, estimate the beta of the market asset. Second, discount the project cash flows using that beta. Unfortunately, convincing analogies are hard to find if the project is a new venture or a financial claim on a new venture. In Chapter 9 we provide empirical estimates of betas for publicly traded corporations that are similar to entrepreneurial ventures.

How the CEQ Method Addresses the Problem

Because the CEQ form of the CAPM does not use the standard deviation of holding-period returns, it avoids the simultaneity problem of the RADR form. To make the transition from the

RADR form to the CEQ form, we start by re-expressing the risky discount rate in a way that depends on the standard deviation of cash flows instead of holding-period returns. Equation (8.6) is the CAPM expression of the risky discount rate.

$$r_j = r_F + \beta_j(r_M - r_F) \tag{8.6}$$

$$\frac{C_j}{PV_j} - 1 = r_F + \frac{\rho(C_j, r_M)(\sigma_{C_j}/PV_j)}{\sigma_M}(r_M - r_F) \tag{8.7}$$

Equation (8.7) makes the appropriate substitutions for r_j and β_j in Eq. (8.6), where C_j is the jth period expected cash flow, σ_C is the standard deviation of cash flow, and $\rho(C_j, r_M)$ is the correlation between the jth cash flow and the market return. For convenience, the rates of return in the above expressions are defined over the holding period for C_j (one year, two years, etc.).

The right-hand side of the equation is the expression for the required rate of return. The left-hand side is the expected return. The two sides are equal at the point where PV_j is the present value of C_j. That is, Eq. (8.7) can be used to find the present value of a future cash flow by using trial and error to search for the value of PV_j that equates the two sides of the equation. Although this obviates the need to assume a standard deviation of holding-period returns, it does not resolve the fundamental problem that the correct risky discount rate depends on the value of the cash flows.

The alternative that is easier to use is to re-express the risky future cash flow as a certainty equivalent and then to discount the certainty equivalent to present value using the risk-free rate of interest. Although the certainty equivalent approach to valuation is general in that it does not impose any particular tradeoff between risk and return, the CAPM can be restated in certainty equivalent form by solving Eq. (8.7) for PV_j.

$$PV_j = \frac{C_j - \dfrac{\rho(C_j, r_M)\sigma_{C_j}}{\sigma_M}(r_M - r_F)}{1 + r_F} \tag{8.8}$$

The numerator in Eq. (8.8) is the CAPM-based certainty equivalent of the risky cash flow, C_j, that corresponds to Eq. (8.2). The denominator is a discount factor that is used to determine the present value of a riskless cash flow.[22]

A certainty equivalent of a risky cash flow is the certain cash flow that, if received at the same time as the risky cash flow, would be equally valuable to the investor. Thus, an investor might regard a risky cash flow with an expected value of $200 and a standard deviation of $50 as being equally valuable to a certain $125 cash flow. If the cash flows are expected to be realized in two years, we can value the project either by discounting the expected $200 risky cash flow at the appropriate risky discount rate or by discounting the safe $125 cash flow at the risk-free rate. When the certainty equivalent form of the CAPM is used to value the project, the risky cash flow is adjusted by a factor that makes the present value of the cash flow equivalent to that derived by discounting the risky cash flow at the appropriate risky rate.

Returning, once more, to the simple wager, it is easy to determine present value by using Eq. (8.8). The standard deviation of cash flows of the wager is $0.50. The other items needed to solve the equation are the same as already enumerated. With those assumptions, the certainty equivalent cash flow, $CE(C_j)$ is \$1.41. This is the numerator of Eq. (8.8). To find PV_j the certainty equivalent cash flow is discounted at the riskless rate, yielding a value of \$1.356 for the wager. Had we continued with the iterations that the RADR approach necessitates, this is where we would have ended up.

Now that we know the present value of the wager, it is easy to determine that the NPV of the opportunity to acquire the wager for \$1.25 is \$.106. It is also easy to determine the true cost of capital. It is simply $C_j/PV_j - 1$, or 10.62 percent.

Because Eq. (8.8) adjusts for risk by using the correlation between project cash flows and market returns, it circumvents the need to determine the risk of the holding-period return. But it does raise another question. How can we estimate the correlation between project cash flows and market returns? A similar information requirement exists if the RADR form of the CAPM is used, but in that case, the need to estimate the correlation is sometimes finessed by analogizing the project to a publicly held corporation and using estimates of beta from published information.

8.6 LIMITATIONS OF THE CAPITAL ASSET PRICING MODEL

There is little disagreement that investors require compensation for bearing risk and that they are concerned particularly with risk that is not diversifiable. The CAPM makes a specific assumption about the kind of undiversifiable risk that is important to investors and about how that lack of diversifiability relates to required returns. There is, however, considerable historical evidence that the CAPM does not fully explain required rates of return for securities of public corporations. For example, historically the returns on investments in small public firms have been higher than what is implied by the CAPM.[23] Other evidence suggests that, when the CAPM is used as a benchmark, the returns on "value stocks" (those that offer high dividend returns) may be better than returns on "growth stocks" (those that offer low dividends but higher potential for capital appreciation).[24]

In some cases, these "anomalies" may have been temporary—the results of regulatory impediments to capital flows, investor oversight, or the lack of sufficient data and analysis to enable investors to recognize systematic valuation errors. Once the barriers are lifted or the anomaly is identified, the market tends to correct the anomaly as investment resources shift until the differential in expected returns disappears. Certainly, a dramatic reallocation of resources to small capitalization stocks occurred after existence of the small firm effect was documented in the academic literature. In other cases, the anomalies may point to persistent limitations of the CAPM. If, for example, as some have suggested, the "value anomaly" is due to differential tax treatment of dividends as compared to capital gains, documentation of the anomaly may not result in much of a resource shift. If true, the implication is that a more elaborate asset pricing model, which factors in tax considerations, would do a better job of pricing capital assets.

The CAPM is not the only model used for valuing investment, but it certainly is the most widely used model.[25] Others tend to add refinements, such as the tax refinement discussed above, but still are founded on the principle that risk that is diversifiable does not affect required rate of return.[26] The implication of portfolio theory for valuing new ventures is that investors cannot expect to be compensated for bearing risk that they could easily avoid by diversifying their investments. As a theoretical proposition, the notion that diversifiable risk should not affect the returns required by investors is incontrovertible. Empirical evidence of market returns is broadly consistent with the proposition.

8.7 RECONCILIATION WITH THE PRICING OF OPTIONS

In contrast to the CAPM and other asset valuation models that are based on the principle of diversification, the Option Pricing Model (OPM) implies that the values of some kinds of claims increase with risk.[27] Because new ventures are, in effect, portfolios of options, you might ask whether the OPM would be a better valuation model for our purposes. To answer, we need to examine the underlying principles of the OPM.

Risk contributes positively to the value of options because options partition risk into the risk of an increase in the price of an underlying asset and the risk of a price decline. An investor who is optimistic about the future performance of a share of stock can buy a call option instead of the underlying share. If the stock value increases, the call option will too. But in contrast to a direct investor in the stock, the call option investor is protected against price declines. If, on the date when the option expires, the stock value has fallen to below the exercise price of the option, then the option is worthless. As long as the stock price is below the exercise price of the call, it does not matter how low the stock price is; the option is still worth zero. Conversely, if, on the day the call option expires, the stock price is above the exercise price, the value of the option will equal the difference between the stock price and the option exercise price. Because the exposure to risk that comes from investing in a call option is not symmetric (only the upside risk matters), the value of a call increases with anything that increases the riskiness of the underlying shares.

Similar reasoning applies to the values of put options. Because puts gain value when the underlying asset loses value, and are valueless if the price of the underlying asset is above the exercise price of the put on the expiration date, they again offer one-sided risk. Consequently the value of a put also increases with the riskiness of the underlying asset.

Can option valuation be reconciled with the CAPM? The key to reconciliation is that an option is a derivative asset. Its value is "derived" from the value of the underlying asset and from the risk characteristics of the underlying asset. Because the underlying asset does not partition risks into good and bad risks, an investor in the asset must bear the risk of loss in order to acquire the potential for gain. In that setting, risk aversion leads to the conclusion that investors will require compensation for bearing risk that is not diversifiable. Thus, there is no inconsistency between using the OPM to value puts and calls, and using the CAPM to value the underlying asset.

Despite the consistency between the CAPM and the OPM, certain aspects of the OPM make its application to valuation of new ventures problematic. One is that the OPM is derived under an assumption of market completeness and continuous trading of assets. A complete market means that the underlying asset, matched pairs of puts and calls (with the same exercise price and expiration date), and riskless debt must all be continuously available and it must be possible to take long or short positions in each. These conditions hold reasonably well for publicly traded options on publicly traded common stock. They also provide reasonable approximations for options on nonpublic assets, such as gold mines, whose values are closely linked to the value of gold, which is a freely traded asset. However, they clearly do not hold for most new ventures. As a consequence, the OPM would tend to overvalue the real options that comprise most new ventures.

Furthermore, as a new venture is an amalgam of many interrelated options, sometimes with complex exercise provisions and controlled by different parties to the venture, use of the OPM quickly becomes impractical. In Chapter 9 we present a simulation approach to valuing new ventures and financial claims based on the CEQ form of the CAPM. The approach provides a convenient way to estimate the effects of embedded real options on the value of a new venture.[28]

8.8 REQUIRED RATES OF RETURN FOR INVESTING IN NEW VENTURES

Early in the chapter we promised a resolution of the paradoxical difference between the sought-for rates of return of venture capital investors and the rates of return they receive. The CAPM helps with the explanation and offers some casual supporting evidence.

Assuming that the CAPM does a reasonable job of estimating the rates of return investors require for investing in new ventures, how high would those rates be? Clearly, a new venture is a risky proposition, which suggests to many that the expected returns for investing should be very high. On the other hand, the point of the CAPM is that only nondiversifiable risk matters.

It seems likely that a great deal of the risk associated with new ventures is diversifiable. Consider, for example, a biotechnology venture. How much of the risk is likely to be nondiversifiable? In many respects, a biotechnology venture is like a lottery. You place a bet today, and at some future date you learn whether you have a winning ticket. The future payoff from such an investment is highly unpredictable and depends on factors such as how significant the innovation proves to be and on market size. The payoff is not likely to depend very much on economic fluctuations or similar factors that would have much greater effects on such products as discretionary consumer durables. Thus, a biotech venture is likely to have a low beta despite its high total risk. This is likely because beta risk depends on how the venture's payoff varies with marketwide fluctuations. Consequently, the cash flows from investing in a portfolio of 100 different biotech ventures might not be very risky at all. Most of the risk is specific to the individual venture and would be substantially reduced by diversifying, even within the same industry. In fact, for a large sample of public biotechnology ventures, we have estimated that the average beta was 0.75. Total risk, however, was almost five times as high.

We will see, in Chapter 9, that estimating the beta of an individual new venture requires judgment. But we can gain some information about the betas of new ventures as a group by studying the market price performance of publicly traded funds that invest in new ventures. The typical betas of those funds are in the range of 1.0 to 2.0.[29] That is, the betas generally are higher than that of the overall market, but not by much.

What do betas in this range of 1.0 to 2.0 imply for the required rates of return on new venture investments? We can answer by looking back at Eq. (8.4) and filling in the other pieces of the equation with some reasonable values. Suppose we use 4 percent as an estimate of the historical average riskless rate of return, r_F, and 9 percent as the historical average market risk premium, $r_M - r_F$.[30] Beta values in the 1.0 to 2.0 range would imply required rates of return in the 13 to 22 percent range. Such low required rates of return seem inconsistent with the earlier mentioned claims that, for investing in new projects, venture capitalists use hurdle rates of return in excess of 50 percent.[31] On the other hand, they are fully consistent with the historical experience of actual returns for new venture investment.

To look more specifically at the rates of return required by venture capital firms, the discount rate for venture capital investing can be disaggregated into four components as follows:

$$r_{Proj}^{VC} = r_F + \beta_{Proj}(r_M - r_F) + Effort + Illiquidity \tag{8.9}$$

where r_{Proj}^{VC} is the discount rate used by the venture capitalist to value a project, β_{Proj} is the beta risk of the project, *Effort* is a measure of the cost of investment management effort committed to the project by the venture capitalist and expressed in returns form, and *Illiquidity* is a measure of the required return differential due to illiquidity of the investment. Note that $r_F + \beta_{Proj}(r_M - r_F)$ is the CAPM applied to the project.

With the model from Eq. (8.9) in mind, an average realized return as high as 25 or 30 percent on venture capital investing is understandable. Using our previous assumptions about the riskless rate of return and the market risk premium, a beta of 2.0 yields a cost of capital for an entrepreneurial venture of 22 percent. Venture capital limited partnerships segregate returns to the general partner (the active investor) from returns to limited partners (passive investors). The general partner's fee is typically 20 percent of returns after initial investment capital has been returned to the limited partners, plus a management fee equal to about 2.5 percent of committed capital.[32] A reasonable estimate, then, is that one-fifth or more of the 25 percent return is actually compensation to the general partner.

This return leaves nothing to compensate for the illiquidity of the investment. However, an adjustment for illiquidity of near zero comports with recent empirical evidence on the cost of illiquidity and with the fact that most investors in venture capital limited partnerships are pension plans and insurance companies. These are investors with long-term investment horizons, at least for some fraction of their portfolios. Therefore, they would demand a negligible return premium to compensate for illiquidity.[33]

Why does the CAPM accurately predict average returns of venture capital investors? In large part, the answer appears to be that assumptions underlying the CAPM are reasonably well satisfied. Most importantly, any venture is likely to represent only a small fraction of the asset portfolio of a large pension plan or life insurance company. For such investors, a substantial component of the total risk is diversifiable, a component of risk that, in a competitive market for venture capital, cannot be used to garner a higher required rate of return.

Then, how do we account for the high sought-for rates of return? Our answer is that those returns represent hurdle rates that investors sometimes use to value cash flow projections that are developed on the presumption that the venture will be successful. In other words, to compensate for the optimism built into the cash flow projections, the investor applies a hurdle rate that is substantially above the required return for investing in the project.[34]

8.9 SUMMARY

Use of the capital asset pricing model for investment decision making in a corporate finance context is widely accepted. However, the CAPM is not as widely used for investment decision making in entrepreneurial finance. Instead, a common practice of investors is to value optimistic forecasts of cash flows using hurdle rates that are biased upward in an effort to offset the optimism in the cash flow projections.

As with any investment decision, investors in new ventures can err by accepting projects that should have been rejected or by rejecting projects that should have been accepted. Biasing the decision rules to minimize the likelihood of investing in bad projects, or of not demanding a large enough fraction of the ownership in exchange for investing, is not a good solution to the valuation problem. Rejecting good investments is just as serious an error as accepting bad ones.

In this chapter we develop the CAPM as a framework for new venture project selection and investment valuation. Careful application of the CAPM can result in fewer and smaller mistakes than more traditional approaches. If we were to study the identities of the venture capital firms that generally outperform the average, we expect that we would find, among other factors contributing to their success, they do a better job of determining project value and structuring investment deals than do their rivals.

There are two forms of the CAPM. In the more familiar form, expected future cash flows are discounted to present value using a required rate of return that depends on the risk of holding period returns. This is the risk-adjusted discount rate form of the CAPM. In the less familiar form of the model, expected future cash flows are converted to their certainty equivalents based on the risk adjustment implied by the CAPM, and the certainty-equivalent cash flows are discounted to present value at the riskless rate of interest. The CEQ form has distinct advantages over the RADR form for valuing investment opportunities in new ventures. The advantage we stress in this chapter is that the CEQ approach does not require knowing the holding-period returns on the investment and does not attempt to infer beta risk from published data or other sources.

QUESTIONS AND PROBLEMS

1. You are considering investing in a new venture. Based on the business plan of the entrepreneur, *if the project is successful,* it is expected to generate the following cash flows for investors:

Year	Cash Flow
1	$0
2	$200,000
3	$2,000,000
4	$8,000,000

The cash flow in the fourth year includes cash flows that would be realized from selling the venture to a third party at that time. After conducting your own due diligence, you have concluded that you agree with the entrepreneur that if the venture is successful, the cash flow estimates are reasonable. The entrepreneur is looking for seed capital of $1 million to undertake the venture. After the initial investment, if it is successful, the venture will be self-supporting.

Using the 50 percent to 100 percent range of hurdle rates for seed and start-up investments, estimate the present value of the venture and the fraction of the equity you would need to cover your investment. Also, determine the hurdle rate that would result in a zero NPV for a 100 percent interest in the venture.

2. Consider problem 1 again. Through your due diligence efforts, you also have concluded that the probability that the venture will be successful through year 2 is about 80 percent, through year 3 is about 60 percent, and through year 4 is about 40 percent. If the venture fails, it will not return any cash to investors. Compute the expected cash flows of the venture and find the discount rates of the expected cash flows that would yield the same ownership fractions as the 50 percent hurdle rate in problem 1. In other words, given the ownership fraction you would require if a hurdle rate of 50 percent is used in problem 1,

what discount rate of expected cash flows would yield a present value of the venture that would imply the same ownership fraction for your investment of $1 million? (Note: Finding this rate may require some experimentation.)

3. Compare the present-value estimates of each of the annual cash flows between problems 1 and 2. What problems can you see with valuing projects using optimistic cash flow forecasts and hurdle rates, as in problem 8-1, instead of expected cash flow estimates and required rates of return, as in problem 8-2?

4. Suppose you can establish that for each annual cash flow of the venture described in problem 1, the correlation between project cash flows and the market is 30 percent. You also have determined that the riskless rate of interest is 4.5 percent, the market risk premium is 6.5 percent, and the standard deviation of market returns is 20 percent for one year, 28 percent for two years, 35 percent for three years, and 40 percent for four years. Use the CEQ form of the CAPM to find the certainty equivalent of each annual expected cash flow, the present value of each annual cash flow, and the present value of the project. How large of an ownership fraction do you need if the CAPM is the correct valuation model?

5. Using Eq. (8.7) and your results from problem 4, find the risk-adjusted discount rate for each of the annual expected cash flows. (Note that the RADRs you compute in this way are cumulative (compounded) rates. To find the annual rate for each cash flow you need to convert the compounded rate back to its equivalent annual rate). Use Eq. (8.6) from the text to find the beta of each annual cash flow.

6. Usually, when people use published information to estimate beta, they assume that the beta is the same for all of the cash flows of the project they are trying to value. Now that you know the present value of the project (from your work on problem 4), find the single discount rate that you can apply to the expected cash flows that yields the same present value. How does the single discount rate compare to the individual discount rates you determined in problem 5? Compare the present values of the individual annual cash flows based on the single rate with the values using rates that are specific to each period. What problems, if any, do you see with trying to value projects such as this one using a single discount rate?

7. Consider the following success-scenario income statement for the next year of operations of a privately owned small business. Figures in the statement are in thousands.

Income Statement	Success
Sales Revenue	$10,000
Cost of Goods Sold	$ 4,000
Gross Profit	$ 6,000
Operating Expenses	$ 4,500
Operating Profit	$ 1,500
Interest Expense	$ 700
Net Taxable Income	$ 800
Income Tax	$ 280
Net Income	$ 520

Develop a companion failure-scenario income statement under the following assumptions:

- Sales would be $6,000,000.
- Cost of goods sold would be $3,000,000.
- Operating expenses would be $2,500,000.
- There is $5,000,000 in debt outstanding, with an interest rate of 14 percent per year, but in the failure scenario the venture will not pay interest beyond what is available from net income.
- The income tax rate is 35 percent.

Assuming that the probability of the success scenario being realized for the next year is 60 percent, generate an expected income statement.

Based on the following assumptions, develop success-scenario, failure-scenario, and expected measures of the cash flow definitions from Figure 8-1:

- Operating expenses includes $2,200,000 in depreciation expense.
- New capital expenditures will be $1,500,000 in the success scenario and nothing in the failure scenario.
- New investment in net working capital will be $250,000 in the success scenario and nothing in the failure scenario.
- In the success scenario, no debt repayment would be due and the venture would borrow an additional $1,000,000. In the failure scenario, the business assets would be liquidated and proceeds of $2,200,000 would be paid to the creditor. The balance of their $5,000,000 loan would be a write-off for the lender.

Discuss your findings for the various cash flow measures, keeping in mind that for the success scenario, the venture will continue in the future, but in the failure scenario, this would be the final year of operation.

8. Suppose the risk-free rate of interest is 5 percent, the market risk premium is 6 percent, and the market standard deviation is 20 percent.

a. Plot the risk-free asset and the market portfolio on coordinates with expected return on the vertical axis and total risk (standard deviation) on the horizontal axis and sketch in the capital market line.

b. Plot both assets on coordinates with expected return on the axis and market risk (beta) on the horizontal axis and sketch in the security market line.

c. Suppose the CAPM is correct and that an asset with a standard deviation of holding period returns of 30 percent has an expected return of 12 percent. Plot the asset on both sets of coordinates. How much of the total risk of the asset is market risk? What is the correlation between the asset and the market portfolio.

d. Explain why another asset with a standard deviation of holding period returns of 30 percent could have an expected return of 10 percent. What would the asset's risk characteristics need to be?

9. Consider the following income statement of a venture that is expected to continue indefinitely but is not expected to grow. The numbers in the income statement are expected to be the same each year. New capital expenditures are expected to exactly offset depreciation expenses so that net income is equal to equity cash flow. The capital structure of the venture is expected to be constant.

Income Statement	Expected
Sales Revenue	$85,000
Cost of Goods Sold	$32,000
Gross Profit	$53,000
Operating Expenses	$32,000
Operating Profit	$21,000
Interest Expense	$ 7,500
Net Taxable Income	$13,500
Income Tax	$ 4,725
Net Income	$ 8,775

Suppose the risk-free rate of interest is 5 percent, the market risk premium is 6 percent, and the corporate tax rate is 35 percent. The venture's equity has a beta of 1.25 and its debt has a beta of 0.25.

a. Compute the cost of equity and the value of a perpetuity of the expected cash flows to equity.

b. Compute the cost of debt and the value of a perpetuity of the expected cash flows to debt.

c. Assuming that the value of total assets is equal to the value of debt plus the value of equity, compute the total value of the venture. Use the total value to compute the cost of capital for the assets and the asset beta.

d. Using total capital cash flows and the asset cost of capital, estimate firm value based on the perpetuity of expected earnings. How does it compare to the value you computed by adding up the debt and equity values?

e. Compute the venture's weighted average cost of capital (WACC). Compute its expected cash flows as if it were all-equity financed. What is the estimated value of the venture if you value the perpetuity of hypothetical cash flows at the WACC?

f. Your value results should be consistent across all approaches. Why do you think they are? What do you think might be different if the venture were expected to grow?

10. Suppose you can acquire a 20 percent ownership interest in a venture for $2.5 million. You anticipate that, if the venture is successful, it will be able to go public in about three years. If so, you estimate that the public-market value of the venture will be about $75 million. However, you believe there is about a 75 percent chance that the venture will fail and your investment will be worthless.

a. Based upon your investment amount, what would be the standard deviation of holding period returns on your 20 percent interest?

b. How does the standard deviation of holding period returns change if you can acquire the 20 percent interest by investing $2.0 million (assume that harvest values and probabilities are not affected by the change)?

c. Suppose the required rate of return for the three-year holding period is 18 percent, the market risk premium for the holding period is 30 percent, the market standard deviation is 35 percent, and the correlation between harvest cash flows and the market is 0.2. Compute the standard deviation of cash flow returns and use Eq. (8.7) to search for the equilibrium value of the investment and the equilibrium standard deviation of holding period returns.

NOTES

1. Venture Economics (1997), p. 51.
2. Charles Tschampion, address, February, 7, 1995 as cited in Bernstein (1996).
3. Baty (1990), p. 63.
4. Roberts and Stevenson (1992).
5. Rich and Gumpert (1992).
6. Poindexter (1976).
7. Hoban (1976).
8. Ibbotson and Brinson (1987), pp. 99–100.
9. Martin and Petty (1983), pp. 401–410.
10. Bygrave and Timmons (1992), pp. 156–158. Returns are based on valuations by the fund managers, and the study is limited to funds in existence for at least five years.
11. The data underlying these IRR estimates are drawn from Venture Economics press releases.
12. It is not uncommon for investors to share their valuation results with the entrepreneur. However, the entrepreneur can never be certain that the assumptions in the investor's valuation model are the ones the investor actually believes are correct. As with any negotiation, a party can be expected to disclose only such information that he expects will help produce a beneficial outcome.
13. The entrepreneur's attitude toward risk is affected by limited ability to diversify. The implications of the entrepreneur's inability to diversify are developed in Chapter 10.
14. See Brealey and Myers (2003), Chapter 4, for elaboration of the relation between share value and expected dividends.
15. If the investor takes on a managerial role and sacrifices salary in order to work on the venture, the salary shortfall, compared to the highest-valued alternative, is considered additional investment in the project.
16. A pioneer of modern portfolio theory, Harry Markowitz, first proposed use of the standard deviation of holding-period returns as the measure of risk. See Markowitz (1952). Harry Markowitz was awarded the Nobel Prize in Economics in 1990 for this contribution to the theory of decision making.
17. In some sources, the term "tangency portfolio" is used instead of "market portfolio." See, for example, Grinblatt and Titman (2001).
18. Development of the Capital Asset Pricing Model from its roots in modern portfolio theory was the contribution of several individuals, working independently. See Sharpe (1964), Lintner (1965), and Mossin (1966). Jack Treynor also contributed to the theory, though his research was unpublished. The theoretical model is based on a number of assumptions, including: homogeneity of beliefs about risk and return, a one-period time horizon, availability of a risk-free asset, and quadratic utility functions for investors or normally distributed risk. Empirical testing of the CAPM is roughly consistent with the CAPM. This suggests that, in most uses, violations of the assumptions are not very important and do not impede its application as a valuation tool.
19. The standard deviation is computed as $(($2 - $1.5)^2 \times .5 + ($1 - $1.5)^2 \times .5)^{1/2}$.
20. The standard deviation is computed as $((60\% - 20\%)^2 \times .5 + (-20\% - 20\%)^2 \times .5)^{1/2}$.
21. Some readers may be wondering why this difficulty of using the RADR form of the CAPM to value real assets did not arise in their corporate finance classes. The answer is that the problem exists in that arena as well, but most texts avoid confronting it by assuming that other

information (such as published estimates of beta) can be used to estimate the cost of capital for an asset. Grinblatt and Titman (2001) is the only corporate finance text we have seen that addresses the difficulty, and their conclusion is similar to ours. In Chapter 9 we suggest some shortcuts that sometimes can be used to circumvent the problem. However, opportunities to use the shortcuts are more limited for new ventures than they are in a corporate finance context.

22. For additional discussion of the CEQ valuation approach, see Robichek and Myers (1966), Brealey and Myers (2003) Chapter 9, and Grinblatt and Titman (2001).

23. The original documentation of the "small-firm anomaly" appeared in the *Journal of Financial Economics* in 1981. See Banz (1981) and Reinganum (1981).

24. The original paper documenting the "value anomaly" is by Lakonishok, Shleifer, and Vishney (1994).

25. For a convenient summary of alternative asset pricing models, see Pratt (1999).

26. The arbitrage pricing model, for example, conjectures that expected returns on capital assets are determined by a multiplicity of factors. The statistical process of factor analysis is sometimes employed to search for the more important ones. *Ex post* examination of the statistically derived factors can be used in an effort to associate the factors to macroeconomic influences, which may or may not include the market *per se*. The important point for our purpose is that factor analysis still only accounts for a fraction of the risk of an asset. Thus, the model implies that other risks are diversifiable against the factors and do not affect required rates of return. See Ross (1976). The arbitrage-pricing model cannot be used to estimate cost of capital in a forward-looking sense unless the factors can be identified. Elton, Gruber, and Mei (1993) use a different approach of identifying macroeconomic factors ex ante, and they use those factors to estimate cost of capital for a group of public utility stocks. Fama and French (1995) develop an empirical three-factor model where firm size and book-to-market value are also priced, in addition to market risk. Whether the additional factors are artifacts in the data or capture risk factors that are omitted in empirical applications of the CAPM is an unresolved issue. However, Jagannathan and Wang (1996) estimate a version of the CAPM where beta can vary over business cycles and where human capital is included in the market portfolio. They find that the unconditional CAPM model implied by their analysis is not rejected by the data and that the Fama-French factors no longer are significant in explaining returns.

27. Fischer Black, Myron Scholes and Robert Merton are the original developers of the option pricing model. See Black and Scholes (1973) and Merton (1973). Scholes and Merton were awarded the Nobel Prize in Economics in 1998 for their contributions. Fischer died in 1996, and the prize is not awarded posthumously.

28. Most proposals for valuing options that are not traded, or where the market is incomplete, involve some means of backing into completeness. For example Mason and Merton (1985) and Kasanen and Trigeorgis (1994) propose that real options that are not traded can be valued by appealing to the existence of a "twin security" that is traded and has risk characteristics that are perfectly correlated with the real option. Short of that possibility, several researchers suggest that untraded options can be valued in the presence of nondiversifiable risk by replacing expected cash flows with their certainty equivalents and valuing the certainty equivalent cash flows at the risk-free rate of interest. But they generally do not state how to determine the certainty equivalent. See Constantinides (1978), Cox, Ingersoll, and Ross (1985); Garman (1977), and Harrison and Kreps (1979). For a current overview and summary of the literature, see Trigeorgis (1996). The valuation method used throughout this text is in keeping with this stream of literature and we use the CAPM assumptions to determine the certainty equivalent.

29. For examples of beta estimates for venture capital funds and indices, see "A Method for Valuing High-Risk, Long-Term Investments," Harvard Business School note 9-288-006, June 1989.

30. These are roughly the long-run historical averages over the 1926–2000 period as estimated by Ibbotson Associates, Inc. See Brealey and Myers (2003), Chapter 7.

31. Bygrave and Timmons (1992) pp. 156–158, for example, note, "A 1984 congressional survey found that independent private venture capital firms expected a minimum annualized rate of return on individual investments that ranged from 75% for seed-stage financing to about 35% per year for bridge financing."

32. See Sahlman (1990) and Gompers and Lerner (1999).

33. For evidence that illiquidity premia tend to be small, see Blackwell and Kidwell (1988), Hertzel and Smith (1993), and Smith and Armstrong (1993). We discuss liquidity further in Chapter 9.

34. Bhagat (1997) makes essentially the same argument.

REFERENCES AND ADDITIONAL READINGS

BANZ, ROLF. "The Relationship Between Return and Market Values of Common Stocks." *Journal of Financial Economics* 9 (March 1981): 3–18.

BATY, GORDON. *Entrepreneurship in the Nineties.* Englewood Cliffs, NJ: Prentice Hall, 1990.

BERNSTEIN, PETER. *Against the Gods.* New York: John Wiley & Sons, 1996.

BHAGAT, SANJAI. "Why Do Venture Capitalists Use Such High Discount Rates?" University of Colorado working paper, 1997.

BLACK, FISHER, AND MYRON SCHOLES. "The Pricing of Options and Corporate Liabilities." *Journal of Political Economy* 81 (May–June 1973): 637–654.

BLACKWELL, DAVID W., AND DAVID S. KIDWELL. "An Investigation of Cost Differences Between Public Sales and Private Placements of Debt." *Journal of Financial Economics* 22 (1988): 253–278.

BREALEY, RICHARD A., AND STEWART C. MYERS. *Principles of Corporate Finance.* 7th ed. New York: McGraw-Hill, 2003.

BYGRAVE, WILLIAM D., AND JEFFREY A. TIMMONS. *Venture Capital at the Crossroads.* Boston: Harvard Business School Press, 1992.

CONSTANTINIDES, GEORGE. "Market Risk Adjustment in Project Valuation." *Journal of Finance* 33 (1978): 603–616.

COX, JOHN, JONATHAN INGERSOLL, AND STEPHEN ROSS. "An Intertemporal General Equilibrium Model of Asset Prices." *Econometrica* 53 (March 1985): 363–384.

ELTON, EDWIN, MARTIN GRUBER, AND JIANPING MEI. "Cost of Capital Using Arbitrage Pricing Theory: A Case Study of Nine New York Utilities." *Financial Markets, Institutions, and Instruments* 3 (August 1993): 46–73.

FAMA, EUGENE, AND KENNETH FRENCH. "Size and Book-to-Market Factors in Earnings and Returns." *Journal of Finance* 50 (1995): 131–155.

GARMAN, MARK. "A General Theory of Asset Valuation Under Diffusion State Processes." University of California, Berkeley. Working paper, 1977.

GOMPERS, PAUL, AND JOSH LERNER. "An Analysis of Compensation in the U.S. Venture Capital Partnership." *Journal of Financial Economics* 51 (1999): 3–44.

GRINBLATT, MARK, AND SHERIDAN TITMAN. *Financial Markets and Corporate Strategy, 2nd ed.* Boston: Irwin/McGraw-Hill, 2001.

HARRISON, J., AND D. KREPS. "Martingales and Arbitrage in Multiperiod Securities Markets." *Journal of Economic Theory* (June 1979): 381–408.

HERTZEL, MICHAEL, AND RICHARD L. SMITH. "Market Discounts and Shareholder Gains for Placing Equity Privately." *Journal of Finance* 48 (1993): 459–485.

HOBAN, JAMES P. *Characteristics of Venture Capital Investing.* Ph.D. diss., University of Utah, 1976.

IBBOTSON, ROGER G., AND GARY P. BRINSON. *Investment Markets.* New York: McGraw-Hill, 1987.

JAGANNATHAN, RAVI, AND ZHENYU WANG. "The Conditional CAPM and the Cross-Section of Expected Returns." *Journal of Finance* 51 (1996): 3–53.

KASANEN, EERO, AND LENOS TRIGEORGIS. "A Market Utility Approach to Investment Valuation." *European Journal of Operational Research* 74 (1994): 294–309.

LAKONISHOK, JOSEF, ANDRE SHLEIFER, AND ROBERT VISHNEY. "Contrary Investment, Extrapolation, and Risk." *Journal of Finance* 49 (1994): 1541–1578.

LINTNER, JOHN. "The Valuation of Risk Assets and the Selection of Risky Investments in Stock Portfolios and Capital Budgeting." *Review of Economics and Statistics* 47 (February 1965): 13–37.

MARKOWITZ, HARRY. "Portfolio Selection." *Journal of Finance* 7 (March 1952): 77–91.

MARTIN, JOHN D., AND WILLIAM PETTY. "An Analysis of the Performance of Publicly Traded Venture Capital Companies." *Journal of Financial and Quantitative Analysis* 18 (1983):401–410.

MASON, SCOTT P., AND ROBERT C. MERTON. "The Role of Contingent Claims Analysis in Corporate Finance." In *Recent Advances in Corporate Finance.* Edited by Edward I. Altman and Marti G. Subrahmanyam. Homewood, IL: Irwin, 1985.

MERTON, ROBERT C. "Theory of Rational Option Pricing." *Bell Journal of Economics and Management Science* 4 (Spring 1973): 141–183.

MOSSIN, JAN. "Equilibrium in a Capital Asset Market." *Econometrica* (October 1966): 768–783.

POINDEXTER, J. B. *The Efficiency of Financial Markets: The Venture Capital Case.* Ph.D. diss., New York University, 1976.

PRATT, SHANNON P. *Cost of Capital: Estimation and Applications.* New York: John Wiley & Sons, 1999.

REINGANUM, MARC R. "A Misspecification of Capital Asset Pricing: Empirical Anomalies Based on Earnings, Yields, and Market Values." *Journal of Financial Economics* 9 (1981): 19–46.

RICH, STANLEY R., AND DAVID E. GUMPERT. "How to Write a Winning Business Plan." In *The Entrepreneurial Venture.* Edited by William A. Sahlman and Howard H. Stevenson. Boston: Harvard Business School Publications, 1992), pp. 127–137.

ROBERTS, MICHAEL J., AND HOWARD H. STEVENSON. "Alternative Sources of Financing." In *The Entrepreneurial Venture.* Edited by William A. Sahlman and Howard H. Stevenson. Boston: Harvard Business School Publications, 1992, pp. 171–178.

ROBICHEK ALEXANDER, AND STEWART C. MYERS. "Conceptual Problems in the Use of Risk-Adjusted Discount Rates." *Journal of Finance* 21 (December 1966): 727–730.

ROSS, STEVEN A. "The Arbitrage Theory of Capital Asset Pricing." *Journal of Economic Theory* 13 (December 1976): 341–360.

SAHLMAN, WILLIAM, A. "The Structure and Governance of Venture Capital Organizations." *Journal of Financial Economics* 27 (October 1990): 473–521.

SHARPE, WILLIAM F. "Capital Asset Prices: A Theory of Market Equilibrium under Conditions of Risk." *Journal of Finance* 19 (September 1964): 425–442.

SMITH, RICHARD L., AND VAUGHN ARMSTRONG "Misperceptions about Private Placement Discounts: Why Market Reactions to Rule 144A Has Been Lukewarm." In *Modernizing U.S. Securities Regulation: Economics and Legal Perspectives.* Edited by K. Lehn and R. Kamphuis. Pittsburgh: Center for Research on Contracts and the Structure of Enterprise, 1993.

TIMMONS, JEFFREY. *New Venture Creation.* 5th ed. Chicago: Irwin, 1999.

TRIGEORGIS, LENOS. *Real Options.* Cambridge, MA: MIT Press, 1996.

VENTURE ECONOMICS. *Investment Benchmarks: Venture Capital,* 1997.

Valuation in Practice:
The Investor's Perspective

I was seldom able to see an opportunity until it ceased to be one. (Mark Twain)

Learning Objectives

After reading this chapter you will be able to:

- Use the CAPM to value an investment by either the Certainty Equivalent (CEQ) method or the Risk-Adjusted Discount Rate (RADR) method.
- Use two common venture capital valuation methods: the First Chicago Method and the Venture Capital Method.
- Recognize the strengths and weaknesses of each valuation method.
- Estimate project betas and required rates of return by alternative methods.
- Estimate the correlation between project returns and market return, the risk-free rate, and the standard deviation of market returns.
- Use multiples to estimate the continuing value of a new venture.
- Recognize and use shortcuts in the valuation process.

As with any other investment, the present value of a new venture can be found by discounting future cash flows using a cost of capital appropriate for the risk. Implementation, however, is challenging. The important challenges are forecasting the relevant cash flows and estimating the corresponding cost of capital.

In this chapter, we address valuation from the perspective of an outside investor. Thus, we maintain the assumption from Chapter 8 that investors are concerned with risks that cannot be eliminated by investing in a diversified portfolio. We begin by setting out criteria you can use to compare approaches to new venture valuation.

9.1 CRITERIA FOR SELECTING A NEW VENTURE VALUATION MODEL

Valuation is critical to the negotiation of financing contracts between entrepreneurs and investors. Not only must you estimate the value of the venture, you also must be able to value specific financial claims.

Standard approaches to valuation are based on applying multipliers to income statement information (such as revenue or earnings) or to balance sheet information (such as asset book value), or on discounting future cash flows to present value. If a multiplier is used, it is common to estimate the appropriate multiplier from market data on comparable public firms, or from primary market transaction data for such companies (e.g., public offering or private transaction values). Discounted cash flow approaches are more likely to be based on market information about the appropriate discount rate.

The primary approaches used in valuing new ventures (especially early-stage, high-technology ventures and those with significant potential for growth) are discounted cash flow approaches. For such ventures, applications of multipliers to current income statement or balance sheet information are not helpful. Those current measures bear little relationship to likely future performance. Furthermore, comparable firm and comparable transaction data are rare.[1]

Several different discounting approaches are commonly used to value new ventures. The main differences among the approaches concern the specific cash flows and discount rates used and the ways uncertainty is taken into account. Each approach has strengths and limitations. The following questions are relevant for assessing the merits of each valuation approach:

- **Is the valuation based on *expected* future cash flows?**
  Some models use biased estimates of cash flows, such as expected accounting earnings or success-scenario cash flows. Approaches that are not based on expected cash flows often are more convenient but can yield erroneous estimates of value for two reasons. First, there is no theoretically sound way to determine the correct discount rate. Second, the values of expected cash flows that will be received at different times can be biased to different degrees and in different directions.

- **Is cost of capital used as the discount rate?**
  Valuing positively biased estimates of cash flow with positively biased hurdle rates tends to cause projects with more distant payoffs to be rejected incorrectly. Similarly, discount rates based on total risk rather than nondiversifiable risk can lead to rejecting projects that should be accepted by an investor who is well diversified.

- **How does the model deal with cash flows that vary in risk?**
  Models that do not distinguish among cash flows that differ in risk can produce distorted estimates of value. Different cash flow streams that occur in the same period can differ in risk. The appropriate discount rates will vary accordingly. Cash flows that occur at different times can also differ in risk. If the discount rates do not account for risk differences, valuation errors can result.

- **Can the model be used to value embedded options and complex financial claims?**
  Complexity affects both expected returns and risk. Choosing a financial structure that includes real or financial options can alter the overall value of a venture. The values of the options depend both on expected cash flows and risk of the option cash flows.

- **How difficult is it to estimate the information required for the valuation?**
  There is virtue in simplicity. Valuation approaches that are complex or difficult to use are sometimes too costly to justify. This is true particularly if the project is clearly worth pursuing, alternative financial contract structures are uncomplicated, and agreements for sharing gains and losses can be reached informally.

We begin by examining how the future cash flows of a new venture normally are projected. With that background, we investigate the traditional approaches to new venture valuation. In this context, we are able to examine valuation approaches based on multipliers as a component of discounted cash flow valuation. We then turn to the CAPM-based approaches first introduced in Chapter 8. We examine both the RADR approach and the CEQ approach.

This chapter should enable you to see how the different approaches to valuation are related. It should also provide a road map you can use to generate the information that is required for each approach. Finally, it should help you decide which approaches will be most useful for addressing a particular valuation problem.

9.2 USING THE CONTINUING VALUE CONCEPT

A common feature of all discounted cash flow approaches to new venture valuation is that cash flows after the first few years are valued implicitly. The overall valuation is divided into two periods.[2] In the first period, explicit cash flow projections are made for each year, quarter, month, or whatever interval is appropriate. We refer to this as the explicit value period because explicit forecasts of periodic cash flows are used in the valuation.

After the explicit value period, instead of projecting cash flows forever, it is common to estimate a continuing value. Normally, continuing value is estimated based on the historical values of market assets similar to the one being valued. For example, suppose the objective is to estimate the continuing value of a new computer software venture at the end of its fifth year of operation. The continuing value could be estimated by applying the average price/earnings ratio for publicly traded computer software firms to a forecast of earnings as of the end of the explicit value period. For most new ventures, continuing value is a very important component of total present value.[3]

We refer to the period after the explicit value period as the continuing value period. Sometimes continuing value is referred to as terminal value. The rationale for "terminal value" is that it is a valuation at a point where existing investments could reasonably be "terminated" by sale to others. It does not mean that the venture is expected to be terminated or the assets liquidated. It does not even mean that the financial claims are expected to be sold, just that they could be sold without unusual difficulty. We prefer "continuing" value because it suggests that the venture is ongoing.

Figure 9-1 illustrates a forecast of the future cash flows of a venture and segregation into explicit value and continuing value periods. In the example, year five is the last explicit forecast. Projections beginning in year six are implicit forecasts based on assumptions about the growth rate from that point forward. Note that the continuing value is an estimate as of the end of the explicit value period (year-5 in the figure). To estimate present value, continuing value must be discounted to present value, as if it were a cash flow that was expected to be received for selling the venture or the financial claim.

Equation (9.1) describes the value of a venture in terms of explicit and continuing value components, based on annual data:

$$PV = \sum_{t=1}^{T} \frac{C_t}{(1 + r_t)^t} + \frac{CV_T}{(1 + r_T)^T} \qquad (9.1)$$

where PV is the present value of the venture; C_t is the annual cash flow in each year, t; CV_T is continuing value as of the last year of the explicit value period, year T; and r_t is the discount rate for year t cash flows. In the following pages we address the problem of estimating present value by this approach.

Estimating Cash Flows During the Explicit Value Period

In Chapter 7, we described the methods you can use to project cash flows during the explicit value period. They include such techniques as scenario analysis and simulation. As we indicated then, if the assumptions are carefully researched and applied, the forecasting model will yield an estimate of expected cash flow that is about as reliable as it can be.

For reasons we already have demonstrated, and others that will become apparent in the next few chapters, it is just as important to do a good job of forecasting the uncertainty of cash flows, as it is to forecast the expected cash flow. A well-constructed model of the venture will yield reasonable forecasts of both the expected cash flows and the uncertainty of cash flows.

Estimating Continuing Value

As Figure 9-1 suggests, continuing value is a discounted cash flow valuation method. However, it does not rely on explicit forecasts of cash flows to be received during the continuing value period. Instead, the cash flow forecast is implicit in the assumptions used to estimate continuing value. In the figure (as in a forecasting model), no explicit forecast is made of the cash flows after year 5, the last year of the explicit value period. Rather, continuing value is estimated on the basis of information from the last explicit forecast along with information on the values of comparable (normally public) companies.

Determining the Explicit Value Period   The length of the explicit value period depends on the nature of the venture. Forecasting of continuing value works best when a firm has established a track record that can be used to estimate value. Continuing value methods do not work well in the early stages of a new venture. Thus, explicit valuation should be applied to value cash

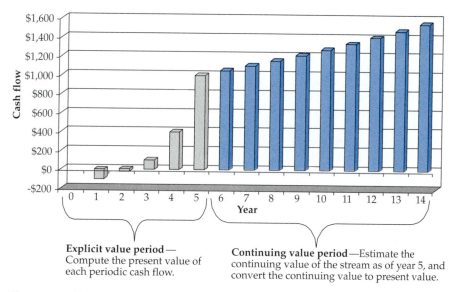

Explicit value period—Compute the present value of each periodic cash flow.

Continuing value period—Estimate the continuing value of the stream as of year 5, and convert the continuing value to present value.

Figure 9-1   Using continuing value to estimate the worth of a new venture

A common approach to discounted cash flow valuation is to divide the cash flow forecast into two periods. During the explicit value period, cash flow projections are valued directly. During the continuing value period, cash flow projections are implicit in a capitalized value that is measured as of the time of the last explicit forecast. Normally the continuing value period begins when the venture is projected to reach a stable pattern of future growth.

flows during development, during periods when the venture has not yet achieved a profitable level of sales, and during periods of rapid growth. Continuing value can be applied at a point beyond which the venture growth rate is expected to be stable. In Figure 9-1, the explicit value period includes years when expected cash flows are negative and when they are growing rapidly. The continuing value period is best limited to years when cash flows are expected to grow at a steady rate.

Sometimes continuing value estimates are applied at earlier stages of development. Rapidly growing ventures with very large capital needs sometimes must seek public equity financing before establishing a stable track record. If similar companies have raised equity at early stages, then underwriters are likely to use a combination of continuing value methods and explicit discounted cash flow methods to estimate the price at which shares will be offered to the public. In such a case, it could be appropriate to use the data from pubic offerings of other early-stage ventures to estimate continuing value at a point before growth is expected to stabilize.

Determining Which Multiplier to Use   Continuing value is estimated by applying multipliers or capitalization factors to aspects of the explicit forecast. Choosing the right multiplier or set of multipliers requires judgment and benefits from practical experience. Multiples of operating cash flow, net income, sales, or assets are most often used. For example, continuing value might be capitalized at 10 times expected cash flow, or 1.5 times expected sales. The relative merits of different multipliers (e.g., sales versus cash flow) are discussed in a variety of sources.[4]

Because present value depends on future cash flows, it may seem obvious that a cash flow multiple is the best one to use. But cash flow multiples do not always yield a precise estimate of value. Continuing value is sometimes estimated on the basis of sales or asset multiples not because investors care about sales or assets, *per se*, but because sales or asset levels at the end of the explicit value period bear a stronger relationship to expected future cash flows over the continuing value period than does cash flow at the end of the explicit value period.

Continuing value methodology works best when the accounting stream on which the valuation is based has stabilized or is normalized and when the relation between the accounting stream and value is strong. Suppose you are considering using a measure of assets (possibly book value, adjusted book value, or replacement cost) to estimate continuing value. The estimate of value is most reliable if it is applied to a venture where the rate of future growth is expected to be stable. Thus, to base the value estimate on a multiple of assets, you should extend the explicit value period to a point where the growth rate of assets is expected to have stabilized.

Similarly, if you are considering valuation based on a cash flow, net income, or sales multiplier, the explicit value period should extend to a point where the expected growth rate of the accounting stream is stable. In addition, if the venture is subject to cyclical variability, the estimate of value is more reliable if the multiplier is derived from data that have been normalized, and where the resulting multiplier is applied to a normalized estimate for the venture. Normalization means that the cash flow, income, or sales numbers used in the calculations are the ones that are expected over the course of the cycle rather than at a cyclical peak or trough.

Even if the accounting stream is stable, its connection to value may be weak. If the relation is weak, then the stream is likely to be a poor basis for estimating value. The strength of the relationship can be evaluated by comparing measures of dispersion of alternative multipliers across a sample of comparable firms. In general, a multiplier with low dispersion, standardized by the mean or median value, yields a better estimate.

Determining the Multiplier   Suppose you can reasonably assume that the cash flows of a venture will grow at an average rate of 5 percent per year after the explicit value period. Moreover, you already have determined that the appropriate discount rate is 12 percent. By applying these assumptions to a forecast of cash flow in the last year of the explicit value period, you can determine the cash flow multiplier that is correct analytically. Equation (9.2) describes the relation between value and cash flow,

$$V_t = \frac{C_t(1 + g)}{r - g} \tag{9.2}$$

where V_t is value at time t, C_t is cash flow at time t, r is the discount rate, and g is the expected growth rate of cash flows.[5]

Equation (9.2) is the standard expression for the present value of a growing perpetuity of cash flows. The equation can be solved for the value of the cash flow multiplier, as shown in Eq. (9.3):

$$\frac{V_t}{C_t} = \frac{(1 + g)}{r - g} \tag{9.3}$$

where V_t/C_t is the cash flow multiplier.

Equation (9.3) shows how the expected growth rate and the discount rate affect the multiplier. Under the assumptions made above, the multiplier is 15 [i.e., $(1 + .05)/(.12 - .05)$]. That is, the continuing value is estimated to be 15 times the cash flow in the last year of the explicit value period. A higher rate of expected growth would increase the multiplier. A higher discount rate would reduce it.

Although the connections between value and other accounting streams are indirect, the same principle applies. Expected growth rates that are high imply high multiples, and discount rates that are high imply low multiples. This suggests a way to use market data to estimate a multiplier. If, relative to the comparable firms, the asset being valued has a high expected growth rate, a higher multiplier should be used. If the comparable firms are selected correctly and if the cash flow used in Eq. (9.3) is the expected cash flow, there is no reason for the discount rate to be different from that for the comparable firms.

If the investor anticipates harvesting by selling the company, it is appropriate to adjust the continuing value estimate for the expectation that underwriters and others in public or private transactions will discount the value. By using data for comparable public transactions, the discount can be implicit in the offer prices of the comparables. If stock price data for established public companies are used, underwriters in going-public transactions normally discount value by 10 to 15 percent compared to market value immediately after the offering.

The other determinant of V_t in Eq. (9.2) is C_t. There are two important issues to keep in mind about C_t. First, the cash flows of comparable public firms are publicly reported information. They have been prepared under Generally Accepted Accounting Principles (GAAP) and have been subject to independent audit. Second, the comparable firms all have survived long enough to have done a public equity offering. Firms that failed or have not gone public are not represented in the sample.

How you should deal with these issues depends on the purpose of the valuation and on your comfort level with the financial projections. Suppose you believe the projections of the venture are prepared according to GAAP, and, though not audited, are unbiased. In this case, it is reasonable to assume that the accounting projections are comparable to the reported numbers of the public companies. It follows that you can apply the public company multipliers directly.

Suppose, instead, that you are considering investing in the venture and that you are using financial projections prepared by the entrepreneur. The projections reflect an unstated assumption that the venture will be successful. In this case, direct application of multipliers from comparable public companies would result in an overestimate of continuing value.

One solution to the bias problem is to base the continuing value estimate on multipliers from private transactions that are derived from accounting information that is likely to be biased to a similar degree. But information about private transactions is difficult to acquire and verify.

A second solution is to adjust the public company multiplier for an estimate of the extent of the bias in the accounting projections for the venture. If, for example, you believe the venture's probability of failure is 30 percent and is not reflected in its projected cash flows, it would be appropriate to adjust the public company multiplier down by 30 percent. This solution is implicit in the actual multipliers that frequently are used in private transaction valuations. Such adjustments often are characterized (incorrectly, we believe) as "illiquidity discounts." We hope this discussion helps you to understand the true nature of the discount. If you understand that the issue is not illiquidity, you can do a better job of applying the data from comparable firms to your own valuation questions.

This leads us to the third solution. If the source of noncomparability is that the financial projections are positively biased, then a sensible way to solve the problem is to develop a set of projections that reflect the true expectations, giving account to the risk of failure. You would then value the asset using the comparable market data without any additional adjustment.

The Effects of Market Timing on Continuing Value

A critical issue concerning the application of multipliers is how market timing should affect the appropriate multiple. To illustrate the importance of timing, in 2001 the aggregate price/earnings (P/E) ratio of the S&P 500 was around 31, nearly an historical high, and the aggregate dividend yield was around 1.3 percent, near an historical low.[6] If the fundamental basis for equity valuation is the present value of expected future dividends, then either the expected rate of dividend growth was very high or the cost of equity capital was very low. More likely, the explanation involves a combination of both factors: optimism about future economic growth (and hence rising dividends) combined with a low cost of equity capital.

Forecasting the Multiple Suppose it is 2001 and you are to value a company based on expected future earnings. You believe the P/E ratio of the S&P 500 is appropriate to use as a benchmark for estimating continuing value. Should you base the valuation on the P/E ratio of the index that exists at the time of valuation? The answer is that you should not. A better approach is to forecast the multiple that will exist at the time of a hypothetical sale of the investment. You do not want the multiple that exists today, because you do not plan to harvest today.

What are the implications of using a 2001 multiplier in deciding whether to invest and in exchange for what fraction of ownership? You would end up investing too much money in exchange for too little ownership during periods when value multipliers are high, and too little in exchange for too much ownership during periods when value multipliers are low. If you try to follow this strategy and are competing against investors who use more forward-looking approaches, you will be outbid during the periods when measures of value are low.

Figure 9-2 shows the P/E multiples of the S&P 500 for the period from 1955–2001. You can see that there is a great deal of variation—from a low of 7.4 in 1979 to a high of 31.5 in 1999. The level from one year to the next is not random. A high value in one year tends to be followed by a high value in the next, and so on.

Suppose you want to use this historical information to help select a P/E multiple for use in estimating continuing value where sale of the investment is expected to occur in five years. We already have established that today's multiple does not yield the best estimate. On the other hand, because the P/E for one year is not independent of the P/E in the prior year, simply using the average P/E of 16.3 over the entire 47-year period may not yield the best estimate either. It would make sense to use the average multiple if there were no realistic expectation of selling the investment. But if the true intent is to sell after a few years, a better estimate of the multiple is possible.

Suppose the investor hopes to sell in about five years. Using the statistical process of regression analysis, it is possible to estimate the expected change in the P/E ratio over five years as a function of the current level. Using this approach, we find that the expected P/E in five years was 9.36 plus 0.395 time the current P/E. Based on this approach, with the P/E ratio in 2001 around 31.1, the ratio in five years is expected to be about 21.6. This is an appropriate multiplier to use for valuing a venture in 2001, where the investment is expected to be sold in 2006 and where the S&P 500 is a good benchmark. For approaches based on other multipliers, the reasoning is similar.

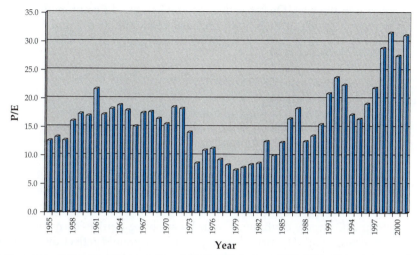

Figure 9-2   Price/Earnings ratio of S&P 500 Index 1955-2001 (Based on trailing-twelve-month earnings)

Price/earnings ratios of the S&P 500 Index have varied from below 10 to above 30. For the purpose of forecasting a price/earnings ratio, it is important to consider time series correlation, such as the correlation that can be observed in the series in the figure.

Source: 2002 Economic Report of the President.

Market Timing   There is evidence that venture capital investors are able to engage successfully in market timing with respect to liquidation of their positions.[7] The evidence implies that the average multiple in the valuation understates true expected cash flows at time of sale. We can get a sense of the potential gains from market timing by examining the range of P/E ratios over a window during which the investor might try to "time the market."

Suppose that instead of selling the investment in five years, the investor would attempt to sell sometime between the fourth and sixth years after investing. The average range of P/E ratios over three-year periods can be used to gain perspective on the expected benefit of market timing efforts. The average difference between the high and low P/E ratio over successive periods of three years from 1955 to 2000 is 4.0. Market timing success would mean that instead of getting the average during the period, the investor might be able to time sale of the investment to achieve a value near the top of the range. If so, the expected benefit of market timing activities would be to raise the multiple of terminal earnings by about 2.0. Thus, to allow for mean reversion of P/E multiples and venture capitalist "skill" at timing the market, we would use the five-year ahead regression-based P/E forecast, plus an adjustment of 2.0 for market timing. Given the 31.1 P/E in 2001, our estimate for a harvest between 2005 and 2007 is a multiple of 22.6.

9.3   NEW VENTURE VALUATION METHODS

In the balance of this chapter, we present four different discounted cash flow methods of new venture valuation. Two are based explicitly on financial economic theory. The other two are practitioner approaches that are based more on experience and rules-of-thumb that have been successful in the past. Our objective is to review the different methods in a way that enables us to reconcile each of them with financial economic theory and to uncover the advantages and disadvantages of each. We begin by defining each of the models and identifying their respective information requirements.

Using the Venture Capital Method

The Venture Capital Method is the traditional approach of venture capital investment valuation. It is also the simplest approach.[8]

> Step 1: Select a terminal year for the valuation and estimate net income in that year based on a "success scenario." A success scenario is one in which the venture meets its performance objectives.
>
> Step 2: Compute continuing value by applying a price/earnings multiple to the earnings projection. The price/earnings multiple should reflect the expected capitalization of earnings for a company that has achieved the level of success reflected in the scenario.
>
> Step 3: Use a very high discount rate to convert the continuing value to present value.
>
> Step 4: Based on present value, compute the fraction of ownership the investor requires in exchange for contributed capital.

You probably can spot some immediate problems with the Venture Capital Method. Most fundamentally, it is based on an optimistic forecast of net income. There is no indication of the likelihood that the success scenario will be achieved.[9] To compensate for the inflated forecast, the hurdle rate used to value net income is well above cost of capital. The approach can easily yield discount rates in excess of 50 percent. However, this does not mean the investor expects to earn 50 percent on the investment.

In addition, the Venture Capital Method (as described above and as normally applied) ascribes all of the value of the venture to cash flows during the continuing value period. It does not consider cash flows in the explicit value period. Although this is easy to address by incorporating cash flows during the explicit value period, the model implies that we would again use projections from a success scenario and would discount them at a high rate. The method's treatment of cash flows before the continuing value period as unimportant implies that continuing value is likely to be estimated at a point before the venture has stabilized. That is, continuing value is likely to be estimated when the venture is expected to be growing rapidly. This suggests that the estimate of continuing value will be more uncertain than if the explicit value period were extended.

Before you reach a conclusion not to use the Venture Capital Method, you should give some thought to the negotiation process. Consider the following scenario: An entrepreneur who is enthusiastic about an idea comes to you with a business plan. You like the concept and believe the team is the right one to undertake the project. However, like many entrepreneurs, this one seems overly optimistic. In particular, the entrepreneur's financial projections are based on a scenario in which the venture develops pretty much according to plan, with no major obstacles or setbacks.

You would like to go forward, but you believe the entrepreneur's projections seriously overstate the likely success. What do you do? Do you engage in a debate with the entrepreneur about the projections, or do you simply try to counter optimism with pessimism by applying a discount rate that is biased upward to compensate for the entrepreneur's inflated projections? At least in the past, the answer has often been the latter. It sometimes is easier to build the valuation on a structure of compensating errors than to work toward projections on which both parties agree.

Liars' Poker   However, envision yourself in the role of the entrepreneur. You know that venture capitalists often use very high discount rates to value investments. Perhaps you have a realistic sense of the future potential for your venture, including the likelihood of failure. What sort of financial information do you put in the business plan? Do you present your true beliefs, or do you try to paint an optimistic picture that you hope will appear credible? As the entrepreneur and the investor are engaged in a game, the choice is a difficult one.

To illustrate, suppose that if the entrepreneur presents her true beliefs and is believed by the investor, the investor will value the project at $100, but if the investor does not believe the entrepreneur, it will be valued at only $50. On the other hand, if the entrepreneur overstates her beliefs, but still is believed by the investor, the project will be valued at $150, but at only $75 if the investor does not believe. The possible outcomes are summarized in the following diagram:

Payoff Matrix: Investor's Valuation Conditional on Entrepreneur's Representations

	Entrepreneur represents beliefs accurately	Entrepreneur overstates beliefs
Investor believes entrepreneur	$100	$150
Investor does not believe entrepreneur	$ 50	$ 75

Suppose, moreover, that the probability of being believed is 50 percent, regardless of whether the entrepreneur is truthful. In that case, the entrepreneur should always overstate, because the expected value of overstating is higher than that of being truthful. The expected value of overstating is $112.5 (i.e., .5 × $150 + .5 × $75), whereas the expected value of being truthful is only $75 (i.e., .5 × $100 + .5 × $50).

But this solution is not attractive to the investor, who will have overvalued the project by $12.5. The overvaluation arises because the investor incorrectly assumes that the probability of the entrepreneur being truthful is .5, when, in fact, the entrepreneur is certain to overstate. On the other hand, if the investor assumes correctly that the entrepreneur always overstates, then the project only ends up being valued at $75, when it really is worth $100. This means projects that really are worth $100 and require investments of more than $75 cannot attract outside funding. For projects that require less than $75 of investment, the ownership stake demanded by the investor will be greater than it has to be.

You can think of the difference between $75 and $100 as additional transaction and negotiation costs the parties must incur because the entrepreneur is unable to commit to be truthful. That differential is an incentive for the entrepreneur to find a way of credibly committing to be truthful. We will return to this issue later in the text, when we take up the subject of contracting.

Valuation versus Negotiation   How are problems of bias-induced valuation error to be avoided? One solution is to rely on experience and elaborate rules of thumb for adjusting the valuations to deal with such errors. This is essentially what the Venture Capital Method purports to do.

A more practical approach is to conduct the real valuation in the back office. The entrepreneur and the investor can build their discussions and negotiations around the cash flow projections and other information shared in the business plan. At the same time, each (but possibly only the investor) may be working separately, with their own private sets of beliefs and true required rate of return, to determine what the project is worth and how best to structure the deal.

Using the First Chicago Method

The First Chicago Method is another valuation approach that commonly is used by practitioners.[10] Under this method, a small number of discrete scenarios are valued using a discount rate that reflects cost of capital. The objective is to select and weight the scenarios in a manner that provides unbiased estimates of the expected cash flows and risk. It follows that the opportunity cost of capital is the correct discount rate to use for valuing the expected cash flows.

The First Chicago Method involves the following steps:

Step 1: Select a terminal year for the valuation.

Step 2: Estimate the cash flows during the explicit value period based on a small number of discrete scenarios. Normally, the valuation is based on a "success scenario," a "failure scenario," and a "neutral" or "sideways scenario." The success scenario may be the same one that would be used in the Venture Capital Method. The failure scenario is likely to be one that culminates in abandonment (possibly during the explicit value period). The sideways scenario can be a scenario based on conditions where the venture would not achieve a track record sufficient for sale of the investment, at least without a substantial discount.

Step 3: Compute the continuing value by applying a multiplier to the financial projection. The multiplier for the success scenario should reflect the expected capitalization for a company that has achieved the level of success reflected in the scenario. The multiplier for the sideways scenario may be different, depending on differences in expected growth rates of the accounting stream used in the capitalization. In the failure scenario, the venture probably is not sold, but the liquidation value, if any, of the assets should be incorporated in the cash flows.

Step 4: Compute expected cash flows by appropriately weighting the scenarios.

Step 5: Compute present value by discounting the expected cash flows, including expected continuing value at their opportunity cost of capital.

Step 6: Based on present value, compute the fraction of ownership the investor should require in exchange for contributed capital.

The First Chicago Method makes fundamental sense, because the goal is to value expected cash flows at a true cost of capital. The scenarios are used to help generate the estimate of expected cash flow and to encourage the analyst to think about the range of possibilities. Information about the uncertainty of the cash flows that is generated by the scenario analysis is not used in the valuation.

Traditional application of the First Chicago Method does not offer much guidance on how to actually determine opportunity cost of capital. It might seem that the dispersion information reflected in the cash flow scenarios should be useful. Later, you will see that it is, but that is in the context of the CEQ model. In fact, if the CEQ model is applied to discrete scenarios, it is the same as the First Chicago Method with the CAPM being used to value the cash flows.

Ultimately, it is not possible to value the cash flows by either the Venture Capital Method or the First Chicago Method without resorting to some asset pricing model to determine the appropriate discount rates. The asset pricing model might be one that is based on experience and rules of thumb. It might be based on simple comparisons to other assets in the market. Or it might be a discount rate derived from a formal asset pricing model, such as the CAPM.

Using the RADR Form of the CAPM

Equation (9.4) is the CAPM valuation model stated in the form of a risk-adjusted discount rate.

$$PV = \sum_{t=1}^{T} \frac{C_{jt}}{1 + r_F + \beta_{jt}(RP_M)} \tag{9.4}$$

In this expression, PV is the present value of all future cash flows. To maintain consistency with the previous discussion, you can interpret the periods from 1 to T as the explicit value period, where the time T cash flow includes continuing value. To allow for the possibility that different cash flows in the same period can vary in risk, C_{jt} represents the value of a particular expected cash flow, j, at time, t. Thus, for example, the total cash flow in a period may be comprised of one part that is risky and another that is riskless. Each cash flow in expression (9.4) is discounted by a factor determined by the CAPM. The elements of the discount factor are the risk-free rate r_F, the market risk premium, RP_M, and beta risk β_{jt}.

Estimating Expected Cash Flow   The cash flow projections required to use Eq. (9.4) are expected cash flows, including risk of failure. They are not the cash flows expected to be realized if the venture is a success. The estimate of continuing value is also an expected value estimate.

When the RADR form is used, uncertainty is addressed in the discount rate. So it is not necessary to make a direct estimate of the uncertainty of cash flows. In practice, this may not be much of an advantage. It is hard to envision good ways of estimating expected cash flows that do not involve assessing uncertainty at the same time.

Equation (9.4) allows for the possibility that different cash flow streams in the same period can differ in risk. For example, except for uncertainties about the tax status of a venture, depreciation cash flows (i.e., the tax savings in each period) are determined at the time the investment is made. Consequently, they are likely to be much less risky than revenues.

When inflows and outflows within a period differ in risk, it is unlikely that you can find a single discount rate that can be used to value cash flows in different periods. It is possible to find a single rate that can be applied to the net cash flows in a given period, but between one period and the next, the relative proportions of cash flows of different risk are likely to change. If they do, then the appropriate discount rate also changes.

Suppose, for example, that the sales are expected to grow over time and that risk is proportionate to sales. It is likely that revenue is more uncertain than depreciation cash flows or fixed expenses, which are not expected to grow. In this case, the proportions of high- and low-risk cash flows change over time. Depending on the nature of the risks, the growth of sales implies a discount rate for valuing net cash flows that is changing. This is a difficult problem to address with the RADR form of the CAPM. Also, it implies that true market comparables for any project or firm are unlikely to be found.

Estimating the Risk-Free Rate of Interest   Suppose the expected cash flows of the venture have been projected in nominal terms, including a forecast of the effect of inflation on revenue growth. To account for the effect of inflation on the required rate of return, the value of r_F in Eq. (9.4) should be based on information that is available at the time of the valuation. If you are trying to value an expected cash flow that will be received in one year, it is reasonable to use the available rate on U.S. government zero-coupon bonds that will mature in one year as an estimate of the risk-free rate. If the cash flow will be received in five years, the rate on five-year zero-coupon bonds is a better estimate. For a project that will produce cash flows in a number of years, you might decide to use a series of risk-free rates corresponding to the duration of each cash flow.

Estimating the Market Risk Premium   The market risk premium is the expected difference between the return on the market and the risk-free rate over the period until a cash flow is received. Hence, the risk premium for a cash flow due in one year is the excess of the expected annual market return over the one-year risk-free rate. The risk premium for a cash flow due in five years is the excess of the expected annual market return over the five-year risk-free rate. In practice, it is difficult to make a forward-looking estimate of the market risk premium that is much better than a long-run historical average. However, recent forward-looking estimates of the risk premium (derived by discounting forecasts of future dividends) suggest that the long-term historical average overstates the market risk premium by 2 to 5 percent. In any case, the market risk premium must correspond to the holding period of the cash flow being valued.

By one estimate, the long-run historical average return on the S&P 500 from 1926 through 2000 is 13.0 percent. Over the same period, the average return on U.S. Treasury bills was 3.9 percent, and the average annual return on long-term government bonds was 5.7 percent. The

Why Are Corporate Bond Interest Rates So Much Higher than Government Bond Rates?

Normally, the so called "promised yield" interest on a corporate bond is significantly higher than on a government bond. To an extent, the difference can be attributed to differences in default risk and the possibility that the bond has an element of systematic (beta) risk. Even very high-quality corporate bonds, however, have rates above government rates.

The primary reason for the difference in promised yields is that most corporate issuers of debt preserve options to call the debt before maturity. The issuer has a call option that is effectively sold to it by the investors. The way investors are compensated for providing the option is through the contractually specified interest rate. No such call option affects the contractually specified yield on U.S. government zero coupon bonds. Thus, the higher interest rates for high-quality corporate debt reflect compensation for options that are sold to issuers by investors. It is not appropriate to include payment for the options in the estimate of the risk-free rate.

average annual rate of inflation was 3.1 percent.[11] Based on this information, a reasonable way to estimate the market risk premium for one year is to find the difference between the return on the S&P 500 and the Treasury bill rate, that is, 9.1 percent per year. To estimate the market risk premium for a cash flow expected in five years, a reasonable approach is to find the difference between the return on the S&P 500 and the long-term government rate, that is, 7.3 percent.[12] You can also see from the above information that, on average, the real risk-free rate for short-term investment is very small—only 0.8 percent. Apparently, for determining the value of an asset, investors have been much more concerned about risk than about time delays.

Our concern with reliance on long-term historical averages to estimate required returns is that the asset mix of investors has changed dramatically since the development of portfolio theory and since the change in the standard of "prudent" investment management for fiduciaries to one that focuses on portfolio risk. A substantially larger fraction of investment capital is now invested in equities, with increasing investments in small-capitalization stocks, foreign equities, and venture capital. Given the structural change, it is not clear that long-run historical averages are the best basis for making estimates of required returns.

Unfortunately, our concern cannot be addressed by using only historical data for more recent years. Because capital has moved from debt to equity in recent years, equity prices have risen dramatically as have real returns on debt securities. The net effect of the shift may be that the expected real risk-free rate is higher than in the distant past and that the market risk premium is lower. Recent academic research supports this view. For example, Fama and French (2001) use dividend and earnings growth rates to estimate the equity premium over 1951–2000, and find equity premia of 2.55 percent to 4.32 percent, compared to the historical average premium of 7.43 percent. Welch (2001) surveys a large number of finance and economics professors and reports that the consensus forecast of the long-term equity risk premium is 5 to 5.5 percent.

In light of the historical and new evidence, we normally assume a market risk premium of about 5 to 6 percent. When we can, we consult with managers of asset allocation funds to learn their current forecasts of the market risk premium. Those estimates usually are based on finding the discount rate that equates their forecast of future dividends to the current stock index value (i.e., dividend discount models of value). You should remain alert to the prospect of better methods of estimating the market risk premium.

Estimating the New Venture Beta   Equation (9.5) is the expression for computing the beta of an asset, A.

$$\beta_A = \frac{Cov(r_A, r_M)}{\sigma_M^2} = \frac{\rho(r_A, r_M)\sigma_A}{\sigma_M} \tag{9.5}$$

The expression implies several different approaches that can be used to estimate β_A.

The middle term in the expression is a regression coefficient that is determined by regressing a time series of asset returns on a time series of returns on a market index. However, because the asset being valued is a nonmarket asset, the information needed to estimate the regression coefficient is not available directly. One common approach for dealing with this problem is to use a regression coefficient that is estimated from data for one or more firms that are comparable to the venture. Beta estimates for the common stocks of public companies are developed from regression analysis techniques and published by several services. A second approach is more conceptual and involves using reasoning to construct scenarios for the assets that are related to the overall market. The asset beta is then inferred from analysis of the scenarios.

The term on the right-hand side of Eq.(9.5) describes the beta of an asset as a function of the standard deviation of asset returns, the standard deviation of market returns, and the correlation coefficient between asset returns and market returns. Thus, a third approach is to derive the estimate of beta from separate estimates of these three elements. We discuss this approach in the context of using the CEQ form of the CAPM. It usually is the most reliable approach for estimating the beta risk of new ventures.

Using the Betas of Comparable Firms   Estimating the beta of a nonmarket asset by regression requires searching for one or more public companies with asset risk that is comparable. The case for using data on comparable firms is strongest if there are public companies with market risk that is comparable to the asset. For example, if the new venture is a grocery store, it could be reasonable to use market information on public grocery store companies to infer the venture's beta risk.

Figure 9-3 contains data on equity betas for a number of different industry groupings. Ranges of equity betas reported in the figure are based on averages for two-digit industries as reported in a study by Kaplan and Peterson (1998). It is apparent that beta values vary in a systematic fashion across industries. For example, the betas of utilities tend to be low, whereas those of professional service providers tend to be high.

One important implication of Figure 9-3 is that for public companies, equity beta values of less than 0.5 or greater than 2.0 are extremely unlikely. Keep in mind that asset betas are lower than equity betas and that they depend on the extent of reliance on financial leverage. The combination of low equity betas and high financial leverage that is typical of public utilities, for example, implies asset betas that are quite low but still materially above zero.

Assuming that public company data are available, they must be converted before they can be used to value a new venture. The beta risk estimate for a public company is estimated from

Equity Beta by SIC Code		
SIC Grouping	**Two-digit SIC Range**	**Equity Beta Range**
Agricultural Products and Services	1	1.63
Extractive	10–13	.80–.94
Construction	15–17	1.26–2.65
Food	20	0.66
Textile	22–23	1.00–1.02
Wood Products	24–27	1.04–1.60
Chemicals and Oil	28–29	.63–1.30
Plastic, Leather, Stone	30–32	.83–1.76
Metals	34	1.89
Manufacturing	35–39	.78–1.75
Transportation	40–45	.69–1.61
Utilities	46–49	.47–.95
Wholesale	50–51	.95–1.38
Retail	52–59	.64–1.34
Financial	60–67	.96–2.23
Consumer Services	70–79	.94–1.72
Professional Services	80–84	1.54–2.00

Figure 9-3   Equity beta by SIC code

Data are pure-play equity betas, derived from a study by Kaplan and Peterson (1998) of over 3000 public companies.

stock market returns. The resulting estimate is an equity beta, β_E. Because equity is a residual claim on the assets of the firm after the claims of debt-holders, the equity beta of a comparable firm is higher than the beta risk of the firm's assets.

To base an estimate of cost of capital on the equity beta of a public firm, it is necessary to determine that firm's asset beta, β_A. Equation (9.6) describes how an equity beta can be used to infer an asset beta.

$$\beta_A = \beta_E \frac{E}{V} \qquad (9.6)$$

In the expression, β_E usually is estimated by regression analysis (possibly from a published source), E is the market value of comparable-firm equity, and V is the market value of comparable-firm assets. The computation in Eq. (9.6) yields only an approximation of the asset beta because it assumes the comparable firm's debt has no market risk (i.e., the debt beta is zero). If the comparable is highly leveraged, the expression will underestimate its asset beta. Also, in practice, because market values of debt usually are not available, it is common to estimate V as the sum of the market value of equity plus the book value of debt.

Assuming comparable-firm data are available for more than one firm, the asset beta normally is estimated as a weighted average of the asset betas of the comparables. The weightings may be equal, or extra weight may be given to the comparables that are most similar to the venture in terms of size, age, or other considerations.

Using Arithmetic or Geometric Average Returns

Suppose an asset that is correctly priced is equally likely to return either 50 percent or zero percent each year. If cost of capital for an investment is inferred by calculating the average annual return, the resulting estimate is 25 percent (i.e., (50% + 0%)/2). If it is calculated as the geometric return it is 22.5 percent [i.e., $((1 + 50\%) \times (1 + 0\%))^{.5} - 1$]. Which one is right?

Consider a one-period investment of $1.00. At the end of the period, it will be worth either $1.50 or $1.00. The average is $1.25. If you discount $1.25 at the arithmetic average rate of 25 percent, you find that the present value is $1.00. If you discount it at the geometric average rate of 22.5 percent, you find that the present value is $1.02. Apparently, the arithmetic average is right.

But consider a two-year investment. Suppose you get a 50 percent return the first year and zero percent the second (or the reverse). The cumulative value is $1.50 for two years. If you discount the $1.50 to present value at 25 percent, you get $.96, whereas if you discount it at 22.5 percent, you get $1.00. It appears that the geometric average is right if you are valuing long-term cash flows. This is the common argument for using the geometric average.

However, look again. The previous calculation does not consider all possible outcomes. If the probabilities remain stable over time, there is a 25 percent chance that the investment will be worth $2.25 in two years (i.e., $1.00 × 1.5 × 1.5), a 50 percent chance that it will be worth $1.50, and a 25 percent chance that it will be worth $1.00. The expected value is $1.56, not $1.50 as in the above calculation. Discounting $1.56 at 25 percent for two periods yields $1.00, the correct present value. Thus, even for a longer holding period, the arithmetic average yields the correct value. Accordingly, we favor using the arithmetic average.

In some cases, the objective is not to value a new venture, but rather a financial claim on the venture, such as the equity. To value the equity, you need to use an equity beta. However, you cannot estimate the equity beta by simply calculating a weighted average of the equity betas of comparables. The equity beta of the venture depends on its financial leverage, which is likely to be different for the new venture than for the average of the comparable firms. To estimate the equity beta, you should first use Eq. (9.6) to estimate the asset beta of each comparable; second, calculate the weighted average asset beta; third, use the asset beta to find the asset value of the venture; and, fourth, deduct the value of the debt. The remainder is an estimate of equity market value.

Our primary concern with using market comparables to estimate beta is that true comparables of the new venture are unlikely. Many new ventures are highly specialized and involve products and market opportunities that are difficult to analogize to existing public companies. Even if a firm is in the same industry, it has survived and grown for long enough to have gone public. The total risk of the new venture is usually much higher than the total risk of a public company in the same industry. Only if the risk of failure is unrelated to overall market risk would it be expected that the beta of the new venture is similar to that of the comparable firms.

While good public-firm comparables for early-stage ventures are uncommon, the late 1990s provides a rare exception. During that period of several years, a large number of "new economy" ventures went public at early stages of development. Based on a sample of over 2600 firm-years of data, Kerins, Smith, and Smith (2003) estimate the equity betas of newly-public firms, including many observations of very small firms, firms that had yet to achieve profitability, and firms that had yet to begin revenue generation. Figure 9-4 summarizes the mean beta estimates

Beta Estimates (S&P 500 as Market Index)		
	Number of Observations	Mean Beta
All observations	2,623	0.993
Industry		
Biotechnology	501	0.747
Broadcast and cable TV	105	0.804
Communication equipment	247	1.157
Communications services	407	1.019
Computer networks	130	1.023
Computer services	440	0.811
Catalog/Mail order (Internet)	39	1.240
Software	754	1.202
Age (years after IPO)		
0–1 years	1,263	0.930
2–3 years	957	0.958
>3 years	403	1.270
Financial condition		
No revenue	102	0.824
Revenue, negative income	1,475	1.139
Positive income	1,033	0.821
Employees		
0–25	187	0.586
26–100	496	0.861
Over 100	1,661	1.138

Figure 9-4 Beta estimates of recently-public new economy firms from IPOs during 1995–2000

Source: Kerins, Smith, and Smith (2003).

from that study. The average beta is very close to 1.0, similar to the total risk of the S&P 500. The evidence also suggests that younger and smaller firms have lower betas. Because these firms tend not to use debt financing, their equity betas are approximately equivalent to asset betas.

Using the Betas of Public Venture Capital Funds   One way to estimate new venture betas is to use beta estimates for publicly traded portfolios of new ventures. Although it is difficult to manage a portfolio of new venture investments in a fund that is publicly traded, several closed-end venture capital funds are public. The typical betas of these funds that invest in the equity claims of new venture are in the range of 1.0 to 2.0.[13]

Estimating Beta from Scenarios   An alternative to using stock market data is to estimate the beta of an asset from scenarios. Because beta is a measure of market risk and not total risk, the scenarios must be related to overall economic performance. To illustrate, suppose the developer of a product for managing the use of energy by manufacturing firms is seeking a $1 million investment from an investor. Demand is subject to an array of uncertainties, including perceptions about value of the product, the possibility of a competing innovation, and publicity about the product. Some of these uncertainties are related to the overall economy; others are not.

On net, the entrepreneur believes the relation between product cash flows and the economy can be described in three scenarios, as shown in the following table:

Scenario	Probability	Return on Market Portfolio	Project Cash Flow per Year	Rate of Return on Investment
Boom	1/3	30%	$200,000	20%
Normal growth	1/2	10%	$170,000	17%
Bust	1/6	−5%	$130,000	13%

The information in the table can be used to estimate the beta of the investment.

Step 1: Compute the expected return on the market portfolio.

$$14.17\% = 30\% \times (1/3) + 10\% \times (1/2) - 5\% \times (1/6)$$

Step 2: Compute the variance of returns on the market portfolio.

$$1.53\% = (30\% - 14.17\%)^2 \times (1/3) + (10\% - 14.17\%)^2 \times (1/2) + (-5\% - 14.17\%)^2 \times (1/6)$$

Step 3: Compute the expected return on the project investment.

$$17.33\% = 20\% \times (1/3) + 17\% \times (1/2) + 13\% \times (1/6)$$

Step 4: Compute the covariance between market and project investment returns

$$0.29\% = (30\% - 14.17\%) \times (20\% - 17.33\%) \times (1/3)$$
$$+ (10\% - 14.17\%) \times (17\% - 17.33\%) \times (1/2)$$
$$+ (-.5\% - 14.17\%) \times (13\% - 17.33\%) \times (1/6)$$

Step 5: Compute beta as the ratio of the covariance to the market variance:

$$Beta = 0.29\%/1.53\% = 0.18$$

Using the beta for the proposed investment and assumptions about the risk-free rate and market risk premium, one can estimate the required return on the investment and the *PV* of the expected cash flow. Suppose the risk-free rate is 4 percent and the market risk premium is 8 percent. The resulting required rate of return for the investment is 5.5 percent. Discounting the expected $173,333 cash flow at this rate yields a present value of $164,310. The total value of the project depends, of course, on the expected cash flows in other years, including an estimate of continuing value.[14] Our point, here, is not to value the project but to illustrate the use of scenario data to estimate beta.

Shortcuts for Estimating Opportunity Cost of Capital You sometimes can back into an estimate of opportunity cost of capital that should be reasonably consistent with the CAPM. Suppose you can find mature public companies that are comparable to the venture you want to value and that pay dividends you expect will grow at a constant rate. If you know the price of the stock, the dividend level, and the expected growth rate of dividends, you can estimate the cost of capital using the dividend model:

$$P_0 = \frac{D_1}{r - g} \qquad \text{so} \qquad r = \frac{D_1}{P_0} + g \qquad\qquad (9.7)$$

where D_1 is the dividend expected next year, g is the expected rate of dividend growth, r is opportunity cost of capital, and P_0 is the current stock price. Suppose the expected dividend is $1, expected growth of dividends is 3 percent per year, and the current price is $12. The resulting estimate of cost of capital is 11.3 percent.

Another possible shortcut is to recognize that if a stock has no opportunity to invest retained cash flows at a rate different from its cost of capital, then the earnings/price ratio is an estimate of cost of capital. If expected earnings is $1 and the current price is $9, the estimated cost of capital is 11.1 percent. If the company has attractive investment opportunities, then the earnings/price ratio will be lower, depending on the value of the growth opportunities.

Both of these shortcuts are ways to estimate the cost of equity. To generate a cost of capital for assets they must be incorporated into a weighted average cost of capital calculation. Realistically, for most new ventures the approaches are unlikely to be of much value as stand-alone methods. Companies that are candidates for using these approaches to estimate cost of capital are much different from new ventures, where the entire value usually depends on prospective growth. Nonetheless, for some private businesses, such as retailing or service businesses, the shortcut approaches can work well. In any case, they can serve as a reality check on the cost of capital estimate you derive using the CAPM.

Using the CEQ Form of the CAPM

Equation (9.8) is the CEQ form of the CAPM, using the notation we already have introduced:

$$PV_t = \cfrac{C_t - \cfrac{\rho(C_t, r_M)\sigma_{C_t}}{\sigma_M}RP_M}{1 + r_F} \tag{9.8}$$

Note that this is the CEQ expression for the present value of a single cash flow that will be received at time t. This is in contrast to Eq. (9.4), which is an expression for the present value of an entire project, consisting of a summation of individual periodic cash flows. We focus on a single periodic cash flow in Eq. (9.8) partly to simplify notation and partly to emphasize the flexibility of the CEQ method.

We already have discussed how you can estimate many of the terms in the expression. To focus on the remaining issues, in Eq. (9.9) we solve for the risk-adjusted discount rate that is implicit in Eq. (9.8).

$$\frac{C_t}{PV_t} - 1 = r_F + \frac{\rho(C_t, r_M)(\sigma_{C_t}/PV_t)}{\sigma_M}RP_M \tag{9.9}$$

Equation (9.9) gives us another way to estimate beta. You can see in Eq (9.10) that beta can be estimated based either on returns, as in the middle term, or based on cash flows, as in the last term.

$$\beta_t = \frac{\rho(r_t, r_M)\sigma_{r_t}}{\sigma_M} = \frac{\rho(C_t, r_M)(\sigma_{C_t}/PV_t)}{\sigma_M} \tag{9.10}$$

Although the last term is stated in terms of cash flows, it is just another way of expressing the beta of the holding-period returns.

Estimating the Elements of Beta   Suppose we try to determine beta by estimating each element in the middle term in Eq. (9.10). If expected cash flows are estimated by scenario analysis or simulation, the information needed to estimate the standard deviation of cash flows is generated at the same time. But as we already have stated, it is not easy to go from the standard deviation of cash flows to the standard deviation of holding-period returns.

If, as in the earlier example, the objective is to determine whether the expected cash flow is high enough to justify an investment of a certain amount, which amount is known in advance, then an approximation of the standard deviation of holding-period returns can be computed on the basis of the required investment.[15] This is how we computed the variance of holding-period returns when we used scenario data to estimate beta. But if the objective is to determine how much a particular risky asset is actually worth, it is not possible to determine the correct standard deviation of holding-period returns without simultaneously determining the value of the cash flows.

Our conclusion is that if you cannot derive a reliable estimate of beta from data for comparable firms, it generally is better to circumvent the problem of estimating beta by using the CEQ form of the CAPM.

Estimating the CEQ Model   The advantage of the CEQ approach is that you do not have to determine the standard deviation of holding-period returns and the present value of the cash flow simultaneously. Look back at Eq. (9.8). We already have discussed methods of estimating all of the information requirements except for two: the correlation between project cash flows and the market, and the market standard deviation. Alternatively, it may be possible to estimate the cash flow beta directly. We illustrate direct estimation of the cash flow beta first.

Using Scenario Analysis to Estimate a Cash Flow Beta We use the previously discussed energy management venture to illustrate how to apply scenario analysis to cash flows instead of holding-period returns. Steps 3 through 5 of the example must be re-computed based on cash flows.

Step 3: Compute the expected cash flow of the project.

$$\$173{,}333 = \$200{,}000 \times (1/3) + \$170{,}000 \times (1/2) + \$130{,}000 \times (1/6)$$

Step 4: Compute the covariance between market returns and project cash flows.

$$\begin{aligned}
\$2{,}861 = {} & (30\% - 14.17\%) \times (\$200{,}000 - \$173{,}333) \times (1/3) \\
& + (10\% - 14.17\%) \times (\$170{,}000 - \$173{,}333) \times (1/2) \\
& + (-5\% - 14.17\%) \times (\$130{,}000 - \$173{,}333) \times (1/6)
\end{aligned}$$

Step 5: Compute the cash flow beta of the project.

$$\text{Cash flow beta} = \$2{,}861/1.53\% = \$186{,}425$$

Now that you know the cash flow beta, you can use it in the CEQ model, Eq. (9.8), to value the expected cash flow.

Step 1: Use the cash flow beta and market risk premium to compute the risk adjustment to the expected cash flow.

$$\text{Risk adjustment} = .08 \times \$186{,}425 = \$14{,}914$$

Step 2: Compute the certainty equivalent cash flow.

$$CE(C_1) = \$173{,}333 - \$14{,}914 = \$158{,}419$$

Step 3: Discount the certainty equivalent cash flow to present value at the risk-free rate.

$$PV = \$158{,}419/1.04 = \$152{,}326$$

Thus, using the previous assumptions of a 4 percent risk-free rate and 8 percent market risk premium, the present value of the cash flow is $152,326, and not the $164,310 value we computed using the RADR approach and an assumed investment of $1 million.[16]

The scenario approach is internally consistent from a mathematical standpoint, but correct implementation is challenging. Consider the example of a genetic engineering venture.

Such a venture is involved in experiments that have very uncertain outcomes. The nature and timing of the payoffs cannot be known with any precision. Investing in such a venture is a lot like buying a lottery ticket, where the expected cash flow payoff has little to do with the overall performance of the economy. A scenario analysis that is based on states of the economy seems to suggest that the scenarios for the venture would be identical (or almost so). If they are, then the cash flows should be discounted at the risk-free rate (or nearly so). If you were to form a large portfolio of biotechnology ventures, it appears that you could reduce the uncertainty of cash flows to almost zero.

Is this a realistic conclusion? We do not believe so. The reality is that the net cash flows of such a venture probably still are affected by the general economy, but in ways that are unlikely to be reflected in a scenario analysis that reduces to questions such as, "How will the venture perform if the economy is booming? Or in recession?" Our concern is that, with scenario analysis, it is easy to underestimate beta. Even projects with cash flow prospects that look like lotteries have positive betas. Recall from Figure 9-4 that there is little evidence of equity betas below 0.5 for public companies. Furthermore, projects with cash flows that are expected to be received farther in the future usually have higher betas than similar projects with shorter duration returns.

Estimating the Standard Deviation of Market Returns   In lieu of estimating the cash flow beta from scenarios, you can estimate the elements of the cash flow beta. The two elements we have yet to discuss are the market standard deviation and the correlation between venture cash flows and the market. We suggest using historical data on market returns to estimate the market standard deviation. In Figure 9-5 we report the standard deviation of a long-run historical average of annual holding-period returns for investing in the S&P 500. Our estimate is an annual standard deviation of 14.1 percent. To compute the standard deviation for a holding period different than one year we assume that holding-period returns from one year to the next are independent of each other.[17] Under this assumption, you can compute the standard deviation for a different holding period either by multiplying the standard deviation by the square root of the time interval in years or by multiplying the annual variance by the time interval and then taking the square root. Thus the two-year standard deviation is

$$19.94\% = 14.10\% \times 2^{1/2} \quad \text{or} \quad 19.94\% = (1.99\% \times 2)^{1/2}$$

Standard Deviation of the Market Return (S&P 500)					
Holding Period Length	Standard Deviation	Variance	Holding Period Length	Standard Deviation	Variance
One year	14.10%	1.99%	Six year	34.55%	11.94%
Two year	19.95%	3.98%	Seven year	37.32%	13.93%
Three year	24.43%	5.97%	Eight year	39.90%	15.92%
Four year	28.21%	7.96%	Nine year	42.32%	17.91%
Five year	31.54%	9.95%	Ten year	44.61%	19.90%

Figure 9-5   Standard deviation of the market return (S&P 500)

Note: The one-year standard deviation is computed from a 1950–2001 average of annual holding-period returns. Returns for longer holding periods are calculated assuming time-series independence of annual returns.

and the six-month standard deviation is

$$9.97\% = 14.10 \times .5^{1/2} \quad \text{or} \quad 9.97\% = (1.99\% \times .5)^{1/2}$$

For convenience, in Figure 9-5 we report market standard deviations for holding periods of up to 10 years.

Estimating the Correlation Between Project Cash Flows and the Market Although Eq. (9.8) circumvents the need to determine the risk of the holding-period return for a cash flow, it does raise another difficult question. How can the correlation between venture cash flows and the market be estimated? One approach is to base the estimate on judgment, in light of the nature of the risks that the venture will face. Alternatively, it may be possible to use stock returns data for public companies to gain perspective on the range of appropriate assumptions.

Although the prospect of estimating a correlation coefficient between a new venture cash flow and the market portfolio may seem daunting, the realistic range of values can be narrowed quite easily. Assuming you can do a good job of estimating total risk, you can use data for comparable firms to generate a reasonable estimate of the correlation coefficient. To begin, it is easy to demonstrate that the correlation of returns between the market and any publicly traded corporation depends on the extent of diversification of the corporation. Large and highly diversified corporations have returns that are more highly correlated with the market than do small and undiversified corporations. Nonetheless, even diversified corporations seldom have correlations with the market that are in excess of 0.7. A more typical level would be 0.3. For a new venture with a high degree of idiosyncratic risk and little diversification, it is unlikely that the correlation of returns with the market will exceed 0.3.

Figure 9-6 shows correlation coefficients with the market for a large sample of recently public firms in new economy industries. Most correlations are in the 0.15 to 0.25 range. Correlations with the market increase with firm financial maturity and size. Given the narrow range of realistic values, attempting to develop a precise estimate of the correlation between project returns and market returns probably is not worth the effort. A number near 0.5 is appropriate for a very market-sensitive venture such as a financial institution or public utility. A number around 0.1 is appropriate for early-stage ventures that have characteristics more like lotteries.

Testing the Consistency of Assumptions If market data for reasonably comparable firms are available, a check can be made on the internal consistency and reasonableness of the assumptions. Compared to public companies, which are normally better established than new ventures and more diversified, a new venture is likely to have higher total risk, but more of the risk is idiosyncratic. Because these deviations are offsetting, Figure 9-4 suggests that the asset beta of a new venture are similar to the asset betas of comparable public companies but comprised of a higher standard deviation and lower correlation. If you think the factors are offsetting, you can use your assumptions about project risk to make an ex post check. Do your assumptions result in an implied beta that is reasonable, in light of what you know about the betas of comparable public companies? If not, you may want to reconsider your assumptions..

If comparable firm data are available, why not just estimate the asset beta from the comparables, such as we report in Figure 9-4? Our answer is twofold. First, it is important to carefully assess the total risk of the venture. It is unlikely that you can generate a good estimate of the expected cash flows without considering risk. A good measure of total risk also is important for

Correlations Estimates (S&P 500 as Market Index)		
	Number of Observations	**Mean**
All observations	2,623	0.195
Industry		
Biotechnology	501	0.149
Broadcast and cable TV	105	0.237
Communication equipment	247	0.215
Communications services	407	0.241
Computer networks	130	0.208
Computer services	440	0.172
Catalog/Mail order (Internet)	39	0.217
Software	754	0.200
Age (years after IPO)		
0–1 years	1,263	0.162
2–3 years	957	0.212
>3 years	403	0.259
Financial condition		
No revenue	102	0.165
Revenue, negative income	1,475	0.197
Positive income	1,033	0.200
Employees		
0–25	187	0.117
26–100	496	0.153
Over 100	1,661	0.231

Figure 9-6 Correlation estimates of recently-public new economy firms from IPOs during 1995–2000
Source: Kerins, Smith, and Smith (2003)

valuing the project in light of the underdiversified position that the entrepreneur may be compelled to accept. Total risk also is critical to the valuation of the complex financial claims and real options that frequently are used in new venture financing. Second, by coming at the question of beta risk from both directions, (that is, by using market comparables for beta, and by inferring a beta estimate from the assumptions used in the CEQ valuation), you gain a way to check the reasonableness of your assumptions.

For an unlevered comparable firm, the estimate of correlation is given by Eq. (9.11).

$$\hat{\rho}(C_j, r_M) = \beta_{Comp} \frac{\sigma_M}{\sigma_{r_{Comp}}} \qquad (9.11)$$

In the above expression, the subscript, *Comp*, stands for comparable firm assets. Because the comparable will generate cash flows in many years, the estimate in Eq. (9.11) is best interpreted as a weighted average correlation over the life of the venture.

A caveat: The CEQ form of the CAPM works well as long as project risk is not too large compared to the expected cash flow and/or as long as the correlation between cash flows is not too great. For very risky cash flows, especially if correlation to the market is high or if value is based on total risk instead of just market risk, CAPM-based valuation models tend to undervalue risky cash flows. Because this problem is more likely to arise in determining value to the entrepreneur, we defer a more complete examination of the problem and possible solutions until Chapter 10. However, sometimes the problem can arise even for a well-diversified investor. If it does, you need to recognize it and modify your valuation to deal with it.

9.4 VALUING THE INVESTMENT

To compare valuation methods, we use a simple example. The example illustrates the valuation process, from determining the required rate of return to calculating net present value. We start with the CEQ, because it most clearly demonstrates the theoretical underpinnings of new venture value. Keep in mind that the valuation is made in the context of an outside investor who can invest in the venture as part of a well-diversified portfolio. Thus, the investor could be a public corporation investing on behalf of its stockholders, a venture capital fund investing on behalf of its limited partners, or even a business angel who is committing a small fraction of wealth to the venture.

An Illustration

Suppose you are employed by Murky Oil, a publicly owned company that is involved in exploration and development of oil fields. The company's plan is to spend five years in exploratory drilling to establish the value of a field that is geologically promising. At the end of the five years, it expects that reserves from the field can be estimated with sufficient precision, based on production at the time, so that it would make sense to sell the field to a vertically integrated petroleum company. You have examined a number of prior transactions and have concluded that established oil fields sell for prices that reflect the values of their reserves. Typically, you conclude, a factor of 10 times trailing cash flows from operations is an appropriate multiple.

Based on geological data for the site, you have constructed three scenarios of what might happen. Under the Likely Scenario, which reflects your beliefs of what is most likely to happen, the field develops at a rate and with yields similar to other oil fields with comparable geology. You estimate that the probability of this scenario being realized is 60 percent. The Success Scenario is patterned after the 20 percent of fields that have developed faster and with higher yields than expected. Finally, the Failure Scenario is that, in spite of five years of exploration, no oil is discovered—a result consistent with the least successful 20 percent of similar projects. In this case, the project cannot be sold.[18]

The following table shows the expected after-corporate tax cash flows each year for the five years of the project, as well as the continuing values. All cash flows are stated in nominal terms. Figures in the table are in thousands of dollars.

Murky Oil—New Field Pro Forma Year	1	2	3	4	5	Continuing Value
Expenditures						
All scenarios	−4,000	−4,200	−4,400	−4,600	−4,800	
Cash Inflows						
Success scenario	0	4,200	6,400	9,600	11,800	70,000
Likely scenario	0	1,200	4,400	6,600	7,800	30,000
Failure scenario	0	0	0	0	0	0

Because expenditures are certain, but cash inflows are risky, we highlight the difference by listing them separately in the table. We also list the continuing value cash flow separately to emphasize that if year 5 operating cash inflows are zero, the project will have a continuing value of zero.[19]

Murky Oil wishes to know the maximum it should be willing to pay to acquire the oil exploration rights to the field. You know that the maximum price depends on the present value of the future cash flows, both the inflows and the expenditures required to develop the field, and you have collected the following information to help determine value.

Current long-term rate on Treasury bonds:	6 percent
Historical average market risk premium:	8 percent
Average asset beta for oil exploration companies:	1.1
Annual standard deviation of market returns:	14 percent
Estimated correlation between oil cash flows and market	0.15

The information in the above listing is essential to every valuation that is based on the CAPM. You should assume that this information was developed using methods described earlier in the chapter.

Valuation by the CEQ Method

We use the CEQ method to derive an estimate of the present value of the oil exploration project that is consistent with the assumptions of the CAPM. To do this, we use the downloadable valuation template in Figure 9-7. In this figure we approach the Murky Oil valuation problem by aggregating all annual cash inflows and outflows. This makes the pattern of cash flows used in the calculation consistent with our assumption that the correlation coefficient applies to the net cash flow on an annual basis. The "Project Information" panel shows the annual cash flows under the three scenarios. The expected cash flow and standard deviations of cash flows are computed from the discrete scenario information and are shown at the bottom of the panel. The expected cash flows, C_t, and standard deviations, σ_C, are two of the inputs to the CEQ valuation model.

The "Market Information" panel is developed from the market assumptions listed in the example. In the description of the problem, we stated the assumptions on an annual basis. In Figure 9-7 we restate them to conform to the holding period of each annual cash flow.[20] Thus, for a one-year holding period the risk-free rate, r_F, is 6 percent, and the expected return on the market portfolio is 14 percent, resulting in a market risk premium, RP_M, of 8 percent. For a year 2 holding period the risk-free rate and expected return on the market portfolio are found by compounding the one-year rates. The two-year market risk premium is the difference between the two-year expected return on the market and the two-year risk-free rate. Because the length of a holding period is arbitrary, in Figure 9-7 we express the rates as their compounded values. Thus, for example, a two-year investment in a riskless asset is expected to yield a total return of 12.36 percent.

Also, in the Market Information panel, we provide information about market risk for each holding period. You can see that the variance of market returns, σ_M^2, increases by a constant amount per year as the holding period is extended. The standard deviation of market returns for each holding period, σ_M, is the square root of the variance for the holding period. Finally, the panel reports the correlation coefficient between project cash flows and the market, $\rho(C_t, r_M)$. We have assumed that the correlation coefficient is the same for all holding periods and that it applies to the total cash flow.

Valuation Template 1						
Diversified Investor Valuation by the CEQ Method **Based on Discrete Scenario Cash Flow Forecast**						
Project Information						
Cash Flows	**Probability**	**1**	**2**	**3**	**4**	**5**
Success Scenario	0.2	−$4,000	$0	$2,000	$5,000	$77,000
Expected Scenario	0.6	−$4,000	−$3,000	$0	$2,000	$33,000
Failure Scenario	0.2	−$4,000	−$4,200	−$4,400	−$4,600	−$4,800
Expected Cash Flow		−$4,000	−$2,640	−$480	$1,280	$34,240
Standard Deviation		$0	$1,399	$2,108	$3,161	$25,912
Market Information						
Risk-free Rate		6.00%	12.36%	19.10%	26.25%	33.82%
Market Rate		14.00%	29.96%	48.15%	68.90%	92.54%
Market Risk Premium		8.00%	17.60%	29.05%	42.65%	58.72%
Market Variance		1.99%	3.98%	5.97%	7.96%	9.95%
Market Standard Deviation		14.10%	19.94%	24.43%	28.21%	31.54%
Correlation		0.15	0.15	0.15	0.15	0.15
Market Value Estimate						
Present Value	**$13,617**	−$3,774	−$2,514	−$719	$446	$20,178
Diagnostic Information						
Required Return		6.00%	4.99%	−33.21%	187.02%	69.69%
Std. Dev. of Returns		0.00%	55.66%	293.24%	708.86%	128.42%
Covariance with Market		0.00%	−1.67%	−10.74%	29.99%	6.07%
Beta		0.00	−0.42	−1.80	3.77	0.61
Weighted Average Beta	1.20					

Figure 9-7 Diversified investor valuation by the CEQ method based on discrete scenario cash flow forecast

This template is designed to value assets with future cash flows projected in the form of discrete scenarios. Value is estimated using the CEQ form of the CAPM. The first panel contains cash flow projections and probabilities. The second contains assumptions about the market and correlation between the project and the market. The beta estimate in the last panel can be compared to other information as a means of evaluating the reasonableness and internal consistency of assumptions. Shaded cells are inputs. Values are in thousands.

In the "Market Value Estimate" panel of the figure, we use the CEQ method to compute the present value of each expected annual cash flow, PV_t. The first two panels of Figure 9-7 contain all of the information needed to use Eq. (9.8) to determine the present value of the oil field. The information requirements of the CEQ are the expected cash flow, the standard deviation of the cash flow, the correlation between cash flow and the market, the standard deviation of market returns, the market risk premium, and the risk-free rate. Total present value is reported in the figure as $13,617 thousand.

The "Diagnostic Information" panel contains information that can be used to help understand the valuation and to assess the reasonableness and internal consistency of assumptions used in the valuation. The first line in the panel shows the required rate of return for each annual cash flow. You can see that the required rates are highly variable and can even be negative. Because each annual cash flow can aggregate positive and negative streams that differ in total risk, the required rate for an annual cash flow cannot normally be determined in advance. Rather, it is inferred in the spreadsheet by comparing the expected cash flow in each year to its present value. The required rate for the year 1 cash flow, for example, is 6 percent and is found by dividing $4000 by $3774. Because the year 1 cash outflow is riskless, the correct discount rate is the risk-free rate of 6 percent. But why is the required rate less in the second year than in the first? The answer is that the discount rate in the figure is actually a weighted average between a (riskless) rate of 12.36 percent applied to the $4200 riskless negative cash flow and a risky rate of 27.50 percent applied to the risky positive expected cash flow.[21] The required rates for years 2 through 5 are, similarly, weighted averages. Because they are, they can be positive or negative and of any magnitude, even though the rates that are implicitly applied to individual cash inflow and outflows within a year are all quite reasonable.[22]

The second line in the panel shows the standard deviation of holding-period returns for each annual cash flow. The important point for comparing the CEQ and RADR approaches is that we could not determine the correct standard deviation of holding-period returns for an expected cash flow until we found the present value of the cash flow. This means that except for a trial and error approach to finding the required rate of return for each annual cash flow, there is no way to use the information from the example problem to find the correct discount rates. The offsetting advantage of RADR is that, if you can determine the appropriate discount rate indirectly, such as from an analysis of comparable firms, you do not need to estimate the correlation coefficient between the project and the market.

The most useful information in the last panel of Figure 9-7 is the beta estimates. The estimate for each year is calculated based on the project and market standard deviations and the correlation coefficient. The weighted-average beta is computed by weighting each annual beta by the ratio of the present value of that year's annual cash flow to total present value. Thus, if the present value of a cash flow is negative, the weight on the beta for the cash flow is also negative.[23]

The weighted-average beta provides a way of checking the consistency of assumptions in the model. In general, it may be reasonable to expect the beta of an individual oil field to be similar to the asset betas of public companies involved in oil exploration and development. Even if the companies are diversified across many oil fields, the effect of such diversification should be to lower the standard deviation of returns but raise the correlation with the market, so that the beta is unchanged. If the weighted-average beta that is derived by the methodology in Figure 9-7 is substantially different from the asset betas of comparable firms, this would suggest the need to reexamine the assumptions about correlation and total risk of the cash flows. In this case, the weighted-average asset beta of the project is 1.20, which is fairly close to the 1.10 average for public oil exploration companies that was stated in the initial assumptions of this example.

To recap, the benefits of the CEQ form of the CAPM are:

- Valuation is based on expected cash flows and not an optimistic forecast.
- Cost of capital is used to value each annual cash flow.
- Cash flows that differ in terms of total risk are handled easily by the CEQ method.
- Cash flows at different times can easily be valued separately.
- Any financial claim can be valued, as long as the CAPM assumptions hold.

- A measure of the total risk of cash flows is generated and will be particularly useful when we address valuation by the entrepreneur.

The main disadvantages of the CEQ approach are:

- An estimate of the full distribution of cash flow possibilities is required, instead of a single estimate.
- The correlation coefficient between venture cash flows and the market can be difficult to estimate, even if data on the betas of comparable firms are available.

Valuation by the RADR Method

Under the RADR method, expected cash flows are discounted to present value using a discount rate that reflects the opportunity cost of capital. The challenge is to determine the correct discount rate. As we have indicated, the only practicable approaches for determining the discount rate are by reference to data for comparable public firms or by scenario analysis. In the example of Murky Oil, we have assumed that comparable oil exploration firm data are available and that the asset beta for those firms is 1.10. This estimate is appropriate for valuing the entire project but is not of much help for valuing cash flows in different periods, even though the risk of the net cash flows differs from period to period. This may or may not be a serious problem.

In Figure 9-8 we use the beta for the comparable firms to value the project. The figure is a downloadable valuation template that contains a spreadsheet similar to the one in Figure 9-7, but modified to conduct the valuation by the RADR method. The Project Information panel is identical except that the standard deviation of cash flows is not computed because it is not used. The Market Information panel is modified by deleting the information on market standard deviation and correlation of cash flows with the market and by adding the comparable firm beta. Consistent with the limitations of comparable firm data, the beta is assumed to be the same in all periods. The information in the panel is used to compute the risk-adjusted discount rates.

The Market Value Estimate panel shows the estimated present value of the project, based on the values of the annual cash flows. The total value, $12,190 thousand is less than the $13,617 thousand value computed by the CEQ method. To establish that the difference is not entirely due to the use of a 1.10 beta, instead of the 1.20 weighted average beta from the CEQ method, we also valued the project using a beta of 1.20. The resulting estimate of value is $11,733 thousand.

The more important factor in the difference is that the RADR method, as applied in Figure 9-8 uses the wrong discount rate to value each annual cash flow. This can be seen by comparing the present-value estimates for the annual cash flows computed by the RADR method to the estimates by the CEQ method, and by comparing the annual cost of capital estimates. All of the information for the comparison is reported in Figures 9-7 and 9-8. The year 1 cash flow is a good one to focus on. We know that the entire cash flow is riskless and that, accordingly, the risk-free rate is the correct rate to use for valuing the cash flow. Yet practical application of the RADR approach results in its being discounted at a rate that is appropriate for a cash flow with beta risk of 1.10. Instead of discounting the cash flow at 6 percent, as is done by the CEQ method, it is discounted at 14.8 percent. Because the year 1 cash flow is negative, the resulting estimate contributes to overvaluing the project. Results for other years have similar problems. The cumulative effect is an undervaluation by about $1,400 thousand.

Valuation Template 2						
Diversified Investor Valuation by the RADR Method Based on Discrete Scenario Cash Flow Forecast						
Project Information						
Cash Flows	Probability	1	2	3	4	5
Success Scenario	0.2	−$4,000	$0	$2,000	$5,000	$77,000
Expected Scenario	0.6	−$4,000	−$3,000	$0	$2,000	$33,000
Failure Scenario	0.2	−$4,000	−$4,200	−$4,400	−$4,600	−$4,800
Expected Cash Flow		−$4,000	−$2,640	−$480	$1,280	$34,240
Market Information						
Risk-free Rate		6.00%	12.36%	19.10%	26.25%	33.82%
Market Rate		14.00%	29.96%	48.15%	68.90%	92.54%
Market Risk Premium		8.00%	17.60%	29.05%	42.65%	58.72%
Comparable firm beta		1.10	1.10	1.10	1.10	1.10
Estimated Cost of Capital		14.80%	31.72%	51.06%	73.16%	98.41%
Market Value Estimate						
Present Value	$12,190	−$3,484	−$2,004	−$318	$739	$17,257

Figure 9-8   Diversified investor valuation by the RADR method based on discrete scenario cash flow forecast

This template is designed to value assets with future cash flows projected in the form of discrete scenarios. Value is estimated using the RADR form of the CAPM. The first panel contains the cash flow projections and probabilities. The second contains assumptions about the market and an estimate of the asset beta. Shaded cells are inputs. Values are in thousands.

Our example exposes the limitations of the RADR method, as against the CEQ method. We do not, however, want you to lose track of its advantages. The principal strengths are:

- Valuation is based on expected cash flows.
- The discount rate is opportunity cost of capital.
- Market data can be used to estimate cost of capital.
- It is unnecessary to estimate the total risk or the correlation with the market.

The main disadvantages of the RADR method are:

- Unless separate information is available on cost of capital, holding-period returns and cost of capital must be determined simultaneously.
- True comparable firms are unlikely to be available for most kinds of new ventures.
- The model works best if applied to cash flows that are segregated according to market risk, but in that case, the appropriate discount rate for valuing a single cash flow cannot normally be determined based on data from comparable firms.

- If information on total risk is not generated, it is difficult to value complex financial claims on the underlying asset.

Valuation by the First Chicago Method

As we have applied the RADR method to value expected cash flows generated from discrete scenarios, it is an illustration of the First Chicago Method, with the specific added assumption that the CAPM is the correct asset pricing model. As such, there is no reason to illustrate application of the method separately. Although the First Chicago Method proposes to discount expected cash flows at their opportunity cost of capital, it does not provide guidance on how to determine cost of capital. A natural approach would be to use comparable ventures, but the method provides no guidance on how to assess comparability. With simple modifications to the Market Information panel of Figure 9-8, you can apply the First Chicago Method without the constraint that the discount rate is determined by the CAPM.

The strengths of the First Chicago Method include:

- Use of discrete scenarios is a simple and easy method of determining both risk and expected return.
- The intent is to value expected cash flows.
- The intent is to discount the cash flows at an estimate of opportunity cost of capital.
- Because information about total risk is derived, the method provides a basis for valuing complex financial claims.

The disadvantages are:

- Discrete scenarios discard information about the risk that could be useful, especially for valuing complex claims.
- No guidance is provided about how to determine the discount rate(s) to be used in the valuation.

Valuation by the Venture Capital Method

We now consider the same project using the Venture Capital Method. We know from the above that, based on opportunity cost, the correct present value $13,617 thousand. In the Venture Capital Method, we focus only on the cash flows of the success scenario. We value them at a hurdle rate that is appropriate for the stage of development of the project. Unfortunately, this approach does not provide much guidance. If the project is considered to be in first-stage development, then the table presented earlier in Chapter 8 argues for a hurdle rate of 40 to 60 percent. Figure 9-9 computes the present values of success scenario cash flows at hurdle rates of 40 and 60 percent. At 40 percent the value is $13,490 thousand, and at 60 it is $6,095 thousand. Both estimates are too low, though the 40 percent rate is close.

Maybe the project should be assumed to be at a later stage of development. But how is it possible to know? Also, in the figure, we search for the single hurdle rate that generates the true present value, as we already have determined it to be. That rate works out to be 39.77 percent.

One problem with the Venture Capital Method should now be obvious. There is little useful basis for selecting the hurdle rate. Furthermore, fairly small errors in the rate (or in success

Valuation of a Success Scenario at Various Discount Rates by the Venture Capital Method						
Cash Flows	**Total**	**1**	**2**	**3**	**4**	**5**
Success Scenario		−$4,000	$0	$2,000	$5,000	$77,000
Valued at 40 Percent						
Present Value	**$13,490**	−$2,857	$0	$729	$1,302	$14,317
Valued at 60 Percent						
Present Value	**$6,095**	−$2,500	$0	$488	$763	$7,343
Implied Single Rate						
Rate	**39.77%**					
Present Value	**$13,617**	−$2,862	$0	$732	$1,310	$14,436

Figure 9-9 Valuation of a success scenario at various discount rates by the Venture Capital Method

Cash flows from a discrete success scenario are valued by the Venture Capital Method, using discount rates that commonly are applied when that method is used. The implied single rate is determined by searching for the discount rate that yields a value similar to that from the certainty equivalent approach in Figure 9-7. Values are in thousands.

scenario cash flows) can dramatically affect the estimated present value. A second problem can be detected by comparing the present values of individual annual cash flows that are shown in Figure 9-9 with the present values of the same cash flows in Figure 9-7. Even though, using a 39.77 percent discount rate, the overall project value is the same as in Figure 9-7, the values of each annual cash flow are wrong, usually more so than when the RADR method is used. There is no good way to generalize about the nature of these errors except to say that they are certain to occur and that the magnitudes of the errors will increase with increases in the variability of cash flows in different years.

It is easy to criticize the Venture Capital Method on quantitative grounds. But the more qualitative advantages are worth noting:

- The valuation can be driven by the financial projections for a success scenario that may be reported in the business plan.
- The negotiation process may be facilitated by centering the negotiations around the projections of the entrepreneur.
- The experience of the investor may be easiest to apply without formal analysis when comparisons of ventures are made on the basis of success scenarios.
- The method is easy to use and may be adequate for simple investment decisions.

The disadvantages include:

- Unnecessary lack of precision due to reliance on limited information and rules of thumb.
- Potential biases resulting from discounting optimistic cash flow projections at a hurdle rate that is above cost of capital.

- Lack of information about uncertainty, which would be useful for valuing complex financial claims.

Although any valuation model has limitations, it generally makes sense to use the best one you can. The "best" model is one that values expected cash flows based on the opportunity cost of alternative investments, giving reasonable consideration to the cost of the valuation and the importance of making a decision quickly. Generally, this points to either the First Chicago Method or the CEQ model. The latter has the advantage of building on the discipline of the CAPM as a basis for discount rate selection and can deal with a more comprehensive description of venture uncertainty.

9.5   WHY IS THERE NO ILLIQUIDITY PREMIUM IN THE DISCOUNT RATE?

As we recognized earlier in the text, venture capital investments are illiquid, yet we make no provision for the RADR-method discount rate to be higher due to illiquidity. The lack of an adjustment may seem surprising, particularly in the face of transactional evidence that observed returns of relatively illiquid assets tend to be higher than returns of more liquid assets. To understand the reasons for ignoring illiquidity in the discount rate it is useful to distinguish between illiquidity that arises from informational asymmetry and regulatory or contractual restrictions on liquidity.

In the market transactions that we can observe some traders are better informed than others. Informed traders try to sell when they know assets are overvalued and buy when they know assets are undervalued. Uninformed traders know that when they buy or sell they may be dealing with an informed trader. To protect themselves, they need to discount the prices at which they buy, compared to what they think an asset is worth. If they discount by the optimal amount, realized returns will, on average, cover their opportunity cost of capital, and informed investors will earn returns above their opportunity cost. Because observed market returns are averages of the returns to informed and uninformed investors, the averages are higher than opportunity cost.[24]

In the equity market, evidence suggests that average returns of relatively illiquid assets are higher than those of more liquid assets.[25] However, this may be nothing more than a manifestation of informed and uninformed traders transacting with each other. The greater the information disparity for an asset, the higher the average return must be in order to provide a normal return to uninformed investors, and the less liquid the market for that asset tends to be. When information differences between investors are important, it does not make economic sense for assets to be traded frequently. Those who buy and hold for long periods can earn higher returns. Hence, even if uninformed investors hold for long periods and just earn normal returns, it will appear from the average returns that the discount rate should reflect an illiquidity discount.

However, informational asymmetry does not mean that the discount rate for new venture investing should be adjusted for illiquidity. The reason is simple—a new venture investment is based on a forecast of cash flows at harvest. Harvest cash flows normally are the proceeds from selling the venture in a private sale or selling the stock in the capital market. If subsequent investors (at the time of harvest) are concerned that the seller may know more than they do, they will discount the harvest-date price. Thus, the expected future cash flow at harvest already reflects this concern. If we were to also adjust the discount rate for illiquidity due to informational asymmetry, we would be double counting the effects of this source of illiquidity on value, just as we would if we were to use a negatively biased harvest cash flow in the CEQ method.

We are left, then, with illiquidity that arises from regulation or contract. In the U.S., for example, holders of unregistered shares of stock are significantly limited in their abilities to sell their shares. The limitations on sale apply even if a prospective seller has no information advantage. Investors in venture capital, similarly, are precluded by contract and regulation from selling their investments.

Here, the argument against increasing the discount rate for illiquidity is an empirical one. Clearly, if the supply of illiquid investments is large relative to demand, then illiquidity could give rise to a higher discount rate. However, most investors in venture capital are well diversified and have other assets in their portfolios that provide sufficient liquidity. Investors such as pension funds and endowments can easily tolerate illiquidity in a small fraction of their total portfolio. Thus, as long as the supply of illiquid assets is a small fraction of the investment funds of such entities, there is no reason to expect a large discount for illiquidity. While there is no good way to observe the compensation institutional investors require for investing small fractions of their portfolios in illiquid assets, the evidence of realized returns to venture capital and willingness of the investors to reinvest suggests that the required return premium for illiquidity is small or nonexistent.

9.6   THE COST OF CAPITAL FOR NON–U.S. INVESTORS IN NEW VENTURES

Perhaps you live in a country other than the U.S., possibly a developed country such as the U.K. or Japan, or maybe an emerging economy such as Mexico or China. If so, you may be wondering about the relevance of diversification and the CAPM as drivers of opportunity cost of capital. While there are differences, the differences are not as great as they appear. Whether you are in a developed or an emerging economy, opportunity cost is always the guiding principle of new venture investing and your ability to invest in a diversified portfolio that includes an investment in the venture is a determinant of opportunity cost.

In all developed countries and many others, investors retain the opportunity to invest in a U.S. market portfolio. However, because of currency exchange rates, doing so could subject the investor to somewhat different risks. In countries like the U.K. and Japan, an investor also can invest in highly diversified domestic portfolios. So, while the market index may be different, the economic principle, only nondiversifiable risk matters, still applies. The problem of estimating opportunity cost may be more difficult because of data limitations. However, the opportunity cost of capital implied by the CAPM for U.S. investors is likely to be similar to the cost of capital implied by well-diversified portfolios throughout the world.

The practical challenge of estimating opportunity cost may be greater in emerging economies. Prohibitions may exist against investments in foreign diversified portfolios, exchange rates may be subject to dramatic swings, investors may have limited opportunities to diversify domestically, and they may face other risks of long-term investing, such as a potential for expropriation. However, the investment principles are still the same. Projections of expected cash flows should incorporate such factors as the risk of expropriation and opportunity cost of capital should reflect the opportunity to diversify to the extent possible. The problem for an investor in an emerging economy, of estimating the opportunity cost of capital for investing in a new venture, can be addressed conceptually by thinking about the risk and expected return the investor can achieve by diversifying to the extent possible and by thinking about how the risk of investing in the venture would limit the investor's ability to diversify or would contribute to diversification. As a first approximation, the investor could still use the CAPM model, but with different assumptions for the risk-free rate, the risk premium on a portfolio that was diversified as much as possible, the total risk of the venture, and the correlation between the venture and the diversified portfolio. In extreme cases, where diversification opportunities are very limited, an analytical approach similar to what we provide in Chapter 10 for the entrepreneur could be appropriate.

9.7   SUMMARY

Sound methods of decision making about investment value are critical to success. Given the intensity of competition among investors, methods of valuation reflect increasing sophistication. The focus of the valuation effort is on the present value of future cash flows the investor would receive.

The four valuation approaches we examine in this chapter differ in several dimensions. The more traditional approaches are relatively easy to use, in a computational sense, and potentially can facilitate negotiation between investor and entrepreneur in simple transactions. On the other hand, they are more prone to result in valuation errors than are approaches based on financial economic theory.

In contrast to the view that high levels of uncertainty reduce the value of forecasting, the exact opposite is true. In addition to forecasting expected cash flows, it is important to do a good job of forecasting risk.

Valuation of investments in new ventures is difficult because the investor can negotiate the relation between the size of the investment and the fraction of ownership that is exchanged for the investment. Valuation also is difficult because of embedded options that affect the riskiness of subsequent investment decisions. To address these factors, it is important for valuation models to recognize how negotiation and embedded options affect required rates of return.

Much of this chapter is devoted to methods for determining the information needed to carry out a valuation. Although we are careful and systematic in coverage of these issues, we also identify shortcuts that sometimes can be used.

QUESTIONS AND PROBLEMS

1.   The following table contains seven years of financial projections for a new venture that is seeking capital to finance the commencement of operations. All dollar figures are in thousands. All cash flow during this period is expected to be reinvested in the venture and is reflected in the table. Assuming the projections represent expected values, including any expected new investments, and given only this information, considering growth rate trends and stability, how would you suggest valuing the venture? How would you estimate continuing value and reflect it in your valuation? Explain your reasoning.

Year	1	2	3	4	5	6	7
Revenue	$0	$850	$2,300	$6,100	$10,700	$13,100	$13,800
EBIT	−$2,000	−$788	−$1,925	−$975	−$325	$275	$450
Assets	$3,000	$1,000	$4,500	$3,525	$6,200	$6,475	$8,925

2. You are considering investing in a venture. Five years from now, assuming the venture is successful, it is projected to have revenue of $52 million, EBIT of $2 million, and assets of $35 million. Three-year compound annual growth of sales as of year 5 is expected to be 20 percent. The venture does not anticipate paying dividends during this period. As a basis for estimating continuing value, you have compiled information on five public companies that are in the same or closely related industries. The comparable firm information is summarized in the following table. Dollar figures are in millions. Analyze the information and use it to estimate the continuing value of the venture. Explain your reasoning.

Comparable Firm	Age in Years	Assets	Sales	EBIT	Dividends	3-Year Sales/Shr CAGR	Asset Market Value
Firm A	4	$ 40	$ 25	−$2	$ 0	85%	$ 85
Firm B	6	$120	$ 65	$2	$ 0	25%	$155
Firm C	9	$ 60	$130	$10	$ 7	3%	$110
Firm D	15	$ 45	$ 70	$4	$ 1	15%	$ 80
Firm E	17	$195	$280	$30	$16	6%	$210

3. Edu-tainment, Inc. is a provider of courses that are delivered over the Internet. The company has developed the concept and worked out a means of controlling access and charging for its services. It expects to contract for content with professors who are recognized for "fun" teaching. These instructors intersperse their lecture material with jokes and anecdotes and use other tactics that help keep students interested. Hence, the company name. The entrepreneur believes that by making Internet education entertaining he can attract and retain a large share of the adult education market.

The following table contains the entrepreneur's financial projections for the venture. Figures are in thousands of dollars. He is seeking to raise $6 million of venture capital (in the form of an equity investment) to initiate the program, contract with content providers, and begin marketing. Successful ventures that are similar have recently gone public at valuations around 12 times trailing net income. Assume you like the concept and are impressed by the entrepreneur. Estimate how much of the equity of the venture you would need to justify your investment. Assume that cash generated by the venture during the forecast period will be retained to finance growth. (*Hint:*You may want to refer back to Chapter 8 for information on the sought-for returns of venture capital investors.)

Year	1	2	3	4	5
Revenue	$0	$1,500	$8,000	$35,000	$80,000
Development expenses	$1,200	$800	$600	$1,500	$2,500
Marketing expenses	$400	$2,000	$3,000	$7,000	$10,000
Content expenses	$0	$150	$800	$3,500	$8,000
Delivery expenses	$500	$1,800	$3,000	$5,000	$7,000
Net income	−$2,100	−$3,250	$600	$8,000	$22,500

4. Suppose you believe that the venture described in problem 3 can be valued by the Capital Asset Pricing Model, using data on several public companies that you regard as comparable in terms of market risk, along with some other market information. The following table contains information on the comparable firms. Assuming the comparable firm debt has a beta of zero, use the information to estimate the beta of the venture.

Comparable Firm	Equity Beta	Share Price	Share Outstanding	Book Value of Debt
Firm A	1.85	$12.00	2,650,000	$4,350,000
Firm B	1.60	$ 8.50	4,750,000	$2,800,000
Firm C	1.42	$20.50	3,280,000	$1,700,000

   In addition, you have the following information on interest rates on U.S. government debt and stock market returns.

   • The current one-year interest rate is 7.5 percent.
   • The long-run historical average one-year rate is 6.5 percent.
   • The current five-year interest rate is 4.0 percent.
   • The long-run historical average five-year rate is 4.2 percent.
   • On average, the S&P 500 has earned annual returns that are 8 percent above one-year U.S. government debt and 7.5 percent above five-year debt.
   • The average historical price/earnings ratio of the S&P 500 is about 14.
   • During the last five years, the S&P 500 has earned compound annual returns of about 20 percent, whereas one-year interest rates on government debt have averaged 5.5 percent.
   • The current/price earnings ratio of the S&P 500 is about 21.
   • The historical standard deviation of market returns is about 14 percent.

   Using the above information, what is your estimate of the required return on assets for the venture? Explain your reasoning.

5. Suppose that, for the venture in problem 3, you develop an expected scenario and a failure scenario to go along with the entrepreneur's success scenario. In the success scenario, you assume the venture is harvested in year 5. You expect to receive no cash flow before harvest. In the expected scenario, the venture has net income of $13 million in year 5, and the expected multiple is 10 times earnings. In the failure scenario, you expect to liquidate the venture in year 5, in which case, your preferred stock claim would be worth about $1.5 million. You believe that the probabilities of results close to success and failure are each 0.25 and that the probability of results close to the expected scenario is 0.5. Using the cost of capital you estimated in problem 4, find the present value of the venture, and determine the fraction of equity you would require (at a minimum) for investing the $6 million.

6. Now, suppose you are comfortable with the multipliers and probabilities as stated in problem 5, but you are uncomfortable with using the comparable firm information to value the

project. In other words, the beta estimate may be fine if you were trying to value the venture as of year 5, but you are concerned that it is not a good measure of beta risk during the early years of the venture. Consequently, instead of using the estimate of beta, you would like to base your valuation on the assumption that the correlation between success of the venture and the overall market is in the range of 0.1 to 0.2. (Your best estimate of the correlation is 0.15.) Using this information, and information from the earlier questions, what range of values would you place on the venture, and what is your best estimate of the value? How much of the equity would you require for investing?

7. You are considering investing $750,000 in software development of a venture that would operate an Internet based video rental business. According to the business plan, the venture will need an additional $1.0 million next year (year one) to acquire the initial inventory of videos it plans to rent. Also according to the plan, the venture will generate no free cash flow in years two and three, $200,000 in year four, $600,000 in year five, and $1.4 million in year six. Suppose you believe there is a 30 percent probability that the entrepreneur will be unable to develop the necessary software and that the venture will fail before the second investment is needed. You also believe that the probability of failing before year four is 50 percent, the probability of failing before year five is 60 percent, and the probability of failing before year six is 70 percent. If the venture fails, you expect that free cash flow in each year after the failure will be zero. If the venture survives to year five, you expect that it will continue to survive and that free cash flow will grow at a rate of 6 percent per year. Because the year-one investment has no beta risk, you believe it should be valued at the risk-free rate of 4 percent. Based on comparisons to other firms, you believe the appropriate rate for valuing cash flows in other years is 11 percent. You wish to determine the fraction of equity that would be sufficient to justify making the first investment assuming that you would receive no additional equity in exchange for making the year-one investment.

  a. Identify the explicit value period, determine the expected cash flows during that period, and determine their present value.
  b. Determine the multiplier that you should use to determine continuing value and use the multiplier to find the continuing value.
  c. Compute the total present value of the venture and determine the minimum fraction of equity you would need to justify making the initial investment.

8. The following table shows average annual returns to venture capital funds as estimated by Venture Economics and the National Venture Capital Association.

Year	1994	1995	1996	1997	1998	1999	2000	2001
Percent Return	11.1	47.4	33.5	28.0	17.8	165.3	37.6	−32.4

  a. Find the arithmetic mean annual return for this series.
  b. Find the geometric mean annual return.
  c. Which do you think would be better for forecasting the future performance of a venture capital fund over eight years? Why?
  d. Test your answer in part (c) by setting up a simulation model where the arithmetic mean return and its standard deviation are used to produce eight independent draws from a normal distribution of annual returns. Use the simulation model to generate

a large sample of cumulative eight-year returns. Is the average from the eight years better explained by geometric compounding of the annual average or by an arithmetic average?

9. The following scenario information describes the harvest cash flows per acre for a new venture that would invest in a plantation forest on public land with the expectation that the trees can be logged and sold for lumber and paper production in 20 years. Compound annual returns for the different scenarios are based on an estimate that the costs of planting and maintaining the forest will be $10,000 per acre.

Scenario	Probability	Return on Market Portfolio	Projected Cash Flow per Acre at Harvest	Compound Annual Rate of Return on Investment
Boom	40%	25%	$164,000	15%
Normal Growth	30%	10%	$96,000	12%
Bust	30%	–10%	$67,000	10%

a. Use the returns information for the different scenarios to estimate the project beta based on the present value of the expected actual investment amount.

b. Use the cash flow information for the different scenarios to estimate the project cash flow beta.

c. Assuming that the long-term risk-free rate is 5.5 percent and the market risk premium is 6 percent, estimate the RADR cost of capital based on part (a) and estimate the present value per acre of the project. Does it appear that you should make the investment?

d. Using the above market information and the cash flow beta, find the CEQ present value. Should you make the investment?

e. Use the results from part (d) to determine the cost of capital implied by the CEQ analysis. Why is the CEQ cost for capital different from the cost of capital estimated by the RADR method?

NOTES

1. Wright and Robbie (1996) survey venture capital firms in the U.K. regarding their valuation approaches. They find that capitalization of historical or prospective earnings is the most widely relied upon approach by a significant margin. Occasionally, early-stage investors base valuations on valuations used in other early-stage transactions that are regarded as comparable. In those cases, the valuation is not so much linked to the accounting statements as to perceptions about the market that is being targeted by the venture. Valuations, however, are sensitive to the specific terms of the financing, which, in the absence of first-hand knowledge, are difficult to establish.

2. For a discussion of new venture valuation, see the note on valuation techniques by Roberts (1994).

3. Application of multiplier-based approaches to valuation is more defensible when the venture is well established than when the venture is at an early stage of development. At later stages, inferences of value from income or balance sheet information are more reasonable and accurate.

4. See Damodaran (1994), Chapters 8 through 12, and Copeland, Koller, and Murrin (2000), Chapter 12.

5. Generally, C is the cash flow generated over a year, and V is value at the end of that same year. This is sometimes referred to as a "trailing" value. It does not imply that value is determined by prior earnings. Rather, it implies that prior earnings can be used in a consistent way to predict future earnings

6. The price/earnings ratio is calculated as the value of the S&P 500 divided by aggregate earnings over the preceding 12 months. Dividend yield is calculated as the latest known annualized dividend rate divided by the current value of the index.

7. Lerner (1994) finds that biotechnology companies with venture capital backing tend to go public when equity valuations are high and that seasoned venture capitalists are relatively good at market timing. When market multiples are low, biotechnology firms with venture capital backing are more likely to place shares privately.

8. For discussion and examples using the Venture Capital Method, see Willinge (1996) and Scherlis and Sahlman (1987). Scherlis and Sahlman describe the Venture Capital Method and illustrate its application. See also Timmons (1999).

9. The relation between net income and cash flow is not explicit. In our discussion, we assume that net income is used as an approximation of steady-state cash flow.

10. The First Chicago Method was developed by the venture capital group of First Chicago Corporation. Scherlis and Sahlman (1987) describes it as a method developed to address valuation biases inherent in the Venture Capital Method.

11. The returns information in this paragraph is obtained from *Stocks, Bills, and Inflation 2001 Yearbook*, (Ibbotson Associates Inc., Chicago), as reported in various sources.

12. Some writers contend that, instead of using arithmetic averages to compute risk premia, as reported here, it is better to use geometric averages. See Copeland, Koller and Murrin (1999) for discussion. On balance, we agree with the school of thought that favors using arithmetic averages. See, for example, Brealey and Myers (2003).

13. As most new ventures do not use much debt financing, the betas of public venture capital funds are similar to asset betas. The main difference is that the claims held by the funds are often preferred shares that are somewhat less risky than the equity held by the entrepreneur. Before you use the beta of a public fund, you should verify the nature of its investments.

14. When a project generates cash flows in more than one period, it is not clear how you should define the holding-period returns for the individual cash flows. The cost of the project is the cost of acquiring the rights to all of the cash flows. To determine the holding-period returns, you would somehow need to allocate the cost over the cash inflows. But there is no obvious method for making the allocation. Because of this, the approach is difficult to apply to projects that pay off in more than one period.

15. The resulting valuations only an approximation of the present value of the cash flow. You can see this by comparing the second and third terms in Eq. (9.10). It is apparent from the third term that the correct holding-period return to use in the calculation depends on the present value of the cash flow. This problem is also recognized by Grinblatt and Titman (2001). Their solution, like ours, is to use the CEQ method.

16. You can use the RADR approach to verify that this is the correct value. Suppose you are offered the right to acquire the expected $173,333 cash flow for $152,326 and calculate the holding-period return on that basis. You will get the same present value. If you try it using $164,310, you will get a different answer. You can also use Eq. (9.8) to ascertain that the true required rate

for the project is 13.8 percent instead of the 5.5 percent we computed earlier and that the returns beta is 1.22 instead of the 0.19 we computed earlier.

17. There is both empirical and theoretical support for assuming independence of the time-series.

18. The use of discrete scenarios to describe the project as an aspect of the First Chicago Method. In Chapter 10 we use simulation instead of discrete scenarios to allow for a richer analysis of risk. In Chapter 11 the valuation model is extended to incorporate the effects of real options on value.

19. Note that although the continuing values are reported separately from year 5 cash flows in the table, they are expressed as year 5 values. See section 9.2.

20. This is merely a convenience for using the spreadsheet. If you were to assume that long-term risk-free rates are different from short-term risk-free rates, you should record the compounded values of the longer-term rates in the appropriate cells of the spreadsheet.

21. To see this result, you must value the inflows separately from the outflows. You can do so by modifying the information in the spreadsheet

22. If the CAPM is the correct valuation model, and our other assumptions are correct, then the required rates shown in Figure 9-7 are correct. We have implemented the assumptions of the example problem exactly. The implication is that aggregating positive and negative cash flows can dramatically affect the appropriate discount rate. If you use a RADR valuation method, it often is better to evaluate positive and negative cash flows separately and to evaluate cash flows that differ in risk separately. Separate evaluation of each cash flow enables you to think about the risk of the cash flow and to select a discount rate accordingly. Unfortunately, since it rarely is possible to observe project cash flows on a disaggregated basis, the actual determination of each rate probably must be based on judgment rather than evidence.

23. This may not be very intuitive. You can understand it by recognizing that a negative weight is analogous to a short position in an asset that has a positive present value.

24. Studies of liquidity premia commonly rely in the liquid investor's ability to exploit an information advantage over uninformed investors. See, for example, Longstaff (1995).

25. Amihud and Mendelson (1986) relate average realized returns to typical investment holding periods.

REFERENCES AND ADDITIONAL READING

Amihud, Y., and H. Mendelson. "Asset Pricing and the Bid-Asked Spread." *Journal of Financial Economics* 17 (1986): 223–249.

Brealey, Richard, and Stewart Myers. *Principles of Corporate Finance.* 7th ed. New York: Irwin/McGraw-Hill, 2003.

Copeland, Tom, Tim Koller, and Jack Murrin. *Valuation: Measuring and Managing the Value of Companies.* 3rd ed. New York: John Wiley & Sons, 2000.

Damodaran, Aswath. *Damodaran on Valuation: Security Analysis for Investment and Corporate Finance.* New York: John Wiley & Sons, 1994.

Fama, Eugene, and Kenneth French. "The Equity Premium," CRSP Working Paper No. 522, University of Chicago (April 2001).

Grinblatt, Mark, and Sheridan Titman. *Financial Markets and Corporate Strategy.* 2nd ed. Boston: Irwin/McGraw-Hill, 2001.

Kaplan, Paul D. and James D. Peterson. "Full Information Industry Betas," *Financial Management* 27 (Summer 1998): 85–93.

KERINS, FRANK, JANET KIHOLM SMITH, AND RICHARD SMITH. "Opportunity Cost of Capital for Venture Capital Investors and Entrepreneurs." *Journal of Financial and Quantitative Analysis.* Forthcoming (2003).

LERNER, JOSHUA. "Venture Capitalists and the Decision to Go Public." *Journal of Financial Economics* 35 (1994): 293–316.

LONGSTAFF, FRANCIS. "How Much Can Marketability Affect Security Values?" *Journal of Finance* 50 (1995): 1767–1774.

ROBERTS, MICHAEL J. "Valuation Techniques." In *New Business Ventures and the Entrepreneur.* Edited by H. H. Stevenson, Michael Roberts, and H. Irving Grousbeck. Homewood, IL: Irwin, 1994.

ROBICHEK, ALEXANDER A., AND STEWART C. MYERS. "Conceptual Problems in the Use of Risk-Adjusted Discount Rates." *Journal of Finance* 21 (December 1966): 727–730.

SCHERLIS, DANIEL, AND WILLIAM SAHLMAN. "A Method of Valuing High-Risk, Long-Term Investments." *Harvard Business School Note,* 9-288-006, 1987.

SICK, GORDON. "A Certainty-Equivalent Approach to Capital Budgeting." *Financial Management* (Winter 1986): 23–32.

TIMMONS, JEFFREY A. *New Venture Creation.* 5th ed. Chicago: Irwin, 1999.

WELCH, IVO. "The Equity Premium Consensus Forecast Revisited." NBER Working Paper (September 2001).

WILLINGE, JOHN. "A Note on Valuation in Private Equity Settings." *Harvard Business School Note* 9-297-050, 1996.

WRIGHT, MIKE AND KEN ROBBIE. "Venture Capitalists, Unquoted Equity Investment Appraisal and the Role of Accounting Information." *Accounting and Business Research* 26 (1996): 153–168.

Valuation: The Entrepreneur's Perspective

There are only two types of people in the world, the efficient and the inefficient. (George Bernard Shaw)

Learning Objectives

After reading this chapter you will be able to:

- Understand how the opportunity to invest in a well-diversified market portfolio determines the entrepreneur's cost of capital.
- Understand why limited ability to diversify affects an entrepreneur's cost of capital.
- Understand how an entrepreneur's cost of capital depends on the fraction of risk capital that is committed to the venture.
- Recognize that an entrepreneur can increase present value by structuring the investment to reduce the need to commit risk capital.
- Use information about venture risk, the market, and the extent of an entrepreneur's investment to compute the entrepreneur's cost of capital.
- Value new ventures that generate cash flows in several periods.
- Estimate the statistical parameters for determining an entrepreneur's cost of capital.
- Understand how the difference between total risk and nondiversifiable risk affects the diversified investor's cost of capital advantage.

Surprisingly, much of the research on entrepreneurial finance focuses on the financing decision and takes the entrepreneur's investment decision as a foregone conclusion. The claim is that the entrepreneur's investment problem is less of a quantitative decision than a qualitative decision, having to do with tastes for being one's own boss, lifestyle preferences, and tolerance for risk. This focus is too narrow. The entrepreneur's decision to invest in a new venture is among the most difficult decisions to make correctly. Furthermore, in some respects, new

INTERNET RESOURCES FOR THIS CHAPTER

As you will see, the entrepreneur's valuation problem is more difficult than that of a diversified investor. The chapter includes several figures based on Excel files that can be used as valuation templates. You can modify the templates to evaluate other ventures and financing arrangements. Experiment with the templates as you read the chapter. To help you master the technical material in the chapter, you can download and work through the valuation templates. The site also contains information relevant to the entrepreneur's valuation problem.

venture investment decisions are more complex than corporate investment decisions. In particular, interactions between investment and financing decisions, which are of minor importance for large public corporations, can be acute for entrepreneurial ventures. Also, because the decisions are almost irreversible, there is an important strategic component to both investment and financing decisions. Lifestyle preferences and similar considerations are easy to factor in once the quantitative valuation has been completed.

As we saw in Chapter 9, venture capitalists and other outside investors routinely address the question of investment value. What generally is not addressed is how valuation is different for the entrepreneur. The entrepreneur's investment decision problem is fundamentally different from the outside investor's problem. Even though the underlying financial economic theory is the same for both, the opportunity cost of capital that is appropriate for the entrepreneur generally is different from that of the outside investor. This is true, even if the financial claims are identical (though usually they are not). Accordingly, the capital value of the venture also is different for the entrepreneur than for an outside investor.

The entrepreneur should take a separate look at value for three compelling reasons. First, as already noted, the entrepreneur has a different required rate of return. A competitive capital market determines the opportunity cost of capital of outside investors. In that market, well-diversified investors vie to participate in ventures based on their evaluations of risk and expected return. Because many investors in the venture financing market are well diversified, investors cannot base their valuations on diversifiable risk. We saw this in Chapters 8 and 9. In contrast, the entrepreneur normally must bear diversifiable risk. Because an entrepreneur usually is sacrificing ability to diversify, the entrepreneur's opportunity cost of capital is higher than that of outside investors. Thus, even if the entrepreneur and outside investors agree about a venture's expected cash flows and risk, their valuations will differ. Other things equal, the outside investor will arrive at a higher valuation.

Second, the ownership claims of investors and entrepreneurs generally are not symmetric. Investors often receive "sweeteners" that make the deal more attractive. Sweeteners are options and preferences that raise the value of an investor's ownership claims. For example, many investor claims are in the form of convertible preferred stock. Preferred stock places investors claims ahead of the entrepreneur if the venture fails and is liquidated. Convertibility enables the investor to share in venture success. Investors may also receive other forms of protection against poor performance and may have control rights that go beyond their fractional ownership interest. Because of sweeteners, an investor will accept a smaller fraction of ownership in exchange for a certain level of investment. Other things equal, provisions that sweeten the deal for the investor make it less attractive for the entrepreneur. However, because the parties value their claims differently, a dollar's worth of benefit for the investor usually costs the entrepreneur less than a dollar's worth of value. Because the costs and benefits of different sweeteners vary, the entrepreneur needs to understand how sweetening affects the value of the deal.

In practice, entrepreneurs and investors refer to the capitalization of a new venture as the value that is derived by dividing the dollar investment of the investor by the percentage of equity ownership the investment buys. So, a $1 million investment for 20 percent of the equity implies a $5 million capitalization. If the ownership claims of the entrepreneur and the investor are identical, then that calculation yields a reasonable estimate of the value of the venture *as if it were owned entirely by diversified investors* (i.e., ignoring the entrepreneur's undiversified risk). However, ignoring the value of sweeteners in computing the capitalization of the venture overstates value, even to diversified investors.

Of course, some differences in financial claims favor the entrepreneur. For example, if the entrepreneur draws an attractive salary (compared with the entrepreneur's other opportunities), that raises the value of the deal for the entrepreneur and lowers it for the outside investor.

The third reason the value placed on the venture by the entrepreneur differs from that of the outside investor is that the two parties are unlikely to agree about the risk and expected return of the venture. Differences in expectations about such things as development timing, achievable sales, and profitability, make contracting to attract investment capital more difficult than it otherwise would be. But a clear understanding of the differences facilitates designing financing arrangements both parties can accept, even if they have different expectations.

In this chapter, we focus on the first of these three concerns: the differences in the required rate of return between the entrepreneur and outside investors. Building on financial economic theory from Chapter 8 and the implementation principles of Chapter 9, we construct a valuation model that addresses the entrepreneur's underdiversified risk. We begin discussion of the second and third concerns, regarding deal-making, in Chapter 11. Thus, for now, we do not consider how the allocation of financial claims affects value. Nor, at this point, do we consider how the allocation of claims affects perceptions of value or incentives of the parties.

10.1   THE ENTREPRENEUR AS AN UNDERDIVERSIFIED INVESTOR

An entrepreneur often must commit most of his or her time for at least a few years, as well as a substantial fraction of available financial capital to the venture. As a result, the entrepreneur *necessarily* bears not just the nondiversifiable risk of the venture, but also the total risk. In a competitive capital market, investors cannot expect compensation for bearing diversifiable risk. But that proposition assumes that the asset under consideration is a market asset that is equally available to all investors.

We assume, in contrast, that the entrepreneur is only able to capture the value of the opportunity by investing his or her own financial and/or human capital in it. This is different from investment by a public company, where financing of an opportunity is raised in a capital market where investors are able to diversify.

The focus on total risk as a determinant of the entrepreneur's required rate of return is appropriate in the new venture setting, in part because entrepreneurial ventures are not market assets. We assume throughout that the venture under consideration is specific to the entrepreneur and cannot be duplicated easily by others. If duplication is possible, then the entrepreneur may face competition from well-diversified investors. In that case, the entrepreneur still should not adopt the required rate of return of a diversified investor, but rather should view the opportunity in light of its return potential evaluated against the total risk of the opportunity. Normally, individual entrepreneurs will not undertake ventures that investors who are well diversified can undertake as successfully.

An Example of Competition between Entrepreneurs and Diversified Investors

To understand the implications of the extent of an entrepreneur's diversification, consider a current example of migration of entrepreneurs away from a market where competition from well-diversified investors may be gaining feasibility. This is the market for automobile dealerships. Traditionally, automobile manufacturers in the United States built their distribution systems around networks of independent dealers. Those dealers have been the entrepreneurs of new vehicle distribution. Successful dealers generally have earned high rates of return based on their abilities to attract customers and to negotiate prices in individual transactions. A vehicle dealer succeeds by understanding the local market and the individual consumer.

But that market is showing signs of change. Consumers can now use new information services, such as Edmund's on the Internet, to shop over broad geographic areas, even without visiting any dealerships, and the intensity of price competition has increased.[1] The net result is that it is harder for individual dealers to earn returns that are high enough to compensate for their undiversified risk. Increasingly, dealerships are being sold to investors who are better diversified.

The change began along traditional lines, with existing dealers acquiring additional franchises. In some cases, these "chain dealers" acquired control of dozens of dealerships of various nameplates over broad geographic areas. Chain dealers gain diversification, and potentially gain economies of scale in some activities, but at the cost of reduced sensitivity to local market conditions.

More recently, there has been a move toward public ownership of automobile dealership chains. Publicly owned firms hope to realize economies of scale and scope by integrating new and used car sales with car rental and service on a scale large enough to permit application of management science concepts, such as "yield management," to motor vehicle distribution.[2] Whether the potential gains and the benefits of diversification of risk can compensate for the potential decline in sensitivity to local market conditions is an open question. If they can, then we expect traditional dealers (the entrepreneurs of automobile distribution) to retreat from the market.

Defining the Entrepreneur's Commitment to a Venture

In this chapter, you will see that the return an entrepreneur should require depends on how much of the entrepreneur's wealth must be invested in the venture. To begin the evaluation, we need a measure of the entrepreneur's wealth. Much of the entrepreneur's investment is likely to be in the form of effort (i.e., human capital) devoted to the venture. That effort has an opportunity cost. The entrepreneur could have devoted the effort to a different occupation than the venture. Accordingly, the entrepreneur's wealth includes both present financial capital and the present value of the entrepreneur's human capital in its highest-valued alternative use.

More specifically, in the context of CAPM-based valuation, we need to measure the entrepreneur's risk capital. We use the term "risk capital" to denote capital invested in risky assets as distinct from capital invested in a risk-free asset. In the CAPM framework, the benefits of diversification derive from investing in a portfolio of risky assets. Investment in a risk-free asset is analyzed separately as a financial leveraging decision. In general, we do not expect that an entrepreneur will have a significant fraction of total wealth invested in riskless assets. Accordingly, analysis and discussion in the next few chapters generally ignores the possibility of investing in a riskless asset. Extending the entrepreneur's choices by including a riskless asset is not difficult, and we will include a few brief comments on it as we proceed. The box "A Closer Look at Entrepreneurs' Wealth, Savings, and Portfolios" contains a review of recent research that supports the propositions that wealthy individuals can more easily justify becoming entrepreneurs because they are better able to diversity risk, and that entrepreneurs tend to invest little in riskless assets.

Given that wealth includes both financial and human capital, we define the entrepreneur's commitment to a venture in terms of the fraction of risk capital committed. Full commitment means that the entrepreneur devotes all financial and human risk capital to the venture. Partial commitment is anything less than full commitment.

In practice, no entrepreneur can make a full commitment to a venture. Doing so would require the entrepreneur to irrevocably commit to work on the venture for the rest of his or her life, no matter how unsuccessful it might prove to be. It would also require, for example, that all existing retirement savings be invested in the venture, something that normally is not possible. Thus, we focus on investment decisions involving substantial partial commitments (i.e., neither a full commitment nor the commitment of a well-diversified investor). To understand how to value partial commitments, we first need to analyze a full commitment.

10.2 REQUIRED RATES OF RETURN FOR FULL-COMMITMENT INVESTMENTS

How can you determine the required rate of return or cost of capital that is appropriate for an entrepreneur's investment? The concept of opportunity cost is the starting point, just as it is for venture capitalists and other outside investors. Prospective entrepreneurs have many alternative uses for their wealth and time. They can invest financial capital, for example, in a diversified portfolio of marketable securities and commit time (human capital) to a career that offers more security than managing a new venture. An individual who is willing to take risk in the hope of a higher return can do so either by undertaking an entrepreneurial venture that requires commitments of both wealth and time or by leveraging an investment in the market portfolio.[3]

The Entrepreneur's Opportunity Cost of Capital

The alternative of leveraging the market portfolio to achieve a higher expected return provides the opportunity-cost basis for pricing the entrepreneur's risk. Setting aside considerations such as job satisfaction, an entrepreneur should not undertake a new venture unless it is expected to provide a rate of return that is at least as high as an investment in the market portfolio that is leveraged to have the same risk as investment in the prospective venture. Thus, if a well-diversified portfolio with high risk is expected to return 20 percent, then an equally risky new venture that requires full commitment of the entrepreneur's time and risk capital must provide an expected return of at least 20 percent to compensate for opportunity cost.

A Closer Look at Entrepreneurs' Wealth, Savings, and Portfolios

Researchers recently have examined the wealth attributes of entrepreneurs, along with their savings behavior and propensity to hold underdiversified portfolios. The following table summarizes some key findings. While definitions of entrepreneurs differ across studies, entrepreneurs generally are defined as those reporting ownership of one or more active businesses or those reporting self-employment income. All findings are relative to nonentrepreneurs, and are based on assets other than human capital:

Entrepreneurial Wealth, and Savings and Investment Behavior

Wealth	Savings and Investment Behavior	Portfolio Diversification
Entrepreneurs are more likely to be wealthy	Entrepreneurs have higher savings rates across age, income, and wealth groups (2)	Entrepreneurs' portfolios are less well diversified: They hold less wealth in liquid assets, bonds, public equity, and housing. They hold more wealth in business assets and nonresidential real estate (2) (3)
Concentration of the wealth increases at higher levels of wealth and income (2)	Wealth-income ratios and saving-income ratios are higher for entrepreneurs (2)	Entrepreneurial investment is extremely concentrated: About 75 percent of all private equity is owned by households for whom it constitutes at least half of their net worth excluding human capital (6)
Inheritance increases the probability of becoming an entrepreneur and remaining one (5)	Saving and investment decisions are interdependent (1) (2) (5)	Portfolios of entrepreneurs grow less diversified over time (2)
Inability to attract outside funding creates a positive relationship between personal wealth and the choice to be an entrepreneur (3)	Reasons for reliance on own wealth include asymmetric information about the value of the venture and moral hazard problems in financing (1)	Wealthy entrepreneurs have a portfolio share in bonds and equity that is half that of wealthy nonentrepreneurs
		Entrepreneurs borrow more heavily than nonentrepreneurs (2)
		Entrepreneurs can benefit "by issuing risky debt and using the proceeds to reduce their equity stake in the firm" (4)

References: (1) Evans and Jovanovic (1989). (2) Gentry and Hubbard (2000). (3) Heaton and Lucas (2000). (4) Heaton and Lucas (2001). (5) Holtz-Eakin, Joulfaian, and Rosen (1994) (1994a). (6) Moskowitz and Vissing-Jørgensen (2002).

We can use the Capital Market Line (CML) that underlies the CAPM to estimate the entrepreneur's opportunity cost of capital as a full commitment. An entrepreneur who makes a full commitment and does not take on any outside investment cannot offset any of the risk by diversifying or allocating risk to outside investors. As a result, the entrepreneur's cost of capital depends on total risk of the venture compared with the total risk of investing in the market portfolio. Thus, the entrepreneur's opportunity cost of capital for investing in a new project P, r_P^E, is:

$$r_P^E = r_F + (\sigma_P^E / \sigma_M) RP_M \qquad (10.1)$$

where σ_P^E / σ_M is the standard deviation of project returns divided by the standard deviation of market returns and other terms are as defined in Chapters 8 and 9.[4] Equation (10.1) looks much like the CAPM (see equations 8.4 and 8.5). In fact, the only differences are that for a venture that requires a full commitment, the entrepreneur does not care about the correlation between venture returns and market returns and the standard deviation of project holding period returns is measured in equilibrium *for the entrepreneur*. So, for example, Eq. (10.1) implies that if a project has a standard deviation of returns of 60 percent, the market standard deviation is 20 percent, the risk-free rate is 4 percent, and the market risk premium is 8 percent, then the entrepreneur's required return on the venture is 28 percent:

$$r_P^E = 4\% + (60/20) \times 8\% = 28\%$$

The opportunity cost of capital is 28 percent because the entrepreneur could use financial leverage to increase the risk of an investment in the market portfolio to match the 60 percent standard deviation of the venture, at which point the expected return for investing in the market portfolio would be 28 percent.

In contrast, if the same venture has a beta of 2.0, then the cost of capital to a well-diversified investor for investing in the venture is 20 percent. To derive the 20 percent required rate of return for a diversified investor, we use the CAPM but substitute β_P for σ_P / σ_M in Eq. (10.1).[5] The difference in required rate of return means that (assuming they agree about the risk and expected return of the venture) the diversified investor values the venture more highly. The implications for new venture financial contracting between entrepreneurs and outside investors are substantial and are addressed beginning in Chapter 11.

Leveraging an Investment in the Market Portfolio to Determine Cost of Capital

An entrepreneur can use market instruments to form a well-diversified portfolio with risk comparable to that of a prospective new venture. To see this, consider the above example, where project risk, σ_P^E, is a 60 percent standard deviation of returns, and market risk, σ_M, is a 20 percent standard deviation of returns. The standard deviation of the entrepreneur's alternative investment in a market index can be increased to match the 60 percent standard deviation of the venture in the following way. For each dollar of the entrepreneur's capital, borrow two more dollars and invest the entire amount in the market index, so that a total of three dollars is invested for each dollar of the entrepreneur's capital. We can calculate the effect of leverage on the riskiness of the entrepreneur's one-dollar investment in the market portfolio by recognizing that the total investment (of three dollars) still has a standard deviation of 20 percent and that the loan to the entrepreneur is essentially riskless. That is, with the total three-dollar investment as security for the lender, the loan should be riskless, so that the standard deviation of returns to the lender is zero.

Mathematically, if the debt is riskless, then the (20 percent) standard deviation of the investment in the market must equal the weighted average of the (0 percent) standard deviation of returns to the lender who financed the leveraged investment, σ_L, and the (unknown) standard deviation of returns to the entrepreneur, σ_P^E:

$$\sigma_M = x_L \sigma_L + x_E \sigma_P^E \tag{10.2}$$

where x_L is the fraction of the total investment that is borrowed by the entrepreneur and x_E is the fraction that is the entrepreneur's own capital.[6] It follows that, in this example, the standard deviation of returns to the entrepreneur is 60 percent:

$$20\% = (2/3 \times 0\%) + (1/3 \times 60\%)$$

Because this is the same as the standard deviation of returns for investing in the venture, we can use the leveraged market portfolio to determine the opportunity cost of capital.

To see the expected return more concretely, the gross expected return on an investment of $300 at the market rate of 12 percent for one year is $36. But to find the return on the entrepreneur's investment of $100, the cost of borrowing $200 must be deducted. Because the borrowing is riskless, it should earn the risk-free rate of 4 percent, or $8 for the $200. The expected net return for each $100 the entrepreneur invests is thus $28 ($36 total, minus $8 of interest). This is a 28 percent rate of return on the entrepreneur's $100 investment. Hence, 28 percent is the entrepreneur's opportunity cost of capital for investing as a full commitment.

How Ability to Diversify Affects Cost of Capital

Figure 10-1 uses the above example to illustrate how differences in abilities to bear risk between entrepreneurs and well-diversified investors result in different required rates of return and different investment decisions. Given the venture's standard deviation of 60 percent, an entrepreneur who must make a full commitment requires a return of 28 percent. This is what the CML implies in the figure. However, given that the venture beta is 2.0, a diversified investor requires only 20 percent. The horizontal line at 20 percent in the figure represents the diversified investor's required return for any venture having a beta of 2.0.

Now consider three ventures that differ in expected return but have the same amount of total risk and market (beta) risk. Project A (in the figure) has an expected return of 16 percent, a beta of 2.0, and a 60 percent standard deviation of returns. Both the entrepreneur and a diversified investor would reject Project A. The expected return is not sufficient to compensate

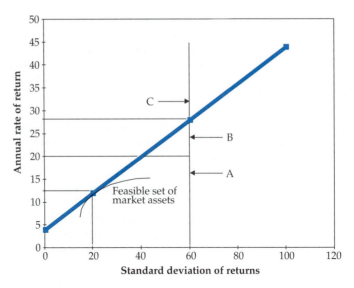

Figure 10-1 Required rates of return for diversified and undiversified investors

The Capital Market Line (CML) represents the opportunities available by investing in the market portfolio and the risk-free asset. The risk-free rate is 4 percent, and the market risk premium is 8 percent. Consider a project with a standard deviation of returns of 60 percent and a beta of 2.0. A diversified investor values the project according to its beta and requires a return of 20 percent. An undiversified investor values the project based on its total risk, which is three times that of the market, and requires a return of 28 percent. Projects like A, with returns below 20 percent, are not acceptable to either investor. Projects like B, with intermediate expected returns, are attractive to diversified investors but not to undiversified investors. Projects like C, with high expected returns, are attractive to both but are more valuable to diversified investors.

for either market risk or total risk. Project B has a 24 percent expected return, a beta of 2.0, and a 60 percent standard deviation. A diversified investor would accept the project, but the entrepreneur would not. Finally, Project C has a 32 percent expected return, a beta of 2.0, and a 60 percent standard deviation. Either party would accept this project, but it would have a higher NPV for the diversified investor.

More specifically, Eq. (10.3) is the expression for a RADR valuation based on the discount rate in Eq. (10.1):

$$PV_t = \frac{C_t}{(1 + r_F + (\sigma_P^E/\sigma_M)RP_M)^t} \qquad (10.3)$$

Suppose it is possible to invest $1 million in a digital television venture with risk characteristics as described above. Suppose, further, that the venture would pay-off at the end of five years. An entrepreneur, who requires an expected 28 percent rate of return per year, is looking for an expected cash return of at least $3.436 million in year 5 (i.e., $1 million x 1.28⁵). A diversified investor would require an expected cash return of only $2.488 million (i.e., $1 million × 1.20⁵).

The following table shows the terminal cash flows of the three ventures in Figure 10-1 over five years, assuming an initial investment of $1 million. It also compares the present values and NPVs by discounting the cash flows at the cost of capital of the entrepreneur and of the investor. Neither party would want to invest in a project like A since NPV is always negative. Projects like B are attractive to the investor but not to the entrepreneur. The question we take up in Chapter 11 is whether, by bringing in an outside investor, the entrepreneur can make the NPV of his or her involvement in a project positive. Projects like C are attractive to both the entrepreneur and the investor. For such projects, in Chapter 11 we begin to examine the potential for the entrepreneur to increase expected cash flow and/or reduce risk by bringing in an outside investor.

Comparisons of Project Values for Entrepreneurs Making Full Commitments and for Well-Diversified Outside Investors

Beta = 2.0, σ = 60%	Project A	Project B	Project C
Project Returns			
Rate of return	16%	24%	32%
Terminal value (year 5)	$2,100,342	$2,931,625	$4,007,464
Entrepreneur Making a Full Commitment (required rate = 28%)			
Present value	$611,280	$853,215	$1,166,325
Net present value	($388,720)	($146,785)	$166,325
Well-Diversified Outside Investor (required rate = 20%)			
Present value	$844,080	$1,178,154	$1,610,510
Net present value	($155,920)	$178,154	$610,510

Factors that Offset the Entrepreneur's Cost of Capital Disadvantage

You may think from the preceding discussion that the entrepreneur's cost of capital disadvantage is hopeless. If a public corporation and an undiversified entrepreneur are equally capable of undertaking a venture, then clearly the venture is more valuable to the corporation. In a competitive market for investing in new ventures, we should find that, because of their lower cost of capital, public corporations spend more resources searching for viable ventures than do entrepreneurs and that corporations often undertake ventures before they reach the threshold of economic profitability for undiversified entrepreneurs.

Offsetting their cost of capital advantages, however, corporations face difficulties when they attempt to engage in entrepreneurship.[7] For example, the rewards a corporation can offer to an employee for perceiving and pursuing entrepreneurial opportunities are likely to be less than what an individual can realize acting alone. This is not because the corporation cannot afford to pay the entrepreneur, but because extreme earnings disparities among workers can cause difficulties in large organizations. Consequently, corporate employees with good new venture opportunities frequently jump ship to pursue them on their own. Incentive alignment problems within large organizations can also offset the cost of capital advantage. As a result, the venture cash flows that are available to entrepreneurs are not always equally available to the shareholders of large corporations. Rather, a tradeoff exists between the organizational efficiencies of entrepreneurial ventures and the cost of capital advantage of a public corporation.

This tradeoff gives initial insight to the kinds of entrepreneurial ventures that are likely to be pursued by corporations rather than individuals. First, the larger the scale of the venture and the more complex the organization that is required to undertake it, the more likely the venture is to be pursued by a corporation. Second, the higher the level of total risk, as compared to beta risk, the greater the cost of capital advantage of the diversified investor and hence, the more likely the venture is to be pursued by a public corporation. Third, with a longer expected holding period between investment and harvesting, the cost of capital advantage of the diversified investor compounds, making corporate entrepreneurship more likely.

There are additional reasons that diversified investors in the market for new-venture investing do not displace entrepreneurs. For any given venture, investors may not perceive the opportunity or may be less optimistic than the entrepreneur. In such cases, the entrepreneur may need to invest more personal resources because money from diversified investors is not available, or the entrepreneur may need to make a larger initial investment to convince prospective investors of the merits of the venture and of her commitment to it.

10.3 LIMITATIONS OF THE OPPORTUNITY COST FRAMEWORK

We infer the opportunity cost for investing in a new ventures from the CAPM, by envisioning an investment in the market portfolio that is leveraged to achieve the same risk. For a well-diversified outside investor, leverage is used to match market risk with the nondiversifiable risk of the investment. For an entrepreneur who is making a full commitment, leverage is used to match market risk with the total risk of the investment in the venture. The total risk of an entrepreneurial venture is often very high.

For two reasons, the opportunity cost reasoning can be problematic for valuing undiversified investments in high-risk, long-term ventures. First, the distributions of projected cash flows for high-risk ventures are likely to be highly skewed. If so, the CAPM can yield biased estimates of value.[8] Second, an investor's ability to leverage the market portfolio is limited. To the extent that venture risk exceeds the risk that leveraging the market can achieve, an investor cannot use the opportunity cost reasoning. In the following subsections, we examine both problems. We then offer a practical solution for dealing with them.

CAPM Valuation Bias Against High-Risk Investments

The CAPM-based model of valuation for an undiversified investment works well as long as the standard deviation of cash flows is not too large compared to the expected cash flow, and/or the assumed holding period is not too long.[9] With high-risk or long holding periods, the CAPM and other mean/variance models can generate negative values for an investment, even if no scenarios involve negative cash flows.

To illustrate, consider a simple project that has a 12.5 percent chance of returning $100 in one year, and an 87.5 percent chance of returning $0. Based on this information, the project has an expected payoff of $12.5 and a standard deviation of $33.07. Now, assume that the risk-free rate is 4 percent, the market risk premium is 8 percent, and the market standard deviation is 20 percent. If we use the CEQ form of Eq. (10.3) to value the venture, the resulting estimate of project value is −$0.70.[10] That is, the equation implies that the entrepreneur would pay $0.70 to *avoid* the project. Clearly, this does not make sense. The worst possible outcome for the venture is a cash flow of $0, so the venture must be worth at least $0. In this case, the asset-pricing model undervalues the venture.

This is a limitation of the CAPM, not just of the modification for valuing an undiversified investment. The CAPM and related models imply that risk only affects value through the standard deviation (or variance) of returns. Such models do not take into consideration the possibility that the actual distribution of returns may have other characteristics that are important to investors. Of particular relevance for valuing new ventures, the actual distribution may be nonnormal and may be constrained not to take on negative values. If other characteristics of risk are important, then mean/variance models can be misleading. Such models are misleading when the standard deviation of cash flows is large relative to expected cash flow and when the market premium for bearing risk is large compared to the standard deviation of market returns. In these cases, mean/variance models can imply negative values for risky cash flows that can never be negative.

This limitation of the CAPM normally is not obvious or particularly important in corporate finance applications, or diversified investor valuations, for three reasons. First, the focus on nondiversifiable risk reduces the bias. Second, required returns usually are estimated from data on holding-period returns of one year or less, so that the market risk premium is small compared to the standard deviation of market returns. If it is small, negative values for assets with only nonnegative cash flows are less likely. Third, project risk usually is assumed to increase over time in such a way that required rates of return for more distant cash flows can be derived by compounding annual required rates.

Limitations of Ability to Leverage Investment in the Market Index

The second area of concern for using the opportunity cost reasoning pertains to limitations of ability to leverage investment in the market index. To be strictly correct in using the opportunity cost reasoning, a well-diversified investor should be able to leverage an investment in the market portfolio to achieve a beta that is comparable to the beta risk of the venture. An undiversified entrepreneur should be able to leverage investment in the market index to achieve risk that corresponds to the total risk of the venture. This raises an important question: To what extent is it really possible to leverage the market portfolio? If it is not possible to match the (market or total) risk of the investment, then the notion that the market can be used to gauge opportunity cost is suspect. Our ultimate concern is how to value entrepreneurial ventures if the risk of the entrepreneur's portfolio (venture or venture and market index combined, if the entrepreneur would hold both) exceeds what he or she can achieve using only a leveraged market portfolio.

The most direct way to invest on margin is to borrow part of the money you use to buy the asset. If you are thinking about investing $100,000 in a venture that is twice as risky as the market, you can duplicate the venture's risk by borrowing $100,000, combining that with your own money and investing the entire $200,000 in the market. In the United States, the Federal Reserve Bank, under Regulation T, restricts the extent to which you can invest on margin directly. Currently, the regulation specifies an initial margin of 50 percent, meaning that you cannot borrow more than half of the money you invest.[11] Thus, by investing in the market index, an entrepreneur could only use the opportunity cost reasoning to infer cost of capital on ventures that are no more than twice as risky as the market.

Option investing is an alternative that can offer higher leverage than can be achieved by investing on margin. By purchasing a call and writing a put on a market index, such as the S&P 500 Index, the entrepreneur can achieve the same dollar variance as by investing in the market but can do so with less money. By investing in options that are "at-the-money" an investor can avoid investing the present value of the exercise price (i.e., the present value of the current market value of the index if that payment were to be made on the date that the option would expire). The present value of the exercise price increases with the time to option expiration and with the risk-free rate of interest. Figure 10-2 shows an estimate of how the achievable leverage of the market portfolio varies with these two factors. Thus, if you were considering a venture with an expected holding period of six years and the risk-free rate of interest was 4 percent, achievable leverage of the market portfolio would be about 4.7 times.[12]

From Figure 10-2, it is evident that for early-stage investments, when the expected holding period is long, the ability to use a leveraged market portfolio to infer opportunity cost of capital generally is limited to risk levels of around three to six times the market. For late-stage investing, where expected time to harvesting is shorter, the opportunity cost of capital reasoning can be used with higher levels of investment risk. For realistically achievable levels of diversification this ability to leverage the market generally is sufficient to support the opportunity cost reasoning. When it is not, we deal with the limitation in the following way.

Dealing with the Limitations

As long as the entrepreneur can leverage investment in a market index to achieve the same risk as the venture or financial claim (or, for a diversified investor, to achieve the same beta), the CAPM framework is a useful way to estimate the opportunity cost of capital. We can simply compare the expected return on the venture (or portfolio) to the expected return on the leveraged market index with the same risk. The opportunity cost concept is more difficult to apply, and more subjective, when the risk of the venture or financial claim cannot be matched by leveraging a market index.[13]

Suppose you are considering a venture with a standard deviation of returns that is higher than you can duplicate with leveraged investment in the market index. What cost of capital should you use to value the opportunity? The answer depends, in part, on individual risk tolerance. Figure 10-3 illustrates the decision problem of an entrepreneur who is considering such a high-risk venture. The figure divides risk and return space into three regions based

Achievable Leverage of the Market Portfolio

Term	Risk-free Rate 2.0%	3.0%	4.0%	5.0%	6.0%	7.0%	8.0%	9.0%	10.0%
1	50.5	33.8	25.5	20.5	17.2	14.8	13.0	11.6	10.5
2	25.5	17.2	13.0	10.5	8.8	7.7	6.8	6.1	5.5
3	17.2	11.6	8.8	7.2	6.1	5.3	4.7	4.2	3.9
4	13.0	8.8	6.8	5.5	4.7	4.1	3.7	3.3	3.0
5	10.5	7.2	5.5	4.5	3.9	3.4	3.0	2.8	2.5
6	8.8	6.1	4.7	3.9	3.3	2.9	2.6	2.4	2.2
7	7.7	5.3	4.1	3.4	2.9	2.6	2.3	2.1	2.0
8	6.8	4.7	3.7	3.0	2.6	2.3	2.1	1.9	1.8
9	6.1	4.2	3.3	2.8	2.4	2.1	1.9	1.8	1.7
10	5.5	3.9	3.0	2.5	2.2	2.0	1.8	1.7	1.6

Note: Achievable leverage of the market portfolio is estimated as the current cost of a long-term at-the-money call less the value of selling a long-term at-the-money put, and with investment in a riskless asset, of the sufficient funds to be able to maintain the position for the expected life of the investment.

Figure 10-2 Achievable leverage of the market portfolio

The table shows approximate ability to leverage the market portfolio, as a function of the risk-free rate, and investment term. If the risk-free rate is 4 percent and the investment is expected to be harvested in three years, options can be used to leverage investment in the S&P 500 Index by approximately 8.8 times.

on achievable leverage of the market portfolio. Projects in Region A have risk levels that the entrepreneur can achieve by leveraging investment in the market and have expected returns above the CML. Such projects or portfolios would have positive NPVs under the CAPM-based opportunity cost of capital framework. Region B defines the area where, for a given expected return, the CML would offer less risk. Accordingly, projects in Region B would all have negative NPVs. Portfolios with risk levels greater than can be achieved by leveraging the market, and with expected returns below the expected return of the most highly leveraged achievable market index, are included in this group of negative NPV portfolios.

Region C defines the area where both the risk and expected return are above what the entrepreneur can achieve by leveraging the market. In this region, a project's acceptability depends on the risk tolerance of the individual decision maker. No high-risk portfolio would have a positive NPV unless its expected return was at least as high as that of the most highly leveraged market portfolio. Beyond that return, the choice is subjective. A portfolio like the one illustrated for the project in the figure would have a positive NPV for the more risk-tolerant entrepreneur in the figure but a negative NPV for the more risk-averse entrepreneur.

Because CAPM-based models can undervalue high-risk projects and we cannot always leverage the market index to determine opportunity cost, we modify the valuation model. Over the range of achievable leverage, we use the CAPM to estimate opportunity cost of capital. Beyond that point, we assume risk neutrality. Our hybrid approach is a sensible middle ground that exploits the opportunity cost reasoning, yet assumes that most entrepreneurs are risk-tolerant with regard to their investment choices.

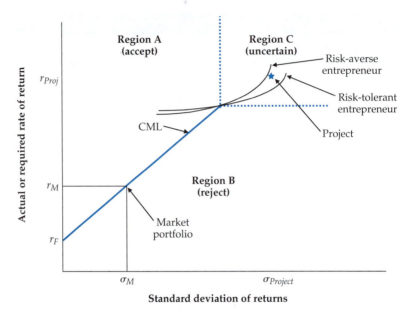

Figure 10-3 Cost of capital for investment in high-risk projects

Achievable leverage of the market portfolio limits ability to infer opportunity cost of capital based on the CML. For riskier projects, required rates are subjective and can differ among investors. All projects with expected return and risk in region A can be accepted, because returns exceed opportunity cost. All projects in region B should be rejected, because they are dominated by market opportunities represented by the CML. Acceptability of projects in region C depends on individual risk tolerance.

10.4   VALUING FULL-COMMITMENT INVESTMENTS

The entrepreneur's valuation problem is significantly more difficult than the investor's problem. However, we have already done much of the spadework in Chapters 8 and 9 to show how you can address it. Here we deal in stages with the remaining difficulties.

In discussion thus far, we have been using the RADR form of the CAPM. That is, we have assumed the entrepreneur already knows the standard deviation of holding-period returns. But it should be clear from earlier discussion that (even if she knows the standard deviation of cash flows) she does not normally know the standard deviation of holding-period returns. Furthermore, although it may be possible to use information about comparable public firms to estimate the beta of a new venture, for the entrepreneur we need a measure of total risk. Because established firms are likely to be less risky and more diversified, data from market comparables may not be helpful. Finally, we have the added complications associated with valuing high-risk projects on the basis of their total risk rather than just their market risk.

We use the following process to value full-commitment investments of entrepreneurs:

Step 1: Use the CEQ form of Eq. (10.3) to value venture cash inflows under the assumption that it is possible to leverage an investment in the market portfolio to achieve the same total risk.

Step 2: Use the maximum achievable leverage estimate from Figure 10-2 to determine a RADR and estimated minimum value of the venture to the entrepreneur.[14]

Step 3: Assuming the entrepreneur *must* either make a full commitment or forego the opportunity, select the greater of the two results as the estimate of project value.

We elaborate on this process in the next section. To postpone dealing with issues of diversification, we focus initially on valuing an entrepreneurial investment as a full commitment.

Using the CEQ Method to Estimate Value

Because the entrepreneur cares about total risk, it is appropriate to modify the CEQ valuation model to be consistent with Eq. (10.3). We do this by deleting the correlation term from Eq. (9.8).

$$PV_t = \frac{C_t - \dfrac{\sigma_{C_t}}{\sigma_M} RP_M}{1 + r_F} \tag{10.4}$$

This expression enables us to address the question of how much the entrepreneur should be willing to pay for the venture if undertaking the venture would require a full commitment and if a leveraged market portfolio can be used to infer opportunity cost of capital.

Equation (10.4) can be used to estimate value in any case where the actual distribution of cash flows is not seriously skewed or where the standard deviation of cash flows is small compared to expected cash flow. When the distribution of possible cash flows is highly skewed, you should interpret Eq. (10.4) as providing a lower bound estimate of value.[15]

Using the Maximum-Achievable-Leverage RADR to Estimate Value

Equations (10.3) and (10.4) yield identical valuations as long as the computed present value is positive.[16] However, given practical limits on ability to leverage an investment in the market, the value estimates may not reflect true opportunity cost. Accordingly, to generate the hybrid estimate of value that we discussed in the previous subsection, we use the maximum achievable leverage estimates from Figure 10-2 to modify Eq. (10.3).

$$PV_t = \frac{C_t}{(1 + r_F + L_{Max} RP_M)^t} \tag{10.5}$$

In this expression, we replace the ratio of venture standard deviation to market standard deviation from Eq. (10.3) by an estimate of maximum leverage of the market, L_{Max}, from Figure 10-2. For the reasons discussed earlier, the value of L_{Max} depends on the holding period and the risk-free rate. Thus, Eq. (10.5) is an estimate of the value of a future cash flow, based on the assumptions that the CAPM accurately describes cost of capital up to the limit of achievable leverage of the market portfolio and that the entrepreneur is risk-neutral beyond that point.

10.5   IMPLEMENTATION—FULL COMMITMENT

Using Simulation to Forecast Expected Cash Flow and Risk

In this section, we demonstrate how to use the RADR and CEQ methods to value full-commitment investments of undiversified entrepreneurs. We also use this section to show how you can use simulation to estimate the expected cash flow and standard deviation of cash flows that are used in the valuation. If you do not plan to use the simulation approach, you can skip over the first subsection.

In Chapter 9, we illustrated the simple approach of estimating risk from discrete scenarios. We now want to introduce the use of simulation to forecast cash flow and risk. Simulation has the advantage of compelling a disciplined investigation of the assumptions that determine value. It also yields a more complete description of risk than can be obtained from discrete scenarios.[17]

To focus on the essential issues of valuation, we abstract from the details of modeling the pro forma financial statements. Figure 10-4 portrays a simple venture in which the entrepreneur makes an initial investment and receives an uncertain cash return in year six, when the investment is assumed to be sold. The year-six cash flow includes continuing value, as well as any accumulated free cash from the first six years of operation.

The figure sets out the simulation model of pro forma cash flows of the venture. All values in the figure are in thousands of dollars. Those actually shown in the figure are from one random iteration of the simulation model.[18] The relatedness of cash flows over time is built into the model by making sales in each year depend partly on sales in the prior year, plus a random growth component. The other assumptions of the model are detailed in the figure. We use a simple assumption for the profitability of sales. The assumption is based on costs that include both fixed and variable components. Furthermore, we simplify by assuming that operating cash flow corresponds to profit. Because growth requires cash for investment in net working capital and fixed assets, we use a simple assumption of the relation between cash needed and sales, and that initial cash of $100,000 is needed for liquidity. In Figure 10-4 we assume the entrepreneur makes an initial investment of $2 million. Free cash is a balance that is computed each year as the free cash balance from the previous year, plus interest on the cash balance computed at 4 percent, plus profit, and less the year-to-year increase in cash needed. Even if the venture accumulates significant free cash before year six, we assume that the cash cannot be distributed until year six. The six-year investment horizon in Figure 10-4 is long enough to enable the entrepreneur, in principle, to harvest the investment by selling or liquidating the venture.

We estimate the value of the venture to the entrepreneur by assuming a hypothetical sale at the end of the explicit value period. At that point, the entrepreneur withdraws any free cash and sells the venture for an estimate of the year-six value of its ability to generate cash flows after year six. In Figure 10-4 we assume that the entrepreneur sells the venture for a multiple of year-six profit. The specific multiple reflects the level of sales in year six and the growth rate of sales in the prior year. Thus, we have built into the multiplier the realistic assumption that ventures with expected high rates of growth generally sell for higher multiples.

New Venture Simulation Model   (Thousands of Dollars)

Forecast of Market Demand

Year	0	1	2	3	4	5	6
Potential Sales	$0.000	$324.241	$436.49	665.175	$1,126.06	1,676.434	$2,475.50

Forecast of Revenue, Profit, Free Cash Flow, and Cash Flow to Investor/Entrepreneur at Harvest

No Options, No Staging		1	2	3	4	5	6
Sales	$0.000	$324.241	$436.489	$665.175	$1,126.056	$1,676.434	$2,475.500
Profit		‾$254.092	‾$203.580	‾$100.671	$106.725	$354.395	$713.975
Cash Needed	$100.000	$162.121	$218.244	$332.588	$563.028	$838.217	$1,237.750
Initial Investment	$2,000.000						
Free Cash	$1,900.000	$1,659.79	$1,466.48	$1,310.12	$1,238.81	$1,367.57	$1,736.71
Out of cash test		0	0	0	0	0	0
Invest	$2,000.000						
Ending Value	$10,542.887						
Ending Cash	$1,736.713						
Total to Investor	$12,279.600						

Assumptions:

Potential Sales is a simulated series including a random starting value in year 1, a random growth rate to year 2, and an element of persistence in growth rates after year 2.

Profit is 45 percent of Sales, less a fixed cost of $400,000.

Cash Need is 50 percent of Sales.

Free Cash is prior year Free Cash plus interest at four percent, plus beginning Cash Needed, plus Profit minus ending Cash Needed.

If Free Cash is negative, the venture is terminated the next year.

Ending Value is a multiple of year-6 Profit. The multiple is an increasing function of sales growth in the last two years.

Ending Cash is year-6 Free Cash and is assumed to be distributed to the entrepreneur.

Total to Investor is Ending Value plus Ending Cash.

Figure 10-4   New venture simulation model (thousands of dollars)

The figure shows a single iteration of the simulation. Required initial investment is $2 million at year zero. The venture is expected to be harvested at year six. Free cash flow before year six is accumulated in the venture, and distributed to the investor/entrepreneur along with the proceeds from selling the equity. "Total to Investor" is the uncertain cash flow the investor receives at harvest. The model can be downloaded from the Web site.

To illustrate how cash flows are related over time, in Figure 10-5 we display the results from 20 iterations of the sales forecast simulation. You can see that if the level of sales is high in one year, it is likely to remain high in subsequent years, but that the rankings of individual series do change, owing to the random elements of the forecast model. To reflect the time series relatedness of cash flows, we calculate the free cash flow in each period and accumulate the free cash balance over time, including an assumption that the balance from the prior year earns interest at the risk-free rate.

Inability to withdraw free cash before the venture is sold reduces value compared to the alternative that free cash can be withdrawn each year, as it is available. However, the assumption approximates reality, as early distributions of cash usually are limited, and many new ventures do not generate much free cash during the early stages.

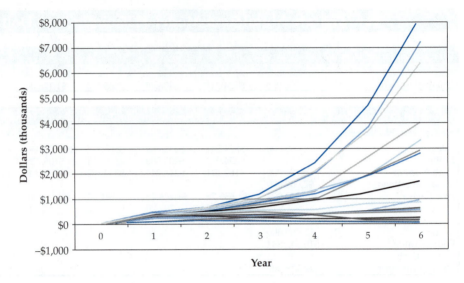

Figure 10-5   Illustration: Sales revenue simulation results

The figure shows twenty random iterations of revenue projections from the model in figure 10-4. The model is structured so sales levels are interdependent. If high sales is achieved in one year, the next year's level also is likely to be high.

As with any valuation problem, it is important to account for all relevant cash flows. For example, if the entrepreneur forgoes other employment to undertake the venture, then differences in compensation, either negative or positive, are among the cash flows that must be valued. The potential for failure and early liquidation is also incorporated in the model in Figure 10-4. This is done by assuming that if cash is not sufficient to meet interim financing needs, the cash balance is invested at the riskless rate until year six.

Using the RADR for a First Look at Value

Suppose, as reflected in Figure 10-4, that to undertake the venture, the entrepreneur must invest financial and human capital having an opportunity cost value of $2 million and must make the entire investment at the start of the venture. Using this information, we ran a simulation of the model in the figure. We found that the expected cash return to the entrepreneur at year six was $8.860 million, with a standard deviation of $5.769 million.[19]

Because the venture holding period is six years, a simple comparison can be made between the venture and the market. First, based on the size of the $2 million initial investment, the expected holding-period return is 343 percent (28.2 percent per year) and the standard deviation of holding-period returns based on the actual investment is 289 percent. In contrast, with a risk-free rate of 4 percent per year and an expected market return of 12 percent, the expected return on the market portfolio over the six-year holding period is 97 percent. The venture has an expected cumulative return that is 3.54 times as high as the market. On the other hand, assuming that the annual standard deviation of market returns is 20 percent per year, and assuming time series independence of returns, the standard deviation of a six-year holding-period market return is 49 percent. Project cash flows at year six are 5.9 times as risky as the market.

Is the expected return high enough to compensate for the added risk? We cannot yet provide a general answer, but we can use Eq. (10.3), along with the actual investment and expected standard deviation of returns on the actual investment, to decide whether the entrepreneur should invest. We use the entrepreneur's $2 million investment and the above result, that the holding-period return of the venture (based on the actual investment) is 5.9 times as risky as the market. It follows from Eq. (10.1) that the required rate of return on the venture as a full commitment of the entrepreneur is 445 percent over the life of the venture, or 32.7 percent per year. Using Eq. (10.3) to discount the expected year-six cash flow of $8.860 million at this rate yields a present value of $1.626 million. Because this is substantially less than the $2.0 million cost of the venture, unless other qualitative considerations outweigh the inadequate return, using the CAPM-based RADR valuation, the entrepreneur should reject the opportunity as a full commitment.[20] The venture might still be worth pursuing if it can be done on a smaller scale or with outside capital, so that the entrepreneur does not need to commit total wealth. We will continue to use this example to explore these possibilities later in this chapter and in Chapter 11.

Valuing a Venture as a Full Commitment

In Figure 10-6 we compute the value of the venture described in Figure 10-4. We do so first from the perspective of a well-diversified investor and second from the perspective of an entrepreneur for whom undertaking the venture would require a full commitment. To evaluate the full-commitment, we estimate value using both the CEQ method in Eq (10.4) and the maximum achievable leverage RADR approach in Eq. (10.5).[21]

The Market Information panel contains details on market returns and risk. For example, the one-year risk-free rate is 4 percent. We derived rates for longer holding periods by compounding, so that the cumulative six-year risk-free rate is 26.53 percent. The market rate of 12 percent is compounded in the same manner. The market risk premium for the holding period is computed as the difference between the market rate and the risk-free rate. Market variance and market standard deviation are computed from the initial assumption of a 20 percent standard deviation of annual returns (4 percent variance) and the assumption that market returns are uncorrelated over time. We assume that the correlation between the venture and the market is 0.2.

The Cash Flow panel in the figure shows the required investments, expected harvest date, and the expected cash flow and standard deviation of cash flows. The CAPM Market Value Estimate panel of the figure computes the value of venture cash inflows to a well-diversified investor, assuming that the CAPM is the correct valuation model. The computations are made using the CEQ form of the CAPM. The resulting present value of $5.683 million indicates that, based on the $2 million investment, the venture would have a NPV of $3.638 million to a well-diversified investor and should be accepted. The implied beta and other information in the panel are included for diagnostic purposes. We use the ratio of expected cash flow to project value to infer the six-year required rate of return. The 55.89 percent return equates to a compound annual return of 7.68 percent. The standard deviation of holding-period returns for the diversified investor is calculated as the ratio of the standard deviation of cash flow to project market value. The required return to a diversified investor is low, even though total risk is high. This is because the nondiversifiable component of venture risk is low. The implied beta of 0.41 is calculated in the usual way from the risk information in the six-year column.

The CAPM Private Value Estimate—Full Commitment panel shows the result of using Eq. (10.4) to compute value to an entrepreneur who is considering a full-commitment. The computed value of $408,000 is well below the $2 million cost. This is the correct value if investments

Valuation Template 3
Valuation of Full Commitment Investment

Market Information	Annual	Holding Period
Risk-free Rate	4.00%	26.53%
Market Rate	12.00%	97.38%
Market Risk Premium	8.00%	70.85%
Market Variance	4.00%	24.00%
Market Standard Deviation	20.00%	48.99%
Correlation		0.2

Cash Flows	Invest Date	Harvest Date
Years Until Expected Harvest		6
Total Investment	$2,000	
Expected Cash Flow at Harvest		$8,860
Standard Deviation of Harvest Cash Flow		$5,769

CAPM Market Value Estimate		
Present Value—Diversified Investor		**$5,683**
Required Return for Diversified Investor	7.68%	55.89%
Equilibrium Std. Dev. of Returns		101.51%
Implied Beta		0.41

CAPM Private Value Estimate—Full Commitment		
Present Value—Undiversified		**$408**
Required Return for Undiversified Investor	67.01%	2069.61%
Equilibrium Std. Dev. of Returns		1412.70%

Maximum Leverage Value Estimate—Full Commitment		
Maximum Leverage (from Figure 10-2: t, r(F))		**4.7**
Required Rate of Return	28.94%	359.53%
Present Value—Project		**$1,928**

VALUE SUMMARY—Full Commitment	
Greater of CAPM or Maximum Leverage Present Value	**$1,928**

Figure 10-6 Valuation of full commitment investment

The spreadsheet is a template designed for valuing investments as full commitments. The panel labeled CAPM Market Value Estimate shows value to a well-diversified investor. CAPM Private Value Estimate—Full Commitment shows CAPM-based value of the venture as a full commitment, assuming the CML defines the opportunity cost of capital. Maximum Leverage Value Estimate—Full Commitment shows value assuming the entrepreneur is risk-neutral beyond the point of maximum ability to leverage the market. Shaded boxes are inputs to the valuation.

in the market can be leveraged to achieve the same total risk as the venture. However, based on the estimated present value of $408,000, the venture is approximately 21 times as risky as an investment in the market. Figure 10-2 indicates that for a six-year investment and a 4 percent risk-free rate, achievable leverage of the market is about 4.7 times. Accordingly, we cannot justify the $408,000 value based solely on market opportunity cost. The value is a reasonable estimate for an investor whose tolerance for bearing risk is similar to that of a representative investor in the market. Other information in the panel is for diagnostic purposes.

The Maximum Leverage Value Estimate—Full Commitment panel is computed by assuming risk-neutrality beyond the point of maximum achievable leverage of the market. We obtained the maximum achievable leverage factor of 4.7 from Figure 10-2 for a six-year holding period and 4 percent annual risk-free rate. Using 4.7 as the value of L_{Max} in Eq. (10.5), the panel shows that 359.53 percent is the attainable expected return over six years on a leveraged market portfolio. The return is computed as 4.7 times the market risk premium, plus the risk-free rate of interest:

$$359.53\% = 4.7 \times 70.85\% + 26.53\%$$

That is, we compute the expected return as if the entrepreneur could borrow 3.7 times the equity investment at the risk-free rate, and invest the entire amount in the market. Discounting the expected $8.860 million cash flow at this rate gives a present value of $1.928 million. Value is substantially higher if the entrepreneur is assumed to be risk-neutral beyond the achievable leverage of the market than if we extrapolate the CML to correspond to the high level of venture risk. However, in this case, the value is still $72,000 too low to justify the $2 million investment.

The Value Summary panel shows the higher of the two entrepreneurial valuations. It is important to recognize, however, that the $1.928 million value is an appropriate measure of value only if the entrepreneur is constrained to pursue the venture as a full commitment, or not at all. If it is possible to pursue the venture on a smaller scale or to bring in an outside investor, then the venture should be evaluated as a partial commitment, even if the entrepreneur might choose to pursue the venture as a full commitment. By not considering a smaller scale investment, the entrepreneur would be ignoring the opportunity of taking a less risky approach to the venture.

10.6   REQUIRED RATES OF RETURN FOR PARTIAL COMMITMENT INVESTMENTS

Suppose the entrepreneur can undertake the venture without committing his or her *entire* wealth. How does this affect the required rate of return? To examine this question, consider an entrepreneur who can allocate wealth between two investment opportunities: the new venture and a fully-diversified market index. In this case, the total portfolio is partially diversified. The entrepreneur's cost of capital for the venture should reflect attained diversification.

Using the RADR Method to Estimate Value

You can estimate the required return for a partial commitment investment by the RADR method using a three-step process.

Step 1: Estimate the standard deviation of holding-period returns of the entrepreneur's total portfolio of risky assets (e.g., the venture and the market portfolio).

Step 2: Use the CML to estimate the required rate of return on the portfolio.

Step 3: Set the portfolio required return equal to the weighted average of the required returns on the market and the venture, and solve for the required return on the venture.

As always, the RADR method requires you to search simultaneously for present value and the standard deviation of holding-period returns. However, in this case, the focus is on the entrepreneur's portfolio rather than just on the venture.

Standard Deviation of the Entrepreneur's Portfolio The following expression describes the variance of a portfolio of two risky assets:

$$\sigma_{Port}^2 = x_A^2\sigma_A^2 + x_B^2\sigma_B^2 + 2x_A x_B \rho_{A,B}\sigma_A\sigma_B \tag{10.6}$$

where A and B are the two assets, x_A and x_B are the value weights of total risky investments in each, and ρ_{AB} is the correlation coefficient between the two assets.[22] Equation (10.6) is a general expression for any portfolio of two risky assets.[23] We are concerned with the special case in which one asset is the new venture under consideration by the entrepreneur (or the entrepreneur's financial claim on the venture) and the other is the market portfolio.

To illustrate, we return to our example from the beginning of the chapter, that is, with $\beta_P = 2.0$, $\sigma_P^E = 60$ percent, and $\sigma_M = 20$ percent. You can infer from this that the correlation coefficient between the venture and the market is at least 0.667. To do this, use $\beta_P = \rho_{P,M}\sigma_P^E/\sigma_M$ where $\rho_{P,M}$ is the correlation coefficient between venture returns and market returns. Solve the expression for $\rho_{P,M}$.[24]

Now, assuming that 25 percent of the entrepreneur's risk capital is invested in the venture and 75 percent is invested in the market portfolio, Eq. (10.6) can be used to find that the variance of the total portfolio of risky assets is 7.515 percent:

$$7.515\% = .07515 = .25^2 \times .60^2 + .75^2 \times .20^2 + 2 \times .25 \times .75 \times .667 \times .60 \times .20$$

The standard deviation, σ_{Port}^E, is the square root of the variance, 27.4 percent.

The Entrepreneur's Required Return on the Portfolio Using Eq. (10.1), continuing with the assumptions that r_F is 4 percent and RP_M is 8 percent, and substituting σ_{Port}^E for σ_P^E, the required return on the total risky portfolio is 14.96 percent:

$$14.96\% = 4\% + (27.4/20) \times 8\%$$

This is the required return on the entrepreneur's portfolio, which includes both the venture and the market. Because the portfolio standard deviation is used, the required return depends, in part, on the value of the entrepreneur's investment in the venture.

The Entrepreneur's Required Return on the Venture To find the required return on the venture, we use the fact that the required return on the risky portfolio is equal to the weighted average of the required return on the venture and the required return on the market. Using this equality, along with what we already know about the expected return on the market portfolio, and the weighting of the entrepreneur's investment value between the project and the market, we can solve for the required return on the new venture investment.

$$r_{Port} = x_P r_P + x_M r_M \tag{10.7}$$

$$r_P = \frac{r_{Port} - x_M r_M}{x_{Port}} \tag{10.8}$$

Using Eq. (10.8), the required return for investing 25 percent of the entrepreneur's risk capital in the project is 23.8 percent.

This is significantly below the 28 percent required return we determined for investing in the venture as a full commitment. The reduction occurs because the entrepreneur can partially diversify between the venture and another asset. Diversification reduces the entrepreneur's risk exposure, which makes bearing the risk of the venture more acceptable.

The reduction in the entrepreneur's cost of capital due to diversifying between the new venture and the market has three important determinants: the ratio of total venture risk to market risk, the degree of correlation between the venture and the market, and the investment weightings between the two assets.

The "Base case" curve in Figure 10-7 illustrates how the entrepreneur's cost of capital for the above venture declines as the fraction of capital invested in the venture declines. As the fraction in the venture approaches zero, the entrepreneur's cost of capital for the venture approaches the 20 percent cost of capital for a diversified investor. The uppermost curve illustrates how the relation shifts if the standard deviation of returns for the venture is increased from 60 percent to 80 percent, with the venture beta unchanged (implying that the correlation coefficient has declined). The lowest curve illustrates how the relation shifts if the correlation coefficient between the venture and the market is reduced to zero (making the required return for a fully-diversified investor equal to the risk-free rate).

In summary, the entrepreneur's cost of capital, while driven largely by the total risk of a venture, depends also on the entrepreneur's other risky assets and on how those risks correlate with the risk of the venture. This is a major departure from investment decision making for a public corporation or a well-diversified investor in new ventures. By controlling the fraction of wealth invested in the venture, the entrepreneur had a degree of control over his or her cost of capital. Thus, an entrepreneur who acts as the sole investor in a project effectively chooses the required rate of return along with the decision of venture scale. The larger the scale, the larger the fraction of the entrepreneur's capital that must be invested, and therefore, the higher the entrepreneur's required rate of return. Later in the text, we explore other issues, such as how the decision to bring in outside investors can affect the entrepreneur's required rate of return.

Using the CEQ Method to Estimate Value

To avoid the need to determine project value and the standard deviation of returns simultaneously, we again resort to certainty equivalents. Valuation of the venture involves two steps.

Step 1: Use the CEQ method to value the entrepreneur's portfolio.

Step 2: Find the value of the venture by deducting the value of investment in the market portfolio from total portfolio value.

Valuing the Entrepreneur's Portfolio by the CEQ Method   Equation (10.9) is the CEQ form of the entrepreneur's valuation model, applied to valuing the entrepreneur's portfolio of risky investments.

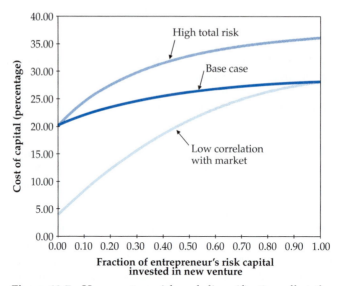

Figure 10-7 How venture risk and diversification affect the entrepreneur's cost of capital

The figure shows how diversification and risk affect required return on investment. If a venture is undertaken as a full commitment (100 percent of risk capital invested), required return is determined by total risk. If a trivial fraction of risk capital is invested, required return depends only on the systematic risk. The higher the total risk, the higher the required return, and the lower the correlation with the market, the lower the required return. The "Base case" venture in the figure has total risk that is three times as high as the market and a beta of 2.0. The risk-free rate is 4 percent, and the market risk premium is 8 percent. The "High total risk" venture has total risk that is four times as high as the market, but a beta the same as the Base case. The "Low correlation with market" venture has the same total risk as the Base case, but a beta of 0.0.

$$PV_{Port} = \frac{C_{Port} - \dfrac{\sigma_{C_{Port}}}{\sigma_M} RP_M}{(1 + r_F)} \tag{10.9}$$

In Eq. (10.9), for convenience, we drop the time subscripts. To use the expression, it is necessary to estimate the expected harvest-date cash return of the portfolio, C_{Port}, and the standard deviation of the portfolio cash flow, $\sigma_{C_{Port}}$. Equation (10.10) gives the expected harvest date cash flow, and Eq. (10.11) gives the standard deviation.

$$C_{Port} = C_P + w_M(1 + r_M) \tag{10.10}$$

$$\sigma_{C_{Port}} = \sqrt{\sigma_{C_P}^2 + (\sigma_M w_M)^2 + 2\rho_{P,M}\sigma_{C_P}(\sigma_M w_M)} \tag{10.11}$$

In Eq. (10.10), we compute the expected cash return for investing in the market index as one plus the expected rate of return, r_M, times the dollar value of the investment, w_M. The expected cash return of the entrepreneur's portfolio is the sum of the expected cash return for investing in the venture and the expected cash return for the investment in the market. The standard deviation of the entrepreneur's portfolio cash flows is computed in Eq. (10.11) using the approach in Eq. (10.6) but is based on dollar-valued cash flows instead of percentages of invested wealth.

Determining the Value of the Venture as a Partial Commitment   Equation (10.12) shows the determination of the value of a venture that is undertaken as a partial commitment of the entrepreneur.

$$PV_P = PV_{Port} - w_M \tag{10.12}$$

Using Data for Public Firms to Estimate The Entrepreneur's Cost of Capital

Because public stock prices and returns are driven by cost of capital of well diversified investors, the entrepreneur's cost of capital is difficult to determine from public firm data. However, with a bit of algebra, it is possible to use market data to infer C_{Port} and $\sigma_{C_{Port}}$ the two parameters we need in order to use Eq. (10.9) to determine the present value of an underdiversified entrepreneur's portfolio, PV_{Port}^E. We then can easily solve for the value of the project to the entrepreneur and for the entrepreneur's cost of capital.

First, we must assume (hypothetically) that a well-diversified investor holds wealth in the venture and in the market and assign value weights in the market and the project similar to what the entrepreneur would have. Because the entrepreneur and the diversified investor value the venture differently, they will not have the same value weights.[25] We can use Eq. (10.13) to compute the expected cash flow:

$$C_{Port} = w_M (1 + r_M) + w_P^I [1 + r_F + \beta_P (r_M - r_F)] \tag{10.13}$$

where w_P^I is based on the diversified investor's equilibrium valuation. For convenience, we assume Eq. (10.13) is standardized so that w_M and w_P^I sum to $1. The result is that C_{Port} is the expected cash return per dollar invested in the portfolio by a well-diversified investor, based on the market risk of the assets.

We compute the diversified investor's equilibrium portfolio cash flow risk, $\sigma_{C_{Port}}$, based on Eq. (10.11):

$$\sigma_{C_{Port}} = \sqrt{(w_M \sigma_M)^2 + (w_P^I \sigma_P)^2 + 2\rho_{P,M} w_M w_P^I \sigma_M \sigma_P} \tag{10.14}$$

Because all variables in Eqs. (10.13) and (10.14) are observable from market data, we now can use market data to solve Eq. (10.9). Then, by subtracting w_M we can find the value of the entrepreneur's investment in the project. We then can use Eq. (10.15) to solve for the entrepreneur's cost of capital:

$$r_P^E = \frac{C_P}{PV_P^E} - 1 \tag{10.15}$$

The other difficulty with trying to use public data is that not much data are available. However, in their recent study of post-IPO data for early-stage high technology ventures, Kerins, Smith, and Smith (2004) report that the average beta of their sample is 0.99, and the average correlation is 0.195, suggesting that total risk is a little more than five times as high as market risk.

Figure 10-8 is a template that can be used to find the entrepreneur's cost of capital by using risk and expected return data for a comparable public firm. In the figure, we use the risk and correlation estimates found by Kerins, Smith, and Smith to estimate venture cost of capital for an entrepreneur who plans to invest 15 percent of wealth in a venture and harvest in two years. In the figure, we assume that the annual risk-free rate is 4 percent, the expected return on the market is 10 percent, and the annualized standard deviation of the market is 14 percent. For the public firm that is comparable to the venture, we assume that beta risk is 0.99 and correlation with the market is 0.195. We also assume (hypothetically) that the well-diversified investor puts 81.3 percent of wealth in the market and the rest in the venture. We selected 81.3 percent in the market because we want to determine the new venture cost of capital for an entrepreneur who put 15 percent of total wealth in the venture. We used the Goal Seek feature of Excel to find the value of the diversified investor's investment in the market that would make the entrepreneur's fraction of wealth invested in the venture equal 15 percent. The template also shows statistics for investment in the venture as a full commitment.

In the template, Eq. (10.13) is used to calculate that the expected cash flow of the entrepreneur's portfolio would need to be $1.21 per dollar invested, 85 percent in the market and 15 percent in the venture. The template uses Eq. (10.14) to compute that the standard deviation of portfolio cash flows is $0.27 per dollar invested. Based on Eq. (10.9), the resulting value of the entrepreneur's portfolio is $0.956, less than the $1 value the portfolio would have for a well-diversified investor. We find the value of the entrepreneur's investment in the venture by subtracting the $0.813, the amount the investor would put in the market per total dollar invested. We find the expected cash flow from investing in the venture by subtracting the expected value of the market investment at the end of the two-year holding period. Finally, we use Eq. (10.15) to infer that 57.6 percent (or 25.6 percent per year) is the entrepreneur's cost of capital for investing 15 percent of wealth in the venture.

Using the Maximum-Achievable-Leverage RADR to Estimate Value

Again, for a partially-diversified entrepreneur, we must allow for the possibility that total risk exceeds the entrepreneur's ability to leverage investment in the market. In this case, the focus is not on the project but on the entrepreneur's portfolio. Equations (10.16) and (10.17) illustrate how to determine new venture value based on maximum achievable leverage.

$$PV_{Port} = \frac{C_{Port}}{(1 + r_F + L_{Max}RP)} \tag{10.16}$$

$$PV_P = PV_{Port} - w_M \tag{10.17}$$

	Per Year	Full Commitment	Partial Commitment
Cost of Capital Template			
Estimation Based on Data from Comparable Public Firms			
Inputs			
Years Until Expected Harvest		2.0	2.0
Hypothetical Fraction of Wealth Invested in Market Portfolio		0.0%	81.3%
Hypothetical Fraction of Wealth Invested in Venture		100.0%	18.7%
Market Data			
Risk-free Rate of Interest	4.0%	8.2%	8.2%
Expected Return on Market	10.0%	21.0%	21.0%
Standard Deviation of Market Returns	14.0%	19.8%	19.8%
Comparable Public Firm Data			
Correlation of Comparable Public Firm with Market	0.195	0.195	0.195
Beta of Comparable Public Firm	0.990	0.990	0.990
Standard Deviation of Comparable Public Firm Returns		100.5%	100.5%
Porfolio Cash Flow Results			
Expected Harvest Cash Flow of Entrepreneur's Portfolio		$1.209	$1.210
Cash Flow Standard Deviation of Portfolio		$1.005	$0.271
Value of Entrepreneur's Portfolio		$0.515	$0.956
Venture Valuation Results			
Value of Entrepreneur's Investment in Venture		**$0.515**	**$0.144**
Expected Cash Flow from Investment in Venture		$1.209	$0.227
Venture Cost of Capital Estimates			
Entrepreneur's Holding-Period Cost of Captial for Venture		**134.8%**	**57.6%**
Entrepreneur's Annualized Cost of Capital for Venture		53.2%	25.6%
Diversified Investors Cost of Capital for Venture		**20.9%**	**20.9%**
Standard Deviation of Entrepreneurs Return from Venture		195.2%	131.1%
Entrepreneur's Wealth Allocation			
Fraction of Entrepreneur's Wealth Invested in Venture		100.0%	15.0%
Fraction of Entrepreneur's Wealth Invested in Market		0.0%	85.0%

Figure 10-8   Cost of capital template

This template can be used with data on comparable public firms to estimate the new venture cost of capital for an entrepreneur who is underdiversified. The template is downloadable from the text Web site.

Because this approach relies on the opportunity cost of capital for a leveraged market portfolio, the portfolio cash flow in Eq. (10.16) should be based on the minimum entrepreneurial investment that is needed. If the entrepreneur decides to pursue the project on a larger scale, involving a larger fraction of wealth, the appropriate discount rate for valuing the project is higher than the rate implicitly reflected in Eq. (10.16) as $C_{Port}/PV_{Port} - 1$.[26]

The Relation Between the Entrepreneur's Wealth and New Venture Value

Portfolio theory leads to the conclusion that for a new venture investment of a given size, the entrepreneur's opportunity cost of capital for the venture is a decreasing function of wealth. As the entrepreneur's wealth increases, holding investment in the venture constant, the entrepreneur's cost of capital declines. This occurs because greater wealth increases the entrepreneur's ability to diversify. As ability to diversify increases, the entrepreneur's cost of capital declines toward that of a well-diversified investor.

The concept of maximum achievable leverage introduces an offsetting effect. Because maximum achievable leverage is applied to the entrepreneur's portfolio, the constraint on leverage becomes binding on a poor entrepreneur at a lower level of investment than on a wealthy one. Thus, for a given size investment where the constraint is binding on a poor entrepreneur but not on a wealthy one, the opportunity cost of the wealthy entrepreneur can be higher. This implies that individuals who are not wealthy and are risk neutral are more likely to find a high-risk entrepreneurial venture of a certain irreducible size attractive. On the other hand, if the venture can be pursued on a smaller scale, or if outside financing is available, the wealthy investor will value investment of a given scale more highly.

10.7 IMPLEMENTATION—PARTIAL COMMITMENT

Returning to the stream of the analysis, suppose that undertaking the venture described in Figure 10-4 does not require the entrepreneur's entire wealth. Rather, the entrepreneur invests effort for the next few years and some financial capital in the venture. We assume that the remainder of the entrepreneur's financial capital is invested in a market portfolio. We also assume that, if the venture fails, the entrepreneur can return to former employment.

Unless the risk of the venture is perfectly positively correlated with the market, the ability to, in effect, hedge some of the risk by holding a diversified portfolio as a second asset reduces the required rate of return. The extent of reduction depends on the correlation between the two assets and the fractions of risk capital invested in each.[27]

Valuing the Venture as a Partial Commitment

Suppose that to undertake the venture described in Figure 10-4 the entrepreneur would have to invest $2 million and that doing so would leave him $4 million to invest in a market index. To estimate the value of the venture to the entrepreneur as a partial commitment, we use the approaches described in the previous section.

The analysis is summarized in Figure 10-9. The Market Information panel shows the same data as in the corresponding panel of Figure 10-6. The Cash Flow panel is expanded to include not just the venture-specific information, but also the expected cash flow and standard deviation of cash flows for investing in the market and for the portfolio that combines the two investments. The expected market cash flow is computed by applying the market rate of return to the $4 million investment in the market. The market standard deviation of cash flows is computed by multiplying the market standard deviation in percentage terms by the $4 million investment in the market. The expected portfolio cash flow and portfolio standard deviation values are computed using Eqs. (10.10) and (10.11).[28] In the CAPM Market Value Estimate panel, we report the values of the venture and the market investments to a diversified investor. The value of the venture is the same as that reported in Figure 10-6.

Valuation Template 4		
Valuation of Partial Commitment of The Entrepreneur		

Market Information	Annual	Holding Period
Risk-free Rate	**4.00%**	26.53%
Market Rate	**12.00%**	97.38%
Market Risk Premium	8.00%	70.85%
Market Variance	4.00%	24.00%
Market Standard Deviation	**20.00%**	48.99%
Correlation		0.2

Cash Flows	Invest Date	Harvest Date
Years Until Harvest		6
Investment in Project	**$2,000**	
Expected Project Cash Flow		**$8,860**
Project Standard Deviation of Cash Flows		**$5,769**
Investment in Market	**$4,000**	
Expected Market Cash Flow		$7,895
Market Standard Deviation Cash Flows		$1,960
Expected Portfolio Cash Flow	$6,000	$16,755
Portfolio Standard Deviation		$6,453

CAPM Market Value Estimate		
Portfolio Present Value		$9,683
Market Investment		$4,000
Present Value—Project		**$5,683**
Project Required Return for Diversified Investor	7.68%	55.89%
Project Equilibrium Std. Dev. of Returns		101.51%
Project Implied Beta		0.41

CAPM Private Value Estimate—Partial Commitment		
Present Value—Portfolio		$5,866
Market Investment		$4,000
Present Value—Project		**$1,886**
Project Required Return for Undiversified Investor	29.64%	374.77%
Equilibrium Std. Dev. of Returns		309.14%

Maximum Leverage Value Estimate—Partial Commitment		
Maximum Leverage (from Figure 10-2: t, r(F))		**4.7**
Required Rate of Return on Portfolio	28.94%	359.53%
Present Value—Portfolio		$3,646
Market Investment		$4,000
Present Value—Project		**−$354**

VALUE SUMMARY—Full Commitment	
Greater of CAPM or Maximum Leverage Present Value	$1,866

Figure 10-9 Valuation—Partial commitment of the entrepreneur

The spreadsheet can be used as a template to value partial-commitment investments. The Cash Flow panel shows the entrepreneur's total wealth (measured at opportunity cost), distributed between investment in a venture and investment in the market. It also shows expected cash flows and their standard deviations at time of harvest, and the expected cash flow and standard deviation of the entrepreneur's total portfolio.

In the CAPM Private Value Estimate—Partial Commitment panel, we value the entrepreneur's investment using the CEQ form of the CAPM-based model, Eq. (10.9). By that approach, the entrepreneur's portfolio is valued at $5.866 million. To find the value of the venture, we deduct the $4 million value of the market index. The resulting estimate of venture value is $1.866 million. In the Maximum Leverage Value Estimate—Partial Commitment panel, we value the entrepreneur's portfolio using the maximum leverage constraint, as in Eq. (10.16). We estimate venture value by subtracting the $4 million investment in the market index. The resulting estimate is negative and less than the CAPM-based estimate. Accordingly, the maximum leverage constraint is not binding, and the Value Summary panel shows $1.866 million as the estimate of project value.

Comparing Full and Partial Commitment Values

The CAPM-based estimate of venture value as a partial commitment is substantially higher than the full-commitment value in Figure 10-6. The CAPM-based required rate of return in Figure 10-9 is 375 percent (29.6 percent per year), as compared to 2070 percent (67.0 percent per year) in Figure 10-6. The reduction in required rate of return reflects the benefit of diversification on the entrepreneur's cost of capital. In Figure 10-9, the total value of the entrepreneur's wealth is $5.866 million, of which $1.866 million, or 31.8 percent, is the value of the venture. In Figure 10-6, the venture accounts for the entrepreneur's entire wealth.

As Figure 10-9 shows, the maximum achievable leverage estimate of value tends to become small and irrelevant as the fraction of the entrepreneur's wealth that is invested in the venture declines. However, paradoxically, the maximum achievable leverage value in Figure 10-6 is higher than the CAPM-based partial-commitment value in Figure 10-9. This difference occurs because the entrepreneur in Figure 10-6 is assumed to be risk-neutral beyond the point of achievable leverage of the market portfolio. In contrast, the entrepreneur in Figure 10-9 can pursue the venture and still have $4 million available to invest in the market. This gives that entrepreneur more ability to duplicate the returns of the venture by leveraging an investment in the market. We cannot invoke the assumption of risk neutrality until we exhaust the entrepreneur's true opportunity to increase expected return by leveraging the market.

Wealth, Diversification, and Venture Value

Calculations aside, the example shows that by using CAPM-based valuation, the entrepreneur's required return declines as the fraction of risk capital he invests in the venture declines. With 100 percent investment, the cost of capital in our example is 67 percent per year. If an entrepreneur invests a trivial fraction of total wealth in the venture, the cost drops to 7.7 percent. This is the return a well-diversified investor would require given the venture's low level of market risk. At the intermediate level of 31.8 percent of wealth invested in the venture, the entrepreneur's cost of capital is 29.6 percent. Using the spreadsheet in Figure 10-9, it can be determined that the venture has a zero NPV at a 28.2 percent discount rate, which corresponds to 30.9 percent of wealth being invested. If the cost of the venture is $2 million, then the entrepreneur needs to invest $4.475 million in a market index.

More generally, Figure 10-10 illustrates the relation between the present value of the venture and the fraction of the entrepreneur's risk capital that is invested in it. The breakeven present

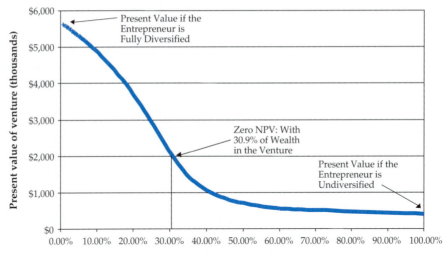

Figure 10-10   Present value and fraction of risk capital invested in venture

For any given dollar investment in a venture, the present value of the investment is greater the smaller the fraction of total wealth that the investment represents. The figure is based on the $2 million investment in Figure 10-9 and shows how present value of the investment changes as the fraction of wealth invested in the venture changes. The venture achieves zero NPV if 30.9 percent of total wealth (in terms of opportunity cost) is invested in the project. The figure reflects only the CAPM-based value and ignores maximum achievable leverage.

value occurs at the point where the $2 million investment accounts for 30.9 percent of risk capital. Venture present value continues to increase as the entrepreneur's total risk capital increases. In the limit, venture value is the same as for a well-diversified investor.

Valuing Ventures that Have Cash Flows in Multiple Periods

The spreadsheet in Figure 10-9 is designed to accommodate valuation of ventures with harvest cash flows that occur in a single period. However, many entrepreneurs are involved in ventures they do not plan to harvest or where they can realize cash flow returns over a number of years. For such entrepreneurs, it is important to be able to value projects with cash flows in multiple periods. Though valuing multi-period investments is easy for well-diversified investors, it is tricky for an entrepreneur who is not well diversified. Ventures that generate cash flows in multiple periods can offer a degree of inter-temporal diversification, which is not taken into account in the valuation framework that we have been discussing.

In Figure 10-9, although different cash flow streams within a period are merged in a way that takes their correlation into consideration, there is no consideration of how to value cash flows correlated over time. This is not a problem if the investor is well diversified, because required rates of return are only affected by market risk. But it is a problem for an underdiversified investor, such as an entrepreneur. By calculating the values of cash flows separately for each period, we, in effect, assume that the benefits of inter-temporal diversification are negligible. For that to be the case, cash flows in different years must be perfectly positively correlated, or nearly so. If they are not, the calculations do not reflect the benefit of diversification over time. Unfortunately, there is no simple way to analyze the value of such diversification. The conceptually correct approach is to treat each annual cash flow as if it were a separate investment and to compute the benefits of inter-temporal diversification from the correlation coefficients between each pair of cash flows. To do so formally, you would need to describe all of the time-series correlations and value the venture as, in effect, a portfolio of projects with single-period cash flows. In recognition of the difficulty of such an approach, we introduce a simplification.

For some multi-period ventures, failing to account for the benefit of inter-temporal diversification is not very important. The effect can be small for two reasons. First, particularly when the continuing value calculation is used, the overwhelming fraction of total value is likely to be concentrated in one period. In such a case, the benefit of inter-temporal diversification is reflected implicitly in the continuing value estimate. Second, the actual correlation of future cash flows over time may be fairly high, particularly for early-stage ventures. Success in one period is likely to lead to success in subsequent periods.

The main concern about intertemporal diversification arises when a venture is an established business that is being managed to generate a long series of cash flows for its owners rather than to be harvested within a concentrated period. For such a business, year-to-year cash flow fluctuations are likely to appear as little more than random fluctuations around a stationary trend. If the deviations are truly random, except for a systematic market component, then, you might think of the beta risk of the business as providing a basis for estimating a lower bound on the entrepreneur's cost of capital. This is overly aggressive, because it implies that the entrepreneur would be indifferent between a venture with only systematic risk and another venture with the same level of systematic risk, but also large nonsystematic annual fluctuations in cash flows.[29]

If you are concerned about the effects of diversification on value, you can take account of diversification by constructing a hypothetical one-period venture that should have a value similar to that of the multi-period venture. This can be done in the following way. First, use the simulation model to generate expected cash flows in each period and use the results to estimate of the duration of the venture. Duration is essentially a weighted average of the timing of discounted cash flows.[30] Second, re-run the simulation but use the risk free rate of interest to shift all of the cash flows from each iteration of the simulation model to the point you determine in your calculation of duration. Shifting the cash flows to a single period implicitly considers inter-temporal diversification. The idea, again, is that instead of valuing the business that generates cash flows in many periods, you can substitute a hypothetical venture that pays off in one period and should have approximately the same value.

Figure 10-11 illustrates the use of duration to address the problem of inter-temporal correlation. We have assumed that the first-year cash flow to the entrepreneur is expected to be $100 and that cash flows are expected to grow at a rate of 20 percent per year, through year 8. Annual cash flows are subject to random surprises and are linked over time, so the result in one year affects the expected value in the next. Because of this link, the risky cash flows are correlated over time.[31] To address this issue, we use the duration approach to devise a hypothetical project that pays off in only one period, takes inter-temporal correlation into account, and is expected to be of equal value.

The first panel of Figure 10-11 shows one iteration of simulated annual cash flows to the entrepreneur. The first step in the valuation is to estimate duration. The second panel shows

Duration Template

Estimating the Single-Period Equivalent of a Project with Cash Flows in Multiple Periods

Period		1	2	3	4	5	6	7	8
Cash Flow to Investor/Entrepreneur		$96	$117	$136	$157	$193	$254	$300	$354
Calculation of Approximate Discounted Present Value of Expected Periodic Cash Flows to Investor/Entrepreneur									
Expected Cash Flow		$100	$120	$144	$173	$207	$249	$299	$358
Preliminary Discount Factor and DCF	0.12	$89	$96	$102	$110	$118	$126	$135	$145
Preliminary Total Discounted Cash Flow (DCF)	$921								
Computation of Approximate Duration (Based on Preliminary DCF)									
Percent of Preliminary Est. of Value		9.70%	10.39%	11.13%	11.93%	12.78%	13.69%	14.67%	15.72%
Duration Weightings		0.10	0.21	0.33	0.48	0.64	0.82	1.03	1.26
Duration (in Periods)	4.86								
Rounded Duration	5.00								
Conversion of Simulated Periodic Cash Flows to Single-Period Equivalent									
Risk-free Rate	0.04								
Time-Shifted Values of Simulated CF		$113	$132	$147	$163	$193	$244	$277	$315
Accumulated Time-Shifted Value of CF	**$1,584**								

The bolded number shown in blue is used in the simulation model to estimate expected equivalent cash flow and risk. Results of the simulation are used in year five in the valuation template from Figure 10-6.

Figure 10-11 Estimating the single-period equivalent of a project with cash flows in multiple periods

The figure demonstrates a way of considering intertemporal correlation. Instead of valuing cash flows from multiple periods, this spreadsheet estimates the duration of the cash flows and constructs a hypothetical single-period venture with approximately the same value as the venture. First, a rough approximation is made of the present value of the expected stream of cash flows. Second, based on this approximation, an estimate of the duration of the cash flows is made. Third, the risk-free rate is used as a lending and borrowing rate to shift the simulated cash flow estimate from each period to the year of the duration estimate. The inter-temporal correlation is taken into account by shifting all cash flows to a single period. The template can be downloaded from the text Web site.

the expected annual cash flows. To estimate duration, the expected annual cash flows should be re-expressed in terms of present value. Unfortunately, because we do not know the correct discount rate, this brings us to a circularity. We cannot compute duration unless we know (or assume) the discount rate. As it turns out, a rough estimate of the discount rate will work well enough for estimating duration. We suggest that you assume a discount rate that seems reasonable. The discount rate used in estimating duration only affects the time positioning of the harvest cash flows from the hypothetical project. For most actual projects, if you assume a discount rate that is too high or too low, the estimated harvest date (duration) will not be affected very much and the present value estimate will be affected only slightly. The higher the rate you use, the shorter will be the duration estimate. We chose to discount the expected cash flows at the market rate of 12 percent. Accumulating the discounted cash flows yields the discounted value of $921, as shown in the figure.

In the next panel, we use the discounted value to compute the percentage of value that is attributable to each period's cash flow. Multiplying those percentages by the number of periods until they are received gives the duration weightings of cash flows. Summing the results gives the estimate of duration. Our estimate is 4.86 years, which we round to 5.

In the final panel, we construct the hypothetical project with all annual cash flows shifted to year five. To do this, we compound or discount the simulated periodic cash flows from the first panel to their values as of year five. Early cash flows are compounded to year five at the risk-free rate, as if they are retained in the venture and invested at the risk-free rate until year five. Late cash flows are discounted to year five at the risk-free rate, as if they are borrowed.

The final estimate of harvest date cash flow that appears in the figure as Accumulated Time-Shifted Value of CF is the estimated cash flow from one random iteration of the model. When we simulated the model in Figure 10-11, we found that the expected cash flow was $1627 and that the standard deviation was $126. We used these results in the Figure 10-6 valuation template and estimated that the value of the venture as a full commitment is $1,211.[32]

10.8 ESTIMATING THE ENTREPRENEUR'S WEALTH AND INVESTMENT

In the preceding example of partial-commitment investment, we determined that, at the breakeven present value for the venture, 30.9 percent of the entrepreneur's risk capital would be invested in the venture. We now want to look more carefully at how to estimate the value of the entrepreneur's risk capital. We also would like to develop a realistic estimate of how much of an entrepreneur's total wealth or risk capital is likely to be invested in a venture.

Estimating the Present Value of Compensation in Alternative Employment

Because required rate of return depends on the fraction of wealth the entrepreneur invests in the venture, we need a way to estimate of the entrepreneur's total wealth. Total wealth includes financial capital and the present value of future compensation from alternative employment. The most difficult aspect of quantifying total wealth is estimating the value of future compensation. However, we often can derive a reasonable estimate using the expression for a growing annuity:

$$PV_{Comp} = \frac{C_1}{r - g}\left(1 - \frac{(1 + g)^t}{(1 + r)^t}\right)$$

(10.18)

where PV_{Comp} is the present value of future compensation over the entrepreneur's work life if the venture is not undertaken, C_1 is first-year annual compensation (i.e., salary and benefits) in the alternative employment, g is the expected growth rate of compensation over the entrepreneur's work life, t is the expected number of years of work life remaining, and r is an estimate of the cost of capital for compensation that is consistent with the riskiness of the compensation.

The Entrepreneur's Total Wealth

Total wealth is the present value of expected total compensation in continuing current employment, plus the present value of the entrepreneur's other assets, net of liabilities. The entrepreneur's total investment in the venture includes the present value of forgone compensation for the length of time the entrepreneur is committed to the venture. This could be the investment horizon (six years in the example we have been using) or a lesser period, if early abandonment is a possibility.[33] The entrepreneur's commitment also includes the value of other assets invested in the venture. Equation (10.18) can again be used to estimate the value of compensation invested in the venture. These are opportunity cost measures of wealth and investment. They are based on the values of opportunities foregone, and not on the present value of the venture.

An Illustration

Consider the venture described in Figure 10-6 at the point where venture NPV is zero. Suppose an entrepreneur's current (year one) compensation is $200,000 and that compensation is expected to grow 3 percent per year until retirement in 20 years. For now, we assume that compensation in alternative employment is riskless. The cost of capital for low-risk compensation is assumed to be the 4 percent risk-free rate of return. The resulting value of total compensation is $3.514 million, and the value of the first six years (the portion committed to the venture) is $1.126 million. The entrepreneur also expects to invest about $0.874 million of cash in the deal to make the total investment $2 million and to retain $4.475 million in an index fund. Thus, based on opportunity cost, the entrepreneur's total wealth is $8.863 million. The fraction of total wealth invested in the venture is 22.6 percent, and the fraction invested in the index is 50.5 percent. The remainder is the present value of the entrepreneur's (riskless) earnings in alternative employment, after commitment to the venture ends. Focusing just on the two risky assets, the venture accounts for 30.9 percent of risk capital, and the market index for 69.1 percent. These are the weights for estimating the entrepreneur's cost of capital for the venture if the RADR approach is used. The resulting cost of capital, as we stated earlier, declines to 28.2 percent per year, owing to partial diversification. This approach works well if the entrepreneur's compensation in alternative employment is low risk.

Human Capital as a Third Asset in the Entrepreneur's Portfolio

Until now, we have assumed that the entrepreneur's portfolio of risky assets includes investments in the venture and in a market index. We have treated the residual value of human capital as a riskless asset. This is an oversimplification. Most entrepreneurs cannot know with certainty what opportunities they will face if they abandon a venture. Also, such things as remaining work-life and the growth rate of compensation are uncertain.

Risky compensation in alternative employment affects valuation in two ways. First, because risk affects an asset's cost of capital, the present value of risky future compensation is less than the present value of safe future compensation. Second, the entrepreneur's portfolio consists of three risky assets instead of two.

Although we can extend the valuation framework to include a third risky asset, doing so would add significantly to complexity. Instead, we deal with the issue by making a few qualitative generalizations.

You can consider treating the value of human capital in one of three ways. First, if earnings in alternative employment would be very safe and predictable, you could assume that the future cash flows from alternative employment are riskless (as we did earlier in this chapter). If so, you would use the risk-free rate in Eq. (10.18) to value the human capital. However, because it is assumed to be riskless, that value would not be included in the portfolio of the entrepreneur's risky assets. Second, if the earnings would be somewhat risky, you could assume that future cash flows are as risky as the market index and that the index is a reasonable proxy for the entrepreneur's risky assets other than the venture (as we do going forward). In that case, you would value future earnings at the market rate and include that value as part of the investment in the market. If alternative employment is very risky, you could consider estimating its present value by using a high discount rate, but still combine it with the market index so that you can continue to value investment in the venture as part of a two-asset portfolio. Obviously, these are shortcut approximations. Which one is better depends on the situation.

10.9 HOW UNDIVERSIFIED ARE ENTREPRENEURS?

It is hard to imagine realistic scenarios in which the entrepreneur could make a full commitment to a venture, in the sense that we have defined a full commitment. A full *current* commitment, in the sense that the entrepreneur resigns from his or her current position and invests all currently available wealth in the venture, is not the same thing. If, should the venture fail, the entrepreneur retains the ability to return to other employment, the commitment of human capital is not a full commitment. Also, if the entrepreneur has financial assets that will not be invested in the venture or used as collateral for loans or if the entrepreneur retains an equity interest in a home or other asset, the commitment of financial capital is not a full commitment. Because the entrepreneur's required rate of return depends so heavily on the extent of commitment, it is useful to consider a couple of realistic scenarios involving full current commitments and see how they relate to our definition of a full commitment.

Scenario 1

The entrepreneur is five years from retirement and is earning $150,000 in current employment, which salary is expected to grow at 5 percent per year. The rate of salary growth is moderately risky (a level of risk that is comparable to the risk level of the S&P 500). The entrepreneur also has $200,000 in liquid assets and a retirement plan with a current value of $1 million. The retirement plan is invested in the market index and cannot be used to support the venture. The entrepreneur is considering resigning to pursue a new venture. Doing so would require investing all liquid assets in the venture. Undertaking the venture is a five-year commitment, so that in the event of failure, the entrepreneur would not be able to return to existing employment. The venture would offer the entrepreneur an expected salary of $50,000 per year for the five years of the commitment.

To measure the entrepreneur's commitment, we begin by computing the present value of future earnings in the current occupation. Using 12 percent as the cost of capital, Eq. (10.18) yields $591,000 as the present value of future compensation. This, together with $200,000 in liquid assets and $1 million in retirement savings, gives $1.791 million as the entrepreneur's wealth. In contrast, assuming the same discount rate, five years of compensation from the venture has a value of $180,000. Thus, investment in the venture totals $611,000 ($411,000 in reduced present value of salary and $200,000 in liquid assets). This makes investment in the venture equal to 34 percent of total wealth on an opportunity cost basis.

The entrepreneur must decide whether the present value of expected cash inflows (excluding the present value of salary during the five years) is worth at least $611,000. Suppose the venture return at year 5 is five times as risky as the market, say, with a standard deviation of returns of 224 percent, and that its correlation with the market is .2. Equation (10.6) can be used to determine that the standard deviation of the risky asset portfolio is 87 percent. Using the three-step method we described in Section 10.6, and assuming the riskless rate is 4 percent and the market risk premium is 8 percent, the cost of capital for the venture works out to about 26.7 percent per year (as compared to 31.6 percent per year if the venture were a full commitment). The reduction is material, but the entrepreneur's required rate of return is still well above the 12 percent return that a diversified investor would require.[34]

Scenario 2

An entrepreneur has just completed college and has an opportunity to begin working in a corporate position with a starting salary (including benefits) of $50,000. Her salary is expected to grow at a rate of 5 percent per year on average, and her expected work life is 40 years. The rate of salary growth is subject to the same degree of risk as in the previous example. The entrepreneur has no savings or other financial assets of any consequence. The venture would require a five-year commitment during which her expected salary would only be $25,000 per year. Should the venture fail, the entrepreneur could take on other employment but would forego the salary growth during the period of involvement in the venture.

The entrepreneur's commitment is measured against the opportunity cost of accepting employment immediately. Using Eq. (10.18), we can find the present value of her employment opportunity, using $50,000 as the time-one salary, 12 percent as the required rate of return, 5 percent as the growth rate, and 40 years as the horizon. The present value of expected future salary works out to $660,000. Now, should the entrepreneur decide to undertake the venture, the present value of her salary during the five-year commitment is calculated as a level annuity of $25,000, a present value of $90,000. The value of future salary after the five years, should the venture fail, is calculated as the present value of a 35-year growing annuity starting at $50,000, as above, but discounting the value of the annuity for an additional five years because it would not begin until five years later. The resulting value is $363,000, making the total $453,000. The present value of the entrepreneur's current commitment to the venture is the difference of $207,000, or 31 percent of the total present value of the entrepreneur's human capital.

Suppose, as in the previous example, the venture under consideration has a standard deviation of returns of 224 percent and that venture returns would be uncorrelated with the value of compensation in alternative employment. Equation (10.6) can be used to find that the standard deviation of the risky asset portfolio is 82 percent.[35] Using the same calculations as in the previous example, we find that the cost of capital for the venture is 26.3 percent per year, compared again to a total-commitment cost of capital of 31.6 percent.

Generalizations

The previous scenarios represent two extremes but yield similar results in terms of the fraction of present-valued wealth invested by the entrepreneur and yield nearly identical required rates of return. Given the specifics of the examples, they also represent reasonable upper bounds on how high the entrepreneur's fractional commitment of wealth is likely to be. They also shed light on the kinds of factors that can be expected to affect required rate of return.

We already have established that the required rate of return increases with the total risk of the venture and with the fraction of the entrepreneur's risk capital that is committed to it. The two previous examples highlight the factors that affect the fraction of risk capital. Generally, the fraction decreases as time to retirement increases and as the shortfall of compensation for involvement with the venture decreases compared to compensation in alternative employment. The fraction of risk capital committed also decreases with shortening the span of time the entrepreneur must commit and with the degree to which involvement in the venture does not reduce the entrepreneur's long-run ability to maintain his or her level of earnings in alternative employment. The fraction of risk capital committed increases with commitment of financial capital and decreases with increases in financial capital that is allocated to other investments.

10.10 BENEFITS OF DIVERSIFICATION

In the preceding examples, it was possible to lower the required rate of return on the venture by diversifying the entrepreneur's risk capital between the venture and the market portfolio. Doing so raises the present value of the venture. Figure 10-12 illustrates more generally how diversification between a new venture and a market index can yield an expected portfolio return that is higher than the required return.

Points on the feasible set are attainable by varying the entrepreneur's total investment between the venture and the market. At one extreme, the entrepreneur can invest all her wealth in the market portfolio. At the other, the entrepreneur can invest all her wealth in the venture. Alternatively, the entrepreneur can use financial leverage to achieve points along the CML. The CML reflects the entrepreneur's opportunity cost of investing some fraction of her wealth in the venture. As the figure shows, the expected return for investing in the venture can also be achieved by leveraging the market but at much lower risk. Accordingly, the NPV of investing exclusively in the venture is negative.

The figure also shows the point where the CML and the entrepreneur's feasible set intersect. That intersection is where the entrepreneur's portfolio has a zero NPV. With smaller percentage investments in the venture, the entrepreneur's expected return is above the CML. Over this gain region, investing in the venture and the market has a positive NPV. Because the market index is

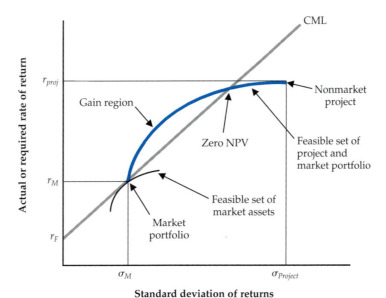

Figure 10-12   Why diversification adds value

A venture can have an expected return that is too low to invest in as a full commitment. However, the venture can have positive net present value if the entrepreneur diversifies by also investing in the market.

expected to earn only its required return, the gain arises because diversification reduces the required return on the venture. Thus, the range of portfolio risk levels where the expected portfolio return is greater than the required return reflects portfolio weights between the venture and the market where the NPV of investment in the venture would be positive.

Although the primary focus of this discussion is on not investing too much in the venture, Figure 10-12 also shows that it is possible for the entrepreneur to invest too little in it, relative to investing in the market. Beyond a point, overweighting the market portfolio reduces the net benefit of diversification. In the extreme, investing everything in the market and nothing in the venture results in a zero NPV for the entrepreneur.

Achieving the Right Balance

You can see that it is much more challenging to formally value a venture from the perspective of the entrepreneur than to assess value to a well-diversified investor. We simplify the task by providing some spreadsheet templates that incorporate the necessary calculations, but the critical factors in making the valuation are the assumptions about the venture and the entrepreneur. We can, and do, offer guidance for thinking about the important assumptions, but ultimately the quality of the valuation estimate is left to the entrepreneur or investor. In some cases, a formal estimate is not critical to deciding whether to go forward. But it still makes sense to try to structure the deal to add as much value as possible.

An essential point in this section is that an entrepreneur who is able to select the amount of investment can reduce the required rate of return by choosing a venture scale and scope that makes diversification feasible. Because the entrepreneur's investment involves both human and financial capital, one way to reduce scale is to limit the amount of time that is committed to the venture. Financial and human capital commitment can be limited by initially pursuing the venture on a small scale and by using milestones that help the entrepreneur decide whether to abandon early. We return to the subject of choosing scale and scope in Chapter 11.

Qualitative Considerations

Up to this point, we have not factored into the analysis anything to reflect, for example, the value to the entrepreneur of self-employment or the psychic income from starting up a new business. Now such considerations can be evaluated in terms of whether they provide benefits that are sufficient to offset any negative NPV of the venture (i.e., How large of a negative NPV would the entrepreneur accept in exchange for being self-employed?).

10.11 A SANITY CHECK—THE ART AND SCIENCE OF GOOD INVESTMENT DECISIONS

Any formal analysis of project value layers assumptions on assumptions. Such a framework can compound the effects of valuation errors—differences between assumed parameters and true parameters. For example, we know, as a theoretical construct, that for any given risky cash flow there is a true cost of capital that yields a correct (value-maximizing) decision to accept or reject the investment. But, in practice, we are estimating the expected cash flow and risk. We are also assuming that the CAPM is the correct model of opportunity cost of capital, and we are using estimates of the risk-free rate, market risk premium, and correlation. For investment by the entrepreneur, we also are estimating the fraction of risk capital committed to the venture. With so many assumptions, the resulting estimate of value can be much different from the true present value. Best-practice decision making involves making sure that the expected valuation error is as small as possible and that it is not biased.

Assessing Sensitivity to Assumptions

The valuation model in Figure 10-9 can be used to gain perspective on the magnitude of valuation errors. One simple approach is to examine the sensitivity of value to individual changes in assumptions about risk and expected return, and about determinants of required rates of return. In the following table, we use the assumptions and model in Figure 10-9 to illustrate the sensitivity of the value estimates to various individual changes. The following table shows the results.

Sensitivity of Venture Present Value Estimates to Key Assumptions

	Range	Low PV	High PV	Average
Expected cash flow	±10%	$1.166	$2.566	$1.866
Standard deviation of cash flows	±20%	$0.598	$3.113	$1.856
Correlation of cash flows to market	±0.1%	$1.669	$2.069	$1.869
Risk-free rate (per year)	±0.5 pct. pts.	$1.478	$2.245	$1.862
Market risk premium (per year)	±2 pct. pts.	$0.263	$3.332	$1.798
Fraction of wealth invested	±10 pct. pts.	$1.523	$2.719	$2.121

We selected the ranges for evaluation in the table casually but with intent to reflect realistic differences in uncertainty about individual assumptions. Evaluating sensitivity in this way suggests that the more critical assumptions, those where errors could most easily result in an incorrect decision to accept the venture, are the market risk premium, standard deviation of cash flows, fraction of wealth invested in the venture, and expected cash flow.

The ranges we use are symmetrical around the assumptions in Figure 10-9. We do this to show that even if the errors in assumptions are symmetrical, the effects on estimated value may not be. In Figure 10-9 present value to the entrepreneur is estimated to be $1.866 million. Compare that to values in the Average column of the table. You can see that the average of low and high present value over the range examined is different from the present value estimate in Figure 10-9. In some cases, the difference is material.

Understanding how uncertainty about assumptions affects expected present value is an additional benefit of sensitivity analysis. With respect to each of the assumptions we tested, the average present value over the range may be a better estimate of value than is the value reported in Figure 10-9. Whether it is better depends on the true degree of uncertainty about the assumptions, something we cannot evaluate by sensitivity analysis.

Using Simulation to Deal with Uncertainty about Assumptions

Sensitivity analysis enables us to study the impact of the assumptions one at a time, but it is not convenient for testing the sensitivity to the key assumptions collectively. By applying simulation to the valuation model, we see how value changes when all key assumptions are permitted to vary at the same time, and can design-in relationships between different assumptions. For example, maybe the standard deviation of cash flows should be positively related to expected cash flow. If so, you can design the simulation to reflect that relationship.

In Figure 10-13, we present a set of results of simulating the valuations to the investor and to the entrepreneur from Figure 10-9. The simulation model is based on assumptions about uncertainty that are similar to those in the table. For example, we assume that the expected cash flow is $8.86 million and that the standard deviation of the estimate is 5 percent. In the figure, we sorted the simulation trials based on present value to the entrepreneur.

There are three principal benefits of simulating the valuation. First, you can determine the combined effect of uncertainty about assumptions on the present value estimate. Second, you can assess the value of trying to get better information that would make your assumptions more precise. Third, you gain perspective to use in negotiating outside funding.

The figure shows the average of the simulated values to the entrepreneur as a dashed line. Under our assumptions, the average present value is $2.37 million, somewhat higher than the value estimate in Figure 10-9—high enough, in fact, that the venture appears to have a positive NPV for the entrepreneur. (The $2 million investment amount is shown as a solid line.) Thus, in this model, simulating the effects of uncertainty could alter the conclusion of whether to invest.

You can also see in Figure 10-13 that, for the entrepreneur, about 42 percent of the time, allowing for uncertainty would lead to the venture having a present value less than the investment. In contrast, for a diversified investor, expected NPV is always positive. The entrepreneur thus could benefit from trying to make more precise estimates of the assumptions. On the other hand, for a diversified investor, there is no apparent reason to expend effort on improving precision.

The decision is more complicated if the entrepreneur and an outside investor share investment in the venture. In that case, if the investor would share proportionately in both the

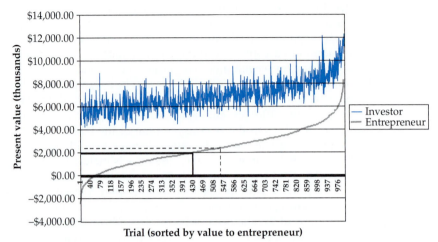

Figure 10-13 Simulation of present values to entrepreneur and diversified investor based on CAPM

The figure shows the results of a simulation analysis of sensitivity to errors in assumptions. Given the base assumptions and assumptions about uncertainty, the venture described throughout the chapter always is attractive to a well-diversified investor. It is attractive to the entrepreneurs in about 58 percent of the 1,000 trials.

investment and the return, then the same principles apply. But the results in Figure 10-13 suggest that, in lieu of trying to generate more information, it could make sense for the entrepreneur to try to shift some of the uncertainty to the investor. This is the focus of Chapter 11.

10.12 USING AND MISUSING SIMULATION AND SENSITIVITY ANALYSIS

In some ways, it is easy to use simulation incorrectly for project valuation. Sometimes decision makers try to value projects by simulating cash flows and converting them to present value by discounting at the risk-free rate. This generally overstates project value. The error is that if the venture is risky, then the risk-free rate usually is not the opportunity cost of capital. A second concern is that if overall risk is used to determine cost of capital, then the ability to diversify is ignored.

One very common mistake is to effectively discount the future cash flows twice. Suppose, for example, you are comparing two projects. You simulate their expected cash flows, and value them using the approach in Figure 10-9. Now imagine that the analysis shows that Project A is slightly more valuable than Project B. However, you notice that A is much riskier than B, and therefore you decide to pursue B instead of A. Doing so is the wrong decision. Your analysis should have ended with the comparison of present values, which indicated that A is more valuable. You took account of the risk differences in the present value calculations. So if you look back at risk again and select B because it is less risky, you have, in effect, discounted for the risk of Project A twice. The same error can arise when a discrete scenario approach is used to assess risk.

Our approach to simulation avoids these pitfalls. First, for the diversified investor, we use simulation to determine the uncertainty of cash flows. But to determine the opportunity cost of capital we use the certainty equivalent version of the CAPM. We do this because it is difficult to infer appropriate discount rates for entrepreneurial ventures simply by looking for public firm data on comparable projects. Second, for entrepreneurs who are unable to diversify fully, we allow for value to depend explicitly on what else the entrepreneur can do with assets that are not invested in the venture. Finally, we avoid the error of discounting twice.

10.13   TREATMENT OF SUNK COSTS IN THE VALUATION

Sunk costs are costs that already have been incurred and cannot be recovered. Not all historical costs are sunk. For example, if you buy lab equipment to pursue a venture, the cost of the equipment is only sunk to the extent that the equipment cannot be diverted to other uses or sold. If you need to learn some accounting to do the bookkeeping for a venture, the investment is only sunk to the extent that you cannot apply the same skills to another project. However, if the alternative activity you are considering is becoming a professional athlete, then perhaps your accounting knowledge would be worthless. In that comparison, the cost of learning accounting is sunk.

Costs that obviously are sunk are expenditures that do not produce any sort of tangible or intangible asset that can be redeployed if the venture fails. Expenditures on specialized equipment and some R and D expenditures, for example, may be sunk from the moment they are expended.

Why be so careful to distinguish between costs that are sunk and costs that are recoverable? The answer is that the decision to invest, or to continue investing in a venture, should not depend on sunk costs. In the example from Figure 10-9 we computed the NPV of the venture by subtracting $2 million from the present value of cash flows. For that to be the valid comparison, the $2 million must be net of any costs that already are sunk. It is appropriate to reflect tangible and intangible capital assets in the comparison but at their alternative use values as opposed to historical costs. The relevant distinction is not between historical and future outlays, but between nonrecoverable historical outlays and those that are recoverable.

Entrepreneurs often err by measuring project value against the total investment the entrepreneur expects to make, including the value of any sunk investment outlays the entrepreneur already has made. We occasionally hear of outside investment offers being turned down because the entrepreneur does not believe the deal would provide enough return to compensate for investments already made. While, as a negotiating ploy, it might be a good tactic to seek a return on the total investment, it does not make sense for the entrepreneur to pass up a venture on the ground that the expected return is not sufficient to compensate for both past and expected future investment. Even as a negotiating ploy, seeking a return on past investment may not be a good tactic: to pull it off, you would have to send a message that you do not understand the irrelevance of sunk costs. Why would an investor want to work with someone who is confused about which criteria should be considered in trying to decide whether to commit to the next milestone?

10.14 SUMMARY

This chapter has developed a framework for evaluating the underdiversified investments of entrepreneurs. This framework recognizes that entrepreneurs, as undiversified investors, should value projects at discount rates that can be substantially higher than the rates appropriate for well-diversified investors. Because the entrepreneur's required rate depends on total risk and not just market risk, a significant opportunity exists to select value-enhancing strategies for undertaking new ventures and to design value-enhancing contracts between entrepreneurs and outside investors.

This chapter begins to explore the opportunities that can derive from regarding entrepreneurial investment in this way. Among other factors, the entrepreneur's required return declines as the fraction of wealth that must be invested in the venture declines. This gives rise to a significant opportunity to create value by selecting the size of investment or, as we study in Chapter 11, bringing in an outside investor to share in the risk of the venture. Doing so can reduce the overall required rate of return.

Given the complexity of the entrepreneur's valuation problem, it is useful to consider some ways to shortcut the decision process. To that end, we offer the following generalizations:

- The entrepreneur's required rate of return depends on the total risk the entrepreneur must bear.
- Because their attitudes toward risk are different, entrepreneurs cannot rely on valuations of well-diversified outside investors.
- Except for differences in beliefs about expected future cash flows and risk, and subjective considerations, there is no way a venture can be more valuable to the entrepreneur than to a diversified investor.
- The main factor that can bring the entrepreneur's value closer to that of the outside investor is that the entrepreneur does not have to commit a very large fraction of total wealth.
- Investments of financial and human capital that are recoverable reduce the size of commitment and increase venture acceptability, as does shortening the length of the commitment.
- Because the entrepreneur cares about total risk but the investor cares only about market risk, the disparity between their valuations is greater the higher is the total risk of the venture, compared with its market risk.
- Relative values also differ if the financial claims differ. Sweeteners that raise the valuation of the outside investor reduce the valuation of the entrepreneur.

QUESTIONS AND PROBLEMS

1. A venture that requires an investment of $5 million is expected to return a total of $20 million in four years. Assume that the venture has a standard deviation of (four-year)

holding-period returns of 120 percent and that its correlation with the market is 0.3. Suppose the risk-free rate is 4 percent per year and the market risk premium is 7 percent per year. The one-year standard deviation of market returns is estimated to be 14 percent.

   a. What is the beta of the venture?

   b. What is its required holding period rate of return to a well-diversified investor?

   c. What is its required holding period rate of return to an entrepreneur who will invest all of her wealth in the venture?

   d. How much is the venture worth to the diversified investor?

   e. How much is it worth to the entrepreneur?

2. Suppose a two-year venture will cost $1.5 million and yield an expected cash flow of $3.2 million. The standard deviation of the expected cash flow is $2 million. Suppose further that the expected market return is 13.5 percent per year, the risk-free rate is 7 percent per year, the market variance is 4 percent per year, and the correlation between the venture and the market is 0.2.

   a. Use the CEQ form of the CAPM to find the NPV of the venture to a diversified investor.

   b. Use your answer in part (a) to find the equilibrium standard deviation of holding period returns and then us the RADR form of the CAPM to find the NPV to a diversified investor.

   c. Use the CEQ form of the CAPM-based model (Eq. 10.4) to find the NPV of the venture as a full commitment.

   d. Use your answer in part (c) to find the equilibrium standard deviation of holding period returns and then use the RADR form of the CAPM-based model to find the NPV of the venture as a full commitment.

3. Consider the simulation model in Figure 10-4. Suppose sales revenue in year 1 is the greater of zero or a normal distribution with a mean of $400,000 and a standard deviation of $250,000. If the forecast of year-1 sales is positive, then the expected growth rate of sales from year 1 to year 2 is 50 percent. After year-2, sales growth rate assumptions are the same as in Figure 10-4, except that if sales in the prior year are zero, then the forecast is for sales of zero. Expected profitability is 55 percent of sales, less a fixed cost of $1000 per year. However, if the venture fails to generate positive sales in year 1, there will be no fixed cost in the subsequent years. Other assumptions in the model are unchanged.

   a. Simulate performance of the venture over the six-year period. What is the expected cash amount that will go to the investor/entrepreneur in year 6, and what is the standard deviation of that cash receipt? How often does the venture fail to generate sales in year 1? How often does it run out of cash by year 6

   b. Using the same model and assumptions, what are the expected sales and standard deviations of year-6 sales and profit? What would expected sales have been if the venture did not run out of cash?

   c. Assuming the required investment is $2 million, the risk-free rate is 4 percent, the market rate is 9 percent, and the standard deviation of market returns is 30 percent per year, try using Eq. (10.3) with the realized holding period return to find the NPV of the investment as a full commitment. What do you find, and what do you conclude?

   d. Now, try using the valuation template from Figure 10-6 to estimate the value of the venture as a full commitment. What do you find for the CAPM-based result? Is your answer the same as in part c? Why or why not?

   e. How does the CAPM-based result compare to the Maximum Leverage result? Why do you think the results are different? How do the results and differences compare to those shown in Figure 10-6? What do you think accounts for the differences?

4. The market standard deviation is 20 percent; and the standard deviation of returns for a new venture is 80 percent. The correlation of returns is 0.4. The risk-free rate is 4 percent, and the market return is 10.5 percent. Find the portfolio standard deviation, portfolio required rate of return, and new venture required rate of return for each of the following.

    a. The entrepreneur invests 40 percent of wealth in the venture and 60 percent in the market.

    b. The entrepreneur invests 20 percent of wealth in the venture and 80 percent in the market.

    Now suppose the correlation is 0.1. Find the portfolio standard deviation, portfolio required rate of return, and new venture required rate of return for each of the following.

    c. The entrepreneur invests 40 percent of wealth in the venture and 60 percent in the market.

    d. The entrepreneur invests 20 percent of wealth in the venture and 80 percent in the market.

5. Return to the simulation results from problem 3. Use the valuation template from Figure 10-9 to evaluate a partial commitment in the venture under each of the following assumptions. (Expected venture cash flows and their standard deviation are from problem 3.) Assume the risk-free rate is 4 percent per year, the market return is 9 percent per year, and the market standard deviation is 30 percent per year.

    a. Correlation between the venture and the market is 0.3; the entrepreneur has total wealth of $8 million and invests $2 million in the venture, with the balance in the market.

    b. Correlation between the venture and the market is 0.3; the entrepreneur has total wealth of $16 million and invests $2 million in the venture, with the balance in the market.

    c. Correlation between the venture and the market is 0.1; the entrepreneur has total wealth of $8 million and invests $2 million in the venture, with the balance in the market.

    d. Correlation between the venture and the market is 0.1; the entrepreneur has total wealth of $16 million, and invests $2 million in the venture, with the balance in the market.

    e. How do you explain the differences?

6. An individual who currently earns $120,000 per year is considering a new venture. To proceed, she must resign and commit three years to the venture. For that, she expects to receive a salary of $50,000 per year. If the venture fails, she can return to her current line of work but expects that her starting salary will drop to $100,000. In either case, her earnings in alternative employment are expected to grow at a rate of 6 percent per year. Her remaining work life is 20 years. She believes it is appropriate to value future earnings using a discount rate of 14 percent. She also has $90,000 of equity in a house and will use the equity to secure a loan of that amount to invest in the venture. Finally, she has retirement savings invested in a market index of $800,000 that she is unable to use in the venture.

    a. What is the present value of the entrepreneur's human capital?

    b. What is the present value of human capital (net of expected compensation) she would need to commit to the venture?

    c. What fraction of her total wealth would she be committing?

7. A public corporation is considering developing a new software application that would enable GPS navigation systems in automobiles to "learn." With the application, the system would be able to update maps when it determined that its initial map file had become obsolete. It also would integrate a clock and calendar, so that over time, it would develop a database of

true expected driving times based on day of week and time of day. This would enable the system to improve its route selections and give more accurate estimates of expected driving time. Company engineers project that it would take four years to develop and commercialize the software. With luck, the corporation would be first to market and would preempt others from entering. If so, the financial planning group estimates that "harvest-date" value of the product would be $60 million. Alternatively, the company's product might not preempt rivals. In a market where several products are competing, the product price would have to be lower. Under that scenario, the financial planning group estimates that harvest-date value would be $35 million. Finally, another entrant could preempt the company's efforts, even after most of the development costs had been incurred. In that scenario, the company would realize nothing on its investment. The annual current risk-free rate is 3 percent. The financial planning group estimates that the market risk premium is 5 percent, the standard deviation of market returns is 14 percent and the venture's correlation with the market is 0.25.

a.   Assuming that the probability of the success scenario is 15 percent, and the probability of the failure scenario is 40 percent, what is the present value of the opportunity to the corporation?

b.   Under the same assumptions, what is the present value of the venture to an entrepreneur who would be willing to invest 30 percent of her $9 million total wealth in the venture, with the remainder being placed in a market index portfolio?

c.   Comment on the relative values to the corporation and the entrepreneur and on who should undertake the venture.

8.   For the project described in problem 7, suppose that the corporate project approval and oversight processes are the main reasons the project is likely to take four years to complete, and that an entrepreneur acting independently could complete the project in three years. Faster completion would increase the likelihood that the innovator would succeed in preempting rivals and would reduce the probability of failure. Assuming that the probability of the intermediate outcome would remain at 45 percent, and the scenario-contingent cash flows would not change despite the faster completion, how much would the probability of success need to increase and the probability of failure decrease to make the project as valuable for an independent entrepreneur as it is to the corporate investor in problem 7?

9.   A public company has a retirement plan where employees can invest a portion of their retirement savings in company stock. Whatever the employee does not invest in company stock can be invested in a diversified portfolio. Whatever is invested in company stock must remain in company stock until the employee retires. To encourage investment in company stock, and in recognition of the resulting underdiversification, the company will match whatever the employee invests in company stock with an additional 15 percent investment on the employee's behalf. Suppose the annual risk-free rate is 4 percent, the market risk premium is 6 percent, and the standard deviation of market returns is 14 percent. Company stock has beta risk of 1.2, and a correlation with the market of 0.4. The annualized standard deviation of returns is 42 percent, based on the beginning investment amount including the employer's matching contribution.

a.   Suppose an employee invests $10,000 in company stock. Considering the employer's matching contribution, what is the expected value of the investment in one year? In two years?

b.   What is the standard deviation of cash flows for an employee's one-year investment of $10,000 by an employee? What is it for a two-year investment? Be sure to incorporate the employer's contribution.

c. Suppose an employee has no other wealth. How soon would the employee need to retire to make investing $10,000 (plus the company match) in company stock equal in present value to investing $10,000 in the market (with no matching contribution)?

d. How would the answer in part (c) be different if the employee had $90,000 of other wealth, all invested in a market index?

e. For an employee who already has $90,000 in the market and five years until retirement, what allocation of a current $10,000 investment between company stock (that cannot be harvested until retirement) and the market index would maximize the present value of the employee's wealth?

10. The annual risk-free rate is 5 percent, the expected return on the market for one year is 11 percent, and the standard deviation of market returns is 14 percent. A prospective venture that would be harvested in one year has an expected cash flow of $2.0 million, with cash flow standard deviation of $1.2 million. The correlation between the venture and the market is 0.25. The venture would require an investment of 1.5 million, which would leave the entrepreneur with $3.5 million invested in the market. Use Equations 10.9 through 10.12 to find the present value of the venture. How would the present value change if the holding period were two years instead of one, with all other assumptions unchanged? Should the entrepreneur invest if the holding period is one year? Two years? Explain.

11. Suppose an entrepreneur is considering a new computer service venture. The entrepreneur believes the venture has risk characteristics similar to early-stage public computer service companies and has asked you how to value the opportunity. The first step in your analysis is to estimate the entrepreneur's opportunity cost of capital. Based on a sample of firms you found on Yahoo.com, you have concluded that computer service firms tend to have beta risk of around 1.10 and that the average correlation of returns with market returns is 0.17. The entrepreneur would plan to invest about 10 percent of his total wealth in the venture. The expected holding period is 1.5 years, the annual risk-free rate is 3 percent, the market return is 9 percent, and the market standard deviation is 14 percent.

12. One of your friends is planning to open a drive-through coffee stand. He expects that the venture will generate around $250,000 in free cash flow each year, as long as no competitor enters the market. Once entry occurs, he expects that free cash flow will drop to around $100,000, which is about what he, or others who are similarly qualified, could make in alternative employment. In other words, once entry occurs, the coffee stand will have no economic value. Suppose the probability of entry is only 10 percent in the first year. From that point on, conditional on entry not having occurred previously, the probability of entry is 30 percent. Your friend is willing to operate the venture for up to six years, after which point, his lease will expire, and renewing the lease will not be worthwhile.

a. Modify the first panel of the Duration Template in Figure 10-11 to simulate the entrepreneur's free cash flows after his assumed annual draw of $100,000.

b. Modify the second panel to compute the cumulative probability of entry in each year and make a rough estimate of the present value of expected cash flows. Generate the rough estimate using an arbitrary 20 percent discount rate. Determine the preliminary estimate of discounted cash flow in this panel. In panel three, what is the estimated duration of the cash flows, rounded to the nearest full year? Does your rounded estimate change if you try different discount rates, such as 10 percent or 30 percent?

c. Assuming that the risk-free rate is 5 percent per year, compute the single-period equivalent cash flow as a simulated value.

d. Run the simulation to determine the mean and standard deviation of the equivalent single-period cash flow. What do you find as the expected cash flow and standard deviation?

e. The market rate is 11 percent per year, and market standard deviation is 14 percent per year. Suppose the venture's correlation with the market is only 0.10, and that, after investing in the venture, the entrepreneur still will have $1,500,000 to invest in a market index. What is the present value of the opportunity? Suppose that, in addition to the investment of effort [which is already provided for by netting it out of the cash flows in part (a)], the venture would cost $150,000 to undertake. Would the venture have a positive NPV for the entrepreneur?

f. In part (e) if you used Valuation Template 4, you should have found the entrepreneur's annual cost of capital for the single period project. If you use this to value the expected multi-period cash flows, as you did using 20 percent in part (b), what do you find for the present value of the project? How does your PV answer in part (e) compare to your PV answer here? What do you think accounts for any difference? Which answer do you think is more accurate?

NOTES

1. The Edmund's Web site contains information on new and used vehicle prices, dealer cost, manufacturer holdbacks, and manufacturer incentive and rebate programs. Using such information, consumers can negotiate more effectively than in the past.

2. The most familiar example of yield management is in the airline industry, where ticket prices are set in various fare classes based on timing of purchase and other restrictions. The airlines continuously revise the allocations of seats to the various fare classes in response to new information about the demand for a particular flight.

3. Clearly, there are other ways to increase risk (e.g., playing the lottery, racetrack betting, etc.). We focus on leveraging investment in the market because, for a passive investor, it offers the highest expected reward, given the level of risk.

4. Equation (10.1) assumes that the entrepreneur requires no additional return for bearing illiquidity risk that is greater than that of the market portfolio.

5. With this substitution, the equation is the RADR form of the CAPM.

6. Equation (10.2), with riskless lending and borrowing, describes how risk varies along the CML. See Brealey and Myers (2003) for elaboration. Note that you cannot use Eq. (10.2) to measure risk if both financial claims are risky and if the correlation between their returns is less than one.

7. Block and MacMillan (1995) provide a managerial perspective on corporate entrepreneurship.

8. When potential returns are skewed, the CAPM can only be precisely correct if investor utility of wealth functions are quadratic. It is well recognized that quadratic utility does not make economic sense. It implies that maximum total utility is associated with a finite level of wealth. Quadratic utility is assumed because it usually works as a reasonable approximation and is easy to use. See Harvey and Siddique (2000) and Kraus and Litzenberger (1976) regarding investor preference for skewness

9. The CAPM is based on the assumption that the possible returns to an investment are normally distributed, or, alternatively, that investors' utility of expected wealth is quadratic (i.e., utility $= a_1 \times$ wealth $- a_2 \times$ wealth^2). High-risk projects are likely to have nonnormal risk distributions, and the assumption of quadratic utility may not reasonably describe value.

10. We determine this using Eq. (10.4) below. We cannot use Eq. (10.3) directly because of the negative NPV.

11. After the initial investment, the required margin for maintaining the investment drops to 25 percent, so it is unlikely that additional equity funds would have to be invested if the value of the market portfolio were to decline.

12. Unhedged positions in options require performance margins. The normal margin for writing an at-the-money put on a market index is the proceeds from sale of the put plus 15 percent of the value of the index. Figure 10-2 assumes that the value of the long position in calls on the index will be sufficient to meet the margin requirement. If this is not so, then a lower degree of leverage is achievable. Currently, long-term options on market indexes are only available for durations of up to three years. To approximate the option strategy underlying a five-year investment, the excess of funds required for five years over funds required for a three-year investment would be invested in a risk-free asset and converted to investment in options when the three-year options expire.

13. The same difficulties arise in corporate investment decision making, but pertain to beta risk. The high levels of risk associated with new venture investing and the importance of embedded options make consideration of the problem more important.

14. In this section, we apply the maximum achievable leverage assumption to the project as a full commitment. This assumes that the entrepreneur must choose to either make a full commitment or not undertake the project. Later in the chapter, we apply the maximum achievable leverage assumption to the entrepreneur's portfolio, including investment in the project. If the entrepreneur can make less than a full commitment, then the choice to pursue the project on a scale that requires a full commitment requires a different analysis of value.

15. Skewness is not a new problem for investment valuation. One valuation approach that has been suggested is to use stochastic dominance to examine the entire distribution of possible cash flows. In essence, this would involve searching for market assets that have similar distributions of possible cash flows and inferring value from the market values of such assets. Another approach that has been suggested is to estimate the standard deviation only over the part of the cash flow distribution that is below the mean (i.e., the "lower partial first moment of the distribution"). Because the distribution of cash flows is skewed, this results in a lower estimate of the standard deviation.

16. Eq. (10.3) can only be used by trial and error.

17. Of course, you can use discrete scenarios to evaluate investment opportunities of underdiversified investors. Our valuation framework depends only on expected cash flows and standard deviation, which you can estimate using discrete scenarios.

18. The spreadsheet for Figure 10-4 is accessible on the Internet site. By uncovering some rows in the spreadsheet that are hidden in Figure 10-4, you can also see the simulation model run with staged investment. We begin to address staging systematically in Chapter 11.

19. Alternatively, we could have used scenario analysis to estimate the expected harvest-date cash flow and standard deviation.

20. Recall from Chapter 9 that, because these calculations are based on the actual $2 million investment, this method does not measure the true CAPM-based value of the project. However, as we discussed earlier, it does correctly indicate whether the NPV is positive or negative.

21. The spreadsheet for Figure 10-6 is a valuation template that is available on the Internet site for the text. It can be modified to examine sensitivity to assumptions and can be applied to the valuation of different financial claims with a single investment date and single harvest date.

22. As we demonstrate below, investment in a riskless asset in addition to the two risky assets can be addressed easily.

23. The expression can be extended to consider any number of risky assets. While doing so can be useful for some new venture valuations, the extension is beyond the scope of this text. For relevant background, see Brealey and Myers (2003).

24. The true correlation would be higher than 0.667. We know this because beta reflects the equilibrium holding period risk of a well-diversified investor. Because such an investor would value the venture more highly than an undiversified entrepreneur, we know that the investor has a standard deviation of equilibrium holding period returns that is less than the 60 percent of the entrepreneur. To achieve the beta of 2.0, correlation with the market must be correspondingly higher. For the purpose of this illustration we use 0.667.

25. We can either start with the investor's value weights (such as 80 percent in the market and 20 percent in the venture), or solve by trial and error for investor weights that yield the target weights for the entrepreneur (such as 85 percent of wealth in the market and 15 percent in the venture).

26. Determining the required rates of return for voluntary increases in entrepreneurial investment above the required minimum is beyond the scope of the text.

27. In reality, the human capital of the entrepreneur is a third asset. Later in the chapter, we consider how the value of human capital affects the analysis.

28. The spreadsheet in Figure 10-9 is a valuation template that is available on the Internet site for the text.

29. Also, even if the pattern seems random, the entrepreneur cannot be certain that a drop in cash flows in one year is not foreshadowing the demise of the business.

30. Most corporate finance texts describe methods of computing duration in the context of debt valuation or hedging.

31. Figure 10-11 is a template that is designed for use in estimating the duration of uncertain cash flow streams. By downloading it, you can test sensitivity to our assumptions.

32. To illustrate the low sensitivity of the value estimate to the assumed discount rate, we tried a rate of 30 percent instead of 12. Duration declined from five to four years. Simulated value increased by about 2 percent, to $1234.

33. Should the venture fail, if the entrepreneur would be unable to return to equally valuable employment as if the venture had not been undertaken, then the potential for lost future compensation also would be "invested" in the venture.

34. With a standard deviation of returns that is five times the market standard deviation and a correlation of .2, the venture has a beta of 1.0 and 12 percent market cost of capitol.

35. For this calculation, we assume that the alternative is to invest the present value of the venture in the market portfolio.

REFERENCES AND ADDITIONAL READING

Blackwell, David W., and David S. Kidwell. "An Investigation of Cost Differences Between Public Sales and Private Placements of Debt." *Journal of Financial Economics* (1988): 253–278.

Block, Zenas and Ian C. MacMillan. Corporate Venturing: Creating New Businesses within the Firm. Boston, MA: Harvard Business School Press, 1995.

BREALEY, RICHARD A., AND STEWART C. MYERS. *Principles of Corporate Finance*. 7th ed. New York: McGraw-Hill, 2003.

BYGRAGE, WILLIAM D., AND JEFFREY A. TIMMONS. *Venture Capital at the Crossroads*. Cambridge, MA: Harvard University Press, 1992.

COOPER, ARNOLD, CAROLYN WOO, AND WILLIAM DUNKELBERG. "Entrepreneurs' Perceived Chances for Success." *Journal of Business Venturing* 3 (1988): 97–108

EVANS, DAVID, AND BOYAN JAVANOVIC. "An Estimated Model of Entrepreneurial Choice under Liquidity Constraints." *Journal of Political Economy* (1989): 808–827.

GENTRY, WILLIAM, AND GLENN HUBBARD. "Entrepreneurship and Household Saving." National Bureau of Economic Research Working Paper, 7894, 2000.

GOLDER, STANLEY C. "Structuring and Pricing the Financing." In *Pratt's Guide to Venture Capital Sources*. 10th ed. Edited by Stanley E. Pratt and Jane K. Morris. Wellesley, MA: Venture Economics, 79–88.

HARVEY, CAMPBELL, AND AKHTAR SIDDIQUE. "Conditional Skewness in Asset Pricing Tests." *Journal of Finance* 55 (2000): 1263–1295.

HEATON, JOHN, AND DEBORAH LUCAS. "Portfolio Choices and Asset Prices: The Importance of Entrepreneurial Risk." *Journal of Finance* 55(2000) 1163–1198.

HEATON, JOHN, AND DEBORAH LUCAS. "Capitol Structure, Hurdle Rates, and Portfolio Choice—Interactions in an Entrepreneurial Firm." University of Chicago Working Paper, 2001.

HERTZEL, MICHAEL G., AND RICHARD L. SMITH. "Market Discounts and Shareholder Gains for Placing Equity Privately." *Journal of Finance* (1993): 459–485.

HOLTZ-EAKIN, DOUGLAS, DAVID JOULFAIAN, AND HARVEY S. ROSEN. "Entrepreneurial Decisions and Liquidity Constraints." *Rand Journal of Economics* 23 (1994a): 334–347.

HOLTZ-EAKIN, DOUGLAS, DAVID JOULFAIAN, AND HARVEY S. ROSEN. "Sticking It Out: Entrepreneurial Survival and Liquidity Constraints." *Journal of Political Economy* 102 (1994b): 53–75.

KERINS, FRANK, JANET KIHOLM SMITH, AND RICHARD SMITH. "Opportunity Cost of Capital for Venture Capital Investors and Entrepreneurs." *Journal of Financial and Quantitative Analysis*, Forthcoming (2004).

KRAUS, ALAN, AND ROBERT H. LITZENBERGER. "Skewness Preference and the Valuation of Risk Assets." *Journal of Finance* (1976): 1085–1100.

MOSKOWITZ, TOBIAS, AND ANNETTE VISSING-JØRGENSEN. "The Returns to Entrepreneurial Investment: A Private Equity Premium Puzzle." *American Economic Review* 92 (2002): 745–778.

RICH, STANLEY R., AND DAVID E. GUMPERT. "How to Write a Winning Business Plan." In *The Entrepreneurial Venture*. 2nd ed. Edited by William A. Sahlman and Howard H. Stevenson. Cambridge, MA: Harvard Business School Press, 1999, pp. 177–188.

ROBERTS, MICHAEL J., HOWARD H. STEVENSON, MICHAEL J. ROBERTS, AND AMAR BHIDE. "Alternative Sources of Financing." In *The Entrepreneurial Venture*. Edited by William A. Sahlman and Howard H. Stevenson. Cambridge, MA: Harvard Business School Publications, 1991, pp. 127–137.

SAHLMAN, WILLIAM A. "The Structure and Governance of Venture-Capital Organizations." *Journal of Financial Economics* (1990): 473–524.

SMITH, RICHARD L., AND VAUGHN S. ARMSTRONG. "Misconceptions about Private Placement Discounts: Why Market Reaction to Rule 144A Has Been Lukewarm." In *Modernizing U.S. Securities Regulation*. Edited by Kenneth Lehn and Robert W. Kamphuis, Jr. New York: Richard D. Irwin, 1992.

Financial Contracting with Symmetric Information

If you want more, make yourself worth more. (Hong Kong Noodle Company)

Learning Objectives

After reading this chapter, you will be able to:

- Determine how bringing in an investor, who shares proportionately in risk and return, affects the entrepreneur's value of an opportunity.

- Evaluate how changing the relative shares of ownership between the entrepreneur and an investor affects the present value of each party's investment.

- Increase the value of an opportunity by designing a financial contract that shifts risk to diversified investors.

- Compare and evaluate financing alternatives that involve passive, active, and subsidized investors.

Entrepreneurs often think of outside investors as a necessary evil—better done without, if at all possible. Although dealing with outside investors can be inconvenient and sometimes even harmful, outside investors can also benefit the entrepreneur. Potential benefits derive from three sources. First, outside investment enables the entrepreneur to invest less in the venture and to increase diversification. Second, because well-diversified investors have lower required rates of return than does an undiversified entrepreneur, increasing the amount of outside investment increases the present value of the venture. The entrepreneur can capture some of the value gain by retaining a larger ownership interest than would be possible if the investor were not well diversified. Third, an outside investor may contribute advice and information that enhances value.

In this chapter, we use a financial contracting framework to study the benefits of outside investment. Financial contracts have three effects: they allocate risk; they allocate expected returns; and they change expected returns. Debt financing, for example, allocates most of the ris to the equity investor, allocates expected returns differently between the equity holder and the creditor, and changes overall returns due to the tax effect of debt financing and possibly due to incentive effects.

To sharpen understanding of how financial contracting provisions affect value, we focus separately on each effect. We begin with a pure risk-allocation provision, one that transfers risk between parties but does not change the allocation of expected returns and does not alter the overall level of expected returns. Next, we consider a pure return-allocation provision. Finally, we consider the ability to affect value by contracting with investors who actively participate in the venture.

We focus the analysis on a project in which all investment by both the entrepreneur and an outside investor is made at the beginning. This is an oversimplification, but it enables us to examine how the structure of financial claims affects value. In this chapter, we assume symmetric information. The investor and the entrepreneur have the same expectations about future performance and risk, and they know that they share the same expectations. Thus, the contracting gains in this chapter derive entirely from parties' differing attitudes toward risk and from the investor's ability to add value. In Chapter 12 we relax the assumption of symmetric information to focus on incentive and information effects related to financial contracts. In Chapter 13 we consider staging of investment.

11.1 SOME PRELIMINARIES

To benchmark the effects of financial contract provisions, we start from the assumption that the entrepreneur and the investor share proportionally in risk and expected returns, based on the relative magnitudes of their investments. This is an arbitrary starting point, but provides an easy transition from Chapter 10. It also enables us to most easily examine the three separate effects of financial contract provisions. Keep in mind that the choice of starting point is arbitrary. In any negotiation, you can think of the effects of a proposed financial contracting provision by examining how the provision affects the allocation of risk, the allocation of expected returns, and the overall expected return.

The valuation effects of any contract provision can accrue to the entrepreneur, the investor, or both. Because the parties have different required rates of return, the clearest picture of the effect of changing a provision is achieved by assuming that one party or the other captures the entire gain. We have adopted the arbitrary convention of allocating the gain to the entrepreneur. This allocation is consistent with assuming that the market for new venture financing is perfectly competitive, so that investors compete to participate in the venture and the entrepreneur realizes the full gain. In reality, the parties are likely to share the gains based on the intensity of competition on each side of the market. If many entrepreneurs with similar opportunities are seeking capital and investors have unique capabilities to add value, then most of the gain is likely to accrue to the investor.

11.2   PROPORTIONAL SHARING OF RISK AND RETURN

In Chapter 10 we reached the conclusion that the entrepreneur's required rate of return increases with the fraction of her wealth that is invested in the venture. In this section we build on these findings to search for ways to use choices about project scale and deal structure to enhance value.

We begin by determining the entrepreneur's optimal scale of a venture when there is no outside investment. For this, we assume the venture is subject to constant returns to scale, so the only factor that affects the choice is the way the entrepreneur's ability to diversify affects required rate of return. With no outside investor, the optimal scale of a venture depends on the entrepreneur's wealth. This is the implication of the partial commitment analysis in Chapter 10.

We finish the section by considering an opportunity that requires a specific size of investment and by introducing an outside investor who shares proportionately in risk and return. With proportional sharing, the entrepreneur's choice of optimal scale from Chapter 10 becomes a choice of optimal ownership share. The entrepreneur makes the same allocation of wealth between the venture and a market index as before. The outside investor provides any needed additional capital.

Choosing the Scale of the Venture

Consider a venture with constant returns to scale, so that proportional increases in inputs lead to proportional increases in output. As the sole investor, the entrepreneur would like to scale to maximize the NPV of her investment. It might seem that, if a venture is subject to constant returns, it should be run on the largest scale possible. That would be correct for a diversified investor but not for the entrepreneur. With no outside investment, the larger the scale, the more underdiversified the entrepreneur's portfolio. Because underdiversification increases the entrepreneur's required rate of return, the largest feasible scale is not the one with highest NPV.

We can use the example introduced in Figure 10-4 to study the effect of project scale on value. Recall that the entrepreneur with total wealth of $2 million was considering an investment of $2 million. Figure 10-6 shows that, as a full commitment, the NPV is negative for the entrepreneur. Because the rate of return does not depend on its scale, the fundamental issue is the tradeoff between project risk and expected return, in the context of the entrepreneur's other assets. The larger the scale, the less the entrepreneur can invest in the market index portfolio.

Figure 11-1 traces out the entrepreneur's feasible set of risk and return combinations. The figure also shows the CML as the opportunity cost of capital for investing at each level of risk. By investing 100 percent of her wealth in the venture, the entrepreneur receives an expected return of 342 percent over the six-year holding period. The total risk that corresponds to investing all wealth in the venture is a 288 percent standard deviation of return. However, as the figure shows, the expected return on the venture as a full commitment is less than the required rate of return. If the entrepreneur were to use financial leverage to increase the risk of investing in the market portfolio to the same level as the risk of the project, the expected six-year return on the market investment would be 444 percent, much better than the expected return for investing in the venture. The expected project return does not adequately compensate for the risk.

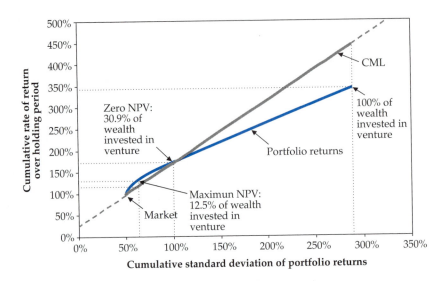

Figure 11-1 Expected portfolio return v. required return of the entrepreneur

The figure illustrates how the value of an opportunity for an entrepreneur is affected by the fraction of wealth invested in the venture. The remainder of the entrepreneur's wealth is invested in a market index. The figure is based on the example of the six-year investment opportunity from Figure 10-4. The vertical axis is the cumulative holding-period return of the entrepreneur's portfolio. The horizontal axis is the standard deviation of the cumulative return. With all wealth invested in the venture, the expected return is below opportunity cost, as implied by the CML. Reducing investment in the venture enables the entrepreneur to benefit from diversification.

At the other extreme, the prospective entrepreneur can invest 100 percent in the market and receive an expected six-year return of 97 percent. The standard deviation of returns for investing entirely in the market is 49 percent. Because the market portfolio is a point on the CML, it is a zero-NPV investment opportunity. These are the end-points of the feasible set of portfolio returns. You can use Figure 10-9 to verify that if the entrepreneur would invest 30.9 percent of wealth in the venture, the result would be a zero-NPV investment in the venture. In Figure 11-1 we show this possibility as the point labeled "Zero NPV." It corresponds to an expected portfolio return of about 173 percent and a level of portfolio risk for the entrepreneur of about 101 percent.

The feasible set of investments implies that an entrepreneur can, by choosing venture size, affect the required rate of return. The smaller the venture, the lower is its cost of capital. Figure 11-1 shows the effect of reducing the size of investment in the venture, holding the entrepreneur's total wealth constant. The vertical distance between the return on the entrepreneur's portfolio and the CML reflects NPV. The NPV of the portfolio reaches a maximum when the entrepreneur invests about $250,000 in the project and the balance of $2 million in a market. You can use the template in Figure 10-9 to verify that, at that point, the project NPV is approximately $205,000.

Figure 11-1 assumes that the entrepreneur can reduce venture scale while maintaining the same profit rate. The figure shows that many investment scales yield positive NPVs. How does the entrepreneur select from among the alternatives? One approach is to value each alternative by discounting at opportunity cost of capital. The cost of capital is the expected return on the market portfolio leveraged to achieve the same risk. The accompanying table displays the results of computing the present values and NPVs of project cash flows by this approach. The calculations are shown for four points corresponding to Figure 11-1: 100 percent wealth invested in the project; 0 percent invested; 30.9 percent invested; and 12.5 percent invested. In making these calculations, we use the underlying data as in Figure 10-4. We assume that the entrepreneur's total wealth is $2 million, so that with an investment of 100 percent in the venture, she would be committing $2 million. NPV is positive at investment levels between zero and 30.9 percent of wealth ($618,000). Maximum NPV of about $205,000 is reached when about 12.5 percent of wealth ($250,000) is invested in the venture and the rest is invested in a market index. Thus, based on the market opportunity cost of capital, with a $250,000 investment, the venture is expected to return almost twice as much as is required.

How the Fraction of Wealth Invested in a Venture Affects NPV

Percentage of Wealth Invested in Venture	Dollars Invested in the Venture	Dollars Invested in the Market Index	Present Value of Investment in Venture	NPV of the Entrepreneur's Portfolio
0%	$0	$2,000,000	$2,000,000	$0*
12.5%	$250,000	$1,750,000	$454,000	$205,000
30.9%	$618,000	$1,382,000	$618,000	$0
100%	$2,000,000	$0	$408,000	($1,592,000)

*The market index is a zero-NPV investment.

Although the above approach provides a reasonable approximation of NPV, it cannot definitively identify the decision that is best for each individual entrepreneur. Because the project under consideration is a nonmarket asset and the entrepreneur's ability to diversify is limited by the magnitude of investment in the project, except at the points where NPV is zero, we cannot appeal to the law of one price to tell us precisely the NPV of the venture to the entrepreneur. Instead, over the range of investment levels where NPV is positive, the highest valued choice depends on the entrepreneur's risk-tolerance. The more risk-tolerant entrepreneur would want to invest slightly more in the venture. The more risk-averse the entrepreneur, the greater the fraction she should invest in the market. Nonetheless the preferences of most entrepreneurs should yield decisions that are close to the results of valuing the venture by discounting expected cash flows at opportunity cost.

Outside Investment with Proportional Sharing

The entrepreneur can affect the size of the investment in two ways: by selecting venture scale or by keeping scale fixed and bringing in an investor. You can reinterpret the preceding analysis assuming that project scale is given. In that case, the entrepreneur's decision of how much to invest also determines how much capital to raise from investors. This view implies that the entrepreneur and the outside investor share project risks and rewards proportionally. Thus, if the project requires a total investment of $2 million, and the entrepreneur invests $250,000, then, with proportional sharing, the entrepreneur is entitled to 12.5 percent of the equity. An investor provides the other $1,750,000 in exchange for 87.5 percent of the equity.

It is easy to interpret Figure 11-1 as illustrating the effects of proportional sharing. Remember that, for convenience, we chose to equate the total investment needed for the venture with the present-valued wealth of the entrepreneur. The figure assumes that the venture requires a $2 million investment and that the entrepreneur can decide how much to invest in the venture versus the market index. For a project that requires an investment that is larger or smaller than $2 million, the total project cash flows and risk would be scaled up or down accordingly. Doing so would not change the value of the entrepreneur's investment in the project. So, for example, if a project requires a total investment of $1 million, the entrepreneur still invests 12.5 percent of wealth to achieve a NPV of $205,000. Under proportional sharing, she would be entitled to 25 percent of the cash flows.

With proportional sharing of risk and return, the entrepreneur's investment decision looks exactly like it did for the choice of project scale. The only difference is that project scale is fixed and the entrepreneur's share of the investment is allowed to vary. The entrepreneur takes scale as given and maximizes NPV by choosing ownership share. In either case, the fundamental choice is the fraction of the entrepreneur's wealth to invest in the project.

11.3 NONPROPORTIONAL SHARING OF RISK AND RETURN

Proportional allocation of risk and return between the entrepreneur and investors is not a likely contractual structure. Investors generally seek a variety of "me-first" provisions and other contractual sweeteners. The contract may specify, for example, that the investor receives warrants to acquire additional shares if performance targets are not met or that the outsider's investment will not be diluted if additional capital must be raised. Conversely, the entrepreneur is likely to draw a salary and may receive supplemental compensation if performance is better than expected. Furthermore, the entrepreneur's investment is likely to be mostly in the form of (hard to value) human capital, whereas the investor primarily contributes financial capital.

In this section, we offer a structured way of analyzing how risk allocation affects value. As you will see, there is a double benefit to bringing in an investor who is well diversified. First, reducing the entrepreneur's investment enables her to realize some of the benefits of diversification. Second, if the entrepreneur and a well-diversified investor agree about expected future cash flows and risk, the investor values the venture more highly than does the entrepreneur.

Generally, each party to a venture seeks to increase the NPV of their investment by shifting as much risk as possible to the other, while retaining as much of the expected return as possible. However, because new ventures combine well-diversified investors with an underdiversified entrepreneur, risk allocation is not a zero-sum game. Because the required return on capital for a diversified investor depends only on market risk, whereas the required return of the entrepreneur depends on total risk, shifting nonmarket risk to the investor can increase value.

Thus, when the entrepreneur's full commitment is combined with investment capital from an outside investor, contract provisions can be used to alter the total risk that the entrepreneur bears. Contract provisions that allocate diversifiable risk to outside investors increase overall value. In cases of partial commitment of the entrepreneur, there is an additional effect. Contract provisions can both alter the total risk that the entrepreneur bears and change the correlation between the entrepreneur's project risk and the market portfolio.

How Shifting Risk Affects the Entrepreneur

Figure 11-2 illustrates the effect of contracting with an outside investor, so that the entrepreneur's total risk is reduced but market risk is unchanged. The illustration extends the previous example by adding a contract provision that reduces the entrepreneur's risk exposure in the project by 20 percent. At the full-commitment level, the contract change reduces the standard deviation from 288 percent to 231 percent. Because the contract shifts only diversifiable risk, the beta risk of each party is unchanged.

The figure shows the shift in risk and return for the entrepreneur's entire portfolio. Because risk of the entrepreneur's investment is reduced but expected return is not altered, the entrepreneur's feasible set shifts to the left. The entrepreneur's gain from shifting risk to the investor does not affect the value of the investor's claim. This is because only diversifiable risk is shifted and the investor is assumed not to care about diversifiable risk.

Thus, contract provisions that shift nonmarket risk to well-diversified investors yield pure gains in NPV. The entrepreneur is better off, and the investor is not worse off. In fact, the more

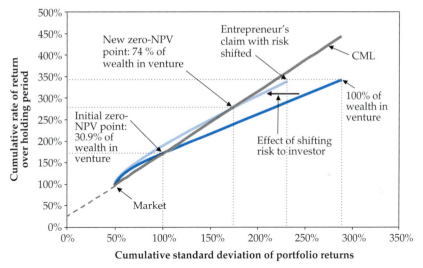

Figure 11-2 Effect of contracting to reduce nonmarket risk borne by the entrepreneur

The figure illustrates the effect of risk allocation on the opportunity set of the entrepreneur. The entrepreneur is able to enter into a financial contract that shifts some nonmarket risk to the investor. Total cash flows and risk of the venture are unaffected by the change. The shifted feasible set of the entrepreneur reflects a 20 percent reduction of total risk. The entrepreneur now achieves zero NPV with a substantially higher fraction of the wealth invested in the venture. The entrepreneur's maximum NPV also is increased.

nonmarket risk that can be shifted, the greater will be the project's NPV. You can see in Figure 11-2 that such a contract can change NPV from negative to positive, as it does in the figure for intermediate levels of entrepreneurial commitment.

The following table shows how shifting nonmarket risk to the investor affects the NPV of the entrepreneur's investment. We continue with the same numerical example. Consider the zero-NPV investment of 30.9 percent of wealth from the previous table; shifting some nonmarket risk to the investor increases the entrepreneur's NPV to $348,000. With proportional allocation, the maximum achievable NPV is $205,000, which occurs when 12.5 percent of the entrepreneur's wealth is invested in the venture. In contrast, with risk shifted, the maximum is $359,000 and is attained when about 24 percent of the entrepreneur's wealth is invested in the venture. Thus, in this example, reducing the entrepreneur's nonmarket risk increases the optimal fraction of wealth for the entrepreneur to invest in the venture. Furthermore, reducing the entrepreneur's nonmarket risk raises NPV at all levels of investment in the venture, without affecting the value of the investor's claim. The venture now has a positive NPV for investment levels up to about 74 percent of the entrepreneur's total wealth.

How Shifting Nonmarket Risk to the Outside Investor Affects NPV

Percentage of Wealth Invested in Venture	Dollars Invested in the Venture	Dollars Invested in the Market Index	NPV of the Entrepreneur's Portfolio	
			Proportional-sharing Contract	Risk-shifting Contract*
0%	$0	$2,000,000	$0	$0
12.5%	$250,000	$1,750,000	$205,000	$294,000
24%	$480,000	$1,520,000	$111,000	$359,000
30.9%	$618,000	$1,382,000	$0	$348,000
74%	$1,480,000	$520,000	($953,000)	$0
100%	$2,000,000	$0	($1,592,000)	($273,000)

*Contract has 20 percent of total risk shifted to the outside investor. All shifted risk is diversifiable.

The Outside Investor's Perspective

Why does risk allocation increase the entrepreneur's ability to invest risk capital in the project? And why would an outside investor agree to such a contract? If proportional risk allocation is used, the entrepreneur and the investor have equal market risk and each bears a high degree of nonmarket risk. To attain a positive NPV for the venture like the one represented in Figure 11-1, the entrepreneur must severely limit the fraction of wealth invested. For a project requiring a fixed amount of total capital, this increases the need for outside capital.

Contracting in a way that shifts nonmarket risk to the investor changes the entrepreneur's incentive to invest. As shown in the above table, with some risk shifted to the investor, the entrepreneur can devote a larger fraction of wealth to the venture, reducing the need for outside investment.

The table suggests why the risk-reallocation would be acceptable to a well-diversified investor. With risk shifted, the zero-NPV point represents a higher degree of total risk in dollar terms for the entrepreneur, as well as a larger investment in the project. At the zero-NPV point, the entrepreneur's investment in the venture is over twice as large as with proportional sharing. As a result, the entrepreneur would be bearing substantially greater project risk under the risk-allocation contract than under the proportional-sharing contract.

The outside investor is bearing more nonmarket risk compared with market risk but has a much smaller total investment in the project. Such a contract should be acceptable given that an outside investor can eliminate nonmarket risk through diversification.

Risk-Allocation Contracting in Practice

This discussion may not seem to comport with conventional wisdom. Venture capitalists, after all, generally try to shift risk toward the entrepreneur, and the investor usually holds financial claims that are less risky than those of the entrepreneur (convertible preferred stock instead of common). There are three responses to this observation. First, remember that the starting point for measuring the effects of contract provision changes is arbitrary. For analytical convenience, we have been comparing proportional allocation of risk to a contract that shifts nonmarket risk away from the entrepreneur. Alternatively, we could, for example, compare an initial proposed contract that shifts considerable nonmarket risk to the entrepreneur with an alternative contract that shifts less risk.

Second, the common wisdom underlying the observation arises from thinking about the negotiation one piece at a time. Generally, the amount the entrepreneur wants to raise from outside sources is predetermined, and negotiations focus on terms for providing that amount of funding. In our analysis, by contrast, both risk allocation and amount of outside funding vary at the same time. The entrepreneur is negotiating to reduce nonmarket risk in exchange for taking on more of the total investment. Such negotiations can be explicit or implicit.

Finally, conventional wisdom is based on observations where the entrepreneur already has made sunk investments in the project. The investor is contributing financial capital in exchange for equity. The entrepreneur's interest is a residual. But if we view the project before any investment has been made, then the negotiation is conducted on the basis of whether the entrepreneur's risk is low enough to justify undertaking the project at all. This assumes that the entrepreneur's funds are not already sunk in the project. If the return to the entrepreneur is not high enough to compensate for opportunity cost on a risk-adjusted basis, then the investor must either take on more of the risk or forego the project.

11.4 CONTRACT CHOICES THAT ALLOCATE EXPECTED RETURNS

When an investor supplies capital to a new venture, the investor usually starts by assessing value. This valuation is made using the investor's required rate of return. If the investor is well diversified, then the required return depends on beta risk. Recognizing that well-diversified investors provide most venture capital and assuming that the market for outside funding is competitive, we refer to value as determined by such an investor as the venture's *market value*.

In a competitive capital market, the ownership claim the investor receives in exchange for contributed capital depends on the venture's market value and not on its total capital needs. Consider, for example, a venture that requires $2 million of total capital and has a market value of $5 million.[1] Suppose a well-diversified outside investor contributes $1.5 million, with the entrepreneur contributing the balance. If there is competition to invest in the venture, then the investor can expect to receive 30 percent of the equity (i.e., $1.5 million/$5 million). With proportional sharing, the investor would receive 75 percent of the equity. But with competition, the investor would not get 75 percent of the equity just because he was investing 75 percent of the capital.

How, more generally, does the competitive market for venture capital allocate risks and rewards between the outside investor and the entrepreneur? And how does outside investment affect the value of the entrepreneur's interest in the venture? To begin to answer these questions, let's examine the investment decision of the investor.

Consider a project that has an expected return on total capital that is above the investor's required return, and where the investor and the entrepreneur plan to hold identical ownership claims (i.e., they both hold common stock and neither party receives any other compensation). If the investor shares proportionally in risk and return (by contributing a given fraction of total capital in exchange for an equivalent fraction of ownership), then the investor's return will be higher than it needs to be. In fact, in a competitive market, the investor would have been willing to pay the entrepreneur just to gain the right to purchase the fractional ownership interest on such terms. In a competitive setting, the investor is compelled to make such a payment and effectively does so by contributing proportionally more capital to the venture than the investor's share of ownership.

As a mathematical convenience, you can think of the investor as purchasing a two-asset portfolio. One asset is a proportional share of the venture. The other is a riskless "asset" with a certain return of minus 100 percent. This second component is effectively a side-payment the investor must make to the entrepreneur for the right to purchase the proportional share. In a competitive capital market, the amount invested in the second component must be large enough so that the NPV of the outside investor's total outlay is zero.

In Figure 11-3, we use this approach to illustrate the competitive market result for the numerical example we have been developing. Note that the horizontal axis in the figure is beta risk, and not total risk. The Security Market Line (SML) in the figure reflects the investor's opportunity cost of capital, based on the CAPM. The other line describes the expected returns and betas for portfolios with varying weights between proportional investment in the venture and a riskless side-payment to the entrepreneur. The project under consideration has beta risk of 1.178 based on the $2 million investment and an expected return of 343 percent over the six-year holding period.[2] However, given the 26.53 percent risk-free rate for a six-year holding period, and the market rate of 97.38 percent, the outside investor's required return on the project is 110 percent. Thus, the investor's expected return is much higher than the required return.

Because the venture has a positive NPV, the investor is willing to pay the entrepreneur for the right to share proportionally in it. The payment actually comes in the form of accepting a smaller than proportional share of the equity in exchange for the investment. The graphical solution in Figure 11-3 is the point where the expected return on the investor's portfolio intersects the SML.

Think of the investor as buying two assets: an investment in the venture, and an investment in a second asset that offers a certain minus 100 percent return. Simple algebra can be used to determine the fraction of the investor's total outlay that goes to acquire the proportional share of the venture. Equation (11.1) is the SML, as shown in Figure 11-3.

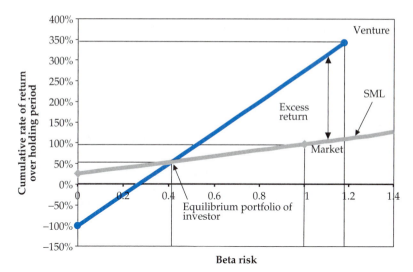

Figure 11-3 Portfolio returns of outside investor compared to required rates of return

This figure continues the illustration, by examining the investment decision of a diversified investor whose minimum acceptable return is determined by the CAPM. The vertical axis is the expected return on investment. The horizontal axis is beta risk. The SML represents the required return of a diversified investor, as a function of beta risk. The expected return for investing in the venture and sharing proportionally in risk and return is well above the investor's required return. The minimum required return is found by treating the investment as a two-asset portfolio, consisting of the venture and a side payment to the entrepreneur. Because the side payment has beta of zero, the amount of equity the investor requires can be determined mathematically. The minimum occurs at the point where the investor's expected return on the portfolio equals the required return on the portfolio.

$$r_{Port}^{Required} = r_F + \beta_{Port}(RP_M) \tag{11.1}$$

The equation is the CAPM measure of cost of capital for the investor's portfolio of the project and a risk-free asset. Equation (11.2) is the investor's expected return,

$$r_{Port}^{Expected} = r_P(x_P) + (-100\%)(1 - x_P) \tag{11.2}$$

where x_P is the fraction of the total investment that notionaly is considered to be invested in the venture with proportional sharing.

To determine the amount of the implicit side payment, we need to find the point where the investor's expected return is equal to the required return. To do this, we note that $\beta_{Port} = \beta_P \times x_P + 0 \times x_{Sidepayment}$. Thus, we substitute $\beta_{Port} = \beta_P x_P$ in the first equation, set the first and second equations equal, and solve for x_P:

$$r_F + \beta_P x_P (RP_M) = r_P(x_P) + (-100\%)(1 - x_P)$$

$$x_P = \frac{r_F + 100\%}{r_P + 100\% - \beta_P(RP_M)} \qquad (11.3)$$

Based on the assumptions about the risk-free rate and market risk premium, x_P is 35.2 percent. Thus, 35.2 percent of the investor's contribution is notionaly an investment in the venture, and the balance is a notional side payment to the entrepreneur.

Given the value of x_P, it is easy to determine the beta and expected return on the investor's total investment.

$$\beta_{Port} = \beta_P(x_P) \ 1.178 \times .352 = .415$$
$$r_{Port} = r_F + \beta_{Port}(RP) = 26.53\% + .415 \times 70.85\% = 55.93\%$$

These results correspond to the equilibrium point shown in Figure 11-3.[3] Given the low beta, the required rate of return on the investor's total investment is only 7.7 percent per year. If this seems unrealistically low, remember that we are working with a hypothetical example and are assuming that the investor and entrepreneur agree about project risk and expected return. An increase in the assumed total risk and a reduction in the expected return on the venture would yield a different result. Also, the market for new venture investment capital is less competitive than we are assuming and is, itself, a costly activity.

The practical interpretation of the example is as follows. If one begins with the actual capital requirement of the project and considers that the investor is planning to contribute 75 percent of the total capital requirement, the investor will do so in exchange for a 26.4 percent interest in the project (i.e., 75 percent $\times x_P$). Of the total $1.5 million investment by the investor, you can think of $528,000 (i.e., 26.4 percent of the $2 million total cost of the project) as a proportional investment in the project and the remaining $972,000 as, effectively, a side-payment to the entrepreneur. The side-payment reduces the entrepreneur's capital contribution for the remaining 74.6 percent interest in the venture to $500,000 (including the investment of human capital).

The investor's capital contribution that is in excess of proportional sharing works like free leverage for the entrepreneur. Figure 11-4 is an Excel spreadsheet valuation of the financial claims of the investor and the entrepreneur. The spreadsheet is based on the same assumptions as discussed earlier. The Outside Investor Allocation panel uses Eq. (11.3) to

Figure 11-4 Valuation–Investor interest and residual partial commitment of the entrepreneur

The figure is an Excel spreadsheet that can be used as a valuation template. It is designed to (1) determine the share of equity a diversified investor requires in exchange for an investment of a given size, and (2) value the residual cash flows of the entrepreneur as one asset of a two-asset portfolio, where the other asset is the market index.

Valuation Template 5

Valuation—Investor and Entrepreneur's Partial Commitment

Market Information	Annual	Holding Period
Risk-free Rate	**4.00%**	26.53%
Market Rate	**12.00%**	97.38%
Market Risk Premium	8.00%	70.85%
Market Variance	4.00%	24.00%
Market Standard Deviation	**20.00%**	48.99%
Correlation		0.2

Project Cash Flows	Invest Date	Harvest Date
Years Until Harvest		6
Investment in Project	**$2,000**	
Expected Project Cash Flow		**$8,860**
Project Standard Deviation of Cash Flows		**$5,769**

Outside Investor Allocation		
Project Beta (based on cost of project)		1.178
Fraction of Investment that is notionally in project		0.352
Outside Investment	$1,500	
Required Percent of Equity		26.39%
Cash Flow to Investor		
Expected Cash Flow		$2,338
Standard Deviation of Cash Flow		$1,523
Outside Investor Value		$1,500

Cash Flow to Entrepreneur		
Entrepreneur's Investment	$500	
Expected Project Cash Flow		$6,522
Project Standard Deviation		$4,246
Investment in Market	$1,500	
Expected Market Cash Flow		$2,961
Market Standard Deviation of Cash Flows		$735
Expected Portfolio Cash Flow	$2,000	$9,482
Portfolio Standard Deviation		$4,452

CAPM Market Value Estimate		
Portfolio Present Value		$5,683
Market Investment		$1,500
Present Value—Project		**$4,183**

CAPM Private Value Estimate—Partial Commitment		
Present Value—Portfolio		$2,406
Market Investment		$1,500
Present Value—Project		**$906**

Maximum Leverage Value Estimate—Partial Commitment		
Maximum Leverage (from Figure 10-2: t, r(F))		4.7
Required Rate of Return on Portfolio	28.94%	359.53%
Present Value—Portfolio		$2,063
Market Investment		$1,500
Present Value—Project		**$563**

VALUE SUMMARY—Partial Commitment	
Greater of CAPM or Maximum Leverage Present Value	$906

determine the fraction of the equity that must be allocated to the investor to compensate for the $1.5 million investment. That allocation is based on the CAPM approach to determining required rate of return. In the Cash Flows of Entrepreneur panel, we show the residual project cash flow that goes to the entrepreneur in exchange for the remaining $500,000 investment. By structuring the deal in this way, we effectively assume that the entrepreneur captures all of the economic rents of the venture. Because the entrepreneur can allocate wealth between the venture and other investments, this panel allows the entrepreneur to invest in a market index portfolio.

The CAPM Market Value Estimate panel shows the value of the entrepreneur's portfolio and of the venture as if they were held by a well-diversified investor. This panel is included only for comparison. The CAPM Private Value Estimate—Partial Commitment shows the value of the portfolio and of the project as the entire risky investment of the entrepreneur. If the entrepreneur is compelled to make an investment in the project of at least the amount shown in the Cash Flows of Entrepreneur panel, the Maximum Leverage Value Estimate—Partial Commitment panel shows the value of the project under the assumption that the entrepreneur is risk-neutral beyond the point of maximum achievable leverage of the market portfolio. In a subsequent discussion, we assume that the entrepreneur can choose the amount of investment in the venture. Thus, we do not consider the maximum attainable leverage estimate.

The Entrepreneur's Gain from Contracting with a Well-Diversified Investor

The following table shows how the entrepreneur's wealth affects the gain from contracting with a well-diversified investor. Consider three entrepreneurs, X, Y, and Z, each of whom has a different amount of wealth. The entrepreneur contributes $500,000 to a venture and invests any additional wealth in a market index portfolio. An outside investor contributes the remaining $1.5 million. (We continue to use the example where the venture requires a $2 million total investment.) The final two columns show the NPV of the entrepreneur's investment for two types of contracts. The first is one in which the parties retain ownership claims that are proportional to their investments. The second is one in which the parties allocate ownership claims so that the outside investor earns the rate of return determined by the CAPM. The entrepreneur captures any excess return.

The table illustrates how the entrepreneur's wealth affects the NPV associated with these two contracts. The lower the percentage of the entrepreneur's wealth that is invested in the project, the closer the entrepreneur comes to holding a well-diversified portfolio, and the higher is the present value of the project. Any entrepreneur, regardless of wealth, will find the project more valuable under CAPM-based allocation than under proportional allocation. The shift enables the entrepreneur to justify investing a larger fraction of total wealth in the project.

The Entrepreneur's Gain from Contracting to Provide the Investor a CAPM-Based Allocation of Ownership

Entrepreneur	Total Wealth of the Entrepreneur	Percentage of Wealth Invested in the Venture	NPV of the Entrepreneur's Investment in the Venture*	
			Investor and Entrepreneur Ownership Shares are Proportional to Investments	Investor Ownership Share is Determined by CAPM
X	$500,000	100%	($398,000)	($199,000)
Y	$1,000,000	50%	($196,000)	$17,000
Z	$2,000,000	25%	$96,000	$406,000

*Under CAPM-based allocation, the NPV of the investor's interest is zero.

How Much of the Entrepreneur's Wealth Should Be Invested in the Venture?

Now consider the entrepreneur's allocation of wealth between the venture and a market portfolio. The change from proportional sharing to CAPM-based allocation for the investor can have a surprising effect on the entrepreneur's wealth allocation decision. To demonstrate, we continue to assume that the venture requires a total investment of $2 million and that (coincidentally) the entrepreneur has total wealth of $2 million. With 100 percent of wealth invested in the venture, the entrepreneur's CAPM-based NPV is very negative.[4]

We established earlier that, with proportional sharing, the zero-NPV point occurs when the entrepreneur invests 30.9 percent of wealth ($618,000) in the venture. With proportional sharing, the entrepreneur reaches maximum NPV at an investment level of about 12.5 percent, or $250,000, and the resulting NPV is $205,000.

Now, let's use the template in Figure 11-4 to compare this with CAPM-based allocation. It turns out that the entrepreneur's present value and NPV are highest when outside investors provide all $2 million of the needed investment capital. In fact, with a zero investment, the entrepreneur's NPV is over $1 million. At the earlier maximum NPV point, with 12.5 percent of the entrepreneur's wealth invested in the venture, CAPM-based allocation increases the NPV of the entrepreneur's investment by about $520,000.

One natural question is, if the entrepreneur is devoting $300,000 of human capital to the venture, how can her contribution be zero? The answer is that the $2 million from the investor is sufficient to purchase the entrepreneur's human capital, in much the same way that any employee is compensated. Compensation for the value of the entrepreneur's time can be an up-front payment of $300,000, or the equivalent present value can be paid out in the form of salary. In short, if the entrepreneur is fully compensated for the opportunity cost of human capital, then the human capital is not an investment by the entrepreneur.

Perhaps you are concerned that with an investment of zero, the entrepreneur will have little incentive to commit effort. This is not the case. Although the entrepreneur contributes nothing, we already have determined that, with CAPM-based allocation, the investor is willing to make the entire $2 million investment in exchange for 35.2 percent of the equity. The entrepreneur still owns the other 64.8 percent of the equity. Thus, even though the entrepreneur's investment is zero, she still has a strong incentive to make the venture a success.

Who Should Own the Venture?

Though our analysis suggests that by investing zero the entrepreneur can achieve maximum NPV, an alternative approach can yield even greater value. With zero investment by the entrepreneur, the present value of the venture (combining the interests of both parties) is equal to the $2 million investment by the investor (in exchange for 35.2 percent of the equity), plus the $1.029 million NPV (and present value) of the entrepreneur's 64.8 percent interest. Thus, total present value is $3.029 million. But in Figure 10-9 we computed the present value of a 100 percent interest in the venture to a diversified investor as $5.683 million. If that is correct, then the approach of asking the investor to commit only $2 million fails to capture $2.654 million of the potential value.

Because the entrepreneur cares about total risk, whereas a diversified investor cares only about nondiversifiable risk, if the parties agree about the expected future cash flows, the investor should buy almost all of the equity from the entrepreneur. If the entrepreneur's capabilities are important to the venture, the investor should hire the entrepreneur as an employee. Under these conditions, Figure 10-9 implies that the investor would be willing to pay $3.683 million to the entrepreneur to acquire 100 percent of the equity and would invest an additional $2 million in the venture. By selling out to a diversified investor, the entrepreneur realizes a NPV of $3.683 million. The entrepreneur's total return is diminished any time she sells less than 100 percent of the equity.

In summary, if the investor is well diversified and requires only a return sufficient to cover opportunity cost of capital per the CAPM, then the entrepreneur can increase expected return and reduce risk by raising equity from the investor. In effect, even though the entrepreneur has only $2 million to invest, she has an asset (the venture) that is worth $5.684 million. The only way she can realize that value is to undertake the venture but sell the ownership to a diversified investor. Equivalently, the entrepreneur could invest the $2 million and immediately sell the venture for $5.684 million.

Reconciling Theory with Practice

Our conclusions from the preceding discussion do not seem to be very consistent with the normal ownership structures of new ventures. Entrepreneurs usually do not sell out entirely, or, if they do, the transactions involve complex structures in which the entrepreneur continues to bear significant risk. If the preceding analysis is correct, why does the entrepreneur ever own any of the risky claims? We now can provide some specific answers.

Setting aside the very real possibility of mistakes, the discussion suggests four answers. First, entrepreneurs often are (rightly or wrongly) more optimistic about success than are outside investors. If so, an investor may not offer enough to fully buy out the entrepreneur. Second, if the market for investment capital is not competitive, then the investor may be able to capture some of the economic rents by offering a below-market price, in which case selling out might not be the most valuable decision for the entrepreneur. Third, if the entrepreneur's effort is important to success, then maintaining significant entrepreneurial ownership is a way of aligning the incentives of the entrepreneur with the interests of the investor. Finally, the entrepreneur may place a subjective value on ownership or control of the venture, beyond the financial calculation.

One other reason that our theory-based conclusions could diverge from practice is that the CAPM employs very specific assumptions about the risk/return tradeoff of investors. Our valuation model for an underdiversified investor also is specific. However, as long as diversifiable risk is more important to an underdiversified entrepreneur than to a well-diversified investor, venture cash flows will be more valuable to the investor. So, although different assumptions would result in different estimates of value, they would not alter the conclusion that the entrepreneur would achieve maximum NPV by selling the venture to a diversified investor.

11.5   CONTRACT CHOICES THAT ALTER VENTURE RETURNS

Given that an entrepreneur requires outside capital, how should she select an investor, and how does the investor's involvement affect value to the entrepreneur? Outside funding can come from either passive or active investors. Some prospective investors may not be well diversified, and others, such as Small Business Investment Companies (SBICs) in the U.S. and state economic development agencies, may accept below-market rates of return. Active investors are likely to demand higher expected rates of return and may insist on mechanisms for directly influencing venture development: On the other hand, they may contribute substantial value. How can the entrepreneur select the best investor from the array of prospects?

Until now, we have focused on a well-diversified, passive investor. In this section, we briefly discuss two other cases: first, a passive investor who is willing to subsidize the project by accepting an expected return that is below the market rate, and second, an active venture capitalist who both adds value and demands a larger share of the business. For convenience, we assume that the contracts involve financial claims that are identical (e.g., both parties receive shares of common stock in exchange for their investments) and that outside investors are well diversified.

Evaluating Investment by Subsidized Investors

SBICs and certain other kinds of U.S. and foreign investors in new ventures receive financing subsidies that are intended to encourage new venture formation or, more generally, to support small business. The forms of the subsidies differ. Some investors receive direct access to low-cost funds, whereas others can use loan guarantees to reduce the cost of borrowing. Subsidized investors often prefer to offer risky debt financing instead of equity. In addition, the extent to which a subsidy for the investor gets passed through to a venture can vary. Consequently, there is no simple way to generalize about the value of subsidized investment. Instead, the effects of a specific subsidy program can be evaluated in much the same way that we evaluated the effects of passive outside investment. While a subsidized investor may be passive or active, focusing on a passive investor enables us to isolate the effects of the subsidy.

How Subsidized Financing Affects the Entrepreneur's NPV   Let's consider how the entrepreneur's risk and return are affected by involving an investor whose cost of funds is reduced by a subsidy. Assuming that financial claims are the same, except for the subsidy, an investor who is well diversified must earn the same return on investment as a well-diversified passive investor. The only difference is that part of the capital supplied to the investor comes at a below-market rate.

Holding the form of investment constant, we can represent this subsidy by reducing the investor's fractional ownership claim to reflect the extent of the subsidy. Suppose, for example, that an unsubsidized investor would invest 40 percent of required financing in exchange for 35 percent of the equity but that a subsidized investor would contribute the same amount in exchange for 28 percent. Thus, the subsidized investor requires a total return that is about 80 percent of what the unsubsidized investor would require. It may seem obvious that this is a good deal for the entrepreneur, who ends up with more of the equity. However, there are two offsetting effects of the subsidy. More equity means that the entrepreneur's expected return is higher. However, the entrepreneur's risk is also higher. Increasing the entrepreneur's share of ownership is beneficial if the entrepreneur would have had a positive NPV with CAPM-based allocation and no subsidy. However, if the unsubsidized position had been negative, then increasing the ownership share would make it even more negative.

In other words, in the CAPM-based framework, this form of subsidy affects expected return and risk. If the entrepreneur would have a positive NPV under CAPM-based allocation, then the expected return effect is dominant. If the entrepreneur would have a negative NPV under CAPM-based allocation, then the risk effect is dominant.

Before you conclude that the effect of subsidized investment is ambiguous, remember that (in purely financial terms) a venture is always more valuable to a diversified investor than to an underdiversified entrepreneur. This is even more true for an outside investor who is subsidized. The entrepreneur in this example can realize an unambiguous gain by maintaining the outside investment level at 35 percent but negotiating for the subsidized investor to provide up to 50 percent of total capital. This would reduce the entrepreneur's investment and enable greater diversification.

Estimating the Required Ownership Share of a Subsidized Investor   The investor's required ownership share is determined by how the subsidy affects the required rate of return. Suppose a venture that is expected to return $10 million in six years requires an investment of $2 million. The risk-free rate is 4 percent per year, the beta is 1.0, and the market risk premium is 5.8 percent. The required annual rate of return of an unsubsidized investor is 9.8 percent. The investor would need an expected cash return of $3.5 million in six years, or 35 percent of the venture's expected cash flow.

Suppose the subsidy to a subsidized investor is a certain 4 percent per year, based on the initial investment. The investor can justify the $2 million investment at an annual return that is 4 percent lower, or 5.8 percent. The subsidized investor would need an expected cash return of $2.8 million in six years, or 28 percent of expected cash flows. If the subsidized investor were to receive 35 percent of the equity, the present value of that interest would be $2.5 million instead of $2.0 million. The entrepreneur's investment could then be reduced by $500,000.

Implications for the Choice of Financing Sources   Other things the same, raising capital from a subsidized investor is preferable to raising capital from one that is not. But because of the nature of many subsidized investors, other things are unlikely to be the same. Subsidized investors often seek relatively low-risk financial claims compared to other investors in new ventures.

They frequently prefer debt (or debt with equity sweeteners) to common or preferred stock. Accordingly, they are better suited to invest in small businesses with positive income and cash flow, and they tend to shift more of the total risk of the venture to the entrepreneur. Compared with raising an equivalent amount of capital from a diversified investor who receives equity claims, this is likely to reduce the entrepreneur's NPV.

Furthermore, it is not always clear that the entrepreneur can realize the benefit of the investor's subsidy. If subsidized investors do not need to compete aggressively with each other to participate in a venture, then the investor is only competing against investors whose opportunity cost of capital is determined by the market. The subsidized investor should be able to capture the benefits of the subsidy rather than using it to reduce the effective cost of capital of the venture.

One factor that mitigates in favor of raising capital from a subsidized investor is that doing so can enable the entrepreneur to retain more control. Subsidized investors who seek low-risk financial claims are more likely to be passive than are investors who seek equity claims, and the less-risky claims normally have more limited voting or other control rights. Thus, even though subsidized financing increases the entrepreneur's risk, the nature of the claims makes it less important that the entrepreneur and the investor agree about the expected future cash flows and risk. Thus, lower-risk subsidized financing may be preferred when the entrepreneur is more optimistic about the prospects for the venture than are outside investors, or when the entrepreneur seeks a capital structure that enables her to retain voting control.

Evaluating Investment by Active Investors

Active investors, such as venture capital firms and business angels, contribute both financial capital and expertise. Typically, they realize the returns on investment of effort through their financial claims. Thus, an active investor, in contrast to a passive investor, demands a larger, more valuable ownership interest to compensate for effort. Because the ownership stake is larger, investor involvement reduces the leveraging effect of outside investment. In addition, if the involvement is constructive, it increases the overall expected return and possibly reduces risk.

How Involvement of an Active Investor Affects the Entrepreneur's NPV   How the combination of factors affects the entrepreneur's feasible set depends on the relative importance of each factor. Figure 11-5 illustrates one possible result. In the illustration, we assume that an active investor increases expected total cash flow by 5 percent and reduces the standard deviation of cash flows by 10 percent (with an offsetting 10 percent increase in correlation with the market). We also assume that the investor requires an expected return that is 20 percent higher than would a passive investor. Thus, if a passive investor would require 10 percent per year, the active investor would require 12 percent.

The figure shows the net effect of these changes. The arrow in the figure shows how the larger equity share of the active investor shifts the entrepreneur's risk and return. It is drawn at the point where 50 percent of the entrepreneur's wealth is invested in the venture and the rest is in a market index. The figure is generated based on the example from Chapter 10, assuming project scale is $2 million. At the arrow, the investor and the entrepreneur each provide 50 percent of required capital. Because the shift caused by active involvement is almost horizontal, involving an active investor primarily reduces the entrepreneur's risk. In this example, although the investor's involvement enhances the expected cash flow, the investor captures most of that gain.

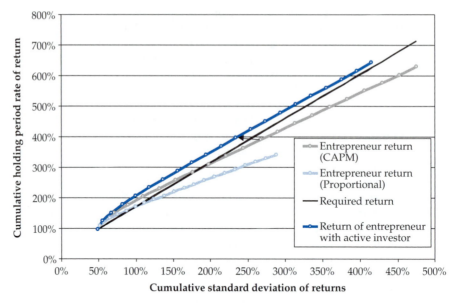

Figure 11-5 Effect of active investor on feasible set of entrepreneur

The figure shows how the risk and return of the entrepreneur's portfolio are affected by involving an outside active investor. The investor requires an ownership share that is large enough to compensate for both the capital and managerial effort the investor commits. The net effect of active involvement depends on how much value the investor adds, compared with the extra return the investor requires.

Even though the entrepreneur's expected return does not increase materially, the NPV of the entrepreneur's investment does increase. The NPV benefit to the entrepreneur arises because active involvement reduces the entrepreneur's risk.

Implications for the Choice of Financing Sources We assume that the objective of an entrepreneur who is deciding among active, passive, and subsidized investors is to maximize the NPV of her position (including investment in other assets such as the market index). Thus, even in this case, a tradeoff must be considered. With respect to venture capital or business angel financing, the critical issue is whether the investor is expected to add enough value (by increasing expected returns, reducing risk, or both) to offset the investor's higher claim on ownership. Both issues can be examined using the modeling approach presented earlier.

11.6 IMPLEMENTATION AND NEGOTIATION

In the preceding discussion, we have examined how to assess the effects of shifting risk, allocating expected returns, subsidizing investment, and active investor participation. The systematic treatment helps us understand the various effects, but the graphical approach is cumbersome. Accordingly, in this section, we adapt spreadsheet Valuation Template 5 (Figure 11-4) to examine how specific financing proposals affect value. For this purpose, we continue with the example introduced in Chapter 10. Suppose the entrepreneur is seeking financing for a venture that requires total investment of $2 million. She plans to invest $500,000 of the total, largely in the form of human capital. Thus, she is seeking $1.5 million from an investor.

In this discussion, we no longer assume that investor claims have NPVs of zero. Rather, the proposals are generated by investors who seek positive NPVs. The entrepreneur knows the proposed terms, and has a sense of how the required return of each investor is determined.

Suppose the entrepreneur is considering the following four choices:

Alternative 1: A well-diversified passive investor will provide $1.5 million in exchange for 75 percent of the common stock.

Alternative 2: A well-diversified passive investor will provide $1.5 million in exchange for 40 percent of the common stock.

Alternative 3: A subsidized passive investor will provide $1.5 million in exchange for 30 percent of the common stock. The investor's cost of funds is 2 percent per year below the CAPM opportunity cost measure.

Alternative 4: An active investor will provide $1.5 million in exchange for 45 percent of common stock. The entrepreneur expects that investor involvement will increase cash flows by about 2.7 percent and will reduce the standard deviation of cash flows by about 9.5 percent.[5]

Now, here is a test of your intuition. Suppose you are the entrepreneur who is faced with these choices. Which one do you think is most attractive and why? How much negotiation room do you think there is for each of them? Don't be surprised if your intuition does not get you far. You probably feel fairly confident that Alternative 2 dominates Alternative 1. But how much can you say about the relative values of Alternatives 2, 3, and 4? Can you come up with any counterproposals that you think the investors would accept?

Evaluating Alternative Financing Proposals

To evaluate each alternative, we used a two-step process. First, we modified the simulation model in Figure 10-4 to reflect the investor's proposed allocation of the year-6 cash flows (the free-cash balance plus continuing value) and re-ran the simulation. For each alternative, we used the simulated results to calculate the expected cash flow and standard deviation of cash flows for the investor and for the entrepreneur. Second, we modified the assumptions in Valuation Template 5 to value the financial claims under each alternative. Figure 11-6 contains a summary of the simulation results and the valuations.[6] Each column in the figure reflects one of the financing alternatives. Under the Active Investor heading, the expected cash flow is higher, and the standard deviation is lower than that for the other alternatives. This reflects the investor's assumed effect on venture risk and return.

The Outside Investor Allocation panel shows the fractions of equity the investor would receive under each alternative, as well as the expected cash flow and standard deviation of cash flows. The last line in this panel is the present value of the investor's investment, assuming that each investor is well-diversified and (except for the subsidized investor) uses the CAPM to value its claim. For the subsidized investor, we assume cost of capital is lower by 2 percent per year. Each investor would contribute $1.5 million to the project.

Based on the valuations in this panel, each alternative yields a positive NPV for the investor. The computed present value is highest for the passive investor who is offering

Comparative Valuation of Outside Financing Alternatives

	Passive Investor (Proportional)	Passive Investor (CAPM)	Passive Investor (Subsidized)	Active Investor
Market Information				
Risk-free Rate	26.53%	26.53%	26.53%	26.53%
Market Rate	97.38%	97.38%	97.38%	97.38%
Market Risk Premium	70.85%	70.85%	70.85%	70.85%
Market Variance	24.00%	24.00%	24.00%	24.00%
Market Standard Deviation	48.99%	48.99%	48.99%	48.99%
Correlation	0.2	0.2	0.2	0.2
Project Cash Flows				
Years Until Harvest	6	6	6	6
Expected Project Cash Flow	$8,679	$8,679	$8,679	$8,910
Project Standard Deviation of Cash Flows	$5,515	$5,515	$5,515	$4,993
Outside Investor Allocation				
Project beta (based on cost of project)	1.126	1.126	1.126	1.019
Fraction of investment that is notionally in project	0.357	0.357	0.357	0.339
Required Percent of Equity	75.00%	40.00%	30.00%	45.00%
Cash Flow to Investor				
Expected Cash Flow	$6,509	$3,472	$2,604	$4,010
Standard Deviation of Cash Flow	$4,136	$2,206	$1,655	$2,247
Outside Investor Value	**$4,199**	**$2,239**	**$1,866**	**$2,655**
Cash Flow to Entrepreneur				
Expected Project Cash Flow	$2,170	$5,207	$6,075	$4,901
Project Standard Deviation	$1,379	$3,309	$3,861	$2,746
Expected Market Cash Flow	$2,961	$2,961	$2,961	$2,961
Market Standard Deviation of Cash Flows	$735	$735	$735	$735
Expected Portfolio Cash Flow	$5,130	$8,168	$9,036	$7,861
Portfolio Standard Deviation	$1,687	$3,530	$4,072	$2,981
CAPM Market Value Estimate				
Portfolio Present Value	$2,900	$4,859	$5,419	$4,745
Market Investment	$1,500	$1,500	$1,500	$1,500
Present Value—Project	**$1,400**	**$3,359**	**$3,919**	**$3,245**
CAPM Private Value Estimate—Partial Commitment				
Present Value—Portfolio	$2,126	$2,420	$2,488	$2,805
Market Investment	$1,500	$1,500	$1,500	$1,500
Present Value—Project	**$626**	**$920**	**$988**	**$1,305**

Figure 11-6 Valuation–residual partial commitment of the entrepreneur: comparison of alternatives

proportional sharing. Assuming the investor is well diversified, the entrepreneur has considerable room for negotiation to reduce the investor's share of equity. However, if this investor is an individual and is not well diversified, then we cannot determine his actual present value. We know, however, that the value is higher the more fully diversified the investor. We assume that the other three investors all are well diversified. The computed present values suggest that each can accept a reduced ownership stake and still benefit. The results suggest that the greatest potential for negotiation from among these three is with the active investor, who has a NPV of $1.155 million under the proposed terms. However, the NPV must also compensate for the investor's effort, which we have not factored into the calculations. If the cost of effort is more than about $400,000, the passive CAPM proposal has the most room for negotiation.

The Cash Flow to Entrepreneur panel shows the projected cash flow and standard deviation that the entrepreneur would receive under each alternative. We generated these results from the simulation trials, based on the entrepreneur's investment of $500,000 in the venture. We assume that the balance of the entrepreneur's wealth, $1.5 million, is invested in a market index.

In the CAPM Private Value Estimate—Partial Commitment panel, the present value of the entrepreneur's total investment (in the venture and the market index) is always greater than the entrepreneur's $2 million total investment. Thus, all four proposals are acceptable to the entrepreneur. The maximum NPV is $805,000 with the active investor (i.e., $1,305,000 present value, less the $500,000 investment).

Developing and Evaluating Counterproposals

The information in Figure 11-6 can be used to formulate some simple counterproposals. Holding the amount of outside investment constant, the investor must be offered a deal that is sufficient to compensate for the opportunity cost of capital and effort. Based on the NPVs of the outside investors in Figure 11-6, and assuming effort cost of $500,000 for the active investor, we consider a counteroffer of 28 percent of equity to the passive investor, 25 percent for the subsidized investor, and 35 percent of equity for the active investor. We also assume $500,000 to be the opportunity cost of the active investor's effort. We do not bother with a counter to the proportional sharing proposal.[7]

Results of modifying the simulation to reflect the counterproposals and recomputing the valuations are reported in Figure 11-7. The Active Investor counterproposal is the most attractive for the entrepreneur, and all three have similar values to the investors.

This comparison of financing alternatives and counterproposals is simplistic. Rarely does an entrepreneur have the opportunity to compare such diverse alternatives, partly because they often are associated with different stages of venture development. In addition, the actual terms of a proposed deal are likely to be substantially more complex, and the negotiations more subtle. Furthermore, we have not explored proposals that would change the amount of outside investment or the scale of the venture. Finally, the analysis does not assess the effects of qualitative considerations that might lead the entrepreneur to prefer one arrangement or partner over another. Still, the power of the quantitative valuation should be apparent from the illustration. As we progress through the next few chapters, we will deal with some of these other qualitative issues.

Comparative Valuation of Outside Financing Alternatives

	Passive Investor (CAPM)	Passive Investor (Subsidized)	Active Investor
Market Information			
Risk-free Rate	26.53%	26.53%	26.53%
Market Rate	97.38%	97.38%	97.38%
Market Risk Premium	70.85%	70.85%	70.85%
Market Variance	24.00%	24.00%	24.00%
Market Standard Deviation	48.99%	48.99%	48.99%
Correlation	0.2	0.2	0.2
Project Cash Flows			
Years Until Harvest	6	6	6
Expected Project Cash Flow	$8,679	$8,679	$8,910
Project Standard Deviation of Cash Flows	$5,515	$5,515	$4,993
Outside Investor Allocation			
Project beta (based on cost of project)	1.126	1.126	1.019
Fraction of investment that is notionally in project	0.357	0.357	0.339
Required Percent of Equity	28.00%	25.00%	35.00%
Cash Flow to Investor			
Expected Cash Flow	$2,430	$2,170	$3,119
Standard Deviation of Cash Flow	$1,544	$1,379	$1,748
Outside Investor Value	**$1,568**	**$1,555**	**$1,565**
Cash Flow to Entrepreneur			
Expected Project Cash Flow	$6,249	$6,509	$5,792
Project Standard Deviation	$3,971	$4,136	$3,245
Expected Market Cash Flow	$2,961	$2,961	$2,961
Market Standard Deviation of Cash Flows	$735	$735	$735
Expected Portfolio Cash Flow	$9,210	$9,470	$8,752
Portfolio Standard Deviation	$4,180	$4,343	$3,468
CAPM Market Value Estimate			
Portfolio Present Value	$5,531	$5,699	$5,335
Market Investment	$1,500	$1,500	$1,500
Present Value—Project	**$4,031**	**$4,199**	**$3,835**
CAPM Private Value Estimate—Partial Commitment			
Present Value—Portfolio	$2,501	$2,520	$2,953
Market Investment	$1,500	$1,500	$1,500
Present Value—Project	**$1,001**	**$1,020**	**$1,453**

Figure 11-7 Valuation–residual partial commitment of the entrepreneur: counter proposals

11.7 SUMMARY

This chapter develops a conceptual framework for evaluating new venture financing alternatives and for developing reasonable counterproposals. The framework recognizes that entrepreneurs, as undiversified investors, should value projects at discount rates that can be substantially higher than the rates appropriate for well-diversified investors. Because the required rate of the entrepreneur depends on total risk and not just market risk, a significant opportunity exists for designing value-enhancing financing contracts between entrepreneurs and investors.

The chapter explores some of the opportunities that can derive from regarding entrepreneurial investment in this way. Among other things, the required return of the entrepreneur is demonstrated to decline as the fraction of wealth that must be invested in the project declines. This gives rise to a significant opportunity for an entrepreneur to contract with outside investors in ways that reduce the overall required rate of return on the venture. Beyond this, the chapter demonstrates that thoughtful design of contracts between entrepreneurs and outside investors can enhance the value of projects and can turn unacceptable projects into attractive ones over a broad range of expected rates of return.

Significant opportunities exist to extend the conceptual framework. For example, with one exception, analysis in this chapter is limited to examination of contracts in which the entrepreneur and the investor hold identical claims. In most real settings, the investor holds a differentiated claim, such as preferred stock, and preserves a variety of rights and options. In addition, investments in many entrepreneurial ventures are multistage, and the outside investor may retain an option to abandon. Most projects also involve some sunk investment by the entrepreneur. You can use the framework developed in this chapter to examine all of these considerations. Doing so can help you to assess, for example, the optimal level of sunk investment before an entrepreneur seeks outside capital, optimal staging of capital infusions, and design of financial contracts with embedded options.

QUESTIONS AND PROBLEMS

1. A venture that will cost $1 million, including $200,000 worth of the entrepreneur's time, is expected to be harvested in three years and to yield $6.5 million at that time. Based on a simulation study, the standard deviation of harvest cash flows is $3.5 million. Assume that the annual risk-free rate is 3 percent and that the expected market rate of return is 9 percent per year. The standard deviation of market returns is 14 percent per year. The correlation between the venture and the market is estimated to be 0.4. Estimate the NPV of the venture to the following individuals, assuming that each makes the entire investment:
   a. An entrepreneur whose total wealth, including human capital, is $1 million.
   b. A well-diversified investor.
   c. An entrepreneur whose total wealth is $2 million, where the balance of total wealth is maintained in a market index.
   d. An entrepreneur whose total wealth is $10 million, where the balance is maintained in a market index.
   e. An entrepreneur whose total wealth is $10 million, where $1 million is in the venture, $3 million is retained in a riskless asset, and the balance is maintained in a market index.

Discuss your results. In particular, discuss how the values of intangibles like self-employment and total control might affect the relative values of the different scenarios, and how the entrepreneur's risk aversion might affect the relative values of the scenarios in parts (d) and (e).

2. Consider the venture described in problem 1, and assume that the entrepreneur has total wealth of $2 million. Evaluate the following financing alternatives in terms of the entrepreneur's NPV.

   a. An investor will contribute $400,000 of the total cost in exchange for a 40 percent share of the equity of the venture.
   b. A creditor will lend the entrepreneur $400,000 in exchange for expected repayment of principal and interest of $700,000 in year 3. The loan is somewhat risky, and reduces the standard deviation of the entrepreneur's cash flow at harvest to $3 million. Assume the correlation of the entrepreneur's risk with the market remains at 0.4.
   c. An investor will contribute $400,000 in exchange for enough equity to generate an expected return equal to the CAPM required return.
   d. An investor will contribute $700,000 in exchange for enough equity to generate an expected return equal to the CAPM required return plus $100,000 of present value.

   Discuss your results, considering also how the entrepreneur's interest in control or private risk aversion might affect the relative values and choice. Also, compare your results to the result in Problem 11-1, part (c).

3. Suppose a venture is subject to constant returns to scale over a range of investment levels from $500,000 to $2.5 million. Above or below those levels, venture rates of return are lower. How should the entrepreneur or a prospective investor use financial considerations to decide on the scale of the venture:

   a. Assuming that the entrepreneur would be the only investor in the venture?
   b. Assuming that the entrepreneur would share risk and return proportionally with an outside investor?
   c. Assuming that an investor would be willing to purchase all of the equity and hire the entrepreneur?

   How would you expect the sizes of the ventures to be different under these three scenarios?

4. Suppose the risk-free rate of interest is 4 percent per year, the market risk premium is 5.5 percent per year, and the market standard deviation is 14 percent. A venture has an approximate beta of 2.0 based on its cost, and a correlation of 0.25 with the market and an expected return on invested capital of 22 percent per year. Total cost is $3 million at time zero. Expected harvest is at year 3.

   a. How much of the equity would a well-diversified investor require in exchange for investing $1.5 million in the venture? What is the true beta of the investor's investment, based on equilibrium holding period returns?
   b. Suppose the entrepreneur needed to raise $800,000 in capital to be used by the venture and was willing to sell 30 percent of the equity. How much more than $800,000 would a diversified investor pay to acquire the equity?
   c. How would your answer change if the entrepreneur were willing to sell 49 percent of the equity? How much would the entrepreneur need to invest, and for what share of the equity?
   d. Assuming the entrepreneur will base his decision to pursue the venture on opportunity cost of capital, how much other wealth would the entrepreneur need to have

available for investing in the market to make the investment in part (c) economically viable?

5. Consider a venture with expected cash flow in year 6 of $10 million and standard deviation of cash flow of $5.5 million. Assume that an entrepreneur plans to invest $1 million in the venture and the remaining $500,000 of her total wealth in a market index. The annual risk-free rate is 4 percent, the annual market rate is 11 percent, and the one-year standard deviation of market returns is 14 percent. The correlation between the venture and the market is 0.3. Use Valuation Template 5 to assess the effects of the following changes on the value of an entrepreneur's interest in a venture. Find the base value and treat each change as incremental to the preceding one.

   a. Time to harvest can be shortened to five years. Doing so would reduce expected cash flow to $8.5 million, and standard deviation of cash flow to $5 million.

   b. The same change would reduce the total required investment to $900,000. The entrepreneur can shift the savings to investment in the market index.

   c. The entrepreneur can bring in an outside investor who offers to contribute $500,000 in exchange for 30 percent of the equity. The entrepreneur would invest the savings in the market index.

   d. The entrepreneur believes the investor would accept a share of equity, in exchange for the $500,000 investment, which would result in a NPV to the investor of $150,000 based on the CAPM required return. Any additional savings would be invested in the market index by the entrepreneur

   e. The entrepreneur also believes that the investor would be willing to purchase 80 percent of the equity on terms that would give the investor a NPV of $250,000 based on the CAPM required return. Any cash generated for the entrepreneur would be invested in the market index.

   f. Finally, the entrepreneur could sell the 80 percent interest to an active investor who would require an annual expected return of 15 percent. The entrepreneur believes that active investor involvement would enable the venture to be harvested one year sooner (in four years instead of five), would yield the same expected cash flow, but would reduce the standard deviation of cash flows to $4 million.

   Discuss your results. Do you think financial structure and the choice of investor are important to the entrepreneur? Assuming the effects of these contract changes cannot be estimated with much precision, what lessons can you still draw?

6. Consider a venture that requires $2 million in capital, including $1.7 million in cash and $300,000 of human capital. Suppose an investor proposes to provide all $1.7 million of the needed cash in exchange for convertible preferred stock with a liquidation preference. The preference would pay the investor 3 times ("3X") her initial investment at harvest, so for each dollar she invested, she would be entitled to receive three dollars before any returns would go to the entrepreneur. The preferred stock is convertible to 20 percent of common equity. At the time of harvest, the investor can choose to receive either three times her initial investment (in cash) or 20 percent of equity (which she sells for cash), whichever is greater. However, if the venture does not do well, she cannot receive more than 100 percent of the total harvest value of the venture. To evaluate the proposed contract, you have constructed the following table, which sets out the likely scenarios of total harvest value, and their probabilities of occurring.

Scenarios	Probability	
Scenario 1: Best case	10%	$40,000,000
Scenario 2	15%	$20,000,000
Scenario 3	20%	$10,000,000
Scenario 4	25%	$4,000,000
Scenario 5: Worst case	30%	$0
	100%	

The risk-free rate is 4 percent per year, the market rate is 9 percent, the annualized standard deviation of the market is 14 percent. Assume that the correlation between market returns and any financial claims on the venture is 0.3.

a. Use the scenario data and contract terms to compute the expected cash flow and cash flow standard deviation of the financial claims of the investor and the entrepreneur. Then use the results along with Valuation Template 5 to value the financial claims.

b. Suppose, instead, that the preferred shares have a 1X preference and are convertible to 35 percent of common equity. Redo the analysis and valuations.

c. Alternatively, suppose the investor receives 40 percent of common equity, with no liquidation preference. Redo the analysis and valuations.

d. Finally, suppose the investor receive 36 percent of common equity with no liquidation preference, but with enough warrants to raise the investor's fractional ownership interest by an additional 30 percent. The warrants can be exercised only if the venture achieves the best case scenario harvest value. Otherwise the investor's interest is 36 percent.

Discuss how the different contracts affect the values of the investor's and entrepreneur's interests. Explain why the values change in the way they do. Given your results, why do you think many new venture financing contracts include liquidation preferences for investors and why do you think entrepreneurs often receive warrants they can exercise if the venture does well?

7. Consider the following three contracts between an entrepreneur and a very wealthy business angel (who would be well-diversified, even after investing in the venture):

• Contract 1: The investor would invest $1 million in exchange for preferred stock with a liquidation preference of two times ("2X") the initial investment. The stock would be convertible at time of harvest to 40 percent of the common equity. The angel would convert if doing so resulted in receiving a higher share of harvest cash flows. The entrepreneur would invest $800 thousand in the venture, including $360 thousand as the value of human capital in alternative use. (You can think of the entrepreneur as drawing no salary, although it would be equivalent for the entrepreneur to fund a salary from his portion of investment in the venture).

• Contract 2: The investor would invest an additional $240 thousand, which would be sufficient to enable the entrepreneur to receive a salary with a present value of $240 thousand. This would enable the entrepreneur to reduce investment in the venture and invest more in the market. The investor still would have a 2X liquidation preference (on a higher total investment) and convertibility to 40 percent of common equity.

• Contract 3: The investor would make the same $1.24 million investment. The liquidation preference would be reduced to 1X. The shares would be convertible to 30% of common equity at harvest. In addition, if total harvest value is more than $10 million, the investor could exercise warrants that would raise his ownership stake to 50 percent. The exercise price of the warrants would be negligible.

Suppose that both parties expect the venture to be harvested in three years, and expect total harvest date cash flows to be exponentially distributed with a mean of $5 million (You can use *Venture.SIM*™ to model this). The risk-free rate is 3 percent per year, the market rate is 9 percent, and annualized market standard deviation is 14 percent. The venture, which is involved in biotechnology, is believed to have a correlation of only 0.1 with the market. Under each alternative contract, the angel investor expects to invest an additional $500,000 of human capital, which is not reflected in the direct investment or the contract terms. To compensate, the investor needs a return on financial capital that has a net present value of at least $500,000. The entrepreneur has total wealth of $3.5 million.

a. Simulate the cash flows of the various claims.

b. Chart the simulation results (sorted by total harvest cash flow) and discuss how the different contracts affect the cash flows and risk of the parties.

c. Value the alternative contracts. Which one would you select, and why?

8. Compare the following three investment alternatives in terms of the percent of equity each investor would need in order to provide a normal (breakeven) return on capital and cover costs related to due diligence, making the initial investment, and ongoing involvement with the venture.

- Alternative 1: A passive investor would provide $1.5 million of the $2.0 million total investment, and would require a return high enough to compensate for $150,000 of due diligence and other costs of evaluating and making the investment. In this case, the expected harvest value would be $14 million, with a standard deviation of $10 million.
- Alternative 2: An angel investor group would provide $1.5 million and contribute significant effort to improving the venture. The investor would need a return high enough to cover the $500,000 present valued cost of these efforts. The involvement would increase the expected return at harvest to $15 million and reduce the risk to a standard deviation of $8 million. Members of the angel group would all be well-diversified after their investments.
- Alternative 3: A venture capital fund would invest $1.5 million. The general partner assesses an annual management fee of 2.5 percent of capital under management (which is revalued annually so you can estimate the total management fee as the first-year fee times the years to harvest). The general partner also retains a carried interest of 20 percent of any capital appreciation at harvest.

Note, in comparing these alternatives rather than simulating the exact contracts you should develop a rough estimate of value to the entrepreneur by assuming that the risk of the investment is prorated; 20 percent of the risk to the general partner and 80 percent of it to the limited partners. With a venture capital investor, expected cash flow would remain at $15 million, but risk would be reduced to a standard deviation of $7 million.

The entrepreneur has total wealth of $1.5 million, $500,000 of which must be invested in the venture. The risk-free rate is 5 percent, the market rate is 11 percent, and market standard deviation is 14 percent. The venture's correlation with the market is 0.2, and it is expected to be harvested in 5 years.

a. Given the impacts of the choices on expected return and risk, how do they affect value to the entrepreneur? Determine the percent of equity each investor would require and the value of the entrepreneur's claim in each case.

b. Which alternative would you select and why?

c. Do you think simulation could produce better estimates of value? If so, explain for each alternative how simulation could help and identify any biases due to focusing on expected cash flows and risk for the entire venture rather than for each financial claim.

NOTES

1. You can see from Figure 10-6 that $5 million is roughly the market value of the hypothetical venture in the example we have been using.

2. The beta can be derived from the beta of .41 that is shown in Figure 10-6. That beta is based on investing $5.683 million in the venture. With only $2 million invested, the standard deviation of holding-period returns on the actual investment is increased by a factor of 2.84 (i.e., 5683/2000), which results in the 1.178 beta.

3. Except for rounding, the .415 beta is the same as in Figure 10-6. Also, note that you could determine the 35.2 percent weight of investment in the venture directly from Figure 10-6. It is the reciprocal of the 2.84 factor described in the previous footnote.

4. See Figure 10-6.

5. We did not develop the expectations for changes in expected cash flow and risk directly. Rather, we modified the sales growth assumptions of the simulation model from Figure 10-4 and re-ran the simulation.

6. The figure is only a summary. To see the full valuation templates for the individual contracts, you need to open the Excel file on the Internet.

7. However, because this structure has the highest total value in Figure 11-6, the entrepreneur could consider a counter that maintains the equity shares but requires the investor to contribute more capital.

REFERENCES AND ADDITIONAL READING

BLACKWELL, DAVID W., AND DAVID S. KIDWELL. "An Investigation of Cost Differences Between Public Sales and Private Placements of Debt." *Journal of Financial Economics* (1988): 253–278.

BREALEY, RICHARD A., AND STEWART C. MYERS. *Principles of Corporate Finance.* 7th ed. New York: McGraw-Hill, 2003.

BYGRAVE, WILLIAM D., AND JEFFREY A. TIMMONS. *Venture Capital at the Crossroads.* Cambridge, MA: Harvard Business School Press, 1992.

GOLDER, STANLEY C. "Structuring and Pricing the Financing." In *Pratt's Guide to Venture Capital Sources.* 10th ed. Edited by Stanley E. Pratt and Jane K. Morris. Wellesley, MA: Venture Economics, n.d., pp. 79–88.

SAHLMAN, WILLIAM, HOWARD H. STEVENSON, MICHAEL J. ROBERTS, AND AMAR BHIDÉ. *The Entrepreneurial Venture.* Boston, MA: Harvard Business School Press, 1999.

Dealing with Information and Incentive Problems

A reputation, once broken, may possibly be repaired, but the world will always keep their eyes on the spot where the crack was. (Joseph Hall)

Learning Objectives

After reading this chapter you will be able to:

- Identify the information and incentive problems that impact new ventures.
- Recognize that three economic phenomena affect contracting: bounded rationality, adverse selection, and moral hazard.
- Understand how adverse selection problems arise in capital raising.
- Understand why an entrepreneur may underinvest in the firm.
- Understand how contracts and other mechanisms can address new venture information and incentive problems.
- Identify the conditions when particular contractual responses to information problems would arise.
- Explain the economic function of relational contracting, reputational capital, certification, monitoring, signaling, and organizational design.

Information and incentive problems are at the core of negotiations between entrepreneurs and investors. New venture markets are highly uncertain and influenced by unanticipated events. The parties may have different expectations about venture success and may have difficulty communicating their expectations to each other. Outside parties often cannot know whether, compared with expectations, venture performance is due to luck or managerial capability and effort. The financial economics literature refers to problems such as these as information problems.

Information problems affect start-ups in many ways. For example, a prospective entrepreneur may have an idea with obvious commercial value but be unable to protect it by patent or copyright. The entrepreneur cannot disclose the idea to prospective investors without risking its appropriation. How do entrepreneurs deal with such dilemmas? Also, how can investors determine the entrepreneur's true expectations or predict the amount and quality of effort the entrepreneur will apply once the investors have committed?

In addition to information problems, incentive conflicts can arise among new venture stakeholders. Conflicts can arise between the investors and the entrepreneur and among different investors. For example, an entrepreneur with a limited equity stake may not always act in the best interest of other shareholders. If outside financing is in the form of debt, the entrepreneur may want to take more risk than creditors would like. How can incentive problems such as these be overcome?

The distinction between information and incentive problems is fuzzy. In fact, every information problem arises because the parties may not have correct incentives to reveal what they know, and every incentive problem arises because the parties cannot costlessly acquire the information they need to evaluate performance.

A useful distinction exists between costs that arise *before* a contract is entered and those that arise *afterward.* Before the agreement, the problem is information. Each party is unsure about what the other knows. If the parties cannot overcome their concerns, they may be unable to reach an agreement.

After agreement is reached, the problem is incentives. A contract is sought in the first place because one party (or both) expects to make an investment in the venture. That investment is, to some extent, nonrecoverable, or "sunk," if the venture fails. Once an investment of financial or human capital is sunk, the investing party can no longer simply "walk away." Sunk investments create opportunities for others to act contrary to the best overall interest of the venture. Thus, incentive problems arise from the presence of the sunk investments.

Our first objective in this chapter is to place information and incentive problems into a general analytic framework. We then provide a structured way of thinking about solutions. Discussion is general and is tied to existing literature on the economics of contracting. In later chapters, we study how specific contract provisions affect the values of financial claims on the venture's cash flows. In Chapter 11, we saw how financial contracts can be used to allocate risk and return and to increase expected return. In this chapter, we view contracts as devices to create value by improving information flows and aligning the interests of the parties.

12.1 INFORMATION PROBLEMS, INCENTIVE PROBLEMS, AND FINANCIAL CONTRACTS

To assess the influences of information and incentive problems on new venture financial contracting, consider the notion of a perfect contract. A perfect contract is complete: It anticipates and provides for every contingency. Its terms bind the parties, so that neither party can try to renegotiate to take advantage of the other. The contract must contain sufficient detail so that a third party, such as a government entity, can fully enforce its provisions. A perfect contract is efficient in the sense that each risk is allocated to the party who can bear it at least cost, and, collectively, the contract terms exhaust the possibilities for mutual gain.

Financial Contracting with Known Symmetrical Beliefs

New venture financial contracts are far from perfect. They often include extensive lists of representations and warranties and complex contingency structures. Such provisions are designed to deal with information and incentive problems. They tend to be complex but incomplete, because they do not address every contingency. Complexity arises from efforts to address information and incentive problems. If the entrepreneur and investor share expectations, then even with uncertainty, their financial contract can be very simple. For a project without staged financing, the contract might reduce to a single statement regarding the fraction of harvest value the outside investor is to receive. For a project with staged financing, the contract needs to describe the conditions for follow-on investing but still can be simple.

Precontractual Information Costs

Information costs are precontractual costs associated with negotiating a contract. However, contracting between new venture parties is likely to be ongoing, and not just a one-time exercise. Information costs arise before any sunk investment is made in the agreement. They arise because the future is uncertain, because the parties may have different information and expectations, and because each party has an incentive to misrepresent their true information or beliefs.

Bounded Rationality   The parties to a venture cannot anticipate all of the contingencies the venture will face. Even if delineating the contingencies were possible theoretically, negotiating contract provisions to deal with each remote contingency would be too expensive to justify. Decision-makers weigh the costs and benefits and rationally stop short of explicitly contracting over all contingencies.

The idea that individuals have limited capacity to process information, deal with complexity, and pursue rational aims is referred to as bounded rationality.[1] To illustrate the implications of bounded rationality for venture financing, consider an entrepreneur who is seeking funding. Product development time may be short or long. Quality of the resulting product and consumer demand may be high or low. Rivals may be successful or unsuccessful in their efforts to compete. Catastrophic events (death of the entrepreneur, war, etc.) may intervene. The funding needs of the venture depend on all of these factors. In some scenarios, the investor will be eager to provide funding, but not in others. In some scenarios, the entrepreneur would prefer to abandon the venture.

If the costs of contracting were low, the parties could develop an elaborate list of contingencies and could design a contract that would specify the response to each. Bounded rationality explains why entrepreneurs and investors do not try to anticipate all contingencies and design contracts that address them.

Information Asymmetry   Each party to a contract has private information that is relevant to the value of the relationship. Information asymmetry means one party has information that the other party lacks and cannot easily acquire. Asymmetric information can prevent a bargain from being struck. If a bargain is struck, asymmetric information can cause risk and return to be allocated less efficiently than if information were shared. The problem is not just that the information is held asymmetrically, but also that each party has an incentive to misrepresent what he or she knows. Consequently, each is concerned with exploitation by the other and is reluctant to commit to the venture. The parties' incentives to misrepresent make asymmetry difficult to overcome.

The used car market is a well-known example of how asymmetric information can disrupt a market.[2] Sellers of used cars usually have an information advantage in that they know more about their cars' quality than do prospective buyers. An owner of a high-quality used car would like to convey the information to prospective buyers but cannot do so easily. Merely claiming that the car is a good one is not enough because all sellers can and do make similar claims, regardless of the qualities of their cars. The result of information asymmetry is adverse selection. Bad products force good ones out of the market. Buyers cannot distinguish high- from low-quality cars. Consequently, both good and bad cars must sell for the same price, a price that reflects the average quality of the cars being sold. At that price, however, owners of high-quality cars will not want to sell. In the extreme, only the lowest quality cars can be sold.

The adverse selection problem applies directly to the market for new venture financing.[3] Most new ventures do not have enough of a track record for an outside investor easily to assess their merits. Entrepreneurs are apt to compete for investment funds by presenting optimistic projections and withholding negative information they may have learned.

To compensate for overly optimistic claims of entrepreneurs, venture capitalists and other investors sometimes use high hurdle rates to value the entrepreneur's projected cash flows.[4] However, reliance on high hurdle rates does not solve the adverse selection problem. Like the owners of high-quality used cars, entrepreneurs with superior opportunities and realistic projections are confronted with undervaluation and may decide not to pursue the opportunities. Those with inferior ventures, but who nonetheless can project overly rosy prospects, remain in the market.

Information asymmetry can also be a problem for entrepreneurs. An entrepreneur usually cannot know why a prospective investor is interested in the venture. The investor may seriously be interested, or may only be seeking to assess it as a competitive threat. Entrepreneurs claim that investors sometimes only get involved in a venture to keep it from reaching the market. This could happen if the investor was involved with another venture that targeted the same market.

Before concluding that you would not want to deal with either of these people, you should note that neither one may be trying deliberately to take unfair advantage. Many entrepreneurs are optimistic. Some are more self-confident than they should be. Many investors have experience with failed investments and are inundated with proposals from overoptimistic, would-be entrepreneurs.

Williamson (1975) refers to the difficulty of communicating private information as information impactedness. Information is impacted when one party is uncertain about what the other knows and the parties cannot easily communicate what they know to each other. Impacted information raises the cost of market exchange and contracting because prospective trading partners fear being taken advantage of. To complete the exchange, one or both parties must expend resources to overcome real or perceived information advantages. For new ventures, the expenditures often take the form of due diligence investigations in advance of contracting or negotiation of contractual contingencies that mitigate the value of information advantages.[5]

Overconfidence and Entrepreneurs

"A large proportion of our positive activities depend on spontaneous optimism rather than on mathematical expectation...if animal spirits are dimmed and the spontaneous optimism falters, leaving us to depend on nothing but mathematical expectation, enterprise will fade and die."—J. M. Keynes

Entrepreneurs enter and persist in businesses despite lower initial earnings and lower earnings growth than they can correctly expect from salaried employment. Hamilton (2000), for example, finds a 35 percent earnings differential for individuals who have owned their own businesses for ten years. Why are entrepreneurs apparently willing to work for so many years for earnings less than their opportunity cost? Similarly, Moskowitz and Vissing-Jørgensen (2002) find that returns to private equity are no higher than returns to public equity. They question why entrepreneurial households willingly invest substantial amounts in a single privately held firm with a risk-return tradeoff that seemingly is unattractive, compared with the public equity market.

Perhaps entrepreneurs make these choices because of their tolerance for risk (skewness preference) and the value they place on nonpecuniary benefits associated with being one's own boss. Bitner, et al. (2002) suggest that entrepreneurs may use their large ownership shares to signal effort and commitment to outside investors. Others point to an apparently common personality trait of entrepreneurs: Over-confidence. Cooper, Wo, and Dunkelberg (1988), using data from nearly 3000 entrepreneurs, report that entrepreneurs, "perceived their prospects as very favorable, with 81% seeing odds of success of at least 7 out of 10. A remarkable 33 percent see odds of success of 10 out of 10." Demonstrating their over-optimism, well over half of the entrepreneurs report that they are more likely to be successful than the average entrepreneur. In a cross-cultural study that included Asian managers of several nationalities, Wright and Phillips (1980) confirm the ubiquity of overconfidence.

Bernardo and Welch (2001) offer a social-Darwinist sorting explanation for why seemingly irrational overconfident behavior persists in society. Entrepreneurs are less likely to imitate their peers (i.e., they ignore the "herd"). By exploring their environment, they reveal private information about themselves or their project. While their over-optimism is not warranted, and many of them fail, the information that is produced through their risk-taking provides a positive externality for society and fosters a more rapid rate of innovation in the society.

Sources: See end-of-chapter references.

Example: Adverse Selection in Capital Raising

Differences in expectations can make capital raising difficult and can cause new venture opportunities to be foregone. Underinvestment occurs when a venture or a public corporation has an attractive opportunity but lacks sufficient capital to pursue it, and when outside investors are uncertain about the value of the existing assets of the venture or corporation. In such cases, raising capital is excessively costly, and good investments may be foregone.

Public companies can mitigate this underinvestment problem by maintaining financial slack. Financial slack is liquidity in the form of cash, near-cash assets, or unused low-risk borrowing capacity. In effect, financial slack is like a small capital market within the organization that can be less expensive to use than the external capital market. However, absence of financial slack is a hallmark of new ventures. Consequently, the underinvestment problem can be more severe for new ventures than for public corporations.

Whose Interest Do Managers Serve?   Not all shareholders of public companies are the same. Some own the stock now, and others will buy it in the future. Even among those who currently own the stock, some can be expected to sell in the near future, others to maintain their current investments over long periods, and still others to maintain their fractional ownership by purchasing new shares whenever the company issues new equity.

In a public corporation, it is unclear which group's managers will try to benefit. If managers act in the interest of current, active shareholders, they will not act in ways that lower short-run value, even to increase value in the long run. If managers act in the interest of investors who try to maintain their fractional ownership, they will accept all positive NPV investments. By doing so, the managers effectively try to maximize the intrinsic value of a share, even if this reduces market value in the short run. If they act in the interest of passive investors who simply maintain their share holdings, then they will attempt to take advantage of differences between market value and intrinsic value by having the company issue shares when the market overvalues them. Doing so successfully benefits existing passive shareholders. These shareholders gain from managers' efforts to take advantage of new investors who are less well informed about intrinsic value.

Outside investors' concern that managers may be acting in the interest of passive shareholders creates an adverse selection problem. An investor who buys when the firm is selling is likely to pay too much relative to intrinsic value.

An early-stage entrepreneur is much like a passive corporate investor, who seeks to raise capital, holding his own interest constant. Closer to harvesting, the entrepreneur (and other existing investors) may be more like an active investor, who is concerned primarily with high near-term value. In either case, the entrepreneur has an incentive to raise capital when the venture is overvalued. Thus, at either point, investors in new ventures face the risk of paying too much.

The Underinvestment Problem   Consider an entrepreneur's decision to seek new equity capital. The entrepreneur may need the money to finance a positive NPV growth opportunity or may desire to capture a gain by selling overvalued shares to outside investors. Because investors cannot be certain why an entrepreneur is issuing new shares, they must assume that the entrepreneur thinks the venture may be overvalued. Consequently, when the entrepreneur seeks new equity, investors may regard the action as an indication that the entrepreneur thinks investors will overvalue the shares. The typical result is that the investor will demand a larger ownership stake in exchange for investing.

The investor's response is problematic for a new venture that is not overvalued and needs capital to finance growth. The investor's reaction raises the cost of capital for the venture and can cause the entrepreneur to forego growth opportunities that would be accepted if the venture could issue shares at a price that reflected their intrinsic value. If the entrepreneur goes ahead with the financing, the investor will realize an unexpected gain in the form of a wealth transfer from the entrepreneur. That is, some of the value of the venture's growth opportunity is transferred to the new investor.

You might think that an entrepreneur could enhance value by stating an intention not to engage in this kind of opportunism. However, the simple claim would not be credible to the investor. Even if the entrepreneur planned not to engage in opportunism, information about the entrepreneur's intent is impacted. Later in the chapter, we examine ways of using contracts to address problems related to impacted information.

A Numerical Example   In Figure 12-1, we use a numerical example to demonstrate why impacted information can cause underinvestment in a new venture. The example concerns a venture in which an entrepreneur already has made a significant investment. Venture assets-in-place reflect the value of the entrepreneur's investment. The venture now has an opportunity to grow but requires $600,000 of outside capital from a venture capital investor to do so. The new financing would be the venture's first round of outside financing. As the figure shows, the values of assets-in-place and the growth opportunity depend on which state of the world (one good, one bad) occurs. At time zero, when outside financing is being sought, the entrepreneur already knows which of the two states will occur. The venture capitalist only knows that the two are equally likely. The venture capitalist will learn the true state at time one.

Suppose the entrepreneur tells the venture capitalist that he plans to pursue the growth opportunity no matter which state occurs. Doing so seems to make sense because the opportunity has a positive NPV in either state. The figure shows that the resulting value of the venture is $850,000 and that the respective values of the entrepreneur's shares and the venture capitalist's shares are $250,000 and $600,000. Because we assume that the venture capital market is competitive, all of the NPV from the investment accrues to the entrepreneur. That is, the venture capitalist realizes a NPV of zero on the first-round investment, and the entrepreneur captures the full NPV of the growth opportunity. The venture capitalist pays $600,000 for an asset (the new shares) that is worth $600,000.

It turns out that this is not the best strategy if the entrepreneur is trying to maximize the value for himself. By looking at the values of the entrepreneur's shares and the venture capitalist's shares conditional on which state of the world occurs, you can see that it is better for the entrepreneur not to raise capital in the good state. The entrepreneur's shares will be worth $300,000 if the growth opportunity is passed up but only $288,000 if the first-round investment is made. Furthermore, the entrepreneur will want to go ahead with the growth opportunity if he knows the bad state will occur, because the value of the entrepreneur's shares will be $212,000 if the new investment is made but only $100,000 if it is not.

This is not an equilibrium. By investing in growth in the bad state and not in the good, the entrepreneur is attempting to exploit an information advantage over the venture capitalist. If the venture capitalist goes along with this, she will be paying $600,000 for an asset that is only worth $508,000. To protect herself from opportunism, the venture capitalist must demand a larger ownership fraction, so that the $600,000 investment is actually worth $600,000. Because, in the bad state, the entire firm is only worth $720,000, this means the entrepreneur's share can only be worth $120,000 in the bad state.

Paradoxically, the entrepreneur ends up worse off than if he could commit to issue no matter what. Faced with the potential for opportunistic behavior, the venture capitalist reacts in a way that reduces the expected value of the entrepreneur's claim to $210,000 instead of $250,000. Consequently, the entrepreneur would be willing to spend up to $40,000 on contractual or other mechanisms to help overcome the problem.

Appropriate mechanisms can take a variety of forms. One is for the venture to maintain enough financial slack to finance the growth opportunity internally. With adequate slack, the entrepreneur can go ahead with his investment plans without concern about adverse reactions to capital-raising efforts. However, maintaining a high level of financial slack is unlikely to be

The New Venture Underinvestment Problem*

Assumptions:

There are two equally likely states of nature: State 1 and State 2.

The entrepreneur learns the true state at time 0.

The venture capital investor learns the true state at time 1.

Asset Values:

	State 1	State 2
Venture assets-in-place (in thousands)	$a = \$300$	$a = \$100$
NPV of first-round outside financing (in thousands)	$g = \quad\$80$	$g = \quad\$20$

The venture has no financial slack ($S = 0$).

The opportunity requires investment ($I = \$600$).

So the entrepreneur must raise equity from a venture capitalist ($E = \$600$).

Suppose the entrepreneur states at time zero that he is seeking outside financing and plans to undertake the expansion no matter which state occurs.

Then the value of the venture at time zero, V', equals $250.

$$V' = (\$300 + \$100)/2 + (\$80 + \$20)/2 = \$250$$

and the value of outside equity, E, equals $600.

Resulting total value of the venture, including the new investment, is $850.

The values of the entrepreneur's shares and venture capitalist's shares when the true state is realized are as follow:

If State 1 occurs, then the total value of the venture, V, is $980, $(a + g + E)$.

$$V^{\text{Entrepreneur}} = V \times V'/(V' + E) = \$980 \times \$250/\$850 = \$288$$
$$V^{\text{Venture Capital}} = V \times V'/(V' + E) = \$980 \times \$600/\$850 = \$692$$

If State 2 occurs, then total value of the venture is $720.

$$V^{\text{Entrepreneur}} = V \times V'/(V' + E) = \$720 \times \$250/\$850 = \$212$$
$$V^{\text{Venture Capital}} = V \times V'/(V' + E) = \$720 \times \$600/\$850 = \$508$$

---

*Adapted from the corporate finance example of Myers and Majluf (1984).

Figure 12-1 The underinvestment problem *(Continues)*

The entrepreneur's shares and the venture capitalists's shares are correctly priced at the outset.

$$V' = (\$288 + \$212)/2 = \$250$$
$$E = (\$692 + \$508)/2 = \$600$$

In this case, the entrepreneur's decision to raise capital tells the venture capitalist nothing about what the entrepreneur knows the true state to be.

Raising capital in both states is not the best deal for the entrepreneur.

Payoffs to the entrepreneur

Payoff	Issue and invest ($E = 600$)	Do not issue ($E = 0$)
$V^{Entrepreneur}$ in State 1	$288	$300
$V^{Entrepreneur}$ in State 2	$212	$100

The entrepreneur is better off if he does not raise capital in State 1, but does raise capital in State 2.

Equilibrium payoffs:

But the venture capitalist will recognize that seeking financing is a signal that the entrepreneur knows that State 2 will occur. The venture capitalist will not invest $600 to receive value of only $508. Instead, the venture capitalist will demand a bigger fraction of the venture's equity in exchange for the $600 investment, such that the entrepreneur's shares are worth only $120 in State 2.

Payoff	Issue and invest ($E = \$600$)	Do not issue ($E = \$0$)
$V^{Entrepreneur}$ in State 1	–	$300
$V^{Entrepreneur}$ in State 2	$120	–

A growth opportunity worth $80 is passed up.
The entrepreneur is worse off than had he been able to commit to always invest, $V'' = \$210$.

Figure 12-1   The underinvestment problem *(Continued)*

possible for most new ventures. Other solutions could include using contract provisions to limit the asymmetry of information or to credibly commit the entrepreneur to pursue the growth opportunity. All such mechanisms involve costs. For example, a contract provision may be inefficient in other respects that limit the flexibility.

Implications for New Venture Financing Typically, an entrepreneur seeks outside financing only after he has developed the venture to a point where investors can estimate its value and when disclosing critical aspects of the venture to outsiders would not result in the opportunity being appropriated. The assets in place are the sunk investment of the entrepreneur. Their value is not necessarily related closely to the amount of financial and human capital the entrepreneur has invested. An investor who receives an equity stake in exchange for providing capital participates in the values of both the new investment and the assets-in-place. As you can imagine, if the investor overvalues the assets-in-place, the entrepreneur will want to sell new equity because doing so enables the entrepreneur to recoup some of the sunk investment.

Prospective investors in ventures with sunk investments are likely to be concerned that entrepreneurs will try to mislead them into overvaluation. They can be expected to respond much the way investors in the capital market react to announcements to issue equity. You can see evidence of this in the bargaining contests that are common between entrepreneurs and investors. Entrepreneurs present optimistic projections, and investors value the projections using discount rates that build in "fudge factors."

The problem is most significant when the going concern value of assets-in-place is highly uncertain and large compared to salvage value. The problem does not arise if the entrepreneur has not already made a significant investment. If a venture with no sunk investment would have a negative NPV for the investor, it also would have a negative NPV for the entrepreneur. There would be little reason for an entrepreneur to propose such a venture to an investor. An entrepreneur with no assets-in-place would not pursue a negative NPV opportunity. However, this is partly because equity shares in the venture are assumed to be proportional to investments. The strong conclusion breaks down once we allow for the parties to contribute and be compensated in different ways. For example, the entrepreneur is likely to contribute primarily human capital and to draw a salary from the venture. If the salary exceeds opportunity cost, then the entrepreneur does have an incentive to pursue negative NPV investments, even if there are no assets-in-place.

The entrepreneur and the investor need to find ways of overcoming investor concern about paying too much (the adverse selection problem). Common solutions include staging investments with abandonment options, allowing the investor to be directly involved with the venture, and other financial contracting provisions that mitigate information advantages. The investor can overcome concern that the entrepreneur may want to pursue a negative NPV venture by ensuring that the entrepreneur's compensation is less than what it would be in alternative employment and that the entrepreneur's return is high only if the venture is a success. When, as is almost always the case, the venture involves a sunk investment by the entrepreneur, the solution is more complex. The entrepreneur might want to pursue the project even at a low salary if doing so could return some of the sunk investment. We explore solutions to information problems more fully next.

Postcontractual Incentive Problems

Once a new venture financial contract has been entered or a sunk investment has been made, incentives change. The parties may act in ways that are not consistent with their original intentions. Incentive problems arise when contracts are incomplete and when parties cannot monitor performance perfectly. Such problems are known, more generally, as moral hazard. Anticipating moral hazard is a first step toward finding ways to use contracts and financial arrangements to minimize their costs.

Health insurance is the classic example of moral hazard.[6] A person who is fully responsible for medical bills makes rational value-maximizing tradeoffs in deciding when and whether to visit a doctor, for example. The person makes expenditures only when expected benefit exceeds expected cost. But with health insurance, the tradeoff changes. A person who is fully insured and does not regard the time spent on doctor visits as a cost will seek medical advice and treatment for every symptom or illness. The use of medical services increases. In some cases, the expected benefit of treatment is below expected cost, including cost the insurer will have to bear. The increased use of doctors due to health insurance is moral hazard.

Financial contracts give rise to similar moral hazard problems. For example, once an investor commits to a venture and shares in the benefits of its success, an entrepreneur may feel less urgency to work toward achieving that success. Equity investors share the benefit of any effort the entrepreneur expends. It makes sense that the entrepreneur would devote less effort than if she were the exclusive beneficiary of her efforts. Shifting from outside equity to outside debt financing changes the entrepreneur's incentives, but if the debt is risky, it does not remove the moral hazard.

Risky outside financing always alters the entrepreneur's incentives. The entrepreneur weighs the cost of effort, not against the benefits to all investors, but against the private benefits of the entrepreneur. Consequently, the entrepreneur may make choices that are not in the best interest of investors.[7]

Moral hazard problems arise from incentive conflicts and from specific investments that are not recoverable. In some cases, the investments give rise to incentive conflicts. In others, contract terms give rise to incentive conflicts even though no prior specific investment has been made. In effect, the contract creates the specific investment.

Specific Investment Specific investments are investments that support a given activity or relationship and are valuable in the activity or relationship but have little alternative use value. Once these investments are made, they are, in effect, sunk.

An example is an entrepreneur's investment in machinery and other resources that are particularly useful for making customized circuit boards for a customer.[8] Suppose the amortized quarterly economic cost of the machinery and other resources is $4000 and the circuit board sales contract between the entrepreneur and the customer calls for the customer to pay $7000 quarterly. This means the economic gain for the entrepreneur is $3000 per quarter. The $3000 gain is an economic rent. Economic rent is an *ex ante* concept that is measured as the excess of expected return over the opportunity cost of resources committed. In deciding whether to make the initial investment to produce the circuit boards, the entrepreneur looks to expected economic rent and commits the resources only if the economic rent is positive. Thus, the economic rent is what makes the NPV of the investment positive.

Now, consider a scenario in which the resource commitment to manufacture the circuit boards already has been made. Economic rent is no longer relevant to any decision of the entrepreneur. Instead, the concern is whether the return is sufficient to cover the alternative use value, or salvage value, of the resources. Suppose the resources have a salvage value of $2500 per quarter. The $7000 quarterly revenue is more than sufficient to justify continuing to use the machine to make customized circuit boards. The $4500 difference between revenue and salvage value is as a quasi-rent. A quasi-rent is an *ex post* concept. It measures the difference between the revenue received and the minimum revenue necessary to justify keeping the machinery in its current use.

Quasi-rents exist because of sunk investments. An asset that generates no economic rent, or even a negative economic rent, still could generate a positive quasi-rent if some of the investment was sunk. Moral hazard problems are related to the existence of quasi-rents. Once a specific investment is made, a customer can try to renegotiate the terms of the contract. In this example, since the entrepreneur will continue to supply circuit boards as long as the quarterly return is at least $2500, the customer who is paying $7000 has an incentive to appropriate the quasi-rent by threatening not to purchase unless the entrepreneur reduces the price. The attempt to appropriate the quasi-rent is an example of moral hazard that arises after a specific investment is made. Note, however, that the entire quasi-rent may not be appropriable. Suppose another customer is willing to buy the same circuit boards if the price is reduced to $5000 per quarter. In that case, only $2000 of the $4500 quasi-rent is appropriable.

The example shows that the parties to a new venture must be sensitive to the presence of specific investments. Such an investment is always potentially appropriable. The potential for appropriation depends on the extent to which the investment is specific to the venture. If the investment is not specific, competition can prevent appropriation. If it is specific, then the investing party faces the risk of appropriation, and the contract structure may need to address the risk. Business (and litigation) history contains many examples of sophisticated firms dealing with problems attributable to specific investments. Later in the chapter, we study how contact provisions and organizational choices can be used to address incentive problems related to specific investment.

Small Numbers Bargaining   Market exchange works best when large numbers of buyers and sellers vie to complete transactions. The market for initial outside financing of some new ventures can be such a market. Many entrepreneurs have ideas and business plans. For any one of them, there may be many potential sources of financing.

It is easy to see how the presence of large numbers of potential investors facilitates exchange. Suppose, as a prospective entrepreneur, you are concerned about losing control of an opportunity if you "shop it around" too early. By making an initial investment of your own, you can advance the venture to a point where it will be clear to others that you have a sustainable advantage in the product market, and the merits of the idea will be more apparent to prospective investors. But any investment you make at this early stage is likely to be nonsalvageable at the time you begin to negotiate for financing.

As the entrepreneur, you must balance the risk of losing control of the opportunity against the risk of losing a return on a sunk investment. With a large number of prospective investors competing to participate in the venture, you do not need to be concerned about making value-enhancing investments before you have agreed to a contract with an investor. If you are right about the merits of the idea, competition among investors will result in terms that more than compensate for the sunk investment. The difficulty arises when the number of prospective investors is small. Then, the entrepreneur cannot rely on competition to give her an opportunity to recover sunk investment. In fact, sunk investment, while it may add to value and help to secure a first-mover advantage, invites appropriation by an outside investor. In the extreme case, if only one prospective investor is positioned to participate in the venture, the entire sunk investment is appropriable.

At the initial stage of securing outside financing, the large number of entrepreneurs and investors vying for deals can limit the potential for opportunism. However, at any given time and for any given venture, the actual number of prospective investors can be low. Although countries like the U.S. and UK have hundreds of venture capital firms, most of them specialize both geographically and by industry. By focusing their efforts, they can be more effective participants in the market for new venture finance. Furthermore, venture capital funds have definite life cycles—periods when they actively seek new investment opportunities and others when they focus attention on managing existing investments or on harvesting. With these restrictions, the number of feasible investors shrinks rapidly, and the potential for opportunism increases.[9]

This partially explains why certain kinds of entrepreneurial ventures and venture capital investors tend to concentrate geographically (e.g., around Boston, the Silicon Valley, and Oxford, England). Geographic concentration increases the number of prospective investors in those areas, mitigating the potential for opportunistic behavior. It also partially explains why countries and regions with limited funds may have difficulty motivating people to undertake new ventures.

Having large numbers of competitors in the market vying for involvement in the initial stage of a venture does not prevent opportunism in later-stage negotiations. Many transactions that involve ongoing activities can evolve from large numbers to small numbers doing the actual bargaining. In general terms, the winner of the first round may gain a first-mover advantage that would make it difficult for rivals to compete in later-stage negotiations. It is not useful to characterize this practice as opportunistic, particularly if the pattern is characteristic of the market.

Still, in new venture financing, the potential for opportunism is large. Investors are unlikely to agree at the outset to provide all needed financing and to place no restrictions on the entrepreneur. To obtain initial financing, the entrepreneur may be asked to provide an abandonment option that the investor can exercise at its sole discretion, and possibly other rights, such as the right to acquire control or to terminate the entrepreneur.

In an exchange with an investor whom the entrepreneur does not know it seems almost inconceivable that the entrepreneur would agree to such provisions. Why do venture financing contracts give so much discretion and control to investors, when it would appear that potential opportunism could be limited by a more complex contract structure that might give similar rights but only under certain well-specified conditions? Apparently, entrepreneurs in such arrangements do not fear opportunism by investors, but why not? The answer is threefold. First, if the venture is successful, the entrepreneur can pursue other financing, even if the investor withdraws. Second, the investor needs to preserve a good working relationship with the entrepreneur to achieve maximum value. Third, any investor who wishes to be involved repeatedly in new ventures must avoid gaining a reputation for behaving opportunistically.

Example: Moral Hazard in Organizations

An entrepreneur must decide how much effort to commit to a venture and how much to commit to other activities. When the entrepreneur does not rely on outside capital, she bears the full costs and benefits of these choices. If investing more effort increases value, the entrepreneur realizes the benefit. If the entrepreneur decides to devote time to other activities, she realizes the cost.

Involving outside investors, whether they are equity holders or holders of risky debt, weakens the link between effort and rewards and causes changes in the entrepreneur's behavior. This change is a moral hazard problem. It arises after the contract is entered.

The Agency Cost of Outside Equity   Jensen and Meckling (1976) explore the effects of increasing outside ownership as a utility-maximization problem. They look first at how the behavior of the entrepreneur (owner-manager) changes when outside equity is added. They extend the analysis to consider the choice between outside equity and outside debt. Figure 12-2 provides a graphical summary of part of their analysis.

Initially, the entrepreneur owns 100 percent of the equity of an all-equity firm. The first panel of Figure 12-2 depicts the choices available to the entrepreneur. By applying all of her effort and other resources to the venture, she can achieve maximum value for the venture of V, measured on the vertical axis in the figure. Think of V as the present value of the entrepreneur's wealth, including human capital. Alternatively, she can allocate effort and resources to other activities (playing golf, other ventures, etc.). If no effort is applied to the venture, it is worthless, and the attained value of other activities is F, measured on the horizontal axis. Jensen and Meckling refer to F as "perquisite consumption." The line segment $\underline{VF}$ describes the entrepreneur's opportunity set. By definition, the value of perquisites is measured in terms of opportunity cost of value foregone in the venture. Thus, $\underline{VF}$ has a slope of -1. The problem for the entrepreneur is to choose the effort that corresponds to the entrepreneur's highest achievable utility. The indifference curve, U_0, reflects the tradeoff of satisfaction the entrepreneur derives from increased value of the venture compared to perquisite consumption. The curve is the one that affords the highest attainable utility. Point D, the tangency between the opportunity set and U_0, is where the entrepreneur's utility is maximized. This point is associated with V^* as the value of the venture and F^* as the value of perquisites.

Suppose that as a means of harvesting some of her investment, the entrepreneur decides to bring in an outside investor.[10] Specifically, the entrepreneur decides to sell a fraction of the equity. Imagine that the entrepreneur retains α percent, and sells $(1 - \alpha)$ percent. Selling part of the equity changes the decision calculus of the entrepreneur. Now, instead of being able to trade one dollar of value in the venture for one dollar of value from other activities, the entrepreneur can trade (α) percent of a dollar of venture value for one dollar of value from other activities. The entrepreneur's incentive to allocate effort to increasing the value of the venture has declined because some of the benefit accrues to the outside investor.

The second panel of Figure 12-2 shows what happens if the investor fails to take account of the change of incentives. In that case, the investor pays $(1 - \alpha) \times V^*$ for $(1 - \alpha)$ percent of the venture. The change causes the entrepreneur's opportunity set to become less steeply sloped. The slope changes from -1 to $-(\alpha)$, and, since the investor has paid a price based on V^*, the new opportunity set passes through V^*F^*. The dashed line shows the new budget constraint. Because the entrepreneur's cost of allocating effort to other activities is now lower, the entrepreneur devotes less effort to the venture and more to other activities. The change is represented by point A, where the new indifference curve, U_1, is tangent to the entrepreneur's new opportunity set. Instead of consuming F^* of perquisites, the entrepreneur consumes F^0. However, the value of the venture is reduced to V^0, owing to the entrepreneur's reduced effort. The investor pays too much for the $1 - \alpha$ share of the equity. Specifically, the investor pays $(1 - \alpha) \times V^*$ for shares worth only $(1 - \alpha) \times V^0$.

The change in the entrepreneur's incentives is an agency cost of outside equity. To the extent that equity ownership is shared, the entrepreneur is an agent of the investor. This is a specific example of moral hazard. Once the contract is changed to reduce the entrepreneur's incentive to expend effort, the entrepreneur changes behavior to make the best of the contract.

The third panel of Figure 12-2 is one in which the investor correctly anticipates the effect of the entrepreneur's changed incentives, and values the venture accordingly. By offering a

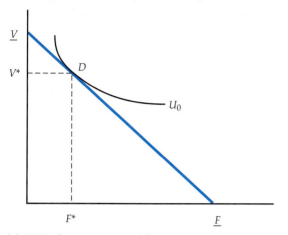

(a) 100% Owner-managed firm

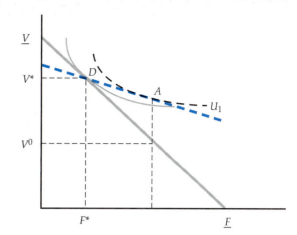

(b) Attempted behavior if the owner sells $(1 - \alpha)$%
to an outside investor

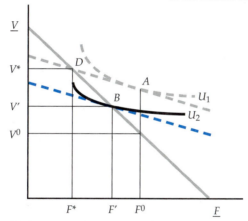

(c) Decision of manager if outside investor
values the firm correctly

Figure 12-2   Agency cost of outside equity

(a) Line $\underline{VF}$ illustrates the feasible combinations of firm value, V, and perquisite consumption, F, that are attainable from a given level of investment. The slope of the constraint is -1. With the manager being 100% owner, the manager maximizes utility at point D, by choosing to consume perquisites of F^*, resulting in a firm value of V^*. (b) The former owner now owns only α% of the firm. If the outside investor values the firm at V^* and pays $(1 - \alpha) \times V^*$ for his share of the firm, the manager acts as if the dashed line (with a slope of $-\alpha$ is the new constraint for trading off firm value and perquisites, and maximizes utility at point A. Firm value declines to V^0 and the outside investor loses a fraction of the investment. (c) The outside investor values the firm at V', recognizing that the manager will increase perquisite consumption once some of the business is sold. The investor pays $(1 - \alpha) \times V'$ for his share of the firm. The manager acts as if the lower dashed line is the new constraint for trading off firm value and perquisites, and maximizes utility at point B. As expected, firm value declines to V'.

*Adapted from Jensen and Meckling (1976).

price consistent with a valuation of V', the investor compensates for moral hazard. Point B is the point of tangency between the entrepreneur's opportunity set and indifference curve U_2, at the intersection of the entrepreneur's new opportunity set with VF. If the tangency is above the intersection, then the price paid by the investor is too high. The NPV of the investor's purchase is negative because of the overpayment. If it is below, then the entrepreneur loses value to the investor.

Suppose the entrepreneur is unusual and is not very interested in consuming perquisites. Demonstrating to prospective investors that she would not reduce effort as much as the average entrepreneur would enable the entrepreneur to sell the interest in the venture for a higher price. But how can the entrepreneur demonstrate that she is different from the others? We discuss ways of addressing this problem later in the chapter.

The Agency Cost of Debt   High-growth, high-risk ventures normally do not use debt financing, but other kinds of ventures often do. Debt financing gives rise to its own kinds of agency problems. As long as the debt is riskless, meaning there is no possibility of default, debt does not create any incentive (or moral hazard) problem. But as riskiness increases, the incentives of the equity holders (the entrepreneur, in our case) change. High-default risk can cause an entrepreneur to underinvest in low-risk activities and/or overinvest in risk activities.

Underinvestment can occur when, in order to pursue a positive NPV opportunity, an entrepreneur must make an investment that is disproportionate to the entrepreneur's share of the return. Consider an entrepreneur who must decide whether to invest in a warehouse and distribution operation to support expansion of his e-commerce business. Suppose, that to pursue the expansion, the entrepreneur would need to invest $100,000. Assume current financing of the venture includes high-risk debt. The expansion has a positive NPV and reduces the risk of the venture. Without the investment, the venture is likely to default on the debt. With the investment, the loan is likely to be repaid. If the change in expected repayment is more than the positive NPV of the expansion, then the entrepreneur is better off foregoing the investment, even though its NPV is positive.

This is an example of underinvestment. A positive NPV investment opportunity is not taken. The reason it is not taken is that much of the benefit accrues to the lender, whereas the entrepreneur (who has the decision right) must make the investment. Clearly, this is not a desirable contract structure, and we might expect to see the entrepreneur renegotiate the loan so that the cost and benefit of the investment are shared. The example illustrates one reason high-risk new ventures tend not to be debt financed.

Overinvestment occurs under conditions that are somewhat similar: The venture is not doing well, and default appears likely. The entrepreneur recognizes that liquidating the remaining assets is more valuable than continuing to operate. Consider a six-year-old, debt-financed pharmaceutical R&D venture that has not yet entered clinical testing and where the likelihood of developing a successful product is now very low. If the entrepreneur shuts down and liquidates the assets, all of the proceeds will go to the lender. However, if the entrepreneur continues to operate until repayment is contractually required, there is a small chance of successful innovation. In the event of success, the venture could easily repay the loan and the entrepreneur would keep a large residual. But if the venture fails, the entrepreneur loses nothing. Even though the NPV of continuing to invest is negative, the entrepreneur will choose to go ahead.

Overinvestment occurs when the entrepreneur is able to invest resources in high-risk activities in which the cost of failure is borne largely by creditors, but the reward of success

Differences Across Countries in Forms of New Venture Financing

U.S. venture capitalists rarely use forms of financing other than convertible preferred equity.* However, other forms of financing are more common in other developed and emerging economies. There are many ways to address the adverse selection and moral hazard problems inherent in new ventures, including mechanisms such as staging, syndication, restrictive covenants, and control rights. The choice of financing depends partly on the other control mechanisms that are available in a particular institutional setting. Among the factors to consider are the specific attributes of a venture (its development stage, investment duration, industry, and so on) and the institutions of the country in which it emanates (such as types of "exit" possibilities, and tax considerations).

As an illustration of the determinants of financing structure, Cumming (2001) studies over 5000 Canadian venture capital finance transactions from 1991 to 1998. He finds that, in Canada, convertible preferred equity is not the most common form of financing. In Cumming's subsample of Canadian deals done by independent, private venture capital firms, straight equity is the most common type of financing (42.6 percent of transactions). Straight debt is the next most popular (15 percent), followed by convertible debt (12.7 percent), and convertible preferred (5.5 percent). Cumming finds that, in contrast to expansion-stage firms, start-up firms tend not to give up straight equity. High-tech firms select away from convertible securities and toward straight preferred equity and straight debt. Gilson and Schizer (2002), adding to the mix of considerations, indicate that because of differences in the Canadian tax system, convertible preferred securities can have adverse tax effects.

To further illustrate the importance of institutions in determining choice of financing, the most widely used instrument in the German venture capital industry is reported to be silent partnerships (a type of debt), followed by straight equity, debt-equity mixes, and lastly, convertibles (Bascha and Walz, 2001). The authors attribute this, in part, to the significant presence of public sector participation in the venture capital market. Public sector investors are more likely to provide financing via guaranteed loans and, hence, are less concerned with high returns and agency costs of equity.

* Kaplan and Strömberg (2002) provide recent data.

Sources: See end-of-chapter references.

accrues largely to the entrepreneur. Suppose lenders know, in advance, that the debt is risky and that the entrepreneur may overinvest in high-risk activities. Under these conditions, lenders are likely to limit entrepreneurial discretion in a variety of ways, such as by shortening the debt maturity or establishing conditions under which lenders gain control over investment decisions. Concern with overinvestment in high-risk opportunities is another reason that debt financing is uncommon for high-risk ventures.

12.2   CONTRACT DESIGN

In this section, we consider contractual and noncontractual responses to information problems and incentive problems. The term "contract" is subject to varying definitions and interpretations. For our purpose, you can consider contracts as spanning a spectrum. At one end of the spectrum, discrete contracts are those that contain very explicit provisions. The transactions underlying such contracts are impersonal, self-contained exchanges, and performance is easily observable and measurable. The contracts are of short duration, and if contingencies are a concern, they are anticipated and provided for explicitly in the contract. MacNeil (1974) characterizes discrete contracts as "sharp in by clear agreement; sharp out by clear performance." At the other end of the spectrum are relational contracts. These are highly flexible, implicit contracts based entirely on ongoing relationships between the parties. A relational contract is like a constitution that describes what the parties are trying to accomplish and how, in general terms, they aspire to share the benefits. Specific implementation is left to be worked out by the parties through what they hope will be a cooperative working relationship.

Discrete Contracting

Discrete contract terms are specific in content and duration. An example is a financial contract between an entrepreneur and a bank, where the venture requires occasional, but small, infusions of cash. If the loan is collateralized, the contract is discrete. The bank does not need to accept the entrepreneur's sales projections or to incur the expense of verifying the venture's financial performance, other than to make sure loan terms are met. The entrepreneur is not concerned that the lender will act opportunistically as long as it is clear that the venture can serve its debt obligations. If the lender does not renew the loan, in spite of the entrepreneur's adequate collateral, it is easy for the entrepreneur to turn to another lender.

Discrete contracting works best for simple exchanges in which the contracting parties have similar expectations, objectives are easy to specify, and performance is easy to verify. But what happens if these conditions are not satisfied? Suppose, for example, that the parties have materially different expectations about the future. It may be possible for them to design a more complex contract that still is essentially discrete but circumvents the need for the parties to have similar expectations.

Our valuation framework implies that if expectations are held symmetrically and incentives are not of concern, then the better-diversified party should bear most of the risk. The contractual solution is likely to be different for risks related to asymmetrically held beliefs. In those cases, new venture financing contracts may shift risk toward the better-informed or more optimistic party. Entrepreneurs often are more optimistic about sales than are outside investors. Suppose the entrepreneur is confident he can achieve $200,000 in monthly sales within 18 months of signing a financing contract. The investor is much less optimistic, projecting monthly sales of $100,000 at that point. A financing contract that provides for equity sharing can be based on the investor's revenue projections but include a provision that if the entrepreneur's revenue expectation is met, he will receive, say, a 15 percent increase in equity. Without the provision, the investor would benefit fully from higher-than expected revenue results. Even though the investor is better able to bear risk, the entrepreneur now accepts some of the risk in order to offset the parties' different performance expectations.

Discrete contracting can also be used to address incentive problems. Suppose an entrepreneur is concerned that an investor who provides the first round of financing may attempt to hold up the entrepreneur when second-round financing is needed. In the first round, the entrepreneur can rely on competition among investors, but afterward, the selected investor may gain an information advantage over rivals and could take advantage of that position. Consistent with our earlier discussion, the incentive problem arises after the first-round financing. It arises because the entrepreneur intends to make a specific investment in the venture and because the value of the specific investment is, to some extent, appropriable by the investor. The

Evidence from Real World Financial Contracts

Venture Capital Contracting

Kaplan and Strömberg (2002) examine the term sheets of 213 investments in 119 portfolio companies by 14 venture capital firms. They find that key attributes of the term sheets address concerns related to asymmetric information and incentive problems that arise in new venture settings. As examples: the entrepreneur's compensation is more sensitive to performance when incentive and asymmetric information problems are more severe; allocation of control rights is a key feature of contracts; although contingency contracting is ubiquitous, the contracts are inherently incomplete, suggesting the importance of reputational capital in enforcing contracts.

Key features:

- Contracts give venture capitalists cash flow allocation rights,* board positions, liquidation, and other control rights.
- Venture capitalist's rights often are contingent on observable performance.
- Staging is common: If the venture performs poorly, the venture capitalist obtains more control. If the venture performs well, the venture capitalist retains cash flow rights but may relinquish control and liquidation rights.
- Contracts include noncompete and vesting provisions that raise the entrepreneur's cost of leaving the venture, mitigating potential hold-up problems.
- Convertible securities are used most frequently (appearing in 96 percent of the financing rounds, with convertible preferred being used exclusively in 80 percent).
- Venture capitalists commonly use optional redemption and put provisions to strengthen their liquidation rights. Redemption provisions are present in 79 percent of the financings in the sample.
- In 95 percent of the financings, anti-dilution provisions protect the venture capitalist against future financing rounds at lower valuations.

Strategic Alliances and Financial Contracting

Robinson and Stuart (2002) analyze 126 strategic alliance contracts between large pharmaceutical companies and small, early-stage R&D companies engaged in genomics research that may be used by the larger companies.

Alliance contracts have key features similar to venture capital contracts:

- Contracts include provisions that reflect the real options of abandoning or waiting associated with resolution of sequential uncertainty.
- Investments are staggered and contingent on milestones and resolution of sequential uncertainty.
- Convertible preferred equity is typical, with conversion typically taking place at IPO.
- Contracts for longer research projects provide the sponsor with warrants and the small biotech firm with puts that force the sponsor to purchase additional shares.

In contrast to venture capital contracts, alliance contracts can sponsor projects inside firms and respond to multi-tasking problems. Contracts have clauses and conditions that are difficult to verify, but rely instead on relational capital.

* Defined as fraction of portfolio company's equity value on which investors and management have claims.

Sources: See end-of-chapter references.

concern can be addressed by discrete contracting. The parties agree in advance on conditions under which the investor will provide second-round financing and on the terms.

Discrete contracting can also cause incentive problems, however. It always is difficult for the parties to state explicit conditions that do not distort incentives. If the entrepreneur's equity share is tied to sales in month 18, then the entrepreneur may devote too much attention to sales and not enough to profitability. If the parties agree on conditions under which the entrepreneur can demand second-round financing, the entrepreneur may concentrate on satisfying those conditions, and not on doing what is best for the venture. On balance, it sometimes is better to leave certain provisions of new venture contracts general or unstated.

Relational Contracting and Flexibility

A relational contract is a more flexible response to information and incentive problems. This may seem paradoxical because relational contracts rely more on implicit mechanisms such as damage to reputation for enforcement of the understanding.[11] Milgrom and Roberts (1992) describe relational contracts in the following way.

> The parties do not agree on detailed plans of action but on goals and objectives, on general provisions that are broadly applicable, on the criteria to be used in deciding what to do when unforeseen contingencies arise, on who has what power to act and the bounds limiting the range of actions that can be taken, and on dispute resolution mechanisms to be used if disagreements do occur. For example, companies entering a relationship to collaborate on a joint research and development project do not attempt to figure out precisely what they will do in every detail as the uncertain project evolves. Instead, they each agree to give their best efforts to developing the project, to share the costs and benefits, to consult with one another as new developments occur, and to bargain in good faith when disputes arise. (p. 131)

The virtue of a relational contract is flexibility. Consider the alternatives of seeking financing from a passive investor who has limited familiarity with the product market of a new enterprise, or from a venture capitalist who is involved in the industry and would be an active participant in the venture's management. The passive investor is more likely to seek a discrete contract that contains specific terms that describe the conditions for funding and sharing ownership. Because of bounded rationality, the contract is likely to rely on crude proxies for states of the world. For example, the contract might specify revenue or profit targets that are only rough indicators of the likely success of the venture. Conditions for later-stage investment, allocations of ownership, and other factors may hinge on whether the venture meets those targets, and only indirectly on the true potential for success.

Many unforeseen conditions could result in failure to meet the targets. If the contract relies too heavily on proxies for future states of the world, the venture loses flexibility that can be important for survival. The problem is exacerbated if the investor is passive and, as a result, has no first-hand knowledge of why a performance target was or was not met.[12] Venture capital financing is likely to be more flexible. Because of industry expertise and active involvement, the venture capitalist often understands the reasons for hits and misses of performance targets. Essentially, the venture capitalist offers a flexible relational contract that provides continued funding as long as providing the funds is in its interest. Provisions in the contract are likely to enable the venture capitalist to monitor the entrepreneur and even restrict the entrepreneur's ability to act without venture capitalist consent. The net effect is that, if additional funds are needed, the venture capitalist is in a good position to evaluate whether to advance the funds. This type of financing contract often can add value to the venture. The net benefit, however, depends on whether the advantages of flexibility offset the cost of the time the venture capitalist must commit.

Venture capital contracts reflect the idea of relational contracting, particularly with respect to commitments by the venture capitalist. In addition to the uncertainty and risk associated with new ventures, the entrepreneur typically does not have a reputation for running a business. The venture capitalist cannot know with certainty how much direct involvement will be required. The result is that the contracts are not explicit about the amount of oversight or monitoring the venture capitalist will provide. That effort depends on how things unfold as the entrepreneur grows the business.[13] Such contracts expose entrepreneurs to the risk of opportunism. Later in the chapter we discuss reasons that entrepreneurs are often willing to accept such risks, rather than insisting on discrete contract terms.

Ironically, an entrepreneur may regard the passive financing alternative as affording more "flexibility." However, a critical distinction exists between the entrepreneur's discretion to make decisions about the direction of the venture and the flexibility of the venture to adapt to its environment. With passive financing, the entrepreneur can have a sense of greater discretion, but for critical decisions, may be constrained by the rigid terms of the discrete contract and inflexibility of the investor. With active financing, there is likely to be more continuous oversight and a requirement of consensus before actions can be taken. However, because the investor is involved and informed, the venture is more capable of responding to threats and opportunities.

Discrete contracts with provisions that are explicit but incomplete and flexible relational contracts are responses to bounded rationality. Which type of contract is better in any particular setting depends on the identities of the parties, the costs and benefits of flexibility, and the ability of the parties to agree on explicit terms that are not overly restrictive.

Incomplete Contracts and Mechanisms for Resolving Information and Incentive Problems

Although relational contracts are more flexible, they do not specifically "solve" information and incentive problems. They are incomplete by design, and rely on broadly stated principles to address uncertainty. Because the contracts are incomplete, other mechanisms that more directly address informational asymmetry and opportunism often accompany relational contracts. Among the mechanisms that complement relational contracts are signaling, screening, monitoring, and bonding. Technically, the terms "signaling" and "screening" apply to mechanisms that address adverse selection (information asymmetry), whereas "bonding" and "monitoring" apply to mechanisms that address moral hazard (opportunism). However, sometimes the terms "signaling," "screening," and "bonding" are used interchangeably. In part this is because adverse selection and moral hazard problems are difficult to distinguish from each other and because they often occur together.

Signaling   It often is difficult for an investor to distinguish high-quality ventures (the "cherries") from the "lemons." The fundamental problem is that the entrepreneur's claims of potential success are costly or impossible for the investor to verify. One way an entrepreneur can convey positive private information is simply to show the information to investors and allow them to draw their own conclusions. But this is risky if an investor who learns the information can decide to appropriate it and not involve the entrepreneur. Suppose, for example, the entrepreneur has figured out how to increase the rate of data transmission over computer modems. The value of the idea is hard for an investor to assess unless the entrepreneur tells the investor how the idea works, at which point the investor might no longer need the entrepreneur's help.

Sometimes, providing the information is not feasible. How, for example, without elaborate documentation, can an entrepreneur convey the knowledge that her efforts to develop

◆ Adverse Selection and Earnouts

One way entrepreneurs and venture capitalists harvest their investments in a business is by selling the business to another firm. In such transactions, asymmetric information problems arise because the current owners may possess information about firm value that is superior to that of outside buyers. One way current owners can avoid the adverse selection problem is by offering to sell with an earnout provision. An earnout is a method of acquisition in which the final price to the seller depends on future performance of the business. The performance target typically is based on earnings or sales from one to five years after the acquisition. An earnout gives the seller an interest in future profits without requiring the seller to maintain ownership.

Datar, Frankel, and Wolfson (2001) report two recent examples of earnout provisions. The first is the purchase of PRN of North Carolina by Medical Industries of America (MIOA). In that transaction, owners of PRN received up to 1 million MIOA shares. Under the terms of the earnout, they received 125,000 shares for each million dollars of pretax profits in the three years after the transaction. The second is the purchase of Miro Computer Products, AG by Pinnacle Systems, Inc. The transaction included an earnout provision tied to sales. Specifically, the sellers received 50 percent of sales in excess of $37 million and 85 percent of sales in excess of $59 million during the year after the acquisition. As the authors report, the contingent payments are designed "to overcome the buyer's difficulty in determining the present value of the future growth rate of the selling company." They also signal the seller's expectations for future sales or profitability.

Agreements vary in terms of whether the seller or buyer manages a target's assets after acquisition. As a result, moral hazard issues may arise. If, for example, the buyer takes over management, the buyer bears the full cost of effort but retains only part of the benefits. The buyer also may have an incentive to manipulate short-run sales or profitability to reduce the ultimate payment to the seller under the earnout. A similar problem arises if the seller manages the assets.

In their study of a sample of mergers and acquisitions in the period 1990–1996, Datar et al. developed a statistical model to determine the relationship between buyer and seller characteristics and the likelihood of an earnout being used. The results show that, earnouts are more likely in acquisitions when the target is a smaller private company in a different industry and different country from the acquirer. Earnouts also are more likely when fewer acquisitions take place within an industry and in the purchase of high-tech firms. In their sample of 17,100 transactions, Datar et al. find that earnouts were used in 2.5 percent of the transactions. If the percentages seem low, remember that many alternative arrangements have effects similar to earnouts.

Source: Discussion is drawn from a paper by Shrikant Datar, Richard Frankel, and Mark Wolfson, "Earnouts: The Effect of Adverse Selection on Acquisition Techniques." *Journal of Law, Economics, and Organization* 17 (2001): 201–238. Also see Hussey, "Earnouts: Motivation and Conflict," *Accountancy,* April 1990, pp. 104–106.

new voice-recognition software have progressed much more rapidly than expected? Conversely, how can a prospective investor convey the knowledge that it is not involved with, or considering involvement with, any competing products that could influence its attitude toward the entrepreneur's product? The challenge is to do so in a way that is convincing, and still preserve the value of the information.

One solution is for the information holder to use a signal. A signal is a credible demonstration that obviates the need to convey the information itself. Sometimes, contract provisions can serve as credible signals. Suppose an investor is concerned that an entrepreneur's financial projections are overly optimistic. By proposing a contract that ties the entrepreneur's return to performance targets, the entrepreneur "signals" his true beliefs.[14]

Economist Michael Spence (1973) first introduced the concept of signaling in a labor market context. In his example, each worker knows his own productivity, but the characteristic is unobservable by prospective employers. Without the ability to distinguish among workers, employers would offer the same (low) wage to all, and an adverse selection problem would result. Spence shows that under certain conditions workers can use educational attainment to signal their productivity. Educational attainment works as a signal because it is observable and separates the workers according to productivity levels. Education does not, as the example is structured, change the productivity of any worker. Thus, the signal is used to address an information problem and not an incentive problem.

There are numerous examples of the application of signaling to finance. It is suggested that, because bankruptcy is costly, taking on additional debt signals that managers are confident about the prospects of the firms. Similar reasoning applies to announcements of dividend increases and to announcements of stock splits.[15]

The idea of signaling can be extended to new venture finance. From an investor's perspective, self-serving proclamations by an entrepreneur of being motivated and energetic are not credible. The attributes investors seek in entrepreneurs are, for the most part, unobservable. Investors would prefer to deal with entrepreneurs who realistically represent their true beliefs and provide accurate information regarding their financial projections and who have the (unobservable) managerial attributes that are needed for success.[16]

Consider the following terms for a contract between an entrepreneur, Miles Stone, and a venture capital firm, Limited Deals, Ltd., concerning financing for an amusement park venture. Upon signing the agreement, Limited is committed to finance the venture up to $4 million for one year, by which time specific benchmarks are to be met. If the benchmarks are met, Limited is committed to invest an additional $2 million. If the venture fails to meet one or more benchmark, Limited has the choice of not investing in the second round. If Limited decides not to invest any additional money, then Miles has 60 days to find a new investor. If he is unable to do so, then Limited can elect to force liquidation. Miles retains ownership of the amusement park idea and the copyrights and trademarks related to the park. If the other assets are sold, the proceeds are to be distributed based on shares of invested capital. Finally, if Limited decides to invest the $2 million even if the venture does not meet the benchmarks, then Limited assumes managerial control of the business.

Willingness to abide by these terms signals several things about Miles. First, the benchmarks are designed to measure performance and are based on his projections. Therefore, adopting the benchmarks signals Miles's confidence that the projections are reasonable. Second, his willingness to relinquish control if performance expectations are not met signals confidence in his managerial skills. A less confident entrepreneur would be less willing to submit to these onerous terms. In this case, the arrangement also affects Miles's incentives to devote effort to the venture. By working harder, he helps ensure that the benchmarks are met. Thus, the signaling device also addresses moral hazard.[17]

Screening   Screening is much like signaling, except that the party without the private information offers a choice of alternative terms such that the party with private information reveals the information by choosing. A classic example of screening is for an employer to offer workers a choice of jobs, some of which are compensated on a piece-rate basis and others on an hourly rate basis. Suppose the productivity levels of workers differ and that an employer must staff two kinds of jobs—those in which the employee has significant control over the rate of output and those in which the rate of output is controlled by a process that the employee cannot influence. Suppose, further, that each worker knows her own productivity level but the employer does not. Assuming that the two kinds of jobs require similar skills, the employer would like to encourage high-productivity workers to take the jobs where they will have a positive influence on the rate of output and would like low-productivity workers to take jobs where they cannot affect the rate of output. To accomplish this, the employer offers two different compensation contracts: piece-rate pay for jobs where workers can affect output, and hourly rate pay where they cannot. If the piece rate and hourly rate are set correctly, the wage contracts will screen employees so that high-productivity workers select piece-rate jobs and low-productivity workers select hourly rate jobs.

In a new venture setting, offering entrepreneurs alternative types of financing can serve a screening function. Entrepreneurs with low expectations for their ventures, for example, are likely to prefer outside financing that minimizes the investor's liquidation preference. Those who are highly uncertain of how the venture might perform also are likely to seek financing that reduces their own risk exposure.

Again, in this example, the screening contract is used to address adverse selection. Piece-rate or hourly rate pay is not assumed to influence worker effort. The contract merely sorts workers based on workers' private information. The sorting works in a way that is advantageous for the employer. If, in reality, the contract terms also affect incentives (as they are likely to do), then moral hazard also is being addressed.

The identity of the actor is the main difference between a signal and a screen. The deal for amusement park financing described earlier as a signal could also be the result of a screening contract. If the entrepreneur (the party with private information) proposed the financing structure in which second-round financing was optional and control could transfer to the investor if performance targets were not met, then it appears that the entrepreneur is signaling. If, on the other hand, the investor (the party without private information) proposed the contract, knowing that alternative deals with more assured financing also were available, then the investor would be trying to screen entrepreneurs based on confidence in their projections.

Bonding   Posting a bond is one way to give credibility to a commitment not to engage in opportunistic behavior. A bond is a penalty that will be paid by the party who makes a promise, in the event the promise is broken. The penalty may go to the other party to the exchange, as it does in the case of a warranty or guarantee, or it may not. The fundamental element is that the party who posts the bond is made worse off if the commitment is violated. Thus, a bond provides an incentive to act according to a commitment. The commitment can be explicit and specific (like agreeing to resign if the investor is not satisfied with the entrepreneur's effort) or implicit (like tying compensation to the attained level of sales).

In a corporate environment, the primary moral hazard problems are shirking and self-interested decision making. An employee who does not realize the entire benefits of his effort can shirk on the job and devote extra time to other activities without bearing the full cost. The concern is that the employee may make investment and other decisions that benefit the employee but not the organization.

Similar problems exist in new ventures. Investors, however, may not be so much concerned that an entrepreneur will not work hard as that the entrepreneur may not focus on the right activities and problems. For example, the entrepreneur may be more interested in working on technical problems related to the product than in managing a rapidly growing organization. Or the entrepreneur may not recognize failure or be open to changing the focus of the venture. This can be an issue of adverse selection, but it also is possible that the untested entrepreneur is just as uncertain about his own capabilities and temperament as is the investor. Consequently, the focus of bonding commitments often is different in new ventures from that in large corporations.

A bond can be provided in several different ways. Sometimes specific contract provisions can function as a bond. Alternatives to using contract provisions include reliance on reputation and certification.

Using Discrete Contract Provisions to Bond Performance   Suppose an entrepreneur seeks funding to begin commercialization of a concept. The entrepreneur has no experience in managing but is hard working and devoted to the venture. Consequently, the entrepreneur wishes to continue as CEO. The investor likes the concept but is concerned that the entrepreneur may not be successful at commercialization. Neither party has a compelling information advantage with regard to the capabilities of the entrepreneur. The fundamental difficulty is that if the entrepreneur proves to be an ineffective manager, then the venture is likely to fail, but the entrepreneur still may be resistant to making the kinds of changes needed to help ensure survival.

The investor would like to select an experienced manager to carry out commercialization, but the entrepreneur does not want to relinquish control. A possible solution is for the entrepreneur to provide a performance bond. One way to do so is to establish performance benchmarks, so that, if they are met, the entrepreneur retains control and, if not, controls transfers to the investor. The bond can be achieved using warrants whereby the investor gains the ability to acquire additional voting shares, culminating in control, if performance targets are not met. Or it can be achieved by giving the investor the right to terminate the entrepreneur as CEO if the targets are not met. The difference between these two approaches is that the former shifts more financial risk to the entrepreneur. Hence, it may be effective as a device for signaling the entrepreneur's expectations, as well as a way of bonding performance.

In this example, the entrepreneur is protected against opportunism by the investor by establishing specific conditions under which the termination right can be exercised. However, as we noted earlier, dependence on specific conditions is not an ideal solution. The question of whether a particular condition is satisfied involves a significant random component that is beyond the entrepreneur's control and is unrelated to the entrepreneur's abilities. Thus, the entrepreneur is not as protected as he would like. On the other hand, explicit conditions are subject to manipulation in ways that are not in the parties' interests.

Using Reputation to Bond Performance   Rather than relying on explicit contract terms, the more successful relationships are likely to be based on trust. To see how reputation is important, consider factors that would induce the parties to a venture to rely on mutual trust

Moral Hazard and the Right to Terminate the Founder as CEO

A common source of discord and discontent between founders of new ventures and venture capital investors is when, if ever, the founder should resign as CEO. Hellmann (1998) considers this issue. A moral hazard problem arises whenever the founder/manager receives capital from investors and therefore shares the residual profits and losses of the venture. An agency problem arises because the founder does not bear all the costs of mistakes or reap all the benefits of wise decisions. As an extension of the problem, many entrepreneurs don't want to be displaced, even if professional managers would increase the value of the business. Because they spearheaded development of the business, they want to continue to manage and oversee its success. Despite this, professional managers often replace founders within the first few months of a company's life. This change often is accomplished by the venture capitalists exercising their control right to terminate the founder/manager. Whether terminations are voluntary or not, the change in management is likely to be traumatic for all involved.

Why don't the founders protect themselves with contractual provisions that are explicit about how and when a founder can be replaced? In principle, the contract with the venture capitalist could specify a generous severance package that is activated if the founder is terminated. Such a provision would work like a "golden parachute" that is activated when a corporation is threatened with takeover. As Hellmann reports, such protection for entrepreneurs is "essentially unheard of in venture capital." Instead, entrepreneurs relinquish the right to appoint the CEO.

What explains the apparent one-sided nature of control rights in venture capital contracts? A possible explanation is that moral hazard and agency costs are high in founder-run businesses. Because the right to appoint a CEO is critical to business value, the founder, along with other investors, will want to create an environment that produces optimal incentives for the venture capitalist to engage in a value-increasing search for a CEO. However, the venture capitalist is unlikely to invest in a search for a professional manager without the right to control the appointment. Hellmann argues that because entrepreneurs are wealth-constrained (otherwise they wouldn't require venture capital), they voluntarily relinquish control, even if their loss is more than the gain to the investors. This is because the equity stake of the founder is not likely to be large enough to obviate concerns that the founder will "hold up" the venture capitalist by pursuing his personal interests rather than the interests of the other owners.

This discussion is drawn from Thomas Hellmann, "The Allocation of Control Rights in Venture Capital Contracts." *RAND Journal of Economics* 29, no. 1 (Spring 1998): 57–76. Harold Demsetz and Kenneth Lehn provide evidence that owners of closely held firms may be concerned with similar hold-up problems. As an example of the problem, they cite the dramatic price increase of Disney stock after the death of founder Walt Disney. See Demsetz and Lehn, "The Structure of Corporate Ownership: Causes and Consequences." *Journal of Political Economy* 93 (1985): 1155–1177.

instead of discrete contract terms. Reputation, or trustworthiness, is key to a relationship in the presence of specific assets that are appropriable. A party can be "trusted" when refraining from opportunistic behavior is the party's higher valued course of action.

The economics literature refers to trust in terms of reputations. Reputational capital is a nonsalvageable intangible asset that is most valuable in its current use. As a result, it functions as a bond. The investors in a firm do not want to lose their sunk investments in reputational capital that could result if the firm were to cheat on product quality or otherwise renege on implicit long-term contracts.

Klein and Leffler (l981) consider expenditures on industry-specific nonsalvageable assets as one means of bonding. Their idea is that a firm can spend resources on advertising and other assets that are specific to continued involvement in the industry, which investment can be recovered only if the firm remains in the industry for a significant period of time. Consumers (or other trading partners) recognize the expenditures as effectively guaranteeing product quality (or performance) and are willing to pay a premium for the guarantee. If the firm disappoints consumers by selling products that are of less than the expected quality, then they discontinue purchasing and the value of the firm's investment in reputation is lost. As long as consumers of the firm's products share information with each other in some way, the firm can damage its reputation even by disappointing a single consumer.[18]

It is easy to see how the Klein and Leffler model applies to new ventures. A venture capital firm that has made a substantial commitment to be involved in the industry does not want to gain a reputation of exploiting either entrepreneurs or prospective investors in the firm's venture capital funds. Reputational damage could impair its ability to attract future entrepreneurs and future investors. Fair dealing with both groups is important. Some entrepreneurs can also have reputational capital. An entrepreneur who has been successful in the past and is continuing to seek opportunities for involvement with new ventures would like to have investors perceive the entrepreneur's decision to join a venture as information that the venture deserves their financial support.

There is more uncertainty about the behavior of a new entrant to the venture capital industry or a first-time entrepreneur. If the venture capital firm or the entrepreneur has not made much of an investment in industry-specific nonsalvageable capital, then others cannot rely on reputation to enforce agreements. The reasoning suggests that relationships involving entrepreneurs and investors with significant industry-specific reputations can rely more heavily on promises and trust.

What happens in relationships where only one party has reputational capital? A venture capitalist with an established reputation, for example, may require that the contract contain explicit provisions regarding the entrepreneur's performance, whereas the first-time entrepreneur dealing with an established venture capitalist may settle for more generally worded promises without explicit enforcement mechanisms.[19]

Using Certification to Bond Performance   There also are indirect means of bonding performance. Consider a first-time entrepreneur who faces investor concern that the entrepreneur's financial projections may be unrealistically high. The entrepreneur recognizes that if investors do not perceive the venture's true potential, then they will require too much ownership in exchange for their investments. Certification is a partial solution. With certification, rather than resorting to elaborate discrete contract terms, the party who lacks sufficient reputation can turn to a third party to certify some aspects of the financial projections.[20] For example, a sales forecast can be supported by a key sales contract or other tangible evidence that a significant customer is interested in buying the product. In effect, the entrepreneur is "borrowing" the reputation of one of its customers and using that reputation to enhance the credibility of projections. Also, bodies of technical advisors can serve to certify aspects of the venture such as technical feasibility. For technical advisors to be credible certifiers, they must have reputational capital at stake.

Another area in which certification plays an important role is public issuance of equity securities. Although a firm can try to market its own securities, success is unlikely. The problem is the one identified by Myers and Majluf (1984). Prospective investors will be concerned that the firm is trying to issue overvalued shares and will react negatively to the issue announcement. To address the problem, the firm likely will use the services of an investment banker. An investment banker is an intermediary between the security issuer and buyers of the securities. Because information about the firm is asymmetrically held, uninformed buyers rely on the underwriter to conduct a "due diligence" investigation of the venture in order to assess the appropriate offering price of the securities and to effectively certify that the offer price is consistent with private information about the firm.

If the underwriter sets an issue price that is too high and the shares lose value after the issue, the underwriter suffers reputational damage. It may incur additional losses if shareholders believe the decline in value is a result of adverse information that the underwriter should have learned through its due diligence efforts.[21] Empirical evidence supports the certification role. When underwriters fail in their certification efforts, not only do they suffer losses of value, so do the firms that previously relied on them for certification of IPOs.[22]

Monitoring   The other way opportunistic behavior is controlled is by monitoring. In lieu of bonding performance, the parties can rely on direct observation. Monitoring can be direct, as in the case of an investor who serves on the venture's board of directors. Or it can be indirect, as in the case of requiring financial statements to be audited (by reputable accounting firms).

The relationships between venture capital firms and their portfolio companies involve elements of both bonding and monitoring. The deal structures frequently involve bonding arrangements such as termination rights or warrants, but the investor also is closely involved in monitoring performance.

Some monitoring arrangements involve formal triggers. For example, staged financing gives the investor specific periodic opportunities to evaluate whether to continue investing. Use of debt covenants is another example of monitoring that employs a trigger. Debt covenants are provisions used by lenders to place restrictions on borrowers. For example, most home mortgages require the borrower to maintain fire insurance. If the borrower fails to insure, the loan is in default and the lender has several options, including foreclosure.

In a business setting, covenants may restrict the borrower from taking on additional debt or from making capital investments beyond what originally was contemplated. They also may require the borrower to adhere to certain constraints with respect to various financial ratios and may limit the borrower's ability to make distributions. Failure to adhere to a debt covenant is a breach of the terms of the loan and can trigger a reaction. The lender can institute changes to protect against loss, such as forcing the company into a bankruptcy-related reorganization.

Debt covenants protect the lender and provide a method of monitoring the borrower without requiring continuous oversight. Such covenants lower the risk of the debt because they provide protection against unfavorable contingencies. As a result, including the covenants lowers the interest rate.[23]

If the lender's concern is that the entrepreneur may take on risks that do not benefit the lender, there are alternatives to constraining the borrower by including debt covenants. One is to issue debt that is convertible at the lender's option to a predetermined number of shares of common stock. That way the lender is positioned to benefit from the firm's performance if it is especially strong. The conversion option reduces the agency cost of debt by aligning the interests of the borrower more closely with those of the lender. It is common for high-risk new ventures to "borrow" using debt or preferred stock that is convertible.[24]

Evidence of Monitoring

Empirical evidence corroborates the observation that venture capital firms play an important role in monitoring portfolio firms. In two studies of 173 start-up firms from Silicon Valley, Hellman and Puri (2000 and 2002) find indirect evidence of monitoring: venture capital is associated with a significant reduction in time to bring a product to market and a greater likelihood that the start-up adopts stock-option plans and hires professional managers. Venture capital-backed firms also are more likely to recruit outside CEOs.

Kaplan and Strömberg (2002) study term sheets and field-based data on investment analysis practices and document the venture capitalist's involvement in shaping and recruiting senior management. In 14 percent of the investments, the venture capitalist plays a role in recruiting the management team before investing, and in 50 percent the venture capitalist expects to play a role after investing. Recognition of the high costs of monitoring is apparent. In more than 33 percent of the investments, the venture capitalist expects to be active in such activities as writing the business plan, networking, and designing employee compensation. In 20 percent, the venture capitalist indicate concern that the investment might require "too much time," again indicative of their monitoring role.

Sources: See end-of-chapter references.

12.3   ORGANIZATIONAL CHOICE

So far we have considered contractual choices and other mechanisms for dealing with information and incentive problems without explicitly considering the broader organizational context. One of the entrepreneur's tasks is to design an effective organization.

Organizational design involves decisions regarding which functions the firm will outsource versus perform in-house. A start-up R&D firm, for example, may have to decide whether to build a manufacturing facility to conduct pilot tests of a new drug, use a subcontractor to conduct the tests, or license the technology to another firm that will undertake testing and development. The right choice involves an array of considerations: protection of the venture's investment in intellectual capital; difficulty of communicating with a subcontractor or licensee; control over product quality; effects of the decision on ability to innovate in the future; and so on.[25]

An Economic Perspective on Organizational Structure

Most economic goods and services are produced through a series of steps. Raw materials are used to produce inputs, which are transported and/or assembled as intermediate goods or services, which are used to produce final goods, which are distributed and sold. Financing at each stage is an input to the production process. Although many e-commerce companies and services challenge aspects of this "value chain" model of the production process, the basic idea (that final goods are produced through a series of sequential or simultaneous steps) still holds. Consequently, every entrepreneur must make choices about which steps to outsource and which to integrate.

How can the basic organizational choices best be made? As a general proposition, the decisions are guided by considering the transactions costs of using markets compared to the costs associated with performing the task internally.[26] Market exchange works best when transactions costs are small. Transactions costs include the costs of searching for trading partners, negotiating prices, and enforcing agreements. Market exchange also is more desirable when buyers and sellers have full information about such things as product quality and availability of substitutes and complements, and when the numbers of prospective buyers and sellers are large so that competitive pressures determine price.

When transactions costs of using markets are high or market competition is imperfect, other organizational options may be more desirable. Complete integration of an activity is one choice, but there are intermediate choices as well. The long-term discrete and relational contracts that we discussed in the previous section make up parts of the continuum from spot-market exchange to complete integration. In this context, a relational contract is a significant shift away from reliance on discrete contracts, toward reliance on organizations. Joint ventures, franchising, strategic alliances, and relational investing all are structures that can be thought of as relational contracts.[27]

Internal exchange also involves transactions costs. Choosing the organizational form involves comparing costs of market exchange with costs of internal exchange. If costs of internal exchange are lower, then transactions-cost considerations favor internalizing the activity within an organization. In such cases, internalizing transactions can lower the price paid by customers, increase gross profit per unit, and increase the quantity of sales.

One aspect of the difference between transactions costs of using markets as compared to internal exchange is how residual decision rights are controlled.[28] Whether exchange occurs in a market or in an organization, the contractual structure of the exchange is necessarily incomplete. Some contingencies will not be addressed with specific discrete terms of the contract. Responses to such contingencies depend on how residual decision rights are assigned. Efficient organization depends, in part, on the efficiency of the allocation rights to control asset dispositions that are not assigned by contract.

One distinguishing feature of organizations is that (in contrast to markets) decision making is hierarchical. In hierarchical organizations, entrepreneurs can be expected to devote some of their time to trying to influence the decision maker. You can think of such efforts as influence costs that are an aspect of the transactions costs of coordinating activity within an organization.[29] Among other considerations, it makes sense to pursue entrepreneurial ventures within organizations when influence costs are small relative to the benefits of the hierarchical decision structure. Thus, for example, a venture that complements the other projects of a large organization can be more efficiently pursued within the organization than can a venture that is in competition with other projects of the organization.

The venture capitalist practice of linking funding to active involvement is a shift away from reliance on market exchange toward an organizational form in which ventures are funded internally. The venture capital financing process is more hierarchical than is raising all funds in the market; it is an example of adaptive sequential decision making by the venture capitalist. As the future unfolds, the venture capital investor can adapt financing commitments to unexpected changes in the development of the venture.[30] Thus, one advantage of internal organization and relational contracts, as compared with discrete contracts, is that they facilitate adaptive sequential decision making. To be comfortable with this process, in which important decision rights are assigned to the venture capitalist, the entrepreneur must have a sense that venture capitalist decisions to provide or withhold funding will be generally consistent with the entrepreneur's interests. If not, then the entrepreneur is likely to seek discrete terms that can preserve access to alternative financing sources.

The relational contracts we observe between entrepreneurs and outside investors are thus consistent with the economic theory of organization. Where small numbers bargaining problems and opportunism can arise, reliance on organizational structure and long-term relationships enables the parties to use simpler contractual provisions than would be expected in discrete contracting exchanges of ownership for investment capital.

Internal organizational structure can go even further to help resolve some incentive conflicts. Potential gains from opportunism can be reduced because, within an organization,

The Contracting Framework*				
Behavioral Assumptions		Asset Specificity	Implied Contracting Process	Comment
Bounded Rationality	Opportunism			
0	+	+	Planning	Without bounded rationality, complete contingent claims contracting is a feasible way to prevent opportunistic behavior.
+	0	+	Promise	Without opportunistic behavior, the parties can cooperate through a series of discrete transactions and rely on cooperation to work out the solutions to problems that arise in the future.
+	+	0	Competition	Without relationship-specific assets, there is no potential for opportunistic behavior.
+	+	+	Governance	When all three concerns are present, the parties may agree on a hierarchical mechanism of controlling the potential for opportunistic behavior.

+ Present to a significant degree
0 Not present to a significant degree

*Adapted from Williamson (1987)

Figure 12-3 The contracting framework

disputing parties can go to third parties for resolution of disagreements. In the case of an entrepreneurial venture that is pursued within a large corporation, the management team responsible for providing financing does not have much reason to behave opportunistically. That team would not be able to capture the gain from opportunistic behavior, as might an outside investor who was involved with a stand-alone venture. In addition, if the team responsible for deciding whether to invest threatens not to do so, the team working on the venture may be able to appeal the decision to a higher level of management.

Hierarchical organization also can help overcome problems of impacted information. Keeping private information secret can be less valuable in an organization than in a market. Communication among parties within an organization can be more complete than in a market. Intellectual property is a good example of private information that may be easier to communicate within an organization than in a market. Divulging trade secrets to trading partners (materials suppliers, for example) exposes the owner of the secret to the risk of opportunism, whereas divulging information within an organization (say, to a division responsible for providing financing) involves less risk.

A Contracting Framework of Organizational Choice

A contracting framework is a useful way to think about the choice of organizational form.[31] The framework is summarized diagrammatically in Figure 12-3. You can use it to determine the organizational form that is most likely to be appropriate for different kinds of new ventures. As shown in the figure, organizational choices can be categorized into four scenarios with respect to the presence or absence of problems of bounded rationality, opportunism, and asset specificity. In each scenario, at least two of these problems are present. Generally, if none of the problems is present, or if only one is, discrete market transactions can be an efficient way to organize.

Scenario 1—Planning Beginning with the first row of the figure, the important concerns are asset specificity and opportunism. Consider a low-risk, high-expected-return venture with limited need for outside financing. Undertaking the venture requires making investments that are specific to it. The specific investments can include the entrepreneur's human capital and tangible assets acquired with the investor's financial capital. Suppose the parties lack reputational capital, such that either one, given the opportunity, might try to renegotiate the deal terms. In cases like this, the normal organizational form is "planning." Planning involves a formal contract that makes extensive use of discrete terms. The parties must be able to describe the possible future states of the world with sufficient precision and completeness that a formal contract structure can be used.

To see where formal contracts are most likely to be used for attracting new venture financing, think of situations where you can describe the payoffs for the investor in a precise way. Bounded rationality always exists, to some extent. But if, for example, under most outcomes, it still would be possible to pay the investor the promised return, then bounded rationality is not a significant concern. If it isn't, then, even if each party would like to engage in opportunism, the discrete contract terms that characterize planning prevent them from doing so.

Scenario 2—Promise "Promise" is the preferred contracting process when the parties are confronted with bounded rationality and asset specificity, but each party can reasonably assume the other will not behave opportunistically. The potential for opportunism, in this case, is both *ex ante* and *ex post*. The parties are not expected either to mislead each other about value or to act opportunistically after agreement is reached. Promise means the relationship is essentially one of trust. The parties agree that they do not know what surprises the future will bring. They recognize that undertaking the venture will require them to invest in specific assets. They are willing to go forward without a complex discrete contract because each believes the other will look for win-win solutions.

To see when promise is most likely, think of factors that would induce the parties to a venture to rely on mutual trust instead of elaborate discrete contracts. Trusting is rational when it is in the economic interest of the other party to be trustworthy. Using the economic paradigm, a party can be trusted when refraining from opportunistic behavior is the higher valued course of action. A party who violates a trust incurs a penalty that is larger than the immediate economic benefit of opportunistic behavior. Accordingly, promise is most appropriate when both parties have significant investments in reputation or when performance is certified by a third party. Performance that is bonded formally through the terms of the contract is a shift in the direction of the planning scenario.

New venture financial contracts often combine planning and promise. The venture capital investor may have a reputation that is sufficient to enable the entrepreneur to rely on promise, whereas an entrepreneur who has no track record may be expected to commit to the more explicit provisions that characterize planning.

Scenario 3—Competition   When the assets invested in a venture are not specific to it, then the potential for opportunism is negligible. Because either party can withdraw from the relationship without incurring significant cost, the parties can rely on the discipline of the market to protect the value of invested assets.

Look for "competition" to be the preferred process whenever there are several parties who could equally well take on the responsibilities of one side of the relationship. The initial round of financing often is such a situation, because there can be many prospective suppliers of financing. For competition to persist as the most effective organization, the parties must be able to continue to rely on the market, even after substantial investments have been made. For this to be the case, either the necessary investments must be small, or they must be salvageable without significant loss of value. Alternatively, the parties must face continuing competitive pressure from alternative prospective parties. Under these conditions, competition can be relied on, even if the venture is subject to considerable uncertainty and neither party has a reputation that would deter opportunism.

Scenario 4—Governance   When bounded rationality, asset specificity, and opportunism all are significant, it is unlikely that the parties can work together effectively without oversight. In such cases, the most efficient contracting process is likely to be "governance." Governance means that the specific transaction is brought within the boundaries of a firm or is "integrated." Reliance on contractual planning as an alternative to governance is undesirable because the future is too uncertain. A contract enforced by promise is undesirable because of the threat of opportunism. And competition cannot be relied on because of the presence of important relationship-specific assets. Governance emerges as the preferred process.

The governance process can be used to resolve disputes more efficiently than if the parties were to rely on external arbiters (who are less familiar with the issues and parties). It also can facilitate efficient redirection of resources in response to information.

Additional aspects of large organizations go beyond the transactional issues. Although much of new venture activity is carried out in hierarchical organizations, the rationale for reliance on governance often focuses on these other aspects. First, some hierarchical organizations, like pharmaceuticals producers, undertake many projects simultaneously. For the employees, there is an element of risk pooling that contrasts sharply with the risk exposure of an entrepreneur. Although the employee's salary and bonus can be affected by successful innovation, gains to employee are not as skewed toward only rewarding success as for an entrepreneur.

Second, the human and physical capital of hierarchical organizations tends to be less project-specific than for ventures that use other contracting processes. Within a hierarchical organization it can be relatively easy to reorganize the teams working on particular projects. In addition, developmental efforts may be capital-intensive, and scale economies may be achievable by using the capital on several related projects. Development of a single microwave tube used in satellite communication or radar navigation normally requires a small team of electrical and mechanical engineers as well as a number of technical support personnel. The tubes also undergo a variety of heat-treating, metallurgical, and testing processes. The entire development effort can require from two to four years to complete. Because the engineering properties of a microwave tube affect its performance (bandwidth, power, etc.), the same engineers, technicians, and equipment can be applied to producing a series of related tubes. Furthermore, multiple teams of engineers can share the developing and testing equipment.

A Recap

Planning is appropriate when the entrepreneur's need for financial capital is limited and the venture is of relatively low risk. If low-risk debt financing is provided, then elaborate delineation of contingencies is unnecessary. Where both the entrepreneur and the investor have established reputations or important nonsalvageable capital, the contracting process can be based on either promise or governance. Governance is more likely when projects involve important team efforts, when it is valuable to be able to set priorities centrally and to alter team composition quickly, and when capital investments are not venture-specific. A mixed form involving both promise (by the investor) and planning commitments (by the entrepreneur) is expected when the entrepreneur lacks sufficient reputation. Reliance on competition is possible only when the number of appropriately suited transacting parties is large or specific investment is small.

12.4 SUMMARY

In the terminology of economics, two kinds of private information raise the cost of market exchange. The first is adverse selection and the second is moral hazard. Information and incentive problems, arising from adverse selection and moral hazard, are important determinants of the financial contract terms and organizational structures of entrepreneurial ventures.

Adverse selection arises when the parties enter a negotiation with asymmetric information and expectations. Information asymmetry is an impediment to effective contracting between entrepreneurs and investors because each may be concerned that the other knows more and is trying to take advantage. Because a party with negative information has an incentive to conceal it and to imitate those with positive information, such problems cannot easily be overcome. Solutions to information problems include signaling and screening. A signal is a mechanism that can be used by parties with positive information to distinguish themselves from those with negative information. Signaling works as long as, for parties with negative information, the cost of imitating is more than the expected benefit of doing so. Screening is a mechanism used by parties without information to induce those with information to reveal whether the information they have is positive or negative. Screening and signaling are similar in that parties with negative information find that it is not economical to imitate those with positive information.

Moral hazard arises after an agreement is entered and sunk investments have been made in the relationship. If a sunk investment is specific to a relationship, a party may attempt to appropriate its value. Techniques for controlling the incentive problems associated with moral hazard include bonding and monitoring. Bonding involves making a commitment or investment such that the party who acts opportunistically would be worse off by exploiting the sunk investment than by not doing so. Bonding can be achieved through formal contract provisions or informally by investing in reputation or by relying on a third party for certification. Monitoring is an activity, undertaken by one party, that is designed to limit the ability of the other party to act opportunistically.

In spite of the information and incentive problems that the parties to a new venture face, the bottom line in negotiations between investors and the entrepreneur is that all parties must expect to come out winners. Of course, each is trying to maximize the size of the gain. However, an important distinction exists between the size of the gain a party expects and the share of the total gain the party expects. Sometimes, it is better to accept a smaller share because doing so is expected to increase the amount of the gain. It is not unheard of, for example, for an investor to ask for less ownership than the entrepreneur is willing to offer. If that happens, it is because the investor is concerned that, while the venture is attractive, it is not likely to meet the expectations of the entrepreneur. If it does not, the investor may be concerned that the entrepreneur will become disillusioned and retreat from a venture that should be pursued, or that without a larger share the entrepreneur will devote insufficient effort.

This chapter also discusses organizational choice as a means of dealing with transaction costs, including information costs. The basic choice for an entrepreneur is whether to organize a particular transaction by using a market-based contract or to integrate the transaction and perform it within the firm. We analyze this variant of a "make or buy" decision in the context of a new venture seeking outside financing. If the entrepreneur decides to use a contractual structure, the choice becomes one of whether to organize the agreement with planning or promise or to rely on competition in the marketplace to enforce performance. This choice is made in a bargaining context. That is, it is not a unilateral decision; the concerns of investors are important, even dominant, considerations. Choices about how to organize a transaction are not one-time, static choices. They are recurring, and the considerations vary with the maturity of the enterprise and the financing stage.

QUESTIONS AND PROBLEMS

1. Discuss how you would expect the contracting process and contract provisions between an entrepreneur and a prospective investor to be different in the following situations:

   a. There are only a few specific possible outcomes that might result from the venture. The parties know what the possibilities are and agree about the probability of each outcome.

   b. Same as (a), except that the parties disagree about the probabilities of the various outcomes.

   c. The future for the venture is highly uncertain, but the parties agree about the risk and expected return of the project, and know that they agree.

    d.   Same as (c), except that the parties do not know that they agree about risk and expected return.

    e.   The future for the venture is highly uncertain, and the parties disagree about the risk and expected return but do not know whether or not they agree.

2. Explain what is meant by "bounded rationality." How would you expect bounded rationality to affect the contracting process between an entrepreneur and an investor? How would you expect the contract terms between the two to be different from a situation where "rationality" was not "bounded"?

3. Explain what is meant by "opportunism." In what sense is opportunism an *ex post* concept? How would you expect opportunism to affect the contracting process and contract terms between an entrepreneur and an investor?

4. How can investments in reputation, explicit contract provisions, and investments in project-specific assets be used to create bonds that facilitate the contracting process? How would you expect the provisions of contracts between entrepreneurs and investors to be different in the presence of nonsalvageable sunk investments by the entrepreneur, the investor, or both?

5. Suppose a venture has existing assets that are worth $360,000 if it is successful but only $60,000 if it is not. The entrepreneur is seeking outside capital of $300,000 to pursue expansion. If the venture is successful, the expansion will have a NPV of $70,000 but only $20,000 if the venture is not successful.

    a.   Suppose the outside investor receives enough equity to return a zero NPV and that the entrepreneur retains the rest. The entrepreneur knows only that the probability of success is 50 percent and that the investor is aware of this. What should the entrepreneur who wants to maximize the value of his ownership do? To answer, analyze the values of the entrepreneur's claims, with and without investment, based on what the entrepreneur knows at the time of the decision to raise the capital and undertake the expansion.

    b.   Suppose the entrepreneur knows whether or not the venture will be successful, but the investor only knows that the probability of the good state is 50 percent. What should the entrepreneur do? How should the investor respond to the entrepreneur if the investor believes that the entrepreneur knows whether or not the venture will be successful? What will be the ultimate result?

    c.   Suppose the expansion opportunity has the same NPVs as above but that the entrepreneur's existing assets are worth $210,000, whether or not the investment in expansion is successful. How does this affect your analysis and conclusions?

    d.   What do you conclude about the role that existing assets play in the investment and capital-raising decision?

6. If an entrepreneur devotes all of her effort to a venture, it will be worth $1.25 million. If she devotes no effort to it, she can consume $1.25 million worth of other goods and activities. Suppose that, as the sole owner, she prefers to devote enough effort to the venture to achieve a value of $1 million.

    a.   Now suppose that she desires to sell 40 percent of the equity to an outside investor and that the investor purchases the equity based on its existing value of $1 million. However, with the entrepreneur's reduced ownership, she would decide to devote less effort to the venture, so that its new value would be only $700,000. Analyze the wealth transfer between the investor and the entrepreneur.

b. Suppose the investor correctly anticipates that the entrepreneur will reduce effort once some of the equity is sold and that with correct anticipation the entrepreneur will devote enough effort to make the venture worth $800,000. How much should the investor pay? What does the entrepreneur end up with instead of the original $1 million of value in the venture and $250,000 of other consumption?

c. Suppose the entrepreneur is a workaholic and will not change effort, but that the investor does not know that she is. The investor believes she would reduce effort to the point where the venture is only worth $600,000. How might the parties use monitoring and bonding arrangements to change the deal? What can you say about how much they would be willing to spend on monitoring and bonding?

7. Alan is a printer and Steve is a publisher. Steve proposes to buy publishing services from Alan for a price of $8,000 per day. To accept the offer, Alan must install a printing press near Steve's location. If he does, the fixed costs, amortized over the life of the press, will be $4,500 per day. If the contract were terminated, Alan would own the press and be able to move it to a new location to realize some salvage value. The salvage value, if moved, is $2,000 per day. Daily operating cost of the press is $2,500 and will be incurred by Alan for operating the press.

a. What is the breakeven price for which it would make sense for Alan to enter into a contract with Steve? How much of the daily service price is economic rent?

b. Of that total service price, how much would be a quasi-rent on the fixed investment and how much would be payment for the variable cost of production?

c. How much of the quasi-rent is appropriable by Steve once the press is in place? Why?

d. Suppose a third party, Ed, is willing to buy printing services from Alan at the same location as Steve and will pay $3,500 per day for the service. How much of the quasi-rent is appropriable?

e. Using this example, discuss the relationship between opportunism and the small numbers bargaining problem.

8. Suppose, in problem 5, that instead of the probability of the good state being 50 percent, it is 70 percent. Answer parts (a) and (b) of the problem with this change.

9. Suppose, in problem 5, that instead of the cost of expansion being $300,000, it is $100,000. Answer parts (a) and (b) of the problem with this change.

10. An entrepreneur who is seeking $1.5 million in outside capital believes her venture can be harvested in about three years. She expects the harvest value to be $8.0 million at that time, and believes the riskiness of the harvest-date cash flow can be represented as a standard deviation of $5.0 million and a correlation with the market of 0.2. From this point forward, she plans to commit $500,000 of her own human and financial capital to the venture. Assume the risk-free rate is 4 percent per year, the market rate is 10 percent, and the market standard deviation is 14 percent per year. The entrepreneur has $1.0 million of other assets she can invest in the market.

a. Suppose she raises the $1.5 million from a well-diversified investor who wants to earn at least $500,000 present value over breakeven to cover the costs of effort the investor expects to devote to monitoring the investment. If the investor agrees with the entrepreneur's cash flow projections, what fraction of common equity will the investor need to justify making the investment? What will be the value of the entrepreneur's claim (Valuation Template 5 is a convenient way to approach this problem)?

    b.   Suppose, that the investor is not as optimistic as the entrepreneur, and, instead, believes the expected harvest cash flow is only $6.0 million. All else the same, how does this change affect the percent of equity the investor requires? How does the change affect the value of the entrepreneur's interest?

11. An investor has been approached by an entrepreneur who is seeking $1.25 million for a venture, claiming that he expects to have the venture ready for harvesting in two years. The entrepreneur claims that harvest value is expected to be $4.0 million at that time, and that the riskiness of the harvest-date cash flow can be represented as a standard deviation of $4.0 million and a correlation with the market of 0.25. From this point forward, he plans to commit $250,000 of his own human and financial capital to the venture. Assume the risk-free rate is 4 percent per year, the market rate is 10 percent, and the market standard deviation is 14 percent per year. The entrepreneur has $1.0 million of other assets he can invest in the market. The investor is concerned that the entrepreneur, like many others, may be claiming he can get to a point where harvesting is feasible faster than he really can. The investor would like to test the entrepreneur's commitment to complete the project in two years instead of three.

    a.   Suppose the investor wants to earn $250,000 in present value to cover her costs of monitoring the investment. Assuming two years until harvest, what fraction of equity does the investor require, and what are the present value and NPV of the entrepreneur's interest (Valuation Template 5 is a convenient way to approach this problem)?

    b.   Suppose the true expected harvest date is three years. How would the investor and the entrepreneur fare if the percentage allocations of ownership from part (a) are used? Everything else is the same. Does the financing plan reveal to the investor whether the entrepreneur really believes harvest will be possible in two years?

    c.   Can the investor test the entrepreneur's harvest date claim by modifying the proposed contract so that the entrepreneur is required to commit $500,000 in financial and human capital, and the investor's commitment is reduced to offset? If the entrepreneur really believes it will take three years to get to harvest, and all else is the same, would the investor expect the entrepreneur to accept the modified proposal? Explain.

NOTES

1.   Williamson's (1975) discussion of bounded rationality in a contracting context draws on work by Nobel Laureate, Herbert Simon. Simon first introduced the concept of bounded rationality in the context of employer–employee relations. See Simon (1957, 1961).

2.   The example was developed and first studied by Akerlof (1970).

3.   Milhaupt (1998) examines the effects of information asymmetry on transactions between entrepreneurs and investors and develops implications for public policy toward small-firm financing.

4.   See the discussion of the Venture Capital method in Chapter 9.

5.   The cost of transacting increases whenever the importance of private information is high relative to the importance of common information. The parties may have different information, but neither may have a clear information advantage. They may even have the same information but be unaware that they do. In either case, an incentive exists to expend resources on information transfer.

6.   See Arrow (1963).

7. For the effects of moral hazard problems on firm value and financing choices see Jensen and Meckling (1976), Myers (1984), Ramakrishnan and Thakor (1984), Darrough and Stoughton (1986), Harris and Raviv (1991), Mello and Parsons (1992), and Fischer (1992).

8. See Klein, Crawford, and Alchian (1978) for an analysis of the risk of appropriation of sunk investments and the choice of organizational form.

9. Smith (1998) provides a comprehensive review of opportunism problems between entrepreneurs and venture capitalists and discusses the implications for venture capital contracting.

10. Alternatively, we could consider expanding the venture using outside capital. Doing so makes the analysis more complex but does not alter the conclusions.

11. For discussion and illustration of the distinction between discrete and relational contracting, see Joskow (1985, 1987).

12. Cornelli and Yosha (1997) offer a contractual approach for dealing with observability issues. Specifically, they consider the use of convertible debt in a relationship in which the investor has an abandonment option. If straight debt is used, the entrepreneur may try to manipulate short-run performance to discourage the investor from abandoning the venture. If debt is convertible, they contend that the entrepreneur has less incentive to engage in this "window dressing."

13. Gorman and Sahlman (1989) report that venture capitalists regularly monitor their portfolio firms but normally are not involved in day-to-day management. Gifford (1997) provides an analysis of the optimal amount of monitoring from the perspective of the venture capitalist. Sapienza and Gupta (1994) report evidence of the determinants of frequency of venture capitalist interaction.

14. The signal also addresses a possible concern that, once the outside capital is committed, the entrepreneur may devote less time to the venture. Tying the entrepreneur's return to attainment of milestones can strengthen the entrepreneur's commitment of effort to the project. Chua and Woodward (1993) analyze the use of stock options to resolve differences in expectations and to align the interests of entrepreneurs and investors.

15. See, for example, Ross (1977), Miller and Rock (1985), and McNichols and David (1990). A substantial literature exists on the mechanisms available to managers for signaling their information to prospective investors. See, for example, Leland and Pyle (1977), Campbell and Kracaw (1980), Heinkel (1982), Truman (1983), Diamond (1985), Flannery (1986), Blazenko (1987), Brennan and Kraus (1987), Diamond and Verrecchia (1991). In general, the existing literature deals with the scenario in which managers are perceived to have superior information, and relates to the case of an entrepreneur who is seeking to raise capital from passive (relatively uninformed) investors. The contracting problem is more complex when, for example, the entrepreneur is negotiating with a venture capitalist and the parties are likely to have different information from each other, but neither has information that clearly is superior.

16. In a startup, the entrepreneur must find a way to reveal the value of the venture to potential investors. Signaling theory suggests that ownership share retained by the entrepreneur helps the investors evaluate the information they receive. See Leland and Pyle (1977). Prasad, Bruton, and Vozikis (2000) reason that because many entrepreneurs have limited personal capital, a preferred signal of project quality is the proportion of the entrepreneur's initial wealth invested in the project. Such information indicates both project value and the entrepreneur's commitment. Signal quality depends on the stage of the venture. As that investment becomes nonsalvageable, the entrepreneur's percentage of ownership is a better signal.

17. Fee (2001) examines motion picture financing arrangements to illustrate how contracting can mitigate incentive problems that arise when outside investors may not value the private benefits of control that accrue to an entrepreneur. While investors will want to monitor the filmmaker's decisions, the presence of outside investors can dampen the entrepreneur's incentives to put effort into the film. Filmmakers (the entrepreneurs) choose between studio funds (losing control over the project) and independent financing (retaining control). Fee finds that using independent motion picture financing is more common when a film requires a high level of creative effort and the filmmaker's specific investment in the film is high.

18. See also Allen (1984) and Bull (1983). For a contrary view, see Bhide and Stevenson (1990). Gompers and Lerner (1999) provide evidence of the effect of reputation on the behavior of venture capital firms.

19. For further discussion, see Ayers and Cramton (1994).

20. For evidence on certification see James and Wier (1990). Thakor (1982) provides a model of third-party certification, and Millon and Thakor (1985) discuss the role of information-gathering agencies.

21. Booth and Smith (1986) provide a formal model of underwriter certification. Beatty and Ritter (1986) provide evidence of the reputational cost to underwriters of mispricing issues. Tinic (1988) examines evidence of litigation related to mispricing.

22. See Beatty, Bunsis, and Hand (1998).

23. See Smith and Warner (1979) for an analysis of bond covenants and flexibility.

24. See Berglof (1994) for an analysis of using convertible securities to allocate control rights.

25. Hellmann (2002) provides a model that predicts that an entrepreneurial company is more likely to be financed by a corporate investor if it is a complement rather than a substitute for the corporation's core business. If the entrepreneurial firm is a complement (substitute), the corporate investor offers a higher (lower) valuation than an independent venture capitalist. The larger the opportunity for the corporate investor to control the strategy of the entrepreneurial firm, the more likely that the entrepreneur will choose an independent venture capitalist. The corporate investor is more likely to make a strategic investment in a particular area when it can commit not to make a rival internal investment in the area.

26. Coase (1937) first espoused the idea that the transaction costs of using markets can be substantial and that productive activity sometimes can be organized by firms to achieve the same productive efficiencies as market exchange. This shifted the focus of economic thinking to a view of the firm as a nexus of contracts for exchange and production, and the choice of economic organization to be one of trying to minimize transaction costs. See also Coase (1960), Williamson (1975, 1985) and Klein, Crawford, and Alchian (1978).

27. Imperfect information is at the heart of the transactions costs identified above. Search costs arise because information is costly. Negotiation costs arise because each party spends resources to discover what the other party knows, to improve their own information, and to control incentive problems that may arise. Finally, enforcement of a contract would be simple if specifying and measuring performance were not difficult.

28. Transactions-cost economics, as articulated by Coase and Williamson, has been criticized for its lack of specific attention to the costs of internal organization. Grossman and Hart (1986) and Hart and Moore (1988) account for the costs and benefits of different organizational forms on the basis of allocation of control rights.

29. Milgrom and Roberts (1992) identify influence costs as internal costs that are incurred by the participants in an organization to influence the decision maker.

30. The term "adaptive sequential decision making" was introduced by Williamson.

31. Williamson (1987) offers this framework for thinking about the nature of the contracting process (broadly defined) between the parties.

REFERENCES AND ADDITIONAL READING

AKERLOF, GEORGE. "The Market for Lemons: Quality Uncertainty and the Market Mechanism." *Quarterly Journal of Economics* 84 (1970): 488–500.

ALCHIAN, ARMEN, AND HAROLD DEMSETZ. "Production, Information Costs and Economic Organization." *American Economic Review* 62 (1972): 777–795.

ALLEN, FRANKLIN. "Reputation and Product Quality." *RAND Journal of Economics* 15 (1984): 311–327.

AMIT, RAPHAEL, LAWRENCE GLOSTEN, AND EITAN MULLER. "Entrepreneurial Ability, Venture Investments, and Risk Sharing." *Management Science* 36 (1990): 1232–1245.

ARROW, KENNETH. "Uncertainty and the Welfare Economics of Medical Care." *American Economic Review* 53 (1963): 941–973.

ASQUITH, PAUL, AND DAVID. W. MULLINS. "Equity Issues and Offering Dilutions." *Journal of Financial Economics* 15 (1986): 61–90.

AYERS, IAN, AND PETER CRAMTON. "Relational Investing and Agency Theory." *Cordozo Law Review* 15 (1994): 1033–1066.

BANKMAN, JOSEPH, AND RONALD J. GILSON. "Why Start-ups?" *Stanford Law Review* 51 (1999): 289–308.

BASCHA, ANDREAS AND UWE WALTZ. "Convertible Securities and Optimal Exit Decisions in Venture Capital Finance." *Journal of Corporate Finance* 7 (2001): 285–306.

BASCHA, ANDREAS AND UWE WALZ. "Financing Practices in the German Venture Capital Industry: An Empirical Assessment." SSRN Working Paper, 2001.

BEATTY, RANDOLPH P., HOWARD BUNSIS, AND JOHN R. M. HAND. "Indirect Economic Penalties in SEC Investigations of Underwriters." *Journal of Financial Economics* 50 (1998): 151–186.

BEATTY, RANDOLPH P., AND JAY RITTER. "Investment Banking, Reputation and the Underpricing of Initial Public Offerings." *Journal of Financial Economics* 15 (1986): 213–232.

BERGLOF, ERIK. "A Control Theory of Venture Capital Finance." *Journal of Law Economics, and Organization* 10 (1994): 247–267.

BERGEMANN, DIRK AND ULRICH HEGE. "Venture Capital Financing, Moral Hazard, and Learning." *Journal of Banking & Finance* 22 (1998): 703–735.

BERNARDO, ANTONIO AND IVO WELCH. "On the Evolution of Overconfidence and Entrepreneurs." *Journal of Economics & Management Strategy* 10 (2001): 301–330.

BHIDE, AMAR, AND HOWARD J. STEVENSON. "Why Be Honest If Honesty Doesn't Pay?" *Harvard Business Review* 68 (September–October 1990).

BITLER, MARIANNE, TOBIAS MOSKOWITZ, AND ANNETTE VISSING-JØRGENSEN. "Why Must Entrepreneurs Hold Large Ownership Shares? Optimal Contracting in Private and Newly Public Firms." University of Chicago Working Paper, 2002.

BLAZENKO, GEORGE W. "Managerial Preference, Asymmetric Information, and Financial Structure." *Journal of Finance* 42 (1987): 839–862.

BOOTH, JAMES R. AND RICHARD L. SMITH. "Capital Raising, Underwriting, and the Certification Hypothesis." *Journal of Financial Economics* 15 (1986): 261–281.

BRENNAN, MICHAEL, AND ALAN KRAUS. "Efficient Financing under Asymmetric Information." *Journal of Finance* 42 (1987): 1225–1243.

BULL, CLIVE. "Implicit Contracts in the Absence of Enforcement and Risk Aversion." *American Economic Review* 73 (1983): 658–670.

CAMPBELL, TIM S., AND WILLIAM A. KRACAW. "Information Production, Market Signaling, and the Theory of Financial Intermediation." *Journal of Finance* 35 (1980): 863–882.

CHAN, YUK-SHEE, DANIEL SIEGEL AND ANJAN V. THAKOR. "Learning, Corporate Control, and Performance Requirements in Venture Capital Contracts." *International Economic Review* 35 (1990): 365–381.

CHUA, JESS H., AND RICHARD S. WOODWARD. "Splitting the Firm Between the Entrepreneur and the Venture Capitalist with the Help of Stock Options." *Journal of Business Venturing* 8 (1993): 43–58.

COASE, RONALD H. "The Nature of the Firm." *Economica* 4 (1937): 386–405.

COASE, RONALD H. "The Problem of Social Cost." *Journal of Law and Economics* 3 (1960): 1–44.

COOPER, ARNOLD C., CAROLYN WOO, AND WILLIAM C. DUNKELBERG. "Entrepreneurs' Perceived Chances for Success." *Journal of Business Venturing* 3 (1988): 7–108.

COOTER, ROBERT, AND THOMAS ULEN. *Law and Economics.* 3rd ed. Reading, MA: Addison-Wesley, 1999.

CUMMING, DOUGLAS. "Adverse Selection and Capital Structure: Evidence From Venture Capital." University of Alberta Working Paper, 2001.

DARROUGH, MASAKO N., AND NEAL M. STOUGHTON. "Moral Hazard and Adverse Selection: The Question of Financial Structure." *Journal of Finance* 41 (1986): 501–513.

DIAMOND, DOUGLAS W. "Optimal Release of Information by Firms." *Journal of Finance* 40 (1985): 1071–1094.

DIAMOND, DOUGLAS W., AND ROBERT E. VERRECCHIA. "Disclosure, Liquidity, and the Cost of Capital." *Journal of Finance* 46 (1991): 1325–1358.

FEE, C. EDWARD. "The Costs of Outside Equity Control: Evidence from Motion Picture Financing Decisions" *Journal of Business* 75 (2002).

FISCHER, PAUL E. "Optimal Contracting and Insider Trading Restrictions." *Journal of Finance* 47 (1992): 673–694.

FLANNERY, MARK J. "Asymmetric Information and Risky Debt Maturity Choice." *Journal of Finance* 41 (1986): 19-37.

GIFFORD, SHARON. "Limited Attention and the Role of the Venture Capitalist." *Journal of Business Venturing* 12 (1997): 459–482.

GOMPERS, PAUL. "Optimal Investment, Monitoring, and the Staging of Venture Capital." *Journal of Finance* 50 (1995).

GOMPERS, PAUL A., AND JOSHUA LERNER. "Reputation and Conflict of Interest in the Issuance of Public Securities: Evidence from Venture Capital." *Journal of Law and Economics* 42 (April 1999).

GORMAN, MICHAEL, AND WILLIAM A. SAHLMAN. "What Do Venture Capitalists Do?" *Journal of Business Venturing* 4 (1989): 231–248.

GROSSMAN, SANFORD, AND OLIVER HART. "The Costs and Benefits of Ownership: A Theory of Vertical and Lateral Integration." *Journal of Political Economy* 94 (1986): 691–719.

HAMILTON, BARTON, H. "Does Entrepreneurship Pay? An Empirical Analysis of the Returns to Self-Employment." *Journal of Political Economy* 108 (2000).

HARRIS, MILTON, AND ARTHUR RAVIV. "The Theory of Capital Structure." *Journal of Finance* 46, no. 1(1991): 297–355.

HART, OLIVER, AND JOHN MOORE. "Incomplete Contracts and Renegotiation." *Econometrica* 56 (1988): 755–786.

HEINKEL, ROBERT. "A Theory of Capital Structure Relevance under Imperfect Information." *Journal of Finance* 37 (1982): 1141–1150.

HELLMANN, THOMAS. "A Theory of Corporate Venture Investing." *Journal of Financial Economics* 64 (2002): 285–314.

HELLMANN, THOMAS. "The Allocation of Control Rights in Venture Capital Contracts." RAND *Journal of Economics* 29 (1998): 57–76.

HELLMAN, THOMAS AND MANJU PURI. The Interaction Between Product Market and Financial Strategy, The Role of Venture Capital." *Review of Financial Studies* 13 (2000): 959–988.

HELLMAN, THOMAS AND MANJU PURI. "Venture Capital and the Professionalization of Start-up Firms: Empirical Evidence." *Journal of Finance* 57 (2002): 169–197

JAMES, CHRISTOPHER, AND PEGGY WIER. "Borrowing Relationships, Intermediation, and the Cost of Issuing Public Securities." *Journal of Financial Economics* 28 (1990): 149–171.

JENSEN, MICHAEL C., AND WILLIAM H. MECKLING. "Theory of the Firm: Managerial Behavior, Agency Costs, and Ownership Structure." *Journal of Financial Economics* 3 (1976): 305–360.

JOSKOW, PAUL L. "Vertical Integration and Long-Term Contracts." *Journal of Law, Economics, and Organization* 1 (1985): 33–80.

JOSKOW, PAUL L. "Contract Duration and Transactions Specific Investment: Empirical Evidence from the Coal Market." *American Economic Review* 77 (1987): 168–183.

KAPLAN, STEVEN N. AND PER STRÖMBERG. "Characteristics, Contracts, and Actions: Evidence from Venture Capitalist Analyses." University of Chicago Working Paper, 2002.

KAPLAN, STEVEN N. AND PER STRÖMBERG. "Financial Contracting Theory Meets the Real World: An Empirical Analysis of Venture Capital Contracts." *Review of Financial Studies* forthcoming.

KAPLAN, STEVEN N. AND PER STRÖMBERG. "Venture Capitalists as Principals: Contracting, Screening, and Monitoring." *American Economic Review Papers and Proceedings* 91 (2000): 426–430.

KLEIN, BENJAMIN, ROBERT G. CRAWFORD, AND ARMEN A. ALCHIAN. "Vertical Integration, Appropriable Rents, and the Competitive Contracting Process." *Journal of Law and Economics* 21 (1978): 297–326.

KLEIN, BENJAMIN, AND KEITH LEFFLER. "The Role of Market Forces in Assuring Contractual Performance." *Journal of Political Economy* 89 (1981): 615–641.

LELAND, HAYNE E., AND DAVID H. PYLE. "Informational Asymmetries, Financial Structure, and Financial Intermediation." *Journal of Finance* 32 (1977): 371–387.

MACNEIL, IAN. "The Many Futures of Contract." *University of Southern California Law Review* 47 (1974): 691–816.

MASULIS, RONALD W., AND ASHOK KORWAR. "Seasoned Equity Offerings: An Empirical Investigation." *Journal of Financial Economics* 15 (1986): 91–118.

MCNICHOLS, MAUREEN, AND AJAY DAVID. "Stock Dividends, Stock Splits, and Signaling." *Journal of Finance* 45 (1990): 857–880.

MELLO, ANTONIO S., AND JOHN E. PARSONS. "Measuring the Agency Cost of Debt." *Journal of Finance* 47 (1992): 1887–1904.

MIKKELSON, WAYNE H., AND MEGAN M. PARTCH. "Valuation Effects of Security Offerings and the Issuance Process." *Journal of Financial Economics* 15 (1986): 31–60.

MILGROM, PAUL, AND JOHN ROBERTS. *Economics, Organization, and Management.* Englewood Cliffs, NJ: Prentice-Hall, 1992.

MILHAUPT, CURTIS, J. "The Small Firm Financing Problem: Private Information and Public Policy." *Journal of Small and Emerging Business Law* 2 (1998): 177–196.

MILLER, MERTON H., AND KEVIN ROCK. "Dividend Policy under Asymmetric Information." *Journal of Finance* 40 (1985): 1031–1052.

MILLON, MARCIA H., AND ANJAN V. THAKOR. "Moral Hazard and Information Sharing: A Model of Financial Information Gathering Agencies." *Journal of Finance* 40 (1985): 1403–1422.

MONOVE, MICHAEL, AND A. GEORGE PADILLA. "Banking (Conservatively) with Optimists." *RAND Journal of Economics* 30(1999): 324–350.

MYERS, STEWART C. "The Capital Structure Puzzle." *Journal of Finance* 39 (1984): 575–592.

MYERS, STEWART C., AND NICHOLAS S. MAJLUF. "Corporate Financing and Investment Decisions When Firms Have Information That Investors Do Not Have." *Journal of Financial Economics* 13 (1984): 187–221.

PRASAD, DEV, GARRY BRUTON, AND GEORGE VOZIKIS. "Signaling Value to Business Angels: The

Proportion of the Entrepreneur's Net Worth Invested in a New Venture as a Decision Signal." *Venture Capital* 2 (2000): 167–182.

RAMAKRISHNAN, RAM T. S., AND ANJAN V. THAKOR. "The Valuation of Assets under Moral Hazard." *Journal of Finance* 39 (1984): 229–238.

RAVID, S. ABRAHAM, AND MATTHEW SPIEGEL. "Optimal Financial Contracts for a Start-Up with Unlimited Operating Discretion." *Journal of Financial and Quantitative Analysis* 32 (1997): 269–285.

ROBINSON, DAVID T., AND TOBY E. STUART. "Financial Contracting in Biotech Strategic Alliances." Columbia University Working Paper, 2002.

ROSS, STEPHEN A. "The Determinants of Financial Structure: The Incentive Signaling Approach." *Bell Journal of Economics* 8 (1977): 23–40.

RUSSO, EDWARD J. AND PAUL J. SCHOEMAKER. "Managing Overconfidence." *Sloan Management Review* (1992): 7–17.

SAHLMAN, WILLIAM A. "The Structure and Governance of Venture Capital Organizations." *Journal of Financial Economics* 27 (1990): 473–521.

SAPIENZA, HARRY J., AND ANIL K. GUPTA. "Impact of Agency Risks and Task Uncertainty in Venture Capitalist—CEO Interaction." *Academy of Management Journal* 37 (1994): 1618–1632.

SIMON, HERBERT. *Models of Man.* New York: John Wiley & Sons, 1957.

SIMON, HERBERT. *Administrative Behavior.* 2nd ed. New York: Macmillan, 1961.

SMITH, CLIFFORD W., AND JEROLD B. WARNER. "On Financial Contracting: An Analysis of Bond Covenants." *Journal of Financial Economics* 7 (1979): 117–161.

SMITH, D. GORDON. Venture Capital Contracting in the Information Age." *Journal of Small and Emerging Business Law* (1998).

SPENCE, A. MICHAEL. *Market Signaling: Information Transfer in Hiring and Related Processes.* Cambridge, MA: Harvard University Press, 1973.

THAKOR, ANJAN V. "An Exploration of Competitive Signaling Equilibria with 'Third Party' Information Production: The Case of Debt Insurance." *Journal of Finance* 37 (1982): 717–739.

TINIC, SEHA M. "Anatomy of Initial Public Offerings of Common Stock." *Journal of Finance* 43 (1988): 789–822.

TRUMAN, BRETT. "Motivating Management to Reveal Inside Information." *Journal of Finance* 38 (1983): 1253–1269.

VAN OSNABRUGGE, MARK AND ROBERT ROBINSON. "A Comparison of Business Angel and Venture Capitalist Investment Procedures: An Agency Theory-Based Analysis." Harvard Business School Working Paper, 1999.

WILLIAMSON, OLIVER. *Markets and Hierarchies.* New York: Free Press, 1975.

WILLIAMSON, OLIVER. "Credible Commitments: Using Hostages to Support Exchange." *American Economic Review* 73 (1983): 519–540.

WILLIAMSON, OLIVER. *The Economic Institutions of Capitalism.* New York: Free Press, 1985.

WILLIAMSON, OLIVER. *Antitrust Economics.* New York: Basil Blackwell, 1987.

WRIGHT, G.N. AND L.D. PHILLIPS. "Cultural Variations in Probabilistic Thinking: Alternative Ways of Dealing with Uncertainty." *International Journal of Psychology* 15 (1980): 239–257.

Financial Contracting

I am treating you as my friend, asking you to share my present minuses, in the hope I can ask you to share my future pluses. (Katherine Mansfield)

Learning Objectives

After reading this chapter you will be able to:

- Understand how and why staging and other real options affect the values of new venture financial claims.

- Value the financial claims of a new venture using either discrete scenario analysis or simulation.

- Use financial modeling and valuation techniques to study game theoretic issues that arise for the parties to a new venture.

- Evaluate the effects of alternative financial contracts on the values of the financial interests of the entrepreneur and outside investors.

- Know how to construct financial contracts to signal information and align incentives.

The objective of financial contract design is to develop contracts that enhance and allocate value. As we have seen in earlier chapters, some allocations of risk and expected returns are better than others. Furthermore, contract terms can enhance value by helping parties overcome information asymmetries and by aligning their incentives. Beyond these considerations, financial contracts can add value through the structure of real options that comprise the venture and the allocation of decision rights to the options.

In short, financial contracts affect value in complex ways. Because the effects are complex, comparing alternative deal structures can be difficult. Nonetheless, deal structure can determine whether a venture is worth pursuing and whether it is likely to succeed or fail. In this chapter, we use the valuation methodology from earlier chapters to examine how financial contract design affects value. Risk allocation, reward allocation, information signaling, and incentive alignment all are elements of contract design that can affect value.

Imagine yourself as a venture capitalist. An entrepreneur, who is seeking investment capital for a telecommunications venture, has approached you. You and the entrepreneur both anticipate that the venture will need substantial outside capital before harvesting will be feasible. You have several concerns. First, you believe the entrepreneur's projections are too optimistic. Second, you are concerned that, although the idea appears sound, the entrepreneur may be more of a visionary than an effective manager. Third, you know that competing ventures are under way and you are concerned that one of them may capture the opportunity before the entrepreneur's venture comes to fruition. Finally, you believe that the entrepreneur will not be motivated to execute the plan unless she can expect to retain significant control and a large fraction of ownership. This chapter focuses on designing financial contracts to deal with such complex issues as these.

Throughout the chapter, we recognize and exploit the fact that investors and entrepreneurs are likely to have different attitudes toward risk and different expectations about performance. We show how financial contracting can address both differences. We extend the discussion from Chapter 11 by considering staging and real options. Toward the end of the chapter, we discuss contracting in the context of information and incentive problems. As always, we adopt the objective of maximizing value for the entrepreneur. We do this by holding the outside investor's return constant and by analyzing impact on the entrepreneur.

13.1 STAGING OF INVESTMENT: THE VENTURE CAPITAL METHOD

Recall that under the Venture Capital Method of valuation, the cash flows of a success scenario are discounted at a hurdle rate that is above cost of capital. The hurdle rate compensates for optimism built into the cash flow projections of the success scenario. Because the probability of failure usually declines as a venture progresses, the hurdle rates that are commonly used under this method are lower for investments made at later stages.

Consider a new venture that has capital needs of $700,000 per year for five years, beginning at time zero. Figure 13-1 summarizes the essential information about the venture. The business plan includes a projection of negative earnings during the first few years, followed by rapid earnings growth. To keep the illustration simple, we assume that the venture generates no free cash flow during the first five years. By the end of year 5, the plan shows earnings of $2.5 million. A public offering of equity is projected at the end of year 5. Because (we assume) the typical earnings multiple of comparable public companies is 15, the projected continuing value as of year 5 is $37.5 million. The figure shows annual hurdle rates for investments made each year. The hurdle rates are generally consistent with the Venture Capital Method rates an investor would use. They begin at 50 percent for investment at time zero and decline by 5

Valuation Template 6
Single-stage Investment—Venture Capital Method

Income Statement Information

Year	0	1	2	3	4	5
Earnings Before Interest and After Tax		($500,000)	($200,000)	$400,000	$1,400,000	$2,500,000

Cash Flow Information

	0	1	2	3	4	5
External Funds Required to Support Operations		$700,000	$700,000	$700,000	$700,000	$0
Equity Capital Raised	$3,240,927					
Beginning Cash Balance	$3,240,927	$2,642,564	$2,020,267	$1,373,077	$700,000	
Uses of Cash	$700,000	$700,000	$700,000	$700,000	$700,000	
Cash Invested in Marketable Securities	$2,540,927	$1,942,564	$1,320,267	$673,077	$0	
Return on Invested Cash	$101,637	$77,703	$52,811	$26,923	$0	
Ending Cash Balance	$2,642,564	$2,020,267	$1,373,077	$700,000	$0	

Investor Valuation and Ownership Allocation

	0	1	2	3	4	5
Investor Hurdle Rate	50.00%	45.00%	40.00%	35.00%	30.00%	25.00%
Continuing Value Earnings Multiplier						15
Continuing Value of Venture						$37,500,000
Required Future Value of Investment						$24,610,789
Ownership Share Required						65.63%

Figure 13-1   Single-stage investment—Venture Capital Method

percent per year. Recall that a hurdle rate of 50 percent means that, for an investment made at time zero, success-scenario cash flows must return 50 percent annually until harvesting; for an investment made at year 3, success-scenario cash flows must return 35 percent annually.

We use this example to see how, based on the Venture Capital Method, staging affects the allocation of ownership in the venture. To establish a baseline, we first determine ownership allocation under single-stage investment.

Single-Stage Investment

Suppose the entrepreneur would like to raise enough cash at time zero to cover projected cash needs for the entire five years. In Figure 13-1, we assume that investment capital raised at time zero but not needed until later can be invested at a risk-free rate of 4 percent until it is needed. On that basis, the entrepreneur is seeking $3.241 million of outside equity at time zero. The cash balance portion of the Cash Flow Information panel demonstrates that this amount is sufficient to generate $700,000 of cash per year over the five-year period.

Our objective in Figure 13-1 is to determine the fraction of equity an outside investor would require in exchange for a single-stage investment of $3.241 million at time zero. Two equivalent approaches are possible. One is to discount the projected continuing value at a rate of 50 percent per year and compare this (post-money) present value to the amount of the investment. The other is to use the time-zero hurdle rate to find the future value of the investment as of year 5 and compare it to projected continuing value. Because the second approach is easier to use when investment is staged (our next step), we use it in Figure 13-1. The figure shows that the $3.241 million investment must generate a year-5 cash return of $24.611 million in the success scenario. Because the continuing value of the entire venture is $37.5 million, the investor would require 65.63 percent of the equity.

If the entrepreneur cares about control and about holding a majority stake of the equity, she will not find this financing arrangement (which leaves her only 34.37 percent of the equity) attractive. However, because we do not know entrepreneur's opportunity cost of capital, we cannot use the computations in Figure 13-1 to value the entrepreneur's financial claim.

Multi-Stage Investment

Suppose, instead of requiring that the entire amount be invested at time zero, the entrepreneur is willing to accept the investor's counterproposal to contribute the capital in stages, if staging will enable her to maintain control and majority ownership.

Figure 13-2 illustrates a staging alternative in which outside capital is invested at time zero and in years 2 and 4. The time-zero investment must be sufficient to finance operation for the first two years. Because some of the capital can be invested at the risk-free rate until it is needed in year 1, the amount required for the first two years is $1.373 million. A like amount is needed at the end of year 2, to finance operations in years 3 and 4, and an investment of $700,000 is required to finance operations in year 5. Thus, the total investment of $3.446 million is somewhat larger than in Figure 13-1. The difference arises because, with staging, the venture has less liquid capital on which it can earn the risk-free rate. Instead, the investor can retain use of the funds for a longer period of time. Because the investor also can earn the risk-free rate, the two financing scenarios have the same present value cost for the investor.

To find the required ownership interest of the investor under the staging scenario in Figure 13-2, we first evaluate each stage separately. Working from the last investment to the first, we begin with the $700,000 third-stage investment. According to the hurdle rates in the

Valuation Template 7
Multi-stage Investment—Venture Capital Method

Income Statement Information

Year	0	1	2	3	4	5
Earnings Before Interest and After Tax		($500,000)	($200,000)	$400,000	$1,400,000	$2,500,000

Cash Flow Information

	0	1	2	3	4	5
External Funds Required to Support Operations		$700,000	$700,000	$700,000	$700,000	$0
Equity Capital Raised		$1,373,077	$1,373,077			
Beginning Cash Balance		$700,000	$1,373,077	$700,000	$700,000	$700,000
Uses of Cash		$700,000	$700,000	$700,000	$700,000	
Cash Invested in Marketable Securities		$673,077	$673,077	$0	$0	$0
Return on Invested Cash		$26,923	$26,923	$0	$0	$0
Ending Cash Balance		$700,000	$700,000	$0	$0	$0

Investor Valuation and Ownership Allocation

	0	1	2	3	4	5
Investor Hurdle Rate	50.00%	45.00%	40.00%	35.00%	30.00%	25.00%
Continuing Value Earnings Multiplier						15
Continuing Value of Venture						$37,500,000

Investor Required Future Value and Equity Share	Required Beginning Share	Required Ending Share	Value
Third Stage	2.43%	2.43%	$910,000
Second Stage	10.30%	10.05%	$3,767,723
First Stage	31.77%	27.80%	$10,426,803
Ownership Required	**40.28%**		**$15,104,527**

Figure 13-2   Multi-stage investment—Venture Capital Method

figure, the investor seeks a return of 30 percent for the investment. Thus, the year-5 future value of the third-stage investment must be $910,000. Given the total continuing value of $37.5 million, the investor requires 2.43 percent of the equity in exchange for the third-stage investment. This is sufficient to cover the investor's opportunity cost.

We can determine the required percentage of ending ownership for the second-stage investment in a similar manner. The desired return on the $1.373 million investment is 40 percent per year for three years, resulting in a year-5 value of $3.768 million. This corresponds to 10.05 percent of continuing value. By the same reasoning, the required ownership percentage for the first-stage investment is 27.80 percent.

Collectively, the investor requires an interest of 40.28 percent of the equity in exchange for the three stages of investment. Thus, with staging, the entrepreneur can retain control and majority ownership of the venture.

Why Does Staging Reduce the Outside Ownership Share?

Comparing Figures 13-1 and 13-2, according to the Venture Capital Method, staging reduces the ownership interest of the investor and apparently benefits the entrepreneur. To understand why you must know why the hurdle rates in the figures change for investments at later stages.

How is the investor's commitment different in Figure 13-2 from what it is in Figure 13-1? For a single-stage investment, the commitment is absolute. Even if it becomes clear, during the five years, that the project is destined to fail, the investor's capital is irrevocably committed. In the event of liquidation, because, in the illustration, the investment is in the form of common stock, the investor would recover only a 65.63 percent share of liquidation value. The balance would go to the entrepreneur as compensation for the entrepreneur's effort.

There is no economic difference between the scenario in Figure 13-1 and an alternative scenario in which investment is staged as it is in Figure 13-2, but made irrevocably at time zero. Because the commitment is made at time zero, the investment must be evaluated as if it were made at time zero. Thus, the 50 percent hurdle rate would apply to investments made at any time during the entire five years.

It follows that the lower hurdle rates in Figure 13-2 for investing in later years arise because some of the uncertainty about venture performance is resolved before the decision to invest must be made. The later-stage investments are made only if the venture continues to be attractive. Unlike the situation in Figure 13-1, the investor's promise in Figure 13-2 is only to make second- and third-stage investments if doing so is in the investor's interest. The actual structure of rights and obligations may be more complex, but the important distinction is that, with staging, the entrepreneur is accepting some risk that the investor will not provide future rounds of financing or that the terms will be different from those originally envisioned.

Because additional risk is shifted to the entrepreneur, it is not clear which of the two scenarios is a better deal for her. In Figure 13-2, the entrepreneur can expect to retain control and majority ownership if the success scenario is realized, but bears more risk that financing will not be available or that the investor will require a larger fraction of equity if the success scenario is not realized. The Venture Capital Method provides no guidance to the entrepreneur for comparing these alternatives. Later in the chapter, we use valuation models from earlier chapters to evaluate the entrepreneur's choice. However, we cannot do so now with only the limited information that the Venture Capital Method uses. The entrepreneur cannot choose between the scenarios in Figures 13-1 and 13-2 simply by comparing the fraction of equity the entrepreneur retains in the success scenario.

Determining Required Ownership Percentage when Follow-on Investment Is Expected

An outside investor often decides to invest during one round of financing and anticipates that the venture will seek additional financing in subsequent rounds. Because additional rounds affect the number of shares outstanding, an investor who bases his decision on the continuing value of the venture at the time of an anticipated liquidity event must take future financing rounds into account. Figure 13-2 demonstrates how, under the Venture Capital Method, anticipated future financing affects the fraction of equity an investor requires at each stage.

Beginning with the third-stage, because no subsequent rounds are anticipated, the required ownership share remains 2.43 percent. A second-stage investor who estimates continuing value as $37.5 million under the success scenario anticipates a third round of financing in exchange for 2.43 percent of the equity. Before the third round, the combined shares of the entrepreneur and investor represent 97.57 percent of ending equity. Since they own 100 percent of the outstanding equity at that time of the investment, an investor who wishes to end up with 10.05 percent of equity at harvest must seek a larger fraction of the equity at the time of investment. Equation (13.1) shows how you can determine the required fraction of equity when future rounds are anticipated.

$$Fraction\ of\ Equity\ Required = \frac{Ending\ Fraction\ of\ Equity\ Required}{(1\ -\ Sum\ of\ Fractions\ Required\ by\ Investors\ in\ Future\ Rounds)} \qquad (13.1)$$

Using this equation, the investor's required share in the second round is 10.30 percent:

$$10.30\ percent = 10.05\ percent/(1\ -\ 2.43\ percent).$$

Similarly, the investor's required share in the first round is 31.77 percent:

$$31.77\ percent = 27.80\ percent/(1\ -\ 2.43\ percent\ -\ 10.05\ percent).$$

This method for determining the investor's required ownership fraction when additional rounds of financing are expected is fundamentally the same when valuation methods other than the Venture Capital Method are used.

How the Capitalization of a Venture Relates to the Stage of Financing

Normally, investors expect the capitalization of a venture to increase at each round of financing. If it does not, or even if the increase from one stage to the next is small, investors sometimes express concern about the venture's prospects. Information in Figure 13-2 demonstrates the basis for such concerns. In the figure, the first-stage investor contributes $1.373 million in exchange for 31.77 percent of the equity. This implies that the investor is capitalizing the venture at $4.322 million (i.e., the post-money valuation).

$$\$4.322\ million = \$1.373\ million/31.77\ percent$$

Because, under the success scenario, the second-stage investor is expected to contribute $1.373 million for 10.30 percent of outstanding equity, the second-stage capitalization is $13.330 million, a substantial gain over first-stage capitalization. Similarly, the third-stage investor is expected to contribute $700,000 for 2.43 percent of equity, a capitalization of $28.807 million.

These increases occur because the venture is progressing according to the projections of the success scenario. The gain is attributable in part to reduced uncertainty and in part to increasing proximity of the liquidity event. Even if the uncertainty were not resolved, capitalization would increase owing to proximity of a harvest opportunity. If the implied capitalization decreases from one round to the next or does not increase very much, it follows that the venture is not performing according to the success scenario. Before committing funds, investors would want to understand why the venture was not meeting its projections.

Limitations of the Venture Capital Method

The Venture Capital Method has two important limitations. First, it provides no fundamental way to determine the appropriate hurdle rates to use for valuing investments made at different stages of development. The rates that are used are based on rules of thumb and experience. Second, it does little to help an entrepreneur decide whether to proceed with a venture or compare financing alternatives. The first limitation can be addressed by incorporating risk into the analysis and focusing on expected cash flows instead of a success scenario. This can be accomplished with either discrete scenario analysis or simulation. The second limitation requires explicit valuation of the entrepreneur's financial claims, in light of her other assets. Hence, we return to CAPM-based valuation.

13.2 STAGED INVESTMENT—CAPM VALUATION WITH DISCRETE SCENARIOS

This section and section 13-3 are difficult, but include core material on structuring contracts that include real options. In order for you to fully comprehend the discussion in these sections, we recommend that you download the Excel files for Figure 13-3 through 13-10, and use them as you read, to examine the cell formulas and the relationships among the figures.

Consider a venture that, according to its business plan, requires cash infusions from an outside investor, totaling $7.5 million over the next few years. At the current risk-free rate of 4.0 percent, the infusions have a present value of $7.159 million. The entrepreneur will resign her current position with another company and will work for the new venture without salary. Her opportunity cost of employment is $100,000 per year on a present valued basis. The entrepreneur proposes to develop a navigation system that will be attractive to private aircraft owners and boat owners. If the venture is successful, pilots and ship captains will be able to download detailed map and navigation information from the Internet and even use the information with a GPS-enhanced PDA for real-time navigation. For aircraft pilots, the system would provide important flight plan and terrain information and information about runway and weather conditions at airports. For ship captains, the system would provide ocean, lake, and river depth information and information on wind and water currents. The entrepreneur and a prospective investor agree that the venture is not expected to generate any free cash flow before harvest. The entrepreneur expects that the venture can be harvested in 3.0 years.[1]

Single-Stage Venture Capital Method Valuation

Cash flow projections in the business plan reflect the entrepreneur's belief that the venture can generate sales from four different customer groups: OEM aircraft avionics suppliers, aircraft owners, OEM marine navigation suppliers, and boat owners. Assuming success with all four groups, the entrepreneur projects that the venture will have a total harvest value of $90 million. Realizing that the historical average annual return to limited partners of venture capital funds has been around 18 percent, the entrepreneur proposes to offer a venture capital investor 20 percent of the equity in exchange for the $7.159 million investment. Discounting the entrepreneur's projected harvest value by 18 percent for three years yields a value of more than $54.7 million. So the offer of 20 percent of the equity seems to the entrepreneur to be sufficient to compensate the limited partners and provide a return to the venture capitalist.

The venture capitalist disagrees for several reasons. First, the investor thinks four years is a much more realistic estimate of time until harvest. Second, the investor believes that the $90 million harvest value is too optimistic by about 10 percent. Third, the investor recognizes that the projected harvest value depends on being successful with all four groups of customers. Fourth, based on projected burn rates, the venture capitalist believes the venture ultimately will require infusions totaling $8.5 million, and having a present value of $8.009 million. Recognizing that the business plan reflects only the scenario of complete success, and considering the early stage of development, the investor believes that a success-scenario projection of $81 million should be discounted at a Venture-Capital-Method hurdle rate of 60 percent for four years. The resulting value, however, is only $12.360 million. Consequently, the investor would require 60.80 percent of the equity in exchange for committing the $8.009 million. Even if the investor were to accept the entrepreneur's more optimistic harvest value, harvest date, and burn rate projections, the 60 percent hurdle rates still would mean that the investor would require 32.58 percent of the equity, an ownership allocation that would be unappealing to the entrepreneur, and, in any case, would not be offered by the investor.[2]

Identifying the Real and Financial Options

Given the disparity of their projections, it may seem that the parties should give up on trying to reach agreement. However, by staging the investment the parties may be able to reach an agreement, even though they disagree about the prospects for success. In this example, we illustrate staging with discrete scenarios. Rather than using the Venture Capital Method (with its ambiguity about appropriate hurdle rates), we use the CAPM-based valuation approach.

Suppose the parties recognize that five outcomes reasonably describe the range of the most likely scenarios. Instead of complete success or outright failure, the venture might fail in its effort to market to boat owners but be successful with all other groups; might fail to penetrate the entire marine market but be successful in the aircraft market; or might succeed only in marketing to aircraft OEMs, which is where it currently is focusing development efforts.

Development and marketing of the software can be staged easily. Efforts to sell the product to aircraft OEMs can progress contemporaneously with efforts to complete software applications for aircraft use. If marketing to aircraft OEMs is successful, the venture can initiate efforts to market to aircraft owners. The more attractive payoffs, however, will come if the software can be adapted to marine use. Development of software applications for marine use only makes sense if success can be established for aircraft use. Thus, software development and marketing to marine OEMs would not begin until success in the aircraft market was established, and marketing to boat owners would not begin until development of marine applications was complete and success with marine OEMs was established.

Figure 13-3 illustrates the interplay between the investor's financial options and the real options of the staged venture.[3] The investor's initial financial commitment (Round 1) will enable the entrepreneur to complete avionics applications and pursue the aircraft OEM market (Stage 1). If those efforts are sufficiently successful, the investor will fund (Round 2) the next stage, which is marketing the software to aircraft owners (Stage 2). Otherwise the venture will

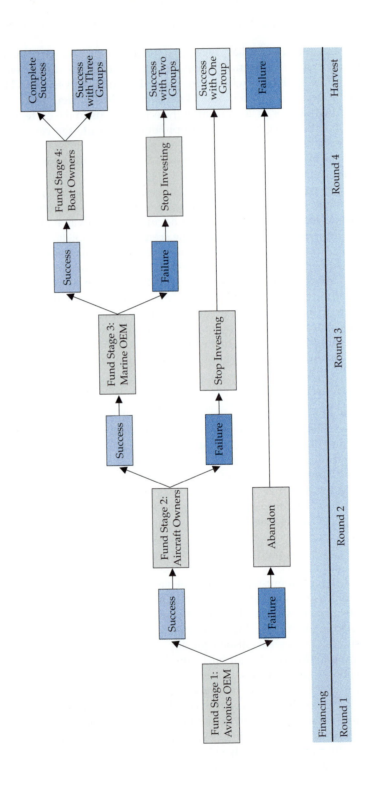

Figure 13-3 Staged investment decision model

Staged investment model of aircraft and marine navigation software venture. The aircraft market is pursued before the marine market, and OEM sales are pursued in each market before end users. Options to invest in development of new markets are exercised only if the prior effort is successful.

be abandoned. Next, if efforts to market to aircraft owners are sufficiently successful, the investor will fund (Round 3) development of marine applications and marketing to marine OEMs (Stage 3). If efforts to market to aircraft owners are not successful, the investor will stop investing and the venture will be harvested based on the value of the aircraft OEM market. If the entrepreneur can develop acceptable marine applications, as demonstrated by OEM sales, the investor will fund (Round 4) efforts to market to boat owners (Stage 4). Otherwise, the venture will be harvested based on the value of the aircraft market. If Round 4 financing is provided, harvest value will depend on whether the venture is a complete success, or efforts to market to boat owners fail.

It should be clear that Figure 13-3 greatly oversimplifies the actual decision process and range of outcomes. At each stage in the figure, there are only two outcomes, success and failure, and the next round investment depends on which of the two occurs. In reality, there could, for example, be outcomes that are successful enough not to abandon, but not good enough to warrant making the next round of investment. There also could be scenarios where the investor would choose not to invest but funding of the round would be provided by a third party.[4] The discrete scenario valuation problem is simplified by using the knife-edged assumption that failure at one stage means that no subsequent investment occurs, and that success at one stage results in investment in the next stage.

Figure 13-3 can be regarded as a rough representation of the parties' understanding. For example, the investor expects that it will be valuable to invest in Round 2 if the entrepreneur is successful in Stage 1, etc. However, while it presents a representation of an agreement, the figure is not representative of a formal contract. The figure suggests that the next round of investment is automatic if the venture is successful in the previous stage, but there is no specific definition of success in the figure, which the entrepreneur could use as a milestone for triggering the next financing round. Nor is there any indication of how the ownership claims to the venture might be reallocated at each financing round. We return to contracting issues later in this section.

Specifying Key Assumptions

The staging structure in Figure 13-3 requires that the parties identify what they believe are the expected harvest values associated with the various scenarios, the probabilities of the different scenarios, and their investment assumptions for each financing round. In Panel (a) of Figure 13-4, we set out the entrepreneur's investment and harvest cash flow assumptions. Based on the assumptions, including the entrepreneur's beliefs about the probabilities of the different scenarios occurring, we compute the expected harvest cash flow and standard deviation of cash flows at each investment round. The expected harvest cash flow and standard deviation by round are inputs to the valuation at each round. The panel also shows the entrepreneur's burn-rate assumption for each stage and the entrepreneur's expectation for the duration of the stage.

Panel (b) shows the same information based on the beliefs of the venture capitalist. As is typical, the investor is less optimistic about the harvest value the venture can realize associated with each level of success, and is less optimistic about the probabilities of various levels of success. In contrast to the entrepreneur, the investor expects that software development will take longer for both aircraft and marine applications, and that cash investments will be higher at the beginning, but will decline as the venture begins to generate operating cash flow.

Panel (a)

Entrepreneur's Assumptions—Financial Model Based on Business Plan

	Conditional Cash Flows	Scenario Probabilities	Round One	Round Two	Round Three	Round Four
Harvest Value Forecast						
Success with All Groups	$90,000,000	20%	$18,000,000	$27,692,308	$32,727,273	$51,428,571
Success with Three Groups	$60,000,000	15%	$9,000,000	$13,846,154	$16,363,636	$25,714,286
Success with Two Groups	$25,000,000	20%	$5,000,000	$7,692,308	$9,090,909	
Success with One Group	$15,000,000	10%	$1,500,000	$2,307,692		
Failure	$0	35%	$0			
Expected Cash Flow at Harvest			$33,500,000	$51,538,462	$58,181,818	$77,142,857
Standard Deviation of Cash Flows			$34,427,460	$29,896,270	$27,738,448	$14,846,150
Investment						
Burn Rates per Year			$2,000,000	$3,000,000	$2,500,000	$3,000,000
Years			1	0.5	1	0.5
Total Investment	$7,500,000					
Present Value of Unconditional Total Investment	$7,159,376					
Present Value of Expected Investment	$4,709,907					

Panel (b)

Investor's Assumptions—Financial Model Based on Business Plan

	Conditional Cash Flows	Scenario Probabilities	Round One	Round Two	Round Three	Round Four
Harvest Value Forecast						
Success with All Groups	$81,000,000	18%	$14,580,000	$22,430,769	$31,695,652	$48,600,000
Success with Three Groups	$54,000,000	12%	$6,480,000	$9,969,231	$14,086,957	$21,600,000
Success with Two Groups	$22,500,000	16%	$3,600,000	$5,538,462	$7,826,087	
Success with One Group	$13,500,000	8%	$1,080,000	$1,661,538		
Failure	$0	35%	$0			
Expected Cash Flow at Harvest			$25,740,000	$39,600,000	$53,608,696	$70,200,000
Standard Deviation of Cash Flows			$31,047,261	$28,371,817	$25,104,545	$13,227,245
Investment						
Burn Rates per Year			$1,800,000	$2,500,000	$2,000,000	$2,500,000
Years			1.25	1.0	1.25	0.5
Total Investment	$8,500,000					
Present Value of Unconditional Total Investment	$8,008,895					
Present Value of Expected Investment	$4,915,173					

CAPM-Based Valuation with Irrevocable Commitment to Invest

To establish a baseline that can be used to isolate the effects of staging on value, it is useful to begin with a CAPM-based valuation where the investor's entire commitment is made at the beginning. Thus, under the entrepreneur's assumptions from Figure 13-4, the investor would commit all $7.159 million at time zero (the present value of the $7.5 million commitment). The entrepreneur would use the money to achieve as much success as possible. By committing at time zero, the parties would be foregoing the abandonment options and could pursue all of the target groups. This unconditional staged valuation is the same as if the venture were not staged and can be calculated using approaches developed in earlier chapters.[5]

In Figure 13-5, we use the assumptions in Figure 13-4 to compute the value of the venture from the perspective of the venture capitalist as a well-diversified investor who also seeks a return on effort. The first panel of the figure shows assumptions about the market and the venture capitalist's contract with limited partners of the venture capital fund. In addition to stated assumptions about the market rate, risk-free rate, market risk, and correlation of venture cash flows with the market, we assume that the venture capitalist seeks a management fee of 2.5 percent based on the value of the investment as well as a carried interest of 20 percent of the value. We implement the contract provisions in an simplified way, by adjusting the harvest-date valuation downward by 20 percent (deducting the carried interest) using the CEQ method and then adding the annual fee (as a percentage) to the discount rate that is used to compute the present value of the CEQ harvest-date value.[6]

With these assumptions about the market and the venture capital contract, the entrepreneur's harvest cash flow assumptions imply that the venture has a present value of $18.794 million (to a well-diversified investor in a venture capital fund), as shown in the third panel. The investor's harvest cash flow assumptions imply a present value of $12.456 million, about two-thirds of the value the entrepreneur's assumptions yield.

In the fourth panel, we use the valuations to compute implicit cost of capital. The entrepreneur's assumptions yield an implicit cost of capital of 21.25 percent for the venture capital investor, about 1.35 percent higher than the 19.90 percent implicit cost of capital under the investor's assumptions. The difference arises because the venture capital carried interest of 20 percent is spread over a longer holding period under the investor's assumptions. Both estimates are computed gross of the venture capitalist's management fee and carried interest. That is, the management fee and carried interest (the returns on the general partner's human capital and fund expenses) are built into the implicit cost of capital. This is the relevant cost of capital for the entrepreneur to consider in seeking capital from the venture capital fund.

As shown in the fifth panel, based on the entrepreneur's valuation, the investor would need 38.09 percent of the equity in exchange for the $7.159 million commitment. Under the investor's assumptions, the investor would require 64.30 percent of the equity in exchange for the $8.009 million commitment. In this example, the CAPM-based valuations are similar to the Venture

---

Figure 13-4   Panel (a) shows the entrepreneur's expectations of harvest cash flows conditional on each scenario and the entrepreneur's belief of the probability of each scenario. These inputs are used to compute the expected harvest cash flow and standard deviation of cash flows at the time of each investment round. The lower portion of the panel shows the entrepreneur's assumed burn rate from each stage and the entrepreneur's expectation of the duration of the stage. The information is used to compute the total investment, present value of the total as an unconditional investment, and present value of expected investment. Panel (b) shows the same information based on the investor's beliefs.

	Entrepreneur's Assumptions	Investor's Assumptions
Valuation of Unstaged Investment—Venture Capital Investor		
Market and Contract Data		
Annual Risk-free Rate	4.0%	4.0%
Annual Market Rate	10.0%	10.0%
Standard Deviation of Market	20.0%	20.0%
General Partner's Annual Fee	2.5%	2.5%
General Partner's Carried Interest	20.0%	20.0%
Correlation of Venture with Market	0.25	0.25
Single-Stage Investment and Timing		
Total Investment Committed	$7,159,376	$8,008,895
Years to Harvest	3.00	4.00
Investor Valuation of Harvest Cash Flows		
Expected Harvest Value	$33,500,000	$25,740,000
Standard Deviation of Harvest Cash Flows	$34,427,460	$31,047,261
Value of Venture at Time of Investment	**$18,794,406**	**$12,456,062**
Investor's Required Rate of Return		
Annualized VC Cost of Capital	21.25%	19.90%
Investor Ownership Requirement		
Ownership Requirement		
Round 1 Investment	$7,159,376	$8,008,895
Value at Round 1	$18,794,406	$12,456,062
Share of Incremental Value Required	38.09%	64.30%
Valuation of Entrepreneur's Interest in Venture		
Entrepreneur's Wealth		
Entrepreneur's Wealth in Market	$1,700,000	$1,600,000
Valuation of Harvest Cash Flows		
Venture (Entrepreneur's Financial Claim)		
Expected Harvest Value	$20,738,805	$9,189,910
Standard Deviation of Venture Cash Flows	$21,312,966	$11,084,752
Market		
Expected Harvest Value	$2,262,700	$2,342,560
Standard Deviation of Market Cash Flows	$588,897	$640,000
Portfolio		
Expected Portfolio Value	$23,001,505	$11,532,470
Standard Deviation of Portfolio Cash Flows	$21,335,812	$11,119,175
Value of Entrepreneur's Portfolio	**$9,161,414**	**$2,866,299**
Value of Investment in Market	**$1,700,000**	**$1,600,000**
Value of Entrepreneur's Interest in Venture	**$7,461,414**	**$1,266,299**
Entrepreneur's Required Rate of Return		
Annualized Portfolio Cost of Capital	35.91%	41.63%
Annualized Venture Cost of Capital	40.60%	64.13%

Capital Method valuations with a 60 percent hurdle rate applied to the success scenario. However, as discussed earlier, you should be more confident of the CAPM-based valuations.

In the sixth panel, we identify the entrepreneur's other wealth, which we assume can be invested in the market. The entrepreneur has total wealth of $2.0 million, and will commit $100,000 per year to the venture, if the venture is pursued. The balance is assumed to be invested in the market.

In the seventh panel, we use the expected harvest cash flows and risk of the entrepreneur's investments in the venture and in the market to compute the entrepreneur's expected portfolio harvest cash flows and risk. As the entrepreneur is underdiversified, the portfolio is valued based on its total risk. The value of the investment in the venture is found by deducting investment in the market. Thus, under the entrepreneur's assumptions, the entrepreneur's 61.91 percent interest would be worth $7.461 million, a NPV of $7.161 million, after the entrepreneur's human capital investment. Under the investor's assumptions, the entrepreneur's 33.70 percent interest would be worth $1.266 million, a NPV of $0.866 million.

In the final panel of the figure we compute the entrepreneur's implicit cost of capital, which, because of underdiversification, is much higher than that of the investor.

Valuing the Staged Venture at each Investment Round

When investment is staged, the investor's financial claims and those of the entrepreneur can be adjusted at each investment round. The value of staging the investment derives primarily from reductions of uncertainty about the likelihood of success or failure.[7] As the uncertainty is resolved and the venture moves closer to harvest, the value of the venture changes. These value changes affect the compensation the investor must receive for investing cash in a financing round. In Figure 13-6, we compute the venture values that correspond to each anticipated financing round. The computed values reflect assumptions in Figure 13-4. Thus, they reflect the entrepreneur's or the investor's expectations as of the time of the initial investment. No doubt, actual results will not be exactly like any of the assumed scenarios. However, the valuations in Figure 13-6 are the best estimates the parties can make at the time of the initial investment decision.[8]

The first two panels in the figure summarize previously discussed assumptions about the market, the venture capital contract, and the parties' beliefs about stage durations and burn rates.[9] Valuations at each possible financing round are computed in the third panel. These valuations are based on the expected harvest cash flow and standard deviation of harvest cash flows at each round, based on the beliefs of the entrepreneur and of the investor (from Figure 13-3). They are values to a well-diversified investor in the venture capital fund, after providing for the venture capitalist's management fee and carried interest. The first-round valuations (and implicit cost of capital estimates, in the fourth panel) are the same as in the single-round valuation in Figure 13-5.

Comparing the Round 1 and Round 2 valuations, you can begin to see the benefit of staging. Consider the column that reflects the entrepreneur's beliefs. The Round 2 valuation is $33.958 million, an 80.7 percent increase over the Round 1 valuation of $18.794 million. To a

Figure 13-5 Single-stage contract using CAPM-based valuation. Valuations are based on the assumption that all necessary capital to achieve success is committed at the outset and that approaching the venture without staging does not affect cash flows of each scenario outcome, the probability of the outcome, or timing.

Valuation Template 8

Valuation of Staged Investment—Venture Capital Investor

	Entrepreneur's Assumptions	Investor's Assumptions
Market and Contract Data		
Annual Risk-free Rate	4.0%	4.0%
Annual Market Rate	10.0%	10.0%
Standard Deviation of Market	20.0%	20.0%
General Partner's Annual Fee	2.5%	2.5%
General Partner's Carried Interest	20.0%	20.0%
Correlation of Venture with Market	0.25	0.25
Single-Stage Investment Timing and Burn Rates		
Round 1—Aircraft OEM		
Burn Rate per Year	$2,000,000	$1,800,000
Years to Complete	1.00	1.25
Round 2—Aircraft Owners		
Probability of Stage 1 Success	65%	54%
Burt Rate per Year	$3,000,000	$2,500,000
Years to Complete	0.50	1.00
Round 3—Marine OEM		
Cumulative Probability of Stage 2 Success	55%	46%
Burn Rate per Year	$2,500,000	$2,000,000
Years to Complete	1.00	1.25
Round 4—Boat Owners		
Cumulative Probability of Stage 3 Success	35%	30%
Burn Rate per Year	$3,000,000	$2,500,000
Years to Complete	0.50	0.50
Valuation of Harvest Cash Flows		
Round 4		
Expected Harvest Value	$77,142,857	$70,200,000
Standard Deviation of Harvest Cash Flows	$14,846,150	$13,227,245
Value to Investor at Time of Investment	**$59,211,238**	**$53,893,465**
Round 3		
Expected Harvest Value	$58,181,818	$53,608,696
Standard Deviation of Harvest Cash Flows	$27,738,448	$25,104,545
Value to Investor at Time of Investment	**$40,431,577**	**$36,534,155**
Round 2		
Expected Harvest Value	$51,538,462	$39,600,000
Standard Deviation of Harvest Cash Flows	$29,896,270	$28,371,817
Value to Investor at Time of Investment	**$33,958,352**	**$23,969,483**
Round 1		
Expected Harvest Value	$33,500,000	$25,740,000
Standard Deviation of Harvest Cash Flows	$34,427,460	$31,047,261
Value to Investor at Time of Investment	**$18,794,406**	**$12,456,062**
Investor's Implicit Cost of Capital at Each Round		
Round 1	21.25%	19.90%
Round 2	23.19%	20.03%
Round 3	27.46%	24.50%
Round 4	69.74%	69.67%

small degree, the valuation increases because the expected harvest date is closer. However, most of the increase arises because of the option value of making the Round 2 investment only if the venture is successful in Stage 1 and otherwise abandoning the project. Based on the entrepreneur's beliefs, the probability is 65 percent that the venture will not fail before the Round 2 investment is made. Thus staging does two things: It reduces the expected investment and it causes the investment to be made only when prior success warrants it. Similar value changes are associated with Round 3 and Round 4. Parallel results obtain when considering the investor's assumptions in the final column.

Determining the Investor's Required Ownership Share

The staged valuation results in Figure 13-6 can be used to determine the minimum equity share the investor would need to justify investing at each stage. We focus on the investor's minimums in order to retain consistency with our general approach of assigning all of the positive NPV to the entrepreneur. Thus, in Figure 13-7, we compute the zero-NPV (after fees and carried interest) ownership percentages of the venture capital investor.[10] For illustration, consider the results based on the entrepreneur's assumptions. We use the backward induction approach to establish the minimum equity allocations that will trigger option exercise of each financing option. Beginning with Round 4, assuming the venture has been successful in the first three stages, the venture will require $1.5 million to attempt Stage 4. Because the venture is worth $59.211 million at the time of the Round 4, in exchange for investing $1.5 million, the investor would need to realize 2.53 percent of the expected harvest value at that time to achieve a NPV of zero. The percentages of harvest value required at the other financing rounds can be calculated in the same way, by comparing the size of the investment to the value of the venture at the time of the investment. Thus, in exchange for making the $2.5 million Round 3 investment, the investor would need 6.18 percent of the expected harvest cash flow at the time.

Concerns with Ownership Dilution

As we saw in the Venture Capital Method example, staged financing with equity normally dilutes the equity claims of earlier investors. That is, the new investment reduces the percentage of firm ownership held by prior investors (including the entrepreneur). However, in this example, to maintain a zero-NPV for the investor at each financing round, we focus on a structure where the early-round investor's claims are not diluted by later round financings. The "Investor's Required Ownership After Investing" percentages in Figure 13-7 are the percentages that result in no dilution of the investor's existing equity claims. Thus, for example, using the entrepreneur's assumption and further assuming the venture is successful in Stage 1, the entrepreneur expects the venture to be worth $33.958 million at the time of the Round 2 financing. At this point, the investor's 10.64 percent of harvest value from Round 1 is worth $3.614 million. This would represent a positive NPV for the investor. However, the positive NPV is offset by what the entrepreneur believes is a 35 percent probability that the venture will fail in Stage 1 and be worth zero. The figure illustrates a way to find the investor's required zero-NPV ownership stake from investing in Round 2, without diluting the value of

Figure 13-6 Venture capital investor CAPM-based valuation by round. Implicit cost of capital estimates are gross of the venture capitalist's management fee and carried interest.

Valuation-Based Contracting Model		
Investor Ownership Requirement		
	Entrepreneur's Assumptions	*Investor's Assumptions*
Investor's Round 4 Investment	$1,500,000	$1,250,000
Venture Value at Round 4	$59,211,238	$53,893,465
Incremental Equity Required	**2.53%**	**2.32%**
Investor's Value from Round 3	$12,577,607	$19,043,975
Investor's Value Required with Investing	$14,077,607	$20,293,975
Investor's Required Ownership After Investing	**23.78%**	**37.66%**
Investor's Round 3 Investment	$2,500,000	$2,500,000
Venture Value at Round 3	$40,431,577	$36,534,155
Incremental Equity Required	**6.18%**	**6.84%**
Investor's Value from Round 2	$6,088,445	$10,409,831
Investor's Value Required with Investing	$8,588,445	$12,909,831
Investor's Required Ownership After Investing	**21.24%**	**35.34%**
Investor's Round 2 Investment	$1,500,000	$2,500,000
Venture Value at Round 2	$33,958,352	$23,969,483
Incremental Equity Required	**4.42%**	**10.43%**
Investor's Value from Round 1	$3,613,666	$4,329,726
Investor's Value Required with Investing	$5,113,666	$6,829,726
Investor's Required Ownership After Investing	**15.06%**	**28.49%**
Investor's Round 1 Investment	$2,000,000	$2,250,000
Venture Value at Round 1	$18,794,406	$12,456,062
Investor's Required Ownership After Investing	**10.64%**	**18.06%**
Required Percentage Increases in Investor's Shares if New Shares are Issued		
Round 4—New Shares to Investor	15.65%	10.53%
Round 3—New Shares to Investor	52.14%	37.14%
Round 4—New Shares to Investor	48.87%	80.75%

Figure 13-7 Investor's incremental required ownership for investment at each round and total ownership, assuming no dilution of earlier round investments

the Round 1 investment. The required ownership stake is computed by adding the new investment to the $3.614 million value of the original 10.64 percent interest. To avoid diluting the initial ownership, the investor would require a total of 15.06 percent of harvest value in exchange for investing in both Rounds 1 and 2. The other investor ownership requirements in Figure 13-7 are determined in the same way.

If the entrepreneur's beliefs are correct and accepted by the investor, and the venture is successful in the first three stages, so that the Round 4 investment is made, the investor would end up with 23.78 percent of the equity. This compares with the 38.09 percent of equity the investor would need if the investment were not staged or the entire amount were committed at the outset.[11] Under the investor's assumptions, the investor's required ownership would increase from 18.06 percent to 37.66 percent, depending on the number of financing rounds provided. Compared with committing all $8.009 million at the outset, from the investor's perspective, staging enables the entrepreneur to retain a much larger share of ownership.

Designing the Investment Agreement

The challenge suggested by Figure 13-7 is to design an investment agreement that enables the investor to realize the intended shares of harvest value depending on which scenario is achieved and on whether the entrepreneur's expectations or the investor's proves to be more accurate. The agreement should also allow for the possibility that different parties may invest in some of the later stages.

Suppose we begin, arbitrarily, with the ownership percentages implied by the investor's beliefs. One way to prevent dilution of the investor's earlier interest is to simply give the investor additional new shares at each round so that the intended new ownership percentage is realized. The percentage calculations in the last panel of Figure 13-7 show the percentage increase in the investor's shares that would be required to accomplish this. Hence, for example, for the investor's stake to increase from 18.06 percent after Round 1 to 28.49 percent after Round 2, the investor would need an 80.75 percent increase in shares owned, assuming that no other new shares were issued. This approach works if the Round 1 investor is also the only investor in each subsequent round. However, in practice, it is likely that new parties will be involved in subsequent rounds.

To illustrate the dilution that could result from raising capital from a new investor when the initial investor is not protected, consider the Round 2 investment under the investor's assumptions. A new investor would not be concerned with dilution of the Round 1 investor's interest. Thus, the valuations in Figure 13-6 imply that a new Round 2 diversified investor would require 10.43 percent of (Round 2) post-money equity, which is equivalent to 11.64 percent of (Round 1) pre-money equity. The 11.64 percent increase in equity would dilute the Round 1 investor's interest from 18.06 percent to 16.18 percent. Total investor equity after Round 2 would then be 26.61 percent, instead of the (ex ante) zero-NPV share of 28.49 percent. The reduction in the first round investor's share would effectively transfer wealth to the entrepreneur, whose share would be 73.39 percent after Round 2, instead of 71.51 percent.

Dealing with Ownership Dilution

The Venture Capital Method, discussed in Section 13.1, seems to suggest that it is possible to neutralize the potential wealth transfer by anticipating the dilutive effects of subsequent financing rounds. However, this approach generally will not work. If the investor's initial equity is selected to produce a zero NPV in the event of complete success, then the ownership percentages will be too high if the later round investments are not made. Only if there are only two possible outcomes, success and complete failure, can the Venture Capital Method with staged investment produce the correct allocation of ownership claims.

For a venture with more than one positive-harvest-value scenario (such as our navigation example), an easy approach to preventing dilution of the ownership share of early-round investments is to maintain the total number of shares outstanding and to compensate the later round investors by transferring equity from the entrepreneur to the new investors. That way, for example, the Round 1 investor's share of harvest value does not depend on which of the five scenarios is realized. Alternatively, the investor's interest could be protected with a form of antidilution right that maintains the investor's share without significant additional investment. With antidilution rights, the venture might issue new shares to a new investor, but the prior investor would receive enough new shares so that the effect is as if no new shares were issued and the new investor received existing shares from the entrepreneur.

Dealing with Parties' Differing Beliefs

Finally, we need to consider the differences in the parties' assumptions. Some of the differences can be addressed and others cannot. For example, with respect to the probabilities of the different scenarios, the parties differ mainly in how likely they think it is that the venture will fail. Because failure is determined in the first investment round and we can never know the true ex ante probabilities, there is no way to address this issue other than by staging the investment. By staging, the parties reduce the fraction of equity and amount of capital that are exchanged at the point when their beliefs are most disparate.

In our example, after Round 1, the parties' assessments of relative probabilities of different scenarios are identical. The remaining differences relate to amounts of cash that will be required, duration to harvest, and amount of harvest cash flows in the different scenarios. The parties can use contingent claims contracts to address these differences. If, for example, the first stage takes less time than the investor expects it will, the investor could agree to give warrants to the entrepreneur to reallocate ownership shares based on the realized amount of Round 1 investment. Warrants could also be exchanged based on time to harvest and harvest value. Alternatively, the base contract could be based on the entrepreneur's assumptions, with the investor receiving warrants that increase the investor's ownership if the venture does not achieve the entrepreneur's projections.

It may appear that, with so many aspects of uncertainty, the contract between the entrepreneur and the investor is necessarily complex. However, that is only true if the parties insist on negotiating the entire contract at the outset. If the parties can operate with a degree of mutual trust, they may only need to contract explicitly for their initial difference in beliefs. After Stage 1 is complete, the parties' expectations are likely to converge and elaborate warrant structures may no longer be important.

Valuing the Entrepreneur's Claim

It is clear from Figure 13-7 that the investor can identify a structure of ownership claims that is sufficiently attractive to justify investment. However, we still do not know the value of the entrepreneur's claim. Based on the investor's ownership percentages in Figure 13-7, the entrepreneur would hold the residual claim on the remaining equity and would be committed to see the venture through to harvest, unless it is abandoned earlier. Under the entrepreneur's assumptions, the entrepreneur would have 76.22 to 89.36 percent of the equity, depending on which scenario was realized. All of these ownership structures are substantial improvements over single-stage investment. In Figure 13-8, the entrepreneur's conditional ownership percentages are used to compute the expected harvest cash flow to the entrepreneur and its standard deviation. Under the entrepreneur's assumptions, the entrepreneur's expected harvest cash flow is $25.793 million. Under the investor's assumptions, it is $16.230 million.

Figure 13-9 shows the computed value of the entrepreneur's claim, taking account of the entrepreneur's total wealth and commitment to the venture. If the investor accepts the entrepreneur's projections as correct, the entrepreneur's claim is worth $9.330 million dollars, a NPV of $9.030 million after the human capital commitment. This is a significant improvement over the $7.161 thousand NPV under the single-stage approach in Figure 13-5. Moreover, as noted before, this improvement in value does not include the value to the entrepreneur of the intangible benefits of self-employment. The value of the entrepreneur's claim under the

Risk and Return of Entrepreneur's Financial Claim

Based on Entrepreneur's Projections

Ownership by Round	Investor Share	Entrepreneur Share
Round 4	23.78%	76.22%
Round 3	21.24%	78.76%
Round 2	15.06%	84.94%
Round 1	10.64%	89.36%

Harvest Value Forecast	Venture Conditional Cash Flows	Scenario Probabilities	Entrepreneur's Conditional Cash Flow	Probability Weighted Cash Flows
Success with All Groups	$90,000,000	20%	$68,602,294	$13,720,459
Success with Three Groups	$60,000,000	15%	$45,734,863	$6,860,229
Success with Two Groups	$25,000,000	20%	$19,689,519	$3,937,904
Success with One Groups	$15,000,000	10%	$12,741,204	$1,274,120
Failure	$0	35%	$0	$0
Expected Cash Flow of Entrepreneur's Claim				$25,792,712
Standard Deviation of Entrepreneur's Claim				$26,144,060

Based on Investor's Projections

Ownership by Round	Investor Share	Entrepreneur Share
Round 4	37.66%	62.34%
Round 3	35.34%	64.66%
Round 2	28.49%	71.51%
Round 1	18.06%	81.94%

Harvest Value Forecast	Venture Conditional Cash Flows	Scenario Probabilities	Entrepreneur's Conditional Cash Flow	Probability Weighted Cash Flows
Success with All Groups	$81,000,000	18%	$50,498,863	$9,089,795
Success with Three Groups	$54,000,000	12%	$33,665,908	$4,039,909
Success with Two Groups	$22,500,000	16%	$14,549,325	$2,327,892
Success with One Groups	$13,500,000	8%	$9,653,388	$772,271
Failure	$0	46%	$0	$0
Expected Cash Flow of Entrepreneur's Claim				$16,229,867
Standard Deviation of Entrepreneur's Claim				$19,311,842

Figure 13-8   Determination of entrepreneur's residual harvest-date cash flow based on investor's required ownership at each round and the scenario probabilities

Valuation Template 9		
Valuation of Entrepreneur's Interest in Venture		
	Entrepreneur's Assumptions	*Investor's Assumptions*
Market Data and Entrepreneur's Wealth		
Annual Risk-free Rate	4.0%	4.0%
Annual Market Rate	10.0%	10.0%
Standard Deviation of Market	20.0%	20.0%
Correlation of Venture with Market	0.25	0.25
Entrepreneur's Wealth in Market	$1,7000,000	$1,600,000
Timing of Staged Investments		
Round 1—Aircraft OEM		
Years to Complete	1.00	1.25
Round 2—Aircraft Owners		
Years to Complete	0.50	1.00
Round 3—Marine OEM		
Years to Complete	1.00	1.25
Round 4—Boat Owners		
Years to Complete	0.50	0.50
Valuation of Harvest Cash Flows		
Venture (Entrepreneur's Financial Claim)		
Expected Harvest Value	$25,792,712	$16,229,867
Standard Deviation of Venture Cash Flows	$26,144,060	$19,311,842
Market		
Expected Harvest Value	$2,262,700	$2,342,560
Standard Deviation of Market Cash Flows	$588,897	$640,000
Portfolio		
Expected Portfolio Value	$28,055,412	$18,572,427
Standard Deviation of Portfolio Cash Flows	$26,297,466	$19,481,699
Value of Entrepreneur's Portfolio	**$11,029,559**	**$3,625,754**
Value to Investment in Market	**$1,700,000**	**$1,600,000**
Value of Entrepreneur's Interest in Venture	**$9,329,559**	**$2,025,754**

Figure 13-9   CAPM-based valuation of entrepreneur's portfolio and residual interest in the venture

investor's assumptions is a more modest $2.026 million present value, compared with $1.266 million without staging. Depending on how confident the entrepreneur is of her assumptions, the true expected value of the entrepreneur's interest likely lies between the two extremes. If, after the Round 1 investment, the investor becomes convinced that the entrepreneur is correct, the investor's subsequent equity shares could be based on the entrepreneur's assumptions. In addition, we have not explored (as discussed in Chapter 11) the opportunity to create additional value by shifting more of the equity to the investor.

13.3 USING CONTRACTS TO INCREASE VALUE, SIGNAL BELIEFS, AND ALIGN INCENTIVES

Assuming the parties to a venture have symmetrical beliefs and that the contract structure does not affect effort or other decisions of the parties, the value of the venture is maximized if all nonmarket risk is borne by a well-diversified investor. However, information and incentive problems operate against the proposition that the investor should bear all risk. We now have the tools to examine this conclusion more systematically.

Returning to the scenarios portrayed in Figure 13-4, and the single-stage valuation in Figure 13-5, under the investor's assumptions, an outside investor would commit $8.009 of capital in exchange for 64.3 percent of the equity. The entrepreneur would retain the remaining 35.7 percent of the equity. Under those assumptions, the value of the entrepreneur's portfolio (venture and market) is $2.866 million. With staging, and with the entrepreneur retaining all equity other than what is necessary to provide a normal return to the venture capital investor, Figure 13-9 shows that the present value of the entrepreneur's portfolio increases to $3.626 million.

Suppose the entrepreneur recognizes the value of shifting risk to the diversified investor and proposes a more extreme allocation. In particular, the entrepreneur proposes that the investor buy her out and hire her back at a salary equal to her opportunity cost. The buy-out arrangement would still enable the investor to stage the venture and to abandon at any point when it appeared that continuing to invest did not make sense. Assuming the entrepreneur's proposal does not change the investor's expectations about performance, the net present value of this offer to the investor can be determined by subtracting from each scenario cash flow, the harvest-date value of the cumulative cash investments the investor would be expected to make. Figure 13-10 shows the resulting valuation of the investor's interest and the entrepreneur's. Under the investor's assumptions, complete ownership of the venture would have a net present value of $9.215 million. If the parties were to contract for sale on this basis, the entrepreneur would be able to invest a total of $11.215 in the market, which would be the present value of the entrepreneur's portfolio. This is substantially higher than if she retains a larger fraction of the equity.

But the investor is likely to be skeptical of the entrepreneur's proposal. First, with all of the value being extracted by the entrepreneur, the investor may interpret the entrepreneur's willingness to sell as a negative signal and reduce the valuation to compensate. Second, the investor may be concerned that, because the entrepreneur has nothing at stake, she may not work as hard to achieve success and the venture may not do as well. Again, this could cause the investor to reduce the valuation. Third, the proposal to sell out leaves the entrepreneur much worse off than if the entrepreneur can find a way to convince the investor that the entrepreneur's projections are correct. In Figure 13-10, if the entrepreneur's valuation were used, the entrepreneur would realize $14.869 million in net present value, instead of $9.215 million.

Dealing effectively with these information and incentive problems is an important aspect of new venture financial contracting. Tying the entrepreneur's return to the venture's performance can preserve the entrepreneur's incentives and can signal the entrepreneur's expectations. Retaining a material fraction of equity, use of warrants linked to achieved milestones, earn-outs, and other devices all detract from value by allocating risk to the entrepreneur, rather than the well-diversified investor. However, the loss due to risk allocation can be more than offset by the increased expected cash flows the entrepreneur can realize by linking her financial return more closely to her own (more optimistic) beliefs.

Valuation of Unstaged Investment—Venture Capital Investor		
	Entrepreneur's Assumptions	*Investor's Assumptions*
Market and Contract Data		
Annual Risk-free Rate	4.0%	4.0%
Annual Market Rate	10.0%	10.0%
Standard Deviation of Market	20.0%	20.0%
General Partner's Annual Fee	2.5%	2.5%
General Partner's Carried Interest	20.0%	20.0%
Correlation of Venture with Market	0.25	0.25
Single-Stage Investment and Timing		
Years to Harvest	3.00	4.00
Investor Valuation of Harvest Cash Flows		
Expected Net Harvest Value	$27,202,464	$20,043,104
Standard Deviation of Net Harvest Cash Flows	$31,935,074	$28,412,132
NPV of Venture at Time of Investment	**$14,869,240**	**$9,214,753**
Valuation of Entrepreneur's Interest in Venture		
Entrepreneur's Wealth		
Entrepreneur's Wealth in Market	$16,869,240	$11,214,753
Valuation of Harvest Cash Flows		
Venture (Entrepreneur's Financial Claim)		
Expected Harvest Value	$0	$0
Standard Deviation of Venture Cash Flows	$0	$0
Market		
Expected Harvest Value	$22,452,958	$16,419,520
Standard Deviation of Market Cash Flows	$5,843,676	$4,485,901
Portfolio		
Expected Portfolio Value	$22,452,958	$16,419,520
Standard Deviation of Portfolio Cash Flows	$5,843,676	$4,485,901
Value of Entrepreneur's Portfolio	**$16,869,240**	**$11,214,753**
Value of Investment in Market	**$16,869,240**	**$11,214,753**
Value of Entrepreneur's Interest in Venture	**$0**	**$0**
Entrepreneur's Required Rate of Return		
Annualized Portfolio Cost of Capital	10.00%	10.00%

Figure 13-10 Calculation of NPV of 100 percent ownership by investor, after providing for conditional investment outlays each round. Entrepreneur's valuation assumes all positive NPV (after investor fees and carried interest) are paid to entrepreneur.

You can assess the effect of revising the investor's expectations if the venture is purchased, by modifying the assumptions in the figures and computing the values. You also can assess how various contract structures might affect value, through their combined effects on risk allocation and expected cash flows.

13.4   USING SIMULATION TO DESIGN FINANCIAL CONTRACTS

To fully understand the discussion in this section and section 13.5, you should download and examine Figures 13-12 through 13-17 as you read. Note that Figures 13-12 and 13-13 contain simulated cells and require that *Venture.SIM*$^{(TM)}$ be installed.

Analyzing discrete scenarios generally is not a very convenient or accurate way to study alternative financial contracts. Each new set of terms requires that you modify the cash flow projections and analyze the reactions of the parties to the changes. Furthermore, limiting the analysis to a small number of scenarios is likely to undervalue embedded real options. Options usually are most valuable when results are either very good or very bad, but extreme conditions often are ignored in discrete scenario analysis. Simulation affords an expedient and insightful way of comparing alternatives. It also has the virtue of providing a more complete description of the risks and returns of a venture and of the financial claims.

The value of any venture depends on how the financial contract is structured, and specific contract alternatives can only be assessed in the context of the venture. Figure 13-11 illustrates a process of designing and evaluating a financial contract from the perspective of the entrepreneur. The process parallels our discussion of building and using simulation models from Chapter 5 but with additional specificity.

Step 1: Model the venture and the financial contract: Build a general financial model that reflects the structure of the venture and any important real options. A financial model is simply a set of mathematical expressions that can be used to project cash flows over time. If a financial contract that is being considered allows for abandonment if sales revenue is low or expansion if it is high, then the financial model must allow for the possible exercise of those options. To be used for valuation, the model should be structured so that it can yield the cash flows that would be committed or received by investors and the entrepreneur under a particular outcome.

Step 2: Specify the assumptions and uncertainties, including terms for exercising the options: The assumptions include such factors as how rapidly sales are expected to grow, and how profitable sales are expected to be, the structure of ownership claims that controls cash flow allocation, and so on. In addition to specifying expected performance, it is necessary to make assumptions about the uncertainty of key financial variables, such as sales and profitability. For any real options it is necessary to make specific assumptions about the conditions under which the option would be exercised. Ultimately, you can use the simulation model to determine when the party with control rights to a real option can be expected to exercise it. Because the best exercise decision is sensitive to other assumptions of the model, initial assumptions about exercise decisions are likely to be educated guesses of how the parties will act.

In the context of negotiation, if each party can have different expectations about cash flows, you can use different sets of assumptions to reflect the different expectations. Specific assumptions may depend on the signaling and bonding aspects of the proposed financial contract.

Step 3: Run the simulation: Based on the assumptions from step 2, you can run the simulation model to generate expected cash flows and standard deviations of cash flows for investors and the entrepreneur. If the real options are modeled correctly, you should also be able to derive estimates of incremental cash flows and the uncertainty of those estimates, conditional on the exercise of any embedded options.

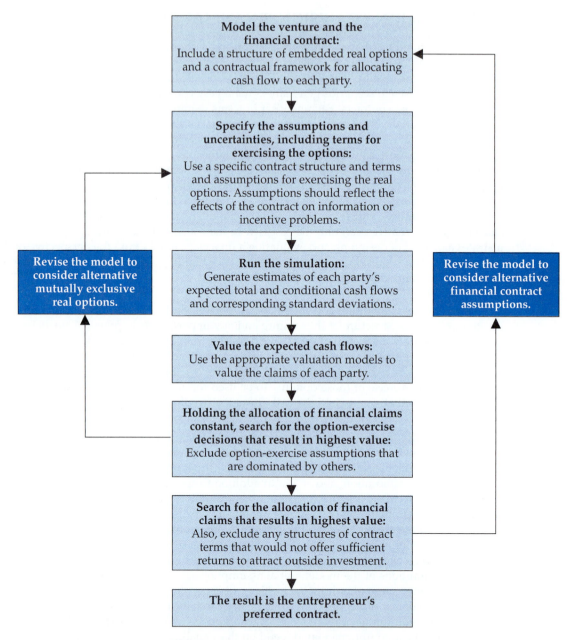

Figure 13-11   The entrepreneur's process of designing and evaluating financial contracts by simulation

Step 4: Value the expected cash flows: Use the appropriate valuation models to evaluate the financial claims and conditional investment decisions of the investor and the entrepreneur, based on the appropriate assumptions about the parties. If the investor is well diversified, evaluate the investment based on the CAPM. If the entrepreneur is poorly diversified, evaluate the financial claim based on the total risk of the entrepreneur's portfolio.[12]

Step 5: Holding the allocation of financial claims constant, search for the option-exercise decisions that result in the highest value: Consider the problem of contract design from the perspective of the entrepreneur. For options where the investor has the control rights, the entrepreneur would like to predict the investor's exercise decision in light of the ownership allocation and would like to understand the implications of the investor's decision for the value of the entrepreneur's financial claim. In addition, the entrepreneur would like to determine optimal exercise decisions for options where she has control rights. Evaluating the option-exercise decisions normally requires you to experiment with a range of possible exercise choices. You should be able to identify a set of exercise decisions that results in the highest value for each party, assuming that the other party also tries to maximize value. Thus, you need to work backward through the game tree to identify the choices that are likely in light of the ownership allocation.

Step 6: Search for the allocation of financial claims that results in the highest value: Now you need to determine whether some other allocation of ownership claims would be better than the one you just considered. Perhaps the investor's allocation needs to be increased or can be reduced. Or maybe the allocation the investor receives for investing at different stages should be different. To evaluate, you need to test different ownership allocations. Thus, you need to modify the financial contract structure and go back through the other steps with the new structure.

In the remainder of this section, we illustrate the model, and discuss its use to evaluate contract alternatives. Because the process of designing a contract that achieves a good alignment of incentives and the best allocation of value is somewhat involved, we illustrate the process in Section 5.

Developing the Financial Model of the Venture and Specifying the Assumptions

To illustrate the use of simulation for designing a financial contract, we use a financial model based on a game tree model. The model provides for some of the uncertainty about the venture's probable success to be resolved by the second year. It allows the investor to make a decision about second-stage investment at that point. The parties can use the model to explore the effects of using different criteria for deciding whether to exercise the expansion option and to explore the effects of different allocations of equity in exchange for first- and second-stage investments. For simplicity, in the illustration, we assume the parties have symmetrical beliefs. You can provide for asymmetric beliefs by using separate model assumptions to study the decisions of the investor and the entrepreneur. You can also adjust the assumptions to reflect use of specific contract terms to signal beliefs or bond performance.

Figure 13-12 shows the results from one trial of the model. The model forecasts the cash flows that the investor and entrepreneur commit and receive. As we addressed financial modeling in detail in Chapters 6 and 7, we abbreviate description of financial aspects of the model.

The model is driven by a forecast of market potential that is subject to uncertainty, where much of the uncertainty is resolved by the end of the second year. The venture's capacity to supply the market depends on the total amount of investment. Time-zero investment is $2.5 million and includes $500,000 of the entrepreneur's human capital. The investor has an option to invest an additional $5 million at the end of year 2. The investment would expand the venture's capacity. In general terms, the investor would want to make the

New Venture Simulation with Conditional Second-Stage Investment **Example Iteration of the Model (Dollar figures in thousands, except unit price)**						
Year	**0**	**1**	**2**	**3**	**4**	**5**
Market Potential		84.12	177.20	381.08	565.77	655.17
Price		$100	$100	$100	$100	$100
Potential Revenue		$8,412	$17,720	$38,108	$56,577	$65,517
Total Investment						
Investment	**$2,500**		**$5,000**			
Cum. Investment	$2,500	$2,500	$7,500	$7,500	$7,500	$7,500
Total Income						
Sales Revenue		$8,412	$17,720	$38,108	$56,577	$65,517
Cost of Sales		$6,729	$14,176	$30,466	$45,262	$52,414
Gross Profit		$1,682	$3,544	$7,622	$11,315	$13,103
Operating Expenses		$1,673	$2,418	$4,049	$5,526	$6,241
Interest Expense		$75	$467	$1,381	$2,287	$2,381
Interest Income		$0	$0	$0	$0	$0
Net Profit		$9	$1,126	$3,573	$5,789	$6,862
Total Cash Flow						
Beginning Cash		$0	$0	$0	$0	$0
Operating Cash Flow		$9	$1,126	$3,573	$5,789	$6,862
NWC Required		$841	$4,654	$10,194	$9,235	$4,470
Free Cash		($832)	($3,528)	($6,621)	($3,445)	$2,392
Borrowing		$832	$3,528	$6,621	$3,445	$0
Repay Loan		$0	$0	$0	$0	$2,392
Ending Free Cash		$0	$0	$0	$0	$0
Loan Balance	$0	$832	$4,359	$10,981	$14,426	$12,034
Total Ending Value						
Continuing Value						$54,897
Plus: Free Cash						$0
Less: Loan Balance						$12,034
Value						$42,863
Total Investment						
Investor's First-Stage Investment						$2,000
Investor's Second-Stage Investment						$5,000
Entrepreneur's First-Stage Investment						$500
Total Equity Share and Return						
Investor's Share in First Stage	10.00%					
Investor's Share in Second Stage	30.00%					
Investor's Total Share	37.00%					$15,859
Entrepreneur's Total Share	63.00%					$27,004

Figure 13-12 New venture with conditional second-stage investment: Example iteration of the model

second round investment only if market potential were expected to be high. The precise conditions under which the investor would want to exercise this expansion option depend on the venture's profitability, its other cash needs, and the financial claim the investor would gain by exercising the option.

In the figure, we assume that the entrepreneur and the investor have agreed on the following terms. In the first round, the investor commits $2 million in exchange for 10 percent of the equity, and the entrepreneur commits $500,000 as the value of human capital. In the second round, if the option is exercised, the investor receives 30 percent of the equity at the time, which, because of dilution, would make the investor's total stake equal to 37 percent. We selected these allocations after we evaluated several alternatives, as discussed in Section 5. We assume the investor exercises the option if year-2 revenue is at least $15 million. We selected this exercise decision after we evaluated several alternatives. Also, as discussed in the next section, for the purpose of evaluating alternative contracts, we assume, arbitrarily, that the investor will not participate unless the investor's NPV is at least $1 million. Thus, the entrepreneur maximizes value subject to a constraint that the investor's claim is worth at least $1 million.

The assumptions regarding ownership claims and the conditions under which the option is exercised are particularly good ones for the entrepreneur. We settled on them only after some experimentation. These assumptions, including investment levels, appear as bolded and shaded cells in the figure. You can evaluate alternative arrangements and exercise decisions by modifying these cells. You can design more complicated allocations by making other simple modifications to the spreadsheet. Other modifications could allow for the possibility that bonding and monitoring aspects of contract terms affect revenue and profitability expectations.

In the model, the cash flows available to the investor and the entrepreneur depend on net profit and annual free cash flow. We compute net profit as operating profit, plus interest income on free cash at the risk-free rate, minus interest expense on any borrowing that is needed to finance working capital. We assume that a liquidity event occurs at the end of the fifth year. Value at that point is computed by capitalizing year-5 earnings, adding the free cash balance and deducting any outstanding debt. The investor and entrepreneur allocate total ending value according to their relative shares of ownership. We assume that the venture pays no taxes.

Using Simulation to Estimate Expected Cash Flows and Risk

Figure 13-12 generates forecasts of expected cash flows and the risk of cash flows for both the investor and the entrepreneur. The investor is interested in two questions. First, assuming that the investor makes the initial investment, under what conditions would it make sense to exercise the option and make the second-stage investment? Second, is the net present value of the investor's financial interest high enough to justify making the first-stage investment? The entrepreneur would like to know the condition under which the investor would make the second-stage investment. Given that condition, the entrepreneur would like to know the value of her financial claim. In this example, we assume that the entrepreneur's commitment is irrevocable for five years. Hence, the entrepreneur has no decision to make at the end of the second year.

To help answer these questions, the Figure 13-13 spreadsheet includes two additional sets of calculations that are not shown. It includes a set of projections in which the second-stage investment is assumed to be zero, regardless of potential revenue and earnings. It also includes the incremental revenue and earnings, and cash flow measured as the difference between the projection from the model in Figure 13-12 and the model with no second-stage investment. Thus, the incremental cash flow is zero when the expansion option condition is not satisfied.

When it is satisfied, the investor commits an additional $5 million in year 2 and receives an increased interest in the venture's cash flow. The entrepreneur makes no additional financial commitment and may receive either an increase or decrease in expected cash flow. The entrepreneur's incremental cash flow can be negative if the investor makes the second-stage investment and gains a higher ownership share in a scenario when the impact of the investment on venture cash flow is small. Thus, if higher sales and profitability dominates the entrepreneur's reduction in fractional ownership, then the entrepreneur gains. If the entrepreneur's reduction in ownership fraction dominates, then the entrepreneur loses.

Figure 13-13 shows a summary version of the three parts of the spreadsheet for one trial of the model.[13] The Total Income panel shows the cash returns to the investor and the entrepreneur, if the investor makes the second-stage investment. The Income—No Second Stage panel shows the cash returns for the same trial, assuming no second-stage investment is made. The Incremental Income—Second Stage panel shows the incremental cash returns due to the investor's second-stage investment decision. We use the results from these three panels to evaluate the conditions under which it would be rational for the investor to make the second-stage investment; to test whether the investor's incentive to invest is aligned with the interest of the entrepreneur; and to evaluate the financial interests of both parties.

To assess the general potential of the venture under a specific set of assumptions, we ran 1000 iterations of the simulation model. The Venture.SIM™ software includes a decision tree simulator that can be used to compile statistics for only the iterations that satisfy a stated condition. In this case, we collected mean values and standard deviations for five variables: For all 1000 iterations, we collected data on Investor's Total Share of cash flows, Entrepreneur's Total Share, and Investor's Second-Stage Investment. Then, looking only at the iterations where the second-stage investment occurs, we also collected data on the mean value and standard deviation for Investor's Incremental Share and Entrepreneur's Incremental Share.

The following table summarizes the simulation results.

Variable	Mean	Standard Deviation	Number of Cases Where Condition Is Satisfied
Investor's second-stage investment	−$2,475	$2,501	1000
Investor's total share	$9,112	$8,483	1000
Entrepreneur's total share	$19,505	$10,842	1000
Investor's incremental share	$14,312	$4,187	495
Entrepreneur's incremental share	$7,824	$5,429	495

Source: Results generated by *Venture.SIM*™ decision tree simulation routine. To see the output table, please refer to the Web site version of this figure.

The table shows the expected second-stage investment of the investor and the means and standard deviations of cash flows for the investor and the entrepreneur from all 1000 iterations of the financial model. In addition, it shows the expected incremental cash flows of the parties and standard deviations, computed over the 495 iterations where the condition for making the second-stage investment is satisfied.

Abbreviated Example: Iteration of New Venture Simulation Model With Incremental Effects of Second-Stage Investment Identified

Year	0	1	2	3	4	5
Potential Revenue		$12,829	$25,796	$53,938	$74,593	$85,848

Total Investment						
Investment	$2,500		$5,000			

Total Income						
Sales Revenue		$12,829	$25,796	$53,938	$74,593	$85,848
Net Profit		$539	$2,096	$5,473	$7,951	$9,302
Total Ending Value						
Value						$61,982
Total Equity Share and Return						
Investor's Total Share	37.00%					$22,933
Entrepreneur's Total Share	63.00%					$39,049

Investment-No Second Stage						
Investment	$2,500		$0			

Income-No Second Stage						
Sales Revenue		$12,829	$25,796	$30,000	$30,000	$30,000
Net Profit		$539	$2,096	$2,600	$2,600	$2,600
Ending Value-No Second Stage						
Value						$26,951
Equity Share and Return-No Second Stage						
Investor's Total Share	10.00%					$2,695
Entrepreneur's Share	90.00%					$24,256

Incremental Investment-Second Stage						
Investment	$0		$5,000			

Incremental Income-Second Stage						
Sales Revenue		$0	$0	$23,938	$44,593	$55,848
Net Profit		$0	$0	$2,873	$5,351	$6,702
Incremental Ending Value-Second Stage						
Value						$35,031
Incremental Equity Share and Return-Second Stage						
Investor's Incremental Share	27.00%					$20,238
Entrepreneur's Incremental Share	−27.00%					$14,793

Figure 13-13   Abbreviated example: Iteration of new venture simulation model with incremental effects of second-stage investment identified

Evaluating the Financial Claims

The Value of the Second-Stage Investment to the Investor   The simulation results can be used to evaluate the various decisions to invest. We follow the conventional approach of evaluating the conditional decisions first. Accordingly, Figure 13-14 concerns the investor's decision to invest in the second stage. A minimum condition for investing is that the investor's NPV for exercising be positive at the time of the decision. To assess this, we use the spreadsheet to compute the value of the investor's incremental cash flow as of the end of the second year. In the figure, we compute discount rates and market risk over the three-year holding period from year 2 to year 5. For the investor, the year-2 value of the expected $14.312 million incremental cash flow in year 5 is $12.121 million. This value is based on the CAPM and on the assumption we made that the correlation between incremental cash flows and the market is .2. The resulting (year-2) NPV of the $5 million investment is $7.121 million.

From the figure, we can determine that exercising the expansion option is beneficial for the investor, whenever year-2 market potential is at least $15 million. However, without testing other exercise assumptions, we cannot determine whether some other trigger value would be even better. Although the NPV is positive for the investor, it may be that the trigger value of $15 million is too low (so that opportunities to add value by investing when market potential is lower are overlooked). It may also be that the trigger value is too high (so that some times the investment is made even though the expected value is negative). To determine the optimal critical value, it is necessary to run the simulation model several more times, with different critical values, and to select the trigger value that offers the highest expected value for the investor.

The Value of the Investor's Second-Stage Decision to the Entrepreneur   One aspect of incentive alignment is whether the investor's decision to invest in the second stage is consistent with the entrepreneur's interest. Ideally for the entrepreneur, the investor should want to make the second-stage investment only in cases where the NPV that derives from the action is also positive for the entrepreneur. In our example, the entrepreneur can negotiate the terms of the option so that the parties' incentives are compatible. To help design terms, the figure includes evaluation of the NPV of the entrepreneur's incremental cash flows over the iterations where the investor makes the second-stage investment. Because total risk matters to the entrepreneur, this assessment value depends, in part, on the entrepreneur's other assets. The computations assume that the entrepreneur expects to have $1.7 million invested in a market index at the point when the investor makes the exercise decision. The $300,000 is the value of the remaining three years of human capital investment.

In the figure, we compute two measures of value for the entrepreneur. The first is a CAPM-based measure in light of the total risk of the entrepreneur's portfolio. The second is a value based on Maximum Achievable Leverage (MAL) of the market portfolio. As discussed in Chapter 10, the first measure is appropriate if the entrepreneur is free to negotiate other arrangements that may involve less risk. The latter is appropriate only if the entrepreneur faces a simple all-or-nothing choice and is willing to accept risk neutrality for risk levels beyond what realistically can be achieved by leveraging the market index. Although we present both figures, we focus on the CAPM-based valuation. In this case, the net value of the entrepreneur's incremental investment is $3.071 million. Thus, the entrepreneur would regard incremental investment with market potential of $15 million as positive. To determine whether this is the best choice for the entrepreneur, we need to test other assumptions, which we do in Section 5.

Valuation Template 10

Valuing the Second-Stage Option Claims by Discounting the Conditional Cash Flows

Market Information		
Risk-free Rate of Interest	0.00%	12.49%
Market Rate or Return	0.00%	40.49%
Market Risk Premium	0.00%	28.01%
Market Standard Deviation	0.00%	34.64%
Correlation Between Venture and Market	0	0.2

Investor Interest and Value—Conditional Second-Stage Investment Only			
Cash Flows			
Expected Cash Flow	$ –	$ (5,000)	$ 14,312
Standard Deviation	$ –	$ –	$ 4,187
Present Value of First-Stage Interest	$ 7,121	$ (5,000)	$ 12,121
NPV of Option to Invest in Second Stage			
NPV of Interest in Venture	**$ 7,121**		

Entrepreneur Interest and Value		
Entrepreneur's Wealth	$ 2,000	
Cash Flows of Investment in Venture		
Expected Cash Flow	$ (300)	$ 7,824
Standard Deviation	$ –	$ 5,429
Cash Flows of Investment in Market		
Expected Cash Flow	$ (1,700)	$ 2,388
Standard Deviation	$ –	$ 589
Portfolio Cash Flows		
Expected Cash Flow	$ (2,000)	$ 10,212
Standard Deviation	$ –	$ 5,577
Maximum Achievable Leverage (MAL)		$ 3,811
Value of Entrepreneur's Investments—CAPM-based		
Present Value of Portfolio		$ 5,071
Present Value of Investment in Market		$ 1,700
Present Value of Interest in Venture		$ 3,371
NPV of Interest in Venture	**$ 3,071**	
Value of Entrepreneur's Investments—MAL		
Present Value of Portfolio		$ 6,340
Present Value of Investment in Market		$ 1,700
Present Value of Interest in Venture		$ 4,640
NPV of Interest in Venture	**$ 4,340**	

Figure 13-14   Valuing the second-stage option claims by discounting the conditional cash flows

The Value of the Investor's Interest in the Venture   Now that we have determined that the investor would exercise the second-stage option and that doing so would be valuable to the entrepreneur, we need to back up one step and determine whether the overall deal is sufficiently attractive for the investor or more attractive than it needs to be. Then we need to determine whether undertaking the venture is worth the entrepreneur's commitment. Figure 13-15 contains the evaluation of the total financial claims. The calculations assume that the second-stage investment is made whenever the trigger value is reached. For the investor, the time-zero NPV of the deal is $1.5 million. This includes the present value of the $5.788 million expected cash flow in year 5 and the present value of the negative $2.288 million expected second-stage investment in year 2. Given the criterion that the investor requires at least a $1 million NPV to cover the investment of effort, the financial structure is acceptable.

The Value of the Entrepreneur's Interest in the Venture   For the entrepreneur, considering total risk and the entrepreneur's other investments, the NPV of the entrepreneur's interest in the venture is $5.177 million. Thus, the venture is acceptable to both. To determine whether it is the best arrangement for the entrepreneur requires searching over alternative financial structures.

As an aside, we have assumed that the correlation between venture cash flows in year 5 and the market is 0.2. In general, we do not believe that much effort should be devoted to assessing separate correlation coefficients for the embedded options. At a maximum, it may be appropriate to consider the nature of the uncertainty that is resolved by waiting. If marketwide uncertainty is resolved, then it may be appropriate to assume that the correlation between the real option cash flows and the market is lower than that between total cash flows and the market. If unique uncertainty is resolved, then the real option cash flows could be more highly correlated. Thus, not changing the coefficient between the two amounts to a neutral assumption about the nature of the uncertainty that is resolved.

The valuation in Figure 13-15 is based on one set of assumptions about when the second-stage investment option would be exercised and one allocation of ownership claims. To determine whether the exercise decision is the highest valued one for the investor and whether some other assignment of ownership claims would be better for the entrepreneur, you must repeat the simulation and valuation steps using other assumptions.

13.5   EVALUATING ALTERNATIVE FINANCIAL CONTRACTS

To identify the financial contract that is most attractive for the entrepreneur (or for the investor), you need to study how particular terms of the contract affect decisions about exercising real and financial options and how the values of the financial claims are affected by the exercise decisions. We use the example from Figures 13-12 through 13-15. Recall that in the illustration we assumed that the investor received 10 percent of outstanding equity in exchange for making the first-round investment and 30 percent of outstanding equity for making the second-round investment. We also assumed that if potential revenue in year 2 was at least $15 million, the investor would exercise the option to invest in the second round. Those terms are particularly favorable to the entrepreneur, given the entrepreneur's desire to make sure the

Valuation Template 11					
Valuing Financial Claims by Discounting All Expected Cash Flows					

Market Information					
Risk-free Rate of Interest			8.16%		21.67%
Market Rate or Return			25.44%		76.23%
Market Risk Premium			17.28%		54.57%
Market Standard Deviation			28.28%		44.72%
Correlation Between Venture and Market			0		0.2

Investor Interest and Value					
Cash Flows					
Expected Cash Flow	$	(2,000)	$ (2,475)	$	9,112
Standard Deviation	$	—	$ 2,501	$	8,483
Present Value of First-Stage Interest	$	3,500	$ (2,288)	$	5,788
NPV of Option to Invest in Second Stage					
NPV of Interest in Venture	**$**	**1,500**			

Entrepreneur Interest and Value				
Entrepreneur's Wealth	$	2,000		
Cash Flows of Investment in Venture				
Expected Cash Flow	$	(500)	$	19,505
Standard Deviation	$	–	$	10,842
Cash Flows of Investment in Market				
Expected Cash Flow	$	(1,500)	$	2,644
Standard Deviation	$	–	$	671
Portfolio Cash Flows				
Expected Cash Flow	$	(2,000)	$	22,149
Standard Deviation	$	–	$	10,996
Maximum Achievable Leverage (MAL)			$	4,919
Value of Entrepreneur's Investments—CAPM				
Present Value of Portfolio			$	7,177
Present Value of Investment in Market			$	1,500
Present Value of Interest in Venture			$	5,677
NPV of Interest in Venture	**$**	**5,177**		
Value of Entrepreneur's Investments—MAL				
Present Value of Portfolio			$	13,271
Present Value of Investment in Market			$	1,500
Present Value of Interest in Venture			$	11,771
NPV of Interest in Venture	**$**	**11,271**		

Figure 13-15   Valuing financial claims by discounting all expected cash flows

NPV for the investor is at least $1 million. In this appendix, we demonstrate how we arrive at this conclusion.

Note that the valuation results in Figure 13-15 are based on the specific assumptions. The investor's claim has a NPV of $1.5 million. The entrepreneur's has a NPV from the venture of $11.271 million. The entrepreneur has total assets of $2 million—the $500,000 investment in the venture and $1.5 million investment in the market index.

An Overview

Contract Allocation and Option-Exercise Assumptions   Figure 13-16 contains a summary of efforts to identify the best set of contract terms and option-exercise assumptions. It is organized like the branches of a decision tree. The first three columns describe the contract and exercise assumptions. Each row in the figure contains the results of simulating the total and conditional values for one set of contract terms and exercise assumptions. Each group of five rows corresponds to a particular set of financial contract terms, with varying exercise assumptions. Starting from the left in Figure 13-16, we considered first-stage investor ownership levels ranging from 10 to 30 percent. For each first-stage ownership level, we considered second-stage investor ownership levels ranging from 5 to 30 percent. The investor only receives the second-stage ownership if he decides to exercise the option to invest in year 2. We experimented with option trigger levels of second-year sales ranging from $12.5 million to $22.5 million. The lower the trigger level, the more likely it is that the investment is made and the expansion option is exercised. For each trigger level, we ran the simulation model (summarized in Figure 13-13) to estimate the probability of exercising the option. The resulting estimates of probability of exercise are shown in the fourth column of Figure 13-16. The shaded row that corresponds to 10 percent first-stage ownership and 30 percent second-stage, and an exercise trigger level of $15 million relates to the assumptions and results in Figures 13-12 through 13-15.

The Investor's Second-Stage Decision   To evaluate the alternatives, our first concern is to determine the conditions under which the investor rationally would want to exercise the option. To determine this, we used the simulation results to determine the investor's conditional NPV for investing in the second stage. Given the specific ownership assumptions, Figure 13-14 shows that the investor's second-stage NPV conditional on exercising the option is $7.121 million. Remember that we computed this NPV as of year 2, when the decision to exercise must be made. The best exercise decision for the investor, however, is not to maximize the conditional NPV. A high conditional NPV is not worth much to the investor if the option is almost never exercised. Thus, to determine the best exercise decision for the investor, we need to weight the conditional NPV by the probability that the option is exercised. When we ran the simulation with $15 million in year-2 sales as the critical value for exercising the option, we found that the investor would exercise in about 50 percent of the trial scenarios. Weighting the $7.121 million conditional NPV by the 50 percent probability of exercise gives the investor an expected NPV of the option of $3.561 million. This value is shown in Figure 13-16 under the heading, Investor Conditional NPV.

Essentially we are working through a game tree. For any given set of contract terms, we assume the investor will select the exercise trigger level that results in the highest expected NPV. With ownership levels of 10 and 30 percent for the investor, $15 million in second-year sales is the best trigger level for the option. You can see from the figure that the best exercise

Search of Contract Terms that Are Most Attractive for Entrepreneur

Assumptions			Simulation Results				
First Round Shares	Second Round Shares	Exercise	Probability of Exercise	Investor Conditional NPV	Investor Total NPV	Entrepreneur Total NPV	Entrepreneur Conditional NPV
10%	5%	12,500	0.68	−$1,588	−$2,550	$3,497	$3,065
10%	5%	15,000	0.50	−$745	−$1,802	$4,174	$5,403
10%	5%	17,500	0.40	−$404	−$1,613	$3,066	$5,033
10%	5%	20,000	0.23	−$66	−$1,231	$2,420	$3,819
10%	5%	22,500	0.09	$30	−$935	$3,321	$2,019
10%	10%	12,500	0.68	−$551	−$1,491	$4,538	$2,298
10%	10%	15,000	0.50	$187	−$1,229	$4,005	$4,165
10%	10%	17,500	0.40	$364	−$905	$3,602	$4,488
10%	10%	20,000	0.23	$388	−$915	$2,618	$3,636
10%	10%	22,500	0.09	$256	−$996	$3,842	$1,771
10%	20%	12,500	0.68	$1,175	−$172	$4,071	$811
10%	20%	15,000	0.50	$1,766	−$371	$4,930	$3,148
10%	20%	17,500	0.40	$1,901	−$36	$4,781	$3,272
10%	20%	20,000	0.23	$1,363	−$183	$4,180	$2,775
10%	20%	22,500	0.09	$663	−$864	$4,389	$1,349
10%	30%	12,500	0.68	$3,045	$1,274	$4,124	−$407
10%	30%	15,000	0.50	$3,561	$1,500	$5,177	$1,536
10%	30%	17,500	0.40	$3,302	$932	$5,507	$1,940
10%	30%	20,000	0.23	$2,293	$229	$5,258	$1,803
10%	30%	22,500	0.09	$1,090	−$666	$5,390	$1,018
20%	5%	12,500	0.68	−$923	−$489	$3,258	$2,585
20%	5%	15,000	0.50	$48	$261	$4,447	$4,399
20%	5%	17,500	0.40	$333	$540	$3,259	$4,712
20%	5%	20,000	0.23	$472	$283	$1,912	$3,388
20%	5%	22,500	0.09	$270	$434	$2,667	$1,713
20%	10%	12,500	0.68	$133	−$8	$3,718	$1,945
20%	10%	15,000	0.50	$791	$879	$4,461	$3,686
20%	10%	17,500	0.40	$907	$897	$3,475	$3,956
20%	10%	20,000	0.23	$802	$648	$2,807	$3,192
20%	10%	22,500	0.09	$452	$366	$3,197	$1,534
20%	20%	12,500	0.68	$1,620	$1,631	$3,378	$843
20%	20%	15,000	0.50	$2,273	$1,779	$4,211	$2,465
20%	20%	17,500	0.40	$2,313	$1,645	$3,983	$2,796
20%	20%	20,000	0.23	$1,673	$1,215	$3,529	$2,338
20%	20%	22,500	0.09	$821	$422	$4,095	$1,223
20%	30%	12,500	0.68	$3,539	$2,839	$3,844	−$279
20%	30%	15,000	0.50	$3,892	$2,895	$4,319	$1,267
20%	30%	17,500	0.40	$3,743	$2,735	$4,580	$1,683
20%	30%	20,000	0.23	$2,549	$1,664	$4,729	$1,539
20%	30%	22,500	0.09	$1,219	$754	$4,409	$842
30%	5%	12,500	0.68	−$19	$1,318	$3,244	$2,061
30%	5%	15,000	0.50	$950	$2,124	$3,219	$3,892
30%	5%	17,500	0.40	$1,064	$2,259	$2,670	$3,971
30%	5%	20,000	0.23	$951	$1,845	$1,777	$3,002
30%	5%	22,500	0.09	$496	$1,641	$2,249	$1,522
30%	30%	12,500	0.68	$3,798	$4,439	$3,604	−$373
30%	30%	15,000	0.50	$4,248	$4,168	$3,921	$1,162
30%	30%	17,500	0.40	$3,971	$4,114	$4,066	$1,414
30%	30%	20,000	0.23	$2,690	$3,477	$4,014	$1,313
30%	30%	22,500	0.09	$1,307	$1,853	$3,894	$689

Figure 13-16 Simulation results under alternative market potential assumptions: Search results for contract terms that are most attractive for entrepreneur

decision for the investor depends on the ownership allocations. In general, the value of exercising is higher for the investor when the investor's first-stage and second-stage ownership levels are high. The higher the investor's ownership levels, the lower is the most favorable trigger level for the option.

Value of the Deal to the Investor   Next, we need to determine that the ownership allocation results in a NPV of at least $1 million for the investor. The figure of $1.5 million in the column labeled Investor Total NPV shows that it does. This value comes from the Investor Interest and Value panel of Figure 13-15. Thus, the contract is one the entrepreneur believes the investor would accept.

Value of the Deal to the Entrepreneur   Finally, we consider value to the entrepreneur. To select the best contract terms, the entrepreneur needs to compare the total value of this contract to the alternatives. The value of $5.177 million in the Entrepreneur Total NPV column comes from the Entrepreneur Interest and Value panel of Figure 13-15. In addition, it makes sense that the entrepreneur would like the investors to exercise the expansion option only when doing so would also be in the entrepreneur's interest. Otherwise, the exercise decision might just transfer value from the entrepreneur to the investor. The last column in Figure 13-A1 enables us to check this aspect of incentive compatibility. The value of $1.536 in the figure is derived from Figure 13-14 by weighting the value of $3.071 in that figure by the 50 percent probability of the option being exercised.

Pruning the Tree

To find the best contract, we need to determine the investor's rational choice under each set of contract assumptions and to prune the other branches that have the same contract assumptions. We also need to prune any branches that do not achieve the return objective we have established for the investor. Finally, from the remaining branches, we need to prune the ones that do not maximize value for the entrepreneur. Let's begin with the first row; there is a probability of approximately 68 percent that market potential will reach at least $12.5 million. However, the contract is not attractive for the investor because the conditional NPV is negative and the total NPV is negative. Both are positive for the entrepreneur but are irrelevant because the investor will not accept the deal. Thus, this branch can be pruned.

Now, suppose the investor is considering a particular set of financial terms. The first question the investor must address is, under what condition would it make sense to exercise the expansion option? The answer is that the investor will select the exercise condition that results in the highest conditional NPV. The conditional choice under each set of contract terms is the highlighted row. Thus, if the contract would give the investor interests of 10 percent and 30 percent, the best decision is to exercise the expansion option whenever market potential reaches $15 million, which we already have discussed. Because we assume the investor will act rationally in deciding to exercise the option, all of the rows that have no shading can be pruned from the tree.

Next, the investor will not accept any financial contract that does not offer a NPV of at least $1 million. Thus, any contract in which the Investor Total NPV of the shaded row is less than $1 million can be pruned. Except for the 10 percent first stage followed by 30 percent second-stage contract, the only surviving contracts have initial ownership stakes for the investor of at least 20 percent. The branches with Investor Total NPV less than $1 million can all be pruned.

Finally, from the remaining branches, the entrepreneur can select the one that offers the highest Entrepreneur Total NPV. As we indicated, the contract with 10 percent initial interest and 30 percent conditional interest for the investor has the highest NPV for the entrepreneur. If the entrepreneur offers this contract, the investor can be expected to accept and to make the second-stage investment whenever market potential in year 2 is at least $15 million.

Refining the Selection

The presentation in Figure 13-16 involves a comparison of discrete contrast choices. The selected contract is not ideal for the entrepreneur for two reasons. First, the investor ends up with a return that is more than required. The entrepreneur should be able to reduce the allocations to the investor somewhat and still reach agreement. Second, the investor's incentive to exercise the option does not align perfectly with the interest of the entrepreneur. The entrepreneur does better if the trigger value for exercising is higher.

Figure 13-17 uses the simulation results to investigate the contracting choices more continuously. The figure shows the smoothed curves through the five discrete exercise choices, with investor shares of 10 and 30 percent from the two stages. The vertical line in the figure is drawn through the apparent maximum point of the Investor Conditional NPV curve. It

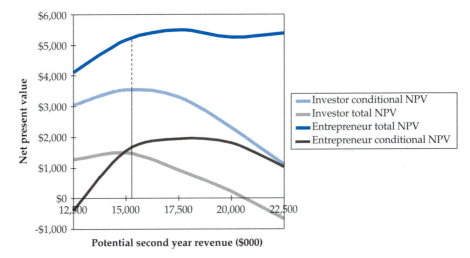

Figure 13-17   Simulation results under alternative market potential assumptions

The investor in this illustration receives 10 percent of venture equity in exchange for a first-round investment and 30 percent of total equity conditional on making a second-round investment of $5 million in year 2. The conditional NPV of the investor for making the second-round investment is maximized if the investor uses a decision rule of investing and if potential year 2 revenue is greater than or equal to about $15.5 million. Under this decision rule, total NPV for the investor is about $1.5 million. The entrepreneur's conditional NPV, given the investor's optimal decision, is also about $1.5 million, and the entrepreneur's total NPV is about $5.2 million, close to the highest attainable NPV for the entrepreneur.

appears that the investor would actually use a trigger level that is slightly higher than $15 million. If the entrepreneur wants to refine the contract terms further, the results suggest that a higher valued alternative can be found by reducing the investor's conditional equity share to something between 20 and 30 percent. Doing so would tend to increase the trigger level and reduce the NPV for the investor.

Considering Alternative Real Options

Our analysis of the entrepreneur's decision problem concerns a single real option. The investor has a choice of committing an additional $5 million to the deal at the end of the second year. We have considered the conditions under which the investor would exercise the option and how these conditions depend on the investor's ownership interest. We have not considered alternative real options that might be more attractive. For example, perhaps the deal would be more valuable if investment could occur in three stages instead of two, or if investments in the first stage and the second stage could be postponed until more market information is obtained. To compare alternative option structures, we would revise the model to reflect the different structure and repeat the analysis of exercise decisions and ownership claims.

13.6   INFORMATION, INCENTIVES, AND CONTRACT CHOICE

In this section, we discuss ways of applying financial modeling and simulation to address other contracting issues. In particular, we consider four broad classes of issues: types of financial claims, number of contracting parties, use of contract provisions to resolve information problems, and use of contract provisions to resolve incentive problems. Because we already have illustrated the systematic process of modeling the claims and simulating their values, our treatment here is more conceptual.

Valuing Different Types of Financial Claims

Thus far, we have only considered examples where the ultimate financial claims of the investor and the entrepreneur are identical, that is, common stock. Nonetheless, in the preceding example, the portfolios of claims of the parties were different. In exchange for the first-stage investment, the investor received common stock plus a call option on additional shares, with a total exercise price of $5 million. For someone to buy a call, someone else must write (sell) it. In that example, since the second-stage investment would increase total shares outstanding, both parties effectively were involved in writing the call. Thus, in the analysis, we did not attempt to value the equity of the venture or to determine the value of a share of stock in the venture. Instead, we valued the complete distribution of cash flows each party would expect to receive, given the financial contract. This principle of valuing the entire distribution of cash flows can be applied to any financial contracting structure the parties to a venture may decide to consider. The following are some examples of common provisions and some considerations for their valuation.

Debt Financing   Straight debt financing is easy to incorporate in a financial model of a new venture. In fact, in the previous example we did include in the model the opportunity for the venture to use temporary debt financing. However, we made an arbitrary assumption

about the interest rate on the debt. We did not derive the rate from the actual risk characteristics of the cash flows. Nor did we analyze whether the rate was higher than necessary
to attract the funding.

Consistent with the example, if the entrepreneur is willing to rely on the market to generate a competitive interest rate, then it is not necessary to value the financial interest of an
outside creditor. This is true even if the entrepreneur is considering alternative debt-financing
proposals. All that is necessary is to model the residual cash flows of the entrepreneur and to
value those cash flows similarly to the way we did in the previous illustration. On the other
hand, if the entrepreneur is involved in a bilateral negotiation over debt-financing terms, there
may be justification for either the entrepreneur or the investor (or both) to estimate the NPV
of the creditor's financial claim. One reason to do so is to design terms for debt financing that
would work to the mutual benefit of the parties.

The primary factors that affect the value of a debt claim are duration, contractual interest
rate, default risk, and market risk. Unlike an equity claim of a new venture, debt normally
generates periodic cash flows from payment of interest and repayment of principal. Thus, it
usually is not reasonable to assume that all of the cash flows are received at the time of a liquidity event. However, the particular cash flow expected each period is not the contractually
specified interest rate. Rather, it is a return that takes into consideration the possibility of default and the cash flows that will be realized conditional on default. You can structure the financial model of a venture to incorporate default states and generate the corresponding cash
flows to the creditor. Thus, you can use simulation of the debt contract to estimate the series
of periodic expected cash flows and standard deviations of cash flows.

The expected cash flows and their standard deviations are inputs to the valuation. If the
investor is well diversified, you can ignore the time series correlations of the cash flows. You
can simply value each periodic expected cash flow by the CEQ method as if it were a separate asset from the others, based on market and riskless return data for the appropriate holding period.[14] If default risk has an element of market risk, you can factor that risk into the CEQ
valuation through the assumed correlation with the market, which can vary over time. If you
assume market risk is zero, then you can discount the expected periodic cash flows at the riskless rate. Unless debt is very risky, correlations with the market are apt to be low.

Personal Guarantees   Until now, we have assumed that the worst possible outcome for the entrepreneur is a return of minus 100 percent. That is, if the venture fails, liquidating the assets
does not return any cash flow to the entrepreneur. However, when debt financing is used, it is
common for the entrepreneur to personally guarantee the venture's obligations or to pledge collateral that is not an asset of the venture. In that case, if the venture fails and the liquidation
value of the assets is less than the venture's financial liabilities, the entrepreneur can have a negative cash flow at the time of liquidation. The issue we address here is how you can treat the
prospect of a negative cash flow in the valuation.

A useful beginning is to recognize that, no matter how poorly the venture may perform,
the entrepreneur's ability to guarantee its obligations is always limited by the entrepreneur's
wealth. A reasonable approach to valuing financial claims that involve personal guarantees
is to consider the amount of the guarantee as part of the entrepreneur's investment in the
venture. In nondefault states of the world, the investment earns a return that is appropriate
for the nature of the assets that are committed by the guarantee. This might be the riskless
rate on a debt instrument, the return on the market, the appreciation on real estate, and so
on.[15] In nondefault states, the entire return accrues to the entrepreneur and is part of the

entrepreneur's total return for investing in the venture and providing the guarantee. In default states, the return on the assets supporting the guarantee is divided between the entrepreneur and the creditor, even to the point that the entrepreneur would liquidate personal assets to satisfy the guarantee.

You can then value the entrepreneur's interest in the venture in the usual way. Any assets that are not committed to the venture are treated as a second asset of the entrepreneur's two-asset portfolio. At a minimum, this includes the present values of assets that cannot be committed to the guarantee (e.g., future human capital, pension assets, etc.).

Convertible Securities   In many cases, the outside investor's financial claim is a hybrid, such as convertible preferred stock or convertible debt. Valuing convertible securities is not fundamentally different from what we have already discussed. The simulation analysis must be based on a financial model that anticipates the conditions under which conversion is expected to occur.[16]

Preferred shares and debt give the investor priority in the event of liquidation. They also may generate periodic dividend or interest payments or accrue rights to dividends or interest, which are to be paid at the time of a liquidity event. The financial model must incorporate the dividend or interest provisions in the parties' cash flow allocations.

With these modifications, the valuation methodology is the same as in the previous example. Each claim is valued based on expected cash flows, standard deviation, and the estimated correlation between the cash flows of the claim and the market.

Warrants   Warrants are long-term call options whereby exercising the option increases the number of shares outstanding. Warrants can be issued to an outside investor as a sweetener for a loan or an equity investment, or to the entrepreneur. Warrants issued to an entrepreneur are usually subject to the condition that a specific performance target is achieved or exceeded. Warrants can also be issued to other parties, such as employees or underwriters, as a form of compensation that is tied to performance.

In the previous example, the first-stage investor effectively received warrants that could be exercised by making a substantial investment in the venture in the second-round financing. Thus, we already have demonstrated how to use simulation to value financial claims involving warrants. The approach for modeling the financial claims of an entrepreneur who holds warrants tied to performance is fundamentally the same.

Ratchets or Antidilution Rights   A ratchet is a right to receive future shares of the venture in the event that value per share is lower in a subsequent round of financing. If valuation per share in the subsequent round is lower, the investor receives additional shares for a nominal price in order to lower the investor's average cost per share. The difficulty of evaluating a ratchet provision is that the financial modeling must yield an estimate of the variable that can precipitate exercise of the ratchet. If exercise is based on price per share in the subsequent round, it is important to recognize that exercising the ratchet would increase shares outstanding without adding to the value of the venture. Consequently, the share price in the subsequent round depends on whether the ratchet would be exercised. Share price and exercise of the ratchet provision are simultaneous outcomes. The model needs to incorporate the simultaneity.

Abandonment   Suppose an investor has committed to make a second-stage investment on the condition that a certain milestone is achieved within a specified period. Otherwise the investor can abandon the venture. Furthermore, if the investor does abandon the venture, suppose the venture will be liquidated before the planned harvesting date. From the investor's perspective, the financial valuation looks very much like the expansion option example.

For the entrepreneur, if abandonment shuts the venture down early, then the entrepreneur's commitment of human capital is different from the example. Specifically, there is a possibility that the entrepreneur would receive a positive or negative cash flow at the time of abandonment. Because the timing of cash flows for abandonment and success is different, the financial claim of the entrepreneur is analogous to a two-asset portfolio wherein the assets yield cash flows at different times. One asset is the success cash flow, including cash flows of zero in the event of abandonment. The other asset is the abandonment cash flows, which are zero in the event that the venture is not abandoned. Rather than attempting to value a two-asset portfolio in the context of the entrepreneur's other wealth, our preference is to simplify the valuation by determining the expected timing of the cash flows over all of the random scenarios.

Control Right, Termination Right, and Other Rights   New venture financing arrangements often involve rights. The value of some rights can be subjective. For example, there is no reason that voting control of the venture must be proportional to shares held.[27] New venture financing arrangements commonly allocate some control rights separately from ownership share. For example, an investor may have the right to appoint some of the directors or the right to terminate the entrepreneur if certain performance targets are not met. The entrepreneur may have an offsetting employment contract or a right to sell out of the venture if she is terminated. An investor may have a right to limit future financings or a first right of refusal on such financings. Both parties may have registration rights in the event of a public offering, and the investor may have rights that can be used to compel a liquidity event of some type.

Sometimes these rights can be valued formally through their effects on the cash flows of the financial claim. Other times, the valuation is subjective. If it is subjective and if the right is conditional, then a reasonable approach to valuation is for the party to assign a value to the right and to add the expected value to the NPV of the financial claim. Suppose the entrepreneur values having control of the venture at $50,000 (i.e., the amount the entrepreneur would be willing to pay in order to have control), and the investor values control at $80,000. Suppose, further, that in 40 percent of the random scenarios the entrepreneur is expected to retain control. By this approach, the entrepreneur's NPV would be increased by $20,000, and the investor's would be increased by $48,000. There is no reduction in value for the scenarios in which a party does not have control. The reason is that the return assumptions of the CAPM valuation methodology are based on market data for small transactions of common stock. Because control rights are not normally being exchanged, the estimates do not reflect the value of control.

Increasing the Number of Contracting Parties

In most discussion up to this point, our focus has been on financial contracts between one investor and the entrepreneur. However, many new ventures involve three or more parties. The nature of involvement can be explicit or implicit and can be direct or indirect. In this subsection, we identify and consider the implications for valuation.

Direct Explicit Involvement of a Third Party   Suppose the first round of financing has already occurred. The venture is seeking funding for a second round. An investor has been identified, who is interested in providing the financing if satisfactory terms can be arranged. Alternatively, the existing outside investor could provide the second-round funding. In such a case, the interests of existing parties may diverge. The entrepreneur may want to bring in a second investor to spread ownership over more parties and reduce the control of the existing investor. Or the prospective investor may be a strategic partner who can aid with distribution of the venture's product. The existing investor may want to retain a larger share of ownership or may regard the prospective investor as a competitor. In addition, both parties may be concerned about the valuation that is used as a basis for allocating shares to the new investor.

To evaluate the alternatives, you would need to model the venture, including the allocations of cash flows to the parties. Using the model, you can experiment with the conditions under which the investment would be made by a new investor or by the existing investor.

Direct Implicit Involvement   Direct implicit involvement occurs when the parties to a negotiation are considering financial terms that could affect the conditions under which a subsequent party would invest. There are many such aspects of negotiation. The most obvious is a ratchet, but other provisions, such as conversion rights or the right to force registration of the shares, can affect the decisions of future investors.

To assess the impact of such provisions, you can develop the financial model to anticipate the possibility of a subsequent financing round. By running a simulation, you can examine the effects of the ratchet on the likely terms of a subsequent investment and can assess the impact of the ratchet on the values of the various financial claims.

A right to invest in a subsequent round of financing at a prespecified price can also be evaluated as possibly affecting an implicit investment by a third party. In the previous example, we assumed that if the investor did not exercise the option to make the second-stage investment, then no investment would be made. We valued the financial claims accordingly. An alternative, possibly more realistic, assumption, is that if the option is not exercised, then some other investor might be found who would contribute the needed capital. In principle, the first-stage investor could forego exercising the option but still be willing to negotiate a second-stage investment.

Indirect Involvement   A venture capital fund is a good example of indirect involvement. The cash flows received by the fund are allocated between the general partner of the fund and the limited partners, according to the terms of the partnership agreement. The general partner must be concerned with the returns to each. By modeling the venture, including the terms for allocating cash flows between the general and the limited partners, you can consider how alternative terms for financing the venture would affect both parties to the partnership agreement.

Contracting to Resolve Information and Incentive Problems

The parties to a venture may disagree about many aspects of the potential for success. They may disagree about when certain milestones are likely to be achieved or about the achievable level of sales or profitability in the event of success. There also may be concerns about incentive incompatibilities. For example, the investor may be concerned that the entrepreneur will want to continue to pursue the venture even after it is clear that failure is almost certain. Conversely, the entrepreneur may be concerned that the investor will take advantage of the bilateral relationship to demand a higher fraction of ownership in exchange for subsequent investment. Many contract provisions help to mitigate information asymmetry and align incentives. Because provisions can have both effects, we cover them under a single heading.

If the parties disagree about the prospects of a venture, they cannot be expected to use the same assumptions, and possibly not even the same financial model. Instead, each party is apt to have its own (possibly very simple) financial model. In general, a negotiation is most likely to be successful if each party attempts to recognize the concerns of the other and to seek financial terms that mitigate the effects of asymmetries and incentive problems.

Actual deal structures demonstrate that information and incentive problems are at the core of new venture financial contracting. Our analysis, in earlier chapters, leads to the conclusion that if the parties have symmetrical expectations, then the highest-valued contract is one in which most of the risk is borne by the well-diversified investor. In effect, the equity interest of the entrepreneur is bought out, and the entrepreneur becomes an employee. Although some aspects of new venture contracting go a long way in this direction, in most cases the entrepreneur continues to bear a large fraction of the total risk. This fact underscores the importance of information and incentive problems.

We already have discussed these problems to a degree. Our objective here is to highlight a few examples and to relate them to financial modeling and valuation.

Debt Financing   Expected cash flows to the entrepreneur usually are higher if outside financing is in the form of debt, but the risk of the equity cash flows also is higher. Substituting outside debt for outside equity shifts total risk from the investor to the entrepreneur. Because the entrepreneur is concerned with total risk, substituting outside debt for outside equity is likely to reduce value.

Why, then, would it ever make sense for an entrepreneur to seek debt financing? The most compelling reason is that with debt financing the investor (creditor) and the entrepreneur can have widely divergent expectations about the prospects of the venture. An entrepreneur may legitimately be very optimistic about the upside potential but be unable to convince prospective equity investors. Consequently, an equity investor would demand more of the equity than the entrepreneur would think necessary to offer. If the failure scenarios are more symmetrically perceived by the parties, then the entrepreneur may be better off with outside debt, even if the risk of the entrepreneur's financial claim increases as a result. Straight debt financing limits the investor's need to incur the costs of evaluating the upside potential of the venture. Debt also obviates the parties' need to reach agreement about the entire distribution of potential cash returns.

Debt maturity can be used to signal the entrepreneur's beliefs about when she expects to reach a milestone. Suppose, for example, that the entrepreneur anticipates having a marketable product within two years but seeks financing for five. The entrepreneur's proposed repayment schedule might be based on her view that even if she is right, it will take five years for the venture to generate positive cash flows sufficient to repay the debt.

However, the entrepreneur's proposal undermines the credibility of her claim that it will take two years to reach the market. If she is correct, then refinancing in two years would be possible at lower interest cost. Consequently, her proposed five-year term suggests that she is not confident about timing. You can expect the creditor to respond by demanding a higher rate of interest. Only an entrepreneur who is not confident should accept the creditor's terms for the five-year loan. An entrepreneur who truly expects to reach the market in two can do better by selecting shorter term financing. Our general point is that shortening the term moves repayment ahead of full resolution of uncertainty about when development will occur. The investor does not need to make a complete assessment of development timing, because in two years there will be an opportunity to reassess.

If the entrepreneur believes the investor is overly pessimistic about the prospects of the venture, then the entrepreneur's financial model alone will not generate results that lead to the highest value for the entrepreneur. The entrepreneur's model cannot be used to generate financing alternatives that will be equally acceptable to the investor. Instead, the entrepreneur must seek financing choices that are achievable in light of the investor's beliefs. However, the entrepreneur should evaluate those alternatives in the context of a model that reflects the entrepreneur's beliefs about the prospects of the venture. Also, if the terms of the financing affect the expectations of either party, then the model's assumptions must be made conditional on the financing contract being evaluated.

Earn-ups   By raising outside capital in the form of debt, the entrepreneur can signal optimism. In addition, because the entrepreneur is bearing most of the risk, she realizes almost the entire return for effort devoted to the venture. But straight debt frequently is not practical. The venture may not be expected to generate positive cash flow for several years, and the tax benefits of debt financing may be negligible. If so, the entrepreneur still may need to find a way to limit the investor's risk. An earn-up is a way to do so. In an earn-up, the entrepreneur's ownership stake depends on the financial performance of the venture. In essence, the investor commits capital based on a pessimistic forecast of performance, but ownership is transferred to the entrepreneur if the venture meets or exceeds certain performance benchmarks.

The specific structure of an earn-up can vary. For example, the investor may receive a large initial fraction, and the entrepreneur may receive warrants to acquire additional shares if benchmarks are met. Alternatively, the entrepreneur may receive a large initial fraction, but the investor may receive warrants to acquire additional shares if performance benchmarks are not met. The net effect can be the same either way. You can structure the financial model of the assignment of cash flows to reflect either alternative.

The information value of an earn-up arrangement is similar to that of debt. The investor and the entrepreneur do not need to agree about the future of the venture. A conservative or an optimistic scenario can be assumed, and warrants can be assigned to deal with the possibility that actual results are different from those envisioned in the initial ownership stakes.

Because the entrepreneur bears substantial risk and participates in the success of the venture, an earn-up also serves to align incentives. Investors often are concerned that the entrepreneur may be a visionary who does not have the disposition to implement the venture concept. If so, the investor seeks a means of replacing the entrepreneur with a proven CEO. If the entrepreneur recognizes the value of professional management, such a change is easier to accomplish if the entrepreneur has a significant equity stake than if the entrepreneur's compensation is mainly in the form of a salary.

Protecting the Entrepreneur   An outside investor may demonstrate good faith in a variety of ways. The simplest is through the investor's reputation of dealing fairly with entrepreneurs. The advantage of reputation is that it mitigates the need to envision an array of contingencies against which the entrepreneur would want to be protected. An alternative to reputation is to specify conditions under which control of key decisions resides with the entrepreneur. If, for example, the entrepreneur is concerned that subsequent financing will be difficult to arrange, the existing investor can agree to give the entrepreneur a call option on additional funds, where the entrepreneur's right to exercise the call is tied to achievement of a verifiable milestone. Such an option can easily be reflected in the financial model of the venture.

13.7 SUMMARY

Many factors contribute to the success or failure of a new venture. Conventionally, the focus of discussion about key drivers of success is on the uniqueness and attractiveness of the idea and on the quality of members of the entrepreneurial team. The thrust of this chapter is on the financial contract as a key driver.

Consider an untested entrepreneur who wishes to pursue an idea and to serve as CEO of the venture. In this case, there is little the entrepreneur can do about the attractiveness of the idea. Given the entrepreneur's desire to remain as CEO, the quality of the team also is, to a significant degree, fixed. With those constraints, the financial contract emerges as perhaps the single most important determinant of success or failure.

A well designed financial contract can contribute dramatically to the value of an idea and can help allay the concerns of outside investors about the capabilities and commitment of an untested entrepreneur. A poorly designed financial contract can just as easily prevent a good idea or product from reaching the market and can keep an entrepreneur from attracting outside funding.

Structuring a deal to help assure venture success and to provide the most attractive risk and return profiles for the parties is not easy. The financial contract brings together issues of real options, incentive alignment, information signaling, and valuation of complex financial claims. The methodology developed in this chapter can be applied to valuation based on discrete scenarios. Simulation, however, generally is easier to use when the contract is complex. Simulation improves the valuations by using a more complete description of the risks of different financial claims.

QUESTIONS AND PROBLEMS

1. Consider a venture to develop a new video game system for babies. The system is designed to be installed in child-safety car seats. If everything goes according to the entrepreneur's plan, the venture can achieve sales of $10 million in four years. At that point, based on market information for similar companies, the venture could be offered to the public at a multiple of six times annual sales. To complete development of the venture, the entrepreneur anticipates needing $1 million in capital immediately, $1.5 million in year 1, $2 million in year 2, and $3 million in year 3. Capital that is raised in advance of when it is needed can be invested to earn an annual return of 5 percent.
   a. Suppose the investor uses hurdle rates of 75 percent for current investment, 60 percent for year-1 investment, 45 percent for year-2 investment, and 30 percent for year-3 investment. How much capital does the entrepreneur need if all of the investment is provided now? How much of the equity would the investor require for making such an investment?
   b. Now, suppose the investor would make annual contributions of the needed amounts of capital (in four stages). How much of the equity would the investor require at each stage? Assuming that the venture is successful and that its projections are on target, how much of the equity would the investor ultimately require?
   c. Finally, suppose the venture survives but is significantly less successful than the entrepreneur projects it to be. At the time of the year-1 investment, the revenue

projection is reduced to $9 million, at the time of the year-2 investment, it is reduced to $7.5 million, and at the time of the year-3 investment, it is reduced to $6 million. All other assumptions are unchanged. What fraction of the equity would the investor ultimately require?

2. Suppose that for the venture described in problem 1, the projected sales level in year 4 is of a success scenario. It is equally likely that the venture will have sales of $2 million at that point. Suppose the investor makes the entire cash commitment at time zero. The entrepreneur plans to contribute $400,000 of human capital, from his total wealth of $1.5 million, and will invest the balance in the market. The expected market return is 11 percent per year. The market standard deviation is 20 percent per year. The correlation between the venture and the market is .25. Suppose the investor and the entrepreneur both receive equity claims.
   a. Assume the market for outside investment capital is highly competitive. How much would the investor require in exchange for the investment? What is the NPV of the investor's interest? What is the NPV of the entrepreneur's interest in the venture?
   b. Now, assume that there is only one suitable investor for the venture and that there are dozens of other people who could develop the concept just as effectively as the entrepreneur. How much equity would the entrepreneur require? What is the NPV of the entrepreneur's interest? What is the NPV of the investor's interest?
   c. Finally, suppose the investor provides the capital at time zero in exchange for a certain payment at year 4, with an annual return of 10 percent. How much is the payment the investor will require? What is the NPV of the investor's financial claim? What is the NPV of the entrepreneur's financial claim?

3. Continue with the same venture as in the previous problems. Try to design a contract for second-stage investment by the investor at year 2. Initially, the investor would contribute enough for the first two years. Later, the investor would contribute enough for the last two years. Suppose that at the time of the second-stage investment, the investor will know that the probability of the success scenario is either 0.8 or 0.2. Assume that if no second-stage investment is made, the venture is terminated with no liquidation value.
   a. Try to select equity stakes of the investor so that the investor will invest if success is likely, but not if failure is likely, and such that the investor's overall decision has a NPV of zero. To do this, you need to compare the investor's NPV from investing or not investing in both the success and failure scenarios. Also, you need to value the investor's claim with rational exercise of the stage-two option.
   b. What is the value of the entrepreneur's financial claim on the venture?

4. Now, suppose a third investor, who has no other investment in the venture, provides the second-stage investment in the previous problem.
   a. Determine the amount of equity the second-stage investor would require to achieve a NPV of zero for investing if success is likely.
   b. Determine the amount of equity the first-stage investor would require to achieve a NPV of zero, assuming the probability of second-stage investment is 0.5.
   c. What is the value of the entrepreneur's residual position?

5. Continue with the same problem and assumptions, except use simulation to evaluate the venture instead of discrete scenarios. Suppose expected sales potential in year 4 is $6 million and is normally distributed with a standard deviation of $5.657 million. Assume that market value at the end of year 4 is six times potential sales revenue, as long as potential sales revenue is positive, and zero otherwise.

a. Suppose the investor provides all outside capital at time zero. How much equity would the investor need to achieve a NPV of zero?

b. What would be the resulting value of the entrepreneur's claim?

6. Suppose, in problem 5, that a second-stage investment can be made at year 2. The investment decision depends on a forecast of year-4 sales, which is made at year 2. Assume that the expected forecast in year 2 is that sales potential will be $6 million and that the forecast has a standard deviation of $4 million. Assume, further, that the actual sales level in year 4 is a normal distribution with expected value equal to the forecast and a standard deviation of $4 million.

a. Suppose a new well-diversified investor who requires a zero NPV makes the investment. What fraction of the equity would the investor need to justify investing whenever the simulated forecast of sales is at least $4 million? $6 million?

b. Suppose the first-stage investor also requires a zero NPV. How much equity would the first-stage investor need at time zero if the second-stage investor invests whenever the forecast of sales is $4 million? $6 million?

c. In both cases, how much equity does the entrepreneur retain? What is the NPV of the entrepreneur's interest?

d. How would you recommend that the entrepreneur try to determine the optimal amount of equity to offer the second-stage investor?

7. Consider the staged discrete scenario investment discussed in Section 13.2. Suppose that, instead of agreeing not to dilute the investor's earlier round ownership when later round investments are made, the parties decide that future rounds will be compensated with new shares so that the dilutive effects will be shared by existing investors in proportion to their ownership fractions at the time. Hence, if the next round would require a 10 percent increase in shares outstanding, each current owner's fraction of ownership would be reduced by $1/(1.10)$.

a. If an investor who plans to invest in each round wants to make sure that the expected ending ownership claim (at harvest) is the same as in Figure 13.7 (so that exercising the financing options and real options is expected to be worthwhile for the investor), how much equity would the investor need in exchange for the financing provided at each round? Base your answer on the investor's assumptions as reflected in Figures 13-4 through 13-7. (You can ignore the entrepreneur's assumptions).

b. Based on the investor's ownership requirements you determined in part (a), recompute the entrepreneur's expected harvest-date cash flow and standard deviation of cash flows, as in Figure 13-8.

c. Recompute the value of the entrepreneur's financial claim, as in Figure 13-9. How much lower is the value of the entrepreneur's claim if (as in part (a)) the parties agree to not protect the investor from dilution? Why is the value lower? Explain. In what scenarios does the investor gain from the dilution protection?

d. Dilution protection is not a common feature of venture capital financing contracts with entrepreneurs, except if the next financing round is at a lower valuation (a "down round"). What reasons can you suggest for the common practice of ignoring dilution except for in down rounds in venture capital contracts with entrepreneurs?

8. Consider the staged discrete scenario investment discussed in Section 13.2. Suppose the entrepreneur is confident of her assumptions but has been unable to convince the venture capitalist that she is correct. If she accepts the investor's first-round valuation and related assumptions, she believes that by the time of the second round it will be clear to the

investor that her assumptions are correct. If so, she believes the investor will agree with her assumptions about incremental financing needs and valuations after the first round.

   a.   Compute the cumulative ownership fractions in Figure 13-7 to reflect the entrepreneur's assumed path of starting with the investor's beliefs in Round 1, but achieving the entrepreneur's projections at each stage with respect to total cash needs, timing, and harvest cash flows. Assume that, after the first round, the investor accepts the entrepreneur's projections.

   b.   How does the assumed path affect the entrepreneur's expected harvest cash flow and risk, compared with if the investor's assumptions are the basis for the entire contract?

   c.   How much more valuable to the entrepreneur is the staged contract with this shift, compared with a contract that is negotiated entirely in advance, where all of the staged investments are based on the investor's assumptions? How much value does the entrepreneur gain by agreeing to the investor's assumptions for only the first round? How much does she lose, compared with if the entire contract were based on her assumptions?

   d.   Compared with the entrepreneur's valuation, how much of the investor's initial (first round) valuation difference is due to the investor's more conservative conditional harvest-date cash flow assumptions? How much is due to the investor's more conservative forecast of success probabilities? Your answers to these questions will not add up to the total difference. Why not?

   e.   How could the investor use warrants to increase the entrepreneur's first-round ownership, provided that it becomes clear that the entrepreneur is correct about the conditional harvest values? Compare your findings with your findings in part (a). How much would the entrepreneur's warrants reduce the investor's initial equity and ending equity compared with part (a)?

   f.   Assuming the entrepreneur's assumptions are correct, how would the warrants affect the entrepreneur's expected harvest cash flow and risk?

   g.   Assuming the entrepreneur's assumptions are correct, how would the warrants affect the value of the entrepreneur's ownership claim?

9. Conditional on success, a venture is expected to have a harvest value of $40 million. Otherwise the venture will be valueless. Some members of a business angel group are considering making the investment (and will still be well-diversified, even after investing). The angels seek a return consistent with the CAPM, plus compensation for their human capital investment at a rate of $120,000 per year. If they invest, they would plan to stage the investment. The investors anticipate a constant burn rate of $100,000 per month over the entire life of the venture. The investors expect to provide the monthly cash needs. The parties agree about risk, expected return, timing, and investment requirements. Stage durations and probabilities of the possible outcomes are as follows:

Outcomes	Probability	Time to Complete	Harvest
Success in Stage 4	30%		$40,000,000
Failure in Stage 4	15%	1.00 years	$0
Failure in Stage 3	15%	1.00 years	$0
Failure in Stage 2	15%	0.75 years	$0
Failure in Stage 1	25%	0.25 years	$0

The annual risk-free rate is 5 percent, the market rate is 11 percent, and the annualized standard deviation of market returns is 20 percent. The venture's correlation with the market is .20.

a. Compute the expected harvest cash flow and standard deviation of cash flows as of the time of each anticipated financing round. Also compute the present value of the commitment, assuming the venture is not staged. (This problem can be completed most easily by downloading and modifying the figures from the chapter).

b. Use the present value of the expected investment required if the venture is successful to determine the value of the venture to the angel investors. What is the fraction of equity the investors would require for committing up-front to provide all of the financing? Be sure to allocate enough equity to the investors to compensate for the human capital they are committing. Assuming that the entrepreneur has $4.0 million of other wealth to invest in the market, what is the value of the entrepreneur's interest?

c. Determine the expected value of the venture at the time of each expected investment round. (Be clear and consistent about how you are dealing with the investor's return on human capital).

d. Determine the minimum fraction of equity the angel investors would require for investing at each stage and determine their cumulative ownership percentage, assuming that ownership percentages are not diluted by subsequent investments. (The percentage must provide for a return on the investor's human capital at each stage). How do the results compare with the results without staging?

e. Compute the entrepreneur's residual expected cash flow and standard deviation of cash flows. How does the entrepreneur's ownership interest compare with the interest if the investment is not staged?

f. Find the value of the entrepreneur's ownership interest in the venture when the financing is staged. How does the value compare with the value without staging?

g. Suppose, at the time of the Round 1 financing, the entrepreneur sells the investor enough additional shares so that, if the venture is successful, the investor's fraction of equity is the same as without staging (the same percentage as in part (b)). Assume the investor pays for the additional equity based on the Stage 1 valuation and that the entrepreneur invests the payment in the market. Compute the value of the entrepreneur's portfolio. How does the expected cash flow and risk of the entrepreneur's ownership claim compare with your answers in part (e)? How does the value compare with the value when the investor receives only the minimum shares necessary at each round (in part (f))?

NOTES

1. All figures used in this section can be downloaded from the Web site and used to study the example or modified for other applications.

2. Calculations for all Chapter 13 examples are available on the Web site in spreadsheet form.

3. Trigeorgis (1993b) examines the relation between financial flexibility and acquisition and exercise of real options. See also Kulatilaka (1993) and Kemna (1993).

4. Smit and Ankum (1993) analyze investment timing decisions as real options in a game-theoretic framework in which waiting to invest affects the likelihood of investing by rivals.

5. To focus only on the effects of staging, we assume that staging does not affect the probabilities of achieving the different scenarios, the scenario conditional harvest values, or the expected time to harvest.

6. This approach to implementing the contract assumes, in effect, the carried interest applies to the entire value rather than just value in excess of the limited partners' investment and that the management fee is based on market value each period, and that the venture is revalued to market each time a management fee is due. While a more accurate modeling of typical venture capital contracts is possible, such modeling would unnecessarily complicate this examination of the value created by staging an investment.

7. Dixit and Pindyck (1995) discuss why investment valuation that ignores embedded options tends to result in undervaluation and incorrect decisions. They focus, in particular, on the timing option. Staging is a special case of a timing option. See, also, Ingersoll and Ross (1992). Berger, Ofek, and Swary (1996) study the value of abandonment options.

8. See Brealey and Myers (2003) for a general discussion of valuing investments with options. Trigeorgis (1993a) examines issues related to valuing projects that include collections of real options, where the options are not additive.

9. This information is included in Figure 13-6 so that the figure can be used independently, by entering investment amounts, stage durations, and harvest cash flow information directly.

10. Note that the zero-NPV increase in ownership is not necessarily the same as the minimum ownership change that would be necessary to cause the investor to want to exercise the financial option to invest. To determine the ownership change that is needed to trigger exercising the option, it is necessary to compare the value of the ownership claim with exercise to an explicit assumption of the value without exercise. That analysis depends on what would happen if the option were not exercised. Not exercising could mean that the real option to go to the next stage cannot be exercised, or that the entrepreneur could raise the necessary funds from another investor either with or without diluting the ownership claim of the existing investor. In this example, if the venture is successful in the prior stage, but the investor does not invest in the next round, we assume that the entrepreneur will raise the funds from another investor on the same terms, but will do so in a way that does not dilute the existing investor's claim. The nondilution assumption assigns all positive NPV to the entrepreneur.

11. The maximum ownership required with staging also is less than what would be found by comparing the expected amount of investment to the expected harvest value at the time of the Round 1 investment. Under the entrepreneur's assumptions, for example, the expected investment (weighting the conditional investments by their probabilities) is $4.710 million. This would suggest that the investor would need 21.44 percent of the equity, similar to the amount that would be required in the success scenario, but higher than what would be required in any other staging scenario.

12. If the entrepreneur is compelled to accept a very high level of risk or else forego the opportunity, the Maximum Attainable Leverage approach from Chapter 10 may be used to evaluate the financial claim.

13. The hidden rows and cell formulas can be studied on the Web site.

14. If the investor is not well diversified, then the time series correlations are relevant to the valuation. In that case, you can generate a reasonable estimate of value by estimating the duration of cash flows, as we illustrated in Chapter 10.

15. Whatever the assets, the return should reflect expected uncertainty and the correlation, if any, with returns on the venture itself.

16. Conversion may be mandatory. Usually conversion is required if the venture makes a public offering of a specified minimum size and a specified minimum price per share.

REFERENCES AND ADDITIONAL READING

BERGER, PHILIP G., ELI OFEK, AND ITZHAK SWARY. "Investor Valuation of the Abandonment Option." *Journal of Financial Economics* 42 (1996): 257–287.

BREALEY, RICHARD A., AND STEWART C. MYERS. *Principles of Corporate Finance.* 7th ed. New York: McGraw-Hill, 2003.

DIXIT, AVINASH K., AND ROBERT S. PINDYCK. "The Option Approach to Capital Investing." *Harvard Business Review* (May–June 1995): 105–115.

GRENADIER, STEVEN R., AND ALLEN M. WEISS. "Investment in Technological Innovations: An Option Pricing Approach." *Journal of Financial Economics* 44 (1997): 397–416.

HARVARD BUSINESS SCHOOL CASE. "Deal Structure." 9-384-186, 1988.

HARVARD BUSINESS SCHOOL CASE. "Note on Financial Contracting: 'Deals'." 9-288-014, 1989.

INGERSOLL, JONATHAN E., JR., AND STEPHEN A. ROSS. "Waiting to Invest: Investment and Uncertainty." *Journal of Business* 65 (1992): 1–29.

KEMNA, ANGELIEN G. Z. "Case Studies on Real Options." *Financial Management* 22 (1993): 259–270.

KULATILAKA, NALIN. "The Value of Flexibility: The Case of a Dual-Fuel Industrial Steam Boiler." *Financial Management* 22 (1993): 271–280.

SMIT, HAN T. J., AND L. A. ANKUM. "A Real Options and Game-Theoretic Approach to Corporate Investment Strategy under Competition." *Financial Management* 22 (1993): 241–250.

TRIGEORGIS, LENOS. "The Nature of Option Interactions and the Valuation of Investments with Multiple Real Options." *Journal of Financial and Quantitative Analysis* 28 (1993a): 1–20.

TRIGEORGIS, LENOS. "Real Options and Interactions with Financial Flexibility." *Financial Management* 22 (1993b): 202–224.

CHAPTER

14

Venture Capital

Venture capitalists do not finance small businesses; they finance young big businesses. (Anonymous)

Learning Objectives

After reading this chapter, you should be able to:

- Describe the structure of a typical venture capital fund and understand how changes in regulations that govern institutional investors influence the structure.
- Explain venture capital fund structure and how the structure influences the kinds of investors who invest in the fund, as well as the kinds of investments the fund seeks.
- Understand how the role of the general partner changes over the life of a fund.
- Understand the contract structure that exists between investors in a fund and the general partner, and how the structure promotes efficient investment and asset management.
- Understand the important role of reputation in defining relationships among venture capitalists, investors, and portfolio companies.

Most people, when they think of new venture financing, think of venture capital. In fact, the term, "venture capital," often is used in a generic sense to mean capital invested in new ventures. But the term also refers to capital supplied by a specific kind of financial institution, the venture capital firm. Venture capital firms have a unique organizational structure and focus on a specific market niche. In reality, most capital supplied to new ventures does not come from venture capital firms, and most new ventures do not have the financial characteristics that would make them suitable for venture capital investing.

Because of the specific orientation of venture capital firms, understanding their nature is important for any prospective entrepreneur. One could easily waste a great deal of time and effort seeking funding from firms that, because of their orientation, are unlikely to find a particular enterprise attractive. Understanding how venture capital firms are organized and how they operate are aspects of a broader issue—where to search most effectively for financing.

Venture capital firms are of interest for other reasons. First, the contract structures they use, both when they invest and when they raise capital from investors, illustrate market-based solutions to many of the information problems we have been discussing in the last few chapters. Second, the market for new venture financing is, by no means, static. The institutions involved in new venture financing are evolving and innovations in institutional form and structure are continuous. The venture capital firm provides a useful frame of reference for examining and evaluating new organizational forms.

14.1 OVERVIEW OF THE VENTURE CAPITAL MARKET

In the broad sense of the term, venture capital has existed for centuries. Queen Isabella of Spain acted as a venture capital investor in the late 1400s, when she financed the voyages of Christopher Columbus. Much earlier, during the time of the Roman Empire, privately financed firefighting teams would rush to the site of a burning building. Only after negotiating a deal to acquire the remains would they extinguish the fire.

In the more specific sense of the term, venture capital is a product of the United States. The first modern venture capital firm, American Research and Development, or ARD, originated in 1946 in Boston. ARD was organized as a closed-end mutual fund. In contrast to an open-end fund, where new investors join at any time by purchasing new shares, the total capital investment of a closed-end fund is fixed. After initial sale of the shares by the fund, a person who wishes to invest must buy existing shares from another person who already owns them and wants to sell.

ARD established the practice, which persists today, of searching for high-risk deals with the potential for big wins. Consistent with this practice, the fund's early-stage investment in just one of its ventures, Digital Equipment Company, accounted for roughly half of the entire returns of the fund over a period of more than two decades.[1] Several other funds during the 1950s and 1960s imitated the structure and orientation of ARD, hoping to realize substantial gains by investing in early-stage ventures. In addition, during that period, the federal government established the Small Business Administration (SBA) and the Small Business Investment Company (SBIC) in order to foster the formation of new businesses. Despite these efforts, the level of new venture investment remained small.

Early growth of the venture capital industry in the U.S. was restricted by regulation, tax policy, and professional investment management practice. Beginning in the late 1960s, closed-end mutual funds, a potential source for venture capital investment, were effectively foreclosed, by government regulation, from investing in venture capital. Closed-end mutual funds are regulated in the U.S. under the Securities and Exchange Acts of 1933 and 1934 (SEC Acts) and under the Investment Company Act of 1940 (ICA). The SEC Acts pertain to companies, including mutual funds, that have broad-based ownership and freely tradable shares. Among other things, the SEC Acts establish procedure for raising capital and requirements for periodic reporting to investors. The ICA pertains, more specifically, to investment companies such as open-end and closed-end mutual funds.

Investment companies are required by the ICA, to periodically report their net asset values (NAV) to investors. NAV is the value of an investment company's assets (primarily equity and debt of public and private corporations) less the investment company's liabilities. For mutual funds, performance commonly is measured and reported as the change in NAV per share. The prices at which closed-end fund shares trade in the secondary market can be higher or lower than their reported NAVs.

In determining NAV, the ICA requires that investments in freely traded shares of public companies be valued at market, based on recent transaction prices. For nonmarket assets (where resale is restricted by provisions of the SEC Acts), such as venture capital, private equity of nonpublic companies, private investments in public equity, and privately placed debt, the ICA requires that the assets be carried on investment company books at their "fair value."[2]

Originally, implementation of the "fair value" standard was left almost entirely to the discretion of fund management. A fund might, for example, simply carry the investments at cost, or at their values as implied by subsequent transactions. Or the fund might gradually accrete the difference between its cost of acquiring an asset and the asset's freely tradable market value. Or it might periodically appraise the values of its nonmarket assets.

In the 1960s, a small group of closed-end funds began to focus their portfolios almost entirely on nonmarket assets. The Securities and Exchange Commission, which is charged with responsibility for enforcing the ICA, became concerned that the lack of more exacting standards for determining fair value could enable the funds to manipulate their reported NAVs. In 1969 and 1970, the SEC issued two Interpretive Releases related to the fair value standard as it applies to investment company investments in nonmarket assets. In these releases, the SEC took two related positions. First, it emphasized that, under the ICA, fair value must be determined "in good faith by the fund's board of directors," and that reliance on others to determine fair value would not absolve the board of its potential liability for valuations inconsistent with fair value. Second, it adopted a very conservative position on the meaning of fair value, essentially equating fair value with current liquidation value, even with regard to assets where the acquirer has no near-term intent to liquidate, and prohibiting arbitrary or formulaic approaches to determining the fair value of any asset.

The effect of the SEC's new emphasis on liquidation value, coupled with the good-faith liability of the fund's board of directors, precipitated a withdrawal of closed-end funds from investing in nonmarket assets. Over most of the ensuing decade, the venture capital market languished. Venture capitalists could avoid SEC Act and ICA regulation by organizing as limited partnerships and only raising capital from investors who are deemed, under the SEC Acts, to be sophisticated investors, not requiring the protections of the SEC Acts.

However, an additional problem impeded the growth of venture capital limited partnerships. Many professional asset managers viewed themselves as constrained not to invest in high-risk or nonmarket assets by an array of state and federal regulations, legal precedents, and investment policies. Consistent with the impact of the SEC's interpretations of the ICA fair value standard on the market for venture capital, Figure 14-1 shows that new capital commitments to venture capital funds declined steadily from 1969 through 1977.[3] To show percentage volatility more clearly, amounts in the figure are shown in log scale. The decline over this period is from $171 million of commitments in 1969 to $39 million in 1977.

Significant changes in the U.S. venture capital market began to occur in the late 1970s, owing to two factors. First, the reduction of the capital gains tax rate in 1978 spurred an increase in entrepreneurial activity. On the demand-for-capital side, the tax-rate reduction increased the values of activities that produce capital gains, relative to ordinary earnings. Hence, workers had

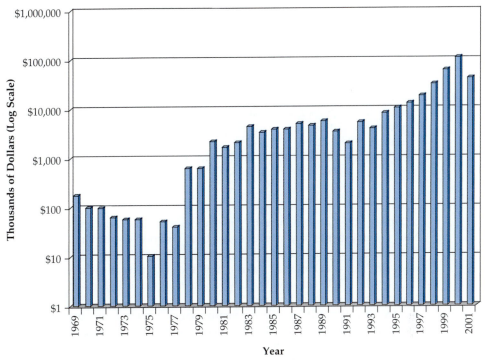

Figure 14-1 Venture capital new commitments (1969–2001)

Sources: Statistical Abstract of the U.S. (various issues), Venture Economics Investor Service, Sahlman (1990)

the incentive to leave salaried employment to pursue new ventures where the principal form of compensation would be capital gain on sale of the venture's stock.[4] On the supply side, the reduced tax rate increased the benefit of capital gains income, compared with dividend and interest income. It thereby increased incentives to invest in assets that produce capital gains.[5]

The second factor that contributed to the increase in venture capital commitments occurred in 1979, when the Department of Labor reinterpreted regulations governing investments by pension funds. Under the 1974 Employee Retirement Income Security Act ("ERISA") and the "prudent person" standard, pension fund managers avoided making significant investments in illiquid and high-risk assets, such as investments in new ventures. The 1979 reinterpretation enabled managers to view the risk of an individual investment in the context of its contribution to the overall risk of the pension fund portfolio. Hence, under the new "prudent investor" standard, pension funds could invest in securities that traditionally were viewed as too risky (imprudent), but, when mixed with other securities, contributed to a diversified portfolio. The result was a rapid increase in the level of pension fund investing in new ventures. Other asset managers with similar fiduciary obligations, such as managers of endowment funds, have adopted the ERISA prudent investor standard.

Corresponding to the 1978 change in the capital gains tax rate, annual new commitments increased from $39 million to $600 million. After 1978, the level increased dramatically, reaching $104.9 billion in 2000, before dropping back to $40.3 billion in 2001, corresponding to the

> ### Greylock
>
> The relatively small amount of total capital under management by venture capital firms may understate their economic significance. Greylock, for example, is one of the earliest organized private venture capital firms to use the current limited partnership structure. The firm was formed in Boston in 1965 and currently has committed capital of $2.2 billion under management. Through 2002, Greylock claims to have provided equity capital and other support to more than 250 ventures. Of those, it reports that more than 120 have become public companies and that another 80 have merged with or been acquired by other companies.
>
> See the firm's Web site at http://www.greylock.com.

collapse of the dot-com industry and more broad-based declines in the public equity markets. New commitments of venture capital bear a strong correspondence to what is happening in the public equity markets at the same time. The early 1980s and much of the 1990s were periods of rising stock market values, high levels of new investment in the capital markets, and high levels of IPO activity. The late 1980s was a period of lower economic growth and a generally less active capital market.[6]

Despite its rapid growth, the venture capital market remains small. The year-2000 high estimate of annual total new capital commitments, $104.9 billion, compares to public and private debt issues totaling $977.6 billion and public and private equity issues totaling $291.2 billion in 2000. Equity private placements, alone, totaled $148.8 billion. However, venture capital commitments are large compared to SBA loans to small businesses, which totaled $12.1 billion in 2000.[7] Furthermore, venture capital funding can dry up very quickly if the equity capital market declines. More importantly, the composition of new commitments has changed over time. In the early years, the commitments went predominantly to seed, start-up and early-stage ventures. However, as Figure 14-2 shows, in more recent years venture capital funds have focused increasingly on expansion and later-stage investments. By 2001, seed and start-up stage investments accounted for a very small fraction of venture capital fund investments. As a rough comparison, in 1999 venture capital funds are estimated to have invested $3.3 billion in seed and start-up stage ventures, whereas business angels invested a total of about $30 billion, much of it going to seed and start-up stage ventures. During the same period, corporations invested around $133 billion in R&D activities, and the U.S. government invested $63 billion, primarily through universities. Compared with these figures, venture capital commitments are a small fraction of the market.[8]

Figure 14-3 illustrates the increasing importance of pension funds and other large institutional investors such as endowments and life insurance companies as sources of new venture funding. The share of total capital commitments from pension funds increased from 20 percent in 1978 to around 40 percent in more recent years.[9] Commitments by institutional investors, as a group, have risen as well. Offsetting this trend, percentages contributed by individuals have declined.

For a small industry, venture capital has a large economic impact. Over the 11 years ending in 1988, about 30 percent of U.S. IPOs had venture capital backing, meaning that a venture capital investor had supplied capital to the firm at an earlier stage and was still invested at the time of the offering. Given the growth of venture capital commitments and

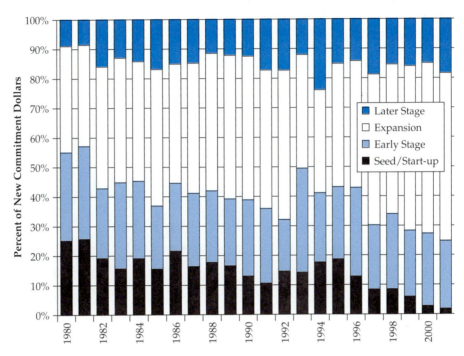

Figure 14-2 Venture capital investments by stage of development
Source: National Venture Capital Association 2002 Yearbook

the changing structure of the economy, the fraction of IPOs with venture capital backing is even higher today. Declining valuations of dot-com and high-technology public firms beginning in April 2000 significantly impacted the venture capital-backed IPO market. Nonetheless, venture capital-backed firms accounted for one-third of the IPOs in 2001.[10]

Why are so many IPOs backed by venture capital? The answer lies in the specialized market niche that venture capital serves. In particular, venture capital investors tend to stay away from early-stage ventures that require modest amounts of capital. Rather, they seek out young companies with the potential for rapid and substantial growth and that will need substantial capital investments to finance the growth. Venture capital thereby fills a niche between early-stage private investment by the entrepreneurs, their friends, and business angels, and the established-company market for public capital or private corporate acquisition. Firms with limited product markets and slower growth potential generally are not candidates for venture capital. Such firms tend to have more modest capital needs. They also may be better suited for risky debt financing than for the equity financing that is characteristic of venture capital.[11]

14.2   THE ORGANIZATION OF VENTURE CAPITAL FIRMS

Successful venture capital investing depends on finding solutions to an array of complex problems. The fund manager must sort through a plethora of business plans, each describing a venture with a negligible operating history. In addition to identifying the few ventures that are

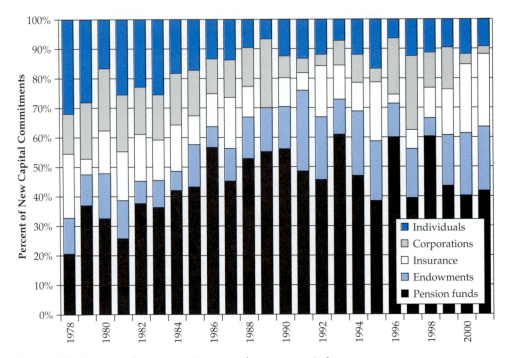

Figure 14-3 Sources of new commitments of venture capital
Source: National Venture Capital Association 2002 Yearbook

likely to be successful, the investor must be able to add enough value to the deals to cover the extra costs of administering the fund's investment portfolio. Beyond these obvious problems, the manager must be able to commit the fund's capital for long periods, with little hard evidence that value is being created for investors. The fund manager must be able to expand, contract, and refocus efforts in response to changes in opportunities and be able to redeploy its human capital when its ability to add value to the venture wanes.

Organizational Structure

The closed-end fund structure first adopted by ARD has important advantages over an open-end structure. In particular, it frees fund managers from unexpected inflows and outflows of capital that could occur if an open-end structure were used. But, it substitutes a fixed supply of capital. The fixed supply, at times, could preclude taking on new opportunities and at other times could saddle the managers with capital that could not be invested profitably. In addition, because the shares of a closed-end fund may be tradable, issues arise related to valuing a portfolio of new venture investments on a continuing basis. Investors who want to buy or sell fund shares will want information they can use to value the shares on a continuing basis. Because of these drawbacks and the ICA disincentives for closed-end funds to invest in fair value assets, the predominant organizational form of venture capital investors is no longer the closed-end fund. The venture capital limited partnership has become the dominant form of fund structure for venture capital investing.[12]

Venture Capital and Private Equity Activity in Europe

Many factors influence the level of venture capital and private equity activity in a country or region. Generally, however, the level of formal activity is higher in developed economies than in emerging economies. While direct comparisons with the U.S. are not possible, Europe clearly ranks as a close second in the overall level of activity. In 2001, a total of 38.2 billion euros in new funds was raised by venture capital and private equity funds. The total was down by 20.4 percent from the year-2000 high of 48.0 billion euros.

European Venture Capital and Private Equity Funds Raised in 2001

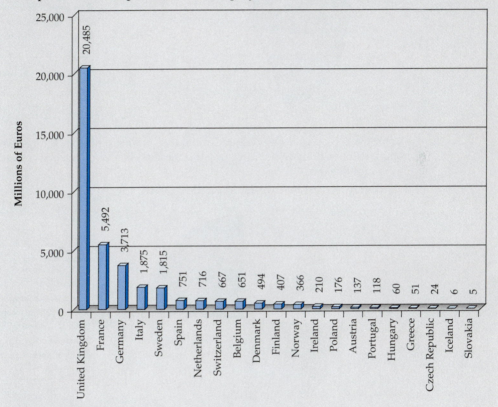

Although the total in 2001 is similar to total U.S. new venture capital commitments, the European total includes all private equity, which is a broader classification than U.S. venture capital. The relatively modest decrease from 2000 to 2001 in funds raised is attributable to the different focus of European private equity and venture capital activity. The focus in Europe tends to be more on later-stage investments and less on high-technology investments. More than half of the funds raised in Europe in 2001 were targeted for buyouts. A total of only 25.0 percent were targeted for early-stage and expansion-stage high-tech ventures, and a total of only 17.6 percent were targeted for early-stage ventures of any type.

(Continues)

(Continued)

Expected Allocation of Funds Raised in 2001

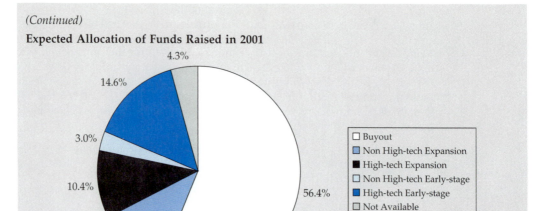

As in the U.S., sources of venture capital and private equity in Europe are concentrated among institutional investors. In contrast to the U.S., banks are major investors in European venture capital.

Private Equity Raised by Investor Type (1997–2001)

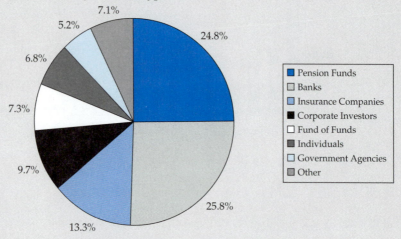

Source: EVCA Network News Supplement, August 2002, European Private Equity and Venture Capital Association.

Figure 14-4 is a schematic representation of the limited partnership form of a venture capital fund. The general partner is the fund organizer and is responsible for raising investment capital from the limited partners and deploying the capital by investing in portfolio companies. On the capital deployment side, the general partner searches through investment opportunities (the "deal flow") and screens them based on quality and compatibility with the general partner's capabilities and with timing of the fund's capital flows. When an attractive investment prospect is identified, the general partner negotiates the terms for investing.

Committing the fund's financial capital to a venture also commits some of the general partner's human capital to ongoing involvement in monitoring and advising. The intensity of these efforts varies across funds. There are different investment philosophies in operation; and some ventures warrant more active investor involvement than others. Finally, the general partner is responsible for harvesting the investment. Harvesting allows the general partner to redeploy human capital to other investments or perhaps to another fund that is managed by the same general partner.

Raising the capital for a venture capital fund is a costly endeavor. The general partner commits a substantial fraction of time to marketing the fund to prospective investors and to managing relations with existing investors. Although the assets of the fund (the investments in portfolio companies) are not tradable by the fund's investors, most investors expect to monitor and influence the investment decisions of the general partner. Most institutional investors require periodic (at least annual) reporting, including valuations and status reports on the fund's portfolio companies.

Returns to General Partners

The general partners of venture capital funds are, themselves, often organized as a partnership. The returns to the individual partners of the general partnership in a venture capital fund can be sizeable, even if the fund performs poorly. Consider a $100 million fund with five members of the general partnership, a 2.5 percent fee for the operating budget, and 20 percent of capital appreciation. Suppose the fund has a 10-year life and a 5-year average holding period, with 20 percent annual appreciation after fees. For simplicity, suppose the fund invests $20 million per year in years 1 through 5 and realizes uniform returns of $49.8 million per year in years 6 through 10 (a 20 percent IRR).

The gross management fee of the fund is $2.5 million per year, or $500,000 per partner. The gross return to the general partnership due to capital appreciation during the harvest years is $5.95 million, or $1.69 million per partner. These returns, of course, are before any partnership expenses. However, even if expenses account for half of the total, the returns to partners still are substantial—annual net fees of $250,000 and annual carried interest returns of $850,000 during the last five years.

Zider (1998) provides a separate estimate of the returns to individual members of the general partnership for a fund with these characteristics. He cites annual salaries of $200,000 to $400,000, and total annual compensation, including carried interest returns, of $1.4 million.

The total return can be higher, because an individual partner may manage assets for more than one venture capital fund. Conversely, if the fund performs poorly, then the partner's career as a venture capitalist may be brief.

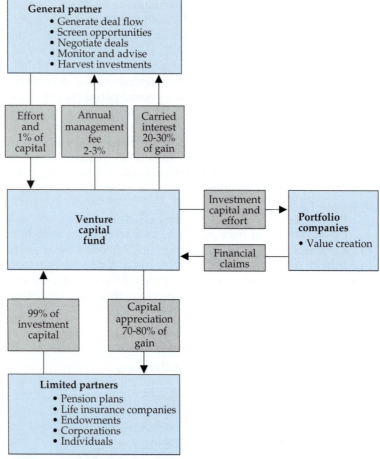

Figure 14-4 Organizational structure of venture capital investment

Venture capital funds usually are organized as limited partnerships. The general partner manages the fund, and limited partners provide investment capital. The fund invests in a portfolio of new ventures.

The general partner's primary contribution to the fund is in the form of effort in managing the investments and raising capital. In addition, though exact practices vary, the general partner normally commits 1 percent of the fund's investment capital. This is an arbitrarily small commitment, given that the general partner normally receives an annual management fee of 2 to 3 percent of committed capital and that the general partner normally is entitled to 20 to 30 percent of the gain of the fund, in excess of the value of committed capital.

Most general partners are themselves organized as partnerships. As such, they can expand or contract in size and can deal with issues of continuity, in the event that a partner leaves the firm.

Figure 14-3 shows that institutional investors are the predominant limited partners of a venture capital fund. Institutions invest in venture capital for several reasons, including the removal of impediments, such as the old "prudent man" standard. A more fundamental reason, however, is that venture capital investing is a long-term proposition. Investors commit to funds for several years, with no convenient means of achieving liquidity. Because institutional investors are long-term investors, the lack of liquidity is not a problem. Furthermore, ability to treat investors symmetrically is important to effective management of a venture capital fund. Limited partnership structures provide that investors contribute capital and receive distributions on the same schedule. Institutions fit the profile of investors who can be trusted to contribute capital on schedule and who are not very sensitive to timing of distributions. This is important because, prior to harvesting (or an IPO that leads to harvesting), there normally is no market test of the values of investments in the fund's portfolio. The potential for opportunism and manipulation would be much greater if investors could enter or exit the fund whenever they chose. Investors would be motivated to devote resources to generating their own estimates of the values of investments in the portfolio and would apply pressure to the general partner to provide more information and try to influence the valuations reported by the general partner.

The upshot of this discussion is that general partners seek investors who reliably can commit their capital for the entire life of the fund. What better place to look for such investors than institutions like pension funds, endowments, and life insurers, all of which have predictable needs for liquidity that are small relative to the overall sizes of their investment portfolios? By extension, if individual investors seek to be involved in a venture capital partnership, the general partner screens for individuals who reliably can commit to maintain their capital investments. Perhaps paradoxically, venture capital is a market where the investor's reputation is as important as the investor's money.

Reputation comes into play in another way. When a new fund is created, the general partner seeks capital commitments from investors at the same time that it assesses new investment opportunities and negotiates deals. Actual investments in new ventures are not made until the fund's "closing." A fund closes when sufficient commitments of capital have been made to warrant going forward with the fund. Each investor's commitment of capital to the fund is conditional on the fund generating sufficient commitments from other investors to reach the minimum total for closing. When the closing occurs, the general partner makes an initial "capital call" of the investors, and the investors have a short time (such as 30 days) in which to deliver the funds. Thus, the general partner has a complex call option on the committed capital of the investors. To achieve the best performance, the general partner makes capital calls only when there are immediately attractive ways of investing the capital. Normally, the investors may receive several capital calls during the first few years of the fund's life. Because each investor is expected to deliver capital in response to capital calls, the investors' reputations are important to effective operation of the fund. Failure to deliver capital when called upon to do so could cause the fund to miss investment opportunities and could otherwise disrupt fund operation.

Use of closing dates and capital calls enables a venture capital fund to operate with very little internal liquidity. However, the need for liquidity does not disappear. Instead, it is shifted to the investors. Consequently, typical investors in venture capital funds are those whose ordinary levels of liquidity are sufficient to enable them to respond to unpredictable capital calls.

The venture capital limited partnership agreement sets out conditions for investing, requirements for closing, general partner compensation, distribution requirements, and the other terms. Figure 14-5 contains a summary of the more important terms and provides examples for a fictional fund, Venture.com Venture Capital Fund, L.P.

Summary of Terms of VC LP Agreement	
Terms	**Venture.com Venture Capital Fund, L.P. (the "Fund")**
Purpose	Identifies the focus and investment objective, such as, to earn superior returns from early-stage investments in e-commerce ventures. May include provisions limiting the amount invested in any one venture and/or restricting the types of investment vehicles.
General Partner	Normally the General Partner is a partnership of individual general partners. Investors in the Fund may seek access to the agreement among the individual general partners, to assess their incentives and may seek further limitations.
Limited Partnership Interests	Specifies the total amount of the Fund that is being offered, such as $250 million, and the minimum per investor, such as $10 million.
General Partner's Investment	The usual contribution is 1 percent, and sometimes may be in the form of a promissory note.
Minimum for Closing	Commitments of a specified amount, such as $100 million, must be received before initial closing. If there is a subsequent closing, it may be restricted to a fixed period after the initial closing.
Payment of Subscriptions	Investors must provide a specified amount of capital at time of closing, such as 30 percent. Subsequent calls may be at specified times, but more often are on short notice to afford maximum flexibility for investing the funds.
Term	Usually ten years, with options to extend on certain conditions to permit orderly liquidation of investments.
Allocation of Profit and Loss	Usually 80 percent to Limited Partners and 20 percent to the General Partner, though sometimes the General Partner share is higher. Other provisions are also possible, relating to how gains and losses are treated.
Distributions	Usually the provisions are intended to assure prompt distribution of much of the cash and all public securities. There may be provisions requiring a full return of capital, or some other hurdle level, before distributions to the General Partner. Alternatively, the General Partner may be required to make up any over-compensation that could result from late realization of a loss.
Service Fee	Normally 2.5 percent of contributed and committed capital, possibly with adjustments for inflation. The fee may be linked to budgeted expenses, may specify specific offsets to be charged, and may be set in light of other funds under management.
Organizational Expenses	The front-end cost of setting up the Fund is usually paid out of the capital contributions to the Fund. The agreement may specify a maximum amount and enumerate items covered.
Conflicts of Interest	Limitations on co-investing with individual general partners or with earlier funds of the venture capitalist.
Other Restrictions and Limitations	Prohibitions on borrowing, organizing follow-on funds, etc. The provisions are intended to control effort devoted to the Fund and to prevent risk-shifting.

Figure 14-5 Summary of terms of venture capital limited partnership agreement

The Investment Process

Figure 14-6 illustrates the venture capital investment process and its relation to the fund's structure. As discussed earlier, after the fund concept is developed, the general partner makes concurrent efforts to secure commitments from investors and to generate deal flow. The fund closing and first capital call marks the point when the general partner begins to build a portfolio of investments. You can think of the closing date as the fund's birthday, even though raising capital and evaluating deals are activities that commence months earlier.[13]

Normally, it takes two to three years before a fund is fully invested. During this period, the general partner is busy screening plans, conducting due diligence on prospective investments, and negotiating deals. Corresponding to these efforts, the general partner makes additional capital calls on committed investors and seeks to place the entire commitment with new ventures.

A fund can have more than one closing. During this funding period, the general manager may bring in new investors and oversee a second or third closing. A closing defines a group of investors who are treated identically as the fund progresses. Managing a fund with multiple closings gives rise to potential opportunism as it enables investors to get into the fund at different times. Existing investors would not want new investors to buy into existing successes at low prices, and prospective investors would not want to buy into existing failures at high prices. Thus, having a second closing elevates the importance of accurate valuations of portfolio companies and existing fund investments in them. Alternatively, the manager can try to address potential opportunism by segregating existing and new investments into separate venture capital funds. Of course, an investor can avoid opportunism by acquiring the right, *ex ante,* to participate in each closing at the same level (e.g., 5 percent of each closing). However, this can increase the investor's financial commitment.

Following investment in a portfolio company, the general partner's responsibility shifts to value creation and monitoring. Service on boards of directors is commonplace, as is continuous performance evaluation. In addition, venture capitalists often are involved in recruiting management-team members, building external relations with prospective trading partners, and helping to arrange financing. Most funds hope to harvest their investments in about five years. Thus, the normal period of active involvement is four to five years.

Value-added Investing—Kleiner Perkins Caufield & Byers

Kleiner Perkins Caufield & Byers is based in Menlo Park, California, in Silicon Valley. Like most venture capital investors, KPCB emphasizes its role of active investor. The firm stresses access to capital, and access to people who can recognize and improve upon the value of the entrepreneur's idea. KPCB identifies its role as building the entrepreneur's vision, strengthening strategic thinking, taking advantage of industry networks, finding and securing managerial and other talent, and arranging additional financing.

In describing the experience of its partners, KPCB reports that it has been an early investor in more than 350 companies, and invested in companies with aggregate market value in excess of $650 billion.

See the firm's Web site at *http://www.kpcb.com.*

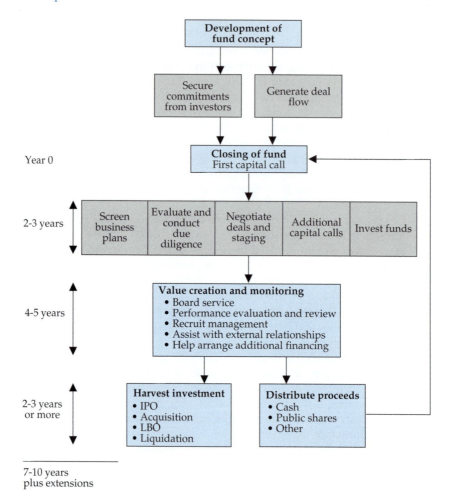

Figure 14-6 The venture capital investment process

Most venture capital funds are intended to last about 10 years. The fund begins on the date of the first closing. The role of the fund manager changes over the life of the fund, from activities related to investing capital to those related to managing and monitoring investments, and finally to those related to harvesting.

Ideally, the general partner continues to work with a portfolio company as long as the general partner is able to add value and until a point when a liquidity event, such as an IPO or private sale, is possible. Harvesting activities enable investors to realize the gains on their involvement with the fund, either through receipt of cash, or of publicly tradable shares. Such distributions are natural milestones for the general partner in its efforts to establish another fund. The harvesting window normally is two to three years. The long window allows the general partner to time the harvest in light of market conditions and company-specific factors.

The periods of investment, value creation, and harvesting within a single venture capital fund overlap, as portfolio companies progress at different rates. Consequently, the normal target life of a fund is seven to ten years. Typically, the general partner can extend the life of the fund for several years to permit management of harvest timing.

The finite life of the fund limits and controls the general partner's behavior. A general partner who is successful in adding value for investors will have little trouble generating commitments to a new fund, whereas one who has not been successful is unlikely to attract new investors. Here, again, long-term relationships and reputation are important. Compared with the public equity market, prospective investors are few and can easily communicate with each other. Concern with reputational damage serves to discipline the general partner and protects investors from short-run opportunism.[14]

Why Limited Partnership Funds?

The limited partnership structure solves many of the managerial problems that arise in new-venture investing. Because investors can participate in multiple funds and can diversify across a broad array of other investments, the general partner is free to concentrate on opportunities in which the partner's expertise adds the most value. In contrast to a closed-end fund, where capital is invested permanently in the fund, the finite life of a venture capital fund subjects the general partner to ongoing market discipline. In addition, it mitigates the need to precisely value each portfolio investment on a continuing basis. In contrast to open-end funds, in which the flow of investment capital is determined by market demand, the limited partnership structure enables the pool of venture capital funds to expand or contract based on the opportunities perceived by the general partners. Finally, the structure makes efficient use of the liquidity that naturally accrues to large institutional investors.

If there is a downside to the limited partnership structure, it is that most individual investors are foreclosed from investing directly in venture capital partnerships. They may, of course, invest in closed-end funds, but for the reasons discussed earlier, such funds are pushed in the direction of more passive investment.

14.3   HOW VENTURE CAPITALISTS ADD VALUE

The general partners of venture capital funds charge substantial fees for fund management and also share significantly in the success of their investments. Although the general partners' return may seem excessive, venture capital funds attract most of their financial resources from sophisticated institutional investors. The investors, either directly or through gatekeepers, continuously monitor the actions and decisions of the general partner. Reputations and relationships play an essential role. The sophistication of venture capital investors suggests that the compensation structures are justified. If so, then the fund managers must contribute significantly to overall performance. Sophisticated investors are cognizant of their opportunity cost of capital and look carefully at actual fund performance. They do not reinvest with general partners in whom they do not have confidence.

General partners, if they are to survive, must be able to add sufficient value to cover their compensation. They seek to work effectively on all margins. Initially, they compete to find the best ventures and those that can benefit from their involvement; and to negotiate deals that adequately compensate investors, while preserving the incentives of the entrepreneur. They also try to time fund creation to correspond to periods of greatest opportunity. Later, they try to add value by making good decisions about follow-on (staged) investments, by monitoring the portfolio companies, and by assisting the venture's managers in a variety of ways. Ultimately, they try to find the harvest opportunities that create the most value for investors.

How Do Venture Capitalists Value the Entrepreneur's Human Capital?

Venture capital firms evaluate thousands of prospective ventures each year. A primary component of the evaluation is assessing the entrepreneur's knowledge and skills, or "human capital." In a field study based on 51 venture capital firms (86 deals), Smart (1998) documents practices related to the methods venture capital firms use to value human capital. The distribution of the sizes of the funds used in the study ranged from $50 million on the low end to greater than $199 million.

Smart reports that venture capitalists devoted, on average, 120 hours per deal to valuing human capital. They spent the greatest number of hours on the "work sample" method in which the venture capitalist "quizzes" the management team regarding the venture. However, the "past-oriented interview" represented the strongest predictor of valuation accuracy. In this type of interview, the venture capitalist interviews members of the management team and focuses on past behavior, accomplishments, and failures, The interviews do not include discussions about present industry trends or strategic planning; instead they measure what the person has done. Only 21 percent of the firms conducted a written job analysis, preferring instead to spend time in face-to-face discussions about business-related topics, such as work samples. The following table shows the number of hours the firms devoted to various methods of valuing managerial skills:

Method	Mean Number of Hours
Job analysis	3.6
Documentation analysis	3.7
Past-oriented interviewing	16.8
Reference interviewing	19.8
Psychological testing	.1
Work sample	63.9
Total hours	**120.1**

Only 31 percent of the respondents reported that they accurately estimated the value of human capital in the projects they evaluated. About 60 percent of the respondents reported that they were less than "very accurate" in their assessments. Even though more hours were devoted to the work sample method, the results indicated that the past-oriented interview is a better predictor of value. Although work samples (for example, discussions about financial projections and working capital needs) provide the prospective entrepreneur with an opportunity to "audition," and "showcase" financial skills and acumen, such auditions do not predict actual job performance as well. In other words, "past behavior" is a better predictor of future behavior than "best behavior." In addition, the study finds that more venture capitalists overestimated the value of the human capital than underestimated it. This supports the much-quoted remark of Arthur Rock, venture capitalist, "Nearly every mistake I've made has been in picking the wrong people, not the wrong idea" (cited in Bygrave & Timmons, 1992, p. 6).

Sources: Geoffrey H. Smart, "Management Assessment Methods in Venture Capital: Toward a Theory of Human Capital Valuation," unpublished dissertation, 1998, Claremont Graduate University, Claremont, CA; William D. Bygrave and Jeffrey A. Timmons, *Venture Capital at the Crossroads* (Boston: Harvard University Press, 1992).

Can the Quest for Home Runs Increase the Risk of Striking Out?

The following (disguised) excerpts from a letter shared by a member of one investment group suggests that sophisticated investors sometimes encourage portfolio companies to take excessive risks and operate in less than ideal ways.

Dear Partners:

The story of XYZ Company and ABC Investment Partners began last year with a presentation from the company. The presentation was impressive and the plan made sense. As a result, we invested a total of $1 million in the deal.

An advisory board was formed by ABC, and descended on the company en masse and proceeded to "help" it. I am sure that everyone involved was well intentioned. I am sure that everyone thought they were helping the company succeed. I am sure some valuable contributions were made. However, the unfortunate reality is that the collective result of our involvement in the management of this company has been overwhelmingly negative. I have no doubt whatsoever that the company would not be in its present position if we had invested the money and walked away. I know that there will be arguments, denials, and rationalizations, but I am absolutely convinced that our hands-on involvement is primarily responsible for the present predicament of the company.

Lots of mistakes were made, some reasonable and some inexcusable. Most, but not all, were the result of extreme pressure from the board and the advisory group. For instance:

- The decision to do TV advertising from the outset was ridiculous and burned a huge amount of the available cash. In addition, all of the advertising was targeted at the users of the service (who use it for free) and essentially none of it reached the vendors (whom we were expecting to pay for the service).

- We changed ad agencies unnecessarily and then proceeded to get into litigation with the first agency.

- We made a number of really stupid mistakes in the development of the database system, the most notable of which was the failure to notice that the information being sent to prospective customers was incorrect.

- There are lots of other notable errors, but in the end it all comes down to the one inexcusable error that makes it difficult to recover from the mistakes cited above: The board of directors completely failed to plan for the future financing requirements of the company. One board member actually told another venture capitalist that the company wouldn't need any additional investment, that it would be growing entirely from cash flow. The primary obligation of the board is the financial oversight of the company. It is their job to make sure the company does not run out of money. They did not do this. . . .

The truly sad part of this story is that the company really deserves to succeed. It is true that the entrepreneur is young and inexperienced, but he is the quintessential entrepreneur. I have no doubt whatsoever that he would have succeeded if ABC, however benevolent, had not meddled so intrusively. He simply would never have run out of money without the help of ABC, and that makes all the difference. You just can't play if you're broke. . . .

Yours truly,

Frank Lee
Partner

Overlaying the attempts to create value for an individual fund, the general partner seeks to maximize value for the venture capital firm. General partners expect to realize the benefits of information economies by operating multiple funds. They also expect to maximize the value of the firm's human capital by deploying experienced partners to work with multiple portfolio companies. This means that when one fund is being liquidated, another often is being formed, so that the firm's human capital is used efficiently over the course of the investment/monitoring/harvesting cycle.

Managing a venture capital fund is complicated because the fund supplies a joint product consisting of investment capital and consulting services. The gross returns on the fund's investment must cover both the opportunity cost of the investment capital and the human-capital services. In addition, the returns must be sufficient to cover the cost of creating the fund, screening investments, negotiating deals, soliciting investment capital, managing relationships with investors, and harvesting.

Adding Value by Selecting Investments and Negotiating Deals

The ideal ventures to include in the fund portfolio are those in which the venture capitalist can add significant value without an excessive commitment of time. Other things equal, an investment is more attractive if the venture appears to be well managed and unlikely to require much assistance. However, such a company should also be able to negotiate a favorable deal with the venture capitalist. Beyond this, a venture is more attractive if its needs meld with the specific capabilities of the venture capitalist. Simple metrics of fit include industry focus, stage of development, and location.[15] Most venture capitalists tend to specialize in each of these three dimensions, though larger firms may be able to support multiple foci.

A prospective venture is more attractive if the timing is right for the required investment. This means that the time interval for venture capitalist involvement corresponds to a time over which the market will come to recognize the value of the venture, so that exit is possible. If the market takes too long to recognize value, the general partner may be compelled to continue to devote time to the venture. This involvement may extend beyond the point of creating value, especially if it causes the venture capitalist to forego work on other ventures.

Breadth of Venture Capital Fund Focus

CROSSPOINT VENTURE PARTNERS

With offices in northern and southern California, Crosspoint Venture Partners exhibits some of the specialization that is common among venture capital firms. Crosspoint describes itself as focusing on two strategic areas—e-business services and broadband infrastructure. The firm proposes to add value based on its knowledge of these industries, including understanding the market and the technologies, and based on its network of executives and entrepreneurs. Investments are concentrated in California and the West. Crosspoint looks for ventures with products or services that offer the potential for sustainable competitive advantage.

Crosspoint indicates an ability to provide incubation space and other support for seed-stage ventures, including assisting with recruiting and developing business partnerships.

For additional information, see the Crosspoint Web site, *http://www.cpvp.com*.

◆ **JAFCO**

JAFCO, established in 1973, is a Tokyo-based venture capital firm that operates on a global scale. In contrast to U.S. venture capital firms, JAFCO is publicly traded and listed on the Tokyo Stock Exchange. At year-end 2002, JAFCO had invested in 2,553 companies. Of the IPOs that JAFCO has backed, 80 percent are by companies based in Japan, 11 percent are by companies from other Asian countries, 6 percent are from the USA and 3 percent are from Europe. JAFCO concentrates on early-stage investment, providing managerial support for portfolio companies. They focus on involvement of overseas offices and arrange business alliances with their contacts in Japan and their portfolio companies. They emphasize the importance of deal flow at the local level and have established both buyout funds and more traditional early-stage investment funds.

In contrast to the U.S., where limited partnership is the most popular form of organization for venture capital funds, some countries do not support the legal institution of partnership (e.g., China). Many countries have adopted the platform of a corporation and attendant limited liability. However, for various reasons, corporations are not as suitable for venture capital investment as are partnerships.

Japan does have a U.S.-type limited partnership construct, known as "toushi jigyo kumiai." JAFCO adopts this format for some of its deals, but at other times acts as a merchant bank making direct investments in companies. When using the limited partnership arrangement, JAFCO generates around 50 percent of investment capital from corporations, with the balance coming from other traditional venture capital sources.

See the firm's Web site *http://www.jafco.com* for additional information.

Because investors in the fund are concerned with earning returns that exceed what they can earn from other investments, the general partner does not want to raise capital before it is needed. Similarly, the general partner does not want to hold a portfolio company after the market recognizes its value. Market conditions affect the decision calculus. Ideally, the manager seeks to create the fund during a period when opportunities to invest capital in new ventures are abundant, and seeks to harvest during a period when the market is receptive to public offerings of new companies. There is some evidence that venture capitalists are able to time distributions to correspond with periods when market values are high.[16]

Adding Value by Allocating Effort Efficiently

Despite ability to expand and contract the investment portfolio, venture capitalists must seek to keep their human capital deployed. Consequently, a venture capitalist usually tries to manage several funds on staggered schedules. Beyond that, the venture capitalist shifts resources from capital raising and prospect evaluation during the early stage of a fund to monitoring and advising in the midyears to harvesting at the later stage.

Recent estimates of how fund managers allocate time to the various activities appear in Figure 14-7. Consulting, monitoring, and managing activities represent approximately 70 percent of time; finding investments and negotiating deals, another 15 percent; and capital raising and harvesting, 15 percent.

The estimates in Figure 14-7 generally are consistent with earlier estimates of time allocations by venture capitalists. Based on a survey from the 1980s, venture capitalists reportedly

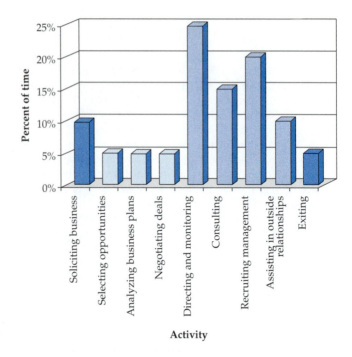

Figure 14-7 Allocation of venture capitalist time

Venture capitalists allocate time to a variety of activities. Managing and monitoring investments account for the largest fraction of time. Activities related to finding and making investments and those related to raising and returning investment capital account for significantly smaller fractions of effort. *Source:* Zider (1998).

spend about half of their time in activities related to monitoring. Most of that effort is devoted to fund-raising for portfolio companies, replacing management, and assisting the management team in other ways. An individual partner spends an average of 110 hours per year on each of nine companies.[17] Activity levels vary, however, as the very good and very bad investments normally do not warrant allocation of much effort by the venture capitalist. Service on the boards of portfolio companies increases during periods of CEO turnover and decreases with geographic distance between the parties.[18]

Deal evaluation is another activity that consumes significant amounts of time. Reportedly, three full-time weeks are spent, on average, over a period of 100 days to evaluate a single deal after it gets through preliminary screening. In contrast, the screening may take only a few minutes.[19]

Adding Value by Monitoring and Advising Portfolio Companies

Venture capitalists can add value by selecting and monitoring portfolio companies or by providing services to the companies. Evidence of the value of service to portfolio companies is

Dismissal of Managers of New Ventures

A recent study of a sample of Silicon Valley portfolio companies (Hellmann and Puri, 2002) finds that professional managers replace more than half of founding entrepreneurs. What factors drive the dismissal of managers of new ventures? Another recent study provides some perspectives on what types of "mistakes" lead to dismissals and what types of contractual covenants are effective in aligning managers' incentives with those of the venture capitalist. Using survey-based data of 205 firms that had received at least one round of venture capital funding, Fiet et al. (1997) examine several hypotheses regarding the likelihood of dismissal.

The primary findings include:

- Contractual covenants limiting salaries paid to the managers of the new ventures reduce the likelihood of dismissal.
- The presence of earnouts in the contract reduces the likelihood of dismissal.
- Sales improvement per employee since first-round funding reduces the likelihood of dismissal.
- Increasing the total number of seats on the venture's board of directors reduces the likelihood of dismissal.
- Increasing the number of venture capital controlled seats on a venture's board of directors increases the likelihood of dismissal.
- Explicit dismissal covenants to force a change in management are not related to dismissal.

The findings point to the power of using "signals" to inform others of expectations for one's own performance. Entrepreneurs who accept lower pay, but negotiate earnouts, are less likely to be dismissed. Willingness to accept these contractual arrangements may signal confidence. The results also point to the importance of board composition, as they indicate that the venture capitalist's participation on the board affects the manager's chances of being dismissed.

These results do not suggest causation. Contractual covenants are negotiated with limited information. Consider the incentives of a venture capitalist who doesn't trust the entrepreneur's management skills or is concerned about poor performance. Under these circumstances, it is more likely that performance-based covenants will make their way into the contract and that the venture capitalist will require more representation on the board. Similarly, an entrepreneur is more likely to secure funding if performance-based covenants are present. A confident entrepreneur wanting to signal confidence may be willing to accept unfavorable board composition in exchange for more funding.

Source: Based on: Thomas Hellman and Manju Puri, "Venture Capital and the Professionalization of Start-up Firms: Empirical Evidence," *Journal of Finance* 57 (2002). James O. Fiet, Lowell W. Busenitz, Douglas D. Moesel, and Jay B. Barney, "Complementary Theoretical Perspectives on the Dismissal of New Venture Team Members," *Journal of Business Venturing* 12 (1997): 347–366.

mixed. One study finds that entrepreneurs do not perceive much value added through venture capitalist service on boards, except, possibly, by the top-ranked venture capitalists.[20] Another finds little evidence that the managers of portfolio companies value the nonfinancial advice of venture capitalists, except when the managers are new or when existing managers are moving into areas where they lack experience.[21]

◆ **Sevin Rosen Funds**

Efforts to strike a balance between investments of capital and managerial effort generally have pushed venture capital firms toward later-stage investment. Nonetheless, there is considerable variation across firms in the approaches they use. Sevin Rosen Funds, for example, describes itself as a firm that actively seeks very early-stage investment. The firm indicates a strong preference for start-up and first-round financing, and actively seeks seed and incubator opportunities requiring investments of $100,000 or less. The rationale is that it can help develop the concept, prepare the business plan, and recruit team members. Through repeated rounds of financing, Sevin Rosen generally invests $4 to $5 million in a successful venture.

Sevin Rosen was founded in 1981 and reports having $1.6 billion under management in 2002. It is best known for its role as lead investor in Compaq and Lotus Development. The firm is based in Dallas, Texas.

See the firm's Web site *http://www.srfunds.com* for additional information.

On the positive side, evidence suggests that venture capital firms foster innovation. Venture capital backing is associated with job creation, higher levels of patent awards, more citations to patents, and more patent litigation.[22] It appears that venture capital backing plays a certification role in the IPO process, as venture capital backing is associated with lower underpricing of IPOs, with lower total cost of going public, and going public sooner.[23]

A typical way to measure underpricing is to compute the difference between the offer price and the closing price of the stock on the first day of trading on an exchange. For example, 5 million shares of Netscape's stock were issued at an offer price of $28 per share. At the end of the day, the stock closed at $58.25, indicating that the original subscription was underpriced by 108 percent. Evidence suggests that IPOs are underpriced, on average, by about 16 percent.[24] Clearly, there are potential gains associated with reducing underpricing.

Other evidence, consistent with the certification role of venture capital backing, shows that the market reacts negatively to distributions of shares of a portfolio company by a venture capital firm.[25] Distribution may suggest that the venture capital investor believes the shares are overvalued by the market or may indicate who the venture capitalist is no longer able to add sufficient value to warrant continued involvement with the company. Although the evidence from these studies suggests that venture capital involvement does create value, it is unclear whether the benefits derive from their involvement or, more simply, from selection of companies in which to invest.

Syndication and Venture Capital

Syndication occurs when venture capitalists co-invest in ventures. Typically, for any given venture, one venture capitalist is the "lead" investor and the others are co-investors. The lead investor normally is the venture capitalist that has the highest level of direct involvement with the venture and is the one most likely to serve on the venture's board of directors. Syndication is a reciprocal, ongoing, informal relationship, in which venture capital funds tend to collaborate by taking turns serving as lead investors or co-investors. The practice enables venture capital firms to pool their human capital resources and to spread their funds over a larger and more diverse portfolio of investments. In countries like the U.S. and U.K., where venture capital investing is well established, syndications among reputable venture capitalists are common. In emerging economies the lack of syndication opportunities (both attractive investments and established venture capital funds) is an important impediment to growth of the industry.

Brander, et al. (2002), identify two primary reasons for syndications: syndications may add value to specific ventures through active managerial involvement of additional venture capital firms, or syndications may emerge as a result of reciprocal certification of investment opportunities. The former hypothesis implies that even the non-lead venture capitalists in a syndicated investment contribute valuable expertise or knowledge to the venture. The latter implies that only the lead investor is responsible for contributing expertise and that syndications merely enable the venture capitalist to economize on the use of their scarce human capital and diversify investments over more projects while still making large aggregate venture capital investments. Using Canadian data, the authors find that syndicated investments have higher-returns than venture capital investments that are not syndicated. They interpret the finding as favoring the value-added rationale.

There may be different reasons for later-round syndication. Lerner (1994), using a sample of 651 financing rounds of biotechnology firms, documents the extensive use of syndication: 41% of first round financings involved syndicates, followed by 28% for second-round, and 30% for third and later rounds. In first-round investments, established venture capital firms tend to syndicate with each other and avoid less experienced firms. Later rounds are more likely to involve syndicated investments by less-established venture capital firms. Lerner interprets the evidence as being consistent with "window dressing" in the syndication of later-round investments.

Admati and Pfleiderer (1994) develop a rationale for late-round syndication based on informational asymmetries, related to our discussion of capital raising in Chapter 12 and staged financing in Chapter 13. Because the first (lead) investor may have an informational advantage over subsequent investors, one way to avoid opportunism is for the lead investor to maintain a constant share of the firm's equity. If the venture needs to raise a large amount of capital in a later round, this can imply that additional investors must provide a portion of the later-round financing. Lerner's evidence supports this explanation, as well.

The lead investor normally is paid for assisting in the syndication; the typical fee is 2 to 3 percent of the money raised from co-investors; sometimes they share the fee with the other syndicate members. As an alternative to venture capital syndication, an investment bank may be retained to put together a large equity private placement for a single investment. Venture capital funds may be among the investors in the private placement. For this service, which is somewhat similar to a public offering, the investment banker collects a fee, typically in the 5 to 10 percent range.[26]

14.4   INVESTMENT SELECTION AND VENTURE CAPITALIST COMPENSATION

The compensation arrangement between the general and limited partners of a venture capital fund is an important determinant of investment attractiveness. In effect, the general partner is a residual claimant on fund value. If portfolio company values appreciate significantly and the fund does well, then the general partner realizes a significant return through its 20 to 30 percent share (or carried interest) of capital appreciation. Conversely, if the investments perform poorly, most of the loss of value accrues to the limited partners, who contribute the bulk of the financial capital. The general partner continues to collect a management fee based on contributed capital.

Perhaps you noticed that the financial claim of the general partner has characteristics of a call option, a limited downside, and significant upside. Because of the structure, investing in high-risk ventures with high *potential* returns can enhance the value of the general partner's carried interest. There are implications of having an option-like payoff as part of the contract between the general and limited partners. The structure can alter the kinds of ventures that attract the general partner's interest, and it can affect the terms of the financial contracts between the fund and its portfolio companies. A venture with an attractive expected return, but limited upside potential, is unlikely to be a prospect for venture capital, even if downside risk is small. Other things equal, such a venture does not offer the potential for the general partner to benefit significantly by sharing in the appreciation.

The attractiveness of the investment to the general partner also depends on the terms of the financial contract. A high-risk venture that is structured to create financial claims that offer safe but reasonable returns to investors is unlikely to attract venture capital funds. On the other hand, a low-risk venture can receive venture capital funding if the structure of the financial claims offers substantial upside potential by shifting project risk to the investor.[27]

The financial claims most commonly sought by venture capital investors are those that align the interest of the general partner with those of the limited partners. Interests are aligned when both types of partners participate in new venture success but are protected against losses if the venture performs poorly. Convertible preferred stock, for example, often is used in venture capital financing. Convertible preferred stock offers some downside protection, and still preserves the potential for significant gain. Other structures, involving staging of investment or put options for the investor, can have similar effects.

14.5 VENTURE CAPITAL CONTRACTS WITH PORTFOLIO COMPANIES

By design, venture capital funds search for high-risk investments with the prospect of very high returns. Consequently, a typical venture capital fund portfolio includes a small number of highly successful investments, combined with a much larger number that are unsuccessful. By one estimate, 6.8 percent of the portfolio companies of venture capital funds account for 50 percent of the returns, whereas 34.5 percent of the portfolio company investments result in partial or total losses.[28]

Because of the quest for high returns, the process by which general partners search for investment prospects can give rise to adverse selection.[29] Consider a process whereby the investor first determines a hurdle rate to screen all prospective projects that are at a particular stage of development. Suppose the venture capitalist develops financial projections for each prospective investment and then applies the hurdle rate to select its investments. Thus, some prospects are screened out on the basis that the venture capitalist's financial projections are too low, given the hurdle rate. Adverse selection arises partly because ventures that are overvalued by the venture capitalist are more likely to survive the screen.

Now, consider the decision of an entrepreneur whose venture has survived the screen. In some cases, the entrepreneur will believe that the venture capital firm has overvalued the opportunity. In other cases, the entrepreneur will believe the venture capital firm has undervalued the opportunity. Entrepreneurs who perceive that their ventures have been overvalued are more likely to accept the financing offered by the venture capital firm. Those who perceive undervaluation are more likely to look elsewhere for financing.[30]

Of course, from the investor's perspective, adverse selection is a problem only if some investors use better decision-making processes than others use. If not, then they all expect to

◆ Corporate Venture Capital

Corporate Ventures

Independent venture capital firms are not the only source of venture capital. By some accounts, more than 100 major U.S. corporations have, at one time or another, implemented an in-house venture-capital program to aid in new-business development for the firm. In many ways, the idea of venture capital within a firm is an oxymoron, as large, established corporations are notoriously nonentrepreneurial. Nonetheless, some firms have found creative ways to supply capital to support ideas that do not "fit" their traditional product or service line but still may have market potential. These internal funds also provide a means to retain creative employees and provide some assurance that great ideas will not "escape." A well-known example of an idea that escaped is William Shockley, of Bell Labs, who took the transistor idea and began a company that eventually became Intel.

Corporate venturing is more likely to occur in firms that depend on innovation to provide competitive advantage. As an example, Xerox sponsors Xerox Technology Ventures, a business unit set up as a venture group. The business unit has money to finance ideas brought to it by employees and possibly others deemed to be market worthy. In exchange, the innovators get a percentage stake in the new ventures. Another example is Bell Labs' New Ventures Group. Any Lucent (Bell Labs) employee can come to the group to pitch an idea. If the idea makes the grade, the venture group provides up to $100,000 to work on a business plan. Larger amounts of money are available to create a prototype and bring the product or idea closer to market. Researchers get shares in their enterprise while continuing to draw a salary from Lucent (but without the usual bonus). The rationale is to encourage more creativity among employees and to do so without much bureaucracy.

Corporate Investing in External Start-ups

In addition to providing funding to prospective "intrapreneurs," a number of corporations provide venture capital for "strategic partners," or external start-ups who are pursing projects that either complement or substitute for their own. Companies that pursue this type of corporate venture capital include large pharmaceutical companies like Abbott Labs and Amgen; food giants, Hormel & Co. and Nestle; and computer-related firms like Intel and Microsoft. These firms set up in-house venture capital divisions that specify investment criteria, evaluate projects, provide funding and monitoring, and perhaps help with the harvesting of portfolio companies.

The magnitude of corporate venture capital investing varies widely from year to year. For example, during the first quarter of 2000, corporate venture capital stood at $6.2 billion, compared to $848 million in the third quarter of 2001. Corporations need not be active investors in new ventures, as they often co-invest with venture capital firms.

Sources: Zenas Block and Ian MacMillan, *Corporate Venturing, Creating New Business Within the Firm,* Harvard Business School Press, 1993; Henry Chesbrough, "Making Sense of Corporate Venture Capital," *Harvard Business Review,* March 2002; *The Economist,* February 20, 1999, pp. 21–22; and A. David Silver, *The Venture Capital Sourcebook* (Chicago: Probus Publishing, 1994).

share the losses that result from investing in overvalued new ventures. Lerner (1994b) points out that syndication is one way of dealing with the problem. When a deal is syndicated, several venture capital firms contribute funds to a venture, sharing in the due diligence efforts of the lead investor and pooling the risk, including risk associated with adverse selection.

Syndication, however, does not substitute for developing methods of project evaluation that deal effectively with adverse selection and other valuation issues. In contrast to risk pooling, improved decision making helps ensure that promising ventures receive financing and those that are not promising do not.

One way to address the adverse selection problem and to improve the overall investment selection process is to adopt contracts that limit investor reliance on *ex ante* due diligence efforts and valuation. Staging is well recognized as a contracting device that has this effect.[31] Staging forestalls the investment decision until the investor gains experience with the entrepreneur and until more information arrives about the prospective success of the venture. Staging preserves some of the strategic options of the investor. In one respect, it affords greater control to the investor while enabling the entrepreneur to retain a larger ownership stake.[32]

Another way to address the adverse selection problem is to employ financial contracting structures that test the beliefs of the entrepreneur, align the interests of the parties, and enable parties with different expectations to transact with each other. One suggestion is to use convertible securities as a screening device.[33] Venture capital investors usually hold convertible preferred stock that gives them a preferential claim in case of liquidation. This shifts the risk of failure to the entrepreneur. Those entrepreneurs who are concerned with failure are likely to be discouraged by the risk exposure. The use of convertible shares by the investor may discourage the entrepreneur from excessive risk-taking.[34] Clearly, use of contingent claims to allocate ownership, such as with performance-based rights or a ratchet, can help screen investment prospects.[35]

Staging and related contractual devices have a downside, however. Staging can encourage myopic behavior by the entrepreneur because later-round investments are contingent, to some extent, on venture performance.[36] The concern is most acute when subsequent investment is guaranteed, provided certain performance benchmarks (a revenue target, product commercialization, etc.) are achieved, or when the allocation of ownership claims depends on realizing specific targets (as in the case of a ratchet or when a contingent right is used). Short-sighted behavior is discouraged if the conditions for making follow-on investments are not explicit and are subject to the the investor's judgment, or where the benchmarks are good proxies for actual success and not easily manipulated. Because of these concerns, some venture capital investors avoid linking follow-on investment or allocation of ownership claims to specific benchmarks.

Venture capital investors protect themselves in other ways. For example, put options, demand registration rights, and similar provisions help ensure that the investor has an opportunity to harvest. Preemptive rights and first rights of refusal enable the investor to maintain an ownership share in the event that the venture is a success. Employment contracts, share-vesting provisions, and noncompete clauses limit the entrepreneur's ability to appropriate the intellectual property and human capital of the venture. Termination rights, on the other hand, protect the investment against the entrepreneur's mismanagement. They also protect the investor from excessive risk-taking by the entrepreneur, which could occur if the venture were performing poorly.[37] Rights to receive information and to board representation ensure that the investor can monitor the venture effectively.

The arrangements described above are not completely one-sided. Granting protection to the investor enables the entrepreneur to retain a larger ownership stake. Some contract provisions also protect the entrepreneur.[38] For example, the investor's right to fire the entrepreneur often is offset by a put option that gives the entrepreneur the ability to sell out of the deal if the termination option is exercised. In addition, demand registration rights may be offset by a call option that gives the entrepreneur the right to repurchase the investor's shares.

In addition, the entrepreneur may have concerns about the quality of the venture capitalist's advisory services. Contracts between the venture capitalist and the entrepreneur, where venture capitalist compensation depends heavily on venture performance, help to screen out incompetent venture capitalists.[39] Such contracts, however, do not prevent opportunistic behavior by the venture capitalist, who may not devote sufficient effort to the investment once the deal is struck. Venture capital firm reputation is, in part, a solution to the problem of shirking. In addition, contracts between the general and limited partners of venture capital funds often limit shirking by establishing specific responsibilities for monitoring investments.

Finally, the IPO process can give a successful entrepreneur the ability to regain control of the venture from venture capital investors, even without achieving majority ownership. Taking a company public usually results in more disperse ownership rights, suggesting that the entrepreneur may re-achieve control, even with a limited ownership stake. Even if the venture does not go public, performance-based rights to acquire additional shares can accomplish much the same result for the entrepreneur.[40]

14.6 VENTURE CAPITAL CONTRACTS WITH INVESTORS

Earlier in the chapter we highlighted some of the complications that led to emergence of the venture capital limited partnership as the predominant organizational form. We also described some of the ways that the partnership structure controls wealth redistribution among fund investors. As noted, the structure of venture capitalist compensation creates an incentive to search for home runs. Next, we discuss how venture capital partnership agreements address a series of concerns related to shirking and opportunistic behavior by the general partner.

A recent study of venture capital partnership contracts classifies covenants under three general headings: overall management, activities of the general partner, and types of investments.[41] Figure 14-8 describes some of the more common covenants. With respect to overall management, investors in a fund may be concerned with the general partner's incentives to take on excessive risk, to favor existing funds over new funds, and to increase management fees by delaying disbursements of investment proceeds.

To address the incentive to take excessive risk, the agreement may limit the amount of investment in a single venture and restrict the ability of the general partner to add leverage by borrowing. Another concern is that the general partner may make investment decisions that favor its existing funds over the new fund it is organizing. Consider a venture capital firm that manages several funds. Suppose an older fund has an investment in a portfolio company that is seeking second-round financing. The general partner may take advantage of limited partners in the new fund by using the limited partners' capital contributions to make a follow-on investment in the venture on terms that benefit the older fund. This may be a particular concern if the venture capitalist is not well established and wants to use the performance of the early fund to attract new capital. To obviate this concern, a fund contract may give investors the right to review the general partner's decisions to make follow-on investments in ventures held by its other funds. Alternatively, the agreement may require that, if the general partner wants to make follow-on investments in portfolio companies of its other funds,

Key Covenant Classes of Venture Capital Limited Partnerships	
Overall fund management	
Investment in a single firm	Limit on amount of investment in a single firm (restricts risk-taking by VC)
Use of debt	Limit borrowing by fund and possibly maturity, may limit borrowing by VC or guarantees by VC (two issues - adding risk to fund, conflict of interest on returns)
Coinvestment by VCs other funds	Monitoring of decision to invest in later stage of existing portfolio company of another fund, or require coinvestment to avoid wealth transfer, or if unaffiliated fund invests (incentive conflict - limits opportunism)
Reinvestment of profits	May be restricted or prohibited after a certain point (relates to conflict of interest on fees of VC.)
Activities of general partner	
Personal investing in portfolio companies	Sizes of investments by partners are limited, or permission may be required (concerns are incentive effects on allocation of VC effort and conflicts about when to harvest). Timing of investment may also be limited to prevent front-running
Sale of interest by general partner	May not be permitted to sell interest separately from those of limiteds, or may require permission (affects incentives of general)
Fund-raising	May limit ability of general to raise new funds until existing funds are substantially committed (avoid dilution of effort to try to increase fees)
Outside activities	May limit outside activities or involvement with outside companies, especially during early stage (to ensure effort)
Addition of general partners	May limit additions of partners (to ensure the quality of effort devoted to fund)
Types of investments	
Restrictions on asset classes	Limit ability to invest in certain classes of assets (usually those requiring less effort, such as public securities, or other venture funds) or into classes where partners lack expertise
Based on Gompers and Lerner (1997).	

Figure 14-8   Key covenant classes of venture capital limited partnerships

it may do so only as a co-investor, along with another first-time investor in the venture. In effect, this covenant uses a third-party investor to validate the general partner's decision.

To avoid fee manipulation, the agreement may restrict the general partner's ability to reinvest fund assets as the fund matures. This limits the ability of the general partner to increase its management fees (which usually are calculated as a percentage of value of assets under management) by postponing distributions to keep the dollar value of assets under management as large as possible. In addition, as a means of controlling potential shirking, the agreement may limit the investment the general partner can make in certain types of financial instruments that offer low expected returns and do not require significant commitments of venture capitalist effort. The rationale for the latter covenant is that the limited partners agree to the general partner's high level of compensation because they expect the general partner to choose portfolio companies that will benefit from significant managerial involvement.

Additional concerns regarding the activities of general partners relate to self-dealing and dilution of effort. To address self-dealing, an agreement may restrict the timing of investments and sales by general partners in the portfolio companies of the fund. Specifically, general partners may be precluded from buying or selling investments in a venture in advance of transactions on behalf of the fund. To control shirking, the agreement may limit the amount of outside investment a general partner can make. It also may restrict the ability of the venture capitalist to raise capital for new funds. Furthermore, it may limit outside activities of the partners, as well as the addition of new partners, and may set expectations for intensity of monitoring activity.

The limited partners have ultimate control of the fund through their ability to withdraw from the partnership or to terminate the agreement. As a practical matter, however, termination is unlikely because substantial sanctions usually are imposed for withdrawal, and because early termination usually is not in the best interest of the partners.

14.7   THE ROLE OF REPUTATION IN THE VENTURE CAPITAL MARKET

Reputation plays a role in the functioning of most markets; the market for venture capital is no exception. Not only does the reputation of the venture capitalist affect the ability of parties to transact, so do the reputations of the investors who decide to participate in the funds and the reputations of the entrepreneurs who seek capital.

Reputation is an important enforcement mechanism for the explicit terms of a contract, such as the commitment by an investor to respond quickly to capital calls. The alternative is to insist that investors place committed funds in escrow accounts until the general partner needs them. But this alternative impedes the limited partners' abilities to invest the funds efficiently until they are needed. Accordingly, there can be significant advantages to working with incomplete, flexible contracts, where reputation substitutes for explicit contract terms. If the venture capitalist can depend on the limited partners not to make opportunistic decisions, then elaborate provisions to limit the choices of the limited partners can be avoided. If the venture capitalist can trust the entrepreneur to act in the interest of the venture, then specific contract provisions designed to shift risk to the entrepreneur are less important.

The overall result is that contractual relationships that are based partly on the reputations of the parties can generate higher returns for the parties. Evidence on this implication is manifested in several ways. First, the preference of venture capitalists to raise funds from institutions demonstrates that the cost of dealing with individual investors is expected to be higher. Second, the ability of established entrepreneurs to raise capital more easily than first-time entrepreneurs indicates that investors rely on the experience of the entrepreneur and demonstrated commitment as an element of the negotiation. Third, that well-established venture capitalists are able to command higher fees and a larger carried interest is evidence that investors anticipate superior overall performance from those venture capitalists.

Evidence from several studies supports the view that firm reputation is important for understanding the functioning of the market for venture capital. One study finds that IPOs with venture capital backing are less underpriced than those without.[42] The findings suggest that venture capital investors perform an important monitoring function. Another study finds that venture capitalist involvement with companies that are going public leads to reduced underpricing and interprets the finding as evidence that venture capitalist backing works as a certification of value.[43]

One economic rationale for a venture capital firm to invest in reputation is that, because the firm's human capital is specific to new ventures, the firm benefits by developing a reputation for not selling shares publicly in IPOs that are overpriced. Compared to a venture capitalist without such a reputation, the reputable venture capitalist is able to sell shares and redeploy human capital with less concern about negative market reaction.[44] Evidence indicates that more-established venture capital firms are better able to bring portfolio companies public at early stages of development than are venture capitalists with less well-established reputations. The data indicate that venture capitalists with established reputations seek to maintain their reputations by selling shares in IPOs only if they expect the IPOs not to be overpriced. Established venture capitalists are more likely to forgo selling shares when IPO shares are overpriced or fully priced, and, in effect, are more inclined than less well-established venture capitalists to sacrifice immediate return for long-run gain.[45]

An earlier study provides evidence that venture capital funds may seek to build reputations in ways that are not necessarily in the best interest of the companies in which they invest. The study reports that venture capitalists that are not well established tend to bring companies public too early. The study concludes that such funds are engaging in "grandstanding," in an effort to demonstrate a track record of high rates of return to attract capital. Consistent with this view, venture capitalists that are not well established tend to raise new funds shortly after IPOs of portfolio companies.[46]

14.8 REPUTATION, RETURNS, AND MARKET VOLATILITY

In our earlier discussion of the venture capital market, we noted that new commitments of venture capital peaked at $104.9 billion in 2000, before declining to $40.3 billion the next year. How are such large variations in new capital commitments possible, and what are the implications for venture capital funds? To understand how new commitments can drop so precipitously, it is important to recognize that an important source of new commitments is the proceeds from harvesting prior investments. If venture capital funds experience a decline in the rate at which they can harvest their investments, then the rate at which capital is returned to limited partners declines. As a significant proportion of new capital commitments is simply rolled-over capital from harvested investments in prior funds, new commitments tend to decline whenever harvest rates or harvest values decline.

The 2001 decline in new capital commitments occurred after several years of very rapid growth in the U.S. venture capital market. Through the year 2000, the average time between venture capital investment and harvest was decreasing and harvest valuations were increasing. As a result, new capital commitments grew rapidly. Well-established venture capital firms could not grow rapidly enough to satisfy demand for investing in venture capital or to pursue all of the new venture investment opportunities. During this period, many new firms entered the venture capital industry, and were able to generate adequate returns for investors. Established venture capital firms were in a good position to attract the best investment opportunities and the most reliable investors. Consequently, they could generate superior returns for their investors. With the market decline in 2001, new entrants to the venture capital industry have found that it is increasingly difficult to find attractive investments or investors. Not surprisingly, the market has tended to consolidate around the established firms with the best reputations.

Among other things, the consolidation has tested the efficacy of venture capital contracts with limited partners and the reputational capital of venture capital funds. Well-established venture capital firms, with good access to deal flow, protect their reputational capital by adapting to the new reality, continuing to work with their existing portfolio companies and, in some cases, returning capital to investors or releasing them from their capital commitments due to the venture capitalist's inability to profitably invest the capital. Some of those with less well-established reputations can be expected to act more opportunistically, holding on to capital commitments (and the related management fees) despite their inability to find attractive investments.

14.9 SUMMARY

Although venture capital has been a source of funding for entrepreneurs for centuries, the modern venture capital firm has its roots in the United States, in the mid-twentieth century. The limited partnership is the most common structure for venture capital investment. The limited partners provide financial capital for promising new ventures, while the general partners locate and cultivate the ventures, and arrange for harvesting the investments. Harvesting usually takes the form of arranging for the venture to go public via an IPO, arranging for a private sale to another company, or arranging a management buyout. Limited partners are precluded from active participation in management of the fund.

The aggregate amount of capital invested in U.S. venture capital funds has increased dramatically in recent decades, largely as a result of institutional investors having more flexibility in their investment decisions. As commitments of capital have increased, so has competition for deals. More intense competition has heightened incentives to improve valuation methods and to develop more sophisticated approaches to generating and structuring deals, marketing them to investors, and designing exit strategies. In spite of the growth of the industry, total venture capital funding available from venture capital firms is still small compared to new venture funding from other sources (including government agencies, corporations, loans, family and friends, and angels).

A notable feature of the venture capital industry is that firms tend to cluster in geographic areas. Prominent examples are the Silicon Valley in California and Route 128 in Boston. In economic terms, geographic concentration suggests the presence of agglomeration economies. Agglomeration economies arise when firms' costs are reduced as a result of being close geographically to their rivals and other market participants, such as suppliers and specialized labor. These characteristics fit the venture capital industry. Value is added through close working relationships between venture capitalists and portfolio firms. For portfolio firms, proximity to rivals is likely to keep them competitive and better informed. When new venture activity is concentrated, venture capital firms can more easily monitor industry trends. In addition, venture capital firms and portfolio companies have specific human capital requirements, such as knowledge of computer technology, biology, or chemistry. It is no accident that the two largest pockets of venture capital firms in the United States are located near large and talented university populations. Consistent with this, it is not uncommon for a venture capitalist that decides to fund a firm outside of its geographic area to predicate funding on relocation of the venture.

Following investment of funds in a portfolio company, responsibility of the general partners shifts from generating deal flow to creating value for portfolio companies. This can mean that the venture capitalist sits on the board of directors, monitors operations, recruits management team members, arranges additional financing, and generally provides expertise and industry contacts. The fund has a limited life, for at some point, usually after about five years, the fund harvests its investments.

We considered two types of contracts that characterize the venture capital industry: contracts between the limited partners and the general partner of the venture capital fund and contracts between the venture capital fund and its portfolio companies. The terms and provisions of both contracts reflect fundamental issues regarding risk bearing and incentive alignment.

Limited partners are passive investors who relinquish control of their investment to general partners who do not bear the full cost of their decisions. Among the issues that arise in this setting are sorting (selecting the portfolio companies from the deal flow) and controlling agency costs and operating costs. Contractual compensation reflects the respective functions of the two types of partners. If the fund does well, the general partner realizes a significant return through its carried interest. If it does poorly, almost the entire loss accrues to the limited partners. In effect, the general partner has a claim on the residual value of the fund. Hence, compensation is linked to value creation.

Contracts used in the industry address incentive and risk-allocation problems with a variety of provisions, including covenants restricting the venture capitalist's ability to add leverage and covenants providing oversight of subsequent investment, and ability to force distributions. In a similar manner, contracts between the venture capital fund and its portfolio companies address potential problems with adverse selection and incentive alignment. Use of convertible securities shifts more of the risk of failure to the entrepreneur. Other provisions that define incentives include put options, demand registration rights, termination rights, performance-based rights to acquire shares, and so on. Finally, the chapter reinforces the role of reputation in the venture capital market.

QUESTIONS AND PROBLEMS

1. The early venture capital funds were organized as closed-end funds. More recently, most venture capital funds are being organized as limited partnerships. What do you see as the key differences between the two forms that help explain the shift?

2. How do the reputations of fund managers, investors, and entrepreneurs bear on the efficient operation of a venture capital fund? How do you think venture capital contracts might be different when a manager, investor, or entrepreneur does not have an established reputation?

3. In the late 1990s, the carried interest of some of the leading venture capital funds increased from 20 percent to 30 percent, and the funds tended to shift more of their focus to making somewhat later-stage investments. These changes occurred at the same time that the number of venture capital funds was increasing, total capital commitments to funds were increasing, and business angel investing was growing and became more organized. Can you think of a competitive reason why the carried interest percentage might increase at the same time these other changes were taking place? Can you explain why investors in the funds might be willing to accept the higher carried interest? Finally, can you think of any way you might be able to test your conjecture?

4. Venture capital firms normally try to solicit investment capital at the same time they are looking for deals. They also can extend the life of a fund for several years beyond its planned liquidation date. How might these practices contribute to enhancing the value of the fund? How might they affect the kinds of investors the fund seeks and the kinds of ventures it invests in?

5. Usually, venture capital firms do not sell their shares when one of their portfolio companies has an IPO. Often, the IPO underwriter precludes them from doing so. Why might underwriters want to limit venture capitalist selling? Under what conditions would you expect them to permit the venture capitalist to sell some of its shares during the IPO? Assuming the underwriter will permit some selling by the venture capital firm, why would the venture capital firm want to sell instead of waiting until after the lockup period (normally 180 days) to sell? How are your answers to these questions related to the extent of underpricing of the IPO?

6. A venture capitalist has a carried interest of 20 percent of appreciation in excess of return of capital. Limited partners get their money back first, and then receive 80 percent of capital appreciation. Consider a venture in which the venture capital fund plans to invest $5 million. The entrepreneur has total wealth of $2 million, $500,000 of which must be committed to the venture. The venture capitalist expects that the venture will have a market value of $15 million in four years, which is when harvesting is expected. The venture capitalist's assessment of uncertainty can be described as a standard deviation of harvest values of $10 million.

   Suppose both the general partner and the limited partners are well-diversified. Assume that the risk-free rate per year is 5 percent and the market rate is 11 percent. The market standard deviation is 20 percent on an annualized basis. The correlation between the venture and the market is 0.3. (You can assume this is the correlation for any investment security of the venture.) Use simulation to estimate the expected cash flows and standard deviations of cash flows for both parties under the following contracts with the entrepreneur. Use a valuation template for a diversified investor to value each party's claim and compare the following contract allocations for each party. Make any other assumptions you need.

   a. The venture capital fund receives interest of 14 percent per year, plus 20 percent of the equity of the venture. The loan principal and the interest are paid in year 4 to the extent that the venture has cash available to do so. (In each year, the loan balance increases by the amount of interest owed.)
   b. The venture capital fund receives interest of 6 percent per year (similar to part a) and 30 percent of the equity.
   c. The fund receives 40 percent of the equity.
   d. Which allocation would the entrepreneur prefer and why (assume the entrepreneur has the same expectations for performance)?
   e. Which of these contracts do you think the limited partners would prefer and why? Which would the general partner prefer?

7. Suppose you are considering whether to launch a new venture capital fund and have decided to build a financial model that can help you make the decision. To begin the analysis, you need to model the relationships among several factors: venture performance, returns to the venture capital fund, and allocation of the returns between the limited partners and the general partner.

   • Portfolio investments: Suppose a typical venture in which your fund might invest would require four years from investment to harvest. To represent the uncertainty of the cash flows of the venture, assume that the harvest cash flow can be described as a normal distribution with mean of $20 million and standard deviation of $40 million, except that simulated negative outcomes imply that the venture fails and generates a harvest cash flow of zero.

- Investment agreements: Suppose, further, that in typical venture capital contracts with portfolio companies of the type you hope to attract, the standard terms are that the venture capital firm receives convertible preferred stock and is entitled to a liquidation preference equal to 1.5 times the initial investment.

- The limited partnership agreement: Finally, suppose that the partnership agreement would provide that the general partner charges an annual fee of 3.125 percent of the net capital invested in each venture. For simplicity, assume that for each $100,000 invested in a venture with four years to harvest, the fund pays a total of $3,125 × 4 or $12,500 to the general partner in management fees. On each investment, the limited partners would be entitled to recoup all of their invested capital before the general partner would share in any of the gains. Once the initial investment is returned from the harvest proceeds of a portfolio company (including the management fee), the general partner shares 20 percent of the gain.

Build a model to simulate the harvest cash flows of a typical venture and the allocation of the cash flows to the limited partners, the general partner, and the entrepreneur. Use the model to simulate the expected cash flows and cash flow risk of the following three assumptions about the size of investment and share of equity. Be sure to incorporate the liquidation preference and the limited partners' right to return of invested capital before any gains are allocated.

a. The venture capital fund commits $2.5 million in exchange for preferred equity convertible to 15 percent of the common stock.

b. The venture capital fund commits $5.0 million in exchange for preferred equity convertible to 25 percent of the common stock.

c. The venture capital fund commits $7.5 million in exchange for preferred equity convertible to 35 percent of the common stock.

Value the various financial claims and discuss the adequacy of returns for the general and limited partners and for the entrepreneur. In valuing the claims, assume that the annual risk-free rate is 3.0 percent, the annual return on the market is 8.0 percent, the annualized standard deviation of market returns is 20 percent, and the correlation of harvest cash flows with the market is 0.15. The entrepreneur has $2.0 million of wealth available to invest in the market.

8. Reconsider problem 7. Model the cash flows of the venture capital fund and use the model to evaluate the general partnership capital account balance and cash returns available to the partners under each assumption for each investment amount in problem 7. Base the cash flow model on the following assumptions:

- There are three members of the general partnership and each can oversee the fund's investments in five ventures.

- The expected life of the fund is ten years. Each partner is expected to add one new venture to the fund's portfolio each year in years two through six. Each venture is harvested four years later (in years six through ten).

- During each of the four years while a fund is invested in a venture, the partnership collects its annual management fee of 3.125 percent of the capital invested in the venture.

- On the expected harvest date for a venture, the fund realizes the carried interest on the investment (i.e., difference between the general partner's expected cash flows of the venture and the cumulative management fees related to investment in the venture).
- The management fees collected in each year plus the carried interest collected in the year comprise the general partnership's revenues for the year.
- Annual operating expenses are expected to be $1.0 million per year in all years, including the initial year (year 1).
- Each partner would like to receive an annual draw of $200 thousand against the capital account balance.
- Assume all figures are in real terms so that you do not need to make adjustments for inflation or interest on capital balances.

Depending on the average size of investment, what initial capital balance would be necessary to keep the fund from developing a negative net cash position at any point during its expected 10-year life? If you think of the initial capital balance as a loan from the partners that is repaid out of the ending balance, how well are the partners expected to do depending on the average size of investment? What do you conclude about how the average investment size bears on the size of the fund and the profitability of venture capital fund management?

9. Continuing with the cash flow analysis from problem 8, suppose that syndication enables each partner to oversee ten ventures instead of five. That is, the firm's partners would only be lead investors in about half of the ventures and would be more passive in the investments where other funds act as lead investors. Assume that the total costs do not change, but the number of investments in each period doubles. How does this affect the economics of making average investments of $2.5 million? How does syndication affect the size of the fund, the required initial capital, and the expected capital balance at the end of the fund?

NOTES

1. See Gompers (1994a) for more information about ARD. Huntsman and Hoban (1980) document the focus of venture capital investors on opportunities with the potential for great success. In their sample, the average compound annual return to venture capital investing was 18.9 percent. However, by dropping the top 10 percent of the investments, the return on the other 90 percent was −28 percent.

2. Private investments in public equity, or "PIPEs," are investments by accredited individual investors or qualified institutional buyers in unregistered shares of public companies. Trading of unregistered shares is restricted for a period of time under Rule 144 of the SEC Act of 1933 or under more recent amendments to the rule. Corresponding to the recent decline in the venture capital market, interest in PIPEs has increased.

3. Smith, Smith, and Williams (2002) provide a more detailed analysis of the SEC's interpretation of the ICA fair value standard on the market for private equity, including investment in nonregistered shares of public companies.

4. In the ongoing debate over expensing and valuation of employee stock options, most of the venture capital industry opposes valuing option compensation on the basis of their present value at the time of issue (irrespective of the particular valuation model). Ascribing a positive value to the options would increase the reported expenses of the venture, but produce no

benefits for most portfolio companies of venture capital funds, as they normally have negative net income and often fail. Positive valuations of employee stock options also would increase the taxable earnings of employees and reduce their capital gains.

5. For discussion and evidence concerning the effects of tax rates on new venture investment activity, see Gompers and Lerner (1998).

6. Gompers (1994) suggests that high rates of return and the "hot" IPO market of the early 1980s attracted a flood of investment capital to new ventures and depressed the returns in the decade. Gomper and Lerner (1998a) examine rates of return to investing in venture capital. They also estimate the elasticity of returns in response to changes in inflows. During the period of the study, doubling the inflow of capital increased valuations of fund investments by 7 to 21 percent. The higher valuations correspond to lower rates of return at harvest.

7. Estimates are as reported in *Statistical Abstract of the United States: 2001.*

8. See the *National Venture Capital Association 2002 Yearbook* and Zider (1998) for additional comparisons on the size of the venture capital market.

9. Gompers (1994a) attributes the venture capital fund change in focus to later-stage investment to the increased importance of pension fund investors.

10. Sahlman (1990) and the *National Venture Capital Association 2002 Yearbook.*

11. Zider (1998) suggests that the venture capital niche exists because of usury laws that prohibit high-risk, high-interest rate loans, and other restrictions on risk-taking by financial institutions.

12. The first venture capital limited partnership, Draper, Gaither, and Anderson, was organized in 1958. However, the organizational form did not reach prominence until the 1980s. See Gompers and Lerner (1996).

13. For discussion of the organization and investment process of venture capital funds, see Bygrave and Timmons (1992), and Sahlman (1990). Sahlman considers the tax advantage of the structure. See also Timmons (1999), Tyebjee and Bruno (1984), and Zider (1998).

14. Institutional investors often delegate the choice of venture capital fund investments to a professional asset manager, referred to as a gatekeeper, who makes the actual investment decisions and is responsible for monitoring performance. Gatekeepers manage assets for several investors and have opportunities to exchange information with others in similar positions. Gompers and Lerner (1996) note that the gatekeeper structure emerged in the mid-1980s.

15. Gupta and Sapienza (1992) and Ruhnka and Young (1991) find that venture capital firms tend to specialize by industry. Barry, Muscarella, Peavy, and Vetsuypens (1990) provide evidence of specialization and suggest that specialization aids in monitoring performance. Ehrlich, deNoble, Moore, and Weaver (1994) offer comparisons on sizes of positions, stages of investments, and locations of portfolio companies. Norton and Tenenbaum (1993) suggest that specialization is paradoxical, given the incentives to diversify risk. The investors in the venture capital fund, however, can still realize the benefits of diversification.

16. See Lerner (1994a).

17. The survey results appear in Gorman and Sahlman (1989). See also Ehrlich, deNoble, Moore, and Weaver (1994).

18. Evidence on board participation appears in Lerner (1995). In a study of venture-backed companies that have gone public, Barry, Muscarella, Peavy, and Vetsuypens (1990) find that a typical company has three venture capital investors, two of whom serve on the board. Collectively, the investments by venture capital firms account for 34 percent of the pre-IPO equity.

19. See Fried and Hisrich (1994).

20. Results are reported in Barney, Busenitz, Fiet, and Moesel (1996).

21. See Fried and Hisrich (1994).

22. See the study by Kortum and Lerner (2000).

23. See Megginson and Weiss (1991).

24. A study by Ibbotson, Sindelar, and Ritter (1994) of nearly 9000 new issues from 1960 to 1987 finds that underpricing averages 16 percent.

25. Gompers and Lerner (1998a).

26. See Gladstone and Gladstone (2002).

27. There is a tendency to think that, because of the desire for home runs, venture capital investors are only interested in high-technology investments. However, companies like Staples and FedEx also have received venture capital funding during rapid growth stages of development.

28. See Gompers (1994). The findings are based on data compiled by Venture Economics.

29. For discussion of the adverse selection problems arising from the venture capital search process, see Amit, Glosten, and Muller (1990).

30. In reality, the entrepreneurs need not have any perception of the correctness of investor valuations. As long as they seek financing from more than one investor, the most optimistic investor with the lowest hurdle rate is likely to win the contest but in doing so, may end up investing too much in exchange for too small of a stake in the venture.

31. Admati and Pfleiderer (1994) demonstrate that multistage investments can result in efficient investment decision making if the venture capitalist invests in fixed proportion over time and receives a fixed share of the total return. This strategy overcomes the entrepreneur's incentive to overinvest if all financing comes from outside investors and the venture capitalist's incentive to underinvest if it makes the entire investment but does not receive the entire return. Lerner (1994a) finds evidence, consistent with Admati and Pfleiderer, that venture capital investment shares tend to remain constant in subsequent rounds.

32. Gompers (1998) finds that staging intervals correspond to the importance of oversight by the investor. That is, staging intervals are shorter when more oversight is warranted.

33. For example, see Sahlman (1990).

34. Berloff (1994), Gompers (1998), and Marx (1998, 1999).

35. Based on a survey of venture capital firms, Trester (1998) documents that convertible preferred equity dominates in early-stage financing choices. Debt and common stock are more common at later stages when there is a lower probability of asymmetric information. Gilson and Schizer (2002) provide a tax-based argument for using convertibles to provide incentives to management. Kaplan and Stromberg (2000) report that convertible preferred stock was used in 95 percent of a sample of 200 financing rounds.

36. See Hellmann (1998).

37. As discussed in Chapter 12, because the investor's financial claims normally are senior to those of the entrepreneur, the entrepreneur sometimes has an incentive to increase risk, even though doing so may lower the expected return of the venture.

38. See Gompers (1994a), and Sahlman (1990).

39. See Smith (1998).

40. See discussion in Black and Gilson (1998).

41. Norton (1995) uses agency theory to describe the structure of venture capital funds.

42. See Barry et al. (1990).

43. See Megginson and Weiss (1991).
44. Lin and Smith (1998).
45. The Lin and Smith (1998) study reports that initial returns average 11.6 percent when venture capitalists with established reputations are among the sellers, compared to only 5.1 percent when they are not sellers. For venture capitalists without established reputations, initial returns average 7.4 percent when they sell and 9.8 percent when they do not.
46. See Gompers (1996).

REFERENCES AND ADDITIONAL READING

ADMATI, ANAT R., AND PAUL PFLEIDERER. "Robust Financial Contracting and the Role of the Venture Capitalist." *Journal of Finance* 49 (1994): 371–402.

AMIT, R., L. GLOSTEN, AND E. MULLER. "Entrepreneurial Ability, Venture Investments, and Risk Sharing." *Management Science* 36 (1990): 1232–1245.

BARNEY, JAY B., LOWELL W. BUSENITZ, JAMES O. FIET, AND DOUGLAS D. MOESEL. "New Venture Teams' Assessment of Learning Assistance from Venture Capital Firms." *Journal of Business Venturing* 11 (1996): 257–272.

BARRY, CHRISTOPHER B. "New Directions in Research on Venture Capital Finance." *Financial Management* 23 (1994): 3–15.

BARRY, CHRISTOPHER B., CHRIS J. MUSCARELLA, JOHN W. PEAVY III, AND MICHAEL R. VETSUYPENS. "The Role of Venture Capital in the Creation of Public Companies." *Journal of Financial Economics* 27 (1990): 447–471.

BERGEMANN, DIRK, AND ULRICH HEGE. "Venture Capital Financing, Moral Hazard, and Learning." *Journal of Banking and Finance* 22 (1998): 703–735.

BERGLOF, ERIC. "A Control Theory of Venture Capital Finance." *Journal of Law Economics and Organization* 10 (1994): 247–269.

BLACK, BERNARD S., AND RONALD J. GILSON. "Venture Capital and the Structure of Capital Markets: Banks Versus Stock Markets." *Journal of Financial Economics* 47 (1998): 243–277.

BRANDER, JAMES A., RAPHAEL AMIT, AND WERNER ANTWEILER. "Venture Capital Syndication: Improved Venture Selection vs. Value-Added Hypothesis." *Journal of Economics and Management Strategy* 11 (2002): 422–452.

BYGRAVE, WILLIAM A., AND JEFFREY A. TIMMONS. *Venture Capital at the Crossroads.* Cambridge, MA: Harvard University Press, 1992.

CHAN, YUK-SHEE, DANIEL SIEGEL, AND ANJAN THAKOR. "Learning, Corporate Control, and Performance Requirements in Venture Capital Contracts." *International Economic Review* 31 (1990): 365–381.

CHIAMPOU, GREGORY F., AND JOEL J. KALLETT. "Risk/Return Profile of Venture Capital." *Journal of Business Venturing* 4 (1989): 1–10.

EHRLICH, SANFORD R., ALEX F. DENOBLE, TRACY MOORE, AND RICHARD R. WEAVER. "After the Cash Arrives: A Comparative Study of Venture Capital and Private Investor Involvement in Entrepreneurial Firms." *Journal of Business Venturing* 9 (1994): 67–82.

FISCHER, DONALD E., ed. *Investing in Venture Capital.* Charlottesville, VA: Institute of Chartered Financial Analysts, 1989.

FRIED, VANCE H., AND ROBERT D. HISRICH. "Toward a Model of Venture Capital Investment Decision Making." *Financial Management* 23 (1994): 28–37.

GILSON, RONALD J. "The Legal Structure of High Technology Industrial Districts: Silicon Valley, Route 128, and Covenants Not to Compete." *New York University Law Review* 74 (1999).

GILSON, RONALD J. AND DAVID SCHRIZER. "Understanding Venture Capital Structure: A Tax Explanation for Convertible Preferred Stock." *Harvard Law Review* (2002).

GLADSTONE, DAVID AND LAURA GLADSTONE. *Venture Capital Handbook.* Upper Saddle River, NJ: Prentice-Hall, 2002.

GOMPERS, PAUL A. "An Examination of Convertible Securities in Venture Capital." Harvard Business School Working Paper, 1998.

GOMPERS, PAUL A. "The Rise of Venture Capital." *Business and Economic History* 23 (1994): 1–24.

GOMPERS, PAUL A. "A Note on the Venture Capital Industry." Harvard Business School Case No. 295-065, 1994a.

GOMPERS, PAUL A. "Optimal Investment, Monitoring, and the Staging of Venture Capital." *Journal of Finance* 50 (1995): 1461–1489.

GOMPERS, PAUL A. "Grandstanding in the Venture Capital Industry." *Journal of Financial Economics* 42 (1996): 133–156.

GOMPERS, PAUL A., AND JOSH LERNER. "The Use of Covenants: An Empirical Analysis of Venture Partnership Agreements." *Journal of Law and Economics* (1996): 463–498.

GOMPERS, PAUL A., AND JOSH LERNER. "The Venture Capital Revolution." *Journal of Economic Perspectives* 15 (2001): 145–168.

GOMPERS, PAUL A., AND JOSH LERNER. "What Drives Venture Capital Fundraising." *Brookings Proceedings on Microeconomic Activity* (1998).

GOMPERS, PAUL A., AND JOSH LERNER. "Venture Capital Distributions: Short-Run and Long-Run Reactions." *Journal of Finance* 53 (1998a): 2161–2184.

GOMPERS, PAUL A., AND JOSH LERNER. "An Analysis of Compensation in the U.S. Venture Capital Partnership." *Journal of Financial Economics* 51 (1999): 3–44.

GORMAN, MICHAEL, AND WILLIAM A. SAHLMAN. "What Do Venture Capitalists Do?" *Journal of Business Venturing* 4 (1989): 231–248.

GUPTA, ATUL K., AND H. J. SAPIENZA. "Determinants of Capital Firms' Preferences Regarding the Industry Diversity and Geographic Scope of their Investments." *Journal of Business Venturing* (1992): 347–362.

HELLMANN, THOMAS. "The Allocation of Control Rights in Venture Capital Contracts." *RAND Journal of Economics* 29 (1998): 57–76.

HUNTSMAN, BLAINE, AND JAMES P. HOBAN, JR. "Investment in New Enterprise: Some Empirical Observations on Risk, Return, and Market Structure." *Financial Management* (1980): 44–51.

IBBOTSON, ROGER G., J. L. SINDELAR, AND JAY R. RITTER. "The Market's Problems with the Pricing of Initial Public Offerings." *Journal of Applied Corporate Finance* 7 (Spring 1994): 66–74.

KAPLAN, STEVEN AND PERS STROMBERG. "Financial Contracting in the Real World." NBER Working Paper 7660 (2000).

KORTUM, SAMUEL, AND JOSH LERNER. "Assessing the Contribution of Venture Capital to Innovation." *RAND Journal of Economics* 31 (2000): 674–692.

LERNER, JOSH. "A Note on Private Equity Partnership Agreements." Harvard Business School Case, No. 294-084, 1994.

LERNER, JOSHUA. "Venture Capitalists and the Decision of Go Public." *Journal of Financial Economics* 35 (1994a): 293–316.

LERNER, JOSHUA. "The Syndication of Venture Capital Investments." *Financial Management* 23 (1994b): 16–27.

LERNER, JOSHUA. "Venture Capitalists and the Oversight of Private Firms." *Journal of Finance* 50 (1995): 301–318.

LIN, TIMOTHY H., AND RICHARD L. SMITH. "Insider Reputation and Selling Decisions: The Unwinding of Venture Capital Investments During Equity IPOs." *Journal of Corporate Finance* 4 (1998): 241–263.

MARX, LESLIE M. "Efficient Venture Capital Financing Contracts Combining Debt and Equity." *Review of Economic Design* 3 (1998): 371–387.

MARX, LESLIE M. "Contract Renegotiation and Renegotiation of Venture Capital Projects." University of Rochester Working Paper, 1999.

MEGGINSON, WILLIAM L., AND KATHLEEN A. WEISS. "Venture Capital Certification in Initial Public Offerings." *Journal of Finance* 46 (1991): 879–903.

NORTON, EDGAR. "Venture Capital as an Alternative Means to Allocate Capital: An Agency Theoretic View." *Entrepreneurship Theory and Practice* 20 (Winter 1995): 19–29.

NORTON, EDGAR, AND BERNARD H. TENENBAUM. "Specialization Versus Diversification as a Venture Capital Investment Strategy." *Journal of Business Venturing* 8 (1993): 431–442.

ROSENSTEIN, JOSEPH, ALBERT V. BRUNO, WILLIAM D. BYGRAVE, AND NATALIE T. TAYLOR. "The CEO, Venture Capitalists, and the Board." *Journal of Business Venturing* 8 (1993): 99–113.

RUHNKA, J. C., AND J. E. YOUNG. "Some Hypotheses about Risk in Venture Capital Investing." *Journal of Business Venturing* (1991): 115–133.

SAHLMAN, WILLIAM A. "Note on the Venture Capital Industry." Harvard Business School Case, No. 285-096 1985, 1981.

SAHLMAN, WILLIAM A. "Note on the Venture Capital Industry—Update." Harvard Business School Case, No. 286-060, 1986.

SAHLMAN, WILLIAM A. "The Structure and Governance of Venture Capital Organizations." *Journal of Financial Economics* (1990): 473–521.

SMITH, D. GORDON. "Venture Capital Contracting in the Information Age." *Journal of Small and Emerging Business Law* 2 (1998): 133.

SMITH, JANET K., RICHARD SMITH, AND KARYN WILLIAMS. "The SEC's 'Fair Value' Standard for Mutual Fund Investment in Restricted and Other Illiquid Securities." *Fordham Journal of Corporate and Financial Law* 6 (2001).

TIMMONS, JEFFREY A. *New Venture Creation: Entrepreneurship for the 21st Century.* 5th ed. Chicago: Richard D. Irwin, 1999.

TIMMONS, JEFFREY A., AND WILLIAM D. BYGRAVE. "Venture Capital's Role in Financing Innovation for Economic Growth." *Journal of Business Venturing* 1 (1986): 161–176.

TRESTER, JEFFREY J. "Venture Capital Contracting Under Asymmetric Information." *Journal of Banking and Finance* 22 (1998): 675–699.

TYEBJEE, T. T., AND A. V. BRUNO. "A Model of Venture Capitalist Investment Activity." *Management Science* (1984): 1051–1066.

WILSON, JOHN W. *The New Venturers.* Reading, MA: Addison-Wesley, 1985.

ZIDER, BOB. "How Venture Capital Works." *Harvard Business Review* (November–December 1998): 131–139.

Choice of Financing

Money often costs too much. (Ralph Waldo Emerson)

Learning Objectives

After reading this chapter, you should be able to:

- Understand the factors that influence the choice of financing.
- Explain why immediacy of financial need limits the range of alternatives and why better planning yields more and less expensive alternatives.
- Understand why the choice of financing depends on the size of the total financing need, duration of the need, and incentive effects of different financing structures.
- Evaluate financing alternatives by considering the venture's financial condition and development stage and the capabilities of alternative providers of investment capital.
- Identify advantages and disadvantages of relational financing arrangements such as strategic partnering and franchising.
- Explain how and why financial distress affects the availability of financing.
- Recognize that financial distress does not necessarily result in failure of the venture.
- Understand how collateral, relationships, and reputations affect availability of financing.
- Recognize that financing usually involves bilateral negotiation between parties who may have differing incentives to complete a deal quickly or draw out the negotiation.

The menu of financing sources for start-ups and privately owned businesses is extensive and growing. We cannot hope to provide a comprehensive survey of the menu in a single chapter. The Internet is a far more convenient and immediate source of generic information on financing. Instead, our objective is to emphasize decision making about the choice of financing and to provide a framework for evaluating financing alternatives. To accomplish this, we introduce and discuss some, but by no means all, financing alternatives.

15.1 FINANCING ALTERNATIVES

Figure 15-1 lists 25 sources of business financing. A comprehensive list would be much longer. Why are there so many alternatives? Part of the answer is that the providers have different objectives, capabilities, and constraints. Some, like banks, seek low-involvement, low-risk investments, usually of short duration. Others, like business angels, seek high-risk, high-involvement investments of moderate to long duration. In some cases, financing is linked to other aspects of the business, such as distribution and marketing. Different financing sources protect the value of their investments in different ways. Some, like venture capitalists, engage in active monitoring to protect their investments. Others, like factoring companies and most lenders, rely heavily on collateral.

The other part of the answer is that businesses have different financing needs. Financing needs may be small or large, and short- or long-term. One business may be capable of offering considerable security, whereas another may require the investor to bear considerable risk. Businesses also differ in their tax exposures, management capabilities, needs for flexibility, and in other dimensions.

Most financing alternatives are market-based responses to demand for financing in the context of tax and regulatory influences. Others are the result of public policies that promote

---

A Partial List of Financing Sources for New Ventures and Private Businesses

- Asset-Based Lending
- Business Angels
- Capital Leasing (Venture Leasing)
- Commercial Bank Lending (various forms)
- Corporate Entrepreneurship
- Customer Financing
- Direct Public Offering
- Economic Development Program Financing
- Employee-Provided Financing
- Equity Private Placement
- Export/Import Bank Financing
- Factoring
- Franchising
- Friends and Family
- Public Debt Issue
- Registered Initial Public Offering
- Research and Development Limited Partnerships
- Relational Investing or Strategic Partnering
- Royalty Financing
- Self (bootstrap)
- Small Business Administration Financing
- Small Business Investment Company Financing
- Term Loan
- Vendor Financing
- Venture Capital

Figure 15-1 A partial list of financing sources for new ventures and private businesses

and subsidize financing for small and new businesses. Although the diverse list in Figure 15-1 may seem daunting to an entrepreneur or small-business owner, the choice actually is very manageable, once financing sources inappropriate for a particular situation are excluded. In the balance of the chapter, we develop a structured approach for identifying appropriate financing sources.

15.2   START WITH THE OBJECTIVE AND BASIC PRINCIPLES OF THE FINANCING DECISION

When evaluating financing choices, we start with the entrepreneur's objective: to maximize the NPV for himself. Other considerations, such as desire to maintain control, can be introduced as factors that mitigate against a source or affect specific terms.

Basic Considerations that Affect Financing Choices

Several principles affect the choice of financing. First, as we have seen, if prospective investors agree with the entrepreneur about the outlook for the venture, externally provided financing normally is preferred to financing by the entrepreneur. Outside investors generally are capable of more fully diversifying risk. Consequently, they can justify lower expected returns for a given level of total risk. One offsetting consideration is that there are costs of managing relations with external providers of financing. Investors expect periodic reporting and access to information. In addition, external financing is likely to affect the entrepreneur's ability to control future decisions.

Second, with symmetric expectations, financing that shifts risk to the investor increases the value of the entrepreneur's financial claim. Well-diversified investors need not be compensated for bearing nonmarket risk. Assuming the CAPM is the correct asset pricing model, allocation of market risk between the parties does not affect the value of the entrepreneur's claim. However, as a practical matter, it is not possible to shift only nonmarket risk. All else equal, the entrepreneur can benefit by using equity for as much outside financing as possible.

Information and incentive concerns limit the entrepreneur's ability to raise outside equity. Some types of financing can ameliorate these concerns. For example, if investors base their evaluations on the entrepreneur's willingness to retain a significant residual equity interest, then value-maximizing financing choices must strike a balance between reducing the entrepreneur's exposure to risk and signaling the entrepreneur's confidence in the venture. Fundamentally, this is an issue of credibility. Similarly, financing that does not maintain the entrepreneur's incentive to commit substantial effort to the venture is unlikely to result in maximum value for the entrepreneur.

Other Considerations that Affect Financing Choices

A number of other issues bear on the desirability of a particular financing choice. Some providers of financing perform advisory, monitoring, or other functions that can enhance value. However, the actual worth of such functions varies. For some ventures, monitoring and advisory functions tied to financing may be of little value or even get in the way. For others, they may be critical to success.

Taxes can also affect the financing choice. The tax effects depend on organizational form. Not all organizations produce taxable income and the applicable tax rate depends on organizational form. For example, tax rates differ for C corporations, S corporations, and proprietorships. Also, the tax treatment of debt differs from that of equity. Interest expenses are tax deductible for C corporations, suggesting a tax advantage for borrowing. Interest and dividends are taxed when investors receive them, but capital gains are not taxed until the gain is realized by selling the asset. This tax-timing option effectively lowers the investor's tax rate on the gain. There is an ongoing academic debate about whether tax deductibility of interest expense reduces corporate cost of capital or whether the tax-timing benefit of equity for shareholders cancels out the advantages of debt financing. However, if a firm organized as a C corporation is unable to take advantage of the tax deductibility of interest (perhaps because it has no taxable income), then this argues against financing with debt. Debt is not attractive for many new ventures, partly because they do not have income to shelter.

Financing that is subsidized through agencies such as the SBA may result in lower cost for the venture. However, the savings must be weighed against possible adverse effects of the financing the agencies offer, and against the time required to complete the financing.

Finally, maximum value for the entrepreneur normally is not achieved by raising all of the anticipated financing needs at one time. The riskiness of successful ventures declines over time, and staging can produce higher expected value for the entrepreneur, especially if the stages are associated with milestones that reduce uncertainty and lower financing cost.

The effects of these considerations on the value of the entrepreneur's claim are complex and sometimes counterintuitive. A sensible approach to making the financing decision is to model the venture and study the effects of alternatives on the value of the entrepreneur's claim. More often than not, the choices realistically available are very limited. But even if the entrepreneur has few options, he will want to evaluate such variables as: the amount of the funding, the form of the commitment the investor plans to make (e.g., debt versus equity; passive versus active commitment, etc.), and the effects of restrictions the investor imposes on future actions (through restrictive covenants or by other means).

15.3 FIRST STEP: ASSESS THE NATURE OF THE VENTURE'S FINANCIAL NEEDS

A useful way to begin paring the list of alternative financing sources is by assessing the nature of the venture's financial needs. In Chapter 7, we studied how financial modeling and simulation can be used to assess the amount and timing of needs. However, we did not consider how the results should bear on the financing choice. We now turn to that issue.

Four Questions the Entrepreneur Must Ask when Choosing Financing

Four critical questions link financial needs to choice of financing.

- Is there an immediate (urgent) need for financing?
- Is the near-term financing need large?
- Is the near-term financing need permanent?
- How does the financing need in the near-term relate to the cumulative need for financing?

These questions break the financial need into three periods: immediate, near-term, and cumulative. The distinction between immediate and near-term needs is based on the time required for negotiation. If financing needs are immediate, there is no time to negotiate over terms that are tied to performance. Instead, financing must be based on the strength of existing relationships, the readily ascertainable value of business, or personal assets the investor can use as security. Near-term financing needs are those required over an intermediate term, such as for going from one milestone to the next but where a need for urgent cash does not constrain the choice. Cumulative financing needs to connect near-term and ultimate financing needs. Cumulative needs may be more or less than near-term needs, but cumulative needs affect future rounds of financing, which in turn influence the near-term decision. For example, if the cumulative need is expected to remain high, it may be appropriate to meet near-term needs with a permanent source of financing.

The Influence of Immediate Financing Needs

If a venture faces an immediate need, many sources are foreclosed. Generally, SBA, SBIC, Export/Import Bank, and economic development program financing sources cannot react quickly to financing needs. The approval processes have many steps and involve many parties. Most SBA-guaranteed loans, for example, have a two-step approval process based on paperwork the entrepreneur is required to complete.[1] In addition, subsidized lending programs may have waiting lists or may base lending decisions on political objectives.[2]

If financial needs are immediate, funding sources that involve equity claims also are foreclosed, unless the entrepreneur has an established relationship with the investor. Venture capital firms and angel investor groups often have lengthy due diligence and approval processes, as they should, because their financial returns depend entirely on the successes of ventures in which they invest. The same is true of venture funds that are operated by corporations. If immediate financing appears to be available from one of these sources, the entrepreneur should question whether the investor actually can deliver. Such funding is unlikely to be available, except from those without established reputations, and then the terms for investing could be adverse to the entrepreneur and could threaten existence of the venture.

Finally, selling equity to passive investors is not feasible if needs are immediate. A registered public offering of equity takes several months to complete. More expedient approaches, like direct public offerings (that attempt to bypass the underwriter), or private placements, are unlikely prospects if needs are urgent. Financing based on selling a patent or other asset (and agreeing to pay royalties or lease payments) also is unlikely, unless the venture has a revenue stream.

The most realistic sources of immediate financing are those for which no negotiation or approval process is required or for which financing is preapproved. A venture that is underway and is generating revenues can bring in immediate cash by taking longer to pay for materials and inventory. Sometimes, it can accelerate collections of receivables by borrowing secured by the accounts receivable or can sell its receivables to a factor. Other business assets can also be used as security or sold and leased back.

The most limited set of alternatives is the one facing a development-stage venture that needs immediate cash. Such a venture normally has few tangible assets that can be used to secure borrowing; and it cannot rely on trade financing because it is not yet generating revenues. The only realistic alternatives are the personal resources of the entrepreneur and financing based on established relationships, such as through friends and families. Even development-stage ventures may have relationships that can be drawn upon. Existing investors, prospective customers, and strategic partners, who are aware of the venture and have a sense of its merits, may provide financing on short notice. Investments from family and friends are based not on the merits of the venture per se, but on the strength of the personal relationship.

◆ **Financing Programs of the Small Business Administration**

The SBA offers both direct loans and loan guarantees. Rules vary with the SBA annual budget. The following are among the SBA's programs.

DIRECT LOAN PROGRAM

Loans under this program are based partly on social policy objectives. Candidates include war veterans, individuals with disabilities, those living in economically distressed areas and areas targeted for disaster relief, and socially and economically disadvantaged individuals. Prior denials of conventional loan requests usually are required.

7(a) LOAN GUARANTEE PROGRAM

The 7(a) program accounts for more than 90 percent of the SBA's lending activity. Loans are funded by private institutions and guaranteed up to 80 percent by the SBA. The maximum guarantee is generally in the $500,000 to $750,000 range. The SBA charges a fee of 2 percent for its guarantee and limits the interest rate lenders can charge. Ideal candidates must be of high enough risk to make the guarantee valuable, but not so risky that the interest rate ceiling makes the loan unattractive to the lender. The loans usually are secured with business assets and guaranteed by the borrower.

7(m) MICROLOAN PROGRAM

Loans under this program are for sums up to $35,000 and are made to promote start-ups and small businesses, where traditional lending is not available. Guarantees can be up to 100 percent, and processing time can be very short.

SMALL BUSINESS INVESTMENT COMPANY (SBIC)

SBICs provide equity, long-term debt, and hybrid debt-equity investments primarily to growth-stage businesses. The SBA licenses SBICs and supplements their capital with government-guaranteed debentures or participating securities.

More information is available on the SBA's Web site, *www.sba.gov*.

The last resort, which is often the first as well, is for the entrepreneur to bootstrap the venture on personal assets and resources. Here is where running credit cards up to their limits and similar tactics can come into play.[3]

The Influence of Near-Term Financing Needs

Financing available from immediate sources can be used to satisfy near-term or long-term needs. However, financing raised in a crisis usually is expensive. Foregoing trade credit discounts, for example, can have an effective interest cost of more than 40 percent. Factoring accounts receivable often is even more expensive, particularly if the venture has developed its own credit management capabilities. Consequently, sources that are appropriate for immediate financing often are not desirable for ongoing financing.

Whether it makes sense to make more permanent use of an immediate financing source depends on the cost of immediate financing compared with the expected future cost of alternatives

Direct Public Offering and Private Placements*

A direct public offering (DPO) is a direct sale of securities to investors that bypasses the formal investment banker underwriting and distribution process. DPOs that involve interstate distribution require filing brief registration statements with the SEC. A Regulation A offering is a short-form registration of an offering under $5 million in a 12-month period. Rule 504 under Regulation D provides for offerings up to $1 million in a 12-month period by filing Form D. The Form D registration also is known as a small corporate offering registration (SCOR) or uniform limited offering registration (ULOR). Rule 147 enables firms that limit their offerings to a single state to avoid federal registration and to offer shares under the rules of the state. Firms engaging in DPOs can solicit investors and advertise their offerings, including on the Internet. There are no restrictions on types or numbers of investors.

Regulation D also provides for private placements without SEC registration. Rule 506 allows for placements of unlimited size with up to 35 accredited investors. Rule 505 allows for placements of up to $5 million with up to 35 unaccredited investors and an unlimited number of accredited investors. Business angels often invest under the guidelines of these rules. The issuer may distribute an offering memorandum but may not advertise or solicit investors.

For all the attention that DPOs receive, their usefulness is limited. By one estimate, there were only about 358 such offerings (including intrastate offerings) in 1996. Furthermore, there is evidence that the majority of DPOs are unsuccessful. Among other things, success of the offering depends on a track record of profitability, an affinity group of customers, employees, or others who recognize the value of the company and have money to invest, and a significant commitment of effort to manage the offering.

Ben and Jerry's used a modest DPO as a stepping-stone for its subsequent public offering. Ben and Jerry's built its first ice cream plant by selling $750,000 of equity directly to Vermont residents. The firm later raised $6.5 million in an IPO. The experience suggests that DPOs can make sense for a firm that has a loyal customer base.

---

*For further information, see Stevenson (1998); Stephanie Gruner, "When Mom and Pop Go Public," *Inc.* (December 1996), pp. 66–70; and Marla Dickerson, "Direct Offerings on Net Can Pull in the Cash . . . at a Cost," *Los Angeles Times,* October 15, 1997, p. 1.

---

available for near-term financing. For example, it may be possible to get immediate financing by paying bills more slowly. As already discussed, this source of financing may involve foregoing prompt payment discounts. The alternative may be to rely on term loans if future conditions warrant. Hence, paying bills more slowly may look attractive as immediate financing, but it does not make sense as permanent financing. Although sources like vendor financing (trade credit) and factoring often are very expensive, some forms of immediate financing may not be. Capital from friends can sometimes be obtained on favorable terms.

A choice of near-term financing may limit the venture's flexibility. For example, if financing requires collateral, then the collateral is not available to secure subsequent borrowing. Another consideration is the present and expected future financial condition of the venture. Financing is less expensive when outside providers of funds recognize the viability of the venture.

More alternatives are available for near-term financing than for immediate financing. Three primary factors influence the venture's choice of near-term financing. First, the choice depends

Research and Development Limited Partnership:

Selling Intellectual Property and Leasing It Back

In a sale-and-lease-back transaction, the venture owns an asset but to generate cash, sells the asset to another party and enters a simultaneous agreement to lease use of the asset. There is nothing fundamentally different between this transaction and venture leasing. In venture leasing, the venture normally enters the lease directly. The lessor acquires the asset from a third party and leases its use to the venture. The transaction also is not much different from borrowing and using the proceeds to purchase the asset, or from using an asset as collateral.*

Not all such transactions must be based on tangible assets. The structure of a research and development limited partnership, for example, is essentially a sale-and-lease-back, where the asset is intellectual property and payments for using the property are in the form of royalties. The main difference is that the agreements often are based on *prospective* intellectual property.

To illustrate, suppose a group of programmers wants to develop and market a new software application and expects that development will cost $2 million. An R&D limited partnership is one way to structure the financing. Under this arrangement, the investors join as limited partners, possibly along with members of the development team. The development team forms a separate organization and contracts to provide R&D services to the limited partnership in exchange for the $2 million. In addition, the development team agrees to transfer ownership to any patents, trade secrets, or other intellectual property to the limited partnership. Finally, the team agrees to pay a royalty to the limited partnership.

Despite their tax advantages, R&D limited partnerships are not a very common way of structuring investments.** To understand why not, consider some of the issues that can arise: What specific intellectual property is the limited partnership contracting to acquire? What conflicts could arise if the limited partnership seeks to license its technology? What conflicts could arise if the limited partnership is not well suited to market the technology?

---

*See Lerner (1994) for a description of venture leasing and the venture leasing industry.

**Losses in early years of the relationship are deductible by limited partners. The partners sometimes can deduct their commitments from taxable income even before the payments are made.

---

on the amount the venture is seeking. For comparatively small amounts, likely sources include the SBA, economic development agencies, banks, and private placements of equity with a few individuals or a group of angel investors. For larger amounts of financing, private placements of debt with institutional lenders, venture capital investors, and strategic partners gain importance. If the required financing is very large, the entrepreneur could consider a registered public offering of debt or equity.[4]

In addition to the entrepreneur's requirements, the investor's financial limitations affect the size of the investment. A venture with large needs cannot turn to a financing source that is incapable of supplying a large amount of capital, at least not as its sole source. Conversely, ventures with modest needs cannot justify the high fixed costs of public offerings.

A study of high-technology ventures provides evidence of the relation between size of financing round and source of financing. Figure 15-2 summarizes the results. Panel (a) demonstrates that individual investors (business angels) concentrate on financing rounds that are

Comparison of Business Angel and Venture Capital Financing

Panel (a)

	Number of Deals		Percent of Deals	
Size of Financing Round	with Business Angel Financing	with Venture Capital Financing	with Business Angel Financing	with Venture Capital Financing
<$250,000	102	8	57.63%	4.62%
$250,000-$499,999	43	14	24.29%	8.09%
$500,000-$1,000,000	15	31	8.47%	17.92%
>$1,000,000	17	120	9.60%	69.36%
Total	177	173	100.00%	100.00%

Panel (b)

	Number of Deals		Percent of Deals	
Stage of Round	with Business Angel Financing	with Venture Capital Financing	with Business Angel Financing	with Venture Capital Financing
Seed	52	11	29.38%	6.36%
Startup	55	38	31.07%	21.97%
First stage	29	56	16.38%	32.37%
Second stage	26	46	14.69%	26.59%
Third stage	10	19	5.65%	10.98%
Bridge	5	3	2.82%	1.73%
Total	177	173	100.00%	100.00%

Figure 15-2   Comparison of business angel and venture capital financing

Source: Freear and Wetzel (1990).

smaller than rounds provided by venture capital firms. Panel (b) shows that angels and venture capital firms concentrate on financing at different stages of development.

The second factor that affects the choice of near-term financing is permanency of the need. If financing need is permanent or long-term, it usually does not make sense to use financing sources that are short-term in nature. Conversely, short-term needs generally are best financed with short-term sources.

The transactions costs of short-term financing usually are lower than those of long-term financing. This is because providers of short-term funds do not need to conduct as extensive due diligence investigations as do providers of long-term funds. Short-term financing generally is debt financing secured by business assets of easily ascertainable value (such as accounts receivable or inventory). Alternatively, short-term financing can be generated by selling business assets (such as by factoring accounts receivable) or by leasing assets. Because the value of the security is clear to the provider of funds, such transactions are comparatively easy to arrange. However, for a venture with long-term needs, repeatedly incurring the smaller transactions costs of short-term financing can accumulate to more than the cost of one round of long-term financing.

Depending on the form of financing and industry conventions, the effective interest cost of short-term financing can be more or less than that of long-term financing. As noted, the cost

The Cost of Vendor Financing

Vendor financing, or trade credit is used by more than 60 percent of small businesses, a rate that exceeds all other financing services except checking. It exists in two primary forms. Sometimes vendors sell on "net terms," such as "net 30." Terms of net 30 mean that payment is due in 30 days. With net term financing, the buyer receives, essentially, an interest-free loan from the seller. If the amount due is material, it would be a mistake for any customer to pay early because, at a minimum, the money could be invested in short-term riskless government debt until the payment was required. Net terms frequently are offered in cases where the buyer is likely to want to inspect the product before paying. Small businesses and young businesses that sell to large and established businesses often find that customary practice includes selling on net terms.

The other form of trade credit is "two-part terms," where the most common arrangement is "2/10 net 30." This means the customer receives a discount of 2 percent if the invoice is paid within 10 days and the entire balance is due in 30 days. If the terms are enforced strictly, this arrangement amounts to an offer of a 20-day loan in exchange for an interest payment of 2 percent. To see the effective interest cost, suppose a customer decides to rely fully on trade credit by always paying on the thirtieth day. Because there are about 18 periods of 20 days in a year, the effective annual interest rate is found by compounding ($1.02^{18} - 1 = 42.8\%$).

At this interest rate, trade credit would not be appropriate for regular financing, except for a very risky business. Smith (1987) demonstrates that setting the terms in this way can function as a screening contract, such that firms that decide to take advantage of the credit period are signaling that lower cost financing is not immediately available. A vendor may respond in a variety of ways. From the customer's perspective, the essential points are that trade credit with two-part terms often is an expensive form of financing. It may make sense to rely on trade credit for unanticipated and transitory cash shortages, but not as a regular financing source. In addition, the customer must be concerned with how the supplier may interpret and react to the customer's failure to take advantage of the discount.*

---

*For additional information on vendor financing, see Biasis and Gollier (1997), Mian and Smith (1992), Ng, Smith, and Smith (1999), Petersen and Rajan (1997), and Smith (1987). Statistics on trade credit use are based on data provided by the 1993 Survey of Small Business Finance, co-sponsored by the Federal Reserve Board and the SBA.

of using vendor financing can be very high. In contrast, formal short-term loans can have very low interest rates. With vendor financing, the effective rates tend to be high partly because the entrepreneur can unilaterally decide to borrow by postponing payment for purchases, whereas a short-term loan is made only after the lender is satisfied with the risk exposure. An entrepreneur may prefer vendor financing if the need is very short-term, because doing so requires little advance planning and the loan can be repaid as soon as cash becomes available. Clearly, however, high interest-rate short-term sources are not attractive for long-term needs.

The third reason to match sources with permanency of needs is that, except for passive equity financing, long-term financing usually comes with more constraints on future decisions. Providers of long-term funds may restrict future borrowing, limit the scope of venture activities, demand control over certain kinds of decisions, and require more access to information about the venture. Sometimes the terms of a long-term financing arrangement can impede a

Issue Cost of Public Offerings

The cost of a public offering includes three components: the spread between the offer price and net proceeds to the issuer; issue costs borne directly by the issuing firm; and underpricing. Lee, Lochhead, Ritter, and Zhao (1995) estimate the first two components (excluding underpricing) for different types and sizes of issues. Their results, as a percentage of net proceeds, appear in the following table.

Initial Public Offering and Bond Issue Cost by Issue Size

Issue Size (Proceeds in millions of dollars)	IPOs	Debt
2–9.99	17.3	4.5
10–19.99	11.8	2.7
20–39.99	10.0	2.3
40–59.99	9.1	1.4
60–79.99	8.6	2.3
80–99.99	8.2	2.3
100–199.99	7.3	2.3
200–499.99	6.8	2.3
500 and up	5.9	1.8

Data in the table are estimated based on Lee, I., S. Lochhead, J. Ritter, and Q. Zhao, "The Cost of Raising Capital." *Journal of Financial Research* 19 (1996): 59–74.

The costs for debt issues are considerably lower than for IPOs at all offering sizes. However, most debt issues are made by established companies that easily can demonstrate their ability to repay. In such cases, investors value the debt almost entirely based on repayment terms stated in the debt contract. The underwriter does not need to devote much effort to due diligence, and investors do not need to devote much effort to valuation. A risky venture that wanted to do a public debt offering would face much higher issue cost.

With regard to IPOs, the table does not tell the full story. In addition to the underwriter's fee and expenses incurred directly by the issuer, it is standard practice for the underwriter intentionally to set the offering price 10 to 15 percent below what the market price is expected to be at the time of the offering. Some studies find that actual underpricing is even higher.* If the underpricing is considered to be part of issue cost, then the total cost of an IPO could be in the 15 to 30 percent range, depending on issue size.

*See the discussion in Chapter 16.

---

venture's ability to raise additional financing. A ratchet provision, for example, can make it impossible for a firm that has performed below expectations to raise more equity without first restructuring the existing claims. In summary, long-term financing can significantly limit flexibility, whereas such limitations can be minimized if financing is short-term.

Finally, addressing short-term needs with long-term financing can reduce expected cash flows and increase the riskiness of cash flows. Long-term financing, for example, can cause

The Mechanics of Factoring

A venture that sells on credit can generate cash by factoring its accounts receivable. In a factoring transaction, the factor buys the receivables at a discounted price and then seeks to collect payment directly from the customer. Receivables may be sold either with or without recourse. If the sale is without recourse and the factor is unable to collect, then the factor bears the loss. If the sale is with recourse, the venture bears the loss associated with uncollected accounts. The discount for factored receivables depends on quality of the receivables, time to expected collection, cost of collection, expected level of defaults, and whether the arrangement is with or without recourse.

Factoring can be either routine or sporadic. In some industries, it is common to factor all receivables. In those cases, the venture can sell on credit but avoids the cost of integrating into the credit management function. Such arrangements are more likely when the factor can manage the credit operation more efficiently than can the venture. In essence, the choice to factor is a choice to outsource functions related to accounts receivable. Sometimes the factor is better able to realize the value of merchandise that is recovered if a customer defaults; sometimes the factor is better able to work with customers who are experiencing cash flow problems; and sometimes the factor serves as an intermediary between the supplier and the customer, on issues such as disputes about product quality. Routine factoring arises in such settings.

Sporadic factoring is more of a financing exigency. The seller turns to the factor to address a cash shortage that it expects will be temporary. Under those conditions, the cost of factoring can be high. The factor may not have an advantage in collecting the receivables, and, if the seller has its own credit management operation, then factoring involves duplicative investments in credit management. Nonetheless, factoring exists in most industries.

Smith and Schnucker (1993) report the results of a survey of 770 firms across a broad span of industries. Of the firms, 19.4 percent report that they use factors. Within manufacturing, firms in all major subcategories of product groupings engaged in factoring receivables.

Percent of Firms by Industry That Offer Factoring

Industry	Percent of Firms That Factor Receivables	Percent of Firm Customers Offered Trade Credit Financing
Mining	17.20	67.20
Manufacturing	19.40	78.00
Transportation and communication	30.60	65.00
Wholesale trade	12.70	80.30
Agriculture, construction, other	7.70	89.00
Total	19.40	77.10

Source: Smith, Janet Kiholm, and Christjahn Schnucker, "An Empirical Examination of Organizational Structure: The Economics of the Factoring Decision," *Journal of Corporate Finance* 1 (1994): 119–138. Based on a 1991 survey of 770 public firms.

the venture to incur interest expenses on unnecessary borrowing. Conversely, the cost of short-term financing can be volatile and, if the financing is used to acquire long-term assets, it can increase the uncertainty of cash flows.

The Influence of Cumulative Financing Needs

The third factor affecting any financing decision is cumulative needs. If the entrepreneur expects the venture will soon begin to generate positive cash flow sufficient to fund growth, then he can make near-term financing choices with little regard to their potential effect on availability or cost of future financing. In such a case, it is not difficult to agree to provisions that limit the venture's ability to raise additional capital. The important scenarios are the extremes. How should near-term financing be arranged if the entrepreneur's cumulative needs may be substantially higher or substantially lower?

If cumulative needs are expected to be higher, current financing must not seriously impede ability to raise capital later. Options to provide additional rounds at pre-agreed prices, first rights of refusal to provide financing, and financing arrangements that include other options and rights can be costly for the new venture. If such terms are agreed to, their effects can be offset by other provisions, such as call options on the financing or buyout options that enable the venture to restore flexibility, such as by paying off the existing provider.

If the entrepreneur expects future needs to be lower than near-term needs, the arrangements should enable the venture to pay off the financing as cash becomes available. Call options and buy-out rights are useful under these conditions, and when the venture is expected to grow rapidly.[5]

15.4 SECOND STEP: ASSESS THE CURRENT CONDITION OF THE VENTURE

In addition to factors like urgency of need and cumulative need, the realistic menu of financing alternatives depends on the current condition of the venture. Considerations include stage of development, value of outside advice, organizational structure, track record, level and stability of earnings and cash flow, asset base, and existing financing.

The Influence of Stage of Development

For early-stage ventures, sources of equity include the entrepreneur and friends, business angels, and venture capital firms. Sources of credit include secured lenders and loans from, or guaranteed by, government agencies.[6] In addition, there are financing sources that operate like venture capital firms, but with ability to access public loan guarantee programs, such as the SBA programs.[7]

An early-stage venture working on product development and not yet generating revenues generally is not a candidate for debt financing. Such a venture cannot service the debt, except with cash generated from subsequent financing. It also cannot realize the tax benefit of being able to deduct interest as an expense.

For an early-stage venture facing a high degree of uncertainty, debt financing puts the entrepreneur and the provider of financing in antagonistic positions. If the amount of debt financing is high, the entrepreneur has an incentive to gamble on high-risk strategies, recognizing that the rewards of success go to the equityholder, but the cost of failure goes to the creditor.[8]

Because creditors recognize this conflict, they seek to encumber the venture with provisions designed to ensure that the debt is repaid, even if the venture fails.[9] By imposing such constraints, the creditor may increase the likelihood of failure.

Appropriate sources of capital to finance expansion are different from those for a start-up. Expansion capital can be debt or equity, but the choice depends on extent of need, expected growth of the venture, expected levels of future income, and amount of risk. Most venture capital firms are more interested in providing expansion financing than early-stage financing. Government-guaranteed sources of loans generally are more appropriate for expansion financing. If capital needs are very large, investment banking firms may act as intermediaries in the process of raising capital via public offering.[10] In some cases, corporate investors or strategic partners are appropriate sources of funds.

Business Angel Groups

Angel investing has been around for centuries, and continues to be a robust source of financing for early-stage companies, especially for entrepreneurs who have exhausted bootstrap financing resources and are not yet ready for formal venture capital. Research shows that the U.S. hosts close to 3 million angels, who invest more than $50 billion in early-stage entrepreneurial firms, which is several times as much as venture capital firms invest in early stages.[11] Some very wealthy business angels invest individually, even to the point of establishing funds with professional management, much like a venture capital firm. Many more are members of angel groups (Investors' Circle, Hub Angels, Tech Coast Angels, etc.). The group structure enables them to increase access to deal flow, make larger aggregate investments, invest in more ventures, and pool their knowledge. While angel investing is, for the most part, a localized activity (investing only in ventures that are close to home), the angel capital industry increasingly is global. Informal private equity markets are emerging in most economies around the world. Many are facilitated by government initiatives. In emerging economies, angel investing often is more prevalent and easier to implement than formal venture capital.

Despite their prevalence, there is little research on business angels. This is largely because angels are disaggregated, and the organizations are only loosely structured. While a few sources help identify angel groups (reportedly around 100 groups in the U.S.), the industry is not currently covered by any reporting service in a systematic way. The angel organizations that do exist have legal structures of varying complexity, most have some full-time or part-time management, a standardized investment process, and a public interface (Web site, public relations activities, etc.). In the U.S., the formality of investment practices is restricted by provisions of the SEC Act, which prevents following any approach to investing that might be construed as "marketed" or a public offering and prevents angel investors from making decisions on behalf of other angels. Angel groups vary in size, but generally are not larger than 80. Membership has to be approved and it is typical for groups to require that members meet requirements (minimum attendance at meetings, evidence of investment, pay dues, etc.) The groups also seek individuals with varying kinds of expertise to gain access to networks and to facilitate making deals.

Angel groups regularly hold breakfast or dinner meetings where members may hear two or three company presentations at a time. The meeting format is very standard: presentations followed by a Q & A session. If there is interest in the deal, angels will discuss among themselves and arrange for a "champion" or small group to take the lead in due diligence. The same

Venture Capital Financing—The Rise and Fall of eToys Inc.

eToys Inc. was incorporated in November 1996 as a Web-based retailer focused entirely on children's products. The company's Web site was launched one year later, in October 1997. Development of the Web site represented the principal costs of initiating the venture. To fund those development efforts, the company raised small amounts of capital from the founders and from idealab!, an early-stage venture investor.

Funds for the start-up of operations were raised from venture capital investors in two rounds of financing. In a December 1997 first-round financing, DynaFund Ventures invested $1 million in exchange for Series A preferred stock valued at $0.207 per share. Intel Corporation (which operates a corporate venture fund) and idealab! also invested $1 million on the same terms. Six months later, in June 1998, DynaFund was joined by two other venture capital firms, Highland Capital Partners and Sequoia Capital, in a $15 million contribution to second-round financing, in exchange for Series B preferred stock valued at $0.701 per share. Of this total, DynaFund invested $2 million, Highland Capital Partners invested $8 million, and Sequoia Capital invested $5 million.* In this round, idealab! invested an additional $1.5 million, and Intel invested $2 million. Generally, funds invested by the venture capital firms were drawn from two or more funds managed by the firm.

Much of the capital contributed by outside investors was consumed in the start-up of the venture. As of year-end 1998, the company had total assets of $23.9 million, including $18.5 million of cash (following the seasonal sales peak) and $5 million of inventory. eToys is a type of business in which growth can be a net source of funds. This is apparent from the fact that its year-end accounts payable balance was $12.3 million. The company reported deferred compensation of $30.1 million and an accumulated deficit of $17.6 million. The company's IPO, in May 1999, generated gross proceeds of $166.4 million by selling 8.32 million shares for $20 per share. The IPO opens the door to harvesting the investments of the venture capital investors only a few months after their initial investments. At the time of the IPO, idealabs!'s investment had a market value of $366.4 million, and Intel's had a value of $154 million.**

eToys, originally a beneficiary of the dot-com exuberance, eventually became a victim of changing market perceptions. After an IPO at $20 per share, and trading in the aftermarket at prices as high as $86 per share, eToys was unable to continue to finance its operations after the dot-com market collapsed. The company filed for bankruptcy in March 2001. The company's stock now is trading for virtually zero and its assets are being liquidated with no anticipated payments to shareholders. In May 2002, eToys filed suit against Goldman Sachs, the investment banker that underwrote its IPO. In the lawsuit, the stockholders blame Goldman Sachs for the bankruptcy, arguing that Goldman deliberately underpriced the IPO for its own benefit and contrary to the interest of eToys shareholders.

---

*Each of the three venture capitalists gained board representation at the time of its initial investment.

**See the eToys Inc. initial public offering prospectus and other public filings for additional information.

champion is likely to be the primary contact that the entrepreneur will have with the angel groups as the firm progresses.

A typical angel deal in the U.S. is an early-stage round where an individual angel invests $25,000 to $100,000 per deal. Angels financing rounds tend to be less than $1 million, raised from six to twelve individuals.

Attributes of Angels

Van Osnabrugge and Robinson (2000) report that U.S. angels tend to be well educated relative to the average population, have successful previous careers in entrepreneurial ventures (75–83 percent have start-up experience), are in their late forties, and are predominantly male (around 97 percent). Counterparts in the U.K. and other countries in Europe tend to be slightly older. Start-up experience is even more prevalent among European angels than U.S. angels: the percent of angels who have started at least one firm is much higher, for example, in Finland and Sweden. Education levels generally are high relative to population averages.

The Influence of the Value of Active Outside Involvement

An important consideration in the choice of financing is whether the venture can benefit from active involvement of an investor. Investors in new ventures can be passive or active to varying degrees. Active involvement may be as limited as simply monitoring the operation and serving on the board. Or it can be as extensive as stepping in as CEO for a period to help get the venture on track, make key strategic and tactical decisions, and help build the management team. In most cases, the investor's return for active involvement comes, at least in part, through ownership participation. For the entrepreneur, the decision to involve an outside investor depends on the cost of the investor's time (in the form of a larger ownership stake) compared with the expected value added by the investor.

Business angels generally are the most actively involved, though some are passive.[12] Those who are active often seek to leverage their experience from a previous venture into another with related product-market overlap. If the entrepreneur is a technical visionary, a business angel may be able to contribute the managerial expertise required for implementation. If the entrepreneur is able to implement the vision without significant outside involvement, then active angel investors may not be worth involving.

Venture capitalists generally are less involved. They may assist with financing and hiring and serve on boards, but for the most part, they are focused on monitoring the investment for their limited partners. It might seem that the investors in the venture capital fund should pay for the monitoring efforts of the venture capitalist. However, investors can always turn to more passive opportunities, which do not require monitoring. Consequently, the cost of monitoring services ultimately must be borne by the entrepreneur.

There are several reasons why it might be worthwhile for the entrepreneur to incur the costs of subjecting the venture to monitoring. One pragmatic reason is that the only way the venture can attract outside capital is if the entrepreneur accepts financing that includes monitoring. This begs the question of why financing is not available from passive sources.

Monitoring adds value for at least two reasons. First, the entrepreneur's willingness to subject the venture to monitoring is a way of overcoming investor concern that the entrepreneur will try to take advantage of the financing relationship for personal gain. Second, a monitoring relationship can enhance the flexibility and adaptability of the venture.

Flexibility of financing is not very important if the assets of the venture are specific to a particular activity. However, new ventures with assets that are less specific may benefit from ability to react rapidly to information. Suppose, for example, that product development efforts are lagging behind business plan projections. How should investors respond to the information that product development is taking longer than projected? At one extreme, it may be increasingly evident that development efforts are unlikely to succeed, in which case the venture

CompuCredit's Accounts Receivable Financing

CompuCredit provides unsecured consumer credit cards under the Aspire and Visa trademarks. It targets consumers who are higher risk than most users of bank-originated credit cards. The company derives its revenues from issuing credit cards to consumers. When a consumer uses the card, a receivable is generated. CompuCredit effectively purchases the receivable from the retailer at a discount. Profitability depends on the company's ability to finance the receivables at low cost, do an effective job of collection, and sell related products such as life insurance and card registration to cardholders.

The company was formed in August 1996 and began soliciting cardholders in February 1997. For the first half of 1998, it recorded net income of $14.2 million on a managed portfolio of credit card receivables of $397.5 million. Yet, its balance sheet at the time shows total assets of only $57.6 million, offset by short-term borrowing of $7.5 million.

CompuCredit's primary means of financing is securitization of its credit card receivables. The company assembles its receivables into portfolios and sells the right to collection of the receivables to a third party. CompuCredit retains a residual interest in the portfolio. Its objective is to earn a return by collecting interest and past-due fees that are in excess of the interest cost of the securitized receivables. If investor required returns are low enough, CompuCredit can sell the interest in securitized receivables for more than it had to pay to acquire the receivables.

The securitized receivables do not appear on CompuCredit's financial statements. Instead, the company records the expected profits at the time of the sale, as securitization income. On the balance sheet, it shows only the value of its retained interest in the receivables.*

---

*See the 1999 initial public offering prospectus of CompuCredit for more information.

---

should be abandoned. At the other extreme, perhaps the delay is due to lack of resources and the venture is likely to be very successful if funds are available. In that case, increasing the financial resource commitment is appropriate. A passive investor may be unable to distinguish between these two very different scenarios, whereas an active investor, who is monitoring the venture is likely to understand the reasons for delay and be able to make a well-informed choice between abandonment and increased commitment.

It is important to recognize that flexibility and survival are different and survival is not the goal. Flexibility includes the ability to close a venture down. It also includes the ability to change focus or change the resource commitment. The ability to abandon a losing venture quickly can benefit both the investor and the entrepreneur. Early abandonment reduces the investor's financial commitment and enables the entrepreneur to redeploy human capital to other activities. Creating the ability to abandon a losing venture quickly can increase the entrepreneur's ownership stake, in the event that the venture is a success.

The need for flexibility depends on the extent to which the value of the venture depends on being able to make timely decisions about exercising, retaining, and abandoning real options. Generally, the value of embedded real options declines as a venture matures, and must commit increasingly to a specific direction. As the importance of flexibility declines, the venture increasingly is able to raise capital from sources that are more passive.

Financing Choices: Angels, VCs, and Corporate Venture Capitalists

Criteria	Angels	Venture Capitalists	Corporate Venture Capitalists
Deal type • **Stage** • **Scale**	Early stage, small scale	Varies, with a focus on later stage, large scale	For a substitute product the entrepreneur may prefer VC. For a complement the entrepreneur may prefer a strategic partner. Scale varies.
Objective	High returns	High returns	Returns to strategic position
Location	Close by	Close if lead investor	Location less important
Managerial involvement/ Monitoring	Active, may share expertise and capital	Active, but focused on monitoring	Sharing of corporate resources
Due diligence and valuation	Generally less sophist-icated than alternatives	Significant due dili-gence and valuation	Complicated valuation due to impact on value of corporation
Exit	Important, but have long horizon	Important	Important, with strategic implications
Contract	Simple, informal, includes valuation, milestones	More complex than angel investment	Added complexity due to strategic position

Based, in part, on discussions in Van Osnabrugge and Robinson, *Angel Investing*, Jossey-Bass (2000), and Hellman, "A Theory of Strategic Venture Investing," *Journal of Financial Economics* 64 (2002): 285–314.

The Influence of the Asset Base

Although borrowing usually is not the best form of financing for an early-stage venture, if eq-uity capital cannot be arranged, debt sometimes is an alternative. A venture with a limited track record, an unproven entrepreneur, and an uncertain future can still attract debt financing if as-sets can be used to secure the loan. If the assets are of sufficient value to repay the loan, the en-trepreneur may not need to convince the financing source of the merits of the venture.

Secured or collateralized lending is one mechanism available to the entrepreneur for assuaging investor concerns with adverse selection and moral hazard. An entrepreneur who is willing to collateralize a loan is unlikely to use the borrowed money to speculate on a high-risk opportu-nity.[13] In addition, because failure likely would result in losing the collateral to the lender, a highly leveraged capital structure still would not induce the entrepreneur to try to increase risk.[14] A per-sonal guarantee by the entrepreneur serves the same function as asset-based collateral.[15]

One advantage of secured lending is that the collateral facilitates enforcing loan covenants and reaching agreement on ways of dealing with financial distress.[16] These advantages to the lender translate into lower borrowing costs, because they commit the entrepreneur to deal

MarketWatch.com and CBS

MarketWatch.com provides real-time business news, financial programming, and analytical tools through its Web properties, CBS.MarketWatch.com, and BigCharts.com. The company was formed in October 1997 as a 50/50 joint venture of CBS and Data Broadcasting Corporation (DBC). In exchange for its ownership interest, CBS agreed to license its name, logo, and some news content to MarketWatch and to provide $50 million nominal value of promotion and advertising business. In addition to its equity interest, CBS also receives a royalty of approximately 30 percent of the banner advertising revenue of MarketWatch. DBC, for its part, contributed initial funding and provides ongoing services and hosting of the Web site. MarketWatch has a staff of full-time and freelance journalists who provide some of the content for the site.

The company's strategic relationships with its primary stockholders, CBS and DBC (now Pearson International Finance Ltd.) are critical to its success. The CBS licensing arrangement expires in 2005, and CBS can terminate the relationship sooner for various other reasons. In addition, CBS has certain controls over editorial content, marketing, and other aspects of the site. Situations could arise where the interests of MarketWatch and CBS are in conflict. If DBC failed to provide its services to the venture, MarketWatch would be forced to develop and replace the resources provided by DBC.*

*See the MarketWatch.com initial public offering prospectus for additional information.

reasonably with future adversity, and because they signal confidence. An offsetting concern is that a secured lender has little interest in the success of the venture. For an entrepreneur who desires active outside involvement, lending (especially secured lending) is unlikely to come with much useful advice, other than on ways to ensure that the loan is repaid.[17]

Aside from collateral and personal guarantees, the primary means lenders have of ensuring that their loans are repaid is to condition the loan on the borrower's willingness to be bound by covenants. These covenants are intended to protect the value of the assets used to secure the loan and to help the lender recognize quickly that a venture is having difficulty. Covenants can be advantageous to an entrepreneur who is confident about the future but can deprive a high-risk start-up of flexibility.

The covenants associated with a loan are not immutable. If it is in the lender's interest, the agreement can be renegotiated. In fact, renegotiation of covenants is common for privately placed loans.[18] However, when a venture faces a high level of uncertainty, future developments can result in conflicts of interest between the entrepreneur and the lender. In such cases, the lender may end up with too much control.[19] Suppose, for example, that revenue is not growing as rapidly as projected. A cautious lender (who will not share in the success if the venture turns around) may decide to force repayment, even if this threatens survival.

15.5   THIRD STEP: ASSESS THE RELATION BETWEEN FINANCING CHOICES AND ORGANIZATIONAL STRUCTURE

Some financing choices are linked to organizational structure. For example, financing by a strategic partner may commit the venture to use the partner's marketing and distribution

GlobeSpan Virata Inc.—Corporate Venture Investing

The company is a developer of digital subscription line (DSL) integrated circuits for use in data transmission over copper-wire telephone lines at rates much faster than a 56 Kbps modem. GlobeSpan was originally organized and operated as the Advanced Transmission Technology Division of AT&T Paradyne Corporation, a subsidiary of Lucent Technologies. As part of a divestiture of Paradyne by Lucent, in 1996 GlobeSpan was organized as an independent company. In the months following divestiture, the company raised capital by selling equity to Lucent and to Communication Partners, L.P., a venture capital fund.

GlobeSpan is a design company and does not produce integrated circuits. Instead, it contracts with Lucent for production. Lucent supported the early-stage development activities of the venture. At the time of the divestiture, GlobeSpan was generating revenues, and those revenues have continued to grow. More recent growth has been financed with debt supplied by BankAmerica Business Credit, Inc. and Communication Partners, L.P. In 2001, GlobeSpan merged with Virata.

capabilities, offer its product only under the partner's brand, or commit to a course of action that eventually transfers control to the partner. In a similar fashion, pursuing a new venture within a corporation can limit the entrepreneur's ability to realize much of the gain.

Franchising is another example of connecting organizational structure to financing. In some industries, entrepreneurs use franchising as a means of financing rapid growth. The franchiser in such a case also is committing to an organizational structure that involves dealing with a large number of more or less independent business operators (franchisees), whose objectives and interests only partly overlap with those of the franchiser. For the venture to rely instead on debt and equity financing, also involves an organizational choice of substituting employees for franchisees.

How is an entrepreneur to select between strategic partnering and a financing relationship that does not restrict product-market choices or between franchising and a financing relationship that does not depend on a network of franchisees? Again, these choices involve cost-benefit comparisons. We use strategic partnering and franchising to illustrate the considerations that bear on the choice.

The Relation Between Financing and Strategic Partnering

Strategic partnering can enable the entrepreneur to take advantage of an investment in resources that the partner already has made. If that investment otherwise would be idle or less productively employed, then strategic partnering can reduce the incremental real resource commitment to the venture. The benefits of the saving can accrue to both parties. In some strategic partnering relationships, the partner is willing to take on more risk than would an outside investor. The entrepreneur may benefit by negotiating financial claims that are of lower risk than otherwise would be possible. Suppose the partner agrees to license the technology of the venture in exchange for a royalty and will bear the cost and risk of manufacturing, marketing, and distributing the product. In addition to the shift in risk, such an arrangement also may add value by enabling the entrepreneur to focus on product development, which, presumably, is the entrepreneur's strength. Corporate venturing has many of the same effects.

Restaurant and Coffee House Chains

WENDY'S INTERNATIONAL

Wendy's is a classic business-format franchise fast-food chain that combines franchisee and company-owned outlets. Company-owned outlets are financed substantially with long-term debt or long-term leases. Financing of franchise outlets usually is up to the franchisee to obtain. In some cases, the company owns the facility and leases it to the franchisee. Wendy's was organized in 1969 and as of early 1994 had a total of 4,168 outlets, including 2,944 owned and operated by franchisees. The geographic pattern of ownership is consistent with the predictions of the economic literature on franchising. Economic theory suggests that where it is not difficult to monitor employees, the franchiser is more likely to own the outlet. In contrast, franchisee-owned outlets are more likely in remote and disperse locations where monitoring costs are high. The cost of monitoring a single site in a remote location may be higher than the cost of monitoring numerous outlets in an urban area. The evidence from Wendy's experience is consistent with theory. Outlets in low-density, insular states like Idaho, Montana, and Nebraska all are owned by franchisees. Those in states with high-density metropolitan areas and high tourism usually have mixtures of company-owned and franchisee operations.* With the exception of Canada, outlets in countries outside the U.S. are owned by franchisees.**

STARBUCKS CORPORATION

Because of its limited menu and direct control over materials, centralized control is possible for operations like Starbucks. Financing is not difficult because each outlet operates in leased space and requires a limited front-end investment. A new location can quickly generate enough revenues to service the lease and cover other expenses. Most of its outlets are company-owned. Licensees operate some outlets, such as those in airports. In many airports, licensing is required and is the only way for Starbucks to gain access. Some international operations are operated by joint-venture partners, who act much like franchisees with chains of outlets.

BUCA, INC.

Buca operates full-service restaurants under the names Buca diBeppo and Vinny Testa's, offering a Southern Italian menu. The company is small and is pursuing a strategy of moderately rapid growth. Because each new restaurant requires an outlay of about $1.5 million, it has settled on an approach of financing each new operation itself and selling a significant ownership stake and share of the profits to the restaurant general manager. Financing is not difficult because, on average, restaurants in operation for two or more years are generating significant free cash flow.***

---

*Within the United States, state laws sometimes compel the company to choose between franchising and company ownership. In most of those cases, the company elects franchising.

**For discussions of economic theory and evidence on franchising, see LaFontaine (1992), and Brickley and Dark (1987).

***See Wendy's International Form 10-Ks, Starbucks Corporation Form 10-Ks, and the initial public offering prospectus of Buca, Inc. for additional information.

Some of the disadvantages of strategic partnering arrangements relate to conflicts of interest. A strategic partner may have other products that are substitutes for the entrepreneur's product. If so, the entrepreneur runs a risk that the partner is investing in order to protect the market for the existing product. Alternatively, the partner may have limited capability to distribute the product but be unwilling to license distribution to competitors because of complementarity between the entrepreneur's product and the partner's other products.[20]

It appears that established corporations have difficulty promoting entrepreneurial activity within the organization because managerial approaches commonly used in large organizations tend to inhibit entrepreneurship.[21] Strategic partnering can overcome some of the organizational difficulties, but concerns remain about conflicts of interest.[22]

The Relation Between Financing and Franchising

Franchising is both a means of implementing rapid growth and an organizational form with decentralized decision making. Rapid growth is possible because decentralized organizations that do not require extensive monitoring are relatively easy to expand and because franchisees contribute to financing their own operations. It is most likely to be an appropriate means of financing expansion in cases where there are distinct advantages to decentralized organizational form and where incentives of franchisees and the franchiser can be aligned.[23]

The difference between a franchise operation and a company-owned operation is that the franchisee is the residual claimant on the success of the operation and makes an investment that would be lost if the franchisee were terminated. Residual claimant status, combined with the sanction of termination, aligns the franchisee's incentives with the interests of the franchiser.[24]

Franchising is advantageous when centralized management cannot serve market demand as effectively as management that is closer to the market.[25] Accordingly, franchise operations are likely to be more effective than company-owned operations in specific types of markets. Franchising is more likely when the prospect of repeat business and the franchisee's reputation in the local market discourage the franchisee from depreciating the quality of the franchiser's product. Franchising also is more likely when knowledge of local market demand is important and when centralized oversight is difficult.[26]

A concern to prospective franchisers is whether the franchise form of organization is as robust as alternative forms where financing and organizational form are more separate. Recent empirical studies find little evidence that franchise organizations have different survival rates than other forms.[27] These studies find that high rates of franchise creation are offset by high failure rates and that exits are more likely for the less well-established franchisers. However, another study demonstrates that termination of the franchise form of organization is a planned-for event, which suggests that failure rates of different organizational forms have different interpretations.[28] The study concludes that ongoing operations of franchise organizations are most effectively governed by a contract structure that is relational but that discrete terms are more effective for franchise initiation and termination. Thus, franchise contracts tend to include discrete terms related to initiation and termination but are less specific about describing ongoing relationships.

15.6 HOW FINANCIAL DISTRESS AFFECTS FINANCING CHOICES

The financial condition of a venture affects its financing opportunities. A profitable business with a steady cash flow can arrange financing more easily than one that is struggling.

◆ Advantages and Disadvantages of Franchising

Advantages to Franchisees

- The business has an accepted product, name, or service that can lead to rapid attainment of sales potential.
- Managerial assistance and training for starting and operating the business often are available from the franchiser.
- Starting a franchise operation may require less capital than starting a new business.
- The franchisee gains access to the franchiser's accumulated knowledge and experience with the market.
- The franchise operation has an established structure of controls that the franchisee can use to manage the operation.

Advantages to the Franchiser

- The franchiser can expand the operation quickly with less capital, lower risk, and minimal commitment to developing a central organization.
- Access to a large-size organization allows the franchisee to quickly attain scale economies in marketing, production, management, and distribution.
- The franchise structure can align incentives of franchise operators and substitute for more intensive monitoring and control.

Disadvantages of Franchising

- The residual claimant status of franchise operators can give rise to disputes between parties.
- Franchisees often have political and legal clout at the state level, and this may impair the franchiser's ability to manage the organization.
- The residual claimant status of franchisees sometimes can lead to holdups and free riding.
- In a franchise organization, the upside potential is shared with the franchisees.

The advantages and disadvantages of franchising are based in part on those identified in Robert D. Hisrich and Michael P. Peters, *Entrepreneurship*, 4th ed. (Boston: Irwin McGraw-Hill, 1998).

However, for many new ventures, at some stages of development, struggling to meet financing needs is normal. The term "financial distress" means more than simply that a venture is in need of cash to fund its operations. A distressed firm is one that is fundamentally disappointing investors. If the investors are creditors, a distressed firm may have violated important debt covenants, or defaulted on its repayment obligations or be about to do so. For equity-financed ventures, financial distress can mean that the venture is so short of cash that it is unable to carry out its business plan. The cash shortage can be symptomatic of missed milestones or other disappointing performance. Such a firm may be compelled to terminate or significantly scale back operations and may be at risk of losing key employees.

Why Turnaround Financing Is Different

Financing distressed firms is different from financing high-risk start-ups for two reasons. First, distress means the entrepreneur already has failed to achieve a level of success consistent with expectations. That failure can undermine the entrepreneur's credibility. Although it is common to seek external causes of underperformance, the evidence suggests that the usual causes are fundamental failures of management.[29] A venture may get into trouble because of strategic issues, management issues, or financial planning and control problems. Strategic issues include such problems as misperceiving the market opportunity or selecting the wrong organizational design. Management issues include lack of critical skills, excessive turnover, and similar deficiencies. Inadequate financial planning and controls can contribute to unanticipated cash shortages, poor pricing decisions, lack of control over costs, and similar problems.

Although any new venture may encounter problems such as these, a financially distressed venture already has faced them. Given that the venture has failed in fundamental dimensions, why should investors assume that projections in a revised plan are achievable or that the entrepreneur is capable of managing the operation? In all likelihood, they will not make such assumptions and instead will start a race for the lifeboats. Without investor support, the venture is almost certain to fail.

In the United States, an entrepreneur who has encountered trouble can take advantage of a legal presumption that the cause of financial distress, if not completely external, is curable. A Chapter 11 bankruptcy offers a window of protection against creditors' demands for repayment of their loans. The underlying concept is that, if a venture is fundamentally viable, then creditors, as a group, are better off remaining on board. The statute gives the entrepreneur time to try to achieve a reorganization plan that creditors find acceptable.[30]

This leads to the second reason financing of distressed firms is different. The financial structure of most firms is based on a premise that the venture will be successful. Creditors, including trade creditors and even employees, expect that they will be paid. When a venture gets into trouble, the orientations of creditors change. Secured creditors look more intently at the value of collateral as a source of repayment. They worry that, if the entrepreneur is allowed to operate the business, the collateral may depreciate. They may press for liquidation as a means of repayment. Suppliers to distressed firms no longer assume that they eventually will be paid for merchandise they sell on credit. They may demand cash payment. Employees may assume that their jobs are at risk and try to protect themselves by seeking new employment. Even customers may become concerned and stop purchasing. After all, what good is a product guarantee from a venture that may be out of business in a few weeks?

Turning around a distressed firm can be more difficult than raising initial financing for a risky venture. This is because the financing already is in place and the threat of financial distress creates conflicts among the stakeholders. In the United States, once a company declares bankruptcy, individual creditors can no longer attach the company's assets. Instead, the assets become part of a common pool, and they are not dispersed unless the creditors reach an understanding about how the various debts will be settled. For example, the assets might be liquidated and the creditors paid out of the proceeds, or the creditors might decide to refinance the failing company.

The rationale for bankruptcy protection is to prevent creditors from participating in a defensive frenzy that destroys the value of the remaining assets. On the other hand, if it appears that the venture's going concern value is greater than its liquidation value, then existing investors may be more willing than new investors to commit resources.

The objective in turnaround financing is to devise a new financial structure such that each party expects to be better off by maintaining or increasing its investment than by collecting the liquidation value of their financial claims. Financial restructuring can involve significant changes in the financial claims held by different investors. Claims of creditors, for example, may be exchanged for common stock or for securities convertible to common. In general, restructuring must achieve three results. It must reduce the cash needs of the venture for servicing existing debt; reallocate the going-concern value to creditors and away from the entrepreneur; and provide a means of raising enough cash to restart the venture.

Even if it is apparent that going-concern value exceeds liquidation value, financial restructuring is not easy. The bankruptcy laws are more complicated than implementing a simple formula. Instead, different parties may dispute the going-concern value. Creditors, in general, have incentives to argue that the going-concern value is low, whereas the entrepreneur has an incentive to argue that it is high. Furthermore, the bankruptcy laws do not require that investors unanimously accept a restructuring proposal. Consequently, groups of investors can attempt to form coalitions to allocate claims in a way that works to their benefit and the detriment of others. Finally, the process takes place in the context of employee concerns about job security and wages, supplier concerns about the future of the enterprise, and customer concerns about the venture's ability to continue to supply products of acceptable quality.

Influence of Financial-Distress Costs on Choice of Financing

Many considerations affect the choice of financing. We have identified risk allocation, information problems, incentive problems, taxes, and a variety of other considerations. The prospect of financial distress and the resulting costs should also be a consideration.[31] For some kinds of ventures, the real costs of financial distress are small. Business assets, though they may be specialized to a particular use or geographic location, are readily marketable, and success or failure of the venture does not depend on the special knowledge or skills of employees. In such cases, financial distress can result in little more than a reallocation of ownership claims and may not materially affect the revenue or profit stream of the venture. Financing for such a venture can be guided primarily by risk allocation and tax considerations.

For other kinds of ventures, even the rumor of financial distress can have important real consequences. Key employees, who would be difficult to replace, may resign. Customers may switch to alternative suppliers to avoid the possible consequences of dealing with a firm that might fail. Managers who anticipate failure may engage in excessive risk-taking or may depreciate the assets of the venture. When the costs of financial distress are large, financing choices should be based, in part, on the value of avoiding financial distress. Among other things, this could imply raising a higher level of capital at the outset and using a financial structure that limits the risk of defaulting or violating debt covenants.[34]

15.7   HOW REPUTATIONS AND RELATIONSHIPS AFFECT FINANCING CHOICES

Reputations and relationships with providers of financing affect the availability of financing for a new venture. Reputation, in the context of financing, is an intangible capital asset that can lose value if the entrepreneur takes advantage of a financing source. An entrepreneur who develops a reputation for treating investors fairly and who values that reputation is unlikely to take advantage of investors after the financing commitments have been made. Thus, reputation operates like a performance bond on the actions of the entrepreneur. Investors who otherwise might be concerned with opportunism may be willing to base financing decisions on the entrepreneur's desire to avoid damage to reputation. For example, a lender may advance funds without requiring extensive collateral if the lender believes the entrepreneur's concern with damage to reputation is sufficient to discourage excessive risk-taking.[33]

Unfortunately, most new ventures are unable to rely on reputation. Although the essential element of reputation is a concern that opportunistic behavior today will impair ability to raise capital in the future, the value of an entrepreneur's reputation is difficult to assess. Commonly, investors assess reputation on the basis of track record. Investors can easily perceive that a venture that has been around for a significant time and has been involved in raising capital repeatedly is likely to continue to need financing. Such a venture is unlikely to try to engage in opportunism toward investors. However, an entrepreneur with a venture on the verge of failure may not place much weight on the venture's ability to secure financing in the future. Survival in the short run is of more immediate concern than damage to reputation.[34]

Related to reputation as a basis for investment, evidence suggests that providers of financing rely, in part, on having an established relationship with the entrepreneur. Banks, for example, are more likely to make loans to customers with whom they have relationships.[35] Through a long-term relationship, a lender can develop private information about an entrepreneur, which serves as a basis for lending. The nature of the information is similar to reputation. The lender may learn that the venture is not as risky as it might appear or that the entrepreneur is concerned about ability to raise capital in the future.

Using data collected in a survey of small firms by the SBA, one recent study finds the primary benefit of building relationships with an institutional creditor is that the availability of financing increases. It appears, however, that the relationship has only a small effect on the cost of the financing. Hence, the primary benefit comes in the form of availability of funds (and other financial services) rather than the price of funds.[36]

The same study documents that small firms organized as corporations are more likely to borrow than are firms organized as proprietorships and partnerships. Twenty-eight percent of corporations and 45 percent of noncorporations have no institutional borrowing. This is partly a size effect—corporations are much larger, on average, than are sole proprietorships and partnerships. For firms that do borrow, the sources of borrowed funds vary with firm size. Based on book value of assets, the smallest 10 percent of firms borrow about 50 percent of their debt from banks and 27 percent from firm owners and families. The fraction borrowed from personal sources (owners and family) declines to 10 percent and the fraction from banks increases to 62 percent for the largest 10 percent of firms. Small firms also tend to concentrate their borrowing in one lender. The smallest 10 percent of firms that have a bank as their primary lender secure, on average, 95 percent of their loans from that bank. On average, the smallest firms tend to have just over one lender, while the largest firms have about three lenders.

15.8 TOTAL AVAILABILITY OF FINANCING FOR SMALL BUSINESSES AND NEW VENTURES

A useful perspective on the availability of financing for new ventures arises from knowing the total amounts of capital supplied by different sources. Although the amounts are difficult to estimate and are uncertain, there is no doubt that public awareness of financing sources for new ventures bears little relation to the amounts of funding available. Venture capital, for example, receives a great deal of attention but represents a small fraction of total financing.

Technology Transfer, Government Sponsorship of University Research, and the Bayh-Dole Act

The Manhattan Project is an early example of the importance of university-sponsored, government-supported research. An early proponent of the promise of technology transfer from university research laboratories, Vannevar Bush, prepared a 1945 report for the U.S. President recognizing the value of universities as a source of knowledge and of the importance of government support of basic science research. His report was instrumental in providing increased research funding through the auspices of the National Institutes of Health, the National Science Foundation, and the Office of Naval Research. However, the federal government, which sponsors much research at universities, was reluctant to permit universities and their faculties and students to retain the rights to their inventions. Instead, the government offered nonexclusive licenses to anyone who wanted to use them. Given the resulting common ownership problem, few companies purchased licenses to government-owned patents.

Much of this changed in the 1980s with the passage of the Bayh-Dole Act and related legislation. The Act provides the basis for current university technology transfer practices. Technology transfer refers to the transfer of research results from universities to the commercial sector. The result has greatly increased the profile of universities in sponsoring and commercializing the research of their faculties.

The Bayh-Dole Act (1980) states that universities may elect to retain title to inventions they develop through government funding and must file patents on inventions they elect to own. The statute and amendments create incentives for government, universities, and industry to invent and develop commercial products based on university and government-sponsored research.

The result of the enabling legislation has been a proliferation of university technology offices and incubators, and an increase in the number of universities actively engaged in technology transfer, as evidenced by increases in the number of patents awarded to universities and in their reported licensing income. University research and technology transfer has been pivotal in spawning the biotechnology industry (arising from Stanford's Cohen-Boyer patent on gene splicing tools), and advancing many industries, including computing, software, and chemical engineering. Commercialization has created thousands of new companies and jobs. As indicators of its impact, one study found that before 1981, fewer than 250 patents were issued to universities per year. Slightly over a decade later, almost 1600 were issued each year. By 1992, 200 universities had at least one patent issued annually.*

---

*Survey of the Association of University Technology Managers, compiled annually by Kathleen Terry, SUNY Buffalo.

Sources: Bayh-Dole Act (P.L. 96-517), and "The Bayh-Dole Act: A Guide to the Law and Implementing Regulations," Council of Governmental Relations Brochure, 1993.

In the most recently available survey article, total estimated financing for small businesses in the United States was compiled for 1992.[37] The findings of that survey are summarized in Figure 15-3. The figure shows that total U.S. small-business financing for the year was approximately $1.6 trillion, divided roughly equally between equity and debt. The single largest category is equity contributions of the principal owner. The second largest, bank debt, is concentrated on small businesses that are capable of generating the cash flows required for debt service and is not a major financing source for early-stage ventures. Trade credit, the third-largest category, is limited to businesses that are past the start-up stage and are generating revenues for operations. Fourth, other equity is a catch-all that includes corporate strategic partners as well as investments by friends and family. According to the survey, those four categories account for nearly 80 percent of small and new business financing. By comparison, financing from venture capital firms and business angels represents (as of 1992) only about 5.5 percent of the total. Such financing is focused on ventures with long-term needs and the potential for very high growth rates.

One noteworthy aspect of the figure is the small amount of financing (less than 0.5 percent of the total) provided to new ventures and small businesses by government sources. This number, however, understates indirect influences of government activities through such means as loan guarantees and government-funded and sponsored research. It also excludes the influence that government has as a purchaser of products developed by new ventures.

Estimates of Financing to Small Businesses and New Ventures as of 1992

Source	Amount	Percent
Principal owner	524.3	31.33%
Angel finance	60	3.59%
Venture capital	31	1.85%
Other equity	215.2	12.86%
Total equity	830.6	49.64%
Commercial banks	313.8	18.75%
Finance companies	82.1	4.91%
Other institutions	50.1	2.99%
Trade credit	264.1	15.78%
Other business financing	82.1	4.91%
Government	8.1	0.48%
From principal owner	68.5	4.09%
Credit cards	2.4	0.14%
Other individuals	24.5	1.46%
Total debt	842.9	50.37%
Total	**1673.4**	**100.00%**

Source: Based on Berger and Udell (1995).

Figure 15-3 Estimates of financing to small businesses and new ventures as of 1992

15.9 AVOIDING MISSTEPS AND DEALING WITH MARKET DOWNTURNS

Anyone who has borrowed to purchase a home understands that financial markets can change abruptly and unexpectedly. During the month or so after applying for a home mortgage and until the mortgage is funded, mortgage rates can easily change by one-half percent or more. Such changes dramatically alter the cash required for repayment. Although not as transparent, the same changes can occur in markets for equity financing, and the consequences can be more severe. It is important for the entrepreneur to recognize that market conditions can change quickly and to factor the risk into the financing decision.

During the late 1990s, the IPO market for high-technology ventures was attractive compared to what it had been. Ventures involved in E-commerce, for example, with short records of accomplishment and negative earnings, were able to go public at high values compared to revenue or earnings. Market valuations sometimes were very high and were based heavily on investor perceptions that such firms were likely to benefit greatly from the rapid growth of the Internet. It is not surprising that, in that environment, many high-tech ventures set their sights on public offering.

Capital market investor perceptions can change very quickly (as they did in April 2000), whereas it can take four months or more to complete a public offering. If the market declines, opportunities to raise capital via public offering can evaporate. Many companies withdraw planned offerings if the stock market declines significantly. In that environment, a company that persists in efforts to issue shares publicly raises questions in the minds of prospective investors. If so many other companies have decided the market no longer is attractive, why is this company going ahead? Could management be going ahead because bad news about the company is about to be revealed?

The net result is that a company that proceeds with an offering may be compelled to accept a price that is much lower than anticipated. One that had planned a public offering but decides not go ahead may find that because of the delay and other market changes, raising capital from other sources has also become more difficult and more urgent.

In deciding where to search for funds, it is important to have a sense of what can go wrong and an awareness of the implications. A public offering might sometimes be attractive for some ventures that have yet to develop much of a track record. But if the market declines before the offering is completed, the venture may end up short of cash and in an adverse bargaining position, needing to complete a deal with someone quickly. If public offering opportunities seem attractive, it makes sense to begin the process far enough in advance that a canceled offering would not result in financial hardship.

Similar issues apply to pursuing financing opportunities that are attractive long shots. If cash is being consumed during the negotiations, then a failed negotiation can leave the venture in a position from which new financing would be difficult to raise.

The Investor's Perspective on Timing

Both parties have some motivation to complete deals quickly. A deal can fail for no other reason than that negotiations have been so protracted that one party or the other has concluded that trying to work together in the future will be more trouble than it is worth. There are other risks of delay. Because the venture and the environment are in a state of continuous change, delay can result in real changes that are sufficient to justify changes in the deal structure or require additional due diligence.

In spite of the these considerations, an investor also has, to some extent, an incentive to delay finalizing the deal. Usually, although negotiations are proceeding, the entrepreneur's ability to pursue alternative financing sources is limited. The investor, for example, may reasonably demand a standstill agreement with regard to other prospective investors as a condition for initiating any serious due-diligence effort. During this period, the venture continues to consume resources, and its ability to arrange alternative financing diminishes. Unless the parties have agreed to a mechanism for solving the short-run cash flow needs of the venture in case of a failed negotiation, the investor's negotiating ability increases as the cash flow concerns of the entrepreneur increase. Sometimes, for high-risk ventures, the investor can treat the deal as a free option. By waiting to invest, the investor can gain more information about the likelihood of venture success. The combination of these factors can be of great advantage to the investor. The entrepreneur needs to recognize that investors sometimes have incentives to delay completing a deal and try to protect against opportunism. At the same time, the entrepreneur needs to recognize that financing decisions require time to complete and that delay is not necessarily opportunistic.

Financing After a Marketwide Downturn in Valuations

When financing of a nonpublic venture is staged, the expectation is that the valuation will increase with each succeeding round. Normally, valuations rise as uncertainty is resolved favorably and as the anticipated harvest date approaches. "Down-round financing" is the term used to describe a financing round that occurs at a valuation lower than the preceding round. A down round can happen either because the venture has failed to achieve the projections reflected in the prior valuation or because, even though the projections may have been achieved, valuations have declined marketwide. The former problem is an aspect of financial distress due to the venture's own shortcomings, as already has been discussed. The latter, rather than being a symptom of distress, can be a cause of distress.

The difficulty of a marketwide decline in valuation arises if the negotiated deal structure impedes negotiating a new round at a lower valuation. If, for example, in an earlier round, the parties have negotiated anti-dilution rights for the investor, it can be impossible for the entrepreneur to negotiate for new financing unless the earlier investor agrees to modify or not enforce the dilution protection. Negotiation of the new round, instead of being bilateral, becomes tri-lateral, and may be very difficult to consummate. The negotiation, much like a bankruptcy restructuring, has many of the same problems, but possibly without the benefit of using bankruptcy laws as a fallback in the negotiation.

One way to limit the potential problems of down-round financing is to avoid complex deal structures in early financing rounds. An early-round investor who does not have dilution protection will necessarily invest at a lower valuation than if the investor's claim is enhanced with a variety of sweeteners. The low initial valuation does two things. First, it reduces the probability that the next round will be a down round. Second, with straight equity, the investor has less ability to impede negotiation of the next round.

Going Private as a Solution to Declining Market Valuations

During the late 1990s, many early-stage high-technology ventures went public. For some of them, the capital raised in the IPO was not enough to finance the venture through to the point of operating cash-flow sufficiency. Rather, such companies depended on the prospect of raising additional equity in a subsequent equity offering. When, after April 2000, the market valuations of these ventures declined dramatically, their abilities to raise additional capital via seasoned offering were lost. It became necessary for these public companies, which had potential but were short of cash, to restructure in order to raise the additional financing. However, public stockholders cannot generally negotiate effectively with creditors and others with claims of company assets. The solution selected by many was for private investors to reacquire the public shares and return the companies to private status. For that purpose, buy-out financing has been a significant focus of venture capital financing activity in recent years.

15.10 SUMMARY

Although the menu of financing sources is extensive, the alternatives that are realistically available to any new venture or small business form a much shorter list. A number of factors influence financing sources that are appropriate for a new venture or small business.

- A venture's financial need includes considerations such as urgency of the need, size of near-term need, permanency of need, and size of the cumulative financing need.
- Financial condition and stage of development relate to completeness of the management team, the value of outside advisors and consultants, the risk/reward profile of the venture, its tax status, and ability to use assets as collateral and to service debt.
- Product market and organizational considerations include the importance of rapid growth as an element of product-market strategy, the nature of relationships with suppliers, customers, and others, and costs and benefits of centralized control.
- Track record, reputation, and relationships of the venture and the entrepreneur bear on the basis for making investments in the venture and on conditions for investing.
- Existing financing relationships affect ability to raise capital in important ways, particularly if the new investment would alter the values of existing claims.

In the chapter, we examine a number of financing alternatives from the perspective of matching the venture's needs and existing financial condition with the capabilities of investors. Although the discussion is qualitative, it fits into the context we have adhered to throughout the text of basing the choice of financing on the principle of value maximization. Debt financing, for example, may be available at a lower cost than equity financing. However, financing with debt instead of outside equity adds risk to the entrepreneur's financial claim, and the entrepreneur usually is less able to bear risk than a diversified investor.

The approach we suggest for analyzing financing choices is one that incorporates insights from previous chapters. The parties involved in a venture differ in ability to bear risk, have different information, and possess potentially conflicting incentives. Because the simulation and valuation tools from earlier chapters are designed to address these considerations, they can be used to evaluate financing alternatives.

QUESTIONS AND PROBLEMS

1. Discuss how you would expect the financing choices of the following firms to differ and explain the reasons for the differences.

    a.   An early-stage research and development venture, compared to an established venture that is generating revenue.

    b.   A venture with revenues that are growing very rapidly and must expand its working capital base to match, compared to a venture with revenues that are growing at the inflation rate.

    c.   A venture that is highly profitable and growing, compared to a venture that is growing at a similar rate but has not yet achieved profitability.

    d.   A venture that is organized as a C corporation, compared to one that is organized as an S corporation.

    e.   A venture that is being undertaken by an entrepreneur who has a significant track record of new venture successes, compared to a venture that is being undertaken by an entrepreneur with no previous new venture experience.

    f.   A venture that requires large investment in tangible assets, compared to one whose assets are all intangible.

2.   What are the advantages and disadvantages of the following financing/organizational choices?
    a.   A strategic partner.
    b.   Factoring of accounts receivable.
    c.   Venture capital.
    d.   Franchising.
    e.   Postponing payment of accounts payable.
    f.   A secured loan.
    g.   Licensing.
    h.   Direct public offering.
    i.   Initial public offering.
    j.   Venture leasing

3.   One advantage of franchising is that standards for product quality and service are set centrally by the franchiser. In the case of fast-food franchising, some standards are left for the individual franchisee to set. Predict the types of decisions that are left to the individual franchisee and those that are determined by the franchiser.

4.   How do the following considerations affect the choice of financing?
    a.   Expected growth is high, but growth prospects are highly uncertain.
    b.   Venture reputation is important to customers and suppliers.
    c.   Employees needed by the venture are not highly skilled or particularly specialized.
    d.   The venture's financing needs are volatile and unpredictable.

5.   Use the following assumptions to develop a simulation model of a venture for a three-year period.

    a.   First month sales revenue is $2 million. Sales revenue in any quarter after the first is expected to grow by 5 percent over the previous month. The actual growth rate is uncertain and is equally likely to be –10 percent, 5 percent, or 20 percent.

    b.   Cost of goods sold in the first period is $2.5 million. Cost of goods sold in each period is expected to be $1.5 million plus 50 percent of sales. The actual variable cost percentage is uncertain. In any period, it is equally likely to be 50 percent, 55 percent, or 60 percent.

    c.   Beginning inventory is $2 million. Inventory is reduced each period by the variable portion of cost of goods sold and is increased each period by purchases. The venture purchases enough inventory each period so that ending inventory is equal to 200 percent of the variable cost for the month that is just completed.

d. Inventory is paid for when purchased, so the venture's accounts payable balance is zero.

e. The company sells on terms of net 30, and all customers pay according to terms. Thus, sales in the month adds to the balance of accounts receivable, and payments are received for sales from the previous month. The venture has a beginning balance of accounts receivable of $1.8 million.

f. The venture requires fixed assets equal to at least three times monthly sales in the month just completed. Assume that capital replacement and depreciation are offsetting so that the venture must provide only enough cash to cover the increase in fixed assets.

g. The beginning cash balance is $0, and the venture must use whatever financing sources it chooses in order to maintain at least a balance of zero. If the venture runs out of cash, it is shut down and has a liquidation value of zero. (Any assets would be used to pay off the debt balance.)

h. The venture is expected to be harvested at the end of year 3, for a multiple of 1.2 times annualized sales in the last month, plus any cash balance and less any outstanding loans.

i. The venture has a line of credit of up to $30 million. Actual borrowing would bear interest at the rate of 1 percent per month on the prior month's balance. The loan can be drawn on whenever funds are needed and paid down whenever cash is available.

Run the simulation with lines of credit of $20, $25, and $30 million. Determine the failure probability in each case and expected harvest cash flows. Value the harvest cash flows to a well-diversified investor and an entrepreneur with $2 million invested in the market. The annual risk-free rate is 4 percent, the annual market rate is 10 percent, market standard deviation is 20 percent (annualized), and correlation with the market is 0.2.

6. Reconsider the venture in problem 5. In addition to the line of credit, the venture can finance its operations by postponing payment for inventory purchases for one month. Doing so would cause it to forego a prompt payment discount of 2 percent. Modify the simulation model from problem 5 and simulate and value the venture.

a. As a conservative way to assess whether deferring payments for inventory purchases would be valuable, suppose the venture postpones all payments and uses the line of credit for any other cash needs.

b. Discuss how you expect your results would change if the venture were to use the line of credit first, and defer payment for inventory only if the line of credit is not sufficient to cover needs.

7. Reconsider the venture in problem 5. Suppose, as an alternative to the $30 million line of credit, the venture can arrange a term loan for a portion of the total. The term loan is non-amortizing and bears interest at the rate of .5 percent per month. To evaluate whether the venture would benefit by financing part of its cash needs with the term loan, consider the following possibilities:

a. a $3 million term loan and $27 million line of credit,

b. a $6 million term loan and $24 million line of credit,

c. a $9 million term loan and $12 million line of credit.

Model the venture with the term loan and line of credit arrangements and simulate the harvest cash flows. Assume that the term loan would be repaid from the harvest proceeds. What do you conclude about the relative cost and failure probabilities of the different alternatives?

NOTES

1. The SBA has taken recent steps to expedite certain kinds of loan approvals. Its LowDoc loan program promises a response within two weeks and streamlines the application process. It is intended as a small loan program, with $100,000 as the maximum loan. Approval is based more on experience with the borrower, credit history, and collateral than on the perceived merits of the venture. FA$TRAK is another SBA program with streamlined documentation, but only 50 percent of the loan is guaranteed. It, too, is limited to loans of $100,000 or less.

2. Some states have established economic development investment programs where assets of the state retirement fund are to be used to fund "economic development" investments in new and ongoing ventures. Although ventures submit funding requests, economic development investments are rare. Although retirement systems are empowered by legislatures to make such investments, they often lack the infrastructure to efficiently process requests and to monitor investments. The example illustrates why entrepreneurs often are frustrated when submitting proposals to agencies that do not have clear objectives and criteria for approving proposals.

3. Bhide (1992) is a practical discussion of bootstrapping and start-up ventures.

4. Based on a sample of recent offerings, Barry and Turki (1998) report that the average offering size of non-biotechnology development-stage company IPOs was $9.8 million and that average firm age was 3.5 years. For development-stage biotechnology ventures, the average offering was $11.7 million and average firm age was 5.6 years. For both groups, the IPOs were substantially underpriced compared to immediate aftermarket value. Non-biotechnology firms were underpriced by 27.1 percent, and the biotechnology firms by 18.6 percent.

5. Bergemann and Hege (1998) consider use of time-varying share contracts between a venture capitalist and an entrepreneur, where the entrepreneur's shares effectively include an option. Their model explains the adoption of convertible securities in venture capital financing.

6. In addition to the SBA, the Farmers Home Administration, the Department of Commerce, the Department of Energy, the Department of Housing and Urban Development, and the Department of the Interior all offer loans or loan-guarantee programs that may be appropriate sources of early-stage financing. Other state and federal government financing sources include State Business and Industrial Development Corporations, the Export-Import Bank, and the Small Business Innovation Research Program.

7. Small Business Investment Companies and Minority Enterprise Small Business Investment Companies generally invest their own money, along with borrowed funds covered by SBA loan guarantees. Small Business Development Companies are consortial arrangements that raise funds from sources that promote economic development. Investments that can be expected to generate steady streams of cash flow are more appropriate for these sources.

8. Concerning the relation between debt financing and moral hazard, see Townsend (1979), Diamond (1984), and Nachman and Noe (1994).

9. Berlin and Mester (1993) find that the use of covenants increases with moral hazard.

10. Fenn, Liang, and Prowse (1997) report that about 30 percent of initial public offerings are venture capital backed.

11. See Frear et al., 1994(a) and 1994(b) and Sohl (1999).

12. Wetzel (1994) describes business angels who are active investors. Barry (1994) notes that many are high-net-worth individuals looking for passive investments with high potential returns. A field study by Freear et al. (1994) documents the heterogeneity of involvement by business

angel investors. Prowse (1998) notes that business angels often work in groups. Current examples are the Breakfast Club in the Boston area and the Band of Angels in Silicon Valley. In our experience, these groups consist of active and passive investors, where the passive investors rely on active investors to identify prospects and oversee the investments. Active investors may value the additional financing capacity created by passive investor participation.

13. Stiglitz and Weiss (1981) note that for a given level of collateral, the interest rate quoted by a lender gives rise to adverse selection. Only those borrowers who regard the interest rate as advantageous will apply for loans. Bester (1985), Chan and Kanatas (1985), and Besanko and Thakor (1987) turn this principle around. They note that, by offering more collateral, a borrower can signal intent to repay.

14. For analysis of secured debt and moral hazard, see Boot and Thakor (1994) and Stulz and Johnson (1985).

15. Avery, Bostic, and Samolyk (1998) find evidence that personal guarantees are more important to small-business financing than is collateral.

16. See Gorton and Kahn (2000).

17. Cornelli and Yosha (2003) study the role of convertible securities in new ventures with staged financing. They suggest that with straight debt, the entrepreneur may have an incentive to "window dress" to attract the next round of financing. Financing with convertible securities reduces the entrepreneur's incentive to engage in such actions because the lender shares in equity returns. In addition, financing with convertible securities compels the lender to weigh the benefits of reducing risk of repayment against the opportunity loss of the equity return.

18. Kwan and Carleton (1993) report that in a sample of privately placed loans by corporations, 47 percent were renegotiated. In fact, one reason for placing a large loan privately is that private placement adds the flexibility of being able to renegotiate covenants.

19. Hart and Moore (1998) analyze short-term loans as equivalent to a long-term loan but with a particularly severe form of covenant in the form of a call. The "covenant" allows the lender to evaluate the loan at the end of the short term (say, every month) and decide whether to keep providing financing. In effect, the short-term loan is callable for any reason at the end of each month. They argue that long-term financing has the distinct advantage of finessing situations in which lender reaction to bad news threatens the survival of a venture that otherwise is worth pursuing. Also see Ravid (1996). However, even though new ventures would like the freedom that comes with longer-term loans, such terms typically are not available. For example, Titman and Wessels (1988) find that small firms are likely to rely on short-term lending.

20. See Hellmann (2002) concerning the effects of conflicts of interest arising in corporate venturing. He suggests that venture capital firms are less prone to such risks.

21. See Sathe (1989); see also Fast and Pratt (1989), who reach a similar conclusion.

22. Zahra (1995) finds that entrepreneurial activity increases following management LBOs. The finding is consistent with the view that corporate organizational structures and practices discourage entrepreneurship. However, the finding also suggests that managers may pursue LBOs to capture more of the gains from the entrepreneurial efforts they expect to pursue.

23. Shane (1996) reports that if decision and ownership rights can be specified clearly, franchise operations are relatively easy to expand internationally.

24. Based on a study of franchise contracts, LaFontaine (1993) concludes that the contracts are designed to align the incentives of the parties. See also Spinelli and Birley (1996).

25. Norton (1988) finds that franchising arises in organizations where separation of management from risk-bearing is inefficient. Michael (1996) describes franchising as a way of allocating decision rights. He notes that the choice of franchising depends on whether a good balance can be achieved between the rights retained by the franchiser and the rights conveyed to franchisees.

26. Brickley and Dark (1987) study organizations that have both franchise and company-owned outlets, and find that franchising is more likely where centralized monitoring and control are difficult.

27. See Bates (1998) and LaFontaine and Shaw (1998).

28. Leblebici and Shalley (1996).

29. See Timmons (1999) for further elaboration of the causes of new venture failure.

30. For discussion of benefits and choices related to bankruptcy for debtors, see Gershun (1984).

31. See Chung and Smith (1987) and Titman and Wessels (1988).

32. Wruck (1990) notes that financial distress can have both costs and benefits. Among the benefits, it creates an opportunity to make changes to management and governance. To an extent, the costs of distress, such as investors jockeying for position, can be avoided by relying on strip financing, where outside investors hold equity claims. Financial structures that minimize default risk are, however, not usually value-maximizing. Among other factors, avoiding debt financing deprives the venture of the tax deductibility of interest payments.

33. See Diamond (1989).

34. Ang (1992) contends that for ventures without track records, the reputation of the entrepreneur gains importance. Even if the venture is likely to fail, an entrepreneur who wants to raise funds for ventures in the future may try to avoid damage to personal reputation.

35. See Cole (1998) and also Berger and Udell (1995).

36. See Petersen and Rajan (1994).

37. Berger and Udell (1995).

REFERENCES AND ADDITIONAL READING

ANG, JAMES S. "On the Theory of Finance for Privately Held Firms." *Journal of Small Business Finance* 1 (1992): 185–203.

AVERY, ROBERT B., RAPHAEL W. BOSTIC, AND KATHERINE A. SAMOLYK. "The Role of Personal Wealth in Small Business Finance." *Journal of Banking and Finance* 22 (1998): 1019–1061.

BARRY, CHRISTOPHER B. "New Directions in Research on Venture Capital Finance." *Financial Management* 23 (1994): 3–15.

BARRY, CHRISTOPHER B., AND L. ADEL TURKI. "Initial Public Offerings by Development Stage Companies." *Journal of Small and Emerging Business Law* 2 (1998).

BATES, TIMOTHY. "Survival Patterns among Newcomers to Franchising." *Journal of Business Venturing* 13 (1998): 113–130.

BERGEMANN, DIRK AND ULRICH HEGE. "Venture Capital Financing, Moral Hazard, and Learning." *Journal of Banking and Finance* 22 (1998): 703–735.

BERGER, A. N., AND G. F. UDELL. "The Economics of Small Business Finance: The Role of Private Equity and Debt Markets in the Financial Growth Cycle." *Journal of Banking and Finance* 22 (1998).

BERGER, A. N., AND G. F. UDELL. "Relationship Lending and Lines of Credit in Small Firm Finance." *Journal of Business* 68 (1995): 351–382.

BERLIN, M., AND L. J. MESTER. "Debt Covenants and Renegotiation." *Journal of Financial Intermediation* 2 (1993): 95–133.

Besanko, D., and Anjan Thakor. "Competitive Equilibrium in the Credit Market under Asymmetric Information." *Journal of Economic Theory* 42 (1987): 167–182.

Bester, Helmut. "Screening v. Rationing in Credit Markets with Imperfect Information." *American Economic Review* 75 (September 1985): 850–855.

Bhide, Amar. "Bootstrap Finance: The Art of Start-Ups." *Harvard Business Review* (November–December 1992): 109–117.

Biasis, B., and C. Gollier. "Trade Credit and Credit Rationing." *Review of Financial Studies* 10 (1997): 903–937.

Boot, A. W. A., and Anjan V. Thakor. "Moral Hazard and Secured Lending in an Infinitely Repeated Credit Market Game." *International Economic Review* 35 (1994): 899–920.

Brickley, James A., and Frederick H. Dark. "The Choice of Organizational Form: The Case of Franchising." *Journal of Financial Economics* 18 (1987): 401–420.

Chan, Yuk-Shee, and G. Kanatas. "Asymmetric Valuation and the Role of Collateral in Loan Agreements." *Journal of Money Credit and Banking* 17 (1985): 85–95.

Chung, Kwang S., and Richard L. Smith. "Product Quality, Nonsalvageable Capital Investment and the Cost of Financial Leverage." In *Modern Finance and Industrial Economics: Papers in Honor of J. Fred Weston. Edited by Thomas E. Copeland.* New York: Blackwell, 1987, pp. 146–167.

Cole, Rebel A. "The Importance of Relationships to the Availability of Credit." *Journal of Banking and Finance* 22 (1998): 959–977.

Cole, Rebel A. and John D. Wolken. "Financial Services Used by Small Businesses: Evidence from the 1993 National Survey of Small Business Finance." www.sba.gov.

Cornelli, Francesca, and Oved Yosha. "Stage Financing and the Role of Convertible Debt." *Review of Economic Studies* forthcoming.

Diamond, Douglas W. "Financial Intermediation and Delegated Monitoring." *Review of Economic Studies* 51 (1984): 393–414.

Diamond, Douglas W. "Reputation Acquisition in Debt Markets." *Journal of Political Economy* 97 (1989): 828–862.

Fast, Norman D., and Stanley E. Pratt. "Individual Entrepreneurship and the Large Corporation." *Journal of Business Venturing* (1989): 443–450.

Fenn, G. W., N. Liang, and Stephen Prowse. "The Private Equity Market: An Overview." *Financial Markets, Institutions, and Instruments* 6 (1997): 1–106.

Freear, John, Jeffrey Sohl, and William Wetzel, Jr. "Angels and Non-Angels: Are There Differences?" *Journal of Business Venturing* 8 (1994a): 109–123.

Freear, John, Jeffrey Sohl, and William Wetzel, Jr. "The Private Investor Market for Venture Capital." *The Financier* 1 (1994b): 7–15.

Freear, John, and William E. Wetzel, Jr. "Who Bankrolls High-Tech Entrepreneurs?" *Journal of Business Venturing* 5 (1990): 77–89.

Gershun, Martha. "Bankruptcy: A Debtor's Perspective." Harvard Business School Note, No. 9-384-119, 1984.

Gorton, Gary, and Jeffrey Kahn. "The Design of Bank Loan Contracts, Collateral, and Renegotiation." *Review of Financial Studies* 13 (2000): 331–364.

Hart, Oliver, and J. Moore. "Default and Renegotiation: A Dynamic Model of Debt." *Quarterly Journal of Economics* 113 (1998): 12–41.

Hellmann, Thomas. "A Theory of Strategic Venture Investing." *Journal of Financial Economics* 64 (2002): 285–314.

Kwan, Simon H., and Willard T. Carleton. "The Structure and Price of Private Placement Corporate Loans." University of Arizona Working Paper, 1993.

LaFontaine, Francine. "Agency Theory and Franchising: Some Empirical Results." *RAND Journal of Economics* 23 (l992): 263–283.

LaFontaine, Francine. "Contractual Arrangements as Signaling Devices: Evidence from Franchising." *Journal of Law, Economics, and Organization* 9 (1993): 256–289.

LaFontaine, Francine, and Kathryn L. Shaw. "Franchising Growth and Franchisor Entry and Exit in the U.S. Market: Myth and Reality." *Journal of Business Venturing* 13 (1993): 95–112.

Leblebici, Huseyin, and Christina E. Shalley. "The Organization of Relational Contracts: The Allocation of Rights in Franchising." *Journal of Business Venturing* 11 (1996): 403–418.

Lerner, Joshua. "Note on the Venture Leasing Industry." Harvard Business School Note No. 9-294-069, Revised 1994.

Mian, Shehzad, and Clifford W. Smith. "Accounts Receivable Management Policy: Theory and Evidence." *Journal of Finance* 47 (1992): 169–200.

Michael, Steven C. "To Franchise or Not to Franchise: An Analysis of Decision Rights and Organizational Form Shares." *Journal of Business Venturing* 11 (1996): 59–72.

Nachman, David C., and Thomas H. Noe. "Optimal Design of Securities under Asymmetric Information." *Review of Financial Studies* 7 (1994): 1–44.

Ng, Chee K., Janet Kiholm Smith, and Richard L. Smith. "Evidence on the Determinants of Credit Terms Used in Interfirm Trade." *Journal of Finance* 54 (June 1999): 1109–1129.

Norton, Seth. "An Empirical Look at Franchising as an Organizational Form." *Journal of Business* 61 (1988): 197–218.

Petersen, Mitchell A., and Raghuram G. Rajan. "Trade Credit: Theories and Evidence." *Review of Financial Studies* 10 (1997): 661–691.

Petersen, Mitchell A., and Raghuram G. Rajan. "The Benefits of Lending Relationships: Evidence from Small Business Data." *Journal of Finance* 49 (1994): 3–37.

Prowse, Stephen. "Angel Investors and the Market for Angel Investments." *Journal of Banking and Finance* 22 (1998): 785–792.

Ravid, S. Abraham. "Debt Maturity—A Survey." *Financial Markets, Institutions and Instruments* 5, No. 3 (1996): 1–68.

Roberts, Michael J. "Alternative Sources of Financing." Harvard Business School Note No. 9-384-187, 1984.

Sathe, Vijay. "Fostering Entrepreneurship in the Large, Diversified Firm." *Organizational Dynamics* (1989): 20–32.

Shane, Scott A. "Why Franchise Companies Expand Overseas." *Journal of Business Venturing* 11 (1996): 73–88.

Smith, Janet Kiholm. "Trade Credit and Informational Asymmetries." *Journal of Finance* 42 (1987): 863–872.

Smith, Janet Kiholm, and Christjahn Schnucker. "An Empirical Examination of Organizational Structure: The Economics of the Factoring Decision." *Journal of Corporate Finance* 1 (1994): 119–138.

Sohl, Jeffrey. "The Early Stage Equity Market in the USA." *Venture Capital* 1 (1999): 101–120.

Spinelli, Steve, and Sue Birley. "Toward a Theory of Conflict in the Franchise System," *Journal of Business Venturing* 11 (1996): 329–342.

Stevenson, Howard H. "Securities Law and Private Financing." Harvard Business School Note, No. 9-384-164, 1998.

Stiglitz, Joseph, and Andrew Weiss. "Credit Rationing in Markets with Imperfect Information." *American Economic Review* 71 (June 1981): 393–410.

Stulz, Rene, and H. Johnson. "An Analysis of Secured Debt." *Journal of Financial Economics* 14 (1985): 501–522.

Timmons, Jeffrey A. *New Venture Creation.* 5th ed. Homewood, IL: Richard D. Irwin, 1999.

Titman, Sheridan, and Roberto Wessels. "The Determinants of Capital Structure Choice." *Journal of Finance* 43 (1988): 1–20.

TOWNSEND, R. "Optimal Contracts and Competitive Markets with Costly State Verification." *Journal of Economic Theory* 21 (1979): 265–293

VAN OSNABRUGGE, MARC AND ROBERT J. ROBINSON. *Angel Investing*. San Francisco: Josey Bass, 2000.

WETZEL, WILLIAM E. "Venture Capital." In *Portable MBA in Entrepreneurship*. Edited by W. D. Bygrave. New York: John Wiley & Sons, 1994, pp. 172–194.

WRUCK, KAREN HOPPER. "Financial Distress, Reorganization, and Organizational Efficiency." *Journal of Financial Economics* 37 (1990): 419–444.

ZAHRA, SHAKER A. "Corporate Entrepreneurship and Financial Performance: The Case of Management Leveraged Buyouts." *Journal of Business Venturing* 10 (1995): 225–247.

CHAPTER

16

Harvesting

There are few ways in which a man can be more innocently employed than in getting money.
(Samuel Johnson)

Learning Objectives

After reading this chapter, you should be able to:

- Understand how early-stage investors can harvest their investments by going public.

- Describe the role of the investment banker in the initial public offering process, including the due-diligence, certification, and marketing functions of the underwriter.

- Explain how an underwriter values a new issue and how the valuation evolves as the time of the offering approaches.

- Describe the ways in which private acquisition transactions can be structured and identify some of the factors that affect the choice of structure.

- Understand when and why an entrepreneur might decide to undertake a management buy-out of outside investors.

- Understand how an ESOP creates liquidity for the owner of a business that is not public and explain how a leveraged ESOP works.

- Describe how roll-up IPOs enable small companies to go public.

- Identify the main factors that affect the choice of harvesting alternatives.

Harvesting is the final stage of the entrepreneurial investment process. It also is a critical component of initial investment decisions. Investors evaluate opportunities based, in part, on the expectation of a liquidity event that will enable them to realize a return and allow them to shift attention to other projects. To estimate value, investors must make assumptions about how and when the investment will be harvested and about the return they will realize.

Harvesting also is of direct importance to entrepreneurs, but the issues may be different. Some entrepreneurs are like investors in their desire to harvest and move on to other endeavors.

Others view the venture as a lifetime commitment. Both types should be cognizant of earning a return that is sufficient to compensate for the opportunity cost of investing capital and effort in other ways.

In this chapter, we begin to explore issues related to harvesting by identifying and examining harvesting alternatives. As with financing, there is a menu of harvesting alternatives. The financing and harvesting menus include some of the same possibilities. However, the harvesting alternatives realistically available to any given venture at any given time are limited. Accordingly, much of the chapter concerns the factors that bear on the decision of how and when to harvest.

Going public and private sale of the venture to another firm (i.e., acquisition) are the harvesting alternatives that normally receive the most attention in business plans and elsewhere. However, other important alternatives include management buy-out of outside investors, sale of the business to employees or other members of the team, and continuing to operate the venture and collect the ongoing free cash flow of the enterprise. We begin by surveying the alternatives, and conclude by examining the factors that affect the harvesting decision.

16.1 GOING PUBLIC

When a venture goes public, an ongoing market is created for its common stock. An initial public offering usually is a primary market transaction. The issuing firm raises capital by selling new shares to public market investors. An IPO is really only the first step in the process of harvesting by going public. By placing freely tradable shares in the hands of investors, the IPO initiates the public market for the shares and allows the "market" to establish a value of the equity. The public market is predominantly a "secondary market." A secondary market transaction is one where market participants transact with each other, based on their different perceptions about share value. Thus, secondary transactions transfer ownership between investors. They do not generate any new funds for the firm that originally issued the shares.

A venture that already has gone public can raise additional capital by issuing new shares in a subsequent primary market offering. The term for such an offering is a "seasoned offering," meaning that shares of the issuer already have gone through a seasoning period of trading in the market. Although the terms sometimes are used interchangeably, a seasoned offering is not the same thing as a "secondary offering," unless the shares that are sold in the offering are not newly issued. In a secondary offering, the shares that are sold were issued previously by the firm and are being resold in a formal pubic offering process. Sellers may include venture capitalists and other early-stage investors, the entrepreneur, and others who acquired shares from the firm.

Market value, or "market capitalization," is the share price (or total equity value) that equates secondary market demand with secondary market supply. Except for primary market transactions (sales of newly issued shares by the issuing firm) and first-time public sales of shares by entrepreneurs and others who invested before the IPO, secondary market supply is fixed. With supply fixed, fluctuations in market value result from changes in demand.

Equity investors can harvest their investments in public companies in four ways. First, existing investors, including the entrepreneur, can harvest a portion of their investment by selling some of the shares they own in the IPO.[1] Second, once the public market has been established, the investors can sell small amounts of shares from time to time directly into the public market.[2] Third, they can sell larger quantities in a secondary public offering after the IPO. Fourth, they can use the public market value to benchmark the price and make a private sale to another investor.[3]

The Initial Public Offering Process[4]

Selecting the Underwriter   The management team that is considering a public offering normally begins by selecting an investment banker or team of investment bankers to underwrite the offering. The underwriter is responsible for advising the issuer, distributing the shares, and "underwriting" the risk of market price fluctuations during the offering. A broader notion of the term "underwriting" is that the underwriter also makes explicit and implicit representations about share value.[5]

Different investment bankers have different underwriting capabilities and have different technologies for carrying out the offerings. Some, for example, are oriented to institutional brokerage clients, whereas others have a retail orientation. That focus affects the kinds of investors with whom the underwriter is likely to place the stock.[6] Several other features may affect the issuer's choice of underwriter: If the issue is to be large, is the underwriter capable of organizing the underwriting syndicate needed to complete a large offering quickly? If promotion of the firm's "story" is important, how active and respected is the investment banker's research staff, and will the investment banker agree to begin research coverage of the stock after the IPO? If secondary market liquidity is important, how strong is the market-making operation of the investment banker, and will the investment banker agree to maintain an active market in the stock? Some investment bankers have established reputations and expertise for handling offerings in particular industries. Some, with more limited infrastructures have more limited capabilities but may be able to underwrite small issues at lower cost.

The choice of investment banker involves matching underwriter capabilities with the issuer's specific interests and objectives. In some cases, one or more investment banker may already have identified the venture as a prospect for public offering and may have initiated a relationship. Sometimes venture capital investors draw upon their relationships with investment bankers as prospective underwriters for the offering. The investment banker may even have a venture capital operation that has invested in the venture at an earlier stage.[7]

An investment banker who is being considered to underwrite an IPO usually undertakes a preliminary valuation of the company.[8] It might seem that a good way to select the underwriter would be to choose the investment banker who arrives at the highest preliminary valuation. However, preliminary valuations are notoriously inaccurate as predictors of final offering prices. An investment banker who competes to underwrite an offering by suggesting a high valuation and who is selected by the issuer has several opportunities to revise the valuation as preparation for the offering goes forward. Consequently, the initial selection of an underwriter usually depends more on qualitative considerations related to "fit" than on the preliminary valuation.

It might also seem that an issuer could use competitive bidding to select the underwriter. That is, the issuer could select the investment banker who bid the lowest fee for underwriting the issue. However, current practice is for the issuer to negotiate IPO fees and other terms bilaterally with the prospective underwriter. Competitive bidding is used in the U.S. primarily for some low-risk debt offerings of regulated firms.[9] However, competitive bidding is not an effective way to select the underwriter of an equity IPO. Providing multiple underwriters with enough information to enable them to bid effectively is not practical, and new information during the process of preparing to market the offering makes negotiation of specific terms infeasible. This is less true of low-risk debt issues, where negotiating the underwriting spread may be all that is needed.[10]

Due Diligence and Issue Pricing   An investment banker who is selected to underwrite an IPO is an intermediary between the issuer and public market investors. The issuer is a well-informed seller of shares. As we discussed in Chapter 12, such a seller can be motivated by the desire to the raise capital for investment opportunities or by a perception that the public market will overvalue the shares. In addition, the seller may want to establish a public market value for the venture. The value can be used as a basis for future transactions, or the public market can enable existing investors to harvest their investments. Public market investors, by comparison, are uninformed about the issuer. They run the risk of being exploited by issuers who expect that the market will overvalue the shares.

Serving as intermediary in transactions between informed issuers and uninformed investors is a difficult challenge. Investors, who are uninformed and concerned about paying too much for the shares, are likely to be conservative in their valuations. Their concern about paying too much discourages prospective issuers. One of the underwriter's responsibilities is to limit the effect of the information disparity. In part, the underwriter addresses the challenge by preparing a prospectus that describes some of the venture's operating history, the market, the management team, and how the proceeds of the offering are to be used. The underwriter verifies the information in the prospectus through an elaborate due-diligence process.

The objective of due diligence is to help ensure that the underwriter discovers any material adverse information about the issuer.[11] The underwriter, however, cannot disclose all of the relevant information in the prospectus. For example, some information is strategically sensitive. Even if the underwriter does not disclose some of the information in a way that it can be processed by investors, the information must factor into the underwriter's decision about pricing the issue. As a result, due diligence sometimes is sufficient to discourage private firms with negative information from issuing shares via public offering. Such firms, if they need equity capital, are more likely to negotiate private transactions.

In addition to publishing a prospectus, the other way the underwriter addresses the information problem between the issuer and public market investors is by establishing the offering price. As a practical matter, information contained in the IPO prospectus is not sufficient to enable investors to arrive at an accurate valuation. Some relevant information is too commercially sensitive to publish. In addition, issuers and underwriters traditionally refrain from making forecasts during the offering process.[12] Based on information acquired in due diligence, the underwriter (in consultation with the issuer) establishes a price for the offering.[13]

The actual process of pricing an issue is more protracted. First, as illustrated in Figure 16-1, the underwriter establishes a "filing range," that is, a range of prices at which the offering is likely to be made. The underwriter publishes the filing range and other information in a preliminary prospectus. At that point, the underwriter and the issuer normally begin a series

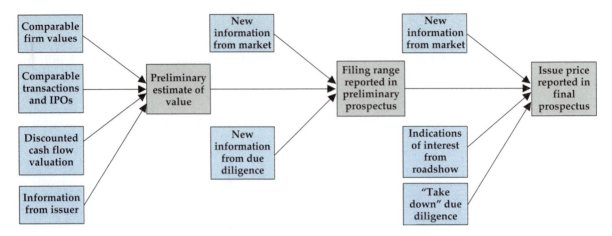

Figure 16-1   The IPO issue pricing process for a firm-commitment underwriting

As part of the underwriter selection process, investment bankers generate preliminary estimates of value. The investment banker who is retained to underwrite the issue prepares a preliminary prospectus that includes a filing range. The filing range is based on the information used in the preliminary valuation but is updated to reflect developments in the market and results of due diligence. The final issue price is a further revision, based on new market information, indications of interest from the roadshow, and a final round of take-down due diligence.

of "roadshow" presentations to brokers and institutional investors. During the roadshow, the underwriter collects information on demand for the shares, in the form of nonbinding indications of interest from prospective investors. The final issue price is determined in light of information from the due-diligence process, indications of interest, and new information that arises between the time of the preliminary prospectus and the final offering.[14]

The offering price represents an opinion about the value of the issue, compared to the contemporaneous market values of other companies. Even though information in the prospectus is incomplete, many investors rely on the issue price as a conservative estimate of what the shares are worth. On average, their reliance is justified, because, as documented in Chapter 14, the immediate after-market price of most IPOs in the U.S. is above the issue price.[15]

Underwriter and Venture Capitalist Certification and Issue Pricing   Why are investors able to rely on the offering price of an issue as a representation of value? The financial economics literature suggests the answer is that one function of the underwriter is to certify the offer price.[16] In effect, an underwriter with an established reputation uses the reputation to guarantee that the offer price is consistent with inside information the underwriter reasonably could be expected to discover through due diligence, and that it is consistent with prevailing market values. The underwriter's fee includes an (implicit) premium for using the underwriter's reputation to certify the issue price. If the issue is overpriced, the underwriter's reputation is harmed, and its ability to charge a premium for future offerings is reduced.[17]

A similar argument is that if an issue is overpriced the underwriter may bear the cost of defending itself (including settlements and damage awards) in litigation brought by investors who purchased shares in the IPO.[18] This is a version of the certification hypothesis, as underwriters must charge premiums to offset the expected cost of litigation.[19]

Underwriter Selection, Issue Pricing, and Distribution

In one recent IPO, the issuer entertained proposals from no less than 15 leading investment bankers over a three-month period, each of whom prepared a preliminary estimate of value. The offering prices inferred from those presentations ranged from $12 per share to $38 per share. At the end of the process, a team of two investment bankers was selected as co-lead underwriters. One of the two had indicated a preliminary valuation of $31 to $36 per share. The other had indicated $16 to $24. Approximately two months later, a preliminary prospectus was circulated, indicating a filing range of $20 to $23. In the interim, the overall market had declined somewhat, and the overall level of IPO activity had fallen. During the roadshow, it became apparent that demand for the shares was not as high as had been hoped. The IPO took place about one month after the preliminary prospectus was circulated. The shares were offered at $20, the bottom of the filing range, and the total size of the offering was reduced in response to information from the roadshow. Immediately following the IPO, the closing price in the after-market was $21, up 5 percent from the issue price. Subsequently, the market for the shares generally languished, with the stock price remaining below the issue price.

The recent IPO of eToys is a counter example (see the box on eToys in Chapter 15). Goldman Sachs was selected as lead underwriter. The preliminary prospectus from spring of 1999 indicated a filing range of $10 to $12 per share. However, in response to indications of strong demand for the shares and overall gains for Internet stocks, the offering was priced at $20, almost double the value indicated by the filing range. The stock closed on the first day of trading, at $80 per share, a gain of 300 percent. The company is now bankrupt. Its shares have a market value of virtually zero, and the stakeholders have filed a lawsuit against Goldman Sachs for allegedly having underpriced the offering for its own purposes.

Venture capital firms also appear to contribute to the certification and monitoring of companies that go public. Venture capitalists and other early investors usually are precluded from selling their positions in or shortly after the IPO. "Lock-up" agreements with the underwriter typically prevent selling for 180 days. Venture capital investors normally remain with their portfolio companies for at least one year after the companies go public.[20] During the period while the venture capitalist is invested, it has an incentive to continue to monitor the portfolio company. Thus, the venture capitalist can provide an important monitoring function that works to the benefit of public market investors. In addition, there is evidence that, in the United States, companies with venture capital backing are less underpriced than other companies.[21] The finding suggests that venture capital firms contribute to certification of value, enabling firms to issue shares at prices that are closer to their market values.

The Cost of Initial Public Offerings   Going public is an expensive process. A venture that undertakes an IPO incurs several costs associated with issuing. These costs include the fee charged by the underwriter, the out-of-pocket costs of the issuer, and the effective cost of underpricing. Historically in the United States, underpricing has averaged about 16 percent of gross issue proceeds.[22] Underpricing tends to be greater for smaller and riskier issues. Many high-tech IPOs in the late 1990s were underpriced to a much greater extent.[23] In Chapter 15, we presented information on typical out-of-pocket costs and underwriter fees. The evidence suggests that those costs range from 6 to about 17 percent of gross proceeds and that the percentage is inversely related to issue size. Based on the difference between net proceeds and first after-market closing price, evidence suggests that a $20 million IPO would be expected to cost the issuer (including underpricing) about 25 percent of after-market value, or about $6 million.

Why are IPOs so expensive, and why do both underwriter fees and underpricing tend to be larger percentages of proceeds for smaller issues? One reason is that there are significant fixed costs associated with underwriting a new issue. Much of the cost of preparing the prospectus, for example, is fixed. The presence of fixed costs contributes to the observed negative relationship between issue size and underwriter fee percentage. Furthermore, the costs of due diligence depend on how fully the issuer hopes to price the offering. The closer to expected market value the offering price is set, the more precautions the underwriter must take to discover information that could adversely affect value, and the more likely a price decline after the offering is to result in litigation.[24] Also, the more fully the offering is priced, the more direct costs the underwriter will have to incur to market the issue. For a small offering, it can be less expensive to underprice more and save some of the costs of due diligence and marketing.[25]

A related view is based on the realization that prospective investors consist of a mix of investors who are informed and uninformed about market demand for the issue.[26] If, on average, issues are priced correctly relative to their market demand after the offering, then informed investors (who have better ability to assess market value) would not participate in overvalued offerings. The result is that informed investors would buy only the undervalued shares and uninformed investors would end up getting 100 percent of overvalued shares, but a smaller fraction of undervalued shares. Thus, when issue pricing is correct on average, but too high or too low in each individual case (and recognizably so to informed investors), the result is losses for uninformed investors. These expected losses would cause the uninformed investors to withdraw from the IPO market. Suppose that it is important to keep uninformed investors in the IPO market. To assure the success of its offerings, an underwriter must set offering prices low enough, on average, so that uninformed investors end up with fair rates of return.

The winner's curse problem seems to suggest that issuers would fare better by using an auction process to sell their shares. That way, the private knowledge of informed investors could influence the offering price. However, auction processes still reward investors for concealing their private knowledge about value, do not eliminate underpricing, and diminish the ability of the market to rely on value representations by the underwriter. As an alternative to auction, underwriters can use their ability to allocate IPO shares to reward investors for revealing their private knowledge or even to encourage investors to produce information about value.[27]

Methods of Valuation and Pricing   Individual underwriters develop their own specific procedures when establishing offering prices. As a common first step, the underwriter estimates the value of the enterprise on a pre-money basis (before the IPO proceeds but reflecting the opportunities facing the venture). That valuation may be based on market values of comparable firms, the prices for other recent IPOs or other transactions of similar companies, or the discounted present value of projected future cash flows. Normally, an investment banker uses several approaches and, based on the results, makes a qualitative assessment of value. Next, to arrive at an estimate of equity market value, the underwriter deducts the value of debt financing. Equity value is divided by the existing number of shares to arrive at an estimate of market value per share. The underwriter determines the number of shares to be offered and price per share based on the estimate of existing value per share.

The Private Investor Securities Litigation Reform Act of 1995

Sometimes, the shares of a company lose significant value within a few months after an IPO. When share price quickly falls below the issue price, a shareholder lawsuit is likely to follow. Attorneys file class action lawsuits on behalf of IPO investors (and possibly investors who bought shortly after the IPO). Defendants generally include the officers and directors of the firm, the underwriter, and the accounting firm that audited the financial statements in the prospectus.

Those filing the suit usually contend that investors were misled because officers and directors failed to disclose information relevant to value, the underwriter either failed to discover or failed to disclose the information, and the accounting firm failed to adhere to generally accepted auditing standards. Defendants usually argue their separate defenses. Collectively, they usually contend that the decline in market value is due to events that occurred after the IPO, that were not reasonably foreseeable, or that are among the "risk factors" detailed in the prospectus.

The SEC took the position that, although either side could be right in individual cases, the aggregate amount of litigation was excessive. On its recommendation, the Private Investor Securities Litigation Reform Act was enacted in 1995. The Act included several provisions that were argued would lead to fewer and more legitimate lawsuits and would address other perceived problems. Among other things, the Act was intended to take some of the initiative for filing lawsuits away from zealous attorneys and to make it more difficult to use vague allegations recited in a complaint as the basis for an expensive fishing expedition. It also was suggested that the Act would make it easier for small and new investment bankers to compete for underwriting business and that reducing the risk of litigation would make it easier to attract members to boards of directors.

For the most part, discussion and debate related to the Act ignored the certification function of the underwriter and the role of litigation as a means of providing certification. Without adequate means of certification by underwriters, the Act could lead to an increase in shareholder lawsuits and to the emergence of alternative means of providing certification.

A *Wall Street Journal* article from mid-1999 provides perspective on the actual effects:

> The number of securities cases filed in federal courts seeking class-action status has risen 50.3% since 1995, to a record 266 in 1998, while the average cost to settle jumped nearly 40% last year to almost $11 million, from $7.8 million in 1997. . . . John Cavoores, president and chief executive of National Union Fire Insurance Co. . . says his company looks for "lock-up" features forbidding insiders from selling stock for half a year or more after the offering, to avoid allegations that management bailed out before releasing bad news. . . . National Union is looking more closely at whether the securities underwriter taking the company public has a successful record of IPOs or whether the offerings tend to crash and burn. . . . The irony is that the pickup in litigation follows 1995 federal legislation aimed at curbing the number of frivolous suits.*

Other factors have influenced some of the changes. IPO activity increased dramatically after 1995, market capitalizations were high compared with historical levels, and high-tech companies with very large capital needs were going public at earlier stages of development than in the past. These may be separate factors, or they may be parts of the same underlying phenomenon.

---

*"Web IPOs: Fees Soar for Liability," *Wall Street Journal,* May 19, 1999, p. C1.

Suppose an issuer hopes to raise $20 million in net proceeds. The underwriter estimates that the market value of equity is $10 per share, based on shares currently outstanding.[28] From this, the underwriter might deduct $1.50 of desired underpricing, and the underwriter fee might be estimated at 10 percent of gross proceeds. Thus, the venture would issue shares priced at $8.50 and would net $7.65 per share. Given the target of $20 million, the venture would need to issue 2.614 million shares. Using this information, the underwriter might specify a filing range of $7.50 to $9.50 per share and report the filing range in the preliminary prospectus, along with the fact that the company plans to issue about 2.614 million shares, to net $20 million. If, at the time of the offering, the market has improved, the underwriter is likely to select an offering price near the top of the range and may issue more shares, depending on how the issuer would like to respond to the change in the market.

The Cost of Harvesting by Going Public   The high percentage cost of an IPO does not translate to a high percentage cost of harvesting by going public. To see why, consider a venture that is seeking to raise $30 million via an IPO. Immediately prior to the offering, the venture's investment banker estimates the pre-money valuation to be $120 million. The offering is expected to raise the other $30 million in net proceeds, making the post-money valuation $150 million.

To assess the cost of the IPO, suppose the venture has been structured to achieve a target after-market value per share of $30.[29] This means that after the IPO, there should be 5 million shares outstanding. Consistent with normal practice, the underwriter builds in underpricing of 15 percent, compared to the estimated after-market value. Thus, the IPO is priced at $25.50 per share. In addition, the underwriter's fee is 12 percent of gross proceeds. So the issuer nets $22.44 per share. To achieve net proceeds of $30 million, the firm plans to issue 1,337,000 shares. Existing shareholders (the entrepreneur, venture capital investors, and others) retain the balance of 3,663,000 shares.

There are several ways to measure the cost of the IPO. First, total cost per share issued is $7.56. This is 29.6 percent of gross proceeds, or 25.2 percent of expected after-market value. Second, in dollars, the cost is $10.1 million. This can be computed as $7.56 per share times the number of shares issued. Alternatively, cost can be measured by recognizing that if the issue could have been done at $30, with no issue cost, the firm would only have needed to issue 1 million shares. Existing shareholders could have retained 4 million. Thus, the 337,000 fewer shares they retain, valued at $30 per share, yields total cost of $10.1 million.

Although the percentage cost of the IPO is substantial, the entire market value of the venture after the IPO is expected to be $150 million. If the $10.1 million is viewed as the cost of harvesting the pre-money value of $120 million, it amounts to 8.4 percent.[30] The percentage cost would be even lower if the venture's pre-money valuation were higher compared to the size of the offering. Therefore, do not be misled into thinking that the high percentage issue cost is the same as the percentage cost of harvesting the investment. The dollar cost is the same, but the percentage cost can be much lower. The best way to think about the cost of harvesting via going public is in dollar terms. If raising new financing is a secondary concern, it could make sense to select the offering size that is expected to minimize the dollar cost of the offering (assuming after-market value is not affected by the size of the offering).

Other Approaches to Public Offering   The public offering approach we have described sometimes is referred to as a "firm commitment" general cash offering. The term firm commitment means the underwriter commits to buy all of the shares the issuer plans to offer, at the net price in the prospectus. The underwriter's compensation is realized by reselling at a higher price. The difference between the gross and net price is the underwriter's fee.[31]

There are other ways of issuing equity. In lieu of a firm commitment, an offering can be done on a best-efforts basis. In a best-efforts offering, the investment banker acts more like an agent of the issuer and does not guarantee net proceeds. You might expect that issuers would select best-efforts offerings when they wish to raise capital but do not have specific concerns about the amount that actually is raised. However, the best-efforts approach also suggests that the issuer is concerned about achieving a high price per share and that the issuer and the underwriter may have differing views about the value of the shares.[32] By proceeding on a best-efforts basis, the underwriter is attempting to provide distribution services to the issuer but not to certify the price. The evidence on best-efforts offerings is not very positive. Generally, it appears that issuers that select the best-efforts approach could have achieved more success with a general cash offering.[33]

The term, "general cash offering" signifies that the shares are being sold to the investment community at large in exchange for cash, and not, for example, only to existing shareholders, in exchange for cash and warrants. The latter approach, generally referred to as a rights offering, is more common outside the United States and is mandatory in some countries.[34] In a rights offering, the issuer raises equity by issuing warrants to existing shareholders. The warrants are call options that enable the shareholders to purchase new shares at a fixed price for a specified period. Shareholders who do not wish to exercise the rights can sell the warrants to others. Assuming that each new share requires one warrant, we find that the effective price of a new share is the fixed exercise price of the warrant, plus the market value of the warrant. The issuing firm receives the exercise price, and existing shareholders receive the market value of the warrants. A public market for the shares is created by first allowing the warrants to trade and then allowing the shares to trade.

The strongest argument for the rights offering approach is that the issuer and underwriter do not need to predict the market price or establish an offering price. Because the effective price of newly issued shares is determined by trading in the market, existing shareholders do not lose if the exercise price of the warrants is below market. Similarly, new investors do not need to worry that the issue price of the shares is set above market value.[35]

An argument against rights offerings is that the approach limits the certification function of the underwriter to warranting the accuracy and completeness of the prospectus. Because the underwriter does not establish an issue price for the shares, information in the prospectus gains importance. However, as mentioned earlier, because of commercial sensitivity and other considerations, it is unlikely that all information relevant to value can be included in the prospectus. In the United States, issuing firms are free to select either a general cash offering or a rights offering. The fact that rights offerings are rare is evidence that, for most U.S. issuers, the issue price certification function of the underwriter contributes more to expected proceeds than concern with mispricing takes away.[36]

Harvesting in the IPO

The IPO is only the beginning of the harvesting process. Existing investors (the entrepreneur, venture capitalists, or others) do not normally sell shares during the IPO. Historical evidence suggests that lead venture capital investors, for example, sell in only about 27 percent of the IPOs in which they invest.[37] When they do sell, they sell on average only about 20 percent of their holdings.

Open IPO—A Test of Efficiency of Current Practice

Under current practice, IPOs are intentionally underpriced by 10 to 15 percent, compared to expected after-market value. The fact that the after-market price is above the issue price indicates that there is more demand for the shares at the issue price than there are shares available. Underwriters normally respond to excess demand by rationing the shares in ways that appear to favor preferred customers, such as those who are willing to buy even when an issue seems to be overpriced, those who refrain from quickly reselling (or "flipping") the shares to make a quick profit, or to those who may be sources of future investment banking business ("spinning").

There are two extreme views of the underpricing phenomenon. Underpricing may be an efficient aspect of the offering process that contributes to the certification activities of the underwriter and reduces the costs of due diligence and marketing the issue. Or it may be an unnecessarily good deal for the underwriters and their preferred customers.

The traditional system of issuing shares in an underwritten offering now is being challenged by a new mechanism, referred to as an "open IPO." W. R. Hambrecht and Company, a split-off from the investment banking firm, Hambrecht and Quist, is the originator of the open IPO process. Under this process, the IPO is carried out via direct submission of bids to the W. R. Hambrecht Internet site. Hambrecht initiates the process by making a preliminary prospectus available on the Internet. The prospectus indicates the number of shares being offered and the filing range. The auction opens when the registration statement for the issue is filed with the SEC, and it remains open until the SEC allows the offering to "go effective." This is normally a period of six to ten weeks. Bidders submit bids of the prices and quantities they are willing to buy. At the point when the offering goes effective, demand information from the bids is matched with the quantity of shares available and the market-clearing price is found. All bidders whose orders are accepted pay the market-clearing price, even if they bid a higher price. Those who bid higher have 100 percent of their order filled. Those who bid the market-clearing price may be rationed to match total supply and demand, but rationing to those bidders is proportional to their bid quantities. The process is modeled after an auction process developed by Nobel Prize-winning economist, William Vickery.

As of this writing, seven offerings have been completed. The first was Ravenswood Winery. The auction price for the IPO was determined to be $10.50, and in the subsequent month, the stock has continued to trade in the $10.50 to $11 range. It appears that the process eliminated underpricing for this issue. Ravenswood was acquired in July 2001. It remains to be seen whether the open IPO process has enabled the issuers to raise as much per share as would have been possible by the traditional approach. Whether investors can rely on the open IPO process for certification of the issue price also remains to be seen. Several years and more data will be required to answer these questions.

There are three reasons for an investor, such as a venture capital investor, to refrain from selling during the IPO of a portfolio company. First, public capital market investors are likely to perceive selling by insiders as a negative signal. If the offering is attractive, why are insiders selling? There are, of course, good reasons to sell. For example, the venture capitalist may be facing expiration of the fund.[38] A second reason for an investor to refrain from selling is that the investor expects to continue to add significant value to the venture. The investor would want to hold the shares until the ability to add value fell below what the investor could achieve by focusing on other ventures. The third reason for not selling is that shares sold in the IPO are likely to be underpriced, as discussed earlier. By waiting, the investor sometimes can obtain a higher price for the shares.

Harvesting after the IPO

Typically, even if an investor does not sell in the IPO, the investor's shares will be registered along with those of the issuing firm. Registered shares are freely tradable in the after-market and can be sold. The main limitation is that existing shareholders normally reach agreement with the underwriter that shareholders will not trade following the IPO, usually for a period of 180 days. This lock-up period serves at least two functions. First, it removes the need for an underwriter, who normally supports the market during an offering, to purchase shares that are being sold into the market at the same time by existing shareholders. Second, it allows enough time to pass so that the sellers cannot easily be accused of trading on the basis of information that should have been disclosed in the prospectus. Once the lock-up period has expired, existing shareholders are free to harvest by sale into the market.

Rule 144 Sales   Shares that are not registered also can be liquidated in the U.S. by sale into the market, but the SEC Rule 144 limits the rate at which the sale can occur. An investor who owns unregistered shares but is not a control person (such as an officer, director, or large block holder) periodically can sell small amounts of unregistered shares. On a quarterly basis, the investor can sell the greater of 1 percent of all shares outstanding, or one-week's average trading volume. After one year of ownership, the restricted shares are freely tradable. If the investor is a control person, the shares remain restricted and subject to the gradual liquidation process.[39]

One consideration behind Rule 144 is a concern that rapid sale of shares into the public market could depress share prices.[40] Gradual sale gives the market time to absorb the shares and reduces concerns about opportunistic selling. The concern is equally appropriate for registered shares.

Seasoned Offerings that Include Secondary Sales   Sometimes existing investors are eager to liquidate quickly. In such cases, gradual sale may not be attractive. The alternatives are to arrange a large private transaction or to participate in a seasoned offering. Issuing firms sometimes use seasoned offerings to lower the overall cost of raising equity capital or to enable investors to harvest. The issuer may undertake a small IPO to enable the market to establish a share price and then follow a few months later with a seasoned offering that will raise the additional capital the issuer is seeking.[41] It is more common for existing shareholders to participate by selling some of their shares in the seasoned offering than in the IPO. Normally, the investment banker's fee for a seasoned offering is less than the fee for an IPO. In addition, seasoned offerings are priced very close to the prevailing market price of the shares at the time of the offering. When a seasoned offering is announced, the market price of the stock drops by about 3 percent on average, but this is far less than the 16 percent average underpricing of IPOs.[42]

16.2   ACQUISITION

When investment in a venture is harvested by acquisition or merger with another company, the transaction can take any of several forms. The acquirer can purchase the *equity* of the venture for cash or exchanged it for shares of the acquiring company. Alternatively, the acquirer can purchase all or some of the *assets* of the venture for either cash or stock. The specific choice is affected by a variety of considerations. Next, we examine the considerations that affect the choice.

Purchasing the Equity of the Venture for Cash

In one form of transaction, the acquiring firm purchases the venture's outstanding equity for cash. By purchasing the equity, the buyer acquires ownership of the assets of the venture and assumes the liabilities.[43] The parties enter a stock purchase agreement that sets out the terms of the purchase and describes the assets and liabilities.

Private acquisition is similar to public sale in that the acquirer normally undertakes some level of due diligence to verify its assessment of value. In addition, sellers normally are expected to provide a series of representations and warranties that go to issues of value. For example, the sellers may warrant that the accounts receivable balance the purchaser will acquire was prepared in a manner consistent with generally accepted accounting principles; that the venture is the legal owner of any intellectual property being transferred; and that the sellers are unaware of any existing or prospective litigation against the venture. The actual list is likely to be much more comprehensive than these few examples.

To an extent, due-diligence efforts and representations and warranties are substitutes. A seller may be reticent to open its records to the due-diligence review of a prospective buyer. This is understandable because, if the transaction is not consummated, the seller could have gained access to confidential information that would be detrimental to the seller. In addition, if the venture is small, the cost of extensive due diligence can exceed the expected benefit. In such cases, the parties may place added weight on the representations and warranties. If the seller can credibly guarantee the representations and warranties, then the potential for litigation after the acquisition can substitute for more due diligence.

If extensive due diligence is not practical and the seller is not able to credibly warrant the assets being acquired and liabilities being assumed, then the transaction price is likely to be reduced. A purchaser who is concerned with overstatement of assets and understatement of liabilities by the seller can be expected to discount the offer to compensate. Thus, due diligence, representations and warranties, and the transaction price are interdependent.

From the perspective of an investor, such as a venture capital firm, sale of equity for cash is likely to be the preferred form of transaction. However, for the acquirer, it may be the most difficult form on which to agree. It also may be unattractive to the entrepreneur. For the outside investor, selling for cash facilitates harvesting. Cash is easily distributed to limited partners. In addition, because most institutional limited partners are not taxed on their earnings, receiving cash does not give rise to adverse tax consequences.

An entrepreneur who is selling equity in a venture may have a somewhat different perspective. If the sale involves a gain, the entrepreneur and members of the management team can be exposed to a significant immediate tax liability. Also, on a more qualitative level, selling for cash has an aspect of finality to it that may not be to the liking of the entrepreneur.

For the purchaser, acquiring equity for cash probably involves the most risk. By acquiring shares and paying cash, the acquirer is giving up a safe asset and acquiring one that is risky.[44] Furthermore, if the acquirer must borrow the cash, then the acquirer's leverage increases. The increase in risk is not particularly important in itself. However, adding leverage can deprive the acquirer of financial slack that could be used for other opportunities.

Purchasing the Assets of the Venture for Cash

Transferring only essential assets of the venture to the buyer can reduce the buyer's risk. In an asset purchase agreement, the seller continues to be responsible for the venture liabilities. Because the buyer does not assume direct liability, the cash price will be higher than for an equity purchase. The seller can use the extra cash to pay off the liabilities.

Automobile dealerships, for example, often are transferred using asset purchase agreements. The buyer acquires the facility, the vehicle inventory, and other essential business assets but does not assume liability for the loan the seller used to finance the inventory. Vehicle inventories normally are financed with "flooring" loans secured through specific claims against individual vehicles in the dealership inventory. When the dealer sells a vehicle, the dealer is supposed to repay the loan amount associated with that vehicle. When new inventory arrives, the dealer can borrow more, based on the specific vehicles received. If a dealer sells vehicles without repaying the loan, a purchaser who assumes the loan obligation can be liable for the repayment. Instead of verifying that all of the inventory securing the loan is still on the dealer's lot, the purchaser simply buys the inventory (possibly arranging new financing) and leaves the seller with the obligation to repay the loan.

For similar reasons, a purchaser may decide to acquire only those assets that are central to future operations. If the venture is a plaintiff in a lawsuit, for example, it may not be worthwhile for the buyer to expend effort trying to estimate the value of the suit. On the other hand, if employees who are key to presenting the litigation evidence would be employed by the buyer, it could be difficult to purchase the business assets and hire the employees separately from acquiring the litigation asset.

The accounts receivable balance is another example. Rather than trying to verify the quality of receivables or requiring the seller to warrant their status, it could be easier not to purchase the receivables. The difficulty is with collection. If the credit management operation is purchased, the acquirer may be in a better position to collect balances that are due. If the acquirer does not purchase the receivables, the acquirer's incentive to use the credit management operation to collect the receivables for the seller might not be adequate.

Exchanging Equity or Assets of the Venture for Equity of the Acquirer

Some transactions are structured as exchanges of the acquirer's stock for either the stock or assets of the venture. Exchanges of stock for assets are difficult because the seller is left with the liabilities and may not have the liquidity to service the debt. Accordingly, we focus on exchanges of stock for stock.

In an exchange of stock for stock, uncertainty about value exists on both sides of the exchange. Not only must the buyer conduct due diligence on the venture, but sellers must also value the shares they will receive. The problem is particularly serious if the acquirer is not a public company. In such cases, there are no public stock prices and no SEC reporting requirements or analyst reports that facilitate agreement. Instead, both parties must rely on their due-diligence investigations and the representations and warranties provided by the other party.

A further issue, if the acquirer is not public, is that the exchange does not directly accomplish the likely objective of the outside investors in the venture, to harvest their investments. For investors like venture capitalists, exchange of nonpublic shares for other nonpublic shares is helpful only if the resulting entity is better able to undertake a public offering in the future or if the acquirer is willing to purchase the holdings of the investor for cash, even though the entrepreneur and members of the management team may receive shares.

If the acquirer is an entity with publicly traded stock, the exchange is easier. The acquirer's shares have an established market value that can be partially relied on by sellers. Furthermore, investors who receive registered shares may be able to liquidate the shares shortly after the transaction is completed. If the shares are not registered, liquidating the holding under the provisions of Rule 144 can take longer, but the path to harvesting is clear.

Exchanges of stock for stock have some advantages over cash transactions. One is that an acquirer who wants to expand rapidly may be able to consummate acquisitions more easily using stock than by having to arrange financing for each transaction. Another is that exchanging shares for shares can address the moving target problem that arises when cash

Going Public by Reverse Merger

The distinction between a merger and an IPO is not as sharp as it might first appear. "Reverse merger" is an alternative way for a private company to become public. In a reverse merger, an existing public company nominally acquires the shares of the private company, and possibly changes its name to the name of the private company. The reason for the term, reverse merger, is that the public company usually is nothing more than a shell—often a remnant of an unsuccessful public company whose only remaining value is that its shares are publicly traded, making it a target for a firm that wants to establish a public market but does not need to raise capital quickly. The notional acquirer (the public company shell) in such a transaction does not need to have any resources to accomplish the acquisition. Rather, through bookkeeping transactions, the owners of the private company simply exchange their shares for shares of the public company.

Reverse merger does not require an underwriter, avoids the cost of an IPO, and can be accomplished relatively quickly. By one estimate, the cash cost of a reverse merger can be $100,000 to $300,000. By another estimate, a reporting OTC public shell can be acquired for $350,000 to $400,000 plus a small amount of private company stock. There is no underwriter fee and no IPO underpricing. On the other hand, as there is no certification of value, the aftermarket capitalization of a company that goes public by reverse merger may be less than of a company that goes public by IPO. Because such companies tend to have little liquidity, lack of analyst following, and few active market makers, the valuation may remain low for a sustained period of time.

Whether, in individual cases, reverse IPO makes sense depends on the firm's circumstances:

- By creating a public market for company shares, reverse merger enables existing investors to eventually harvest their investments, creates a medium of exchange that can be used in other merger and acquisition transactions, and may enable the formerly private firm to use market-based incentive compensation more effectively.
- Because it does not generate any immediate capital for the issuer and may result in lower valuations for sustained periods, reverse merger is not suitable for near-term capital raising, and may not be ideal for near-term harvesting when the firm is large enough and well enough established for an IPO or a true acquisition.

In the U.S., reverse mergers have come under increasing SEC scrutiny. While new requirements may limit the market and slow the rate at which a reverse merger can be achieved, they also may contribute to the legitimacy of this approach to going public.

(Continues)

(Continued)

Some Recent Examples

- **Siebert Financial Corporation** is a holding company for Muriel Siebert and Co., Inc., which engages in discount brokerage, investment banking, and trading on its own account. Muriel Siebert, the first woman to purchase a seat on the NYSE, transformed Siebert Financial into a public company by reverse merging the brokerage into a furniture company, **J. Michaels, Inc.** Company shares, which traded as high as $60 per share in 1999, were trading around $2.50 as of the end of 2002.

- **Telmais S. A.**, a Brazilian telcom operator, became a U.S. public company, subject to U.S. GAAP and SEC Act reporting requirements by reverse merging into **NetBet.com**, an out-of-business public dot-com. The company expects the transaction to give it increased access to private and public capital that it could not otherwise achieve, given the state of the IPO market and public appetite for technology ventures.

- Seeking to "awaken the giant within," in 1999, motivational speaker, Tony Robbins, reverse merged his company, **Dreamlife,** into a medical company shell, **GHS, Inc.** The company, which subsequently was renamed **EOS International, Inc.,** launched a Web site in February 2000, devoted to personal and professional improvement. The then-public venture failed and became the corporate shell in the next round. In July 2001, EOS acquired all of the outstanding stock of nonpublic **Discovery Toys, Inc.** After the transaction, former holders of Discovery Toys stock held a majority of the voting shares of EOS. The company now is in financial distress.

is used. Changes in public equity market values probably imply corresponding value changes for nonpublic companies. This is especially true if the parties have similar product-market orientations. In a volatile market, the parties, knowing that value can fluctuate before the deal is completed, can have trouble agreeing on a cash price. When a transaction is structured as an exchange of stock, marketwide value changes tend to affect the values of both parties similarly. Consequently, abrupt changes in the market are less likely to disrupt the transaction. Another advantage is that, in some cases, exchanging shares enables the seller to postpone recognizing a capital gain. The ability to defer taxes adds to the value of the exchange.

After the Acquisition

In some transactions, the acquirer wishes to retain the services of members of the venture's management team. Team members may be expected to enter employment agreements for some period. Employment agreements protect the acquirer from loss of value due to resignations of team members who have specialized knowledge. The acquirer may also seek to align the incentives of team members with the interests of the acquirer. Approaches for doing so include asking the team members to accept restricted shares of the acquirer (so their ability to trade the shares and defeat incentive alignment is limited), compensating team members partly with equity claims or options on the acquiring firm, or simply offering incentive pay.

The acquirer also may be concerned that once the venture is sold and the team members are free to pursue opportunities of their choosing, they will decide to reenter the market as competitors. Accordingly, sellers sometimes are asked to accept noncompetition agreements as a condition of the transaction.

Agreeing to Disagree

When the sellers of a venture are more optimistic about the venture than is the acquirer, reaching agreement on fixed terms of exchange is difficult. The parties can try to address the difference by encouraging the acquirer to devote resources to due diligence or by strengthening their representations and warranties. Conceivably, the additional effort will lead to valuations that are more consistent. The parties also can use an earn-out provision to make the acquisition price contingent on its future performance. The compensation can be adjusted whether or not the seller is still associated with the venture. If the seller is no longer with the venture, contractual compensation can be adjusted to reflect performance. If the seller has stayed on as an employee of the acquirer, then the employee's bonuses can be tied to performance.

Valuing Private Transactions

How much is a venture worth in a private transaction? The answer depends on a myriad of factors, but the overriding considerations are its value in the next best alternative and the costs of the transaction. We consider the transaction costs first, followed by opportunity cost.

Costs of the Transaction   We have shown that the cost of raising capital in the public market can be substantial. Public issue costs are related to due diligence, marketing the issue, supporting the offer price, and expected cost of litigation (for issues that experience significant losses of value shortly after the offering). The costs of private transactions are of a similar nature but less directly observable. For an IPO, we know the underwriting spread and the extent of underpricing. For a private transaction, we usually only know the net proceeds the sellers receive. Hence, there is no convenient measure of the costs of the transaction.

One way to gain perspective on the transaction costs of private sales is to examine the pricing of private equity sales by companies that have public equity outstanding. One study of equity private placements that includes data for a sample of small public companies finds that, on average, share of private transactions are priced at an average discount of 20.1 percent of contemporaneous public market values. The discounts are larger for smaller firms, when small amounts of proceeds are raised, and when a placement is large relative to firm size. Discounts also are larger when uncertainty about value is high, such as when a firm is involved in speculative product development or is threatened with financial distress.[45] Assuming that the private value of a venture is similar to its public market value, these discounts are estimates of the purchaser's cost of due diligence. Private transaction prices may also reflect a discount for illiquidity of shares purchased. However, discounts for illiquidity generally are small.[46] Comparing these results with total issue cost for IPOs, including underpricing, shows that the average transactions costs for private sales are somewhat lower.

Opportunity Cost   The value of a venture to a prospective acquirer depends on its stand-alone value, plus the value of any synergistic gains, less the costs of the transaction.

For a private venture that is acquired by a public firm, value also can be created by transfer of ownership from underdiversified investors to the capital market. Whether sellers are able to capture any or all of the synergistic gains, or the gains from movement to a public market, depends on comparison of opportunities. If the venture is unique and multiple public acquirers

Estimating the Cost of Private Transactions

Suppose it is possible, using comparable public firms or other data, to estimate the value of a venture as if it were a public company. Assuming the acquirer is public and values the acquisition on the basis of comparable firms, the acquisition price can be estimated by deducting the expected discount to reflect the cost of the private transaction:

Acquisition Price = Public Company Market Value − Private Transaction Discount

The following table summarizes some of the statistical evidence of private transaction discounts:

Variable	Mean Discount	Variable	Mean Discount
Proceeds (millions)		*Market Value of Equity (millions)*	
≤$1.0	43.7%	≤$10.0	34.6%
$1.0–$5.0	33.1%	$10.0–$25.0	35.6%
$5.0–$10.0	15.1%	$25.0–$75.0	17.2%
$10.0–$20.0	10.1%	>$75.0	7.6%
>$20.0	0.2%	*Single Investor*	
		Yes	11.7%
Book-to-Market		No	23.3%
Equity Ratio			
≤0.1	31.3%	*Speculative Product*	
0.1–0.4	25.0%	Yes	32.2%
0.4–0.7	21.9%	No	14.7%
0.7–1.0	5.0%		
>1.0	3.3%	*Financial Distress*	
		Yes	34.8%
		No	16.5%

Consider a biotechnology venture that has begun to generate revenues but is not yet profitable and where there is significant potential that the firm ultimately will lose out to rivals. The venture has book assets of $5 million and no debt. Suppose, based on comparable public firms, market value is around $20 million. Given the market value estimate, the Proceeds data above suggest an acquisition price of about $18 million (a discount of about 10.1 percent). The Book-to-Market Equity Ratio of .25 suggests an acquisition price of $15 million (a discount of 25 percent). The Market Value of Equity estimate of $20 million suggests an acquisition price of about $13 million (a discount of about 35.6 percent). The average discount for single-investor transactions is 11.7 percent, suggesting an acquisition price of about $17.5 million. The average discount for speculative products is 32.2 percent, suggesting an acquisition price of about $13.5 million.

Although some of these estimates are likely to be more accurate than others, a simple equal-weighted average suggests an acquisition price of $15.4 million, or a discount of about 23 percent. Based on this estimate, the entrepreneur can begin to consider the relative merits of private acquisition or public offering.

Source: Hertzel and Smith (1993). Although the study uses data from private placements of public companies, the findings capture many of the qualitative considerations that are likely to affect the costs an acquirer would incur in the acquisition of a private venture.

are competing to acquire it (and could benefit equally from any synergies), then sellers should realize most of the full public market value, including synergies, less the buyer's transaction costs. Conversely, if there is only one prospective buyer, and there are no good private market alternatives, and if other ventures would be similarly attractive to the buyer and would substitute for each other, the buyer should be able to capture most of the value that is created. These are the extremes. In other cases, the gains are likely to be shared on the basis of availability of substitute buyers and sellers.

Thus, a reasonable approach to valuation is to estimate public market value, assuming gains are captured by the seller, and estimate stand-alone private market value. These are the bounds to the transaction value before subtracting the buyer's transactions costs. The transaction value can be estimated by considering how the parties are likely to share the gains.

Noncash Transactions   What if the venture is sold for financial claims other than cash? How should the entrepreneur and other sellers value the claims they receive? Clearly, if freely tradable stock is received, then (except for tax considerations) there is little difference between receiving stock and receiving cash. However, the stock often is restricted from trading for a significant period. Sometimes, the restriction is designed to align the entrepreneur's incentives with the acquirer's interests. Restricting resale also is a way of making sure the entrepreneur's gain from selling is related to the acquirer's subsequent performance (including the acquirer's interest in the venture).

Stock that is not freely tradable leaves the entrepreneur with a financial position that is still underdiversified. Consequently, this form of compensation is less valuable than if the entrepreneur were to receive cash or freely tradable shares. The valuation methods developed in earlier chapters can be used to assess the impact of trading restrictions on the value of shares the entrepreneur receives. For a diversified investor, such as a venture capital firm, it is reasonable to value the shares as if they were freely tradable.

16.3   MANAGEMENT BUY-OUT

Harvesting opportunities are of critical importance to venture capitalists and other outside investors. They are often less important to the entrepreneur and key members of the management team. In the recognition that harvesting is a source of potential conflict, the parties normally negotiate harvesting options at the time of the initial outside investment. The investor may negotiate the right to demand registration of shares, which could be tantamount to compelling the venture to go public, or may have other, less onerous, registration rights. Short of the ability to force a public offering, the investor may have the right to insist on being bought out by the entrepreneur on terms that are related to the value of the venture.

Sometimes a management buy-out (MBO) is an optional response of management to investors' insistence on exercising demand registration rights or rights that could trigger an acquisition. Suppose, for example, investors wish to sell and have located a buyer. The prospective acquirer wishes to retain the management team but purchase their existing equity. Suppose, however, that members of the management team value their status as equityholders. Perhaps they believe the venture has more potential than is reflected in the transaction terms under consideration. One response is to counter with a proposal to buy out the investors' equity interest.

In most cases, MBOs are financed with debt. The investors' equity is valued and borrowing is arranged, so that the venture, the entrepreneur, or other members of the management team can repurchase the investors' shares. Regardless of how the transaction is implemented, the venture normally ends up with a capital structure that is more highly leveraged than before the MBO.[47] A management buy-out is feasible only if the venture is reasonably successful. Value must be high enough to justify the price the investors receive. In the case of a leveraged transaction, the venture must be capable of generating enough cash flow to service the debt.

Valuing MBO Transactions

The advantage of an MBO is that the buyer (the management team) already knows almost everything there is to know about the venture. Because due diligence is not necessary, the transactions cost can be low. If outside debt financing is used, the buyers must be able to demonstrate that repayment is likely, or must be able to secure the loan. However, because the lender only needs to assess repayment potential, and not overall value, even that aspect of the transaction can be low cost compared to a public offering of equity.

Offsetting the cost saving, the entrepreneur and members of the team continue to be underdiversified. This makes MBO transactions paradoxical. Investors, who are well diversified are selling to management team members, who are not as well diversified. Saving of transactions costs is one factor that can help explain such transactions. The other factors include differences in expectations about future performance and the subjective value team members place on continuing to own and manage the venture. Generally, the rationale for an MBO is stronger if management expects that capital market investors will recognize and accept its assessment of value within a short period, thereby enabling a public offering.

16.4   EMPLOYEE STOCK OWNERSHIP PLANS OF PRIVATE AND FAMILY BUSINESSES

In many private businesses, the entrepreneur has little desire to harvest in any formal sense. Instead, the entrepreneur's objective is to realize a return through the stream of free cash flows the enterprise produces. The need for liquidity is reduced if the venture has no outside equity investor who is pressing for a liquidity event. In some cases, enterprises such as these are family businesses, and family members expect that, over time, management will pass from one family member to another.[48] In others, there may be no specific line of succession.[49]

Even family businesses with no outside investors, however, need liquidity from time to time. The most obvious liquidity need is associated with estate management. When an owner dies, the owner's estate is obligated to pay taxes.[50] The amount of the tax liability depends on asset market value, and not on current earnings or cash flows from operations. Sometimes the tax liability can be large, whereas no cash flow is available for paying taxes. Businesses with positive earnings and cash flow sometimes can satisfy the tax liability by borrowing. But what if the venture's earnings and cash flow are too limited to support the level of borrowing that is needed?

A closely related problem is that, following the death of the owner, venture shares may be distributed to heirs. However, what if some or all of the heirs are not interested in the business, or they have important disagreements about direction? These problems are difficult to solve without some means of introducing liquidity.

Employee stock ownership plans (ESOPs) are used widely in public corporations to allocate ownership to employees, for a variety of purposes. However, the ESOP was originally conceived as a means of providing liquidity to private businesses, in lieu of alternatives such as public offering or acquisition.

The ESOP Process

The ESOP of a private business creates liquidity by establishing an internal market for its shares. It does so by providing a mechanism that enables employees to invest their retirement funds in equity of the business and to liquidate their investments at retirement or upon a change of employment. ESOPs can be leveraged or unleveraged. A leveraged ESOP is more complex and provides liquidity more quickly than does an unleveraged ESOP.[51]

In Figure 16-2, we describe the structural elements of a leveraged ESOP. Panel (a) of the figure describes ESOP formation. The process begins when the company establishes an ESOP trust. The trust is responsible for administering all of the share transactions and for assuring that the transactions are based on fair valuations. In a leveraged ESOP, the trust acquires ownership of enough shares to meet the expected needs of the company retirement plan for several years. If the company is publicly traded, the trust can purchase the shares in the market or directly from specific stockholders. For a private company, the trust purchases shares from one or more of the existing owners. To ensure that employees receive equitable treatment, the company or the trust normally arranges for an outside party, such as a valuation consultant, appraiser, or accountant, to value the equity.[52] Based on the valuation, the ESOP trust agrees to purchase an appropriate number of shares from the entrepreneur or an investor who wants to harvest. To pay for the shares acquired in a leveraged ESOP, the trust arranges for a bank loan. The loan is a primary obligation of the trust and is secured by the shares the trust acquires. In addition, the bank loan normally is guaranteed by the company, which commits to make annual retirement contributions of cash to the trust on behalf of its employees.

Initiation of the leveraged ESOP is the primary liquidity event for the entrepreneur. The bank loan is used to purchase the entrepreneur's shares. From that point forward, the entrepreneur is not directly involved in ESOP transactions. The same structure can be used to deal with liquidity issues arising among different owners. An investor who desires liquidity, be it a venture capital firm or a family member who disagrees with the direction of the company, can be bought out via a leveraged ESOP.[53] The main difference between a leveraged ESOP and one that is unleveraged is that, in the latter, the trust purchases shares from the existing owner(s) as needed, over a period of several years.[54]

Panel (b) of the figure illustrates how annual retirement contributions are funded. The amount of contribution is determined by the company's retirement plan and is a function of total compensation to employees who are plan members. The company transfers the required funds to the trust, based on a new valuation of company equity. The money the company pays is used by the trust to pay interest and a portion of the principal of the bank loan. Based on the repayment, the bank releases its claim to some of the securities. The trust then is free to assign appropriate numbers of shares to the retirement accounts of the employees.[55] This process of valuation, funds transfer, and loan repayment continues each year until the loan is repaid.

Because there is no market for company shares, employees must have a means of converting their equity holdings into cash. As shown in panel (c), this is accomplished by allowing employees to sell shares back to the ESOP trust at the estimated value at time of retirement (or resignation). Thus, in any given year, the cash retirement contribution of the employer goes partly to repay the loan and partly to repurchase shares from retiring employees.

Valuation Considerations

Although the ESOP provides liquidity needed for certain critical transactions, the company remains private. The entrepreneur's underdiversified position can be improved by liquidating

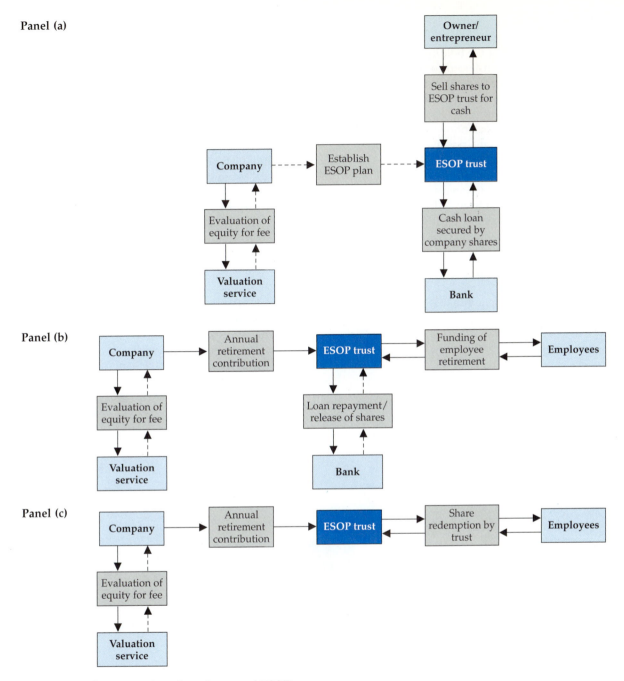

Figure 16-2 Structure of a private leveraged ESOP

In Panel (*a*), the privately owned company establishes an ESOP plan managed by an ESOP trust. The company owner contributes shares and receives cash obtained via a bank loan. Terms of the transaction depend on an independent valuation. In Panel (*b*), the company makes its annual retirement contribution, which is used to repay the loan. Shares of company stock are assigned to fund the retirements of employees. In Panel (*c*), retiring employees sell their shares back to the ESOP trust and receive cash through the continuing contributions of the company.

some of the holdings and reinvesting the proceeds. The values at which shares are purchased and transferred to the ESOP and to employees usually reflect discounts from public market value. Discounts are appropriate because employees are relying on a valuation estimate rather than a verifiable market transaction and because an employee's retirement fund is underdiversified. Even if the company is public, employee investments of retirement funds in company stock normally are made at discounts to reflect underdiversification.

On the positive side, it is argued (but has not been demonstrated convincingly) that giving employees equity interests in their organizations aligns their incentives, which enhances the value of the organization. On purely technical grounds, it does not appear that a small ownership interest in an organization with many employees can do much to align incentives. The cost to an individual employee of shirking and free riding is spread over all shareholders and is negligible for an employee who is deciding how hard to work. On the other hand, stock ownership may give rise to feelings of esprit de corps and result in more effective teams.

16.5 ROLL-UP IPO

A company that is too small to go public by itself may be able to do so by combining with others to create an organization that is large enough to make efficient use of the public offering process. A roll-up IPO is a device that enables this to occur. Figure 16-3 illustrates the process. Normally, a roll-up combines several smaller firms that are similar in orientation and have track records of profitable operation. The owner of each firm exchanges exiting shares for shares of the new company. Each seller may also receive cash and frequently enters an employment contract that ties her to the new company for several years.

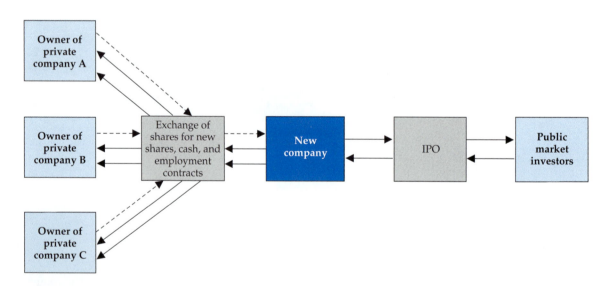

Figure 16-3 Roll-up IPO

In a roll-up IPO, several private entities merge to form a corporation large enough to go public. Owners of the companies normally receive cash from the IPO and hold equity in the new company.

The new company goes to the capital market with an IPO based on the consolidated financial statements of the rolled-up companies. The new company may operate essentially as a portfolio of the smaller companies, or some centralization may be sought. Funds from the IPO provide any cash that is distributed to owners of the rolled-up companies, and the IPO leads to a public market, in which shares of the new company eventually can be sold.[56]

Valuation Considerations

Although most roll-up IPOs advertise the benefits and synergies the new company hopes to achieve, many of those benefits could have been realized through mechanisms short of consolidation. For example, the individual firms could have entered reciprocal referral arrangements or consolidated their accounting operations without a formal merger. Thus, the driving force in a roll-up is not synergies, but the value created by transition from private, undiversified ownership to public ownership. Detracting from this is any loss of operational efficiency that may result from conversion of entrepreneurs to employees of a larger corporation.

The concept of a roll-up is not new. Companies in the 1960s and early 1970s sometimes are criticized in finance texts for playing a "price/earnings multiple game." A public company with a high price/earnings ratio would acquire smaller private companies in the same industry, paying a substantially lower price, relative to earnings. The hope was that the earnings of the targets would be capitalized by the market at the price/earnings ratio of the acquirer. The academic criticism is that it should not be possible to create value by simply transferring earnings from one company to another. Thus, the P/E multiple of the consolidated firm should be a weighted average of the individual firm P/E multiples. The criticism is correct when both firms already are public. Combining their earnings, without creating synergies, does not create market value. However, if the target is a private company, then value is created by enabling the owner of the private company to achieve diversification.

16.6   THE HARVESTING DECISION

Going public generally is perceived to be the harvesting alternative that yields the highest valuation. Whether it does in any given case depends on a variety of factors. Public market investors can diversify easily so that market value depends on systematic risk. This is in contrast to private transactions, where the investor may have limited ability to diversify. The gain associated with transferring ownership to diversified investors argues in favor of harvesting by going public or merging with a public firm. Other factors also are important and weigh against IPO.

Decisions regarding how and when to harvest are complex. Not only does the menu of choices include alternatives that are substantially different from each other and difficult to compare, but also harvest timing involves a choice of whether to exercise an option or to wait. In the following discussion, we review factors that bear on the decision.

Company Size

Public offering is more cost-effective for large firms than for small ones. Many of the costs of a public offering are fixed, and some of the benefits of being public depend on the firm's ability to achieve a reasonable volume of trading activity in the market.

A small firm can achieve a public market valuation and liquidity for its investors if it is acquired by a public company. Acquisitions also involve significant fixed costs, but private contracting provides more ways to limit the costs. The parties can, for example, structure the transaction so the seller's return depends on how the acquired firm performs after the acquisition. This is more difficult to achieve for a public sale of equity. In a public sale, the entrepreneur's return does depend on the market price of the shares. Because the entrepreneur usually cannot begin selling her shares until a few months after the offering, after-market performance can affect the return.

The Value of a Public Market for the Shares

Going public subjects the firm to periodic reporting requirements and the need to commit resources to maintaining relations with investors. On the other hand, the public market provides a continuous measure of value that facilitates the firm's use of its shares as a medium of exchange in future acquisitions. Also, the fact that there is a public market for the stock facilitates using incentive compensation and means that the company's managers are subject to the discipline of the market.

Another benefit of going public is that the process may raise consumer and investor awareness of the company's products and may enhance the company's image. Public offering also can have strategic significance for a company and its rivals. Because public offering is expensive and because the offering prospectus commits the firm to a fairly specific course of action, going public is a way to credibly commit the firm. The commitment can be attractive to customers and suppliers, and can discourage rivals.

Going public also gives existing investors flexibility over harvest timing. In a private transaction, the ownership interest of the entrepreneur is bought out. If the company is public, the entrepreneur can sell shares according to a schedule that potentially is more attractive. Gradual sale of shares of a public company is both an opportunity and a necessity. In some cases, even if the entrepreneur would like to liquidate quickly, going public can delay liquidation, due to lock-up provisions and other restrictions on selling.

Synergies

An important benefit of going public is the transition from private, underdiversified ownership to public ownership. Opportunities to create additional value by selling to a company that can make complementary use of the firm's resources and capabilities are not directly achievable via public offering.

Generally, if synergies are significant, the harvesting choice is likely to be influenced by the owner's ability to capture as much of the gain as possible. A private firm that "should" be merged with a public firm (because of synergies) might, for example, go public as a way of establishing public market value as a floor on the acquisition price.

Track Record and Ease of Valuation

Going public at a reasonable valuation is not always possible. The most important factor affecting a venture's ability to go public is its record of accomplishment at the time of the offering. A venture with a solid operating history of steady revenue and earnings growth and predictable future growth is relatively easy for public market investors to evaluate. A less well-established venture that is at an early stage of development is hard for investors to value reliably. For such a venture, small deviations from expected performance and small changes in the market or in competitive conditions can trigger precipitous changes in market value.

For a variety of reasons, investors in public companies do not receive full information about companies that elect to go public. In part, investors must rely on investment bankers for their valuations. The more difficult it is for public market investors to evaluate a company, and the more they must rely on the investment banker's reputation rather than specific information, the stronger is the case for private sale. In a private transaction, commercially sensitive information can be shared. The buyer may be particularly well suited to evaluate the company.

Timing

As we noted in Chapter 15, an initial public offering cannot be completed quickly. From the time that a venture decides on public offering until the offering occurs, market conditions can change dramatically and can drastically affect the market values of early-stage companies.[57]

Particularly for going public, timing is a factor that is closely related to track record. During expansionary periods, it is relatively easy to convince investors of a venture's need to raise capital. However, if market values have declined and other firms have postponed or canceled their offerings, a company that proceeds with an offering is regarded with skepticism by investors. During such periods, it can be advantageous for the firm to wait, or if waiting is not possible, a private market transaction may be warranted. The venture should be better able to communicate the reasons for its decision to a private acquirer than to the market at large. It should also be better able to structure the deal.

Ownership and Control

The various harvesting alternatives have different implications for control. In an acquisition (except for reverse merger), the entrepreneur is almost certain to lose control to the acquiring firm. In a public sale, the entrepreneur may be able to maintain control, even if the entrepreneur's investment is significantly reduced. Dual class ownership, where the entrepreneur's shares have superior voting rights, is increasingly common.

Even if public market investors have very limited control, however, they can exert influence over the venture by making some courses of action more expensive and time-consuming than they otherwise would be. Private ownership by the entrepreneur is a way of preserving a high level of control, with minimum outside intervention, but comes at the cost of continuing underdiversification for the entrepreneur.

Taxes

For some investors, such as pension funds, tax considerations have little influence on the choice of harvesting alternatives. However, for the entrepreneur, the tax implications of harvesting are likely to be important. It is difficult to generalize about the tax advantages of the alternatives. An ESOP can yield a tax deferral, but whether it does depends on a variety of factors that are beyond the scope of this text. Private sale in an acquisition may or may not generate an immediate tax obligation. Going public provides the entrepreneur with a tax-timing option, inasmuch as shares can be sold during periods when the tax consequences of the transaction would be most favorable for the entrepreneur.

Transactions Costs

Generally, private market transactions are less costly and have lower fixed cost components than going public. Consequently, transactions costs and firm size are related. Small firms are more likely to remain private or be harvested in a private transaction than are large firms. The main exception is that if small firms can be consolidated without significant loss of operational efficiency, then a public offering may be possible.

16.7 VENTURE CAPITAL HARVESTING AND THE INTERNET "BUBBLE"

Figure 16-4 shows daily closing values of the Dow Jones Composite Internet Index over the five years from 1998 through 2002, with index values standardized by their March 9, 2000 high value. From the end of 1998 through mid-March 2000, the value of the index increased by a factor of more than four. By mid-April 2002, the index had lost more than half its value. By the end of 2002, the index was at only 7.5 percent of the March 2000 high. Over this period, broader indexes, such as the S&P 500 and NASDAQ followed a similar, but less severe, pattern.[58] This rise in market valuations, followed by a precipitous decline, has been referred to as the "Internet bubble," suggesting that market valuations during the period were irrationally exuberant.

In earlier chapters, we discussed how the booming market of the late 1990s affected new capital commitments of venture capital and the market for new venture financing. Here we address two further questions. First, can we necessarily infer from a pattern like the one in Figure 16-4 that stock market valuations are driven by irrationality? Second, what are the implications of stock market declines for harvesting of investments in new ventures?

Investor Irrationality

At the height of the Internet episode, market valuations of high-technology firms were extremely high, compared with conventional indicators of value. Microsoft, the firm with the highest market capitalization of any firm, was selling for 23 times annual sales and $17,000

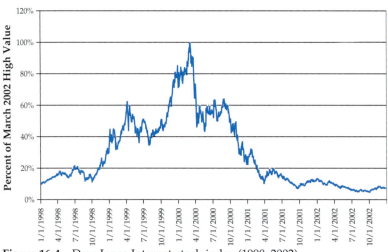

Figure 16-4   Dow Jones Internet stock index (1998–2002)

per employee; whereas General Electric, with the second highest market capitalization, was selling for only four times annual sales and $1,300 per employee. Amazon.com, with only 2,000 employees (compared to 293,000 at General Electric) was not profitable, and was selling for 37 times annual sales or $11,000 per employee.

Could any rational economic theory justify such extreme valuations? And could the same theory justify the rapid rise and precipitous decline in valuations? Conceivably, the answer is "yes." In early 2000, the high valuations of Internet businesses were based on a belief that the Internet potentially would displace conventional means of marketing and distributing. People were referring to that transformation as "from bricks to clicks," implying that many of the marketing and distribution-related tangible assets of established businesses were becoming liabilities, and that new economy businesses, which were not saddled with large investments in brick and mortar, could potentially be the winners in the economic transformation. That view, even today, is not necessarily wrong. In fact, the gyrations in market valuations can be rationalized by a theory that market value is the present value of expected future cash flows, but where the investors' assessments of the probability that commercial and retail markets would be transformed to Internet-based markets was changing dramatically. If the Internet were to quickly displace traditional marketing and distribution, then companies like Amazon, which were building market share and had developed effective Web sites, could conceivably become very profitable. If the Internet transformation were slower than expected or if the Internet became simply another path to consumers, then early movers (with only Web sites) might easily fail.

The Internet episode is only the latest of a number of historical episodes when the capital markets have been confronted with the potential for major transformations. The computer hard-drive boom, the telecommunications boom, and the biotechnology boom are other recent examples where new technologies had the potential to transform the economy and where market prices rose in the face of potential transformation and subsequently declined when the transformation either did not happen or happened more slowly or than anticipated. Only if investors chronically were over-optimistic would it be possible to conclude that valuations are irrational. However, there are not enough market experiments on which to base such a definitive conclusion. In each of these periods, the stocks of the innovator companies are essentially call options on the transformational technology. Just like with other options, when the transformation does not materialize or is slow to materialize, the riskiest stocks are likely to end up "out of the money" and worthless. However, these same stocks are the ones that would produce the greatest returns for investors if the transformation did materialize. Hence, more often than not, we should expect to see stock price patterns that look like the Internet bubble, but occasionally we should find that even the high valuations prove to be much too conservative.

Economic transformation is always a matter of degree. Averaged over the 5-years from late 1997 to late 2002, some stocks like Qualcomm, Amazon, Dell, Apple, Microsoft have generated positive returns while some notable blue chip stocks, including Campbell Soup, Ford, Eastman Kodak, Boeing, and Gillette, have posted striking losses. This evidence suggests that some gains in the tech sector were legitimate and created long-term value for investors.[59]

In one fundamental way, it does appear that valuations during the Internet episode were influenced by irrationality. During the period, many venture capital-backed companies went public at very early stages, including pre-revenue. Those IPOs, which enabled venture capital investors to harvest very quickly, were driven by the desire of public market investors to participate in venture capital investing related to the Internet, and did not make much sense at a fundamental level. Public-market investment in very early-stage ventures is difficult to justify on economic grounds. Normally, such firms need financing from sources that can stage financial commitments and can respond quickly and correctly to new developments. The public equity market lacks the needed flexibility and access to private information about company successes or failures. As we discussed in Chapter 15, for an early-stage company, going public can reduce flexibility and can contribute to ultimate failure. It appears from the low level of IPO activity in recent years, that public market investors may now have learned this lesson.

Public Market Valuation and Harvesting Choices

Figure 16-5 shows that IPO activity by venture capital-backed firms correlates with market valuations. By comparing IPO activity in the figure with the market index in Figure 16-4, you can see that IPO activity is high when market valuations are high and have been rising. IPO activity declines when market values decline. Systematic fluctuations in IPO activity may be another indication of irrationality in market valuations. If market values are a random walk, why should IPO activity decline when market valuations decline?

To a degree, systematic changes in IPO activity can be traced to the backward-looking valuation practice of investment bankers and the way issuers and investment bankers respond to changes in market prices after the IPO filing range has been published. Generally, if market values rise after the preliminary prospectus is issued, the IPO goes forward, but with an upward adjustment of the offer price. However, if market values decline, IPOs tend to be cancelled. This asymmetric practice means that IPO activity will tend to increase when the market values rise and decline when market values decline. When market value changes correspond to positive or negative economic news or changes in real interest rates, the asymmetry may imply that the issuing firm's need for capital depends on the state of the economy.

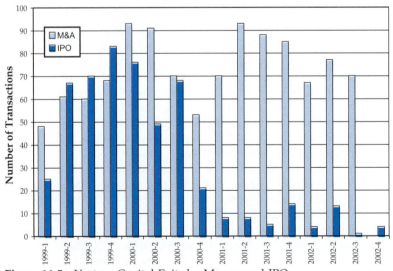

Figure 16-5   Venture Capital Exits by Merger and IPO

If market values decline, perhaps the reasons underlying the firm's need to raise capital also have declined, leading to cancellation of the IPO.

However, what about firms that go public mainly to enable investors to exit? It is apparent from Figure 9-2 that marketwide average price/earnings ratios do not follow a random pattern. Rather, price/earnings ratios appear to be mean reverting. If so, investors who are not under pressure to exit and who believe company earnings are not sensitive to economywide changes may be better off by trying to time IPOs to occur when price/earnings ratios are high. As we discussed earlier, if declining market values cause firms not to issue, then a firm that goes forward with an IPO is likely to be viewed skeptically by investors. What does this imply for firms with good prospects for success and that want to facilitate harvesting by investors? The answer is that IPO is only one exit strategy available to existing investors. Merger and acquisition (M&A) is another. In fact, in recent years, despite the decline in the IPO market, M&A has remained a popular liquidation strategy. Figure 16-5 shows the total number of M&A exits by year by venture capital-backed firms. The advantage of M&A, when IPO activity is low, is that a single investor may be able to better understand the basis for the sellers' optimism about the firm or may be able to agree to a contract, such as an earn-out, that ties the sellers' return to actual performance. Even during periods of high IPO activity, M&A activity also has been high. Over the four-year time span from 1999 through 2002, mergers outnumber IPOs in all but three quarters.

16.8   SUMMARY

Harvesting is an essential aspect of entrepreneurial finance. Harvesting strategies are considered when investment decisions are made. Harvesting is factored into the valuation of financial claims and often is provided for explicitly in deal structures.

Frequently, the business plan of a new venture envisions an IPO within a few years after the first significant outside investment. However, going public is only one of several harvesting alternatives. For many kinds of ventures, it is an unlikely possibility. Other alternatives include private acquisition, management buy-out, creation of an ESOP to provide liquidity to a venture where harvesting of the entire investment is not an objective, and indirect approaches to public offering, such as a roll-up IPO.

The costs and benefits of the alternatives differ markedly. Going public requires an IPO. An IPO usually is expensive as a percentage of proceeds received. However, harvesting by going public normally involves selling a small percentage of the venture's outstanding shares. Therefore, cost can be a small percentage of firm value. Furthermore, existing investors in the venture normally do not sell significant fractions of their share holdings during the IPO. The actual cost of harvesting by going public depends on the process that is used by investors to sell their shares. Developing a public market for company shares has some distinct benefits that can influence the choice of harvesting alternatives.

Private acquisitions also can be expensive. However, acquisition may enable the selling shareholders to realize some of the gains arising from synergies with the acquirer. MBOs, ESOPs, and roll-ups all have distinct advantages and disadvantages. The correct choice in any instance depends on factors such as transactions costs, firm size, track record, timing, tax implications, and other factors.

QUESTIONS AND PROBLEMS

1. The investors in Generation.com, a company organized to sell fashions to the current generation of teenagers over the Internet, are interested in harvesting their investments. Based on a lengthy meeting with an investment banker, they believe the pre-money valuation of Generation.com is $80 million. The investment banker is recommending an IPO that would yield gross proceeds of about $12 million. The investment banker would try to set the issue price at about 85 percent of the expected market value per share after the offering and would charge a total fee of $900,000. In addition, Generation.com would incur out-of-pocket costs of about $400,000.
    a. Assuming the venture currently has 2 million shares outstanding, what is the pre-money valuation per share?
    b. What is the expected after-market valuation per share?
    c. How many new shares would the venture issue in the IPO?
    d. What is the total issue cost in dollars and as a percentage of gross proceeds?
    e. What is total issue cost as a percentage of post-money market value of equity?

2. Suppose the current investors in Generation.com intend to harvest by using Rule 144. Based on the agreement they expect to enter with the investment banker, they cannot sell anything for six months. Assume that the market standard deviation is 14 percent per six months, the risk-free rate is 2 percent per six months, the market risk premium is 3 percent per six months, the equity beta is 1.5, and the standard deviation of the stock value in six months is 45 percent of the expected stock price.
    a. After the six months are over, a well-diversified investor expects that it would take one year to completely harvest her investments by gradual sale into the market under the Rule. (Thus, the average time required per share is 12 months after the IPO.)
        (1) Compute the expected stock price in 12 months, assuming there are 2 million shares of Generation.com outstanding and the expected appreciation depends on the CAPM.
        (2) Compute the standard deviation of share values as of month 12, assuming returns are uncorrelated over time.
        (3) Suppose the investor, who is well diversified, owns 8 percent of the outstanding equity. Modify a valuation template to reflect this information, and use it to estimate the present value of the investor's equity.
    b. Another investor, who is not well diversified, has 70 percent of his wealth invested in a market index; the remainder is invested in the venture. This investor also owns 8 percent of the equity and, therefore, would also require one year to completely harvest his investment under Rule 144.
        (1) Modify a valuation template to reflect this information, and use it to estimate the present value of the investor's equity. (*Note:* You can do the analysis based on an average holding period of 12 months after the IPO.)
        (2) How would you expect the value of each investor's holdings to be affected if more than one year would be needed to completely harvest the investment? Explain.

3. As an alternative to Rule 144 liquidation, the investors in Generation.com are considering a secondary offering six months after the IPO. They expect the stock to appreciate according to the CAPM during the six months but to lose about 3 percent of its value when

the seasoned offering is announced. They also anticipate that total issue costs will be about 5 percent of gross proceeds. Market and stock price appreciation assumptions are all as stated in problem 2.

    a. Evaluate this harvesting alternative from the perspective of the well-diversified investor in problem 2.

    b. Evaluate the alternative from the perspective of the underdiversified investor in problem 2.

    c. Compare your results in this problem to your results in problem 2. Why do the values differ? Which harvesting alternative do you recommend? Why?

4. Private placement is another alternative for the investors in Generation.com. The investment banker believes an investor can be found who would be interested in acquiring the venture for its public market value, less a normal private placement discount. As indicated in problem 1, the venture's pre-money valuation is about $80 million. In addition, its book-to-market equity ratio is about 0.5. The product is selling well, and the venture is approaching breakeven profitability.

    a. Use the information from the private placement discussion in the chapter to develop an estimate of the private placement discount percentage. Explain your reasoning. Also develop and explain an estimate of the uncertainty of the percentage.

    b. How does the value of the private placement alternative compare with the other possibilities for harvesting?

5. An outside investor in a new venture is eager to harvest its investment and has just notified the entrepreneur of its intent to exercise its demand registration rights. The entrepreneur believes that if the venture were to go public at this time, it would be substantially undervalued by the market, owing to its slow progress over the most recent three years. She expects that the venture would be worth substantially more in two years than it is today. Consequently, the entrepreneur is considering a leveraged buy-out of the investor.

    Currently, the entrepreneur has 20 percent of her wealth invested in the venture and 80 percent in a market index. If she were to buy out the investor, her borrowing would effectively change her ownership to 35 percent of wealth invested in the venture and 65 percent in the market index. The entrepreneur's current wealth is $7 million. The expected market risk premium is 6 percent, and the risk-free rate is 4 percent per year. The standard deviation of market returns for one year is 20 percent. The entrepreneur expects that her wealth invested in the venture will be worth $5 million in two years, with a standard deviation of $2.5 million. Correlation between the venture and the market is 0.4.

    a. Suppose, initially (and counter-factually) that the investor agrees with the entrepreneur's forecast of cash flows in two years. Use Valuation Template 5 to determine the fraction of equity the investor would need to own in order to be indifferent between holding the shares for an additional two years or selling out to the entrepreneur for $1,050,000 (15 percent of the entrepreneur's current wealth).

    b. Under the assumption in part (a), what is the value of the entrepreneur's ownership interest and what is the value of the entrepreneur's portfolio?

    c. If, with agreement between the parties, as in part (a) the entrepreneur were to acquire the investor's interest, what is the value of the entrepreneur's investment in the venture and the value of the entrepreneur's portfolio?

d. Suppose, instead, that the investor owns 30 percent of the equity, and values the claim at $1,050,000, due to lower projections of harvest value in two years. Assuming the entrepreneur buys the investor out, what would be the value (to the entrepreneur), of full ownership of the venture, and of the entrepreneur's portfolio.

6. Based on data for comparable public firms, the equity of a private firm would be worth $50 per share. The entrepreneur is considering using an ESOP plan to provide liquidity. Under the ESOP, the trust would buy shares from the entrepreneur at their public-market value and use the shares as a retirement investment vehicle for employees. Employees would be free to choose between investing their annual retirement contributions in company stock or investing in mutual funds of public securities. Recognizing that the company shares could only be redeemed at retirement or resignation, the company would partially match the an employee's retirement contribution to the ESOP in an effort to make the company plan as attractive to employees as investing in the market. As a basis for the analysis, the company is examining three representative employee profiles:

- An early career employee, with a ten-year expected term of employment and 5 percent of total wealth invested in the business
- A mid-career employee with a seven-year expected term of employment and 10 percent of total wealth invested in the business
- A late career employee with a four-year expected term of employment and 15 percent of total wealth invested in the business

The risk-free rate is 0.4 percent per month, the market rate is 1.0 percent per month, the monthly standard deviation of the market is 4.0 percent, and (based on comparables) the business has a correlation of 0.25 with the market and beta risk of 0.80.

a. Find the annual expected return and annualized standard deviation of returns. Develop a model to simulate monthly stock values per share. Use the model to simulate harvest value per share at the ends of four, seven, and ten years.

b. Determine the amount of supplemental investment that would be needed to compensate each of these representative employees for not putting their retirement savings into the market.

c. Under what conditions (time to retirement and fraction of wealth invested) would you want to invest in the ESOP as opposed to in the market?

7. Discuss the reasons that periodic valuation is important when ownership of a private company is transferred to employees via an ESOP. What factors do you think would lead an entrepreneur (whose shares an ESOP was purchasing) to favor a leveraged ESOP over an unleveraged ESOP?

8. From the perspective of the entrepreneur, what are the pros and cons of an IPO as opposed to private sale of the venture to a public company in exchange for stock?

NOTES

1. In this case, the IPO combines a primary market transaction to raise capital for the firm and a secondary offering by investors.

2. SEC Rule 144 governs the rates at which such sales can occur in the United States.

3. Private transactions of unregistered shares in the United States are subject to SEC Rule 144A.

4. This discussion pertains to the general cash offering process, which is the process used most often for offerings in the United States. The rights offering process, which is more common in some other countries, is discussed below.

5. Smith (1992) discusses the history of thought related to underwriting.

6. The actual sale is handled by a group of securities dealers working together as a syndicate. The orientation of the lead underwriter is only one factor that affects the mix of investors.

7. From the narrow perspective of a single transaction, integration of the investment banker into venture capital seems to create a conflict of interest. Might the investment banker be motivated to overprice offerings where it also is a venture capital investor? Gompers and Lerner (1999) examine this possibility but find no evidence that such issues are priced differently from other issues where the investment banker is not an investor. Apparently, the investment banker's interest in maintaining reputation is sufficient to overcome the concern.

8. For this valuation, the underwriter normally relies on information supplied by the issuer and assumes the information is complete and correct. Before the IPO, the investment banker will verify the information as an aspect of due diligence.

9. Sometimes, certain regulated firms in the United States are required by state or federal laws to use competitive bidding. Competitive bidding is rarely used when it is not required, and then only for low-risk debt issues.

10. Smith (1987) analyzes of the relative costs of competitive and negotiated underwriting of public utility debt issues.

11. Due diligence for IPOs in the U.S. normally takes several weeks. The final stage occurs just before the offering. This final "take-down" due diligence usually is a request by the underwriter, asking that the issuer disclose any new information that could materially affect value. At this stage the venture's accounting firm issues a "cold comfort letter," stating whether they are aware of any material changes in the business. Such information could affect issue pricing.

12. The concern is that if, for any reason, the forecast is not achieved, investors may claim that they relied on the forecasts, and may seek compensation for any resulting loss of the value of an investment. U.S. legislative changes in 1995, supported by the Securities and Exchange Commission, are intended to encourage issuers to make fuller disclosure and to include "forward-looking statements" or forecasts in the prospectus. For the most part, the new legislation has only been used to protect issuers and underwriters against liability for inadvertently making such statements. See the Private Securities Litigation Reform Act of 1995.

13. Deeds, Decarolis, and Coombs (1997) find that, for a sample of biotechnology firms, public information about the venture also affects the amount of capital raised in the IPO.

14. The actual offering may be priced in the filing range, or above or below it. Hanley (1993) documents that offering prices only partially adjust for differences between expected demand (as reflected by the filing range) and actual demand.

15. Studies of IPOs in other countries also generally find that offering prices are below closing prices in the after-market. See, for example, Jenkinson (1990) regarding offerings in the United Kingdom and elsewhere, and Kutsuna, Cowling, and Westhead (2000), and Packer (1995) regarding offerings in Japan.

16. Booth and Smith (1986) formally develop the hypothesis that investment bankers certify the prices of the issues they underwrite.

17. Benveniste and Spindt (1989) make a similar argument. Beatty and Ritter (1986) provide evidence that underwriters who frequently underprice too much or too little tend to lose market share. Hansen and Torregrosa (1992) contend that, in addition to certification, the underwriter

monitors the firms that it brings public and that the monitoring is costly for the underwriter and value enhancing for the issuer.

18. See Tinic (1988).

19. The Private Securities Litigation Reform Act of 1995 changed the liability standard in U.S. securities litigation cases in a way that reduces the ability of plaintiffs to recover damages from underwriters. An unanticipated consequence of the Act is that insurance premiums of officers and directors increased. Apparently, insurers are concerned that protecting underwriters from liability could increase judgments against officers and directors. The change suggests that when one means of certification is restricted, other (possibly less efficient) means will be sought by the market.

20. This finding is reported by Barry, Muscarella, Peavy, and Vetsuypens (1990).

21. See Megginson and Weiss (1991).

22. For additional evidence on underpricing, see Ritter (1987).

23. Underpricing normally is measured from the issue price to the first after-market closing price. Somewhat longer-term measures indicate that price can change dramatically after the IPO. The following are the most extreme cases from 1998: On September 23, eBay was offered at $18 per share. It closed on December 31 at $241.25, a gain of 1240.3 percent. Inktomi was offered at $18 on June 9 and closed the year at $129.375, a gain of 618.8 percent. Overpricing also is possible. The worst performer of 1998 was BMI Medical Management, which was offered at $7 on February 4 and closed the year at $0.08, a loss of 98.9 percent. USN Communications is a close second: Offered at $16 on February 3, it closed the year at $0.19, a loss of 98.8 percent.

24. Choe, Masulis, and Nanda (1993) find that underpricing is less during periods of economic expansion. They interpret the finding as evidence that expected costs of adverse selection are less during periods when the economy is growing when firms are more likely to be motivated to issue because of the need to raise capital to fund investment opportunities.

25. Ruud (1993) offers an alternative view. She notes that market value declines at the time of the IPO are not observable, owing to the market stabilization activities of the underwriter. By extending the window over which returns are studied, she finds that overpricing takes longer to be reflected in aftermarket stock prices, whereas underpricing is immediately observable. Benveniste, Busaba, and Wilhelm (1996), on the other hand, point out that price stabilization is one way the underwriter can bond (guarantee) the valuation.

26. See Rock (1986).

27. The literature related to this view is extensive, beginning with Benveniste and Spindt (1989). For a more recent treatment that includes a review of the literature, see Sherman (2000).

28. If there are outstanding options to acquire additional shares, the underwriter may estimate "fully diluted" value assuming that all of the options are exercised.

29. Before the IPO, the number of shares can be adjusted by splitting or reverse splitting, to achieve the target value per share.

30. This does not include costs investors would incur by selling shares in the secondary market or in a seasoned offering. Such costs are considerably smaller than the cost of an IPO.

31. Sometimes underwriters also receive warrant compensation. The reasons for using warrants are complex. Barry, Muscarella, and Vetsuypens (1991) contend that warrants enable underwriters to circumvent legal limitations on compensation. Dunbar (1995) suggests that issuers select between warrant compensation and cash compensation to minimize issue cost. Ng and Smith (1996) also argue for issue cost reductions, and suggest that warrant compensation is a way that underwriters who lack established reputations can certify new issues. Ng and Smith find empirical support for all three reasons.

32. Consistent with this view, Bower (1989) suggests that high-quality firms (undervalued firms) select firm commitment, but low-quality firms (overvalued firms) select best efforts because the effective cost of certification is too great.

33. See Booth and Chua (1996). Sherman (1992) notes that best-efforts underwritings tend to be more underpriced than firm-commitment underwritings. Ritter (1987) finds average underpricing of 48 percent for best-efforts issues compared to 15 percent for firm-commitment issues.

34. Rights offerings enable issuers to raise capital without circumventing the preemptive rights of existing shareholders. Preemptive rights enable current stockholders to maintain their ownership percentage by participating in subsequent equity issues. In the United States, shareholders normally waive their preemptive rights. Doing so makes cash offerings feasible.

35. Smith (1977) offers an explanation of the rights issue process.

36. Hansen (1988) examines the reasons for the declining use of rights offerings.

37. Lin and Smith (1998) look specifically at selling by the lead venture capital investor.

38. Related to this, Gompers (1996) contends that venture capital firms that are not well established may urge companies to go public too soon as a way of building a track record that will facilitate raising additional venture funds.

39. Implementation of Rule 144 is highly technical, which results in unintended Rule violations. For more information, see Lipman (1994).

40. A seller under Rule 144 must file Form 144 and represent that she is unaware of any nonpublic information that should be disclosed and could adversely affect value.

41. Several studies argue that the two-stage process is used by high-quality firms (undervalued firms) to signal quality. See, for example, Allen and Faulhaber (1989), Chemmanur (1993), Grinblatt and Hwang (1989), and Welch (1989). Other research disputes the signaling interpretation. See Jagadeesh, Weinstein, and Welch (1993).

42. Mikkelson and Partch (1985) and Smith (1986) provide evidence on market reactions to offering announcements.

43. Before the acquisition, the venture may restructure its assets and liabilities to make the acquisition more attractive to the purchaser. For example, the venture might draw down current asset balances and use the proceeds to liquidate some outstanding liabilities. It might also "clean up" the structure of equity claims by converting preferred shares to common and eliminating or exchanging any outstanding stock options.

44. As noted, the assets, in addition to being risky, are subject to overstatement by the seller, and the liabilities are subject to understatement.

45. Hertzel and Smith (1993) estimate that the liquidity discount is approximately 13.5 percent. For shares that are not restricted, they find an average discount of 15.6 percent.

46. See Wruck (1989), Silber (1991), Hertzel and Smith (1993).

47. An MBO is a leveraged buy-out where management is the buyer. Arzac (1992) examines the financial theory related to leveraged buy-out financing.

48. Morris, Williams, Allen, and Avila (1997) find that, among other factors, the success of family transitions and survival of family businesses depend on financially planning for the transition.

49. Chami (1997) examines some of the issues of risk allocation and incentive conflict in the context of family owned businesses.

50. Similar needs for liquidity can arise from transfer of ownership interest as gifts.

51. Leveraged ESOPs are argued to be an inexpensive source of borrowing. As our focus is on harvesting and providing liquidity for owners, we do not address this issue. See Weston, Chung, and Siu (1998) for an overview of ESOPs as a source of financing.

52. Valuation services can be contracted by the company or by the trust. In the figure, for convenience, the company is shown as contracting for valuation.

53. The transaction can result in a tax advantage for an individual seller because sometimes the proceeds can be rolled over into other investments and capital gains can be deferred.

54. This suggests that one consideration in the choice between a leveraged and unleveraged ESOP is how the existing owner expects valuation of the shares to change over time. If the owner expects value to increase significantly, an unleveraged ESOP may be preferred.

55. Funding and vesting of retirement benefits are separate events. Vesting practices do not materially affect the role of the ESOP as a harvesting mechanism.

56. Usually, trading by sellers of the rolled-up companies is restricted for several months by the lock-up provision of the IPO and may be explicitly restricted for a longer period by terms of the roll-up agreement.

57. See Shah and Thakor (1988).

58. The general stock market decline started a few months later than the Internet crash—the S&P 500 index fell by 23 percent between August 2000 and December 2000. This general stock market "crash" was uneven: prices fell by 11 percent on the Dow Jones but by as much as 49 percent on the NASDAQ, with higher-risk stocks losing the most value.

59. See E.S. Browning. "Why Some Tech Stock are Still Breathing." *Wall Street Journal,* Nov. 18, 2002, C1.

REFERENCES AND ADDITIONAL READING

ALLEN, FRANKLIN, AND GERALD R. FAULHABER. "Signaling by Underpricing in the IPO Market." *Journal of Financial Economics* 23 (1989): 303–323.

ARZAC, ENRIQUE R. "On the Capital Structure of Leveraged Buyouts." *Financial Management* (1992): 16–26.

BARRY, CHRISTOPHER, CHRIS MUSCARELLA, AND MICHAEL VETSUYPENS. "Underwriter Warrants, Underwriter Compensation, and the Cost of Going Public." *Journal of Financial Economics* 29 (1991): 113–135.

BARRY, CHRISTOPHER, CHRIS MUSCARELLA, JOHN PEAVY, III, AND MICHAEL VETSUYPENS. "The Role of Venture Capital in the Creation of Public Companies: Evidence from the Going Public Process." *Journal of Financial Economics* 27 (1990): 447–476.

BEATTY, RANDOLPH P., AND JAY R. RITTER. "Investment Banking, Reputation, and the Underpricing of Initial Public Offerings." *Journal of Financial Economics* 15 (1986): 213–232.

BENVENISTE, LAWRENCE M., WALID Y. BUSABA, AND WILLIAM J. WILHELM, JR. "Price Stabilization as a Bonding Mechanism in New Equity Issues." *Journal of Financial Economics* 42 (1996): 223–255.

BENVENISTE, LAWRENCE M., AND PAUL A. SPINDT. "How Investment Bankers Determine the Offer Price and Allocation of New Issues." *Journal of Financial Economics* 24 (1989): 343–361.

BOOTH, JAMES R., AND LENA CHUA, "Ownership Dispersion, Costly Information, and IPO Underpricing." *Journal of Financial Economics* 41 (1996): 291–310.

BOOTH, JAMES R., AND RICHARD L. SMITH. "Capital Raising, Underwriting, and the Certification Hypothesis." *Journal of Financial Economics* 15 (1986): 261–281.

BOWER, NANCY L. "Firm Value and the Choice of Offering Method in Initial Public Offerings." *Journal of Finance* 44 (1989): 647–662.

CARTER, RICHARD, AND STEVEN MANASTER. "Initial Public Offerings and Underwriter Reputation." *Journal of Finance* 45 (1990): 1045–1067.

CHAMI, RALPH. "What's Different about Family Businesses." IMF Working Paper, 2001.

CHEMMANUR, THOMAS J. "The Pricing of Initial Public Offerings: A Dynamic Model with Information Production." *Journal of Finance* 48 (1993): 285–304.

CHOE, HYUK, RONALD W. MASULIS, AND VIKRAM NANDA. "Common Stock Offerings Across the Business Cycle." *Journal of Empirical Finance* 1 (1993): 3–31

DEEDS, DAVID L., DONA DECAROLIS, AND JOSEPH E. COOMBS. "The Impact of Firm-Specific Capabilities on the Amount of Capital Raised in an Initial Public Offering: Evidence from the Biotechnology Industry." *Journal of Business Venturing* 12 (1997): 31–46.

DUNBAR, CRAIG G. "The Use of Warrants as Underwriter Compensation in Initial Public Offerings." *Journal of Financial Economics* 38 (1995): 59–78.

GOMPERS, PAUL. "Grandstanding in the Venture Capital Industry." *Journal of Financial Economics* 42 (1996): 133–156.

GOMPERS, PAUL, AND JOSH LERNER. "Conflict of Interest in the Issuance of Public Securities: Evidence form Venture Capital." *Journal of Law and Economics* 42 (1999): 1–28.

GRINBLATT, MARK, AND CHAUN Y. HWANG. "Signaling and the Pricing of Unseasoned New Issues." *Journal of Finance* 44 (1989): 393–420.

HANLEY, KATHLEEN WEISS. "The Underpricing of Initial Public Offerings and the Partial Adjustment Phenomenon." *Journal of Financial Economics* 34 (1993): 231–250.

HANSEN, ROBERT S. "The Demise of the Rights Issue." *Review of Financial Studies* 1 (1988): 289–301.

HANSEN, ROBERT S., AND PAUL TORREGROSA. "Underwriter Compensation and Corporate Monitoring." *Journal of Finance* 47 (1992): 1537–1555.

HELLMANN, THOMAS. "IPOs, Acquisitions and the Use of Convertible Securities in Venture Capital." Stanford Law Working Paper (2002).

HERTZEL, MICHAEL G. AND RICHARD L. SMITH. "Market Discounts and Shareholder Gains for Placing Equity Privately." *Journal of Finance* 48 (1993): 459–485.

JEGADEESH, NARASIMHAN, MARK WEINSTEIN, AND IVO WELCH. "An Empirical Investigation of IPO Returns and Subsequent Equity Offerings." *Journal of Financial Economics* 34 (1993): 153–175.

JENKINSON, T. J. "Initial Public Offerings in the United Kingdom, the United States, and Japan." *Journal of Japanese and International Economics* 4 (1990): 428–449.

KUTSUNA, KENJI, MARC COWLING, AND PAUL WESTHEAD. "The Short-run Performance of NASDAQ Companies and Venture Capital Investment Before and After Flotation." *Venture Capital* 2 (2000): 1–25.

LIN, TIMOTHY H., AND RICHARD L. SMITH. "Insider Reputation and Selling Decisions: The Unwinding of Venture Capital Investments during Equity IPOs." *Journal of Corporate Finance* 4 (1998): 241–263.

LIPMAN, FREDERICK D. *Going Public.* Rocklin, CA: Prima Publishing, 1994.

MEGGINSON, WILLIAM, AND KATHLEEN WEISS. "Venture Capitalist Certification in Initial Public Offerings." *Journal of Finance* 46 (1991): 879–903.

MIKKELSON, WAYNE H., AND MEGAN H. PARTCH. "Stock Price Effects and Costs of Secondary Distributions." *Journal of Financial Economics* 14 (1985): 165–194.

MORRIS, MICHAEL H., ROY O. WILLIAMS, JEFFREY A. ALLEN, AND RAMON A. AVILA. "Correlates of Success in Family Business Transitions." *Journal of Business Venturing* 12 (1997): 385–401.

NG, CHEE K., AND RICHARD L. SMITH. "Determinants of Contract Choice: The Use of Warrants to Compensate Underwriters of Seasoned Equity Offerings." *Journal of Finance* 51 (1996): 363–383.

PACKER, F. "What Improves the Credibility for the Offering Price? Empirical Results on Japanese OTC Markets." *Securities Analyst Journal* (March 1995).

RITTER, JAY R. "The Costs of Going Public." *Journal of Financial Economics* 19 (1987): 269–281.

ROCK, KEVIN. "Why New Issues Are Underpriced." *Journal of Financial Economics* 15 (1986): 187–212.

RUUD, JUDITH S. "Underwriter Price Support and the IPO Underpricing Puzzle. "*Journal of Financial Economics* 34 (1993): 135–151.

SHAH, SALMAN, AND ANJAN V. THAKOR. "Private Versus Public Ownership: Investment, Ownership Distribution, and Optimality." *Journal of Finance* 43 (1988): 41–59

SHERMAN, ANN. "IPOs and Long Term Relationships: An Advantage of Book Building" *Review of Financial Studies* 13 (2000): 697–714.

SHERMAN, ANN. "The Pricing of Best Efforts New Issues." *Journal of Finance* 42 (1992): 781–790.

SILBER, WILLIAM L. "Discounts on Restricted Stock: The Impact of Illiquidity on Stock Prices." *Financial Analysts Journal* 47 (1991): 60–64.

SMITH, CLIFFORD. "Investment Banking and the Capital Acquisition Process." *Journal of Financial Economics* 15 (1986): 3–29.

SMITH CLIFFORD W. "Alternative Methods of Capital Raising: Rights Versus Underwritten Offerings." *Journal of Financial Economics* 5 (1977): 273–307

SMITH, RICHARD. "The Choice of Issuance Procedure and the Cost of Competitive and Negotiated Underwriting: An Examination of the Impact of Rule 50." *Journal of Finance* 42 (1987): 703–720.

SMITH RICHARD L. "Underwriting of New Issues." In *The New Palgrave Dictionary of Money and Finance*. Edited by Peter Newman, Murray Milgate, and John Eatwell. New York: Macmillan, 1992.

TINIC, SEHA M. "Anatomy of Initial Public Offerings of Common Stock." *Journal of Finance* 43 (1988): 789–822.

WELCH, IVO. "Seasoned Offerings, Imitation Costs, and the Underpricing of Initial Public Offerings." *Journal of Finance* 44 (1989): 421–449.

WESTON, J. FRED, KWANG S. CHUNG, AND JUAN A. SIU. *Takeovers, Restructuring, and Corporate Governance*. Upper Saddle River, NJ: Prentice Hall, 1998.

WRUCK, KAREN H. "Equity Ownership Concentration and Firm Value: Evidence from Private Equity Financings." *Journal of Financial Economics* 23 (1989): 3–28.

The Future of Entrepreneurial Finance: A Global Perspective

Adaptive efficiency . . . is concerned with the kinds of rules that shape the way an economy evolves through time. It is also concerned with the willingness of society to acquire knowledge and learning, to induce innovation, to undertake risk and creative activity of all sorts, as well as to resolve problems and bottlenecks of the society through time. (Douglas C. North, 1990)

Learning Objectives

After reading this chapter, you will be able to:

- Review conceptual differences between entrepreneurial finance and corporate finance, and describe methods for addressing the unique challenges of entrepreneurial finance.

- Recognize some of the unresolved issues of entrepreneurial finance and the potential for new research to address these issues.

- Understand the importance of international differences in financial and regulatory institutions and how the differences contribute to variations in entrepreneurial activity.

- Understand that change in the market for new venture creation and financing is inevitable and recognize the implications of change for new venture investors and entrepreneurs.

As a field of study, entrepreneurial finance builds on the concepts and methodology of financial economics. In particular, we have stressed methods of financing, investment decision making, valuation, and contract design, in the context of new ventures. The concepts and methodology are helpful not only to prospective entrepreneurs, but also to those who supply funds to entrepreneurs—business angels, venture capitalists, lenders, employees, friends of the entrepreneur, trading partners, universities, government agencies, and so on.

The study of entrepreneurial finance is not limited to the start-up stage of a new venture or even to small or privately owned-businesses. A great deal of entrepreneurial activity is carried out by corporations and by faculty members working in universities. We have discussed how financial problems vary depending on the source of financing and how they vary

www.wiley.com/college/smith

INTERNET RESOURCES FOR THIS CHAPTER

The Web site identifies a number of sources related to financial markets in various countries. The site also points to new research and information on topics related to entrepreneurial finance, including print and electronic journals, as well as academic programs that produce research and seminars. For those who care to respond, we also provide an opportunity for your feedback on the book and the Internet resources.

over the life of the venture. Thus, we address the financial aspects of a venture, up to the point where the teachings of corporate finance can be applied directly.

Much of our analysis has stressed the importance of incentive and information problems that face the participants in the market for entrepreneurial finance. These problems explain many features of the market, including staging of investments, terms of financial contracts, the role of reputation, and trade practices and valuation approaches that emerge.

Entrepreneurs and investors who understand the financial determinants of new venture organizational and contractual structure, including the incentive and information structure, can more effectively design their own contracts to reflect deal-specific issues and to increase the value of an opportunity.

In this final chapter, we highlight the essential concepts and tools that have emerged from the study of entrepreneurial finance. We also identify areas where more data and research would provide clearer understanding of unresolved issues. We then study factors that contribute to the level of entrepreneurial activity and survey differences across international markets. We consider such questions as: Why has entrepreneurship thrived in some regions of the United States? Can other regions or other countries be effective in imitating the success formula? We conclude with a discussion of the future of entrepreneurial finance.

17.1 COMPLETING THE CIRCLE

In the introductory chapter, we identified eight fundamental differences between entrepreneurial finance and corporate finance. To solidify what you have learned, we return to that list for a final review.

Entrepreneurial Investment and Financing Decisions Are Interdependent

- The decisions entrepreneurs and investors make concerning allocation of outside and inside ownership have important implications for the venture and for the values of its financial claims. You now are able to evaluate the interdependence and design financial contracts that deal effectively with it.

In corporate finance, we usually assume that a firm makes its investment decisions without regard to choice of financing. This is because we assume that corporate investors care only about nondiversifiable risk. Although the assumption may be reasonable for a publicly held corporation, it is not appropriate for a new venture.

An entrepreneur often is compelled to choose between being underdiversified or not pursuing the venture. Underdiversification exposes the entrepreneur to risk that is specific to the venture. Opportunity cost reasoning implies that an underdiversified entrepreneur should require compensation for bearing venture-specific risk. As well-diversified investors do not care about venture-specific risk, the entrepreneur's required rate of return should be higher than that of an investor who can diversify.

When an entrepreneur participates in a venture along with an investor who can diversify, the parties place different values on the same financial claims. The diversified investor values the claims more highly. This means that the value of an opportunity depends on how the financial claims allocate risk and expected return. All else being the same, allocating more non-market risk to the diversified investor increases the value of an opportunity. Effective use of financial contracts to allocate risk can enhance the value and can change negative-NPV opportunities into positive-NPV opportunities.

Earlier, we analyzed how to value of financial contracts that allocate risk in different ways. From that analysis it is clear that entrepreneurial investment and financing decisions are not separate. The merits of an opportunity are sensitive to how risk is allocated.

Investment Value Depends on the Entrepreneur's Ability to Diversify

- For the entrepreneur, ability to diversify increases the value of a new venture opportunity. You have the tools to estimate the entrepreneur's wealth and to value a new venture opportunity in light of the entrepreneur's diversification.

Even if no outside investor is involved, the entrepreneur's ability to diversify affects value. The entrepreneur's required rate of return for investing in a venture depends on the fraction of total wealth the entrepreneur commits. The larger the fraction that is committed, the higher is the entrepreneur's required rate of return.

The entrepreneur's total wealth includes more than just financial wealth. It also includes the present value of human capital. You can use methods illustrated in the book to estimate the entrepreneur's total wealth and the fraction that is invested in a venture. Project value also depends on how the risk of the investment in the venture relates to the risk of the entrepreneur's other investments. You can value an opportunity when the entrepreneur's other wealth is invested in a market index portfolio or in another risky investment.

The same venture is more valuable to an entrepreneur who is wealthier because more wealth enables the entrepreneur to achieve greater diversification. It follows that reducing the investment in the venture also can enhance the value of the opportunity to the entrepreneur. Pursuing an opportunity on a smaller scale, bringing in an outside investor, or finding ways of reducing the duration of the entrepreneur's commitments can reduce the size of the entrepreneur's investment. The methods you have learned allow you to evaluate the effects of such changes on the value of the entrepreneur's interest in the venture.

Some Outside Investors Are Actively Involved in Their New Venture Investments

- Active involvement by investors can add value to a venture. Different types of investors contribute in different ways and are compensated in different ways. Your understanding of the ways active investors can contribute enables you to evaluate financing alternatives.

New ventures raise capital from a variety of sources. Some provide only financial capital; others provide both capital and managerial skills. Business angels and strategic partners often are involved in managerial aspects of the enterprise. Venture capital firms are involved at critical junctures and continuously monitor their investments. Investors such as these seek returns on both their financial capital and their human capital investments. An important theme of the book has been to illustrate how managerial and monitoring efforts affect investment and financing choices and the structure of financial claims.

Investors, who are actively involved, can add to the overall value of a venture by changing both expected returns and risk. You can use the tools and techniques you have learned to study how financial sources impact expected return and risk and how different types of investors are likely to affect the values of the parties' financial claims.

Financial Contracts and Other Devices Can Be Used to Address Information Problems

- Entrepreneurs and investors face serious information problems. Signaling, reputation, and certification can be used to overcome information problems and entrepreneurs can use the business plan and financial contracting to overcome information problems.

Information problems present a significant obstacle to raising outside financing. Entrepreneurs often are overly optimistic and presume that their venture ideas will be successful. Consequently, investors often severely discount the entrepreneur's projections.[1]

In this environment, both parties have trouble credibly communicating their true beliefs to each other. The communication difficulties not only impede capital raising, but also can result in two types of investment mistakes: investing in ventures that should be foregone and failing to invest in those that should be pursued.

The parties to a new venture financial contract can use the provisions of the contract to signal their beliefs to each other. An entrepreneur, for example, can lend credibility to projections that otherwise would seem optimistic by tying ownership interest or other compensation to future attained performance, and by using milestones that give the investor the opportunity to postpone some of the investment until more information is received.

Well-chosen provisions of financial contracts help convey the beliefs of the parties. Reducing information asymmetry results in better decisions about when to pursue a venture and when to forego it. However, contract provisions sometimes shift additional risk to the entrepreneur, a result that works against the risk-allocation benefits of contracting with a diversified investor. Alternative ways of signaling beliefs can be compared, and contract structures can be designed that are likely to be advantageous for both parties.

An investor's assessment of the value of an opportunity depends on more than the terms of the financial contract. The business plan also can signal the entrepreneur's capabilities and commitment to the venture. By carefully supporting and documenting the assumptions behind the plan's financial projections, an entrepreneur can narrow the information gap between the parties. By identifying critical milestones and assessing the financing needs to move from one milestone to the next, the parties can limit the financial commitment the entrepreneur seeks from the investor. This enables the entrepreneur to preserve a larger ownership stake in the venture.

An advantage of thinking about information problems in this way is that it focuses thinking on how best to use contractual provisions and other means to signal beliefs and how to design contracts that are advantageous for both parties. Dealing with information problems is an ongoing concern. Information asymmetry affects subsequent financing arrangements, even through the harvesting stage. Throughout the process, financial contracting, signaling, and certification can be used to deal with informational concerns.

New Venture Financial Contracts Can Align Incentives

- Understanding the tradeoff between risk allocation and incentive alignment contributes to optimum design of organizational structures and financial contracts that address the tradeoffs. Well-structured contracts anticipate and provide for incentive conflicts that can arise as the venture progresses.

The direct effect of transferring the risk to a diversified investor is to increase the value of the opportunity. However, risk allocation also affects incentives. An entrepreneur whose reward is not tied sufficiently to success may not be motivated to work toward that success. Also, the incentives of investors sometimes can be in conflict with the entrepreneur's interests. A creditor, for example, may emphasize safety, even to the detriment of overall value.

Providers of financing sometimes have options to increase the total amount of financing or to call for repayment. They also may have options to force a sale of the venture or a public offering and may have options to terminate the entrepreneur.

You now have insights about how to use financial contracts to align incentives and enhance value. One approach we have considered is to identify the advantages and disadvantages of alternative financing sources. The tradeoffs often are complex. For example, working capital policy affects the venture's returns, its ability to respond to events, perceptions of suppliers and customers, and the need to seek financing from other sources.

Real Options Are an Important Source of Value for New Venture Stakeholders

- Decision trees and game trees are particularly useful for describing the real options that are embedded in new ventures. You can use simulation, scenario analysis, and other approaches to study and evaluate the real options involved in alternative new venture organizational structures, financial contracts, and strategic choices.

Often, in corporate finance, investment opportunities are treated as one-time decisions. The decision is made at the beginning, as if there is no opportunity to abandon the project, expand it, or change direction. In such cases, projects are evaluated using simple discounted cash flow methods. However, this approach does not reflect the nature of new venture opportunities, which are structured as portfolios of real options. The portfolios provide opportunities to raise additional capital, abandon the venture, and change direction. Existing investors also may have options to contribute additional funds in exchange for additional ownership, terminate the entrepreneur, and make various other choices.

The real option structures of new ventures are complex, and the options are interdependent. Exercising one option precludes exercising others or changes the values of others. In addition, the conditions that support using standard option pricing model approaches to valuation are not satisfied. Because a venture is a portfolio of real options, riskiness can change dramatically over time. As the venture progresses from one milestone to the next, risk is likely to decline. A decision tree is useful for modeling the real option structure of a venture. You can use financial modeling and forecasting to project the cash flows, assess uncertainty, and value complex financial claims under different assumptions about exercising or abandoning the options.

Harvesting Is Critical to the Investment Decision

- You now recognize the various alternatives for harvesting and are able to compare their effects on investment value for the entrepreneur and for investors.

Harvesting is an important aspect of the decision to invest in any new venture. This aspect contrasts sharply with corporate investment decisions where capital market investors are not specifically concerned about how the corporation will harvest its investments. We have reviewed the harvesting alternatives that are available to a venture and the primary factors that influence the choice of harvesting.

An IPO is only the first step in the harvesting activities of investors in a venture that has gone public. It establishes the public market for the venture's securities, in which the investors ultimately will sell their ownership interests. We have reviewed evidence on the costs of various harvesting methods, including IPO and private acquisition. Because existing investors usually do not sell many of their shares in the IPO, the cost of an IPO is not the same as the cost of harvesting an investment in a public company.

A new venture can be valued as of the time when harvesting is expected to take place. That value can be incorporated into the valuation at the time when the investment decision is made. Doing so enables the parties to agree on the fraction of equity an investor would need to receive in exchange for making an investment. Parties to a venture may have different interests and incentives when it comes to harvesting. Solutions can be designed, such as formation of an ESOP, that enable each party to pursue his or her own objectives.

New Venture Organizational and Financing Choices Can Be Compared Based on Their Effects on Value to an Entrepreneur or to an Investor

- You understand the difference between value to the entrepreneur and value to a well-diversified investor. You know how to evaluate financial claims from either perspective and how to design financial contracts based on their implications for value allocation.

There is a critical difference between value to stockholders and value to an entrepreneur. Depending on your perspective, either as a entrepreneur or as a diversified outside investor, it is possible to assess the value of financial claims and to evaluate alternatives with regard to their expected benefit. The allocation of value between the parties can be conceptualized, and financial contract structures can be developed that allocate value in ways that reflect the realities of the market for new venture financing. If the market is very competitive, the entrepreneur can capture most of the value. Conversely, if many similar entrepreneurs are competing for scarce financing or the skills of a few active investors, then investors can capture most of the value.

17.2 BREAKING NEW GROUND

Entrepreneurial finance is a new field in financial economics. Much of the academic research is recent. A large portion of it is descriptive and provides a better understanding of institutions and practices. Considerably less research focuses on tools for improving decision making and for adding value to new ventures. The underlying motivation for this text is to emphasize the latter type of research, by drawing on the fundamentals of financial economic theory to generate applications for the practice of entrepreneurial finance. The following are a few areas in which theoretical and empirical advances have the potential to contribute significantly to our understanding of the field.

How Can Portfolio Theory Best Be Adapted to Evaluate High-Risk Opportunities with Significant Probabilities of Failure?

In the evaluation of new venture opportunities, we have relied on the principle of risk aversion. We have assumed that a mean/variance approach to evaluating return and risk (such as the Capital Asset Pricing Model) is a reasonable representation of how risk aversion maps into value. However, the mean/variance framework can yield nonsensical values for opportunities that are highly risky, where horizons are long, and there is significant probability of losing the entire investment. No simple solution to this problem occurs to us, particularly because value to the entrepreneur depends on how risk relates to the entrepreneur's other holdings.

What Is the Opportunity Cost of Capital for High-Risk, Long-Term Investments?

The standard approach to valuing investment opportunities assumes that the investor can leverage the market portfolio to achieve comparable risk. We employ this opportunity-cost concept to value investments in new ventures. However, for high-risk, long-term projects, risk levels can exceed practical limitations on the ability of investors to leverage the market. We have assumed the investor is risk-neutral beyond the point of maximum leverage. The assumption is generous concerning project value but offsets the tendency of the mean/variance framework to undervalue high-risk opportunities. New research may suggest a better alternative to estimating the opportunity cost.

What Is the Best Way to Value Investment Opportunities Involving Portfolios of Complex and Interdependent Real Options?

Recognizing that new ventures are portfolios of real options, we employ decision trees to describe option structures. We use simulation and scenario analysis to describe how uncertainty changes over time and how it changes with different organizational, product-market, and financial strategies. We value uncertain cash flows using discount rates that reflect risk aversion. We do not value the cash flows at the risk-free rate, and we do not try to estimate "risk-neutral probabilities." We have not used valuation approaches based on option pricing theory because the assumptions that support those approaches are not satisfied for new ventures. Also, new venture option structures are too complex and interdependent to value as if the options were independent. The result of applying the mean/variance assumptions to investment portfolios of real options is unclear. More practical and consistent methods of valuing structures of interdependent real options are needed.

What Is the Best Way to Estimate the Uncertain Cash Flows of a New Venture and the Correlation of Those Cash Flows with the Market?

Required rates of return and standard deviations of holding-period returns are determined simultaneously. Corporate finance techniques finesse simultaneity by valuing cash flows at discount rates that are inferred from market data on firms with comparable systematic risk. However, when total risk affects value, as it does for the entrepreneur, data on other firms are useful only if both total risk and systematic risk are comparable. Although data on public companies are readily available, early-stage ventures are likely to be riskier and less diversified.

To avoid both the simultaneity problem and the need to rely on comparable firm data, we have adopted the certainty-equivalence approach to value new venture cash flows. However, the CEQ approach is sensitive to assumptions about the total risk of venture cash flows and the correlation between venture cash flows and the market. Users of this approach would benefit from new data and evidence that could be used in estimating the risk of an investment and its expected cash flows.

What Is the Best Approach for Valuing Multiple-Period Cash Flows for an Underdiversified Investor?

In corporate finance, the present values of cash flows in different periods are additive. This facilitates valuation of investments that generate cash flows in multiple periods. The intertemporal correlations only matter if they are correlated with the market . The discount rate applied to each cash flow accounts for correlation with the market. By contrast, the intertemporal correlation of cash flows does matter for an underdiversified investor. Currently, we have no easy way to address the effect of intertemporal correlation on value to an underdiversified investor. We have addressed the problem by simulating the risk and return of a single-period project that has approximately the same duration as the venture and where risk of the single-period cash flow depends on the time series correlation of cash flows. A tractable and intuitive alternative would be of significant practical value.

What Kinds of Investment Opportunities Are Most Effectively Pursued by Individual Entrepreneurs and what Kinds Are Most Effectively Pursued by Corporations?

Corporations owned by diversified investors have a cost of capital advantage over individuals. However, experience shows that large organizations have difficulty managing entrepreneurial ventures. Little is known about how the tradeoff is resolved in individual cases. Research on this topic could generate insights regarding the organization of entrepreneurial activity and could enhance the ability of corporations to undertake entrepreneurial ventures.[2]

How Do Financial Wealth and the Opportunity Cost of Human Capital Affect an Individual's Decision to Undertake a High-Risk Entrepreneurial Venture?

We expect the decision to pursue a venture to be a decreasing function of the fraction of total wealth the entrepreneur must commit. However, we do not know much about how individuals assess the opportunity cost of the time they must devote. Research could generate insights as to which types of individuals choose to become entrepreneurs and how variations in the required commitment of human capital affect their decisions.

How Can Organizations that Engage in Research and Development Promote Entrepreneurial Activity While Preserving the Right to Realize Some of the Rewards of the Activity?

A common concern of research-oriented firms and universities is that employee researchers will work for the firm until they discover an attractive idea and then leave to pursue the venture individually. Such behavior discourages firms to invest in research. Scholarship may reveal mechanisms that would enable established firms to invest more aggressively in research and to participate more fully in research successes.

What Social and Economic Institutions Foster Entrepreneurial Activity and Can Communities Proactively Develop Such Institutions?

Entrepreneurship is thriving in some regions of the United States. The success is due partly to the institutional environment. However, it is not clear that simply transferring the U.S. environment to other countries or regions would foster similarly significant entrepreneurial growth. It also is possible that fostering entrepreneurship gives rise to other problems.

How Will a Decrease in the Rate of Innovation Affect the Allocation of Resources Devoted to Entrepreneurial Activity?

In the recent past, the rate of technological progress in such areas as the Internet, computer software, medicine, and telecommunications has generated a growing stream of investment opportunities. Many entrepreneurs and investors in these new ventures became wealthy quickly. Many companies that receive early financing made rapid transitions to the public capital markets.

But what is likely to happen to institutions such as venture capital firms and angel investor groups now that the rate of technological progress has slowed and the industry orientation of new venture activity has changed? Will the same kinds of institutions function as well when the focus of entrepreneurial activity has changed? Can existing institutions efficiently downsize as the flow of investment opportunities slows? Alternatively, will institutions continue to search for opportunities even if the expected investment returns are low?

Existing institutions facilitate the growth of entrepreneurial activity, but technological shocks, such as the rapid development of E-commerce, also play a significant role in affecting the level of entrepreneurial activity. How the industry will react to a long period of slower progress is an open question.

17.3 AN INTERNATIONAL COMPARISON OF ENTREPRENEURIAL ACTIVITY

By all accounts, the United States generates more entrepreneurs and start-up businesses than any other country in the world. Understanding the causes of the extraordinary amount of entrepreneurial activity in the United States may have economic payoffs for other countries. On the other hand, there may be significant cultural, social, and economic costs of policies designed to foster entrepreneurial activity, including costs of bankruptcy and litigation. Bankruptcies and litigation in the United States are omnipresent. Bankruptcy is a way of life for many individuals, who repeatedly try new ventures and fail. The court system adjudicates numerous lawsuits, initiated by stockholders, lawyers, and private investors, against new companies, their underwriters, accountants, and managers, for allegedly misrepresenting facts about the companies or mismanaging assets.

Researchers have produced a vast literature on economic development and industrialization. Policy-makers across the globe have an intense interest in finding ways to facilitate and encourage innovation and entrepreneurial activity. However, economic growth should not be confused with an active entrepreneurial climate. Although entrepreneurial activity can contribute

Entrepreneurial Activity, Prosperity, and Economic Growth

The relationship between entrepreneurial activity and prosperity is complex. Based on the U.S. experience, it might seem that countries with high levels of entrepreneurial involvement tend to be wealthy and growing. The U.S., after all, has the highest level of per capita income and a high level of entrepreneurial involvement. Data compiled annually by the Global Entrepreneurship Monitor ("GEM") project shows that, after the U.S., the next tier of countries in terms of per capita Gross National Product ("GNP"), those with 1999 per capital GNPs above $20,000, displays widely varying levels of entrepreneurial involvement. For these countries, the levels of entrepreneurial involvement generally are lower than in the U.S. However, many of the countries with the highest involvement levels are countries with low per capita GNP.

In part the pattern is explained by taxonomy. The GEM project, on which this discussion is based, uses a broad definition of entrepreneurship that includes virtually all family-owned businesses. Thus, more agrarian economies show high levels of entrepreneurial involvement, whereas industrialized economies with many low-wage factory jobs show low levels of entrepreneurial involvement.

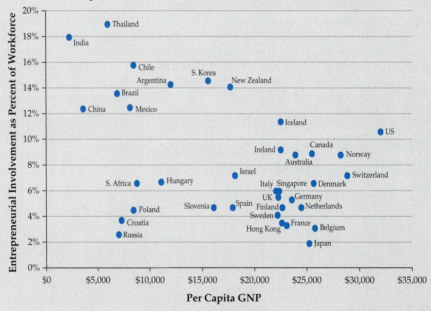

Entrepreneurial Involvement and Gross National Product

Sources: Global Entrepreneurship Monitor 2002 Executive Report, Statistical Abstract of the United States: 2001.

(Continues)

(Continued)

In some Latin American and Asian economies, entrepreneurial involvement is high because employment opportunities are scarce, or what the GEM project refers to as "necessity-based entrepreneurship." The study finds evidence that necessity-based entrepreneurship is symptomatic of infrastructure problems: necessity-based entrepreneurship is high when the institutions that support financial entrepreneurship financially are weak; when government policies impede business entry and expansion; and when research is not supported and intellectual property rights are not well protected.

Whether, on net, entrepreneurship fosters economic growth is an open question. It is clear that entrepreneurial opportunities and infrastructure supportive of entrepreneurship can soften an economic downturn, energize a stagnant economy, or enable resources to flow quickly into new opportunities. Thus, for example, the GEM project demonstrates a short-run relationship between entrepreneurial involvement and subsequent economic growth. However, in some respects, a climate supportive of entrepreneurship can interfere with the smooth operation and growth of established businesses. As yet, there is no definitive understanding of the tradeoff.

Entrepreneurial Involvement of Workforce: 2001

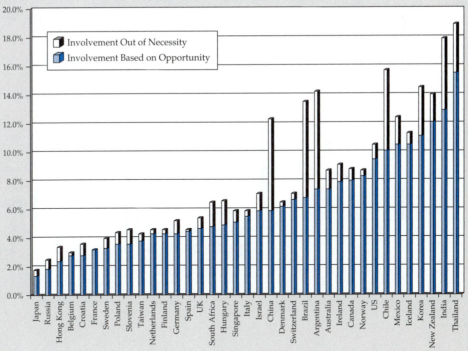

Source: Global Entrepreneurship Monitor 2002 Summary Report.

to growth, it also can be symptomatic of lack of economic opportunity in conventional areas. Individuals tend to move into entrepreneurship when their opportunity cost is low. Some countries, like the United States and the United Kingdom, have been extremely successful at incubating and growing firms. Others have been successful in more limited ways, by developing institutions that encourage growth in specific sectors, such as basic manufacturing. Those institutions provide less support in service industries and R&D-intensive industries.

Access to venture capital is a primary determinant of entrepreneurial activity. A recent study analyzes determinants of venture capital for a sample of countries, and considers the importance of IPOs, GDP growth, labor market conditions, accounting standards, private pension fund investment, and government programs.[3] Some factors may have influences that extend across countries, and the influence can vary with the stage of the venture. For example, a factor could affect early-stage funding but not later-stage. Results indicate that the rate of venture capital investing is positively correlated with IPO activity, although IPO activity does not explain differences in early-stage venture capital investing across countries. Private pension fund investing also is a significant determinant over time but not across countries. Labor market rigidities negatively impact early-stage venture capital investing but not later-stage. The authors of the study conclude that while patterns in later-stage venture capital investing are well understood and largely explained by IPO activity, early-stage investing and the impact of government-funded investments require more research.

Figure 17-1 shows cross-country differences in the allocation of venture capital funds to early-stage ventures as opposed to later-stage. The figure is based on data for the single year,

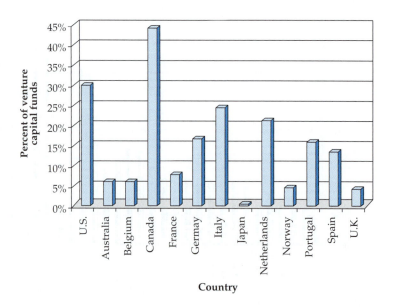

Figure 17-1   Allocation of venture capital funds to early-stage ventures

Countries differ in the fraction of total venture capital funds allocated to early-stage ventures. The figure includes data for venture capital in 1995. Based on Jeng and Wells (2000).

1995, and includes only countries with at least 50 million in total new commitments of venture capital. The U.S. level (approximately 30 percent) is substantially higher than the levels for most other countries.

Numerous features contribute to differences in entrepreneurial activity across countries and regions. Based on empirical research, we identify below several features that appear to explain international patterns of activity. Understanding these features helps answer the question of whether employing specific policies to foster entrepreneurial activity is possible and/or desirable. We identify these features in general terms first, followed by more specific discussion of U.S. financial structures compared to the financial structures of other countries.

The Role of Financial Structure in Stimulating Entrepreneurial Activity

Financial structure is a general term for the mix of financial markets, institutions, and contracts that characterize an economy. Financial structures vary across countries and as countries develop.[4] The following attributes of a financial structure are likely to stimulate new venture activity:[5]

- The financial structure facilitates assessment of the risks and rewards.
- The financial structure limits exposure to risk and increases expected rewards.
- The financial structure both facilitates and limits risk-taking by the entrepreneur.
- The financial structure includes patient investors with minimal need for liquidity.
- The tax structure favors capital investment.
- The financial structure facilitates diversification and pooling of risk.
- The financial structure provides easy access to public capital markets.
- Investment decisions are predominantly market-driven.

The Financial Structure Facilitates Assessment of Risks and Rewards

The decision to pursue or invest in a venture depends on ability to assess the risks and potential rewards. Reliable information is critical to making an accurate assessment. Among the important determinants of risk and reward are market size, costs of production and distribution, and the activities of competitors. Entrepreneurs and investors in the United States have relatively good information and information networks upon which to base their assessments.

The United States is an information-rich economy and generates tremendous amounts of information relevant to new ventures. Entrepreneurs and investors who target a U.S. market as well as firms planning to produce in the United States, have access to information from public and private sources on market size and market characteristics, and on production and distribution costs. The data generally are accurate, current, and inexpensive. Moreover, it generally is possible to assess market responses to new products quickly and comprehensively. In contrast, market information in many countries is very costly or difficult to obtain. Consequently, risks and potential rewards often are more difficult to assess.

For many high-technology fields, as well as other fields such as motion picture production and publishing, the United States is on the frontier of economic activity. Within the United States, activity is clustered in small geographic areas (Silicon Valley, Route 128, Los Angeles, New York). Clustering facilitates information flow among industry participants and helps each to do a more effective job of assessing market potential and competitive actions and reactions. As such, clustering improves the accuracy of risk-reward assessments. The economic benefits of clustering are not easy to nurture or replicate in other regions.

The Financial Structure Limits Exposure to Risk and Increases Expected Rewards

For products where the United States is on the technological frontier, U.S. entrepreneurs have a competitive advantage in controlling risks and rewards. Clusters that include industry leaders not only increase information flow, they also reduce risk and increase expected rewards for activities that are pursued. Individuals who have capabilities critical to success often reside in the cluster already. Or they easily can be persuaded to move to it. It is more difficult to persuade a key individual to move away from an area that complements her expertise.

More fundamentally, an entrepreneur who is close to the nexus of economic activity in a particular field can learn of, and react quickly to, changes in competitive conditions. An entrepreneur who is isolated or removed from such information is at a great disadvantage. Location advantages enable entrepreneurs and investors to take deliberate actions to alter risk and reward structures in response to, or anticipation of, competitive actions.

The other way the financial structure can limit risk and increase rewards is by establishing and enforcing property rights. Property rights are established both formally (through the legal system of patents, copyrights, and trademarks) and informally (through credible commitment, bonding, and reputation). The U.S. structure fares well on both fronts. Formal legal property rights are relatively easy to establish and enforce. Good information flows promote reliance on reputation as a means of enforcing property rights.

The Financial Structure Both Facilitates and Limits Risk-Taking by the Entrepreneur

A society that insulates entrepreneurs against some of the consequences of adverse outcomes facilitates risk-taking. The U.S. financial structure achieves insulation through several channels. First, U.S. bankruptcy laws enable entrepreneurs to avoid destitution if their ventures fail. The entrepreneur's assets are protected, to a point, from the claims of creditors. Entrepreneurs are precluded from entering contracts that could indenture them to lenders and from using pension fund assets or rights to social security payments to secure obligations.

It sometimes is argued that the U.S. bankruptcy laws encourage entrepreneurs and others to take excessive risks. Examples of abuses of the U.S. bankruptcy laws are numerous. However, an important effect of the laws is on risk *allocation*. Risk that otherwise would be borne by the entrepreneur is borne instead by others (including creditors, customers, suppliers, and employees). Our analysis of the relative differences in risk tolerance of the entrepreneur compared to well-diversified investors leads to the implication that, as long as the effect of bankruptcy laws is purely on risk allocation, the laws are socially beneficial. This is because bankruptcy laws allow risk to be transferred to others who can bear it more easily.

Compared to many countries, business failure or bankruptcy in the United States carries little social or financial stigma. Individuals who have failed at one venture, nonetheless, often are able to attract support for subsequent ventures. Attitudes toward failure carry over to the corporate level. In the United States, we expect pharmaceuticals producers to fail in many of their development efforts and oil drillers to fail in many of their explorations. Consumer products firms occasionally market things that no one wants to buy.

The Climate for New Venture Formation in Japan

There are, of course, shining examples of successful entrepreneurs in Japan—Sony's Akio Morita, Matsushita Electric's Konosuke Matshushita, and Honda's Soichiro Honda. However, the Japanese economy has not witnessed much entrepreneurial activity arising from individual effort. A number of features of the economy contribute to the low levels of activity.

Bank Financing   According to the Japan Small Business Corporation, 90 percent of venture financing comes directly from banks, securities, and insurance companies. These traditional institutions often rely on the borrower's ability to post collateral and adhere to a regular schedule of payments. However, collateral and regular payments are not arrangements that commonly are sought by companies with no track record or new ventures that are oriented to long product development times and rapid growth.

Government Support   Although the Japanese government provides a network of services for small firms, government programs do not facilitate rapid growth. Bank financing may be withdrawn as firms enter rapid growth. Thus, firms must look elsewhere to fund growth. In the United States, venture capital firms often supply several rounds of equity as firms mature. In Japan, venture capital firms are rare. Those that exist generally concentrate on debt. If a venture capitalist makes an equity investment, the ownership stake usually is small.

The Japanese government has made several efforts to subsidize and encourage venture capital firms. However, the firms that have been formed are affiliated with banks or security companies that are members of a keiretsu. A keiretsu is a group of companies in different industries held together by an extensive cross-ownership structure. The structure is similar to strategic-partnering relationships in the United States but is more extensive and intensive. The structure can facilitate cooperative relationships among firms but often impedes individual entrepreneurial activity. Member firms may resist dealing with new ventures that are pursuing opportunities that could infringe on opportunities of keiretsu members. This resistance forces new venture activity into the corporate structure, even though it is difficult to foster entrepreneurial activity in large organizations. Furthermore, venture capital firms in Japan typically are captives of Japanese banks. In addition, the staffs of venture capital firms tend to have conservative orientations toward risk and may not have the necessary industry experience to add value to the ventures they fund.

The Japanese Ministry of International Trade and Industry created the Venture Enterprises Center in 1974 in order to provide loan guarantees to "ventures." In Japan, there are formal criteria to classify as a venture enterprise. Most of what is classified as venture capital in Japan is longer-term debt. These programs aim to make small and medium-size businesses more productive and to encourage new enterprises. There does appear to be momentum in Japan to change the policy objectives to ones that could better fit high-growth ventures.

A further limitation on venture capitalists in Japan is that they have limited ability to fire an ineffective manager, even if they own 100 percent of the company. Managers and banks often carry more weight in decision making than do shareholders. Policies such as these impede financing for new ventures. Also, restrictions on foreign investment and foreign ownership constrain the ability of foreign venture capital firms to invest.

Bankruptcy   As in many countries, bankruptcy in Japan is very costly and carries a social stigma. Consequently, it is not common. Arbitration of bankruptcies in Japan can take up to a decade, and top executives bear personal responsibility for company debts. The Japanese culture, which

(Continues)

(Continued)

produces a bias against risk-taking, contrasts with the U.S. culture where entrepreneurs frequently and unabashedly tell stories of their failed enterprises. Many U.S. entrepreneurs adopt the adage that, "You can't expect to succeed until you've failed at least three times." The underlying notion is that there is something of value to learn from mistakes.

High Start-up Costs   The cost of incorporating is high in Japan. The tax and legal codes discourage a number of financial mechanisms that U.S. entrepreneurs commonly use. Japan law, for example, discourages stock option distributions, limited partnerships, stock swaps, initial public offerings for companies that have yet to report a profit, and takeovers (unless minority shareholders approve).

Michael Porter's (1990) assessment of the strengths and weaknesses of the Japanese economy reflects the effects of Japanese culture. He describes entrepreneurial management in larger firms:

> A new generation of managers is taking the helm in Japanese industry. They are replacing, in many cases, the founders and entrepreneurs who built up the companies after the war. The risk is that stewardship and conservatism may replace vision and institution building.

> Postwar Japanese managers had little to lose economically by taking entrepreneurial risks. The opportunity cost becomes much higher as the economy becomes more robust.

The primary issue is not with innovation arising within large corporations, but with the incentives for individual innovation and creation of new businesses. Reinforcing this is statistical evidence (Hawkins, 1993) that the number of new enterprises has declined sharply.*

Harvesting   The Japanese bank-centered financial structure impedes harvesting by going public. Milhaupt (1997) cites evidence that the Japanese process from start-up to IPO can take over 15 years. Furthermore, until recently, Japanese firms have faced listing requirements that deprive high-growth firms of access to public equity markets. The Japanese Ministry of Finance also rations the aggregate amount of IPO activity on a weekly basis.

Sources: *Del Hawkins, "New Business Entrepreneurship in the Japanese Economy." *Journal of Business Venturing* 8 (1993): 137–150. Michael Porter, *The Competitive Advantage of Nations* (New York: Macmillan Press, 1990); Curtis J. Milhaupt, "The Market for Innovation in the United States and Japan: Venture Capital and the Comparative Corporate Governance Debate," *Northwestern University Law Review* (1997): 865–898; Mark Magnier, "Entrepreneurship Hits a Cultural Wall," *Los Angeles Times*, section C, April 25, 1999.

The financial structure not only facilitates taking risk, it also limits the extent of risk the entrepreneur must take. If an entrepreneurial endeavor is likely to fail, financing and development activities accelerate discovery of the likely failure and allow the parties to abandon the project quickly. This aspect of the U.S. financial structure can be imitated in other countries by using the same or similar contract terms. However, while the contracts directly limit financial investment, the limitations on human capital investment are only indirectly related to the contract. To pursue a venture, an entrepreneur normally must resign from current employment. When an entrepreneur makes the calculation about how much human capital to invest in a venture, the entrepreneur must consider the opportunity cost of the time it will take to determine whether the venture is going to succeed or fail. Beyond this, if the venture fails or the entrepreneur is terminated, the entrepreneur must find new employment. Thus, the total commitment of human capital depends on how quickly the entrepreneur can find new employment and on how adversely the entrepreneur's earnings would be affected by failure of the venture or termination. In the United States, labor markets are fluid, workers are mobile, and midcareer moves are common. Consequently, the costs associated with human capital investment are lower than in economies like Japan, where midcareer moves are hard to make.

The Financial Structure Includes Patient Investors with Minimal Needs for Liquidity

Most private money invested in entrepreneurial activity in the United States comes from two sources: public corporations for research and development activities and institutional investors such as pension plans and endowments. Normally, these corporations and large financial institutions can manage their liquidity needs from other sources, such as the dividends and interest on their other investments, and large corporations can manage liquidity needs with operating cash flows. Consequently, these investors are able to commit significant amounts of funds to new ventures quickly, without interfering with their other activities. They also can maintain investments for years without realizing any significant cash flow.

A prominent feature of the U.S. market for venture capital is the pivotal role that pension funds play. U.S. rules for pension fund investing have had a positive influence on generating funds for new ventures. The 1979 ERISA revision of the "Prudent Person" standard enables pension funds to make high-risk investments, including investments in venture capital. In addition, a 1980 ERISA "safe harbor" regulation states that venture capital fund managers are not considered to be fiduciaries of pension fund investors when the pension funds invest in the venture capital portfolios they manage. The 1980 regulation removed a source of risk exposure for venture capital firms that accept pension funds as investors and contributed to the growth of the venture capital industry over the past two decades.

Pension funds have become the largest source of venture capital funding in the United States, United Kingdom, Ireland, and Denmark, all of which have capitalized pension funds and rules that facilitate investing in venture capital.[6] This type of pension regulation contrasts sharply with that of many countries that either do not have capitalized pension funding or have prohibitions against investing in venture capital. Switzerland, for example, traditionally has taken a very conservative position on pension fund investing. Swiss funds average only 10 to 13 percent of assets invested in equities, let alone in venture capital, compared to over 50 percent in the United States and the United Kingdom. Swiss funds generally do not invest in venture capital. To a significant degree, U.S. pension funds have contributed to venture capital investing outside the United States. U.S. pension funds and insurance companies supply over 30 percent of the total funds of independent venture capital firms in the United Kingdom. U.S. pension funds and insurance companies also supply a large fraction of venture capital in France (due partly to the absence of pension funds in France). In several OECD countries, pension funds are not permitted to invest in the private equities market. Japanese pension funds also do not normally contribute to venture capital funds.

In many industrialized countries, banks are the primary source of financing for new ventures.[7] Banks are primarily lenders, as opposed to equity investors.[8] Reliance on debt rather than equity reduces the funding available to ventures that do not generate regular cash flow. Countries that lack significant private retirement savings programs or large endowment funds also do not have resources to support illiquid investments in new ventures.

For funding of new ventures, equity has significant advantages. In particular, many ventures that are capable of rapid growth are unlikely to generate positive cash flows in the near-term. They also typically need flexible forms of financing. Flexibility allows managers to reinvest cash in the business rather than paying off debt contracts.

Furthermore, equity financing of new ventures often is tied-in with nonmonetary support. Most entrepreneurs are not versatile enough to come up with a good idea *and* implement it *and* manage it to maturity. Instead, the principle of comparative advantage suggests that they should rely on others to help implement the idea or to provide managerial advice. In the United States, business angels, venture capital firms, and other equity participants provide managerial expertise, industry knowledge, advice, contacts, and other types of support. Frequently, the investors use their own first-hand experience.

This type of participatory financing is rare in most other countries. For example, except through connections with lenders (who may also hold small amounts of equity), Japanese entrepreneurs are less likely than U.S. entrepreneurs to benefit from the experiences of other entrepreneurs in the same industry. Japan does not have an active angel investor community. Furthermore, Japanese venture capital firms generally are staffed with individuals from banking, who do not have entrepreneurial experience.[9] The United Kingdom has a market for entrepreneurial finance that operates much like the U.S. market. However, U.K. business angels are not as actively involved in management as angels in the United States. This difference is surprising, especially because estimates suggest that early-stage investments in ventures by U.K. business angels are twice as important as early-stage investments by formal venture capital firms.

One indication of the value-added by outside investors is the amount of time a venture capitalist devotes to each venture in the portfolio. Figure 17-2 compares time commitments in the United States and three European countries. Effort levels in the United Kingdom are similar to those in the United States. Those in France and the Netherlands are substantially lower.

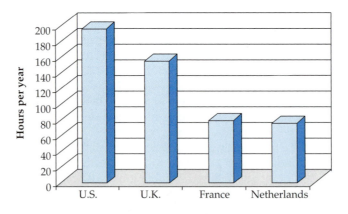

Source: Sapienza, Manigart, and Vermeir (1996)

Figure 17-2 Venture capitalist time commitment to each portfolio company

The extent of active venture capitalist involvement with portfolio companies differs materially across countries.

The Tax Structure Favors Capital Investment

The U.S. tax structure encourages investment in new ventures in several ways. First, the primary tax in the United States is based on income, and not revenue or value added. A U.S. entrepreneur who attempts a venture that fails and collects no salary, pays no income tax. His living expenses, in effect, are subsidized compared to a system where the primary tax is on sales or value added. In such a system, a failed entrepreneur who draws no salary still spends money on living expenses. Because the entrepreneur's expenditures include a large component for taxes, entrepreneurial activity in countries that emphasize value-added or revenue-based taxes are not subsidized.

Second, in the United States there is a differential between the individual tax rates on capital gains and ordinary income. This differential, combined with the benefit of being able to

The Climate for Entrepreneurship in Germany

In Germany, most firms rely very little on private capital for financing. Most venture capital funding comes from subsidiaries of financial institutions such as commercial banks, insurance companies, and investment banks. Captives of the large banks and insurance companies account for 55 percent of venture capital funding. Insurance companies account for 12 percent. German firms also rely very little on equity financing. Only about 6 percent of total capital is invested in equity, compared to 21 percent in the United States.

The public capital market has limited importance in Germany. The German stock market is among the largest in the world. However, in the first six years of the 1990s, when there were only 77 new listings in Germany, there were over 3,000 in the United States. Germany also requires that new shares be issued by rights offering instead of general cash offering. In addition, German public companies require that half of the members of the external board be representatives of employees, a significant disincentive to going public. The overall evidence supports the relative inability of German investors to diversify risk, resulting in lower economic value. One study estimates that large block holdings by individuals, families, and others account for 60 percent of total stock holdings in Germany. In the United States only 10 percent of the stock holdings are in the hands of individuals and families. Correspondingly, total market capitalization of public firms is about 25 percent of GDP in Germany, in contrast to about 70 percent in the United States.

Gilson (2002) argues that German government involvement in developing the venture capital market has "failed miserably." The government program, WFG, was funded by a consortium of German banks. The banks were induced to participate by a government guarantee against significant losses. In addition, the WFG's return on successful investments was capped, which diminished incentives to make good investments. Over its life, WFG produced a return of –25.0 percent.

Sources: Carl W. Kester, "Governance, Contracting, and Investment Horizons: A Look at Japan and Germany," *Journal of Applied Corporate Finance* (1992): 83–98; Jim Martin, presentation on "Financing the Entrepreneurial Venture in the UK and Continental Europe," at NYU conference, The Economics of Small Business Finance (1997); Stephen D. Prowse, "Corporate Finance in International Perspective: Legal and Regulatory Influences on Financial System Development," *Economic Review,* Federal Reserve Bank of Dallas, 3rd quarter, 2–15. O' Shea, Special Features: Venture Capital in OECD Counties, l996. Gilson, Ronald. "Engineering a Venture Capital Market: Lessons from the American Experience." Stanford Law School Working Paper, 2002.

defer realization of gains, encourages investing in equity that does not generate cash flows. The entrepreneur is better off by taking a larger equity stake or stock options and drawing a smaller salary.

The tax structure also encourages early-stage ventures to raise capital in the form of equity instead of debt. A venture that generates no taxable income cannot take advantage of the deductibility of interest payments. The net effect is that for some ventures equity can be a less expensive form of financing than debt, on a risk-adjusted basis.

Finally, many venture capitalists believe the differential between capital gains and ordinary income tax is an important determinant of incentives to invest in new companies. The tax structure encourages individuals to save through tax-deferred programs, such as pension funds. However, the net effect of the capital gains tax structure on venture capital investment is not clear. Although tax deferral makes the pension fund indifferent between dividend income and capital gains, the more important effect may be that pension funds are patient investors who do not need to invest in assets that can be liquidated easily. Several studies have found no statistically significant relationship between capital gains taxes and new venture funding. One reason is that a large percentage of venture capital comes from tax-exempt investors.

A recent study suggests a different avenue of influence of capital gains taxes on business creation.[10] Prospective entrepreneurs face an opportunity cost of quitting their income-producing jobs. Reductions in the capital gains tax rate lessen the opportunity cost and make entrepreneurial careers more attractive, because much of an entrepreneur's compensation can be in the form of a capital gain.

International differences in tax treatment of entrepreneurs' incomes are likely to play a role in determining the creation and likely success of new ventures. In the United States, wealth accumulated through stock and stock option ownership is taxed as a capital gain when the securities are sold. In many European countries, including Germany and France, options are taxed as income, when granted, even though the holder may not be able to exercise the options for several years. Stock options often represent a large part of the financial incentive for entrepreneurs and other managers of start-up companies.[11]

The Financial Structure Facilitates Diversification and Pooling of Risk

Ability to diversify lowers required rates of return. Wealth that is insulated from bankruptcy, rapid assessment of venture potential and abandonment, and efficient labor markets all facilitate the entrepreneur's ability to diversify. Venture capital funds and public corporations represent investors who are well diversified. Even business angels have begun to organize in ways that facilitate diversification, though usually across a limited number of industries. Furthermore, most angel investors devote small fractions of total wealth to venture investments and can diversify with the remainder of their wealth.

There are differences across countries in firm ownership structure. In many cases, the differences affect ability to diversify, to take risks, and to reward risk-taking. State ownership is more extensive in Continental Europe than in the United States or the United Kingdom. Family ownership and cooperatives/mutual organizations also are more prevalent on the Continent.[12] These differences are consistent with less firm reliance on private investment and equity funding. Because there are significant advantages of private investment and equity, the differences may partly explain the lower levels of entrepreneurial activity. For example, many important innovations in Germany originated from large companies such as BMW and BASF rather than from start-up firms. The same is true for Japan, where a few dominant firms are responsible for a majority of significant innovations.

The Financial Structure Provides Easy Access to Well Functioning Public Capital Markets

A well functioning capital market is essential to many areas of new venture investment. Capital markets enable investors to diversify, which lowers the cost of outside capital. They also enable entrepreneurs to diversify (depending on total wealth and size of commitment to the venture), thereby lowering the entrepreneur's required return for investing in the venture. Larger, more liquid, markets make is easier for an investor to profit from information. Well functioning markets include institutions and contracts that provide for monitoring and disciplining managers. The markets also provide exit mechanisms for entrepreneurs and investors.

Capital markets that are well functioning have low transactions costs for raising capital and for secondary market trading. The market value of a financial asset is reduced by the present value of expected future transactions costs. Thus, public equity is less valuable if the costs of secondary market transactions are high, and private equity is less valuable if the cost of gaining access to public capital markets is high.

Transactions costs includes costs that investors incur to evaluate opportunities. If a firm incurs due-diligence and certification costs as an aspect of going public, and if it is required to provide financial information that is certified by a reputable accounting firm, then costs investors would otherwise incur decrease.

The United States has developed significant disclosure requirements that facilitate trading of securities.[13] There are public good aspects to information production by firms that are seeking external finance. Requirements for the firm to disclose information reduce duplicative search efforts and ensure that the least-cost producer of information will provide it. Requirements to disclose can reduce of the public good problem and move the market closer to optimal information production. Thus, capital markets that make efficient assignments of responsibility to produce information tend to have lower transactions costs.[14] Transactions costs also are lower in markets where large numbers of investors participate and where trading volume is high. By these criteria, the U.S. capital market is the largest and most efficient capital market in the world.

Well functioning capital markets promote entrepreneurial activity in other ways. Information and certification functions enable companies to transition to public ownership at earlier stages than otherwise would be possible. If ventures go public at earlier stages, entrepreneurs are able to harvest more quickly. Hastening the process reduces the adverse effect of the entrepreneur's higher required rate of return. Also, outside investors liquidate their positions more quickly and are able to redeploy their human capital more efficiently. They can make larger, but shorter-term, commitments of human capital to the ventures in which they invest.

The U.S. capital market includes the New York Stock Exchange, several smaller exchanges, and the dealer or over-the-counter (OTC) market. The main differences between the exchanges and the OTC market relate to the execution of secondary market trades. There is little to suggest that one trade execution mechanism (exchange specialist or OTC market makers) is significantly more efficient than the other. Although the NYSE is the largest equity stock exchange in the world, most small companies go public on the OTC. In the United States, the OTC market hosts public trading of some of the most remarkable entrepreneurial successes of the century, including Microsoft, Intel, and others.

Other countries have launched similar markets and exchanges in the last two decades.[15] These include new OTC markets in countries with established stock exchanges and entirely new exchanges in the "emerging market" countries.[16] However, efforts to develop new markets and exchanges have not been particularly successful. The mere existence of the market is not enough if transactions costs of using the market are high and trading volume is low, as often is the case. Partly in response to the problems experienced by the secondary markets in other countries, venture capitalists around the world, most notably from Israel, have opted to bring companies to the U.S. capital market for their IPOs. Doing so commits the companies to the information requirements of the U.S. market and gives the issuer better access to U.S. underwriters and accounting firms.

Investment Decisions Are Predominantly Market-Driven

Financial structures that foster entrepreneurial activity reward entrepreneurs and investors for good decisions about which projects to pursue, when to abandon, and when to harvest. In this context, government programs that promote entrepreneurial activity can be constructive or destructive. Subsidy programs that lower the cost of funds for investors may foster entrepreneurial activity. They are more likely to do so if the profit motive still guides fund allocation decisions and if those directly involved in investment allocation must compete for the subsidized funds in ways that preserve some benefit for the entrepreneur.

The main arguments for more proactive government involvement are that private processes fail to achieve certain social objectives and that some individuals or groups need protection from potential abuses. However, private mechanisms can promote and capitalize on positive externalities that may be related to public policy goals. Silicon Valley, for example, emerged as a private structure to capitalize on high-technology opportunities. It is not the result of any government program to nurture high technology in that region. Other industry clusters also are predominantly private market responses to opportunities.[17]

Capital markets are less likely to address other social objectives, such as fostering minority- or women-owned businesses. However, it still is possible to retain competitive processes for selection of opportunities within the bounds of social objectives.

The Climate for Entrepreneurship in the United Kingdom

The U.K. approach to financing entrepreneurial enterprises closely resembles that of the United States. Among the shared characteristics is the reliance on sweat equity, friends, and family financing at early stages, the presence of numerous "seed funds" sponsored by universities and government programs, reliance on formal venture capital firms to supply several rounds of financing, access to pension fund investing, and access to stock markets for harvesting. In addition, the U.K. experience with new ventures has been much like the Silicon Valley experience. Both are closely tied to universities and commercialization of academic research. The "Cambridge Phenomenon" started in the early 1980s and resulted in the launch of a number of biotech and information technology companies. Many of these companies were unsuccessful, but the experience improved efforts at assessing technologies and recruiting quality management to the technology companies.

Sources: Discussion is drawn from several sources, including Jim Martin, presentation on "Financing the Entrepreneurial Venture in the UK and Continental Europe," at NYU conference, The Economics of Small Business Finance (1997). See also Murray (1999).

Public policy efforts to protect individuals from abuses can stimulate or impede entrepreneurship. Policies that lower information costs for investors and are not excessively burdensome are likely to be beneficial. Policies that restrain the contracting choices between the general and limited partners of a venture capital fund are more likely to impede investment than to ensure that all the parties are compensated fairly.

17. 4   THE FUTURE OF ENTREPRENEURIAL FINANCE

Much of what we have discussed concerns entrepreneurial finance as it is today. There is great potential for dramatic change. Twenty years ago, the market for venture capital investing barely existed. Twenty years from now, the market is likely to be very different from what it is today. Ten years ago, biotechnology was a major focus of new venture investment. The recent focus has been on electronic commerce. No one can know what the focus will be ten years hence.

Here are a few thoughts and conjectures about the future of entrepreneurial finance.

Methods of Selecting New Venture Investment Opportunities Will Improve

Financing of entrepreneurial ventures occurred long before entrepreneurial finance existed as a field of study. The field is young, but is evolving rapidly, as academic research grows and innovations occur in the private sector. As these contributions increase, methods for selecting investment opportunities are certain to improve.

Both Investors and Entrepreneurs Will Develop Better Methods to Evaluate and Decide Whether to Pursue Opportunities   Both parties will likely pay more systematic attention to the opportunity costs of investing resources in a new venture and to the merits of the opportunity. Improvements in the technology for evaluating entrepreneurial investments are certain to continue.

The most successful investors will be those who can most accurately value and beneficially structure the promising new ventures. This suggests increased competition not only in screening opportunities, but also in valuing and structuring deals. Although these qualities have always been integral to smart investing, the market increasingly reflects the use of more sophisticated valuation tools. These tools include valuing real options and recognizing the value of strategic commitment. Modern valuation tools, including simulation, offer promising ways to reflect uncertainty in valuation.

In addition to tools aimed at improving the *ex ante* aspects of deal-making, there also is competition in post-deal development. Most investors, such as venture capitalists and angels, devote considerable time to working with their investments. In the future, we expect that venture capitalists will compete to improve portfolio company performance. Financial instruments will be designed to facilitate transactions by lowering the monitoring and enforcement costs that impede efficient investment.

Data Available for Assessing Potential Rewards and Risks Will Improve   Corresponding to improvements in valuation technology, availability of data that are relevant to selecting and valuing new ventures will improve. All asset pricing models and methods have information requirements. For example, the CAPM normally requires an estimate of beta and the market risk premium. When the model was introduced, its users had to devote effort to estimating both pieces of information. It now is possible to retrieve estimates of equity betas of public companies from dozens of sources and to retrieve estimates of the market risk premium from several sources. If an approach to asset valuation is useful, companies that specialize in providing financial information will begin to generate the information that complements the valuation approach.

Better Ways to Structure Deals Will Be Developed   The value of a new venture investment opportunity is extremely sensitive to how the deal is structured—how it is staged, the flexibility options that are retained or excluded, the amount of financing provided, how risk is shared, and so on. We have a fundamental understanding of how such factors affect the value of an opportunity, but designing value-enhancing deal structures is hard work, and the value of the effort depends on the quality of the valuation technology and information used. As the models and information sources improve, so will the quality of the deal structures.

Changes in the Set of Entrepreneurial Investment Opportunities Threaten Existing Institutions

The amount and nature of entrepreneurial opportunities are certain to change over time. Some of the changes will significantly threaten the viability of existing institutions, including the current division of entrepreneurial activity among individuals, corporations, universities, venture capital firms, angel investor groups, strategic partners, and other entities.

The Rate of Technological Progress Will Change   Technological progress does not occur at a constant rate. Economies go through periods when investment opportunities are plentiful and periods when they are severely lacking. Based on Schumpeter's view of dynamic economics, a healthy economy is constantly "disrupted" by technological innovation.[18] The upswing in a cycle of economic activity starts when a set of innovations is adopted and becomes generally used. After a period of rising adoption of technology, the innovation and related entrepreneurial activity begin to decline. Historical examples include innovations in water power, iron, textiles (late eighteenth century); steam, railroads and steel (mid-nineteenth century), electricity, chemicals, merchandising, and internal combustion (early twentieth century), petrochemicals, electronics, aviation (mid- to late-twentieth century).

During expansionary periods, it seems that almost anyone who has money to invest can expect to profit. During slow periods, only the strongest competitors survive. Marginal competitors, faced with unacceptably low returns, tend to exit.

The latest wave in new venture activity and investment peaked in 2000. E-commerce, telecommunications, and computer software industries were booming, attracting high levels of interest in the public capital market. As the rate of entrepreneurial activity slowed, the importance of making good entrepreneurial investment decisions increased. In the current environment, firms need to reassess their existing human capital allocations. Even if good investment prospects diminish, it may be appropriate to increase the allocation of resources to investment selection and evaluation. It may become appropriate to maintain existing investments for a longer period of time so harvesting can occur when the venture has a successful history backing it.

The Direction of Technological Progress Will Change   Not only will the aggregate level of technological progress change, so will the focus of technological activity. The current institutional structure suits the kinds of new ventures emerging in the high-technology sectors. The next technological shock may require an entirely new structure and set of institutions.

In the past, some innovations have occurred in the corporate sector, where they were financed and developed. In contrast, some of the more recent innovations were hatched in college dormitories and were easier to pursue by new entities that did not have the baggage of established physical distribution and retailing structures. There is no reason to assume that the progression over the last century represents a trend toward innovation being concentrated in this particular way. The next wave could be one for which the large corporate structure is essential.

The Frontier for New Opportunities Will Be Global   Despite the differences that exist across countries, the capital markets of the world are growing together. Foreign investment capital flows into the U.S. capital market, and U.S. investors invest in foreign securities. At a more basic level, corporations are diversifying internationally. Even an investor who only holds securities of U.S. firms has a significant international risk exposure through the international holdings of U.S. companies.

Countries throughout the world are adopting institutional structures that have been proven successful elsewhere, particularly those of the United States. Entrepreneurs increasingly can select between their local institutions for funding and those that exist in other countries. As the constraining effects of local financial structures are removed, the local financing environment becomes less limiting in terms of when and where technological progress occurs. Other factors, such as education, wage rates, natural resources, and distribution capabilities, gain importance as determinants of the nexus of activity. The result is that technological progress is likely to be less constrained by political boundaries or local financial market conditions.

Clustering of Entrepreneurial Activity Will Persist   Nonetheless, clustering of activity will persist. Clustering, such as in Route 128 and Silicon Valley, is not driven by artificial or political constraints. It is an endogenous response to the advantages of agglomeration. Globalization of capital markets for new venture financing will not diminish the economic advantages of clustering. This fact has significant implications for policy-makers, who decide whether and how to invest resources in promoting economic development and entrepreneurship.

From a policy perspective, it is useful to recount what experience and economics have taught about building infrastructure to facilitate growth. First, developing markets, including entrepreneurial markets, require a range and coordination of talents. Clustering makes coordination of activity less costly to accomplish. Michael Porter and others point out that close working relationships with suppliers spark innovation and that proximity to rivals enhances effective competition. Such clustering results in more efficient and quicker transfer of technical knowledge and skills.[19] In entrepreneurial markets, participants require financing and hands-on managerial help. An entrepreneur decides to locate near venture capitalists and business angels in order to increase the likelihood of personal contact with the venture capitalist, rivals, and prospective partners and employees. The proximity allows the entrepreneur more frequent monitoring and arguably higher quality managerial advice.[20]

Agglomeration economies that arise from clusters suggest that a community may develop a comparative advantage as an entrepreneurial location if it attracts a broad spectrum of specialized firms and individuals, including venture capitalists, input suppliers, technically trained workers, accountants, lawyers, consultants, and so on. Typically, entrepreneurial "hot groups" locate near research universities that supply a stream of talented individuals with innovative ideas and connections to facilities such as libraries, computers, and research labs.

As there are scale economies associated with clusters, it is likely that only a few communities will be successful at capturing them. Success depends on building a competitive advantage that is sustainable. Strategic efforts to transplant or mimic the product-market orientations of existing clusters of new venture activity (such as Silicon Valley) and that do not leverage existing strengths, are poorly conceived.

Changes in the Competitive Climate Are a Threat to Existing Institutions

Separately from changes in opportunities to pursue and invest in new ventures, the competitive environment will change in ways that threaten existing institutions.

Competition Among Investors Will Intensify   As demand for opportunities to invest in new ventures grows, competitors will have access to better information and analytical capabilities. Competitors who can easily identify prospects and rapidly and accurately evaluate them will win the contests to select and invest profitably in new ventures. As a result of such competition, superior ability to identify and evaluate opportunities will become valuable. Nonetheless, such an advantage is likely to be small and easily lost to competition.

New ventures are often highly technical in nature. Providers of financing compete to build the technical skills needed to assess the viability of the concepts. The nature of venture capital firms reflects this. Evidence indicates that venture capital firms frequently specialize in particular industries and develop complementary human capital.

As we have witnessed over the last decade, creative use of financial instruments, including derivatives, has revolutionized the way people think about managing risk. Innovations in financial instruments and contractual provisions are likely to continue and will be applied more systematically to the market for new venture finance. Competition will require both entrepreneurs and investors to develop good working knowledge of how these devices can add value to deals.

Competition Among Investors Will Be Increasingly Global   U.S. venture capital firms are developing funds that focus on entrepreneurial activity in specific foreign countries. Moreover, foreign investors are significant investors in U.S. venture capital funds. Some countries, such as the United Kingdom and Israel, already have achieved success with new venture financing capabilities that parallel those of the United States. Other countries are pursuing similar objectives. There is little to deter any venture capital firm from locating in one country, raising capital in another, and investing and deploying some of its human capital in a third.

Consistent with the integration and globalization of the market for venture capital, the European Union (EU) is developing plans to change Europe's economic structure to make it more conducive to new and small business. The EU is initiating efforts to solve a perceived venture capital shortage by integrating the venture capital markets, eliminating regulatory barriers to venture capital funds, and increasing the tax incentives for venture capitalists. In addition, they are addressing some deep-rooted cultural characteristics that may impede risk capital formation in Europe. The EU says efforts are needed to promote development of high-tech firms, increase the pool of skilled workers, and promote a culture of entrepreneurship.[21]

The Rate at Which Capital Flows to New Opportunities Will Increase   There is broad-based capital market recognition of the economic advantages of diversification. Individual investors increasingly are moving away from direct selection of investments and delegating stock selection and bond selection to portfolio managers. The result is that an increasing share of investment capital is under professional management in mutual and pension funds. Furthermore, investors less frequently allow professional asset managers to engage in stock selection. In recent years, index funds have grown significantly in comparison to actively managed funds. The force driving these changes is a recognition that stock selection is expensive, whether carried out individually or by professional asset managers. It usually accomplishes little more than random selection. Although there always will be a role for some investors to devote resources to investment valuation, most investors are better off accepting the market return.

One aspect of investment management that is lagging is asset allocation across classes of assets. For the most part, asset allocation decisions are made either by individuals, as they decide how much to invest in equity funds versus debt funds, or by pension fund managers, as they select allocations across different kinds of asset managers. Reallocating investment funds across different asset classes is relatively difficult. Indexing across (as opposed to within) asset classes, except for debt and equity, is not feasible. This is especially true for new asset classes (small-capitalization firms, international equities, emerging market equities, real estate securities, venture capital, and other alternative investments) that continue to be identified.

New Competitive Structures Will Emerge   Historically, public corporations and universities have been unable to develop structures that sufficiently reward innovation within the organization. As a result, entrepreneurs have tended to create independent new ventures to develop their ideas. For the most part, the new venture finance industry exists because of this unsolved problem. The differential between required rates of return for diversified and underdiversified investors provides significant incentive for public corporations and universities to work on possible solutions. Although we do not know that a comprehensive solution is achievable, it is likely that improvements will occur. As they do, corporations and universities will likely displace individual entrepreneurs to an increasing degree.

What Will Be the Drivers of Success?

For dealing with the uncertain future of entrepreneurial finance, the drivers of success fall into two categories: short-run and long-run. The drivers are the same for entrepreneurs as they are for investors.

Success in the short-run depends on three primary factors. Entrepreneurs and investors, for whom success is likely in the short-run, will use the best available methods and information to decide which ventures to pursue and how to structure the deals. These entrepreneurs and investors will be able to add the most value to the ventures they pursue. They will form the best teams and deal most effectively with suppliers and customers.

Succeeding in the long-run also depends on three primary factors. Entrepreneurs and investors, for whom success is likely in the long-run, will develop organizational structures that are agile and capable of reacting quickly to changing environments and opportunities. They will perceive changes in the environment and distinguish between fundamental changes and transitory fluctuations. Finally, they will have an orientation to the future. They will abandon practices that are ill suited for the future and replace them with plans that should be effective in the new environment.

NOTES

1. Manove and Padilla (1999) describe a similar response by bank lenders to pervasive optimism of entrepreneurs.

2. For a perspective on the puzzle of why start-ups are observed when investors have lower required rates of return than entrepreneurs, see Bankman and Gilson (1999).

3. See Jeng and Wells (2000). Their sample consists of 21 countries.

4. As Levine (1997) documents, economists have different opinions regarding the importance of the financial structure to economic growth. Schumpeter (1912) contends that well-functioning banks spur technological innovation by identifying and funding the entrepreneurs with the best chances of implementing innovative products and production processes. In contrast, Joan Robinson (1952, p. 86) states that, "Where enterprise leads finance follows." The reasoning is that economic growth development creates demand for financial institutions that facilitate growth. Levine reviews the literature. His findings indicate that many types of studies (cross-country studies, case studies, industry- and firm-level analyses) document "extensive periods when financial development crucially affects the speed and pattern of economic development" (p. 689).

5. Milhaupt (1997) identifies five "traits of the active venture capital market" that correspond with our list of structural attributes: existence of large and independent sources of funding, liquidity, highly developed incentive structures, labor mobility, and risk tolerance.

6. In the United States, United Kingdom, Ireland, and Denmark, 1994 pension funds investment as a percentage of total venture capital funding represented 47 percent, 30 percent, 36 percent, and 32 percent, respectively. See O'Shea (1996) OECD, "Special Features: Venture Capital in OECD Countries, Paper No. 63, February 1996, appearing in *Financial Market Trends* (Bern: OECD, 1996).

7. In Mediterranean countries, for example, firms often borrow from state-owned industrial finance agencies, which in turn borrow from state banks. In Germany and most northern European countries, state-sponsored industrial finance is used less and corporate debt largely consists of long-term bank credits. Compared to the United States and United Kingdom, the magnitude of the bank credit is larger and the terms of the debt contracts are longer.

8. In some countries, notably Japan and Germany, banks are the most important large shareholders in firms. Prowse (1996) reports that in Japan, they own over 20 percent of outstanding common stock of nonfinancial firms. In Germany, they own 10 percent, and they have the additional flexibility of being able to vote common stock owned by individuals that is held by banks in trust for them. Therefore, banks in those countries have powerful positions as active monitors through their presence on boards and their votes in shareholder meetings. In the United States, more severe legal and regulatory restraints on equity ownership and active involvement limit the behavior of large investors. In the United States, banks own negligible amounts of nonfinancial firms' equity. As of 2000, 50 percent of equities in the United States were held by other financial institutions, including mutual funds, pension funds, insurance companies (*Statistical Abstract of the United States*, 2001).

9. See Milhaupt (1997) for elaboration on the Japanese new venture environment.

10. Gompers and Lerner (1998).

11. There are other important structural differences as well. For example, in Japan, there currently is no organizational form comparable to the U.S. limited partnership, which allows flow-through tax treatment and limited liability.

12. In Italy, Greece, and Portugal, state-owned businesses account for over 15 percent of nonagricultural value added. In France, Ireland, and Belgium, they account for over 10 percent. In the United States, they account for less than 5 percent.

13. U.S. disclosure requirements generally are more comprehensive than those of other countries. See Prowse (1996) for discussion of the requirements in Japan and Germany. He also notes that, until recently, both countries imposed significant taxes on capital market transactions.

14. Although it is common for small-business owners to complain about paperwork and other costs of doing business, these costs generally are smaller in the United States, and regulations are less likely to be biased toward the status quo than they are in many other countries.

15. Jeng and Wells (2000) examine the factors that influence venture capital fundraising internationally. They find the strength of the IPO market is an important determinant of venture capital commitments. *See also* Black and Gilson (1998).

16. A number of European countries have created new OTC markets, including Brussels-based EASDAQ, London's AIM, France's Nouveau Marche, Frankfurt's Neuer Markt, Begium's Euro NM and Amsterdam's NMAX. (See Martin, 1997.) However, the amount of capital raised by firms traded on NASDAQ (a part of the U.S. OTC market) was approximately seven times more in 1997 than that raised on all equivalent European OTC markets combined.

17. As an example of public intervention, Lerner (1999) examines award recipients U.S. government's Small Business Innovation Research programs and finds the awards contribute to certification of firm quality, but there also appear to be distortions from the award process.

18. See Schumpeter (1934).

19. See Porter (1990).

20. As Dennis Weatherstone, former CEO of J.P. Morgan, once quipped, "Financial centers would not exist without lunch." This insight is equally applicable to entrepreneurial centers.

21. "EU Unveils 6-Point Plan to Boost Weak Venture-Capital Market." *Wall Street Journal,* April 2, 1998, p. C1.

REFERENCES AND ADDITIONAL READING

BANKMAN, JOSEPH, AND RONALD J. GILSON. "Why Start-Ups?" *Stanford Law Review* 51 (1999): 289–308.

BLACK, BERNARD, AND RONALD GILSON. "Venture Capital and the Structure of Capital Markets: Banks versus Stock Markets." *Journal of Financial Economics* 47 (1998): 243–277.

FRANKS, JULIAN R., KJELL G. NYBORG, AND WALTER N. TOROUS. "A Comparison of US, UK, and German Insolvency Codes." *Financial Management* 25 (1996): 86–101.

GILSON, RONALD. "Engineering a Venture Capital Market: Lessons from the American Experience." Stanford Law School Working Paper, 2002.

GOMPERS, PAUL, AND JOSH LERNER. "The Venture Captial Revolution." *Journal of Economic Perspectives* 15 (2001): 145–168.

GOMPERS, PAUL, AND JOSH LERNER. "What Drives Venture Capital Fundraising?" *Brookings Paper on Economic Activity,* 1998.

HAWKINS, DEL I. "New Business Entrepreneurship in the Japanese Economy." *Journal of Business Venturing* 8 (1993): 137–1950.

HYDE, ALAN. "Silicon Valley's High Velocity Labor Market: When Labor Markets Work Like Information Markets." *Journal of Applied Corporate Finance* (1998):

JENG, LESLIE A., AND PHILIPPE C. WELLS. "The Determinants of Venture Capital Funding: Evidence Across Countries." *Journal of Corporate Finance* 6 (2000): 241–289, 1998.

KAISER, KEVIN M.J. "European Bankruptcy Laws: Implications for Corporations Facing Financial Distress." *Financial Management* 25 (1996): 67–85.

KESTER, W. CARL. "Governance, Contracting, and Investment Horizons: A Look at Japan and Germany." *Journal of Applied Corporate Finance* (1992): 83–98.

LERNER, JOSH. "The Government as Venture Capitalist: The Long-run Effects of the SBIR Program." *Journal of Business* 72 (1999): 285–318.

LEVINE, ROSS. "Financial Development and Economic Growth: Views and Agenda." *Journal of Economic Literature* 35 (1997): 688–726.

MANOVE, MICHAEL, AND A. JORGE PADILLA. "Banking (Conservatively) with Optimists." *RAND Journal of Economics* 30 (1999): 324–350.

MARTIN, JIM. "Financing the Entrepreneurial Enterprise—the UK and Continental Europe." Presentation at New York University Conference on Small Business Finance, New York, May 1997.

MASON, COLIN AND RICHARD HARRISON. "Editorial: Venture Capital—Rationale, Aims, and Scope." *Venture Capital* 1 (1999): 1–46.

MILHAUPT, CURTIS J. "The Market for Innovation in the United States and Japan: Venture Capital and the Comparative Corporate Governance Debate." *Northwestern University Law Review* (1997): 865–898.

MURRAY, GORDON. "Early-Stage Venture Capital Funds, Scale Economies, and Public Support." *Venture Capital* 1 (1999): 351–384.

NORTH, DOUGLAS C. *Institutions, Institutional Change and Economic Performance.* New York: Cambridge University Press, 1990, pp. 80–82.

O'SHEA, MARGARET. "Venture Capital in OECD Countries." Financial Affairs Division of OECD paper 63, in *Financial Market Trends.* Bern: OECD (1996).

PORTER, MICHAEL. *The Competitive Advantage of Nations.* New York: Macmillan Press, 1990.

PROWSE, STEPHEN D. "Corporate Finance in International Perspective: Legal and Regulatory Influences on Financial System Development." *Economic Review,* Federal Reserve Bank of Dallas, 3d quarter, pp. 2–15.

ROBINSON, JOAN. "The Generalization of the General Theory." In *The Rate of Interest, and Other Essays.* London: Macmillan, 1952, pp. 67–142.

SAPIENZA, HARRY J., SOPHIE MANIGART, AND WIM VERMEIR. "Venture Capitalist Governance and Value Added in Four Countries." *Journal of Business Venturing* 11 (1996): 439–469.

SCHUMPETER, JOSEPH A. *Theorie der Wirtschaftlichen Entwicklung* [The theory of economic development]. Leipsig: Dunker & Humblot, 1912. Translated by Redvers Opie. Cambridge, MA: Harvard University Press, 1934.

SINGH, AJIT. "Corporate Financial Patterns in Industrializing Economies: A Comparative international Study." International Finance Corporation, The World Bank, Technical Paper Number 2.

ZUCKER, LYNNE, MICHAEL DARBY, AND JEFF ARMSTRONG. "Geographically Localized Knowledge: Spillovers or Markets?" *Economic Inquiry* (1998): 65–86.

ZUCKER, LYNNE, MICHAEL DARBY, AND MARILYN BREWER. "Intellectual Human Capital and the Birth of U.S. Biotechnology Enterprises." *American Economic Review* (1998): 290–306.

Index

Page numbers for Tables and Charts are shown in **Bold.**